A History
of Soviet Russia

THIRD EDITION

A History of Soviet Russia

M. K. Dziewanowski

University of Wisconsin, Milwaukee

PRENTICE HALL, Englewood Cliffs, New Jersey 07632

LIBRARY OF CONGRESS
Library of Congress Cataloging-in-Publication Data

Dziewanowski, M. K.
   A history of Soviet Russia / M.K. Dziewanowski. -- 3rd ed.

   Includes index.
   ISBN 0-13-392275-8
   1. Soviet Union--History--20th century.   I. Title.
DK246.D9 1989
947.084--dc19   88-5998
                                                        CIP

Editorial/production supervision and
   interior design: *Jenny Kletzin*
Cover design: *Ben Santora*
Manufacturing buyer: *Ed O'Dougherty*

Photographs on pages 38, 42, 48, 57, 71, 93, 100, 106, 137, 145, 154, 159, 166, 189, 198, 202, 225, 242, 245, 272, 280, 282, 285, 291, 299, 309, 329, and 339 are used with the permission of the National Archives.

Photographs on pages 26, 65, 180, 214, 303, 326, 330, 337, 352, 359, and 367 are reproduced from the Collections of the Library of Congress.

The photograph on page 184 is used with the permission of the United Nations.

The photograph on page 383 is used with permission of Leslie Deeb.

Photographs on pages 258, 264, 265, 273, and 378 are used with the permission of the Soviet Embassy, Washington, D. C.

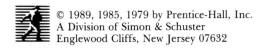 © 1989, 1985, 1979 by Prentice-Hall, Inc.
A Division of Simon & Schuster
Englewood Cliffs, New Jersey 07632

Printed in the United States of America

10 9 8 7 6 5 4 3 2 1

ISBN 0-13-392275-8

Prentice-Hall International (UK) Limited, *London*
Prentice-Hall of Australia Pty. Limited, *Sydney*
Prentice-Hall Canada Inc., *Toronto*
Prentice-Hall Hispanoamericana, S.A., *Mexico*
Prentice-Hall of India Private Limited, *New Delhi*
Prentice-Hall of Japan, Inc., *Tokyo*
Simon & Schuster Asia Pte. Ltd., *Singapore*
Editora Prentice-Hall do Brasil, Ltda., *Rio de Janeiro*

To my Harvard teacher
of things Soviet: Professor Merle Fainsod

Contents

Part Three: LENIN'S SOVIET RUSSIA

CHAPTER 7
The Brave New World at the Creation   97

CHAPTER 8
The Ordeal of the Civil War, 1918–1921   109

CHAPTER 9
From War Communism to the New Economic Policy   124

CHAPTER 10
Between the Comintern and the Narkomindel: Early Soviet Foreign Policy

139

CHAPTER 11
The Formation of the USSR and Lenin's Death

152

Part Four: THE STALIN REVOLUTION

CHAPTER 12
The Struggle for Lenin's Mantle: The Stalin-Trotsky Controversy

163

CHAPTER 13
The Industrialization Debate and the Five-Year Plans

178

CHAPTER 14
The Purges

CHAPTER 15
A New Nationality Policy
and the Soviet Cultural Revolution

CHAPTER 16
From Isolation to Collective Security

CHAPTER 20
The End of an Epoch:
Stalin's Death and the Twentieth Party Congress

Part Six: POST-STALIN SOVIET RUSSIA

CHAPTER 21
The Khrushchev Years: The Upward Trend

CHAPTER 22
Khrushchev's Decline and Fall

CHAPTER 23
Soviet Russia Under Brezhnev's Leadership

351

CHAPTER 24
Soviet Russia Since Brezhnev

374

Appendix

396

Index

401

Preface

The third edition is an updated and expanded version of the second. The last chapter has been rewritten to cover the Andropov and Chernenko interludes, as well as Gorbachev's reforms. Some new maps and illustrations were added as to better reflect the historic narrative.

A German historian, Otto Hoetzsch, writing his history of Russia, which included a significant segment devoted to the postrevolutionary period, gave his book the title, *The Evolution of Russia.* According to his interpretation (which initially seemed rather fantastic!), the Bolshevik revolution did not constitute a total break in historic continuity. His thesis, however, has been vindicated by subsequent developments. The historic and geopolitical origins of the Soviet state have been increasingly visible; this has been especially true during the post-Stalin period. One of the most characteristic features of this era has been the revival, not only among the intellectuals and artists, of the historic roots of Russian culture. Seventy years after the Bolshevik coup d'état, most of the Soviet leaders are better understood as Russians than as communists. The present author agrees with this interpretation and stresses in this new edition the increasingly visible continuity of Russian history.

This approach does not mean that the author has underestimated the role of Communist ideology and the role of the Communist Party of the Soviet Union (CPSU). Quite the contrary! The achievements of an organization that has fostered a profound transformation of some one-sixth of the globe over more than seven decades has to be treated with due consideration. Consequently, the story of the Party and its ideology has been one of the predominant themes of the book. But it is obvious to the present writer that the Party has been undergoing a profound evolution since its triumph in November 1917. Communist evangelic sectarianism, strong until the 1930s, has been rapidly fused with traditional Great Russian nationalism, although carefully camouflaged by Marxist verbiage. These two elements—nationalism and Communism—initially antagonistic, are now being synthesized by the rulers of the Soviet Union. These attempts are strikingly opposed to the sentiments of many other ethnic groups of which the USSR is composed. This book pays a great deal of attention to the multi-national character of the Soviet Empire and to the centrifugal and centripetal forces whose interplay has been an essential thread in Muscovite-Russian-Soviet history. A large part of the book is devoted to the twenty-nine-year period of 1924–1953, to the phantasmagoric era of Stalin, who, even from his second, more modest grave, still influences much of the political reality of contemporary Soviet Russia.

Any history of Russia that has to straddle the imperial and the Soviet periods faces many problems. Among them is the unavoidable issue of the calendars. Until February 1918, Russia used the Julian calendar, which in the twentieth century was thirteen days behind the Western, or Gregorian, calendar. Hence, the Russians speak of the "February Revolution" when referring to the downfall of the Tsarist regime in Petrograd (February 27), while for us it is the revolution of March 12. The abdication of Tsar Nicholas II, which according to the old-style calendar took place on March 2, for us occurred on March 15. Lenin returned from Switzerland to Petrograd on April 3, according to the Julian calendar, but on April 16, according to ours. Finally, the "Great October Proletarian Revolution,"

which, according to the Julian calendar, was carried out on October 25, for us was accomplished on November 7. In order to avoid confusion, both dates are given for events prior to January 1918.

Another problem is that of the spelling of Russian words. There is, unfortunately, no universally accepted system of transliteration of Russian into English. On the whole, the book favors transliteration rather than phonetic transcription, but tends to accept well-established traditional spelling of East Slavic names as easier on the student.

While preparing my book, I was ably and unselfishly assisted by Bill Myers, my graduate student at Bostoin University. I am also grateful to Kathy Reck, to Chuck and Annabelle Sherba, and to my wife, Ada, for helping me with the preparation of the third edition. My warm thanks go to my friend and colleague, Professor of Geography at the UWM, Dr. Paul E. Lydolph, for kindly allowing me to use a statistical table from the 1979 supplement to his excellent *Geography of the U.S.S.R.* and to professors Wolfgang Leonhard of Yale, Daniel Brower of the University of California, and Neil Weissman of Dickinson College for their critical remarks.

I am greatly indebted to the Russian Research Center of Harvard University, with which I was connected from 1949 to 1968. The stimulating atmosphere of the Center and the contacts provided by it have been very helpful in preparing this basic survey of Soviet history.

M.K. Dziewanowski
University of Wisconsin, Milwaukee

A History
of Soviet Russia

CHAPTER 1

The Geopolitical Personality of the Soviet Union

Modern science and technology have considerably liberated contemporary Western civilization from subjugation to the forces of nature and geography. But this freedom from natural environment is far from complete, even in the most technologically advanced countries of the West. In backward Russia, dependence on geography has always been of great importance. Hence this introductory chapter on the physical environment and its persistent influence on Russian history.

SIZE, SHAPE, AND RESOURCES

First, one must start with the size and shape of the USSR. There is a unique signpost in Vladivostok that reads: 9,329 kilometers (5,789 miles) to Leningrad. That sign is curbstone confirmation of what a glance at any map of the world would show: the Soviet Union represents the largest national land mass on the face of the earth. The map would also reveal two other characteristics of the USSR—its basic flatness and its northern location.

The enormity of the Soviet Union is perhaps the most striking feature of its geographic personality. It takes the Trans-Siberian express ten days to cover the distance between Leningrad and Vladivostok. The USSR covers eleven time zones. To cross the Soviet Union from its western to its eastern extremity, the traveler must span nearly 7,000 miles and reset his watch ten times. When the long summer day draws to an end on the Baltic shore of the Soviet Empire, it is already dawn of the next day on its Pacific coast. The sun never sets on the Soviet Union.

Covering 8.6 million square miles, or about one-sixth of the firm surface of the globe, Soviet Russia encompasses more land than all of North America. Indeed, it is about as large as the United States (3.6 million square miles), China (3.7 million), and India (1.2 million) *combined*. The size

1

and continental character of the United States and Russia are common features of the two countries. Space (and hence colonization) has been an important geohistorical phenomenon in both. It provided what had once seemed an ever-receding frontier, and one which engendered certain common attitudes and national policies. Muscovy's march (the name *Russia* was first coined by Peter the Great at the beginning of the eighteenth century) to its Pacific was similar in both execution and purpose to America's march to its Pacific. Both countries provided an outlet for the socially restless, opened new lands for an excess population, and had migrations of gigantic scope.

The Soviet Union, though the largest, is not the most populous country in the world. With some 285,000,000 people, it is well behind China with over 1,000,000,000, and India with some 700,000,000, but ahead of the United States. The USSR with over 100 ethnic groups, is far less ethnically homogeneous than the United States or even China, and has one of the lowest population densities in the world (ten persons per square kilometer). Its very size and heterogeneity create formidable political, cultural, communication, and transportation problems —all of which make administration an onerous task. For the same reason, national defense is also a troublesome matter. The job of conquering territories, integrating them, and keeping them subdued has proved to be a heavy drain on the Great Russian people, the founders and real masters of the Muscovite-Russian-Soviet imperial structure.

Soviet Russia's size is matched by its resources. The Soviet Union has on its territory every raw material it needs for its economic development, except natural rubber and quinine, and there exist substitutes for both. It is estimated that about one-half of the known deposits of iron and one-fifth of the world's hard-coal deposits are located within its territory. It is the largest producer of oil in the world. It also contains 33 percent of the world's water power, 25 percent of the world's forests, and 10 percent of

the world's oil reserves. Potentially, Soviet Russia is the richest country in the world. Yet the resources of the USSR are not without certain limitations. First, most of the soil is poor, especially in ethnic Russia. Second, rainfall is erratic and often comes not in the spring but in the summer, during harvest time. Third, the Soviet Union has the highest percentage of marshland in the world; marshes and extensive peat bogs cover roughly one-fifth of its land surface. Finally, 88 percent of the total area of the USSR is unsuited for cultivation; rain shortages, severe subarctic climate, and the nature of the soil permit a mere 12 percent of the land to be used for farming. As a consequence, the agricultural season is on the whole as short as it is hectic. Where Western European farmers enjoy a farming season of eight to nine months, their Russian counterparts have only four to six. This has traditionally resulted in low yields and a low level of animal husbandry.

In addition, Russia's resources are located largely (with the exception of the Urals and Siberia) on its periphery—in the Ukraine, the Caucasus, Turkestan, and Siberia. Furthermore, a considerable part of its water power lies in the frozen wastes of northern Siberia where it cannot effectively be used. The valleys of the great Siberian streams—the Yenisei and the Lena, for instance—contain large deposits of coal and iron ore, but for the most part they are buried in a frigid area where the earth, permanently frozen to a depth of several hundred feet, makes exploitation uneconomical. Hence, besides its persistent structural and organizational troubles, the Soviet economy has to cope with difficulties inherent in the nation's geographic and climatic conditions.

Almost as striking as Russia's size is its location. The USSR's southernmost point, Kushka in Turkmenistan, lies on the latitude of Memphis, Tennessee. The southernmost harbor of the Soviet Far East is due west of Portsmouth, New Hampshire. Most of the USSR is on the same latitude as Canada; next to it, Soviet Russia is the

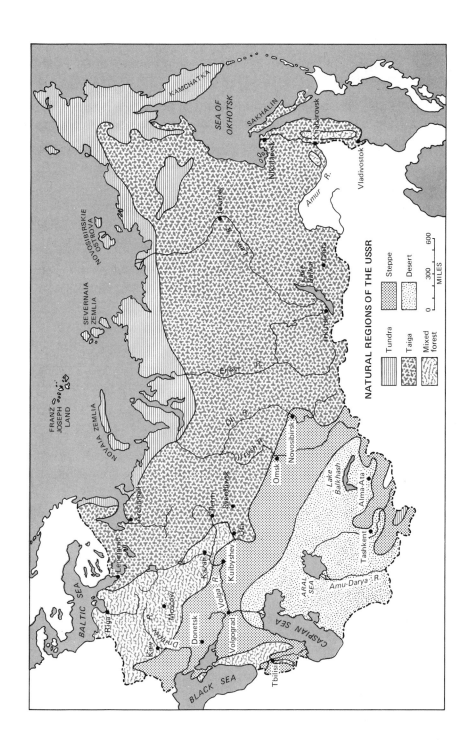

NATURAL REGIONS OF THE USSR

Tundra

Taiga

Mixed forest

Steppe

Desert

0   300   600
MILES

FRANZ JOSEPH LAND

NOVAIA ZEMLIA

SEVERNAIA ZEMLIA

NOVOSIBIRSKIE OSTROVA

KAMCHATKA

SEA OF OKHOTSK

SAKHALIN

Khabarovsk

Vladivostok

Amur R.

Nikolhevsk

Chita

Lake Baikal

Irkutsk

Yakutsk

Enisei R.

Ob R.

Irtysh R.

Novosibirsk

Omsk

Lake Balkhash

Alma-Ata

Tashkent

ARAL SEA

Amu-Darya R.

CASPIAN SEA

Archangel

Perm

Sverdlovsk

Leningrad

Kazan

Kuibyshev

Volga R.

Volgograd

Moscow

Kiev

Donetsk

Riga

BALTIC SEA

Dnieper R.

Don R.

Tbilisi

BLACK SEA

3

northernmost country in the world. Moscow is north of Edmonton, Alberta; Leningrad lies as far north as Anchorage, Alaska; and the Crimean resort town of Yalta is as far "south" as Bangor, Maine. Nor surprisingly, then, the Russians have developed agriculture and industry in the north to a far greater extent than have the Canadians.

Nearly three-quarters of the USSR has an extremely cold winter. The average January temperature is below zero degrees Fahrenheit. During the late autumn and winter, icy, biting winds, unchecked by mountain ranges, sweep from that gigantic icebox, the Arctic Ocean, through the vastness of Siberia and over the East European plain. The extremes of heat and cold are greatest in the Eurasian heartland.

The relative flatness of the Soviet Union, and especially of European Russia—its amorphous, sprawling boundlessness—is another characteristic of its geopolitical personality. By and large, the Soviet realm is one huge plain that extends from Central Europe deep into Asia. This broad stretch of land, where for hundreds of miles one may search in vain for a hill, let alone a mountain, has also profoundly affected the Soviet mentality.

GEOGRAPHIC REGIONS

The Soviet Union can claim a greater variety of geographic regions and climates than any other country in the world. It is the only land that harbors both tigers and polar bears. Actually, the Russian heartland is characterized by a certain uniformity; the variety is on its fringes. The territory of the Soviet Union may be divided into four main climatic and botanical zones or regions. Running essentially east to west, these are: the subarctic tundra, the forest, the steppe and desert, and the mountain region.

The subarctic tundra is the northernmost; it spreads along the Arctic Ocean from Finland to the Bering Sea. Frozen most of the year, it is a bleak region of marshes, moss, crawling shrub, dwarf trees,

and grass. Its soil yields practically no crops, and its subsoil is perpetually frozen. To the hunter and trapper, however, the tundra is a paradise, for it is rich in fur-bearing animals, including polar fox, sable, and ermine.

The tundra, which covers a large part of the Soviet subarctic territory, merges with the taiga, or the coniferous forest. Here spruce, pine, cedar, and fir predominate, with a sprinkling of ash, aspen, and birch. Leningrad (St. Petersburg, 1703–1914; Petrograd, 1914–1924) lies not far to the south of the tundra zone. With some 5 million inhabitants, the city is the second largest and most important in the Soviet Union. A great port at the juncture of the Baltic and the Neva and a vital railway terminal, Leningrad is also a cultural and industrial center of considerable importance. Culturally, it is the most Western city in Russia proper.

Further south, beyond the taiga, lies the zone of forests and fields, some 5,000 miles long and 1,200 miles wide. Most of the woodlands are mixed: a blend of coniferous and deciduous trees. They contain one-quarter of the world's forest preserves. Moscow, with some 8 million inhabitants, is situated in the middle of this zone, near the sources of the Western Dvina, the Dnieper, and the Volga, in approximately the same latitude as Labrador. Besides being the capital of the Union, and hence the political as well as the cultural focus of the realm, Moscow is a major industrial center in its own right. It is responsible for about 20 percent of the industrial output of the USSR. It is also the most important communication center of the Soviet Empire. Eleven main railways converge on the capital city—the heart and the brains of the USSR.

Forests have played a considerable role in Russian history. The early civilization of Russia, and for that matter of Eastern Europe as a whole, has been profoundly affected by the extensive forests that once covered areas much larger than they do now. Timber has always been widely used throughout Eastern Europe. Besides serving as fuel, the forests have provided material for weapons and ploughs, for dwellings, palisades, furniture, and for all sorts of domestic utensils. Moreover, forests provided meat and fur-bearing animals, berries, honey, wax, and mushrooms. The northern regions have an abundance of timber, but they do not produce enough food, especially grain. On the other hand, the southern regions like the Ukraine yield sufficient food but possess relatively little timber. The forest reserves (soft and hard wood) of the USSR account for about 20 percent of all standing timber in the world.

There are no sharp transitions between Russia's various botanic and climatic zones; they merge undramatically, almost imperceptibly. The mixed forests gradually become the wooded tracts to the south, which in turn slowly give way to the broad, seemingly endless, prairie or steppe. The steppe is a flat, treeless region covered with grass; it extends for a distance of some 2,600 miles from the Western Ukraine to Central Asia and is about 600 miles wide. Kiev, the capital of the Ukraine, lies in the northern part of this steppe region. Its population is over 2 million, and it is the third most important city in the Soviet Union. The city is situated on hills picturesquely rising four hundred feet above the Dnieper. Some of the best farmland in the world lies south and southeast of Kiev. Its rich black soil is three to five feet deep and contains 8 to 20 percent organic mold. Since the end of the eighteenth century, the Ukraine has been the grain belt, the breadbasket, first of the Tsarist empire and then of the Soviet Union. However, the fertility of the soil is counterbalanced by the scarcity and capriciousness of the rainfall, which frequently causes serious droughts and often comes in July and August. Ukraine's industrial position is equally prominent: it produces nearly 25 percent of Russia's electricity, nearly one-third of its coal, natural gas, and fertilizers, about 40 percent of its steel, and about 70 percent of its sugar. The Ukraine's output of beet sugar is about two-thirds that of Cuba's average production of cane sugar

and exceeds that of all the United States. Its balanced industrial–agrarian economy makes the Ukraine the only potentially self-sustaining republic of the USSR.

The contrast between the forest and the steppe has been significant not only geographically but historically as well. The open fertile spaces have been an invitation both to invaders and to those seeking land and freedom. The nomadic tribes of Asia— the Polovtsy, the Petchenegs, the Tatars— have often invaded Eastern Europe by passing through the open flat gap between the Urals and the Caspian Sea. For centuries the lush grassland of the steppe has attracted adventurous souls bent on escaping tyranny. It was the steppe that produced the typical frontiersmen of Eastern Europe, the Cossacks. The superb horsemanship and daring of these people were largely the result of the challenge of their geographical environment. In the long run, however, the steady, tough, and hard-working inhabitants of the forest prevailed over the mercurial, less reliable men of the steppe, and Muscovy conquered the Ukraine in the seventeenth and eighteenth centuries.

As the steppe extends south and southeast toward the Caspian and Aral seas, the amount of rainfall diminishes. Here dry winds from the east often bring severe droughts. In many parts of the steppe zone, cultivation without a great deal of artificial irrigation is risky. This requirement is particularly vital around the northern end of the fast-shrinking Caspian Sea, which is now some ninety feet below sea level, where the dry steppe is giving way to the advancing sand dunes of Central Asia. The enormous desert region, larger than the state of Texas, is interspersed with oases and pasture land. It stretches eastward beyond the Caspian Sea toward Turkestan and Mongolia and ends only at the Chinese border, in Manchuria. Since the 1950s, the Soviet government has tried to plow and cultivate the virgin lands of western Siberia, northern Kazakhstan, and the southern Urals, thus adding some 90 million acres of arable land.

Three small subtropical zones—the

southern segment of the Crimean peninsula, the eastern coast of the Black Sea, and the region south of the Caucasus Mountains—extend over barely 2 percent of Soviet territory. These areas have a mild, pleasant climate similar to that of northern California or the Mediterranean. They enjoy heavy rainfalls, which give them a lush vegetation that includes grapes, oranges, and palm trees. The small enclaves of this Soviet Mediterranean world owe their existence largely to the protective mountain ranges that shelter them from the arctic gales that sweep into the Ukraine.

The fourth geographic region is the mountains, most of which are situated in the southern sectors of the USSR. As has been already noted, European Russia is a huge, flat saucer with few hills and no mountains worth climbing. Western Siberia has the same terrain. The Ural Mountains, picturesque and rich in mineral wealth, are really a chain of gently sloping hills. They form a purely conventional and symbolically low frontier between the European and Asiatic segments of the Soviet Empire. On the other hand, much of the southern frontier areas of the USSR are mountainous, such as those bordering Turkey, Iran, Afghanistan, China, and the Mongolian People's Republic. The highest ranges of the Soviet Union, the Tien Shan and the Pamir, are in the Kirhgiz and Tadjik Soviet republics. The Pamirs are known as "the roof of the world"; they include the 24,590-foot Mount Communism (formerly Mount Stalin). The Caucasus Mountains, between the Caspian and Black seas, can boast of the highest peak in Europe, Mount Elbrus, at 18,470 feet. These mighty mountain ranges circle eastward around the southern fringes of the Caspian Sea into Asia. The lower ranges reach eastward along the Iranian frontier; further east, in Afghanistan, the Hindu Kush peaks merge with the snow-capped Pamirs close to the Indian and Pakistani borders. The numerous streams in these mountains supply ample water for the irrigation of the cotton-growing lands of Soviet Central Asia.

The land between the Caspian Sea and the Tien Shan presently supports some 40 million Muslims. It was once the springboard of the Turkic peoples, the seat of a brilliant Muslim civilization that rivaled those of Cordova, Damascus, and Baghdad. Almost in the heart of Asia, far removed from the great oceans, it is comprised of two regions usually called Russian (or Western) Turkestan and Chinese (or Eastern) Turkestan; the latter is now part of China's Sinkiang province. These areas are bordered to the south by high peaks and to the west by the Caspian Sea. To the north of Turkestan is a desert and the great inland bodies of water, the Aral Sea and Lake Balkhash, the fourth and seventh largest lakes in the world.

Thus in terms of altitude, the Soviet Union is divided into three regions: (1) the low-lying plains of the Baltic lands, Belorussia, the Ukraine, Russia proper, most of Soviet Turkestan, and western Siberia; (2) the low mountains that separate the European plains from those of Siberia (the Urals) and the hills of Kazakhstan; and (3) the mountain regions in the south (the Crimea, the Caucasus, and finally the western region of the Pamirs, the Altai and Sayan ranges, and the hilly regions of the Baikal, the Amur, and the Pacific coast).

East of the Urals, the plain continues into western Siberia to the valley of the Yenisei River, where it turns into the central Siberian upland. Surrounding the east European and west Siberian plains on the south and east are young, rugged mountains. In the very southwestern part of European USSR are the lands acquired during World War II from Romania and Czechoslovakia: Bessarabia, Bukovina, and Carpatho-Ukraine, which separate the bulk of the Soviet Union from the Danubian regions. The Carpathian mountains in these regions are somewhat higher than the Urals and often exceed 6,000 feet. Further to the east, on the Crimean Peninsula, mountains of about 5,000 feet plunge abruptly into the Black Sea. The Great Caucasus, with peaks of about 18,000 feet and no low passes, presents formidable obstacles to both communication and northern climatic influences.

SOVIET ASIA

The broad lowlands to the north of the central Asiatic mountains are deserts punctuated by river valleys, oases, and three large bodies of water: the Caspian Sea, the Aral Sea, and Lake Balkhash. In the north, this desert gradually merges with the western Siberian upland, which is traversed by the basin of the River Ob. Further to the northeast, between the sources of the Irtysh and the Ob rivers, are the northwest–southeast oriented Altai Mountains, which reach heights of about 16,000 feet. Rich in mineral resources, these mountains continue eastward along the borders of the Soviet Union, Mongolia, and China, and encompass the Sayan, Yablonoi, and Stanvoi ranges, which stretch along the Amur River. Lake Baikal, believed to be about 25 million years old, is one of the deepest lakes in the world; it contains nearly one-fifth of the globe's lake water. More than one thousand varieties of plants, fish, and animals are unique to the lake. To its north, sandwiched between the Sayan and Yablonoi ranges and the Yenisei and Lena rivers, is the broad central Siberian plateau. Although its altitude is generally about 2,000 feet above sea level, it occasionally rises to 6,000 feet. The plateau is dissected by numerous mighty rivers, including the 2,500-mile-long Ob and the 2,300-mile-long Yenisei.

Further to the east, along the eastern Arctic Ocean and the Sea of Okhotsk, in the valleys of the Lena, Kolyma, Amur, and Ussuri, stretches eastern Siberia, or the Soviet Far Eastern Region. Eastern Siberia, the traditional destination of large numbers of Russian political and criminal exiles, has become an area of growing strategic importance. It has been a source of discord between China and Soviet Russia since the 1960s. The Far Eastern Region, on which China has made sizable territorial claims, is the largest territorial unit of the Soviet Union. It includes southern Sakhalin and the Kurile Islands (seized from Japan after World War II), as well as the autonomous republic of Birobijan, where Stalin tried to establish the Jewish Autonomous Region in 1928. The northern tip of the Soviet Far Eastern Region is within 20 miles of Alaska; the southern tip comes close to the Japanese islands and borders on China. The chain of the Kuriles, stretched between the Sea of Okhotsk and the Pacific, forms a stepping stone between the Kamchatka peninsula and Japan.

The Soviet Far Eastern Region is the land most distant from the main centers of the USSR. To link it with Moscow, the double-tracking of the Trans-Siberian Railroad was completed in 1937; the 1970s have seen the Baikal–Amur branch connect Lake Baikal with the Pacific coast. The development of jet-plane communication has also helped to diminish the isolation of the Soviet Far Eastern Area. Even so, its strategic position—because of its proximity to the United States, Japan, and China—and its underpopulation make its status rather precarious. Twelve times the size of France, the region is still populated by only about 7 million people.

The dwindling numbers of the original inhabitants have been overtaken in the twentieth century by the Russians and Ukrainians. The Chinese, once found throughout the Amur and the Maritime Territory with its 4,000 miles of Pacific seaboard, were expelled at the end of World War II to Manchuria and other parts of China. The population is unevenly distributed and tends to be centered in large towns like Khabarovsk, Komsomolsk, and Vladivostok. The population concentration in the industrial centers is due to the same conditions that make agriculture very difficult throughout most of the Soviet north: permafrost, scarcity of rain, and brevity of the agricultural season. The only large expanses of cultivated land in the region are the Amur Basin and the southern Pacific coastal area. Despite some economic progress, the

Far Eastern Region is still far from self-supporting in terms of either manufactured goods or food, with the exception of fish. The maritime region has the largest fisheries in the Soviet Union.

The Far Eastern Region also contains considerable mineral wealth, which the Soviet government is trying to develop with the help of foreign capital. Besides huge resources of timber, oil, water power, furs, and fish, the region contains diamonds, gold, mercury, mica, tin, and tungsten. Some 60 percent of Soviet gold is mined in the Far Eastern region, with the Kolyma mines the most productive. The USSR is the second largest producer of gold after South Africa. The inaccessibility of many of these minerals and the high cost of their production, however, reduce their practical value.

RAINFALL AND CROPS

The dearth of rainfall is one of the USSR's most serious natural handicaps. More than a third of its territory has an average annual rainfall and snowfall considered insufficient for agriculture or successful stock-rearing. Indeed, few districts enjoy the average North American rainfall. As a consequence, in many places even a slight shift of the moisture balance or a delay of spring rains can spell famine. Moreover, the available moisture is not well distributed. In the south, where the soil is good, much of the desperately needed rain comes in the form of heavy thunderstorms, which cause short, lush springs that soon fade into hot, arid summers. Throughout most of the extreme north, especially in the tundra regions, the cold and lack of rain are the two climatic enemies of the Soviet people. Verkhoyansk, in northern Siberia, is the coldest human settlement on earth; the thermometer there often drops to minus 120 degrees Fahrenheit. Only where a chain of mountains blocks off the arctic winds and intercepts the rain clouds does the climate change dramatically, as in the Crimea and the Caucasus.

Climate and soil determine the character of farming. The long severe winters mean short growing periods and so dictate the nature of the crops. Winter wheat, for example, is grown in the region of Rostov-on-Don and along the northwestern coast of the Caspian Sea; in eastern Siberia there are no winter crops whatsoever. Some 40 percent of the Soviet soil lies within the permafrost zone where the subsurface soil is permanently frozen to a depth of several hundred feet. Thus Soviet agriculture is greatly hampered by three crucial factors: the scarcity of precipitation, the short harvest season, and the nature of the soil.

Each Soviet geographic zone has its own form of vegetation. In the tundra there is neither forest nor agriculture; only primitive cattle breeding (mostly reindeer farming) is possible. Likewise, in the northern forest zone there is little agricultural development. In contrast, the black soil belt, which has its widest expanse in the Ukraine and from there stretches eastward in a narrowing triangle into western Siberia, is blessed with fertile humus, rich in organic matter and minerals. A wide variety of crops is cultivated throughout this belt: wheat, beet roots, flax, tobacco, sunflowers. There are large deposits of minerals—iron ore and coal—and some oil in the Ukrainian portion of the black soil. The steppe is more favorable to cattle breeding because agriculture would require intense irrigation. The grass desert region of Turkestan (similar to areas of South America and Australia) has for many centuries supplied pastures for innumerable herds of cattle. In irrigated areas of this region, cotton and subtropical fruit are now being successfully cultivated.

SEAS AND WATERWAYS

The Soviet Union is surrounded by ten seas, most of them frozen over during a good part of the year. The Baltic gives the northwestern part of European Russia indirect access to the North Sea and thus to the Atlantic Ocean. The main Baltic ports are Leningrad, Tallin, Riga, Memel (Klaipeda), and Kaliningrad. Through the Turkish straits (the Bosporus and the Dardanelles), the Black Sea connects the southwestern part of the Soviet Union, its Ukrainian and Caucasian domains, with the Mediterranean. Through the Suez Canal, it connects with the Indian Ocean. The principal ports on the Black Sea are Odessa, the naval base of Sevastopol, Nikolaev, Zhdanov, Novorossisk, Poti, and Batum. Five seas of the Arctic Ocean touch the northernmost lands of the Union, and three of the Pacific Ocean (Bering, Okhotsk, and the Sea of Japan) wash Russia's Far Eastern maritime frontiers. There are also the two landlocked seas—the Caspian and the Aral—but they are, for all practical purposes, large, salty, shallow lakes. The principal Caspian ports are Astrakhan, Krasnovodsk, and Baku. Except for the Baltic and Black seas and the Pacific Ocean, most of the waters around the Soviet Union are of little practical value because they are icebound most of the time.

The Soviet Union's long coastline is rather deceptive, for the bulk of Soviet land is located far from seas and oceans. Paradoxically, despite the ten seas that surround it, the USSR is the most landlocked nation in the world: the furthest point from the ocean in central Kazakhstan is about 1,600 miles. "The urge to the sea," to use Robert Kerner's well-known expression, the desire to reach a warm-water outlet, has been one of the drives motivating Muscovy–Russia.[1] The Soviet designs on the eastern Mediterranean and Iran and Afghanistan have been partly inspired by this urge.

The Soviet Union's maritime coast is split into four main sectors: the Black Sea, the Baltic, the Arctic and its subsidiary, the White Sea, and the Pacific Ocean. The Arctic Ocean and the White Sea have been a negligible factor, both politically and economically, in Russia's development. And it was not until the eighteenth century that the Russians reached both the Baltic and the

Black seas. Maritime communications between the Black Sea and the Baltic are difficult enough, but between them and the Pacific the problems are formidable. The Imperial fleet learned this fact firsthand in 1905 during the war with Japan when its Baltic squadron tried desperately to rush to the Far East to rescue its comrades-in-arms in the Pacific. Even the recently built and expanded canals between the Baltic and the White Sea do not permit the passage of seafaring craft. The route from the White Sea to the Far Eastern waters along the northern shores of Siberia, some 4,000 miles, also involves considerable hardship despite such new technological developments as the atomic icebreaker. One drawback of the Soviet naval position is the distance that separates the Baltic and the Black seas from the three oceans, a problem that compels the Soviet Union to maintain separate fleets in the Baltic, the Black Sea, the Arctic, and the Pacific.

It is a severe strategic and economic handicap that most of the Russian ports are icebound for a considerable part of the year. Oddly enough, Murmansk, the northernmost Soviet harbor, is an exception, for the benign Gulf Stream washes this sector of the Arctic coast and makes it generally accessible. On the other hand, the shores of the Gulf of Finland, including the ports of Leningrad, Kronstadt, and Tallin, are frozen from November to April. As a rule, the harbors of the Black Sea are ice-blocked throughout January and February. Vladivostok, precariously suspended at the end of the long trans-Siberian railroads and situated in a region now claimed by China, is icebound for four months in the winter.

The lands where Russia has access to the moderate Baltic and Black seas are inhabited by non-Russian people: the Finns, the Estonians, the Latvians, and the Ukrainians. The outlets from the Baltic are held by the Danes and the Germans, and those from the Black Sea by the Turks. Relatively unhampered access to the Atlantic is through remote Murmansk and the Kola Peninsula. Until recently, these factors have both inhib-

---

[1] Robert J. Kerner, *The Urge to the Sea; the Course of Russian History* (Berkeley and Los Angeles: University of California Press, 1942).

Seas and Rivers of the USSR

ited the development of naval forces and maritime trade and made Russian expansion a painstaking, costly proposition. One of the paradoxes of the Soviet Union's geopolitical situation, therefore, is that although it has some 35,000 miles of coastline—the longest coastline of any nation in the world—it is also the most landlocked of the world's major states.

If until the 1960s the seas have played a relatively small part in Russia's history, the rivers have not. They have had a decisive influence on the nation's destiny. All told, Russia has about 180,000 miles of rivers. The intricate system of rivers that intersects the Eurasian plain has been an important channel of communication. In the past, long, swift, navigable rivers have enabled the Russians to travel more widely than the people of Central or Western Europe. By cutting through forest and marshes, the rivers have deprived these natural obstacles of much of their forbidding character. They have always provided highways for boats and barges in the summer and for skis and sleds in the winter. The main rivers of European Russia (the Dvina, Dnieper, Don, Donets, and Volga) all radiate from the Great Russian plain, not far from Moscow; they originate from either the Valdai Plateau of some 1,000 feet or the marshes and lakes of the central region. Most of them flow in a north–south direction. The city of Moscow started its fantastic imperial career as a settlement at the crossroads of the two greater waterways and trunk lines of trade: the Caspian-Baltic axis of rivers and portages and the west–east route from the Western Dvina to the Volga. Thus the city eventually became a natural pivot of the Eurasian empire that its rulers founded.

Of the half-million rivers and streams of the Soviet Union, the longest are the Amur (2,900 miles), which stretches along most of the Soviet–Chinese frontier and empties into the Sea of Okhotsk, the Lena (2,860 miles), the Ob (2,287 miles), and the Yenisei (2,300 miles). The longest European river, the Volga, is about the same length (2,300

miles); the Dnieper (1,400 miles) and the Don (1,100 miles) are a good deal shorter. Most Russian streams, with their western banks higher than the eastern, meander lazily through the plains. When the snows melt, the rivers often flood the low-lying areas and cause much damage. In European Russia, the economic value of the main rivers is largely curtailed by the nature of the seas into which they empty: The Northern Dvina flows to the icy White Sea, the Dnieper and the Don both empty into the Black Sea, whose outlets are controlled by Turkey, and "Mother Volga" reinforces the dwindling water resources of the Caspian. The Volga has more than a thousand tributaries and drains an area the size of Germany, France, and England combined. As Russia's Mississippi, it winds leisurely from the Belorussian forests to the shores of the Caspian, and through its tributary, the Kama, it extends far to the east, beyond the Urals, and approaches the proximity of the powerful west Siberian river, the Ob. The Volga is, in a way, a symbol of the Eurasian nature of Russia. A remarkable network of canals, especially in European Russia, has tied many of these rivers together.

SLAVIC FAMILY OF NATIONS

The absence of serious natural obstacles in European Russia permits an easy flow of people and invites their control by the strongest, best organized, and most enterprising group. The Russians are the largest branch of the Slavic race, which altogether numbers well over 200 million people. The next largest Slavonic peoples are the Ukrainians and the Poles, over 42 million and 37 million people, respectively. The Slavs belong to the Indo-European family. The origin of the Slavic settlements in Europe is a controversial issue because conclusive evidence is still lacking on the date of the settlements and on the areas the Slavic tribes initially occupied. For our purposes, it is enough to say that by the sixth century they lived in an area of Europe bounded by the Carpathians, the Dnieper, and the Elbe. By that time they had begun to evolve higher forms of social and political organization and had to set up the first tribal principalities under princes of their choice. Probably at the same time these Slavic tribes settled along the principal rivers of the region—not only the Elbe and Dnieper, but the Oder, the Vistula, and the Danube.

The Russians, together with the Ukrainians, Belorussians, Serbs, and Bulgarians, constitute the eastern segment of the Slavonic family. Their ethos, mores, and mentality have been deeply permeated with the Eastern, Greek Orthodox brand of Christianity. For more than a millennium, the Eastern Slavs have been using a modified Greek alphabet while the Western Slavs— the Poles, Slovaks, Croats, Slovenes, and Czechs—have clung to the western variety of the Christian religion (mostly Roman Catholicism) and use Latin script.

The cultural split of the Slavonic race has had a substantial impact on East European history. It has lent a specific coloring to the rivalry between the two most dynamic and ambitious Slavic nations, the Russians and the Poles. For a thousand years each has viewed itself as the champion of its respective brand of civilization and way of life. For a thousand years Russians and Poles have argued and fought over the territory between them, for these two antagonists are not, and never have been, immediate neighbors. They have always been separated by a chain of four peoples: the Letts (or Latvians), the Lithuanians, the Belorussians, and the Ukrainians. The perennial question has been which country shall control, organize, and lead the peoples of the transition zone.

The Russians' feud with the Poles, of course, has not been the sole source of unrest and wars in Eastern Europe. Another great conflict has been that between the Great Russians and the restless and mercurial Ukrainians—the Catalonians of the USSR. The Ukrainians are the second largest Slavic group of the Soviet empire and control vast natural resources placed in a highly strategic location.

Since the sixteenth century the Muscovite–Russian state has been a multinational structure. For as Kliuchevsky stresses in his monumental *History of Russia,* migration and colonization have been fundamental facts of Russian history. When faced with open "frontiers," or large empty spaces such as Siberia in the sixteenth and seventeenth centuries, or the Ukraine (which literally means "frontier") in the eighteenth century, Russian expansion has been both swift and dramatic. When faced with tough opponents, however, the Russians' progress has been rather slow. The Swedes, the Poles, the Tatars, the Turks all barred Russian encroachment for centuries. On these various fronts, fierce battles were fought.

Ethnically, the Soviet Union is the result of several centuries of Muscovite conquests and the absorption of well over a hundred peoples of diverse racial and cultural stock. No single factor can adequately explain this steady, truly phenomenal Russian expansion. Neither the relative weakness of the neighboring peoples, nor the lack of natural barriers confronting the Russians, nor their compulsion to reach the sea and acquire warm-water ports, nor even the Muscovite sense of messianic mission tells the whole story. The restless, elemental impulses that have compelled the Russian people to wander further and further in search of new lands and fresh conquests are among the most controversial subjects of modern psychohistory.

The present-day frontiers of the USSR are a result of spectacular triumphs of Soviet arms in World War II and a series of wartime diplomatic conferences in Teheran (November–December 1943), Yalta (February 1945), and Potsdam (July–August 1945). By the end of the war, the Soviet Union had acquired considerable territory in Europe at the expense of Finland, Estonia, Latvia, Lithuania, Poland, Czechoslovakia, and Romania; and in the Far East, at the expense of Japan. (For a detailed discussion of Soviet territorial gains after World War II, see Chapter 21.)

The largest of the families of people in the Soviet Union are the Great Russians who now make up slightly more than one-half of the population, the Ukrainians, the Belorussians, and the Turkic peoples. The Ukrainians, the second most numerous nationality, possess a separate though similar language and a substantial literature distinctive from the Russian. The Ukrainians' long historic tradition dates back to the ancient Kievan state of the early Middle Ages. The Ukraine has little tradition of full, independent statehood, however, for Ukrainian history is one of centuries of futile revolts and severe repression. Even so, a nationalist movement grew among the Ukrainians of Tsarist Russia (as it had under the Hapsburg Empire) and eventually won a partial victory in the form of the Ukrainian Soviet Socialist Republic. World War II unified all Ukrainian territories under Soviet rule. Stalin's desire to increase the role of the USSR in the international arena and to have three votes instead of one in the United Nations led to the proclamation of the Ukraine and Belorussia as charter members of the United Nations. Both are also represented separately in other international bodies.

The USSR's third most numerous ethnic group is the Belorussians. Belorussia, with Minsk as its capital, covers an area between ethnic Poland, Lithuania, and Russia proper. The Belorussian language resembles that of the neighboring Slavs, yet it is distinct enough to have been recognized as a separate language by the founders of the USSR. The economy of the Belorussian SSR is not so rich and varied as that of the Ukraine; it centers primarily on agriculture, but the lumber and textile industries are becoming increasingly important. As with the Ukrainians, all Belorussians were unified within the Soviet Empire as a result of World War II.

OTHER ETHNIC GROUPS

The large Turkic (or Turko-Tatar) family of nations inhabits a huge region extending from the Mediterranean to Siberia, though most of these people live in Soviet Central Asia. The Turkic ethnic groups are related to the Osmanli Turks of Anatolia. They are also related linguistically, although they speak various dialects. All are united, however, by their Moslem faith, to which they are firmly attached. The most numerous of the Turkic peoples are the Uzbeks, who number over 4 million and live in the south central part of Soviet Turkestan bordering on Afghanistan. Uzbekistan has Tashkent as its capital city and contains such ancient cities as Bukhara and Samarkand, once the capital of Tamerlane's empire. It is the main Soviet cotton-producing area and also has large textile and chemical industries.

Another Turkic group, the Kirgiz, live to the east of the Uzbeks along the border of Sinkiang, or Chinese Turkestan. For centuries the Kirgiz have been nomadic horsemen. Even today their occupation consists largely of tending their herds in mountain pastures. A similarly nomadic Turkic ethnic group, the Kazakhs, inhabit the plains to the north of Kirgizia and Uzbekistan. Following Moscow's decision to cultivate the vast, dry virgin lands of Kazakhstan, their traditional pastoral economy has been undermined by the heavy influx of Russian and Ukrainian settlers. To the southwest of the Kirgiz SSR, in the highlands of Pamir, live the Tadzhiks, a Persian people of Moslem faith who engage in agriculture, animal husbandry, and mining.

To the west of Uzbekistan and north of Iran and Afghanistan, on the desert lands around the southern shore of the Caspian Sea, are the Turkmens; their capital is Ashkhabad. On the western shores of the Caspian Sea live members of another Turkic Moslem ethnic group, the Azerbaijani. Their land possesses remarkable variation. Oil is found in their capital city, Baku;

cotton, rice, tea, fruit, and fish (including sturgeon, the source of caviar) make Azerbaijan a most precious bridge between the Caucasus and Soviet Asiatic possessions.

Other peoples who make up the varied Turko-Tatar family are the Bashkirs—some 1 million strong, who live south of the Urals—and the three Tatar groups—the Volga Tatars, the Siberian Tatars, and those of Crimea. All three Tatar groups are descendants of the various hordes that invaded the Ukrainian-Russian lands in the thirteenth century and exercised a sort of overlordship for more than two hundred years. The Volga Tatars are to be found along the middle reaches of the Volga and around the city of Kazan. The Siberian Tatars live in the western parts of Siberia near Tomsk and in the Tyumen, Tobolsk, and Tara regions. The Crimean Tatars lived in Crimea until World War II, when Stalin ordered them deported to various distant parts of the USSR because of their alleged pro-German sympathies. Only after 1957 did they begin to return individually to their former homes and settlements and to clamor for complete rehabilitation.

The Caucasus, broken into innumerable isolated valleys, is a colorful and baffling mosaic of ethnic groups, some of them numbering only a few thousand people. Besides the Azerbaijani, the two most resilient and dynamic are the Georgians and the Armenians. The Georgians live in a picturesque region on the eastern shores of the Black Sea; their capital city of Tiflis (Tbilisi in Georgian, meaning "warm springs") is rich in manganese deposits, wineries, citrus fruit, and tea plantations. Converted in the fourth century to Orthodoxy by Byzantine missionaries, the Georgians boast of a culture far older than that of Russia. The Armenians of Russia, who inhabit the region north of Turkey and Iran are, like the Georgians, heir to an ancient Christian civilization that predates the Russians'. Enterprising and better educated on the whole than most other Soviet peoples except for the Jews, the Armenian diaspora involved

not only neighboring Georgia and Azerbaijan but the whole of the USSR.

The Jewish population, numbering now over 2 million people, became part of Russia during the partition of the Polish-Lithuanian Commonwealth in the eighteenth century. Most of the Jewish minority of Poland–Lithuania had been originally expelled from German lands and sought shelter in Poland, where the kings granted them considerable liberties. With the annexation of the Lithuanian, Belorussian, and Ukrainian lands in the eighteenth century, the Russians confined the Jewish population to a *Pale of Settlement,* and passed other discriminatory legislation that was abolished only with the downfall of the Tsarist regime in 1917. Today the Jews, survivors of the Nazi extermination policy practiced in the western German-occupied lands of the USSR during World War II, live throughout the Soviet Union, with heavy concentrations in urban centers. Since 1948–1949, they have again been subject to discrimination and, consequently, have tried to leave the USSR.

In addition to these ethnic groups, who were living in Soviet territory prior to World War II, four other nationalities should be mentioned. These peoples were incorporated into Russia when it annexed the three Baltic states of Lithuania, Latvia, and Estonia and took over Bessarabia from the Romanians. While the Lithuanians and Latvians are Baltic peoples and speak a similar language, the Estonians are related to the Finns, the Hungarians, and the Turks. They speak a Finno-Ugric tongue. The Estonians and the Latvians are mostly Lutherans; the Lithuanians are overwhelmingly Roman Catholics. Although Estonia and Latvia were part of the Tsarist empire following Peter the Great's victories at the beginning of the eighteenth century, they throve as small, independent countries between the two world wars. The capitals of the three Soviet Baltic republics are ancient and attractive cities with a great historic tradition: Vilnius (Vilna, in Russian) for

Lithuania, Riga for Latvia, and Tallin for Estonia. The Romanians of Bessarabia, officially referred to as Moldavians, live in the land between the rivers Dniester and Pruth, and their capital is Kishinev. A part of greater Moldavia until 1812, Bessarabia then belonged to the Tsarist empire until the Revolution of 1917, when it was reunited with the rest of Romania until World War II.

Among the major remaining ethnic groups of the Soviet Union are the Germans, the Poles, the Bulgars, the Greeks, the Hungarians, the Koreans, the Kurds, and the Gypsies. Altogether, the USSR officially lists more than 120 ethnic groups, some of them very small. In spite of the Soviet Union's efforts to distribute its population more evenly throughout its vast empire, nearly 75 percent of the people are still found in the European part. Soviet Asia, with 75 percent of the land area of the USSR, supports only about 25 percent of the population.

The Soviet Union possesses the longest frontier of any state in the world. It borders on more countries—thirteen—than any other state in the world. Of these thirteen countries, seven are Asian (Turkey, Iran, Afghanistan, China, Mongolia, North Korea, and Japan), and six are European (Norway, Finland, Poland, Czechoslovakia, Hungary, and Romania). Since the non-Russian ethnic groups of the Soviet Union inhabit its frontier regions and often spill over into bordering states, some of them actually constitute potential national irredenta.

SUMMARY

What is then the gist of the Soviet Union's geopolitical personality? Peninsularity and mosaics of land and sea mark the western extremities of this Euro-Asian land mass. But the outstanding features of the USSR are its northern location, its massiveness, its position astride Europe and Asia, and its continental isolation from direct maritime influence.

Russia is the only major country of Europe that has never even temporarily been a part of the Roman Empire, and it has relatively little in common with the cultural and spiritual heritage of the West. Russia is a typical frontier country and has always lived on the margin of the Western world. In the global view, and in the terminology of the British political geographer Sir Halford MacKinder in his *Democratic Ideal of Reality,* Russia might be said to be a pivotal part of the "World Island" of which Europe forms merely a fringe. Culturally, the Russians have absorbed both European and Asiatic influences, and in so doing they have produced a unique Euroasiatic politicocultural world of their own that is distinct from both Europe and Asia.

SUGGESTED READING

For a list of the basic books, atlases, and bibliographic references about the history and geography of Russia and the Soviet Union, see Paul L. Horecky (ed.), *Russia and the Soviet Union, a Bibliographic Guide to Western Language Publications* (Chicago: University of Chicago Press, 1965), and Horecky, *Basic Russian Publications: A Selected and Annotated Bibliography on Russia and the Soviet Union* (Chicago: University of Chicago Press, 1965).

More specific information may be derived from the following books:

CAMPBELL, ROBERT WELLINGTON, *Soviet Economic Power: Its Organization, Growth, and Challenge.* Boston: Houghton Mifflin, 1960.

CHEW, ALLEN F., *An Atlas of Russian History: Eleven Centuries of Changing Borders.* New Haven and London: Yale University Press, 1970.

CRESSEY, GEORGE B., *Soviet Potentials: A Geographic Appraisal.* Syracuse, N.Y.: Syracuse University Press, 1962.

DUBINSKAYA, LIDIYA, *The Soviet Union. A Guide and Reference Book.* Moscow: Raduga Publishers, 1985.

GREGORY, JAMES, *Russian Land, Soviet People.* London and New York: Pegasus, 1968.

HOLZNER, LUTZ AND JEANNE M. KNAPP (Eds.), *Soviet Geography Studies In Our Time. A Festschrift for Paul E. Lydolph.* Milwaukee: The University of Wisconsin, 1987.

HOOSON, DAVID J. M., *The Soviet Union.* Belmont, Calif.: Wadsworth Publishing Company, 1966.

JACKSON, WILLIAM A. D., The Russo-Chinese Borderlands. Princeton, N.J.: Princeton University Press, 1962.

KATZ, ZEV, R. ROGERS, and F. HARNED, eds, *Handbook of Major Soviet Nationalities.* New York: Free Press, 1975.

KERNER, ROBERT J., *The Urge to the Sea.* Berkeley and Los Angeles: University of California Press, 1942.

LYDOLPH, PAUL E., *Geography of the U.S.S.R.* Elkhart Lake, Wis.: Misty Valley Publishing, 1979.

MELLOR, ROY, *The Soviet Union and Its Geographic Problem.* New York: Macmillan, 1982.

MIKHAILOV, NIKOLAI N., *Glimpses of the USSR: Its Economy and Geography.* Moscow: Foreign Language Publishing House, 1960.

Oxford Regional Economic Atlas: U.S.S.R. and Eastern Europe. New York: Oxford University Press, 1963.

PARKER, W. H., *An Historical Geography of Russia.* Chicago: Aldine Publishing Company, 1969.

SHABAD, THEODORE, *Geography of the U.S.S.R.: A Regional Survey.* New York: Columbia University Press, 1951.

SHIMKIN, DIMITRI B., *Minerals: Key to Soviet Power.* Cambridge, Mass.: Harvard University Press, 1953.

WESSON, ROBERT G., *The Russian Dilemma: A Political and Geopolitical View.* New Brunswick, N.J.: Rutgers University Press, 1974.

CHAPTER 2

The Russian State Tradition

Human beings are shaped not only by their physical environment, but also by generations of historic experience. Without entering into intricate controversies about the origins of Russia as a state, one may say that the first large-scale organization to function on the territory of the present-day Soviet Union was the work of the Norman warrior-traders (known as Vikings), interacting with local Slavic and Finnish elements.

By 862, the Vikings, or Varangians, whom the Finns called *Ruotsi* and the local Slavs *Rusi,* had managed to organize the hitherto rather amorphous host of Slavic and Finnish tribes along the Dvina–Dnieper waterway into a loose federation of towns and trading stations that actually resembled more the East India or Hudson Bay Companies than a medieval feudal state. The federation, often called by its Finnish-Norman name of *Rus,* centered around the most important commercial emporium, Kiev, strategically situated at the junction of the

Dnieper and the Desna rivers. The Dvina–Dnieper waterway was a major trade route that connected Scandinavia with the richest and most powerful center of the early medieval world—the East Roman or Byzantine Empire, with its capital in Constantinople. The Byzantine Empire was at that time a large market for furs, wax, hides, amber, and slaves, and attracted merchants from all over the world. Among them were the adventurous Norman Vikings, who tried to get there from Scandinavia not only through the Mediterranean, then infested by the Arabs, but also through the combined overland and water route leading from the Gulf of Finland through the Western Dvina and the Dnieper to the Black Sea. The Slavs and Finns through whose area the Vikings passed must have been impressed by the superior skills and discipline of the Scandinavian warrior-traders, because in 862 they submitted to their rule without much opposition.

KIEVAN RUS

One of the crucial events in the early period of Rus was the acceptance of Christianity in 988 by Prince Vladimir, a descendant of Rurik, the Varangian prince and ruler of Novgorod. Unlike what had happened to the Western Slavs, the Gospel came to Kiev not from Rome, which was becoming an important cultural and political center of the Western world, but from the decaying Eastern Greek or Byzantine Empire, which was already involved in an ecclesiastic schism with Rome. Along with Greek or Orthodox Christianity, Kievan Rus acquired from Constantinople its written language, its art, and its philosophy of government and State–Church relations. These relations were based on the concept of the unity of secular and religious authority, symbolized in the person of an autocratic ruler, or Caesaropapism. The language the Greek missionaries brought with them to Kiev was a Bulgarian-Macedonian dialect of the region of Saloniki and a modified Greek alphabet. The dialect, which the two chief missionaries of the Southern Slavs, Cyril and Methodius, had used in preaching the Gospel to the Slavic tribes in the Balkans and Moravia, soon became the literary and ecclesiastic language of the Kievan state, the present-day Church Slavonic.

The Kievan Rus was a loose federation of Finnish and Slavic towns and trading stations stretching through the region between the Baltic and Black seas along the Dvina–Dnieper waterway. The Kievan state was controlled by an oligarchic elite, which was largely of Norman-Varangian stock. The Norman rulers considered Rus as their property and limited their exercise of power to the collection of tribute. Soon the pirate-traders settled down, intermarried, and gradually merged with the natives and produced the upper social stratum of Kievan nobility. Only they were entitled to own land and to bear arms. They also supplied candidates for higher ecclesiastic offices that initially had been overwhelmingly occupied by Greeks. Although the northern segment of

the Kievan Federation, centering around Novgorod, developed a mixture of urban oligarchy and democracy exemplified by popular assemblies of all free citizens; this system, after the Mongol invasion, was largely limited to Novgorod and a few cities in the north like Pskov. Kiev, more under Byzantine influence and in danger of constant raids by the nomadic tribes of Asia, stuck to a more autocratic system of government.

In the eleventh and twelfth centuries, Rus reached a high level of economic and cultural development. While agriculture and handicraft played some role in the life of the federation, trade with Byzantium, Persia, and Scandinavia was the life blood of the Kievan state. Trade, however, especially with the south, was constantly hampered by raids by the barbarian tribes that emerged from the steppes of Central Asia, one wave after another. During the twelfth century, these constant attacks by the nomadic tribes undermined the Kievan federation's commerce and depopulated and ruined its eastern approaches. Consequently, the population of Kievan Rus began to migrate in two directions. One stream flowed west, toward the region of the western Bug and the upper Dniester, to Volhynia and Galicia; another migratory movement flowed northward toward the lands of the Oka, the Moskva and the upper Volga, where marshes and forests provided a natural shelter against the raids of the nomads. The nomadic invasions chased the population from the devastated southern regions and thereby contributed to the settlement of the central forest lands, destined to be the heartland of the future Muscovite-Russian state.

The final blow to the decaying Kievan federation was dealt by the Mongol or Tatar invasions of the thirteenth century. The Tatars, who originally inhabited the Mongolian plateau north of the Gobi desert, were a savage, quick, and fast-growing group of horsemen, herdsmen, and hunters. One of the Tatar chieftains, Ghengis Khan, united the quarreling tribes and marched against his overlord, the Emperor of China. The Tatars broke through the Great Wall and captured Peking in 1215. After having enlisted the services of Chinese military and administrative experts, they turned toward Central Asia, Iran, Northern India, and, finally, Europe. In 1236, they appeared on the Volga, and in the spring of 1237 invaded the Dnieper valley. Kiev was captured and razed in December 1240, while most of its people were slaughtered. The Tatars devastated the land—burning, pillaging, and taking thousands of slaves, mostly women and children. The main city of northern Rus, Novgorod, was spared through the payment of tribute.

After having destroyed Kievan Rus, the Mongols proceeded westward toward Poland, Bohemia, and Hungary. In April 1241, they crushed a mixed Polish-Bohemian-German force at Legnica (Liegnitz) in Silesia. In 1242, a struggle for succession after the death of Ghengis Khan prevented the Tatars, who had meanwhile reached the Adriatic Sea, from exploiting their unprecedented victories. The Mongol invaders withdrew to their base in Mongolia, abandoning Poland, Bohemia, and Hungary, but not the bulk of the Kievan Rus. Soon the empire of Ghengis Khan split into several segments. Meanwhile, Ghengis Khan's grandson, Kubla Khan (1260–1294), had subdued all of China and established the Mongol dynasty on the throne of Peking. Another segment of the Tatars, with its capital at Sarai on the lower Volga, the "Golden Horde," kept the northeastern Rus, including Novgorod, as its tributary.

THE EMERGENCE OF MOSCOW

The Tatar raids were one of the worst plagues that Eastern Europe as a whole suffered during the Middle Ages. For the lands of Kievan Rus, they were a catastrophe. Devastated, depopulated, and for generations separated from stimulating contacts with Western civilization, the lands of the Dnieper valley, as well as the territor-

ies to their northeast around Vladimir and Moscow, stagnated under the Tatar yoke. The Tatars, who themselves converted to Islam only in the fourteenth century, were tolerant in religious affairs but greedy for tribute and slaves, especially women and children. As a result of Tatar raids, the lands of the Dnieper valley were devastated and depopulated. Many survivors fled to the north and northeast. As a consequence, during the thirteenth and fourteenth centuries the lands around present-day Moscow were settled by refugees from the south who sought shelter in the northern forests from the repeated Tatar raids. The city of Moscow stood on the Moskva River, which had great economic importance because it connected the river system of the middle Oka with that of the upper Volga. The population attracted to its lands and the large volume of trade on the Moskva River brought in taxes and customs duties.

The princes of Moscow skillfully profited from the location of their capital at the intersection of two important migration and trade routes that went from the north to the northeast and from the north to the south. To facilitate the collection of tribute, the Tatar Khans would appoint one of the native princes to act as their instrument in administering the conquered lands on behalf of the Golden Horde. Since the princes of Muscovy struck the Khans as the most ruthless and obsequious of the princes of Rus, they were appointed tax collectors and administrators of justice. This gave to the Muscovite princes definite advantages over the other regional rulers and descendants of Rurik and thus launched them on an unprecedented imperial career.

While enjoying the favors of the Tatars as their agents, the rulers of Muscovy took advantage of their position to enhance their power and enlarge their domain. Their policy combined shrewd marriages with conquest and purchase of surrounding territory. While princely domains around them were subdivided, Muscovite rulers as a rule willed their inheritance to the oldest son. Freedom from Tatar raids and relative prosperity attracted settlers, commerce, and gave Moscow political prestige. In the fourteenth century, the privileged and sheltered city attracted the Metropolitans of Kiev, who eventually settled in Moscow. Thus, by the end of the fourteenth century, Moscow had emerged as the most important political and ecclesiastic center of the Tatar-controlled portion of the former Kievan Rus.

The other parts of the now atomized former Kievan federation had a different fate. The city-republic of Novgorod, far away to the north and fairly secure from the Tatar raids behind the belt of forest and marshes, developed into an affluent trading center. The city soon joined the German commercial league, the Hansa, and prospered on fur, hides, wax, and all sorts of naval stores, until the close of the fifteenth century. The westernmost fringes of the former Kievan federation—present-day Belorussia, the western Ukraine, or Volhynia, and Galicia—fell under the influence of Lithuania and Poland, both better able to protect their inhabitants from Tatar encroachments. At the end of the fourteenth century, Poland and Lithuania established a personal union, and set up a confederation known as the Polish-Lithuanian Commonwealth, which was to last for about four centuries, until its partition at the end of the eighteenth century. During the fourteenth and fifteenth centuries, by skillfully combining dynastic marriages and conquests, the Lithuanians and Poles acquired most of the Dvina–Dnieper waterway. The Grand Duchy of Muscovy and the city republic of Novgorod, however, remained outside their reach.

MUSCOVY AS HEIR OF THE TATARS AND BYZANTIUM

The middle of the fifteenth century opened great vistas to the ambitious Muscovite rulers. The Turks captured Constantinople in 1453, while the decaying Golden Horde split into three Khanates: Kazan and As-trakhan on the Volga, and Crimea. Each of these opportunities was in turn exploited by the princes of Moscow. By far the most important was the final disintegration of the Golden Horde. Seeing the growing weakness of the Tatars, Ivan III (1440–1505) simply refused to pay his annual tribute and homage in 1480. The Tatars, divided among themselves, were unable to reassert their power. Thus the "Mongol yoke" undramatically disappeared overnight. Yet it left as lasting an imprint on the people and lands that had been under their overlordship as any other single factor in Muscovite-Russian history. The Mongol yoke lasted in Rus for some 240 years, roughly from 1240 to 1480, longer than any other epoch in the history of the land. (The subsequent Muscovite period lasted only 223 years, from 1480 to 1703; the later imperial era stretched for 214 years, from 1703 to 1917.)

The "yoke" has had a far-reaching and lasting effect on Muscovite mentality and institutions. First, Rus, isolated from Western influences, never used Roman law or partook in the great religious movements of the West. It was not affected by the Renaissance, the Reformation, and the development of flourishing urban centers and universities. Second, for nearly ten generations the Russian princes watched with awe and envy the military skills and political efficiency of the Tatars. They tended to ascribe the Tatars successes primarily to the discipline and slavish obedience enforced by the Khans not only on their conquered peoples, but also on their own subjects. This bolstered the latent autocratic tradition taken over from Byzantium. Medieval Muscovite society was overwhelmingly dependent on the autocratic ruler who, following the Tatar patterns, subjugated all social groups and made them serve his purposes.

Moreover, the Muscovite rulers took over from their masters many political and administrative institutions. For instance, the census, tax collection, and postal system of the Muscovite state, as well as its methods of spying and torturing, were borrowed from

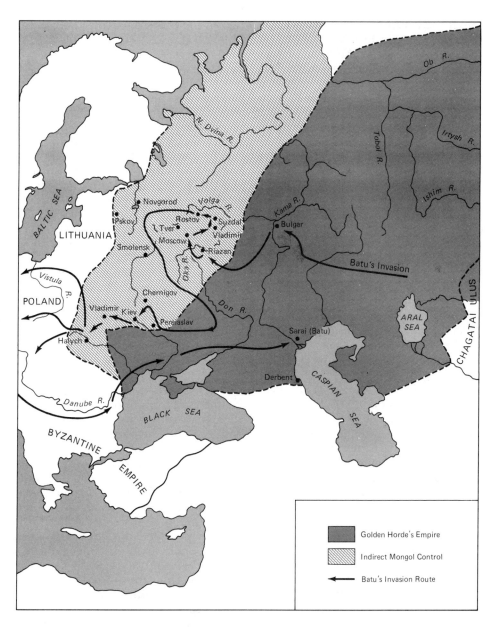

the Mongols. Since they admired Tatar military efficiency, the Muscovite princes tried to imitate their pattern of army organization, training, and tactics. Up to recent times these traditions were still visible, for example, in the scouting tactics of the Cossacks. The Tatar influence could for centuries also be observed in a variety of details: in the long, oriental dress of the Muscovite people, in their cooking, in their vocabulary. For instance, the Russian words for whip, shackles, inn, horse, money, and treasury are of Mongol origin; so too is the word cossack. Finally, during centuries of coexistence, a great deal of Tatar blood has been injected into Muscovite veins. A considerable segment of the Russian aristocracy traced its origins to the Tatar princes.

After the overthrow of the Mongol yoke in 1480, Muscovite princes continued to follow the Tatar examples: they regarded the persons and possessions of their subjects as their property, and the entire land as a source of tribute and recruits. The tribute the Muscovite rulers used to levy for the Tatars was now collected for their own benefit. The main purpose of their despotic regime was to continue squeezing the maximum income out of the people, as the Tatars had done. Thus, Tatar rule shaped a society deficient in those political, economic, and cultural institutions the existence of which is a precondition of a pluralistic body politic of the Western type. This was a bad civic school for the Muscovites, both the rulers and the ruled.

The second important event of the fifteenth century was the capturing of Constantinople by the Ottoman Turks in 1453 and the downfall of the Byzantine Empire. Moscow's connections with Constantinople were largely limited to the recognition of the traditional primacy of its Patriarchate over all other Orthodox Churches. With passing generations, the umbilical cord uniting the Orthodox Church of the Rus–Muscovy had become weaker. The cultural–spiritual dependence of Muscovy on Constantinople was largely channeled through the Orthodox hierarchy; traditionally, the bishops and metropolitans, although actually chosen by the Grand Prince, were endorsed by the Byzantine Patriarchs. This began to change after 1439, when the Muscovite Church rejected the accord of the Union of Florence between the Greek Orthodox Church of Constantinople and Rome as an act of apostasy. The Grand Duke of Muscovy immediately took advantage of the break and began to appoint his own bishops without any reference to the Patriarch of Constantinople. The last vestiges of traditional dependence on the senior Orthodox patriarchate disappeared almost automatically when the capital of the Byzantine Empire fell into the hands of the "infidel" Turkish Sultan in 1453.

As a consequence of the fall of Constantinople and the overthrow of the Tatar yoke, the Grand Dukes of Muscovy emerged as the only fully sovereign Orthodox rulers of importance. Ivan III married a daughter of the last Emperor of Byzantium, took over his coat of arms, the black double-headed eagle, and assumed the title of Caesar, or Tsar in Russian. The old theory that the church and state could not exist without one another was now re-emphasized in Moscow with increased vigor and given new meaning. After 1453, Muscovy came to regard itself as the sole citadel of the Orthodoxy, beleaguered by infidels, heretics, and apostates, while the Grand Duke of Muscovy was its sole secular shield. This was immediately acknowledged by the Muscovite hierarchy, eager to assure itself a protector against internal and external dangers: a reform movement at home, and the Catholic Church of Poland–Lithuania in the West. In return for this protection, the Muscovite clergy, brought up in the centuries-old tradition of Byzantine Caesaropapist submission, gave the autocrat its full support. The popular saying, "One God in Heaven, one Sovereign on Earth," was strongly backed by the hierarchy. As a Muscovite monk, Joseph of Volokolamsk, put it: "In his mortal form [the Tsar] resembles all men, but in his power he is like unto Almighty God." Moreover, the Orthodox Church provided the Muscovite monarchy with a whole array of convenient legends, one of which traced Rurik's ancestry to Emperor Augustus of Rome. The crowning piece of this mythmaking was the allegation that Moscow was the "Third Rome." This was suggested in the greetings sent to Ivan III in 1475 by Monk Philotheos, Abbot of Pskov monastery:

The Church and ancient Rome fell because of the Apollinarian heresy; as the second Rome, the Church of Constantinople, it has been hewn by the axes of Ishmaelites; but this third new Rome, the Holy Apostolic Church, under Thy mighty rule, shines throughout the entire world more brightly than the sun. All the Orthodox Christian realms have converged into their own. Thou art the sole Autocrat of the Universe, the only Caesar of the Christians. . . . Two Romes have fallen, but the Third stands, and no fourth can ever be. . . .

Soon the Messianic message of Abbot Philotheos, combined with the dynastic claims of the Rurik dynasty and Slavic nationalistic urges, became the program of the Muscovite Tsars, and later of the Russian Emperors. The doctrine of Moscow as "the Third Rome" evolved into a highly complex national and religious philosophy and survived to modern times, accompanied by various historically conditioned interpretations. Up to the time of the Revolution of 1917, all Russian rulers—autocratic heads of State as well as secular heads of the Orthodox Church of the Empire—embodied the Caesaropapist concept of power, both spiritual and temporal. As temporal heads of the Orthodox Church and its protectors, they were surrounded by a semi-religious halo, and their persons were treated as sacred.

THE MUSCOVITE SYSTEM

The second half of the fifteenth century produced in Muscovy a unique political system, a blend of Mongol despotism, Byzantine Caesaropapism, and local Slavic-Finnish tradition. This peculiar system was already striking at the time of Basil III (1505–1533), son and successor of Ivan III, and father of Ivan IV, or "the Terrible" (1533–1584). This phenomenon puzzled Baron Sigmund Herberstein, who traveled to Russia as the Ambassador of Holy Roman emperors Maximilian I and Ferdinand I. Herberstein noted in his diary that the Tsar had unlimited control over the lives and property of his subjects. Nobody dared to oppose him. His will was God's will. "These people enjoy slavery more than freedom."

Marquis de Custine, who went to the Russia of Nicholas I in 1839, summed up his observations by concluding that "The political state of Russia may be defined in one sentence: it is a country in which the government says what it pleases, because it alone has the right to speak. . . . In Russia fear replaces, that is, paralyzes thought."

Parallel to the consolidation of the Tsarist theocratic absolutism was a social system, the foundation of which was the attachment to the land of most of the rural population. The primitive conditions of Russia's economy resulted in a shortage of ready cash. This made the rulers of Muscovy pay their servants not in money but in landed estates. For their services as officers and officials, the ruler would grant landed estates on the condition of service, which terminated only by death or severe illness of the grantee. The estates could be sold, exchanged, or even passed from father to son only with the prince's permission, and only on condition of continuing service by the new owner. To allow the gentry to serve the sovereign, the gentry had to be assured that their lands would be duly cultivated. Hence peasants were assigned to the estates and obliged to cultivate the master's land. In return, the masters would leave a certain amount of that land to the peasant for his family's support.

The right of freedom to roam about had been firmly rooted in the customary law of the early Rus. The Russian peasant could go where he pleased at a time when his Western counterpart was still tied to the land. But as Tatar raids and exactions caused a severe scarcity of manpower, the princes and landowners resorted to all sorts of tricks to limit the right of movement and fix the fluid population to the land. This came to be applied ultimately not only to the peasants but also to the members of the prince's retinue, who had customarily been free to enroll in the service of a prince of their choice. Thus the enserfment of the peasants was closely intertwined with the attachment of the gentry to their estates. Since the masters were also magistrates for their peasants, the power of the lord over his "souls" (as the serfs were called) was for all practical purposes complete, despite the vestigial legal limitations. By the middle of the seventeenth century, the serfs were already treated like chattel; they were bought and sold, exchanged and pawned; they lost the right to appeal to the state against the injustices of their owners. The only exception to this was high treason. Since they owned serfs, the Muscovite gentry were in turn bondsmen of the all-powerful Autocrat. As his vassals, they were at the mercy of the despot; they owned the land only as long as they served their sovereign; like the serfs, they also could be deprived of land, moved from one job to another, or transferred to a different place.

Let us reexamine the peculiarities of Muscovy's social development, which was largely shaped by a mixture of Byzantine and Tatar traditions. The forces that opposed the rise of royal absolutism in the West were either very weak or altogether absent in Muscovy–Russia. The Church was a captive of its Greek Caesaropapist heritage; unlike the Western Church, it never claimed equality with, let alone superiority over, secular rule. The Orthodox hierarchy never produced its Gregory VII or Innocent III. It had experienced neither its struggle for investiture nor its Canossa.[1] This political dependence had far-reaching consequences. Pressed by Islam and by Roman Catholicism, the Orthodox Church became withdrawn, intolerant, and largely ignorant. It never developed an intense intellectual life or a deeper involvement in vital social issues. Unlike the Western churches, it never founded universities. As early as the sixteenth century, it was no longer an autonomous body that could counterbalance the power of the state, but was rather more like its agency. Until the end, in Imperial Russia the Church was the subservient instrument of the State.

The feudal lords were another social force that could have challenged the autocracy, but in Muscovy they were never as strong and well organized as in Central or Western Europe. Hereditary property in landed estates existed for a short period of time in Muscovy prior to the consolidation of the ducal absolutism at the close of the fifteenth century. After 1480, as soon as the Grand Duke strengthened his power, he proceeded to replace private property with tenure conditional on service. Between the end of the fifteenth century and 1785, Russian squires held their land on the Tsar's sufferance. Consequently, the Muscovite-Russian nobility was largely composed of shifting elements without deeper local roots; the "serving gentry" was moved from place to place in accordance with the needs of the state or simply at the whim of the Autocrat.

Another social stratum that played a considerable role in the West—the merchants—constituted in Muscovy an overwhelmingly rural society, a relatively small and weak group. Moreover, they were also compelled to serve the State, or, more exactly, its ruler, who treated the State as his property. The only two independent trading communities with an oligarchic tradition, the northern, largely commercial city-republics of Novgorod and Pskov, were overwhelmed and destroyed in the fifteenth century by their Muscovite rival. The rest of the Russian merchant class did not reveal much appetite or ability for self-government even when offered it during the eighteenth and nineteenth centuries. Alliances between burghers and other social groups or the Crown, so characteristic of West European development, were never seriously attempted in Muscovy–Russia. The weakness of Russian liberalism, so striking during the period of the "Great Reforms" of the late nineteenth century and during the constitutional period of 1905–1917, can be largely traced to the anemic

---

[1] A humble pilgrimage to beg papal forgiveness was made by the Holy Roman Emperor of the German nation to Canossa in 1077.

weakness and passivity of the Russian middle class, especially the urban bourgeoisie.

MUSCOVITE EXPANSION

Besides the quick consolidation of Tsarist absolutism and the enserfment of the peasants, another characteristic feature of Muscovite–Russian development was the phenomenal territorial expansion of Muscovy in all directions. With the annexation of the Tatar city-states Kazan and Astrakhan during the sixteenth century, Muscovy acquired its first major non-Slavic territory. From the Volga bases a rapid, largely spontaneous, movement developed; it proceeded eastward beyond the Urals and toward the Caspian Sea, Central Asia, and the Pacific Ocean. Siberia, a subcontinent larger than the United States, was conquered in a short sixty-two years by groups of Cossack adventurers and common criminals. By 1643, the Muscovites were already on the Pacific coast. Muscovy's territorial expansion was unprecedented in history. In 1300 the Duchy of Muscovy covered approximately 20,000 square kilometers; in 1462 when Ivan III ascended the throne, it reached 430,000 and continued to grow at the rate of 35,000 square kilometers a year for the next century and a half. As early as 1600 it was as large as the rest of Europe, and by the middle of the seventeenth century—even before the conquests of Peter the Great—Muscovy was the largest country in the world.

There are many reasons for Muscovy's expansion that go far beyond the loudly proclaimed desire to "gather the lands of Rurik," or the overrated "urge to the sea." Not the least important of these was the perpetual hunger for fresh resources, especially agricultural; in a primitive, extensive economy, more and more land was needed. Every new conquest was usually followed by the deportation of large groups of the local population and by Muscovite peasant colonization. As the great Russian historian,

Vasily O. Kliuchevsky, bluntly put it: "Colonization is the essence of Russian history." Colonization was accompanied by distribution of landed estates to deserving officers, officials, and Orthodox monasteries. Of some 800,000 serfs whom Catherine II (1762–1796) presented as gifts to her supporters and lovers during her reign, well over half came from the lands seized from the partition of Poland–Lithuania. These expansive and centralistic tendencies were paralleled by the desire to proselytize and spread the Russian language and culture and the Greek Orthodox faith to the furthest Tsarist domains.

By the beginning of the nineteenth century, with the incorporation of Finland (1809) and Poland (1815), about half of the Empire's population was composed of ethnic minorities. Yet the autocracy insisted on treating the Empire as if it were a unitary state and tried to impose its absolutist system on all its subjects. Whatever special powers St. Petersburg was compelled to concede to certain parts of the Empire (like the constitutions of the Grand Duchy of Finland between 1809 and 1899 or of the Kingdom of Poland between 1815 and 1831) were reluctantly given and only under pressure. Moreover, these concessions were made in view of existing peculiar conditions, and were regarded as temporary expedients necessitated by the wish to accommodate these new peripheral acquisitions to the essentially centralistic structure of the state. The Russians moreover resented the liberties granted to "the conquered peoples" and considered those concessions unjustified, discriminatory, and hence humiliating to the Russians themselves. Hence the tendency to cancel or at least curtail these liberties.

Largely as a result of its westward expansion, by the second half of the sixteenth and the beginning of the seventeenth century, Muscovy—like Japan in the nineteenth century—came into ever closer contact with the more advanced outside world, especially Sweden and Germany. The Tsars' realization that Western civilization was technologically superior made them launch a series of reforms aimed mainly at modernizing their backward instruments of power and imperial expansion. Consequently, most reforms were limited to military and naval matters and rejected Western ideals and the political institutions that stood behind them.

The most striking representative of the new dynasty that ascended the Muscovite throne in 1613—the Romanovs—was Peter I, known as "the Great," (1682–1725). Impatient, restless, and often reckless, Peter brought a large number of Western teachers and technical experts to Muscovy, and with them embarked upon a policy of streamlining his antiquated domains. His reforms were not so much introduced as inflicted on his subjects. Those who opposed them, he punished harshly. He reorganized the old Muscovite Army and founded the Russian Navy. Peter fostered education by means equally as ruthless as those he employed in his other reforms. It was he who laid the foundation of modern Russian industry. The brunt of his reforms was borne by the peasant masses already firmly shackled by serfdom and assigned to the land to serve the serving gentry. Peter went one step further and put all of the peasant's property, as well as his body, at the master's disposal. He also granted to the gentry the right to increase the peasant's obligations at will, and even to send him to penal servitude. Beards, a symbol of the old mores, were forbidden. For Peter, the Muscovite beard was as much a symbol of tradition as the Turkish fez was for Kemal Atatürk in 1920s.

The rule of Peter the Great marked the last stage in the process of chaining the Orthodox Church to the state. In 1721, Peter abolished the office of the Patriarch and substituted a Church Council, the Holy Synod, composed of bishops, but headed by a lay official appointed by the Tsar. The clergy became simply a part of a huge bureaucratic machine by means of which Peter ruled his expanding realm. The treatment of Russian Orthodox clergymen as

Emperor Peter I

government officials continued after Peter's reign. This included the payment of salaries as well as the award of ranks and orders. Until 1863, junior members of the clergy were submitted to flogging, like enlisted men in the armed forces.

Peter's desire to obtain access to the sea, to open "a window to the West," implied a challenge to Sweden, then the master of the Baltic. The protracted conflict, known in history as the "Great Northern War" (1699–1721), was concluded by the Treaty of Nystadt (1721). As a result of his triumph over Sweden, Peter acquired the entire south coast of the Gulf of Finland, including Ingria, Estonia, and Livonia. Peter, who hated Moscow as a symbol of the old, largely medieval traditions, built a new capital in the Finnish marshes at the mouth of the Neva River on the land newly conquered from Sweden. From 1703 to 1918, St. Petersburg, not "Holy Moscow," was the capital of the Empire. The Tsardom of Muscovy was meanwhile officially renamed the "Russian Empire," the new term "Russia" being the Latinized form of Rus.

Peter the Great desperately attempted to bridge the gap between his country and the

West and tried to civilize his country by barbarous means. With his ferocious passion for modernization, his contempt for tradition, and his ruthless methods, he has often been called "the first Bolshevik."

PETER'S SUCCESSORS

Under Peter's successors, reformatory zeal slackened considerably for two generations or so, but was felt strongly by Catherine II (1762–1796). Her long rule, brilliant in the international arena, was marred, however, by her neglect of socioeconomic issues, especially of the soaring peasant problem. By the close of the eighteenth century the issue of serfdom became the dominant issue of the Tsarist Empire. Elevated to the throne by a camarilla of aristocratic officers, Catherine freely distributed estates and serfs to her supporters and lovers. Since peasants working on the estates belonging to the Crown enjoyed a better legal and economic status, their transfer to private hands meant a considerable worsening of their lot. During Catherine's reign, the lot of the serf population and its legal and economic situation hit bottom, for Catherine not only confirmed the decrees of Peter the Great, but enlarged upon them. For all practical purposes, the status of the serfs was equalized with that of the slaves. No wonder, therefore, that in 1773–1775 her Empire witnessed the greatest and most horrible of all the peasant rebellions so characteristic of Muscovite-Russian history. The uprising, led by a veteran Cossack, Yemelian Pugachëv, shook the very foundation of the Empire, and only the use of a large army crushed the rebellion.[2]

While Peter the Great established Russia firmly on the shores of the Baltic, Catherine

II wrested from the Turks the northern littoral of the Black Sea, including the Crimea. During two brilliant campaigns, the Russian fleet roamed the Mediterranean. Catherine was the first Romanov ruler to proclaim loudly that Constantinople was her goal and to claim openly a protectorate over the Christians of the Ottoman Empire.

A special feature of her reign was her Polish policy. While Peter the Great considered Poland–Lithuania as Russia's protectorate and as a buffer in the West, Catherine partitioned the ancient Commonwealth three times (in 1772, 1793, and 1795), in partnership with Prussia and Austria. The two Teutonic powers annexed most of ethnographic Poland, while Catherine appropriated not only the lands that had formed part of the old Kievan state, like Belorussia and the Ukraine, but also ethnic Lithuania, which had never belonged to "Rurik's patrimony."

Later, in 1815, after the Napoleonic Wars, the acquisition of Central Poland by Alexander I (1801–1825) created a highly explosive "Polish problem," which became one of the endemic issues of the Tsarist Empire. A series of Polish uprisings (in 1794, 1830–1831, and 1863–1864) had an adverse effect on Russia's domestic stability as well as on its international relations. First, the existence of the highly explosive Polish question created a certain community of interest with the other reactionary partitioning powers, Prussia–Germany and Austria, thus strengthening within the Empire the conservative, Teutonic elements. The German influence became very powerful in Tsarist Russia beginning at the time of Peter the Great with his acquisition of the Baltic provinces and their rich and influential German landowning and merchant class. All this created internal tensions and affected

---

[2] Some historians trace the origins of the modern Russian revolutionary movement to the peasant rebellions that were such a striking feature of the Tsarist realm in the seventeenth and eighteenth centuries. All of these uprisings, however, including the fiercest of all–the rebellion of Pugachëv at the close of the eigh-

teenth century–were merely anarchic outbursts devoid of any concrete political program. Moreover, practically all of these peasant revolts were directed not against the institution of Tsardom, but in defense of the monarch, allegedly misled by his corrupt officials and the greedy gentry.

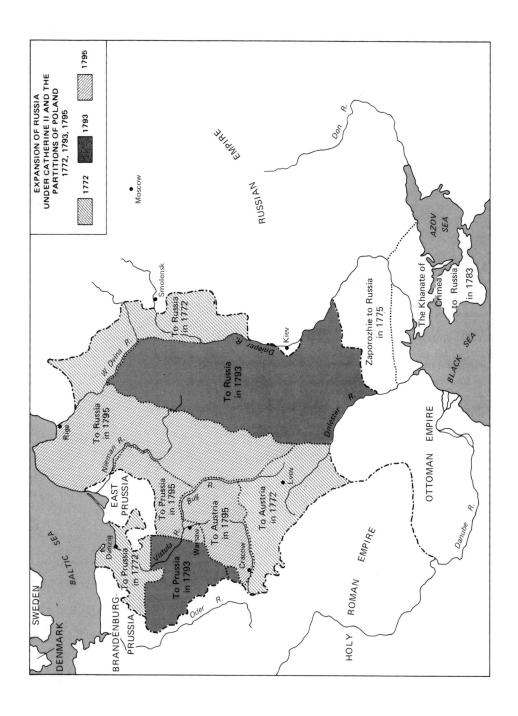

EXPANSION OF RUSSIA
UNDER CATHERINE II AND THE
PARTITIONS OF POLAND
1772, 1793, 1795

1772

1793

1795

RUSSIAN EMPIRE

Moscow

Don R.

Smolensk

To Russia
in 1772

Kiev

Dnieper R.

Zaporozhie to Russia
in 1775

AZOV
SEA

The Khanate of Crimea
to Russia
in 1783

BLACK SEA

W. Dvina R.

Riga

To Russia
in 1795

To Russia
in 1793

Dniester R.

OTTOMAN EMPIRE

Niemen R.

EAST
PRUSSIA

To Prussia
in 1795

Lvov

To Austria
in 1772

Bug R.

Danube R.

BALTIC SEA

Danzig

BRANDENBURG-
PRUSSIA

To Prussia
in 1772

Vistula R.

Warsaw

Cracow

To Austria
in 1795

To Prussia
in 1793

Oder R.

HOLY ROMAN EMPIRE

SWEDEN

DENMARK

Russia's freedom of movement on the international scene, especially toward Prussia–Germany. Second, Russia's rule over most of ethnographic Poland hampered the Empire's internal evolution; one of the chief arguments of reactionary forces against any liberalization was that national minorities, especially the Poles, would seize such an opportunity to claim autonomy and thus undermine the unity of the Empire. Meanwhile, in 1809, Russia annexed Finland and, in 1812, Romanian Bessarabia. As a result, the Tsarist Empire came to control a belt of territories on its western front that stretched from the Gulf of Finland to the mouth of the Danube. Most of these lands had a much higher level of civilization than Russia, and their people were reluctant subjects of St. Petersburg, eager either for independence or at least broad autonomy. By hindering the process of peaceful reform, nationality problems pushed Russia toward a violent upheaval.

For all practical purposes, up to the middle of the eighteenth century the Tsars claimed all the lands of their realm as their patrimony and all its inhabitants as servants of the State. This began to change in the second half of the eighteenth century as far as the nobility was concerned. The succession crisis that followed the death of Peter the Great in 1725 allowed the gentry, through a series of palace revolutions, to strengthen its position. By placing on the Tsarist throne several inexperienced monarchs, mainly women and adolescents, the Russian nobility wrested from them important concessions which somewhat limited imperial absolutism. In 1762, the gentry was formally exempted from obligatory state service by Peter III. They were allowed to pursue their interests and even to travel abroad. Nearly all the monopolies on trade and industry were abolished. In 1785, Catherine II allowed the gentry and the townsmen to form their respective corporate organizations. Moreover, they were given full and unconditional title to their estates.

Despite these concessions, and despite the influence of the enormous and unwieldy bureaucratic machine, the old authoritarian and patrimonial system never disappeared completely. Although allowing many of its subjects to become rich and educated, the autocracy insisted on preserving its monopoly of political authority and refused to share it in the form of truly representative institutions. This created a paradoxical situation: an increasingly enlightened and prosperous society was forced to tolerate a paternalistic state that rejected any freely elected representative institutions of the Western type. This basic contradiction was a source of tension between the politically minded members of the society and the authorities. By the end of the eighteenth century the Russian gentry, more economically secure, freer from being constantly ordered about, and better informed as a result of exposure to Western ideas, began to think for itself.

Under Catherine's rule, the abolitionist movement was born. In 1790, the son of a gentry family and a customs official, Alexander Radishchev (1749–1802), published his critical volume *Journey from St. Petersburg to Moscow*. In the form of letters to an imaginary friend, Radishchev presented the tragic lot of the serfs and urged abolition of this immoral, inefficient, and degrading institution. The book was confiscated and its author imprisoned and sentenced to ten years in Siberia. Radishchev's *Journey* greatly influenced all subsequent radical and socialist writings of the nineteenth century. He is generally considered a forerunner of the peculiarly Russian phenomenon called *intelligentsia*.

Unlike the present Soviet definition of *intelligentsia*, which equates it with the white-collar class, the old term, which had become a household word by 1860, had a more restricted meaning. Prior to the Bolshevik triumph, the term *intelligentsia* comprised only those critically minded and educated people who were in opposition to the establishment and dedicated to selfless work on society's behalf. Both missionary spirit and a critical attitude toward the powers that be were regarded as essential features of an *intelligent.* Inspired by a guilt complex and a preoccupation with the messianic, promethean idea of social redemption, the members of the intelligentsia devoted themselves to the cause of social revolution. The revolutionary movement of the Tsarist Empire was inspired, organized, and led overwhelmingly by the intelligentsia.

SUMMARY

Like the Golden Horde or the Ottoman Empire, the old Muscovite state was organized more for warfare than welfare. A sense of responsibility for public well-being came very late, only in the second half of the nineteenth century. Unlike Western or Central Europe, no reception of Roman law ever took place in Russia. Following the Tatar example, law was equated with the will or whim of the ruler. Until the Great Reforms of the 1860s, Tsarist jurisprudence did not distinguish between laws, decrees, and administrative ordinances. Only in the nineteenth century was Russian law codified, and even then the codification was inadequate. Until the judiciary reform of 1864, justice was a branch of the administration, and its first concern was not defense of the individual but protection of state interests and enforcement of public order, as interpreted by an autocratic ruler.

The Russian autocratic system, as it existed with some modification until March 1917, made one individual the central pillar of the Empire. The Tsar was not only the symbol of state sovereignty and unity but also its absolute ruler, its supreme executive of government. In this task he was assisted by cabinet ministers who were merely his personal agents. The Emperor was also the supreme legislator, the sole source of law. In this task he was assisted by the Council of State, an institution modeled on the French by Tsar Alexander I in 1810. The Council was composed of high administrative officials and legal experts appointed by the Tsar to help him in drafting legislation. The existence of the Council, like that of the

ministers, did not limit the absolute power of the Emperor. The ministers did not share in his power; they were called in only to assist with advice and legal-administrative technicalities. Besides being the supreme executive and the only source of law, the Russian monarch was also the supreme judge. All verdicts in the Empire were pronounced in his name. In his capacity as supreme judge, the Emperor was assisted by the Senate. In addition to its judicial functions, the Senate exercised supervision over the administrative machinery. Thus the Russian Senate combined some of the functions exercised in the United States by the Supreme Court with those of the administrative tribunals provided for by some European constitutions. The Tsar was also the Supreme Commander-in-Chief of the armed forces, the army and navy. As if all these powers were not sufficient, the Tsar was also the secular head of the Orthodox Church of his Empire. His person was regarded as sacred, and on state occasions he was surrounded by a semireligious ceremony. The Tsar was also the richest land owner of the country: on the eve of the Revolution of 1917, the crown properties numbered some twenty million acres of cultivated and timbered land.

Imperial Russia, however, was never a totalitarian state as we understand the word. It lacked both the will to become one, largely because of its lingering respect for traditional Christian values and for private property, as well as the technical means available to modern dictators.

The scope of the Tsarist reprisals against the opposition was on a relatively small scale by contemporary standards. Between 1823 and 1861 only a dozen or so people were executed and only some 14,000 to 15,000 people exiled for political reasons. From the hanging of the five leaders of the "Decembrist" revolt against Nicholas I in 1826 to the downfall of the Tsarist regime in 1917, the number of all death sentences actually carried out on the territory of the Empire amounted to 14,000, according to Lenin. Many of these executions took place under the martial law prevailing between September 1, 1906, and May 3, 1907, when the regime was fighting the unprecedented wave of terrorism that was responsible for the death of 1,969 state officials and 2,535 private individuals. In 1880 there were in the whole Russian Empire only 1,200 people exiled for political crimes. In 1901 the total number of political exiles amounted to 4,113, and most were living in relative comfort in faraway places assigned to them by the police. Mass executions without trial or mass deportations to Siberia or other remote places were unknown to the prerevolutionary Russian regimes after the cruel and despotic rule of Peter the Great.

Yet the lack of autonomous political, socioeconomic, or even cultural–religious institutions, the almost total absence of any give and take relations between State and society until the constitutional era of 1905–1917, was a bad political and civic school for the Russian people in general. The intolerant attitude of the autocracy that rejected outright, on principle, any idea of compromise or any partial political adjustment—the all or nothing approach—was taken over by opponents of the regime, the revolutionary movement. When the constitution was granted in October 1905, it was already too late to change the deep-rooted habits of most of the Russian people.

SUGGESTED READING

BILLINGTON, JAMES, *The Icon and the Axe: Interpretive History of Russian Culture.* New York: Random House, 1970.

BLUM, JEROME, *Lord and Peasant in Russia.* Princeton, N.J.: Princeton University Press, 1961.

CURTIS, JOHN S., *Church and State in Russia, 1900–1917.* New York: Columbia University Press, 1940.

CUSTINE, ASTOLPHE L. L., *Journey for Our Times,* New York: Pellegrin and Cudahy, 1951.

DANIELS, ROBERT V., *Russia. The Roots of Confrontation.* Cambridge, Mass., and London: Harvard University Press, 1985, Chs. 1–4.

KLIUCHEVSKY, VASILY O., *Peter the Great.* New York: St. Martin's Press, 1958.

KUCHARZEWSKI, JAN, *The Origins of Modern Russia.* New York: Polish Institute of Arts and Sciences in America, 1948.

MADARIAGA, ISABEL DE, *Russia in the Age of Catherine the Great.* London: Weidenfeld and Nicolson, 1981.

MASSIE, ROBERT K., *Peter the Great.* New York: Knopf, 1980.

MILIUKOV, PAVEL N., *Outlines of Russian Culture* (Michael Karpovich, ed.). Philadelphia: University of Pennsylvania Press, 1942. 3 vols.

——, *Russia and Its Critics.* New York: Collier Books, 1962.

MULLER, ALEXANDER V., *The Spiritual Regulations of Peter the Great.* Seattle, Wash.: Washington University Press, 1972.

PIPES, RICHARD, *Russia under the Old Regime.* London: Weidenfeld and Nicholson, 1974.

PUSHKAROV, SERGEI, *The Emergence of Modern Russia, 1801–1917.* New York: Holt, Rinehart and Winston, 1963.

RAEFF, MARC, ed., *Russian Intellectual History: An Anthology.* New York: Harcourt Brace Jovanovich, 1966.

RIASANOVSKY, NICHOLAS V., *A History of Russia,* 4th ed. New York: Oxford University Press, 1984.

ROBINSON, G. T., *Rural Russia under the Old Regime.* New York: Longmans, Green, 1949.

ROGGER, HANS, *National Consciousness in Eighteenth Century Russia.* Cambridge, Mass.: Harvard University Press, 1960.

SETON-WATSON, HUGH, *The Russian Empire, 1801–1917.* New York: Oxford University Press, 1967

STARR, FREDERICK S., *Decentralization and Self-Government in Russia, 1830–1870.* Princeton, N.J.: Princeton University Press, 1972.

VERNADSKY, GEORGE, *The Mongols and Russia.* New Haven, Conn.: Yale University Press, 1953.

VINOGRADOV, PAUL, *The Legacy of the Middle Ages* (G. G. Crump and E. F. Jacob, eds.). New York: Oxford University Press, 1926.

VUCHINICH, VANE S., ed., *The Peasant in Nineteenth Century Russia.* Stanford, Calif.: Stanford University Press, 1968.

WALLACE, DONALD M., *Russia on the Eve of War and Revolution.* Princeton, N.J.: Princeton University Press, 1984.

WARE, TIMOTHY, *The Orthodox Church*. New York: Penguin Books, 1963.

WITTFOGEL, KARI A., *Oriental Despotism*. New Haven, Conn.: Yale University Press, 1957.

WREN, MELVIN C., *The Western Impact upon Russia*. New York: Holt, Rinehart and Winston, 1971.

ZAIONCHKOVSKY, PETER A., *The Russian Autocracy under Alexander III* (ed. and trans. by David R. Jones). Gulf Breeze, Fla.: Academic International Press, 1976.

ZERNOV, NICHOLAS. *Eastern Christendom*. New York: G. P. Putnam's Sons, 1961.

CHAPTER 3

The Russian Revolutionary Tradition

The first instance of a modern Russian revolutionary group acting against the Tsar in the name of a more or less coherent program was the revolt of a handful of aristocratic guard officers against the autocracy and the iniquities of the age-old socioeconomic system. Since the revolt took place in December 1825, its members are known as *Decembrists.*

The uprising has to be viewed against the background of its epoch. The Napoleonic period saw Russia deeply involved in the affairs of Europe. A grandson of Catherine II, Alexander I (1801–1825), had ambitious plans for restructuring the European community in accordance with his visionary, idealistic, but impractical schemes. Preoccupied primarily with international affairs, Alexander had abandoned his early plans for enlightened domestic reforms. This deepened the dissatisfaction of the expanding, restless intelligentsia with Russia's backwardness and fostered their further alienation from the system based on serf-dom, repression, and censorship. The young Russian officers roaming Europe during the campaigns against Napoleon brought home the liberal and revolutionary ideas of the West and formed a number of secret societies dedicated to the implementation of these ideas.

In December 1825, within a month of Alexander's death, a group of officer-conspirators staged a coup d'état, the aims of which were the abolition of the autocracy and serfdom and the introduction of either a liberal constitution or a centralized republican system of government. The improvised revolt was promptly and ruthlessly suppressed by Alexander's younger brother, Nicholas I (1825–1855). The five ringleaders of the conspiracy were hanged and several others banished to Siberia.

The uprising of the Decembrists was the first Russian revolt directly inspired by Western liberalism and the first to have a political program. Hastily organized, deprived of determined and experienced leadership, and with no support from the masses, it was doomed to failure. The Decembrists were trying to reap before they had sown, to stage a revolution before they had organized a revolutionary movement. But the revolt of the Decembrists provided the mounting opposition to the Tsarist autocracy with two important elements: a revolutionary legend and a group of martyr-heroes to worship.

Shaken by the revolt of the Decembrists, who were almost exclusively aristocrats and guard officers enjoying all the privileges of their class, the sulking Tsar Nicholas sought safety by suppressing even the idea of fundamental reform. Soon after the trial, he established a corps of gendarmes of some 10,000 men and a new branch of the secret police, the "Third Section" of his personal chancery, to deal with political problems and the repression of dissent. In 1845, Nicholas I also promulgated a new Criminal Code, which has become a milestone in the evolution of Russia as a police state. The new code made all attempts to limit the authority of the Tsar, to alter the existing system of government, or even to fail to denounce anyone guilty of these offenses, criminal offenses carrying the death penalty and the confiscation of all property. The propagation of ideas that in any way spread doubt about the authority of the Tsar was punishable by the loss of civil rights, from four to twelve years of hard labor, and, in addition, corporal punishment and branding. The Criminal Code of 1845 made politics a monopoly of the establishment and gave to the Third Section and its auxiliary organs a perfect instrument for the arbitrary repression of all forms of political dissent.

The system of Nicholas I was undermined not by domestic political opposition but by foreign adventures. The Tsar's ambition to extend Russia's influence over the Balkans and the Middle East and to partition eventually the Ottoman Empire caused him to stumble into a war against a powerful coalition composed of Great Britain and France. Apprehensive of his bold designs, they supported Turkey as a dam against further Russian encroachments in the area. The Crimean War (1853–55), which centered largely around the peninsula of Crimea, resulted in a humiliating defeat for the Russian forces, which were badly armed, indifferently commanded, and composed of ignorant and sulking serfs.

THE GREAT REFORMS

Nicholas's son and successor, Alexander II (1855–1881), ended the Crimean War by the Treaty of Paris (1856) and turned his attention toward neglected domestic issues. The educational system was liberalized; access to higher education was granted to all classes, primary as well as secondary education was expanded, and in 1863 institutions of higher learning were granted a measure of autonomy. Preventive censorship was abolished. By the Imperial decrees of 1861 and 1864, the serfs (both those privately owned and those belonging to the State) were emancipated from the power of their masters. The peasant was to remain a member of the existing local village commune, or *mir*, organized on the basis of the collective ownership of land. The landowners were to be compensated from State funds, while the peasants were to repay the State over a period of forty-nine years. The liberation of the Russian serfs, parallel to the emancipation of the slaves in the United States, involved a huge mass, nearly 52 million people. Unlike the American slaves, the Russian peasants retained most of the land they were cultivating at the time of the emancipation.

Following the liberation of the serfs in 1864, Alexander established elected self-governing bodies on the communal, district, and provincial levels. Although the landowners were largely in control, the peasants also participated. Soon these local bodies, or *zemstvos*, became schools for responsible, day-to-day, grass-roots civic work. The only outlet for semiindependent social activities, the zemstvos soon became a breeding ground of liberal and reform sentiments. In addition, in the same year independent judiciary and public trial by jury were introduced. In 1870 a measure of municipal self-government was granted. Four years later, the antiquated structure of the military service (in which a man had to serve for twenty-five years) was streamlined, somewhat humanized, and the length of service shortened. The principle of universal military service was introduced. During the period of the *Great Reforms,* Alexander II attempted to put an end to the arbitrary rule of the police and to transform his Empire into a state grounded in law. The Great Reforms, carried out against the bitter opposition of the conervatives and the well-entrenched bureaucracy, were considered by Russian liberals as a significant step toward eventual establishment of a constitutional system of government, or a "crowning of the edifice."

Yet the reforms of the 1860s not only did not eliminate the tension between state and society; rather, they intensified it. While conceding its people significant economic opportunities, basic civil rights, and some intellectual freedoms, the autocracy insisted on keeping its monopoly of political power and continued to regard itself as the only legitimate source of authority. The growing disappointment with the shortcomings of the Great Reforms, especially the stiff terms of the emancipation of the peasants, caused a great deal of vocal criticism and public manifestation during the early 1860s and resulted in the birth of the Russian agrarian socialist movement, *Populism.*

RUSSIAN AGRARIAN SOCIALISM

One of the earliest Russian socialists was Alexander I. Herzen, a brilliant publicist. Through his voluminous and persuasive writing, Herzen, in exile after 1847 in France, England, and Switzerland, tried to adapt the European socialist concepts to the conditions of his native country. His London-based periodical *Kolokol (The Bell)* attempted to demonstrate that backward, agrarian Russia was actually riper for Socialism than advanced, industrialized Western Europe. With Herzen, the Russian agrarian socialists of the 1860s and 1870s believed that if the peasants could be educated to socialist ideas, the native Russian form of agrarian cooperative, the village commune, or *mir,* would be transformed into the basic cell of a new society. In this way, Russia could escape the miseries of capitalism and pass in a relatively short period of time from her feudal state to socialism; in their plans, the village commune would be the main instrument of the socialist reconstruction of the country.

Populism was based on two premises: first, faith in the significance of the commune as a key institution of the socialist transformation of Russia; and, second, mistrust of liberalism and capitalism. Both assumptions were connected with the belief that Russia's backwardness was an advantage over capitalist Western Europe and a way of bypassing the capitalist stage of development. Yet Herzen and his followers believed that Russia was essentially a part of the Western world. Unlike their opponents, the Slavophiles, the Westernizers rejected the uniqueness of their country's civilization and regarded Russia merely as a retarded segment of Europe, the segment that should try to catch up with the rest of the Western world.

Paradoxically, it was the emancipation of the serfs and other progressive reforms, the realization of some of the age-old progressive dreams, that gave birth to the revolutionary activities of the Populists. There were numerous reasons for the spread of their protest movement. First, emancipation gave the peasants too little land, saddled them with high redemption payments, and left them on the margin of the society, almost as a separate caste. Second, some of the reforms—such as those of the press and the education system—were abandoned halfway. Moreover, educational reform, which gave access to higher education to sons of peasants and merchants, soon produced a considerable body of educated people of radical political views. This new breed was anxious to help the strata of population from which it had emerged.

One characteristic phenomenon of the 1870s was the emergence of the *going-to-the-people* movement, or a tendency of the Populist intelligentsia to live and work with the peasantry in order to help in its education and eventual emancipation. The movement reached its peak in the "mad summer" of 1874. Thousands of young and not-so-young members of the intelligentsia flocked to the villages to preach the gospel of social revolution. Yet the peasants were indifferent to abstract political ideas and hostile to those who wanted to inculcate them with strange concepts. The main preoccupation of the peasants was the acquisition of more land and the betterment of material conditions in general. The idea of a revolutionary overthrow of the Tsar, whom the peasants tended to view as their father and protector against the greedy landowners and corrupt officials, was alien to the rural masses. In many cases the peasants simply handed over the strangers from the cities to the local police as dangerous agitators against the Tsar. The foolishly idealized image of a "good peasant" was shattered almost overnight. The going-to-the-people movement ended in failure.

Disappointed in their pet dream of galvanizing the peasant masses into revolutionary action by means of propaganda and agitation, the radicals turned to terror. Violent protests involving the use of pistols and bombs were begun in 1878 by a small body of some thirty or forty people who called themselves the *People's Will*. Their terror and sabotage, conducted with breathtaking courage for some three years, aimed at shattering the bureaucratic machinery and inciting the peasants to rebellion by exposing the Tsar's helplessness and his unwillingness to carry out more radical land reform ("the black partition"), or to summon a Constituent Assembly representing the real desires of the people, or the "people's will."

Failures in the international forum soon added to domestic tensions. The humiliating setbacks of Russian diplomacy at the Congress of Berlin that ended the Russo-Turkish War of 1877–1878 were bitterly resented by the nationalistic public opinion at home. The dismantling of Greater Bulgaria, sponsored by St. Petersburg but opposed by London, Berlin, and Vienna, was followed by the occupation of the Slavic provinces of Bosnia and Herzegovnia by Austria–Hungary; these were bitter pills for the increasingly Slavophile-minded Russian patriots to swallow. Soon a more politically minded outgrowth of the Slavophiles began to preache the idea of Russia as leader and future unifier of all the Slavic peoples.[1]

The mood of patriotic enthusiasm generated by the war against the Turks, considered a traditional enemy of the Orthodox Slavs, had temporarily silenced domestic opposition against the soft-pedaling of the Great Reforms. In 1878, after the Congress of Berlin, the revolutionaries, especially the terrorists of the People's Will, redoubled their efforts. The battle of wills between the Tsarist security apparatus and the terrorists lasted for three years. Finally, on March 13, 1881, a bomb thrown by one of them in St. Petersburg killed the "Tsar Liberator." A few hours before Alexander was killed, he had signed a quasi-constitutional project devised to involve elected representatives of a consultative assembly in legislative tasks.

---

[1] The *Panslavic* school of thought was greatly stimulated in 1869 by the publication of a theoretical study, *Russia and Europe*. Its author, Nicholas Y. Danilevsky (1828–1885), was an eloquent exponent of Russian nationalism who advanced a theory of the unique and superior character of Slavic destiny. According to him, Slavic civilization, as embodied in its most representative Russian variety, was virile, creative, and dynamic, as contrasted with the decaying Western civilizations. In the inevitable contest, the Slavs (led by their senior brothers, the Russians) were bound to win. Danilevsky outlined in his book a future Russo-Slavic Empire comprising most of Eastern and Central Europe as far as the Oder River and the Turkish Straits, including Constantinople. As a poetic spokesman of the Panslav ideas, Alexander Pushkin, put it: "The Slavic rivulets are to merge in the Russian sea."

THE BIRTH OF RUSSIAN MARXIST SOCIALISM

The assassination of the "Tsar Liberator" was the peak of the activites of the People's Will. Alexander III (1881–1894), the embittered son of Alexander II, never published his father's quasi-constitutional charter. Quite the contrary: acting under the influence of his narrow-minded, reactionary advisor, a professor of law at the University of St. Petersburg, Constantine Pobedonostsev (1827–1907), the new Tsar proclaimed his unmitigated devotion to absolutism in his accession manifesto and initiated a repressive course of action. Its main victims were not only the radical and liberal opposition, but also religious and national minorities, especially the Jews, who suffered numerous pogroms. The press was muzzled, the zemstvos hampered in their activity, and intellectual life stifled.

To the terror of the People's Will, the government responded by a series of systematic countermeasures. One of them, already taken in 1878, empowered the Corps of Gendarmes to detain and even exile administratively (without trial by a law court or permission of the Attorney General) anyone suspected of a political crime. Whereas under the Criminal Code of 1845 a citizen had to actually commit a subversive act before being liable to exile, now a suspicion of subversion was enough to have him suffer that fate. Trial by jury was done away with in political cases; now all political cases were to be dealt with by "administrative methods," that is, by the gendarmes and police, to the exclusion of the law courts. In addition, Alexander III reorganized the branches of the police dealing with political crimes by giving them further arbitrary powers. The law of August 1, 1881, introduced two institutions: the state of "Reinforced Safeguard," which corresponded to a minor state of seige, and that of "Extraordinary Safeguard," which in the West would equal a major state of seige. The law of 1881 gave to the police and administrative authorities powers unparalleled in the civilized world. The law placed the fate of the people in the hands of uncontrolled police officials and made them entirely dependent on their whim, thus making Russia a full-blown police state. From then on, a majority of the Tsarist Empire was under the state of Reinforced Safeguard with occasional recurrence to Extraordinary Safeguard, as, for instance, during the revolution of 1905 and its aftermath.

As a consequence of this series of measures, the opposition was temporarily paralyzed. Soon, however, the revolutionary movement revived. The excesses of the burgeoning Russian industrial revolution; the plight of a peasantry suffering from high taxes, redemption payments, and high-handed governmental paternalism; the oppressive though erratic censorship; the spread of Great Russian chauvinism—all these produced increasing resentment and at the close of the century gave birth to several new revolutionary groups, most of a socialist variety.

One reason for the upsurge of the revolutionary groups was the deteriorating situation of the peasant masses. Agricultural production, hampered by the collectivist *mir,* was lagging. According to an official census of 1877, the average landholding of a Russian peasant family was about thirty-five acres; in France in 1884 the average size of a peasant farm was about nine acres. But the colder, drier, and more capricious climate, in addition to the backward cultivation methods, for instance the existence of communal holdings, made the position of the rapidly increasing Russian peasantry incomparably worse. Since the shortage of land was relative, it was technological backwardness that was mainly responsible for Russia's agricultural retardation. The threat of periodic repartition hampered initiative and prevented peasants from investing in land that could be taken away at any time. All these factors inhibited productivity and resulted in the progressive impoverishment of the countryside during the second half of the nineteenth and the beginning of the twentieth century.

The plight of the Russian worker, largely an unwilling and homesick migrant from his native village, was equally bad. Fascinated by the machine and the profit it provided to those who mastered it, the Russian entrepreneurial class, like its Western counterpart at the early stages of the industrial revolution, was blind to the human side of economic progress. At the end of the century, the workers' barrackslike living conditions were quite similar to those Marx's collaborator Engels had observed in England in the 1840s. Wretched working conditions, long working days of about twelve to sixteen hours, arbitrary fines, compulsory workers' canteens run by the factory owner—these were commonplace phenomena in Russia in the 1880s and 1890s. To this one should add the shortage of labor inspectors to check on the rudimentary labor legislation hastily enacted in the 1880s, and a ban on strikes, although not on lockouts. These grievances were sullenly nurtured by the rapidly growing working class, who could not express them in a legitimate way, let alone much improve their wretched condition.

The task of defending the interest of the laboring masses of the Tsarist Empire was taken over by the increasingly radical intelligentsia. This new revolutionary mood was more directly inspired by the followers of Marx and Engels than that of the 1860s and 1870s. The Russian translation of *Das Kapital* was published in Russia in 1872, five years after its German edition but earlier than in any other foreign country. Marxism spread among the Russian intelligentsia like wildfire. This was in part because the doctrine gave to the people who had rejected religious dogma a sense of scientific certitude for which they had been longing, and also because it represented what seemed a panacea for the ills of contemporary society. The classic Marxist ideas, however, which were formulated on the basis of West European experience, were hardly applicable to the condition of a heterogeneous and overwhelmingly rural–pastoral Tsarist Empire. Transplanted to Russia, the Marxist theories had, of necessity to be adapted to suit the new, strange environment.

GEORGE PLEKHANOV

The transformation of orthodox Marxism into Soviet Communism was a long, gradual, and involved process. The first systematic explanation of Marxist doctrine in Russian was given by a repentant nobleman, George Plekhanov. As a student at the Mining Institute of St. Petersburg, Plekhanov had participated in the going-to-the-people movement of the 1870s. Disappointed with the passivity of the peasant masses and the fruitless terrorist activities of the radical wing of Populism, he emigrated to Switzerland and began to study Marxism. Plekhanov, together with three former Populists, Paul Axelrod, Lev Deutsch, and Vera Zasulich, was the founder of the first Russian Marxist group, "Liberation of Labor" (1883).

During the forty years of exile, Plekhanov wrote many books and pamphlets.

Karl Marx

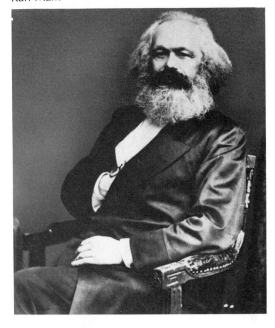

Owing to his intellectual capacities, he soon became the leader of the slowly forming Russian Social-Democratic movement. Plekhanov believed that the main failing of the Populist creed lay in its uncritical worship of the passive peasant masses, at the cost of doctrinal and organizational weakness. The chief strength of Marxist Socialism, on the other hand, lay in its intellectual discipline and its "scientific" formulation of a program of political as well as social action. Along with Marx and Engels, Plekhanov argued that not the numerically superior peasant masses spread over the vastness of the Tsarist Empire, but the workers concentrated in the strategic points of modern industrial societies should form the core of a modern revolutionary organization. The working-class movement, acting in a still semifeudal country, argued Plekhanov, should proceed through two phases: a bourgeois upheaval followed by a socialist revolution. First, a political revolution should destroy the Tsarist autocracy and establish a liberal bourgeois regime; such a regime would create conditions more favorable for the proletarian masses (an eight-hour working day, trade unions, social security, educational facilities, and so on). After an indeterminate period, the working class, by then ready for its historical role, would strike out, abolish bourgeois rule, and establish the dictatorship of the proletariat. The revolution would place control of the means of production in the hands of the workers and establish a socialist system, a steppingstone toward the final goal of the historic process, which is Communism.

To achieve these objectives, argued Plekhanov, it was necessary to create an instrument that would direct the struggle, that is, a regular social-democratic party. The party would be composed essentially of workers but led, at least in the beginning, by the intellectuals. Following the tradition of Marx and Engels, and in accordance with the pattern set by the largest and most prestigious Social-Democratic Party in the contemporary world, the German party, Plekhanov emphasized democratic principles and minimized the leadership role of the intellectuals. Their function was merely to serve the working-class movement. Plekhanov stressed that a socialist revolution should wait until the working class was ready to assume its high responsibilities, which is to say, when "objective" socioeconomic conditions would be ripe for the introduction of a complex socialist system suitable only to highly developed industrial societies. Thus, Plekhanov was a rather scrupulous interpreter of orthodox Marxism to his countrymen and wanted to transplant it to his native country without major adaptations.

THE SHAPING OF SOCIALIST MASS PARTIES

While Plekhanov was laboring abroad to lay down the theoretical foundations of the Russian Marxist movement, the industrial revolution in the Tsarist Empire was advancing rapidly. Actually, the first socialist parties of the Empire were formed on its multinational periphery, in Russian Poland, and in the socioeconomically more advanced western provinces of the Tsarist domains. As far back as 1882, an early socialist party called "Proletariat" was organized in Warsaw. Ten years after its suppression by the police, a group of Polish intellectuals and workers who were forced to emigrate to Paris formed there the Polish Socialist Party (1892). The next year a splinter group, protesting its native party's emphasis on patriotism, established a party of its own, the Social-Democratic Party of Poland (soon to be renamed Social-Democratic Party of Poland and Lithuania). This was the party of Rosa Luxemburg, Feliks Dzerzhinsky, and Karl Radek. And it was in the Lithuanian regions of the Tsarist Empire, in Vilna (Wilno, Vilnius), that in 1897 the delegates of various Jewish Marxist debating clubs and underground cells gathered to set up the General Jewish "Workers' Union" in Lithuania, Poland, and Russia. This representation of the Jewish, Marxist proletarian masses was to be known by its colloquial Yiddish abbreviation of *Bund.* Owing to the high educational level of its membership, the qualities of its leaders, and the oppressive conditions under which the Jewish proletariat vegetated in the towns and cities of the *Pale of Settlement,* to which they were limited by the authorities, the Bund developed into a mass party sooner than the socialist organizations of other ethnic groups. In Livonia and Kurland, the Lettish social-democratic movement achieved considerable influence among the local workers, both in the urban centers and in the countryside. At the same time, in the Transcaucasia, especially among the Georgians and the Armenians, various socialist groups were also formed. Lack of political freedom continued to favor conspiratorial activity.

In 1898, on the initiative of the Jewish Bund, nine delegates of these scattered socialist conspiratorial cells congregated in the Belorussian city of Minsk and proclaimed the foundations of the Russian Social-Democratic Workers' Party (RSDWP). While the immediate objective of the party was the establishment of a constitutional regime, its ultimate goal was to be public ownership of the means of production, including land. Soon after this meeting, declared to be the first congress of the new party, most of the delegates were arrested by the Tsarist political police. Thus the seemingly stillborn party suffered its first heavy blow, which seemed to spell its end. Yet the unrest that prompted the formation of these groups was a symptom of deep-seated socioeconomic and political malaise that proved impossible to extirpate. The ferment was soon to be aggravated by the severe economic depression of the years 1899–1903. Since the famine of 1891, which had brought widespread death from starvation in many regions of the Empire, unrest among peasants had also worsened.

The plight of the peasantry was a challenge to the Populist-inclined intelligentsia. A few former members of the agrarian socialist groups Land and Liberty and the People's Will, began to re-form their scattered ranks, and at the close of 1901, they formed the *Social Revolutionary Party.* The *SRs,* as they were colloquially called, were dedicated to the defense of the peasant interests and subscribed to the main tenet of the Marxist doctrine: the necessity of public ownership of the means of production, including the land. Yet, while preaching close cooperation between workers and peasants, they rejected the hegemony of the urban proletariat in an overwhelmingly agrarian society. This factor, as well as the distinctive mentality of the village people, argued the Social-Revolutionary leaders, necessitated a specifically Russian interpretation of the doctrine involving acceptance of a leading role for the peasantry. Moreover, argued the SRs, the elemental land hunger of the peasant, his fierce attachment to the soil he tilled, ought to be respected. Hence the agrarian program of the SRs provided for nationalization of the land that should be owned by the State; the State, however, would lease the land to local peasant communities, which would in turn sublease it to individual peasant families for long periods of time.

While devoting the bulk of their energies to grass-roots work among the peasants (as social workers in the ranks of the local zemstvos, as teachers, doctors, or agrarian instructors), the Social Revolutionaries propagated the theory of propaganda by acts of terror, when necessary. Whenever Tsarist officials were especially obnoxious and all other means of persuasion and pressure failed, such representatives of the oppressive regime had to be assassinated in the name of the higher interest of the people. The SRs were convinced that such a punishment of hated officials, often called "propaganda by deeds," would spur on the revolutionary spirit and eventually frighten the regime into concessions. Thus the doctrine of the SRs was a compromise between collectivist doctrine and common sense, between the going-to-the-people movement and the terrorist traditions of the People's Will.

The principal leaders of the SRs were Catherine Breshkovskaya, called the "grandmother of the Russian Revolution"; Victor Chernov, its main theoretician; Gregory Gershuni, the first leader of its Fighting Organization; and Boris Savinkov, his successor, a man who combined reckless courage with considerable literary talent. The SRs, despite their loose organization, were strikingly appealing not only to the peasant masses but also to many students and intellectuals. Soon the Social Revolutionary Party became the largest and the most deeply rooted political party of pre-Soviet Russia. This was to be dramatically revealed during the November 1917 elections.

LEGAL MARXISTS

Meanwhile, the already differentiated Marxist movement began to undergo further evolution. By the end of the nineteenth century, the revisionist, gradualist ideas of a prominent member of the German Social Democratic Party, Edward Bernstein, had also penetrated into Russia. By the close of the century some early, more scholarly Russian students of Marxism, like Peter Struve and Sergei N. Bulgakov, began to formulate a theory of nonviolent social change similar to that of Edward Bernstein. Struve, in his *Critical Notes on the Problem of the Economic Development of Russia,* published in 1894, had come to the conclusion that capitalism would offer to backward Russia a great many practical advantages, and that his countrymen should learn from Western liberalism. The Tsarist authorities did not suppress the writings and activities of this type of harmless, scholarly Marxist, and tended to regard such people as "thieves falling out." Despite these hopes, the ideas of the "legal Marxists," as they were called, found a considerable following among intellectuals and university students. By and large, gradualism had no significant appeal to the masses of the Russian people. In a society shaped by the forces described in the pre-

vious chapter, any idea of a partial adjustment, of give and take, tended to be regarded with suspicion; radical slogans were likely to find more support than those advocating patient, step-by-step solutions to the burning, everyday problems

Parallel with legal Marxism, an ingenious secret police officer, Sergey Zubatov, convinced Tsarist authorities that they should fight the revolutionaries by infiltrating the labor movement. He advocated spreading slogans that would stress economic demands and thus would be attractive to the workers, yet largely harmless to the government. As a consequence of this strategy, the wrath of the workers would be directed against the local factory owners and other capitalists, who were largely foreigners or Jews. The idea of channeling and deflecting the wrath of the workers was temporarily accepted by the regime. For a number of years the movement, soon to be called "police socialism," spread in a series of urban centers, including St. Petersburg and Moscow. Some of the Zubatov methods were soon taken over by a son of a Ukrainian peasant, a Greek Orthodox priest named Gregory Gapon, to form his Assembly of Russian Workingmen, a nucleus of a Christian Socialist movement. He was to play a significant role during the revolutionary events of 1905.

THE EMERGENCE OF LENIN

Among the members of the lingering Russian Social Democratic Workers' Party was the son of a school inspector, Vladimir Ulianov, whom we know better by his revolutionary pen name of Lenin. Vladimir Ulianov was a gold medal graduate (which would correspond to our summa cum laude) of the University of Kazan on the Volga. Together with his greatly admired older brother, Alexander, Vladimir Ulianov early joined a Marxist conspiratorial cell. Soon his brother became involved in an attempt on the life of Alexander III. While Alexander was sentenced to death, Vladimir was exiled to Siberia, and later, in 1900, expelled from Russia. His revolutionary experience had taught Vladimir the specific weaknesses of his countrymen: anarchic tendencies, proclivity to loose talk, endless theoretical hairsplitting, lack of discipline, and inability to keep secrets. All this he contrasted against the skillful and ruthless operations of the Tsarist secret police. The story of the First Congress of the RSDWP was a good example of this contrast. Vladimir Ulianov concluded that under the circumstances, the revolutionaries had little chance of success unless they radically changed their methods.

Analyzing in exile the existing situation and the prospects for the future, Ulianov wrote a booklet that he published in 1902 under the pseudonym Lenin, entitled *What Is To Be Done?* In his polemical pamphlet directed against the reformist trend of the Russian Socialist movement, Lenin forcefully stated his views. The only remedy to the many ills of the Russian revolutionary movement would be to set up a tight, hierarchically organized party composed of dedicated people devoted body and soul to the task of the proletarian revolution; they must be a match for the repressive instruments at the disposal of the establishment. The nucleus of the party, he argued, should be a small compact core united by the bonds of reliable and hardened workers connected by strict secrecy. Only such a strong and disciplined organization could prevent the danger of premature outbreaks before the ferment and anger of the workers had ripened. He argued that, because of the need for restraint and secrecy, democratic management was inapplicable to a revolutionary organization in Russia. According to *What Is To Be Done?*, the proposed party should act as a "vanguard of the revolutionary forces," or a small detachment of soldiers preceding a larger body of troops and doing scouting work for them. This quasi-military formula chartered the elitist and antidemocratic course of the movement Lenin established.

The concept of a small, select revolution-

V. I. Lenin

ary party was not a novelty in the Russian revolutionary tradition. There had been in the past some Russian Populists of a Jacobin variety who advocated a similar approach. The most significant were Pyotr Tkachëv and Sergey Nechayev; both preached violent overthrow of the Tsarist order and establishment of a revolutionary dictatorship. In 1868–1869 Nechayev together with Tkachëv drafted a "Program of Revolutionary Action" which spoke of "social revolution as our final aim, and political revolution as the only means of achieving this aim." The essence of Russian Jacobinism was the insistence on the dictatorship of a minority group with the object of carrying out by force the socialist transformation of the country's political and socioeconomic system. Nechayev, in his booklet *Revolutionary Catechism*, stressed the need for total dedication, and wrote: "The revolutionist is a doomed man. He has no personal interests, no affairs, sentiments, attachments, property, not even a name of his own. Everything in him is absorbed by one exclusive interest, one thought, the revolution."[2] Lenin's spiritual links with Nechayev and Tkachëv were close. With Tkachëv, Lenin shared three vital concepts: (1) the belief in the decisive role of a disciplined, hierarchically organized conspiratorial elite; (2) the necessity of a violent revolution to be launched as soon as possible, irrespective of socioeconomic conditions as prescribed by Marx and Engels; and (3) the insistence on the establishment of a determined minority dictatorship that would introduce socialism, imposing their reforms by force if necessary. Nechayev and Tkachëv, but especially the latter, form a vital link between revolutionary Populism and Bolshevism. This makes Lenin a continuer of the native Jacobin trend.

MENSHEVISM VERSUS BOLSHEVISM

Lenin's seminal book, *What Is To Be Done?*, was published in 1902. The next year the resurgent Marxist groups decided to resume their broader organizational activities and arrange for their second congress. It gathered some fifty delegates, first in Brussels, and then, again detected by the Russian police, the group moved its deliberations to London. During the crucial second congress, two main issues agitated the delegates: that of the party structure and organization, and that of its affiliations and allegiances.

The first problem focused on two issues: who can be a member of the party, and what

should be his duties? Some delegates, like Yulii O. Martov, Lenin's associate and coworker from the émigré paper *Iskra* (*The Spark*), advanced a broad formula: every person who agreed with the movement should be considered a member. According to Lenin, the acceptance of this formula would make the party a broad, amorphous mass movement with many people loosely connected but not really belonging to it. His counterformula was: a member of the party is one who, besides paying his dues, submits to its discipline and actively works in one of the party cells, doing a job assigned to him.

Despite Lenin's vigorous opposition, the supporters of the broad definition, who were in the majority, prevailed. Soon, however, another difference polarized the reborn Social-Democratic movement. Everyone realized that the working class of the Tsarist Empire, then numbering about two and a half million people, was still too weak to gain power single-handed and had to have allies in its struggle. The question was, with which social stratum should the workers cooperate in their struggle against the autocracy allied with the capitalists? Plekhanov and Martov and most of their followers, true to the teachings of Marx and Engels, were for supporting the struggle of the most progressive and educated segment of the middle class, the liberal bourgeoisie. On this point they again clashed with Lenin, who rejected Marx's condemnation of the peasantry as a petty bourgeois class and advocated close cooperation with the poor and landless peasants. Lenin claimed that the latter were actually closer to rural workers; hence, for all practical purposes, also proletarians like the urban workers. According to Lenin, while the liberal bourgeoisie at the decisive moment always would side with the autocracy against the socialists, the rural proletariat, land-hungry and revolutionary by instinct and tradition, was the only reliable ally of the workers. And here Lenin found supporters among most of the Congress delegates. Delighted to be finally in the majority, despite his contempt for the

---

[2] The very title of Nechayev's work, *Catechism*, has obvious religious connotations, and a mixture of religion and politics permeated with Byzantine traditions has been a part of the Russian ethos. The advice to abandon permanently one's name while entering a revolutionary conspiracy was observed by many followers of the movement, including Ulianov–Lenin himself. Iosif Djugrashvili soon became Joseph Stalin, and Lev (or Leon) Bronstein, Leon Trotsky.

democratic process, he called his followers the "majority faction"—*Bolsheviki* in Russian. Lenin's adversaries, actually a numerically stronger group on most other issues, meekly gave up this term while accepting the psychologically debilitating name of *Mensheviki*, or members of the "minority faction." The nicknames stuck.

The second congress of the RSDWP, besides voting the party rules, also formulated its program. The immediate or "minimum" program dealt with the short-range goals of the movement, those objectives to be achieved before the establishment of socialism. The minimum program comprised the overthrow of Tsarist authority and the establishment of a democratic republic that would abolish all remnants of serfdom in the countryside and the introduction of progressive social reforms benefiting both workers and peasants, including an eight-hour working day. The original program of the RSDWP included a point about an agrarian reform that would allot more land to the peasants. Later, however, the Bolsheviks replaced this postulate with a demand for the outright confiscation of all landed estates, while the Mensheviks came to advocate control of the land by local, freely elected peasant committees.

As a consequence of its second congress, the RSDWP split into two factions, which soon solidified. They established themselves into two antagonistic parties, each with a different program, leadership, methods of operation, and a contradictory vision of the future. While the Bolsheviks represented a centralist, elitist, authoritarian concept, the Mensheviks were inclined to model their party after the social-democratic movements of Central and Western Europe, especially the German Social Democratic Party. The Mensheviks attached considerable importance to trade unions and to democratic and parliamentary activities. They were motivated by the desire to work gradually with and for the masses. Until the crisis of the autumn of 1917, they had more of a mass following than the Bolsheviks.

The Bolsheviks, on the other hand, were more efficiently organized, more firmly led, and inclined more toward clandestine activities.

The programmatic clashes that split the RSDWP had their origins in the difficulties of adapting Marxist doctrine, which was a product of West European thought and environment, to specific Russian conditions. The Menshevik theories, which tried to follow rigidly Marxist doctrine and West European patterns, were to prove more alien to the Russian working masses than the simpler teachings of Lenin, whose dogmatic and authoritarian approach was so much closer to the native Russian mentality. This was especially true of the theses about the two-stage revolution to take place in a still semifeudal country like Russia. One of the basic assumptions of the Mensheviks was that a bourgeois revolution should precede Socialism by an unspecified but lengthy period of time. This meant that the revolutionary party would act as the chief agent of the bourgeois revolution, yet after the overthrow of Tsarism would refrain from participating in the new government that would be established on the ruins of the old. Power would be left to the partner in the victory, or the liberals. Meanwhile, during the period of transition between the two stages, the party would remain in opposition in order to prepare itself for its future role under Socialism. This meant in practice that the party would work for the proletarian cause, contribute to its triumph, and then leave power to its fellow-traveling bourgeois ally for an indefinite period of time.

SUMMARY

The compulsive revolutionary, as some of his biographers called Lenin, rejected the two-stage concept as unnecessary procrastination incomprehensible to the simple-minded workers of Russia. Already, during the revolution of 1905, he jettisoned the orthodox Marxist two-stage scheme and decided that the workers and peasants of Russia should seize power as soon as possible, and thus break the capitalistic chain at its weakest point as the first step toward the world proletarian revolution. Thus, while paying lip service to Marxism, Lenin proceeded to construct a doctrine that was actually a revision of the original theory. The three most significant aspects of Lenin's "revisionism" were (1) his attempt to make Marxism applicable to rural Russia by preaching an alliance of industrial workers with the landless and poor peasantry; (2) his theory of the hierarchic, centralist, authoritarian party as an indispensable tool of the proletarian revolution or "the vanguard of the proletariat," which was unable to fulfill its historic role alone; and (3) the rejection of a two-stage revolution.

As we have seen, at the beginning of the twentieth century the Russian revolutionary movement represented a plethora of clandestine parties, factions, and small debating groups. The Bolsheviks, although very vocal and active, were merely a minor segment of the movement. Most of the revolutionaries shared with the mass of the Russian intelligentsia its characteristic features: a principled, abstract, often highly doctrinaire approach to most issues at stake and the rejection of any compromise with the hated Tsarist regime. It was not to be reformed but destroyed.

SUGGESTED READING

ASCHER, ABRAHAM, *Pavel Axelrod and the Development of Menshevism*. Cambridge, Mass.: Harvard University Press, 1972.

BARON, SAMUEL H., *Plekhanov: The Father of Russian Marxism*. Stanford, Calif.: Stanford University Press, 1966.

BERDYAEV, NICHOLAS, *The Origins of Russian Communism*. Ann Arbor: University of Michigan Press, 1960.

BERLIN, ISAIAH, *Karl Marx: His Life and Environment*. New York: Oxford University Press, 1948.

BILLINGTON, JAMES H., *Mikhailovsky and Russian Populism*. New York: Oxford Press, 1958.

FISCHER, LOUIS, *Lenin*. New York: Harper and Row, 1965.

HAIMSON, LEOPOLD H., *The Russian Marxists and the Origins of Bolshevism*. Cambridge, Mass.: Harvard University Press, 1955.

KROPOTKIN, PETER, *Mutual Aid*. Boston: Porter Sargent, 1976.

MALIA, MARTIN, *Alexander Herzen and the Birth of Russian Socialism, 1812–1855*. Cambridge, Mass.: Harvard University Press, 1961.

MEYER, ALFRED G., *Leninism*. Cambridge, Mass.: Harvard University Press, 1957.

NAIMARK, NORMAN M., *Terrorists and Social Democrats. The Russian Revolutionary Movement under Alexander III*. Cambridge, Mass.: Harvard University Press, 1983.

POSSONY, STEPHEN, *Lenin—A Compulsive Revolutionary*. Chicago: Regnery, 1964.

PUTNAM, GEORGE F., *Russian Alternatives to Marxism*. Knoxville: University of Tennessee Press, 1977.

RADKEY, OLIVER, *Agrarian Foes of Bolshevism*. New York: Columbia University Press, 1958.

RIASANOVSKY, NICHOLAS V., *A Parting of the Ways: Government and the Educated Public in Russia. 1801–1855*. New York: Oxford University Press, 1976.

ROGGER, HANS, *Russia in the Age of Modernization and Revolution*. New York: Longman, 1983.

STITES, RICHARD, *The Women's Liberation Movement in Russia: Feminism, Nihilism, and Bolshevism, 1860–1930*. New York: Columbia University Press, 1977.

SZAMUELI, TIBOR, *The Russian Tradition*. London: Secker and Warburg, 1974.

TREADGOLD, DONALD W., *Lenin and His Rivals: The Struggle for Russia's Future, 1898–1906*. New York: Praeger, 1955.

TUCKER, ROBERT C., *Stalin as a Revolutionary, 1879–1929*. New York: W. W. Norton, 1973.

ULAM, ADAM, *The Bolsheviks*. New York: Collier, 1965.

———, *In The Name of the People*. New York: Viking Press, 1977.

VENTURI, FRANCO, *Roots of the Revolution: A History of the Populist and Socialist Movements in Nineteenth Century Russia*. New York: Knopf, 1960.

WILLIAMS, ROBERT C., *The Other Bolsheviks. Lenin and His Critics, 1904–1914*. Bloomington: Indiana University Press, 1986.

WILSON, EDMUND, *To the Finland Station*. Garden City, N.Y.: Doubleday, 1947.

WOLFE, BERTRAM D., *Marxism: 100 Years in the Life of a Doctrine*. New York: Dial Press, 1967.

——, *Three Who Made a Revolution*. New York: Dial Press, 1948.

YARMOLINSKY, AVRAHM, *Road to Revolution (A Century of Russian Radicalism)*. New York: Collier Books, 1962.

CHAPTER 4

The Russo-Japanese War and the Revolution of 1905

When, Tsar Nicholas II ascended the ivory throne of Ivan the Terrible in 1894, he inherited a huge and heterogeneous empire of some 130 million people, beset by a host of pressing problems. His economically fast-progressing realm was saddled with an obsolete centralistic structure unsuited for a dynamic country inhabited by over one hundred ethnic groups, many of them craving political and human rights as well as national autonomy, and some of them, like Finland and Poland, striving for independence. By the end of the nineteenth century it was obvious that most of the politically minded subjects of the new Tsar, irrespective of their origin, had outgrown the existing political structure and were eager to establish a legal order based on civil liberties and human rights. Also, the geopolitical situation of the Russian Empire was deteriorating rapidly, and the Euroasiatic realm of Nicholas II had to face two dynamic powers on its Western and Eastern extremities: a united Germany and a modernized Japan.

The new monarch possessed many features praiseworthy in an ordinary citizen but fatal in an autocratic ruler. He was modest, frugal, and very polite, a good son, husband, and father; yet he was weak, moody, had an untrained, undisciplined mind, and lacked the primal energy of will so essential in a leader. At the same time, Nicholas II was a fatalist; he believed that, since he was born on the day of St. Job the Sufferer, his life was bound to be marked with tragedy. Politics inspired him with aversion. He disliked serious discussions of theoretical problems because he could not cope with them. His former tutor, Konstantine P. Pobedonostsev, the Ober-Procurator of the Holy Synod, a reactionary Slavophile and narrow-minded fanatic who firmly believed in the traditional autocratic system and in Russia's historic mission, inculcated Nicholas with a profound suspicion of the dynamic forces of the epoch of liberalism and democracy. Pobedonostsev's influence strengthened the native conservatism of the young monarch and his belief in the divinely ordained mandate of the autocratic Tsar; he was determined to preserve his power intact. Consequently, in the liberal and progressive ideas of the times Nicholas saw nothing but stupidity and malevolence—vain, unhealthy dreams of intellectuals, manipulated by international Jewry and Freemasonry.

Nicholas II was married to a German princess, Alexandra of Hesse, a granddaughter of Queen Victoria. His wife was a striking contrast to him, intense and ambitious. Nicholas was dominated by his spouse and often tended to follow her advice in matters of the highest importance. As one of his critics, Leon Trotsky, put it, he was a henpecked husband and a chicken-headed monarch.

THE PEASANT PROBLEM

The man so badly equipped to exercise his office was confronted with a host of stupendous problems, the most important of which was the land question. It was crucial because of its magnitude and age-old neglect; it affected nearly 80 percent of the population, or over 100 million peasants. Yet for centuries the Tsarist regime had considered the issue from the point of view of its own fiscal and military interests and that of the nobility, the class regarded as the main support of the throne. The Emancipation Decrees of 1861 and 1864 were the first partial breach in the traditional neglect of the peasantry. The decrees freed the peasants from their masters but not from the village commune; if anything, the com-

Tsar Nicholas II (sitting on the left) and his family on a visit to King Edward VII of Britain, in 1910

mune's hold over it members was strengthened. The village commune existed throughout most of ethnic Russia, but not in the multinational borderlands of the Empire. The commune had three characteristic features. First, within the commune the land belonged not to individuals but to all its members collectively; individual peasants had no right of property, but merely a right of use as determined by the commune. The land was allotted not to individuals but to families, and was periodically repartitioned in accordance with the changing size of the families. Second, the commune was collectively responsible for taxes. This necessitated restriction of the peasant's right of withdrawal from the commune; the right was to be granted only if the departing peasant would undertake to continue paying his share of taxes. Third, the peasant was subject to a form of paternalism embodied by the state-appointed officials called "land captains," who were usually retired army officers. Moreover, the peasant was subject not to the general laws of the country but to local custom and was liable to corporal punishment. Consequently, the village commune hampered peasant economic initiative, inhibited experimentation, and kept the peasantry as a class apart, almost a caste. The communal system of land tenure was protected by the Government because the village commune facilitated collection of taxes, the commune being jointly responsible for each member's obligations.

To the inferior legal status, one must add the gradually worsening economic situation of the large masses of the peasantry. Heavy taxes and high redemption payments set up by the Emancipation Decrees compelled a large percentage of the fast-multiplying peasantry to hire themselves as farm labor, to seek outside earnings, or simply to migrate to the cities in search of gainful employment. The population explosion that followed the Emancipation was not paralleled by technical progress or the introduction of modern cultivation methods. This was due to a lack of capital and to an attachment to the communal system that tended to reinforce the traditional farming methods, like the scattered-strip or three-field system, in which one field lay fallow each year. This, more than the shortage of land, was mainly responsible for peasant poverty. The land hunger was only partly alleviated by migration to distant parts of the Empire like Southern Siberia, where village communes did not exist, or by purchase of land from the disintegrating large estates. In both cases, however, the difficulties were considerable. The outgoing peasant had to assume his share of his commune's taxes in addition to those he would be paying on his new farm.

THE NATIONALITY PROBLEM

The second most important problem confronting Nicholas was the nationality question. About half of the Empire was composed of ethnic minorities. Prudence dictated a cautious and conciliatory policy toward ethnic groups, especially those constituting large and compact segments of the Empire like Finns, Poles, or Ukrainians. This policy was, however, not practice. Following his father's slogan, "Russia for the Russians," Nicholas II pursued a policy of centralization and Russification.

Finnish autonomy, respected by the previous rulers, was restricted in 1898. In 1901 the Finnish Army was disbanded and military conscription into the Russian armed forces was extended to the Grand Duchy of Finland. The Finns, hitherto loyal to the Empire but fiercely attached to their constitutional privileges, resented these encroachments. In protest against them, a Finnish patriot assassinated the Russian Governor-General, Nicholas Bobrikov in 1904. The centralizing policy boomeranged and eventually turned the hitherto peaceful Finns into supporters of the revolutionaries. The Finns provided them with shelter and assistance while nurturing their own irredentist aspirations. In the Empire's Polish provinces, the policy of Russification initiated after the uprising of 1863–1864 continued unabated.

The Tsarist regime did not recognize the existence of a separate Ukrainian nationality or Ukrainian language. According to official doctrine, there was one Russian nation composed of three branches: Great Russians, Little Russians (Ukrainians), and White Russians (Belorussians). Also the endemic anti-Semitism of the Russian autocracy continued under Nicholas II in a more virulent form. Legislation concerning the Pale of Settlement, where some 3 million Jews were located, was tightened. Their access to higher education and liberal professions was restricted; they were also discriminated against in economic life and subject to special taxes. The authorities tolerated vicious forms of anti-Semitism, including violent pogroms. The most infamous took place in Kishinev in April 1903, in Gomel in August 1903, and the largest in 1905 in Odessa. No wonder, therefore, that Jewish emigration from Russia to the United States, Palestine, and Western Europe continued to increase, while at home the Jews constituted a considerable segment of the revolutionary movement. At the same time, treatment of other national minorities, especially the Caucasian peoples and the Baltic Germans, was harsh and often trampled on their ethnic feelings unnecessarily. The Russifying tendencies of the Tsarist administration in the Baltic provinces, initiated by Alexander III, were not only maintained but even intensified after 1894. These policies tended to alienate large strata of the non-Russian majority of the Empire's population; the percentage of non-Russians in the revolutionary movement was remarkably high.

INDUSTRIAL EXPANSION

The close of the nineteenth century saw the first phase of the industrial revolution in Russia. Large deposits of coal and iron were discovered in the Ukraine, especially in the basin of the Donets River, and oil was found in the Caucasus. From 1880 on, the output of iron and steel showed a remarkable increase. The Civil War in the United States made cotton export difficult and thereby stimulated its production in Russia, where the newly acquired Central Asiatic provinces supplied ample quantities of raw material. In northern Russia, production of flax grew by leaps and bounds. Soon Moscow and Lódz in Russian Poland became important centers of the textile industry. The rapid expansion of industrial production was paralleled by the mushrooming of private trade, banking, and insurance companies. The swift growth of industry, trade, communication, and various services resulted in the appearance of a large mass of urban workers and in the quick expansion of the stratum of professional people.

Economic development of the Tsarist Empire was given a powerful stimulus in 1892 with the appointment of Sergius Witte to the key post of Minister of Finance. This self-made former railroad engineer proved to be a technocrat with great energy and a clear vision of Russia's future as an industrial giant. As Minister of Communication, he had already greatly developed the Empire's infrastructure, beginning with the railroad system—a precondition for industrialization. The climax of the railroad building came in the years 1896–1900, when over 10,000 miles of rails were laid. Witte controlled the Ministry of Finance for eleven years, until August 1903. For a decade he was the most powerful man in Russia. Through his administrative empire-building, the Minister of Finance managed to control education and agriculture as well as foreign policy. Witte saw Russia as a part of European, indeed, world economy. Although a fierce patriot, he nevertheless believed that for a decade or so Russia should forego its great power pretentions in order to devote its energies and resources to the vital task of modernization.

Witte realized that to remain a great power the Empire had to industrialize at all costs. To this objective he was determined to subordinate other considerations. He was, for instance, in favor of a highly protectionist trade policy that would allow infant Russian industries to develop and mature. Consequently, he set up stiff tariffs and introduced heavy taxes on such articles of common use as alcohol, matches, tobacco, and kerosene. Witte was aware of the scarcity of Russia's native capital. Consequently, he tried to attract foreign investments with prospects of high profit and financial stability. Arguing that all major powers including Japan had adopted the gold standard, at that time a symbol of respectablity, he introduced it in Russia in 1896. As advantageous as Witte's policy was for industrialization, it was a deterrent to agrarian progress; high tariffs, while protecting big industrial trusts and syndicates, drove the price of agricultural machinery and other products needed for modernization of the backward Russian farms to prohibitive heights.

On the other hand, under Witte's leadership Russian industry increasingly attracted foreign credits and investments. The alliance with France, concluded in 1892–1893 under Alexander III, was followed by a rapid influx of French capital. With its aid, the Trans-Siberian Railroad connected St. Petersburg with Vladivostok, although initially with only a single line. Soon British, Belgian, and American capital, lured by lavish concessions and huge profits, followed the French example.

As a consequence of rapid yet uneven progress and of rural overpopulation, the number of industrial workers was expanding rapidly. By the end of the nineteenth century they numbered over 2.5 million, and well over 3 million on the eve of the Revolution of 1917. Their economic position was unenviable: they had to subsist on one of the lowest wages in Europe. They lived mostly in wretched, barracks-like dwellings or in miserable wooden cottages, where the lack of sanitation and pure water caused frequent outbursts of dysentery and typhoid fever. In 1897 the standard working day was eleven and a half hours. Because the workers had no right of association and no right to strike, they often had to suffer abuses by foremen as well as by factory owners. Only in 1912 would a rudimentary security system for industrial workers be introduced by the government. Attempts at strikes were ruthlessly suppressed.

In view of these actions, the proletarians of Russia felt that the Tsarist government was not their protector but their coexploiter, who tended to side not with the workers but with the capitalists, many of whom were foreigners. Initially the workers' restiveness was not explosive; however, gradually stimulated by revolutionary agitation, they awakened to the value of group action, and industrial strikes and riots soon paralleled the traditional sporadic peasant mutinies. The situation worsened in 1901–1903 when Russian passed through an economic depression that resulted in widespread unemployment and a rapid fall in stocks, in bank capital, and in prices. In 1902, for instance, no less than 2,400 enterprises went bankrupt and over 90,000 workers lost their jobs. The situation improved only slightly in 1904.

POLITICAL FERMENT

The second half of the nineteenth century, marked by rapid socioeconomic transformation and freer access to education in Russia, produced an expanding group of professional people. By the close of the century, they numbered some half a million. The industrial revolution, the expansion of the bureaucratic machine and of educational facilities, the functioning of rural self-government, all provided this group with considerable economic opportunities and broader political vistas. The growing aspirations and expectations of these people were bound to clash with the autocracy's monopoly of political power. To close the gap between the establishment and the educated, and hence politically minded, strata of the population seemed logical. This was not the case, however. The autocracy, after a brief period of relative liberalization that lasted for over a decade from 1855 to 1866, returned to tighter controls on intellectual actitivites; the autonomous status of institutions of higher learning was abolished and censorship of publications tightened. Constant administrative interference with the often enlightened and beneficial work of the local self-governments, which had been functioning in the countryside since the 1860s, heavy-handed censorship, tight control of the otherwise neglected educational institutions, and frequent arbitrary arrests irritated the Russian liberals. As a consequence, many members of the educated classes, denied legitimate active participation in political life, increasingly assumed the radical attitudes characteristic of the hard core of the intelligentsia. Many intellectuals, professional people, and even some of the gentry supported the working classes' demands for shorter hours, social security, and the right to organize. The early hopes that the Great Reforms initiated by Alexander would be brought to their logical conclusion, that the autocratic regime would be gradually transformed into a constitutional monarchy, were cruelly disappointed under Alexander III. In 1896, Nicholas II also condemned these aspirations as "vain dreams."

The Russian Liberal movement began to crystallize at the beginning of the twentieth century. In 1901, the progressive zemstvo circles established in Stuttgart, Germany, a journal called *Liberation,* under the editorship of a former Social Democrat, later a "legal Marxist," Peter Struve. The journal's first issue expressed the hope of "uniting all those groups of Russian society that cannot find an outlet for their feelings of indignation either in class or in revolutionary struggle." In 1903 some of the readers of the journal formed a *Union of Liberation* led by an eminent professor of history, Paul N. Miliukov, author of the impressive *Studies in the History of Russian Culture.*[1] Miliukov postulated that the subjects of the Empire

should not be treated in a less favorable manner than the people whom they helped to free. He argued that the Russians, no less than the Bulgarians liberated by Russian arms from the Turks in 1878, deserved a bill of rights, including *habeas corpus,* and a constitutional charter providing for political representatives elected by universal suffrage. However, the program was rebuked by the Government as unsuitable to Russia. This intractable attitude tended to push the frustrated Russian liberals to the left, toward the radicals and socialists. Consequently, to the ferment among the politically more advanced ethnic groups (the Jews, the Finns, the Poles), as well as the peasants and the workers, now were added many frustrated Russian liberals.

By 1902 the Empire was experiencing an economic depression and industrial unrest flared markedly. That summer the Ukrainian provinces witnessed the worst outbreak of peasant violence since 1880. The highly explosive situation alarmed Tsarist authorities. The reactionary Minister of the Interior, Vyacheslav von Plehve, talking to Witte in 1903, said bluntly: "The country is on the verge of revolution. The only way to avert it is to make a small victorious war." The tense situation in the Far East soon provided the military–bureaucratic clique at the Court with opportunities to engineer such a military clash as an outlet for domestic difficulties.

RUSSIAN FOREIGN POLICY

To understand the Russo-Japanese war of 1904–1905, one must understand Russia's international position. At the Congress of Berlin in 1878, the united front of Britain, Austria, and Germany deprived Russia of the main fruit of her victory over Turkey. Rebuffed in the Balkans, the Russians turned their energies toward Central Asia and the Far East, where they continued to press against the decaying Empire of China and gained considerable stretches of territory along the Amur River, as far as the

---

[1] The work appeared in English as *Outlines of Russian Culture,* edited by Michael Karpovich (Philadelphia: University of Philadelphia Press, 1942), 3 vols.

Pacific. Drive in that direction was urged not only by a group of Russian thinkers and writers of the Eurasian school, who preached Russia's expansion in Asia, but also by a cousin of Nicholas II, the German Emperor William II. He was anxious to divert Russia's energy from the Balkans, where her Pan-Slavic ambitions conflicted with the interests of Germany's chief ally, Austro-Hungary, while in Asia, Russia was bound to cash with Britain, Germany's chief commercial and naval competitor.

Prussia had been Russia's traditional ally throughout most of the nineteenth century, and the two countries were linked by a network of royal intermarriages as well as by a common fear of the twin dynamic forces of the modern era: nationalism and social revolution. Germany, united under Prussian leadership in 1871, continued to be Russia's chief trading partner and main provider of technical know-how. Nevertheless, the requirements of the European balance of power, the fear of the growing might of a powerful Germany allied with Austro-Hungary, pushed the Tsarist Empire toward France, then sulking after her defeat by Prussia in 1870–1871.

The spectacular German naval, commercial, and colonial expansion also threatened the British. As a consequence, London gradually abandoned its traditional mistrust of the French and established an informal understanding with them known as the *Entente Cordiale.* Yet even the *Entente* was not sufficiently strong to counterbalance the might of Germany and Austria, and Russian aid was needed.

Rapprochement between autocratic Russia and the liberal Third Republic was not a simple matter. It was opposed in Russia by many conservatives, including Witte, who favored alliance with Germany, as well as by some economic vested interests. Nevertheless, believing Russia to be isolated and menaced by the growing German ambitions, Alexander III was increasingly leaning toward the French. The Russian need for French capital and the generous loans offered by Paris to St. Petersburg paved the way toward a politcal understanding in 1893–1894. The military agreement between Russia and France provided that, if France were attacked by Germany or by Italy supported by Germany, Russia would use all its available forces to fight Germany. On the other hand, if Russia were attacked by Germany, or by Austro-Hungary supported by Germany, France would launch an offensive against the aggressor with all its forces.

The signing of the alliance with France was designed to protect the Tsarist Empire from both Germany and Austro-Hungary. Vienna and Budapest resented Russia's close ties with the Balkan Slavs, especially with small but ambitious Serbia, whose leaders dreamed of unifying all southern Slavs. In view of the circumstances under which World War I broke out, it is worth bearing in mind that the French promised to help the Russians against Austro-Hungary only in case the latter were supported by Germany. The alliance with France was the cornerstone of St. Petersburg's policy from 1894.

RUSSIAN EXPANSION IN THE FAR EAST

Meanwhile, the progressive distintegration of the Chinese Empire, which reached bottom at the end of the nineteenth century, created a power vacuum in the Far East. This tempted Russia and Japan to fill the gap. Nicholas II believed in Russia's "Asiatic mission," and circumstances seemed to favor the idea. The Trans-Siberian railroad brought the Pacific within eight days' journey from Moscow. Russia's export of textiles and metallurgical products to Far Eastern markets expanded. Southern Siberia and the Maritime Provinces around Vladivostok were gradually settled with the surplus population from the Empire's European provinces. The Trans-Siberian railroad passed along southern Siberia but made a great detour around Manchuria's northern frontier in order to reach the main Russian port of the Pacific, Vladivostok, which in Russian means "Rule of the East."

China's growing weakness was an invitation to Russian expansion. Largely spontaneous, the drive that had begun in the fifteenth century assumed a more systematic character around the middle of the nineteenth century. At the same time, however, the reformed and revitalized Japan was nurturing imperial ambitions around Manchuria and Korea—so close and hence believed to be vital to Japan's security. Since meanwhile, the Russians had also developed a foothold in Korea, the interests of these two dynamic powers clashed with those of the Chinese trying to protect their old hegemonic sphere.

In 1894 an armed conflict broke out between China and Japan over Korea. The freshly modernized Japanese army and navy easily prevailed over the antiquated Chinese forces. In 1895 Peking was compelled to cede to Japan the island of Formosa (now Taiwan), the Pescadores Islands, and the peninsula of Liao-Tung, which has two harbors: Port Arthur and Dairen (known in Russian as Dalny). Both powers now recognized Korea's independence. Soon, however, an international conference summoned by Nicholas II deprived the Japanese of the strategic Liao-Tung peninsula. Instead the Japanese were given a considerable indemnity and kept Formosa and the Pescadores. China's territorial integrity was otherwise guaranteed by Russia. For its alleged services to China, Russia extracted an important concession for the construction of a railroad running from Chita across Manchuria to Vladivostok. The concession put a consierable strip of Chinese territory under Russian administration for a period that might extend to eighty years. Russian troops organized as an "international defense force" were to protect the "East Chinese Railway."

Meanwhile, the Russians were also trying to replace China as Korea's protector. Simultaneously with the penetration of both Manchuria and Korea, St. Petersburg extracted from Peking another concession in the form of the right to keep Russian warships in Port Arthur and Dairen. This gave the Russians unhampered, ice-free access to the Pacific through the Yellow Sea, outside the enclosed Sea of Japan. As a consequence of these encroachments, China's patriotic feelings were aroused and a wave of xenophobia swept the country. In November 1897, two German missionaries were killed by a mob in Shantung. To this the European powers replied by wholesale spoliation of China. Germany, Great Britain, and France each annexed a port city, while Russia, guarantor of China's integrity, imposed on Peking another of those "unequal treatie" about which the Chinese have been complaining ever since and wrested Port Arthur. The annexation was camouflaged as a "lease" for twenty-five years.

The humiliated and desperate Chinese replied to this vivisection with another outburst of xenophobia and a revolt led by a military organization known as "Boxers." In 1900 numerous massacres of "the foreign devils" were perpetrated throughout the Middle Kingdom. The Western quarter in Peking was besieged. The European powers retorted with a naval and military expedition and a cruel revenge. Now the Chinese were compelled by St. Petersburg to prolong the "lease" of Port Arthur from twenty-five to ninety-nine years. The harbor was connected with the Trans-Siberian Railway through the "Chinese Eastern Railway" running through Manchuria.

Meanwhile, at the Russian capital two factions were fighting over the best course of action to be taken in the Far East. One was headed by Witte, who argued that Russia should take into consideration Japan's vital interest at least in Korea and slow down its headlong expansion. In a memorandum presented to the Tsar in 1902, he urged him to strive for a rapprochement with Japan on the basis of mutual economic advantages in developing the resources of the Far East. Witte advised Nicholas to strike a bargain with Tokyo that would consolidate Russian influence in rich and strategic Manchuria while leaving Korea to Japan. This cautious

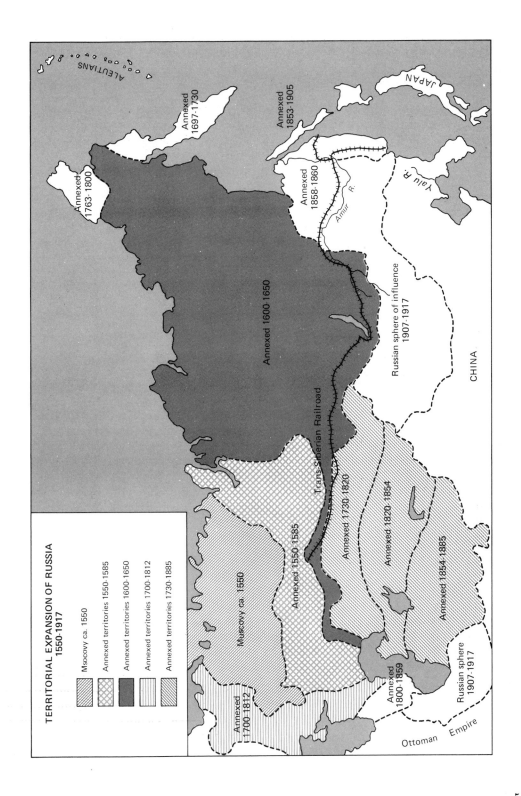

TERRITORIAL EXPANSION OF RUSSIA
1550-1917

Muscovy ca. 1550

Annexed territories 1550-1585

Annexed territories 1600-1650

Annexed territories 1700-1812

Annexed territories 1730-1885

Annexed 1763-1800

Annexed 1697-1730

Annexed 1853-1905

Annexed 1858-1860

Annexed 1600-1650

Amur R.

Yalu R.

JAPAN

Russian sphere of influence 1907-1917

CHINA

Trans-Siberian Railroad

Muscovy ca. 1550

Annexed 1550-1585

Annexed 1730-1820

Annexed 1820-1854

Annexed 1854-1885

Annexed 1700-1812

Annexed 1800-1859

Russian sphere 1907-1917

Ottoman Empire

ALEUTIANS

policy of "peaceful penetration" was opposed by a group of the Tsar's advisors, who played on the Emperor's proclivity toward spectacular schemes and on the greed of some Grand Dukes who had been involved in a timber concession on the Yalu River. Supported by the influential Minister of the Interior, von Plehve, the hawks won the day. In August of 1903, Witte was dismissed from the key post of Minister of Finance and appointed Chairman of the Council of Ministers; this was actually a form of honorary retirement. His economically inspired pacifism was only one of many disagreements between the Tsar and Witte, who was a paragon of efficiency and an often brutally frank opponent of some of the Emperor's hare-brained schemes.

While recklessly pursuing an expansionist policy and rejecting Japanese overtures, St. Petersburg neglected military and naval preparations in the Far East, where its forces were inferior to those of its opponent.

THE RUSSO-JAPANESE WAR OF 1904–1905

After completing their preparations, the Japanese, without declaring war, launched a surprise attack on the Russian Pacific squadron lying at anchor off Port Arthur on the night of January 26 (Februrary 8 NS), 1904. Several Russian vessels were destroyed and several others damaged. The remnant of the cripple fleet was compelled to seek shelter in the inner harbor, there to be blockaded for months. This early Pearl Harbor left the strategic initiative in the hands of the Japanese.

In view of this disaster, it was decided in St. Petersburg that the Russian Baltic squadron should be send to Far Eastern waters to restore the naval balance there. The squadron, unable to sail through the Suez Canal controlled by Japan's ally, Great Britain, had to travel almost nine months; they covered 18,000 miles, or two-thirds of the earth's circumference. Sailing around

the Cape of Good Hope, the Baltic squadron finally reached the Far Eastern theater of war in May 1905. There in the straits of Tsushima that separate Korea from Japan, the naval battle of Tsushima was fought. The encounter of the two fleets, in which nearly a hundred ships took part, lasted only about forty-five minutes. The more maneuverable and better commanded Japanese fleet annihilated the Russian Baltic Squadron almost completed. Only two cruisers and two destroyers managed to escape to Vladivostok. Having seized command of the sea, the Japanese transported their superbly trained troops, full of patriotic fervor, onto the Asian mainland. Fighting with reckless bravado, they proceeded to inflict on the Russians a series of humiliating defeats, first in the valley of the Yalu River and then in Manchuria. The Russian Far Eastern stronghold, Port Authur, surrendered in December 1905 after 148 days of siege.

Despite the catastrophe of Tsushima and the capitulation of Port Arthur, and despite the defeats in Manchuria, the total potential resources of Russia were still far superior to those of Japan, exhausted by her costly victories. What prevented Nicholas II from continuing the war was the situation at home. From the very beginning the distant Far East war was almost as unpopular among the Russian people as the war in Vietnam was in the United States. By the summer of 1905, large-scale political manifestations and mutinies by soldiers, sailors, peasants, and workers, acts of terror, and sabotage assumed menacing proportions. Under the circumstances, Tsar Nicholas decided to accept President Theodore Roosevelt's suggestion of peace. Witte was sent to the United States to negotiate a settlement. At the presidential summer home in Portsmouth, New Hampshire, the peace treaty between Russia and Japan was signed on August 23 (September 5 NS), 1905. Witte acknowledged Korea and southern Manchuria as Japan's sphere of influence. The Japanese annexed the southern part of the island of Sakhalin. Russia ceded to Japan the rights it had recently acquired in Port Arthur and Dairen on the peninsula of Liao-Tung. Northern Manchuria, however, with its important East Chinese railroad, remained within the Russian orbit.

The underlying cause of Russia's defeat was its failure to match its imperial drive in the Far East with adequate diplomatic planning and to balance its new commitments with military resources. St. Petersburg had underestimated the rising power of Japan and its own strategic vulnerability in the Orient. While provoking Tokyo by encroaching on Japan's spheres of influence in southern Manchuria and Korea, the Russians had failed to draw proper conclusions about the possible consequences of their acts. Lack of adequate military supplies, antiquated training, obsolete transport facilities, and the corruption and inefficiency of Russian civil military admin-

istration were all significant factors that hampered the Russian war effort. But political and social unrest played a crucial role in the Russian acceptance of the Japanese peace terms.

UNREST AT HOME

From the very beginning, the Russian people suspected that the adventures had been engineered as a substitute for domestic reforms. Yet as long as there was a chance for a military victory, the population of Russia proper did not protest very actively. Initially, it was in the nationally heterogenous borderlands—where ethnic grievances were compounded by political and socioeconomic issues—in the Baltic provinces and in Russian Poland that the opposition to the war assumed very threatening proportions.

In Russia proper, the first major

President Theodore Roosevelt with S. J. Witte and Baron Roman Rosen of Russia and the Japanese Delegates before the signing of the Treaty of Portsmouth

symptom of discontent came somewhat later; the assassination of the unpopular Minister of the Interior, von Plehve, in July 1904 was one of the first signals of the unrest. Von Plehve was replaced by a mildly liberal bureaucrat, Prince Sviatopolk-Mirsky, who immediately made a series of minor concessions. This failed, however, to satisfy the mounting opposition. Since any public discussion of fundamental reform of the Empire was still taboo, in September—October 1904 representatives of seven underground opposition groups—Russian liberals, Social Revolutionaries, Polish National Democrats, and delegates of the Polish Socialist Party—got together in Paris with delegates of Finnish, Georgian, and Armenian revolutionary groups. The conference issued a common declaration that provided for cooperation of these groups in their fight for constitutional reform and national self-determination.

This statement had a profound effect on the opposition movement at home. From late autumn of 1904, most of the educated, politically active middle and upper classes were in an uproar, loudly condemning the war and urging immediate reforms: legal justice for all without discrimination and an elected legislative body. As political meetings were forbidden, the action of the opposition was expressed in a series of professional conferences and banquets not dissimilar to those held in France on the eve of the Revolution of 1848. The worsening situation at the front and the defeats of Russian forces in Manchuria inhibited the Tsarist authorities from suppressing these manifestations. When in December 1905 the fortress of Port Arthur capitulated under humiliating circumstances, a wave of protest against the war broke out.

Meanwhile, the opposition movement initiated by the professional people spread to the proletarian masses in the cities and to the countryside. When in December 1904 four members of a labor group were dismissed from the Putilov Steel Works in St. Petersburg, several thousand workers went on strike. Soon other factories in the capital joined them. By the beginning of January 1905, the number of strikers had reached 140,000. Most of the industrial life of the capital was paralyzed.

Aware of inflation and unemployment among the workers of the capital and sympathizing with their plight, the hitherto loyal Christian Socialist Assembly of the Russian Factory Workers, led by an Orthodox Priest, Father Gapon, decided to stage a mass demonstration. His idea was to submit the grievances of the workers in the form of a humble petition to the Tsar, asking for an eight-hour working day, an increase in workers' wages up to one ruble per day, a bill of rights, and free universal education. Despite police warnings that the planned mass demonstration would not be tolerated in the vicinity of the Palace and that the delegation would not be received by the Tsar, Gapon insisted on carrying out his original plan.

On Sunday, January 9 (22 NS), 1905, large crowds of workers singing patriotic and church songs and carrying pictures of the Imperial family and holy icons converged on the Winter Palace. On the order of Grand Duke Vladimir, military governor of the capital, the police and some 20,000 soldiers barred all roads leading to the Palace. When, despite two successive warnings to disperse, the demonstrators pressed their march forward, several volleys were fired into the crowd. Then a cavalry charge dispersed the demonstrators. According to the official figures, 96 people were killed on the spot and 333 wounded, of whom 34 died subsequently.

Prior to that Bloody Sunday, often called "the Gaponade," the old myth of the Tsar as "Little Father" had lingered among the people. The massacre of January 22 dealt a severe blow to the legend of the "good Tsar" separated from his children by the "bad bureaucrats." The expulsion of a large number of unemployed people from the capital ordered by authorities after Bloody Sunday merely helped to disseminate the news about the massacre to the remote corners of the Empire. This resulted in an epidemic of strikes, mutinies, and other violent demonstrations that soon spilled over the Tsarist domains. Now the initiative shifted from the liberal professionals to the workers. Acts of sabotage and terror against police officers were committed in increasing numbers, with most of the assailants escaping. In February 1905, Grand Duke Sergius, uncle of the Tsar and Governor General of Moscow, was murdered at the Kremlin in broad daylight by a Social Revolutionary. Prince Sviatopolk-Mirsky was dismissed and the crucial Ministry of the Interior was taken over by his Deputy, Alexander G. Bulygin, a colorless bureaucrat.

Meanwhile, in March 1905, the Russian forces were beaten at the eight-day battle of Mukden, in Manchuria, bloodiest battle of the war. The Russians alone suffered casualties amounting to nearly 100,000 men. Again the Government offered some concessions to appease the people and issued a series of partial concessions. In April a toleration edict was issued: religious teaching was declared free, and dissenters from Greek Orthodoxy were allowed to abandon the established church. The Jews were also given some minor concessions. When news of the Tsushima catastrophe reached the capital, the Government outlined a scheme for a consultative assembly to be elected on a limited franchise in four stages.

The opposition took advantage of this scheme, which seemed to foreshadow elections to a consultative *Duma* (an assembly), to form open political parties, trade unions, and other associations. From "the Mukden Spring" on, hitherto secret groups, like the Constitutional Democrats (or Cadets), the Social Revolutionaries, the two Social Democratic factions, as well as innumerable minor groups and trade organizations, operated quite freely. On the initiative of these parties, pamphlets and leaflets were published, and meetings and mass demonstrations were organized. All the while, political unrest was spreading and numerous mutinies

in the armed forces took place; for instance, the sailors of the battleship *Potemkin* rebelled in Odessa in June 1905. During the spring and summer of 1905, Russian, Ukrainian, and Latvian peasants began to help themselves to the landlords' estates, to cut timber, and to appropriate grain, cattle, and implements. There were numerous cases of the peasants paying off old scores with bludgeon and torch.

THE ST. PETERSBURG SOVIET AND THE CONSTITUTIONAL MANIFESTO

It was in the midst of his ferment that Witte returned home with the Treaty of Portsmouth in his pocket. This meant that now the Tsarist regime would be able to withdraw most of the Far Eastern contingent of troops and assume a stiffer posture toward the opposition. By October the Government regained its self-confidence and ordered the entire Congress of Railroad Workers, then deliberating in St. Petersburg, to be arrested. In protest against this move, nearly all the railroads went on strike. As a result, many factories had to stop work because of the lack of supplies. In a few days the strike had spread and paralyzed most communication, industry, trade, education, and even entertainment within the Empire. It was especially effective in St. Petersburg, essentially a northern frontier city overwhelmingly dependent on transport for food, fuel, and other necessities.

Amidst the mounting wave of protest was born the idea of a working-class coordinating council to direct the originally spontaneous protest movement. The nucleus of the first such council (*soviet* in Russian) was set up by the strikers of some fifty printing shops in the capital. They elected deputies to represent them in dealing with the authorities. These deputies, joined by delegates from other similar bodies, formed a Council, or Soviet, of Workers' Deputies composed of some 122 members; 26 of them were delegates of the organized trade unions, while 96 represented various industrial plants. The St. Petersburg Soviet elected an Executive Committee. Its vice-chairman was a young member of the Russian Social Democratic Workers' Party, Leon Bronstein (best known by one of his pen names, Trotsky). The St. Petersburg Soviet of Workers' Deputies issued a manifesto that not only repeated the demand for a Constituent Assembly, but also appealed for unity of the working class under "the glorious Red Flag of the proletarians of all lands," an echo of the Communist Manifesto of Marx and Engles.

The majority of the Soviet belonged either to the Menshevik faction of the RSDWP or, like Trotsky, were close to it; the rest were affiliated either with the Bolsheviks, the Social Revolutionaries, or various minor revolutionary groups. Overthrow of the autocracy and setting up a democratic republic in Russia were their common objectives. For this purpose, the Soviet urged the workers to form fighting squads, or "Red Guards." Soon similar Soviets were formed in several hundred provincial places. From the very beginning there were differences of opinion between various groups as to the course to be followed. The Bolsheviks and some of the Social Revolutionaries considered an armed uprising as the only means of overthrowing the Tsarist regime; the Mensheviks saw a possiblity of at least a temporary accommodation with the liberals and were less inclined to plot an armed uprising. At the bottom of this attitude of the Mensheviks was the classic Marxist theory of a two-stage revolution and a hope for a legal workers' party modeled after the German Social Democratic movement.

Frightened by the general strike, Nicholas II surrendered. On October 17 (30 NS), 1905, he decided upon a step that he regarded as a betrayal of the promise he had made to his father on his deathbed: to preserve the autocratic power intact. He reluctantly issued a manifesto that promised most of the concessions demanded by the liberal opposition. The concessions included a bill of rights and a Legislative Assembly (Duma), without which no law would be passed. The Duma was to comprise two houses. The lower house was to be composed of deputies elected for five years on a fairly broad franchise; the upper house, the old but now reshaped Council of State, was to be composed of an equal number of appointed and elected representatives. Cabinet ministers were to be appointed by and responsible to the Monarch.

According to the supplemental Fundamental Laws, the Monarch—not the people—was the source of sovereignty. The budget rights of the Duma were strictly limited, with certain segments exempted from its control, including the budget of the Imperial House and certain sections of the armed forces appropriations. Budget and foreign policy were to be controlled largely by the Sovereign. Article 87 of the Fundamental Laws granted the Government the right to issue decrees in case of emergency or when the Duma was not in session. Such decrees, however, were technically invalid unless confirmed by the Duma within three months. In short, the Russian system was a crossbreed between Western constitutionalism and Russian autocracy. Significantly, the Tsar not only retained numerous prerogatives but also his title of "Autocrat of all the Russias."

The last major revolutionary event of that fateful year was another general strike proclaimed by the Moscow Soviet in December to protest against the reprisals. Soon the strike turned into an armed uprising in the working-class Presna district of Moscow and was brutally suppressed. It took two years and a series of stern measures to bring the minor, smoldering fires of 1905 under control. Peasant unrest continued throughout 1906 and was only suppressed by large-scale summary executions of ringleaders of the rebellion. But with the collapse of the Moscow rebellion, the task of breaking the back of the revolutionary movement was accomplished.

THE BALANCE SHEET

The balance sheet of the crisis of 1905 is complex. As a result of it, no new ruler ascended the throne, no socioeconomic upheaval took place, no power was transferred from one class to another, and no radical shift in Russia's foreign policy was brought about. The revolt of the workers and peasants was suppressed without the achievement of their final objectives. The widespread unrest and the series of mass demonstrations, mutinies, and acts of terror resulted merely in a partial reshaping of the autocratic system, which became a halfway house between Western liberalism and Russian autocracy, a hybrid combining Western constitutionalism with native autocracy. The compromise reflected the balance of political forces that existed within the Empire at that time.

It was true that under pressure of the revolutionary movement, the autocracy had had to make some concessions to the opposition, but the opposition was not strong enough to make absolutism capitulate undoncitionally. The two pillars of the regime, the armed forces and the bureaucracy, although badly shattered, remained basically loyal to the Tsar. The peasants, previously frightened by the punitive expeditions, were now temporarily bribed by the abolition of the redemption payments. The revolutionaries provided to be weak because of their division among at least three major groups, the Social Revolutionary Party, the Mensheviks, and the Bolsheviks, each advocating different tactics.

Nevertheless, the events of 1904–1905 should be looked upon as the first rumblings of the storm that was to come twelve years later, a "dress rehearsal for 1917," as Lenin put it. The crisis of 1905 brought about a series of novel phenomena that foreshadowed future events. One of them was the active participation of millions of people in political life. Another was the emergence from underground of the first legal political parties in Russian history; the most important were the Cadets, the SRs, and the Social Democrats, by that time already irrevocably split into two rival factions. From now on these parties, together with other emerging organizations like the legalized trade unions and other professional associations, made Russia a different place. Finally, October 1905 saw the appearance of the Petersburg Soviet, a broadly representative council of the working class. The institution of soviets was to play a significant role in the Revolution of 1917. The controversies between the Mensheviks and the Bolsheviks were intensified during the crisis of 1904–1905. The Bolsheviks were especially deeply affected by this crisis. By July 1905, Lenin, impressed with the strength of the revolutionary upsurge of the working masses, had already rejected the Menshevik—Marxist concept of a two-stage upheaval to take place in semi-feudal Russia and began to insist on a direct jump from bourgeois democracy to the class rule of the proletariat.

The crisis also gave a powerful stimulus to the more mature and restless ethnic groups of the Empire to express their own dissatisfaction. As a result, the Poles and the Baltic peoples, and to a lesser extent the Jews, gained some religious and cultural concessions. The crisis of 1904–1905 also hastened the evolution of the national consciousness of the Ukrainians and the Muslim peoples.

The revolutionary crisis of 1905 had, moreover, considerable impact on the outside world. The changes brought about in Russia demonstrated that significant concessions might be wrested from an autocratic ruler even by backward, agrarian people Besides stimulating the growth of radical and socialist forces in Europe, the Russian storm contributed substantially to the subsequent awakening of nationalism and the development of constitutional regimes in Turkey, Persia, and China. The Russo-Japanese War was fought largely on Chinese territory, in Manchuria, and around the Liao-Tung peninsula. This further stressed the helplessness of the Manchu dynasty, speeded its downfall in 1911, and prepared the way for the proclamation of the Chinese Republic with Sun Yat-Sen as President.

The Russo-Japanese War, which represented the first major defeat of a great European power at the hands of an Asian nation, was also a major stage in the process of undermining the supremacy of the white man on the globe. The Russian storm of 1905 contributed significantly toward preparing the ground for a tidal wave of anti-white, anticolonial sentiment, which spread from Asia to Africa and in our day has swept away most of the colonial regimes.

SUGGESTED READING

BONNELL, VICTORIA, *Roots of Rebellion, Workers' Politics and Organizations in St. Petersburg and Moscow, 1900–1914.* Berkeley and Los Angeles: University of California Press, 1986.

BUSHNELL, JOHN, *Mutiny Amid Repression: Russian Soldiers in the Revolution of 1905–1906.* Indiana—Michigan Series in Russian and East European Studies (edited by Alexander Rabinowitch and William G. Rosenberg). Bloomington: Indiana University Press, 1985.

DALLIN, DAVID J., *The Rise of Russia in Asia.* New Haven, Conn.: Yale University Press, 1949.

DZIEWANOWSKI, M. K., *The Communist Party of Poland: An Outline of History.* Cambridge, Mass.: Harvard University Press, 1959 and 1976, Chs. 1–3.

GREENBERG, LOUIS. *The Jews in Russia: The Struggle for Emancipation.* New Haven, Conn.: Yale University Press, 1965, 2 vols.

HARCAVE, SIDNEY, *First Blood: the Russian Revolution of 1905.* New York: Macmillan, 1964.

LEDERER, IVO J. (ED), *Russian Foreign Policy.* New Haven, Conn.: Yale University Press, 1962.

MALAMAZOFF, ANDREW, *Russian Far Eastern Policy, 1881–1904.* Berkeley: University of California Press, 1958.

PAVLOVSKY, GEORGE, *Agricultural Russia on the Eve of the Revolution* (reprint). New York: Howard Fertig, 1968.

ROMANOV, BORIS A., *Russia in Manchuria, 1892–1906.* Ann Arbor, Mich.: J. W. Edward, 1952.

RUBINOW, ISAAC MAX, *Economic Conditions of the Jews in Russia.* New York: Arno, 1975.

SCHWARZ, SALOMON M., *The Revolution of 1905: The Workers' Movement and the Formation of Bolshevism and Menshevism.* Chicago: University of Chicago Press, 1967.

SABLINSKY, WALTER, *The Road to Bloody Sunday.* Princeton, N.J.: Princeton University Press, 1976.

SAVINKOV, BORIS, *Memoirs of a Terrorist.* New York: A. & C. Boni, 1931.

SPECTOR, IVAR, *The First Russian Revolution and Its Impact on Asia.* Englewood Cliffs, N.J.: Prentice-Hall, 1962.

TROTSKY, LEON, *1905.* New York: Random House, 1971.

TROYAT, HENRI, *Daily Life in Russia under the Last Tsar.* New York: Macmillan, 1962.

VON LAUE, THEODORE, *Sergei Witte and the Industrialization of Russia.* New York: Columbia University Press, 1963.

WITTE, SERGEI, *Memoirs of Count Witte.* Garden City, N.Y., and Toronto: Doubleday, 1921.

CHAPTER 5

The Aftermath
of the Revolution of 1905:
The Constitutional Experiment

The crushing of the Moscow uprising set the stage for the elections to the first Duma. Meanwhile, fortified by a large loan of 400,000,000 rubles that France had granted to bolster its tottering ally, and with the aid of the troops returning from the Far East, Witte gradually proceeded to pacify the rebellious western and central provinces. The peasants were appeased by the abolition of the redemption payments and the soldiers by an increase in allowances to privates and noncommissioned officers and the allowance of bonuses to those who participated in police duties. The main centers of the rebellion were repressed. Although some acts of terror and agrarian disturbances and riots, especially in the western borderlands, continued for over a year, the exhausted country was gradually settling down to a more normal existence.

Having restored a semblance of order, Witte made his bid to the liberals. He issued a decree that made the franchise for the Duma practically universal; it was to include all taxpayers, nearly all lodgers, and factory workers. Unimpressed by the October Manifesto, the Fundamental Laws, and Witte's gambit, the Cadet leader Pavel Miliukov declared, "Nothing has changed, the struggle goes on." He believed that no reform short of the establishment of a parliamentary system of the British type would be good enough for Russia. Many of his colleagues did not share that view, however. Consequently, the Cadet party split; its right wing seceded and formed a party of its own led by a moderate liberal businessman, Alexander I. Guchkov. The new party represented the progressive stratum of the upper middle class, which approved of the October Manifesto and was determined to implement it; hence their colloquial name, the *Octobrists*.

THE FIRST DUMA
AND WITTE'S DISMISSAL

The Duma elections were an unprecedented phenomenon in Russian history. The voting took place in March 1906, in a tense and uncertain atmosphere punctuated by acts of terror. Because both the reactionaries and the radicals had been discredited by their excesses, public opinion favored the middle-of-the-road parties. Moreover, boycott of the elections by most of the socialist groups benefited the well-organized Cadets, whose slogan, "Political Freedom and Social Justice," appealed to many people. And indeed they won well over one-third of all the seats and emerged as the largest party in the Duma. The Cadets were the only nonsocialist group that had vitality, vision, and good organization. Consequently, they dominated the first Duma.

As soon as the ailing Witte had completed the tricky task of transition from autocracy pure and simple to a half-autocratic, half-constitutional regime, he was dismissed by the Tsar. Witte's place was now taken by an old bureaucratic conformist, Ivan L. Goremykin, a former Minister of the Interior.

Witte was the dominant personality of Russia's politics of the late nineteenth and early twentieth century, its virtual Prime Minister for over a decade, from 1892 to 1903. A man of great energy and considerable political skill, he was determined to push industrialization at all cost. He boldly tried to overcome Russia's backwardness by modernizing her economy from above without destroying the traditional foundations of the Imperial regime. Under his administration the Empire's industrial production more than doubled. He was convinced that enlightened, modernized absolutism was more suitable for Russia than Western parliamentary systems. Yet once the constitutional remedy appeared to him as an expedient necessity, he did not hesitate to sponsor it with the zeal so characteristic of all his undertakings. With the dismissal of Witte passed one of the rare statesmen of the Empire's sunset.

The business of the first Duma, which gathered in the Tauride Palace in St. Petersburg in May 1906, was largely in the hands of the Cadets. On their initiative the House put forward a program of comprehensive reforms, including a scheme for agrarian reform that provided for segments of private large estates to be expropriated at a fair market price and divided among peasants under state supervision. However, the program was rejected outright by the Government as "inadmissible" and violating "the sacred right of private property." In reply, the House declared its lack of confidence in the Government, a move contrary to the Constitution. This provoked the Government to issue a statement warning the country not to trust the Duma. To this the House replied by passing an appeal to the people denouncing the Executive, another gesture denoting lack of familiarity with the system as defined by the October Manifesto and the Fundamental Laws of 1906. Unable to work with the Duma, Goremykin dissolved it in July 1906 after less than three months.

The night of the dissolution some two hundred deputies, most of them Cadets, crossed the Finnish border to Viborg. There, under the protection of Finnish autonomy, they drew up another public appeal urging passive resistance, including refusal to pay taxes and supply recruits to the armed forces until the Duma was restored. The opposition also disclaimed responsibility for all foreign loans concluded by the Executive without the Duma's approval. The Government denounced the Viborg Manifesto as a revolutionary step and disenfranchised its authors. The manifesto fell flat because the apathetic country would not respond to its appeal.

THE ASCENT OF STOLYPIN

Piotr Stolypin, the strong man of Goremykin's cabinet, was chiefly responsible for the dissolution of the Duma, and he now replaced the aging Goremykin as Premier. Although a moderate constitutionalist by conviction, Stolypin was determined to interpret the October Manifesto and the Fundamental Laws in a restrictive sense and refused to go any further because he believed that Russia was not ready for a fully parliamentary system. Another Duma was called for March 1907, within the legal time limit of nine months. Stolypin used the intervening period for accomplishing two tasks: to restore "law and order" and to implement moderate reforms. The pacification, however, he considered as priority number one.

Both tasks were to be accomplished by means of extensive use of Article 87 of the Fundamental Laws, which allowed the Government to issue decrees when the Duma was not in session. In September 1906, Stolypin instituted special military tribunals to deal with flagrant violations of the law. The proceedings of these tribunals were to be completed within four days. In case of conviction, the standard sentence was death, usually by hanging. Where the disorder assumed threatening proportions, as in Russian Poland or in the Baltic provinces, large-scale "punitive expeditions" were dispatched. The most savage reprisals took place in Estonia and Latvia, where some 3,000 attacks had been made by the local peasants on the powerful German landlords, Russian officials, and soldiers, and where entire districts had been taken over by Lettish and Estonian insurgents. From the day of their institution in September 1906 to the day of their cancellation in May 1907, these tribunals executed 1,144 persons. Hence the hangman's noose became known as "Stolypin's necktie." To understand the severity of Stolypin's reprisals, one has to bear in mind that during the year 1906 alone, no fewer than 738 state officials and 645 private individuals were murdered by revolutionaries and common criminals, while 1,719 were wounded. In 1907 about 3,000 people all told were killed and nearly 1,734 wounded. Only in 1908 did these figures drop dramatically.

The terrorist activities of the leftist groups were matched by the extreme right-wing groups, who set up armed squads of all sorts and perpetuated numerous acts of violence. The "Fighting Squads" of the Right became known under the blanket name of *Black Hundreds.* The rightists were convinced that the Constitutional Manifesto

Anton P. Chekhov

was an unwarranted mistake, a concession wrested from the Autocrat in a moment of weakness by the revolutionary movement secretly instigated by the Jews. The Black Hundreds staged several pograms. Soon the rightists founded a political party called *The Union of the Russian People,* which insisted on the revocation of the Manifesto. In 1907–1908, at the peak of its activity, the Union had about 200 branches with some 30,000 members.

The Russian conservative movement, of which the Black Hundreds was merely a segment, was shaped largely by the negative qualities of its opponent. The conservatives shared with the leftists their preference for physical violence, their contempt for Western liberalism and parliamentary procedures, and their all-or-nothing attitude. Both groups were, in different ways, authoritarian and intolerant. If one adds the elements of racism inherent in their glorification of their own people, their anti-Semitism, and their love of "direct action," the Black Hundreds were in many ways forerunners of Fascism. The groups reflected two trends common to many Great Russians: first, instinctive, spontaneous loyalty to the Tsar as the central pillar, the essence of the autocratic system and the symbol of the Empire; second, a profound nationalism mixed with xenophobia, of which anti-Semitism was an integral part. The Union found ready support among many officers, officials, and even among some governmental and Court circles.

STOLYPIN'S AGRARIAN REFORMS

The new strong man of the constitutional period, Piotr Stolypin, a landowner of gentry origin, was by education a natural scientist with a strong interest in agriculture. He acquired extensive administrative experience as governor of Grodno and Saratov. Despite his social origins, Stolypin was aware that an inept, indolent, and impoverished rural nobility could not be a sufficient base for the Imperial regime. Even the addition of the bureaucracy and the small, largely foreign, entrepreneurial and merchant groups could not sufficiently broaden the social base of the regime. Stolypin understood that the welfare of the largest stratum of the country was a prerequisite for its overall economic well-being and political stability. To rebuild the prosperity of peasant Russia, a task neglected by Witte, now became Stolypin's main objective.

Simultaneously with the repressive measures, between September and November 1906 Stolypin issued a series of decrees that constituted a virtual agrarian revolution. First, he made large tracts of Crown and State land available for sale at moderate prices to the peasants. Second, he allowed them to leave the village communes and claim their allotment in private property consolidated in one parcel outside the mir, and thus become individual farmers, like those of Western and Central Europe. Finally, Stolypin swept away most of the vestiges of feudalism still affecting the peasantry, like special domestic passports,

arbitrary jurisdiction of the land captains, and degrading corporal punishment. The peasants were now eligible for offices in local administration. Thus the peasantry ceased to be a separate caste and was made equal with other classes.

Stolypin's objective was to encourage the more enterprising, hard-working, thrifty peasants, those who had enough savings and energy, to take advantage of his reform, which, under Russian conditions of inveterate collectivism, had a rather revolutionary tinge. "The sober and the strong," as he put it, were to remain in the countryside, set up their individual farms, and become the backbone of the new, orderly, prosperous, and powerful Great Russia about which he was dreaming. Those who had neither resources nor skills to accomodate themselves to the new conditions were either to be driven to the cities to provide a surplus labor force for fast-growing industry or be left in the countryside as cheap hired labor available to the squires and the prosperous peasants, or *kulaks*.

Of all the Russian political parties, only the Octobrists backed Stolypin's reforms. For opposite reasons, both the conservatives and the revolutionaries desired to maintain the village commune. The former, permeated with the Slavophile concept of an idealized mir, wanted to preserve this decaying institution as an alleged embodiment of the old Russian tradition. The socialist parties, on the other hand, wanted to keep communal ownership of the land because, they calculated, it would be easier to transfer to State ownership the already collectively owned land than to wrest it from millions of individual farmers. Both factions of the Social Democrats rejected the Stolypin reform because they realized that the creation of a strong stratum of yeomanry would imperil the cause of the revolution. The reform, they argued, would not solve the land problem but merely deepen the differences between rich and poor, since only the rich would be able to pay the high market prices for land. The Social Revolutionary Party held that the land was to be handed over to the local organs of self-government for lease to peasant families. The Cadets criticized the reform as not radical enough; it avoided the crucial issue of the compulsory division of private large estates against proper compensation to the owners. Moreover, the Cadets joined in leftist criticism of the reform because they needed the support of the left for their pet project, the transformation of the lame constitutional system into a full-scale parliamentary one.

Thus only the masses of the peasantry enthusiastically responded to the decrees of the Premier. The response was strongest in the Ukraine along the right bank of the Dnieper, where the tradition of individual ownership was strongest. There about half of the former communal land soon passed into private ownership. Between 1907 and 1915, when the reform was suspended because, as it was explained, of the absence of huge numbers of drafted men, over 2 million peasant households left the mir and became individual owners of their allotments. This amounted to 22 percent of the total number of commune members. Since, in addition to that, there were over 2.8 million peasant families, mostly in the western and southwestern provinces of the Empire, who owned their plots as individual farmers before Stolypin's reform, by 1915 about half of the whole peasantry was already free of its debilitating collectivist fetters.

THE SECOND DUMA

While pacifying the country and reshaping its agrarian structure, Stolypin was at the same time engineering the elections to the second Duma. This was a difficult task because, for the first time, various socialist parties were to participate in the elections. The Senate, by arbitrary interpretation of the Electoral Law, disenfranchised large categories of voters. This included the two hundred signatories of the Viborg Manifesto. The attempts at influencing the election to the second Duma by "administrative means" boomeranged, however, and the second Duma was considerably to the left of the first. Although the Cadet representation was reduced by one-third, various socialist groups entered the second Duma in force; together they represented an impressive force of about two hundred deputies. The two factions of the RSDWP together with their sympathizers had 65 votes, of which 35 were Mensheviks or their hangers-on, while the Bolsheviks had only 18 deputies. The Populist Labor Party, or the *Trudoviki,* was the largest segment, numbering 104 deputies. The remaining 12 Social Democrat deputies oscillated between the two factions but more often than not voted with the Mensheviks. While the Mensheviks plunged into parliamentary activity with gusto, the Bolsheviks regarded the Duma merely as an arena for the dissemination of revolutionary propaganda. By blocking orderly legislative activity, the Bolshevik Duma faction persistently interfered with the enactment of various reforms. The constant filibustering provided an additional argument for the enemies of the constitutional system. One of them, the *Union of the Russian People,* was led by a former co-worker of von Plehve, Vladimir M. Purishkievich. The Union tried to prove that in Russia the constitutional system was unworkable and should be abolished. Here they clashed with the Octobrists, who represented a small but compact club of thirty-two deputies led by the dynamic Guchkov, who, while supporting the Government, refused to enter it.

The life of the second Duma was no smoother than that of the first. The question of terror and sabotage and the measures to be undertaken to curtail them soon resulted in another political stalemate between the Duma and the Government. While the opposition denounced Stolypin's method of pacification, the Government, in turn, condemned indiscriminately most of the Duma factions for stirring up civil disobedience. Stolypin, who was an authoritarian personality, found it difficult to establish a working compromise with a popular representative body. Unable to achieve a modicum of cooperation, in June 1907 he dissolved the three-month-old second Duma under the convenient pretext that a group of deputies had participated in a plot against the life of the Emperor.

Nicholas II, who had granted the Constitution with revulsion and regret, now toyed for a while with the idea of restoring his autocratic prerogatives. Stolypin nevertheless was too much of a realist to accept such a solution. He wanted neither to abolish the Duma nor to restore the unrestricted autocratic system, but desired a modernized monarchical system of the Prussian or Japanese type.

Before the Duma's dissolution, a new electoral law had been carefully prepared by the Ministry of the Interior. The law was a flagrant violation of the Constitution, which provided that no change relating to the status of the Chambers was to take place without their consent. But Stolypin, bent on having a more cooperative legislature, proceeded to engineer the elections to the third Duma to suit his purpose. The original electoral law had been framed in a way that would assure a large peasant representation, because Witte believed that the peasants were essentially conservative and loyal to the Tsar. In the first and second Dumas, however, the peasant deputies surprised the Government by their advocacy of several radical schemes, including the abolition of large private estates. Consequently, the new electoral law was so constructed as to give predominance to the gentry and the upper middle class, as well as to reduce the representation of ethnic groups. On Stolypin's instruction, the local governors were given a free hand in manipulating the electoral process. The slightest failure to observe the formalities of a complicated registration system was used by the authorities as an excuse to cancel the voting rights of those suspected of supporting the opposition. The main victims of the "administrative measures" were among the leftist groups; thirty-one Social Democratic deputies were arrested and sent to Siberia.

THE THIRD DUMA

Elections to the third Duma, conducted in an atmosphere of repression, finally satisfied Stolypin's expectations. The Cadets obtained only about half of their former representation and had only about fifty votes. On the other hand, the number of deputies belonging to conservative and reactionary groups increased considerably. Under the leadership of the Octobrist Guchkov, they would dominate the third and also the fourth Dumas. Representation of the multinational borderlands in the third Duma was cut down drastically; for instance, the Polish Circle was reduced from 34 to 14 deputies. The Octobrists, with 153 deputies, took over the role of the Cadets in the previous two Dumas. The third Duma was as submissive as the previous ones were rebellious. Most of the attacks on the Government now came not from the Left, reduced to an insignificant representation, but from the extreme Right, from such groups as the Union of the Russian People, which were anxious to mitigate Stolypin's reformatory zeal.

A ruthless, resolute, and incorruptible Stolypin had many enemies within his own administration, and even among the Imperial family, who considered him too progressive and too much bent on experimentation. To his numerous political enemies, one should add his personal enemies, for his bluntness did not make him popular in government circles. At the court, Stolypin had antagonized those who supported a charlatan and impostor named Grigory Y. Rasputin. Rasputin had come to St. Petersburg at the end of 1903 from the Siberian city of Tobolsk, posing as a wandering saintly beggar and hermit. He was actually an unordained religious teacher wandering from place to place, living often by his wits. Grand Duke Alexis, the only male in the Imperial family and hence heir to the throne, was suffering from acute hemophilia, and Rasputin was the only man who could stop the frequently recurring bleedings. This gave the alleged miracle worker ascendancy over the anxious mother and through her considerable political influence. Stolypin early perceived that Rasputin was an unscrupulous and self-seeking crook and repeatedly warned the Emperor against him.

On September 14, 1911, under mysterious circumstances, Stolypin was fatally shot at a gala performance at the Kiev opera house in the presence of the Tsar. The assassin was an individual who was connected both with the police and the revolutionary underground.

Stolypin's record was ambivalent. He was the first Russian statesman since the emancipation to pay serious attention to the plight of the peasantry. He favored modernization of the government. Yet he held steadfastly to his concept of bureaucratic paternalism and made only token concessions to popular desires. On the other hand, he recognized the importance of improving education and the standard of living. He was not opposed to a modicum of popular participation in government, but firmly believed that the locus of political power ought to reside in the central administration. He always treated the Duma with a mixture of suspicion and condescension. While he declared, from time to time, his willingness to find a workable compromise with it, he was determined to compromise only on his own terms.

Stolypin's conservative political views were profoundly tinged with Great Russian nationalism, which made him a firm centralist impatient of ethnic dissent. He understood the necessity of streamlining Russia's antiquated socioeconomic structure, but his concept of modernization had to do not so much with people's welfare as with Russia's strength as a great power and with the survival of the monarchy. In short, he was an able bureaucrat and an enlightened yet ruthless despot-administrator. Being a Great Russian nationalist, he dreamed about a powerful and centralized but economically progressive Empire. Turning to the socialist deputies of the second Duma,

Stolypin said: "You want a Great Change, while I want a Great Russia." Despite many errors, his ingenuity, boldness, and strong will were impressive. Stolypin was the last statesmanlike figure of prerevolutionary Russia, and his policies represented a desperate effort to bolster the Imperial regime by providing it with a broader social base.

THE RECORD OF THE THIRD AND FOURTH DUMAS

The third Duma was the only one to die a natural death (in 1912), and the first that was permitted to examine the budget and engage in systematic parliamentary work. Although both the third and fourth Dumas were based on a very narrow foundation and were grossly unrepresentative, simply the fact that the Chamber was the only forum where elected deputies could voice popular grievances and desires gradually made many people forget its limitations. One of the instances when public opinion rallied behind the Duma was the bill voted in 1908 to provide for universal free, obligatory education for children aged eight to eleven. The scheme also provided for the reorganization and expansion of teacher training and school construction so as to liquidate illiteracy in Russia by 1922. The whole plan was to be financed by the Treasury. Whether the scheme was realistic, in view of the shortage of funds and competent personnel, is doubtful. As is the trouble with many blueprints in Russia, the vision was greater than the capacity to put it into practice. Yet considerable progress was made. By 1914 almost every populous settlement in European Russia had some type of primary school, and between 1907 and 1914 the number of children in the elementary schools more than doubled. While in 1894 the incidence of literacy among military recruits was 38 percent, in 1913 it improved to 73 percent, which was roughly equivalent to that of Italy at that time. During the period of 1907–1914, enrollment in institutions of higher learning more than tripled, while the number of students in secondary schools nearly quadrupled.[1]

THE "SILVER AGE" OF CULTURE

The life of the third and fourth Dumas coincided with a renewed phase of economic progress and considerable artistic and scientific creativity. At the close of the nineteenth century, Russia entered a period usually referred to as the "Silver Age." This period was characterized by a general rise in the cultural level and the expansion of an intelligent and often highly appreciative public. Unlike the present-day Soviet policies, Tsarist censorship was purely negative and limited in focus. It tended to suppress material the authorities considered either directly offensive or subversive, but it did not exact positive conformity to a set of ideological, let alone esthetic, principles. The censors concentrated their attentions mainly on political books, pamphlets, and periodicals, while treating fiction, poetry, and literary criticism more lightly. Consequently, while Tsarist censorship hampered the expression of radical political views, it did not seriously interfere with artistic creation.

Although the great genius of Russian prose Leo Tolstoy lived until 1910, the religous experience he had undergone in 1880 separated him from the main current of the Russian literary scene. But meanwhile a number of talented writers arose in vari-

ous corners of the vast Empire. The most prominent and best known in the West was Anton P. Chekhov (1860–1904). Chekhov came from a family of former serfs. Brought up in Taganrog on the Sea of Azov, he graduated from the Moscow University medical school. Soon, however, he deserted his profession for literature and published a series of sketches about peasant life that often contained subtle, subdued humor. Later he moved from short stories to theater and developed an extraordinary gift for penetrating psychological insight and for portraying moods and attitudes characteristic of the Russian intelligentsia. The two most striking examples of his mature work are the plays *The Seagull* (1896) and *The Cherry Orchard* (1904). A mixture of quiet, philosophical pessimism and subtle irony permeates his later works. They usually end on a minor key—"not with a bang but a whimper."

The first director to become interested in Chekhov's plays was Konstantin S. Stanislavsky (1863–1938), who launched Chekhov's early plays in Moscow on the stage of the newly created Moscow Art Theater. Rejecting established routine and repertoire, Stanislavsky insisted upon staging only plays of the highest artistic value and originality. Experimenting with various methods, he finally arrived at an approach that he called "psychological realism." His was the theater of moods, capable of projecting subtle psychological nuances. Stanislavsky's dramatic school provided new cadres of the Russian theater and has had many followers in the West.

In 1890, Russia witnessed the rise to fame and great popularity of a self-educated worker, Alexis M. Peshkov (1868–1936), who became known under his pen name of Maxim Gorky (or Maxim the Bitter). This initially little known provincial journalist soon produced a series of books and stories, some of them autobiographical, like his trilogy *Childhood, In the World,* and *My Universities.* Gorky ran counter to the predominant trend of nineteenth-century literature that

---

[1] "The social mobility accompanying the growth of the higher education is reflected in the fact that the proportion of children of peasants, craftsmen, and workers enrolled in the universities grew from 15.7% in 1880 to 38.8% in 1914, and in the higher technical institutes was 54% in the latter year. The officer corps was no doubt the most conservative branch of the bureaucracy, but it appears that by the end of the Empire a majority of the new officers came from non-noble families, as did some of the leading generals in the First World War." C. E. Black, "The Nature of Imperial Russian Society," *Slavic Review,* 20 (December 1961), 579.

Russian Prima Ballerina, Anna Pavlova. Portrait by Dorothea Cordes

sympathized with morally perplexed and overly sensitive people. Many of his heroes are rough but dynamic daredevils, reckless tramps, and resourceful revolutionaries, some of them forerunners of the "positive heroes" of Soviet literature. By the beginning of the twentieth century, Gorky had achieved world fame. By 1900, Gorky had become perhaps the most popular prose writer of Russia. Politically, he was a member of the RSDWP and often sympathized with the Bolshevik wing, while quarreling with them from time to time.

The close of the nineteenth century witnessed the appearance of a neoromantic trend in Russian letters. Its ideals and aims were best expressed by the group known as *Symbolists*. The Russian Symbolists were inspired by the French group of the same name (Mallarmé, Verlaine, Rimbaud) and also by Edgar Allen Poe. Nevertheless, na-

tive inspiration was not lacking. The real meaning of the neoromantic trend was a partial return to the long-discarded and often ridiculed romantic ideals of the first half of the nineteenth century.

It should be stressed that the neoromantic movement started as a protest against the established standards of artistic naturalism, realism, or "civic art" so fashionable during the 1860s to 1890s and so popular with many revolutionaries, including Lenin himself. *Civic art* was initially introduced by such nineteenth-century writers as Vissarion G. Belinsky, Nicholas G. Chernyshevsky, Nikolay A. Dobroliubov, Dmitri I. Pisarev, and Nicholas A. Nekrasov, who considered all forms of artistic expression as mere tools of social reform. In the field of plastic art, one of the main instruments of civic art was the society of Circulatory Exhibitions, which tried to propagate all forms of artistic creativity, especially painting, among the masses. Some of the pictures of Ilya I. Repin, for instance his well-known "Volga Boatmen" or his "Arrest of a Revolutionary," are typical examples of this trend, so influential among the radicals at the close of the nineteenth century.

The fundamental reason for the neoromantic revolt was psychological. It was a protest by the more romantically inclined younger artists, fed up and frustrated by the often drab, dreary, moralizing civic art of the older ones. Raising again the old romantic standard of "art for art's sake," the neoromantics ridiculed literature saturated with sociological verbiage, science, and politics. While the naturalist school paid more attention to prose, the young generation returned to poetry as "the language of the gods."

The most significant among the Russian Symbolists were Dmitri S. Merezhkovsky, Andrey Bely (Boris N. Bugayev), and Alexander A. Blok. In 1892, Merezhkovsky, who was also a literary critic and a poet, wrote a book entitled *Symbols,* which revealed the influence of the poetic concepts of Charles Baudelaire and Edgar Allen Poe. Merezhkovsky saw as the goal of history the synthesis of the Hellenic principle of the purity of the flesh with the Judeo-Christian principle of the purity of the spirit. He was also one of the prominent figures in the religious revival, or "God-seeking," that became prominent in the early twentieth-century Russian intellectual life. Merezhkovsky and Nikolai A. Berdiaev, a talented philosophical writer, were among the first in Russia at that time to devote themselves to the search for a new form of ecumenical Christianity.

Another contributor to the neoromantic trend, Andrey Bely, was a rather esoteric and extravagant writer of a "symphonic" poetry full of ingenious but often puzzling polyphonic experiments. He is best known for his novel *St. Petersburg* (1913) and for the four volumes of his memoirs, which are a valuable record of the Symbolist movement.

The most original and the deepest of the group was, however, Alexander A. Blok, a philologist by training. Blok quickly gained renown because of his musical poems, lyrical dramas, and a cycle of historical verses that sprang from his deep love of Russia. Although Blok reached the peak of his creativity and fame after the Boshevik upheaval with the publication of two allegorical poems, "The Twelve" and "The Scythans" (1918), the bulk of his work belongs to the preceding period. Like most of the Symbolists, Blok was initially sympathetic to the revolutionary movement but was quickly alienated from the Bolshevik regime. He died of hunger in 1921, a bitterly disillusioned man full of tragic forebodings.

A powerful stimulus was given to the neoromantic movement by the appearance of a richly illustrated artistic magazine called *The World of Art (Mir Iskustva).* Although it lasted for only five years (1899–1904), *The World of Art* helped considerably to popularize the ideas of the Symbolists and to refine the artistic tastes of the general public. In particular, the magazine contributed to the advancement of graphic art, book illustration, and stage design. While the group of gifted and imaginative people who gathered around the paper did not neglect native Russian sources of inspiration, it was also in touch with the West as well as with the Orient. Generally, *The World of Art* had a stimulating effect on all branches of the arts, on public interest in them, and on the popularization of Russian artistic achievements abroad. In 1900 the paintings of some Russian artists were displayed at the Paris Exposition. Six years later a special exhibition of Russian art was organized in the French capital, and it scored a remarkable success. The ikons were particularly admired by the Western public for their originality and power of expression.

The contribution of the Symbolists to Russian literature was impressive. New imagery was introduced; poetic language was renewed and revitalized; new rhymes, rhythms, and forms were sought after; and the musicality of Russian poetry was strikingly enriched. The Symbolists also influenced by their work a large group of younger writers, including Boris L. Pasternak, whose talents were to blossom fully during the Soviet period.

Of the artistic-literary schools of prerevolutionary Russia besides the Symbolists, the *Acmeists* should also be mentioned. This group was both an outgrowth of the Symbolists and at the same time a reaction against them. The name of the group comes from the Greek word *acme,* which means blossoming or attaining a high stage of perfection. By 1911, the Acmeists had rebelled against the Symbolists' affected estheticism and often excessive verbosity. The Acmeists urged a return to precision and simplicity in the use of words, in short, to a greater harmony of artistic expression. The leading Acmeists were Nicholas S. Gumilev, Anna A. Akhmatova, and Osip E. Mandelshtam. All three were highly individualistic poets who emphasized a sensual, vitalistic, and nostalgic perception of the world. All of them continued to create during the Soviet era.

The neoromantic trend quickly spread from literature to other artistic media, including music and dance. One of the most prominent and influential musicians of the twentieth century was Igor Stravinsky. His versatility, originality, and endurance were amazing. His works comprise operas, ballets, orchestral pieces (including several symphonies), concertos, and chamber and piano music. Three of his ballets produced during the prerevolutionary period are "The Firebird" (1910), "Petrushka" (1911), and "The Rite of Spring" (1913). Stravinsky's teacher at the St. Petersburg Conservatory of Music was Nicholas Rimsky-Korsakov. He wrote some fifteen operas, numerous cantatas, and choral pieces. His best-known operas are "Sadko" (1895) and "The Tsar's Bride" (1898). Rimsky-Korsakov also relied on native sources; he collected Russian folksongs, which were an important source of his creativity. Perhaps the most popular of the Russian composers of the prevolutionary era was Alexander N. Scriabin. He wrote numerous piano concertos and orchestral works, among them "The Poem of Ecstasy" (1908) and "Prometheus" (1909–1910). Scriabin aimed at a synthesis of all the arts that would transform the world of creativity. He worked in the mystical vein of many of Russia's writers and was a believer in the philosophy of Merezhkovsky.

The beginning of the twentieth century also marked a new epoch in the history of the Russian ballet, which culminated in the achievements of an ingenious and resourceful impresario and director, Serge Diaghilev. Diaghilev's central idea was to bring about an organic integration of ballet, music, and scenery, including costumes. The roster of pictorial talents that Diaghilev employed in his twenty-year career (1909–1929) is most impressive: it includes Picasso, Braque, Derain, and Rouault. This integrative concept was the basis of the remarkable dancing ensemble known as the *Ballets Russes,* which Diaghilev organized, directed, and took to Paris and London in 1910, there to score great artistic successes. Diaghilev was the first to present to the Western public Stravinsky's "Firebird," "Petrushka," and "The Rite of Spring." The Ballets Russes had many stars, but Vaslav Nijinsky (Wacław Nizyński) and Anna Pavlova were perhaps the most brilliant. The Ballets Russes was not only the first modern ballet company; it also embodied for a whole generation of European intellectuals the very expression of the refined, yet largely nostalgically decadent culture of prerevolutionary Russia.

To complete the picture of the artistic scene of prerevolutionary Russia, we should mention a small but highly vocal group of writers and painters known as the *Futurists.* In the years 1909–1913 the manifestoes of the Italian founder of the futurist movement, F. T. Marinetti, were published in Milan. They were translated into Russian and published in Moscow already in 1914. They stimulated the growth of artistic groups that identified themselves with Futurism. Never in their history were the Russian educated strata so close to Europe as on the eve of World War I. The leading representative of Russian Futurism was a young poet, Vladimir V. Mayakovsky. Born in Georgia, he started his career, together with Boris Pasternak, Andrey Bely, and Alexander Blok, just on the eve of World War I. Influenced by the Italian pioneers of Futurism, Mayakovsky sympathized with the Bolsheviks and revolted against all established traditions and accepted artistic forms. He tried to experiment with words as pure sound apart from their meaning, often shocking the "bourgeois" public by unexpected, brutal associations, bizarre metaphors, and startling alliterations. In the plastic arts, the Futurists toyed with geometric designs that expressed the massiveness and speed of the machine age. They attempted to create a "dynamic art of the future." They were, in a way, the forerunners of abstract art. Of these Russian pioneers of abstract art, Vasily V. Kandinsky is the most important. He emphasized the significance of color and form, regardless of subject matter. He taught for a time during World War I at Moscow University and the Moscow Academy of Arts, but then he returned to Germany and became an active member of the German group known as the Bauhaus. Another painter, Kazimir Malevich, starting as a follower of the impressionists, passed through expressionism, fauvism, cubism, and eventually evolved a style of his own, which he called Suprematism, pictures consisting of arrangements of geometrical elements. Malevich attempted to re-create the two-dimensional spirituality of icons through the medium of abstract painting. After the 1917 revolution and the Bolshevik *coup,* when many painters accepted utilitarian social functions of art as the only true ones, Malevich continued to insist on the priority of the spiritual values of abstract paintings. Unlike Kandinskiy or Chagall and many other artists, Malevich remained in Russia and neglected and forgotten, died there in 1935.

By the late nineteenth and early twentieth centuries, Russian scholarship had reached a respectable level and also maintained close ties with the West. In 1869, Dmitri I. Mendeleyev compiled his periodic system of chemical elements, corrected the atomic weight of nine elements, and predicted the existence of four new ones. Perhaps the most famous Russian scientist at the end of the Imperial regime was Ivan P. Pavlov. In 1904 he won the Nobel Prize for his theory of conditioned and unconditioned reflexes. He advanced his theory on the basis of his experiments with dogs. Pavlov discovered that a conditioned reflex could be established by applying sound stimuli over a period of time to an animal before it ate. He noted that the dogs would salivate when the stimuli were reapplied, even if food was no longer offered to them. Pavlov also made contributions to medical science and chemistry; for instance, he discovered the existence of fermenting enzymes in gastric juices. Ilya Metchnikov was awarded the Nobel Prize for medicine in 1916 for his achievements in bacteriology. He was the first to postulate that white corpuscles and leucocytes devour bacteria in the blood, and that inflammation in infected parts of the body is caused by the struggle between white corpuscles and germs.

Vassily Kliuchevsky, the greatest Russian historian, produced at the turn of the century a monumental five-volume synthesis of his country's history, as well as a number of excellent monographs comparable to the best Western works. But no Russian social scientist has reached greater fame than the jurist and historian Pavel G. Vinogradov. In 1903 he left the University of Moscow because of a conflict with the Tsarist authorities, went to England, and was appointed Professor of Jurisprudence at Oxford. There he introduced the seminar system and produced the nine-volume *Oxford Stud-*

ies in Social and Legal History (1902–1907), as well as numerous other works.

THE TSARIST EMPIRE ON THE EVE OF WORLD WAR I

This artistic and scientific creativity during the twilight of the Empire blossomed against the background of an expanding economy and a latent revolutionary movement. The movement revived, however, in 1912 after the violent Lena gold mine disturbances during which some two hundred workers were killed. The crest of the new wave of protest and rebellion was reached on the eve of the war. Yet, the surface seemed to be fairly placid. There had been several good harvests, per capita agrarian production had scored sizable gains, and the Empire was able to export a substantial quantity of food products, especially grain. Industrial growth, while not as spectacular as under Witte, was impressive enough. Both the metallurgic and textile industries were advancing rapidly. Only the production of oil was lagging behind, and this was due partly to the ravages wrought in the Baku region by the Revolution of 1905 and partly to the depletion of the oil wells there. The Empire's fast economic progress was a result of several factors, the most important of which were a huge population living within a single customs area, the general advance of science and technology following the rising educational level, and a considerable inflow of foreign capital.

After 1907–1908, with the pacification of the country under Stolypin, the influx of foreign—mostly French—capital again became a significant factor in the process of industrialization. By 1914 French investors owned 22 percent of the stocks of the major privately owned Russian banks. About one-quarter of the total French income from long-term investments came from Russia. In 1913 about one-third of all capital in private industries was foreign. By 1914 Russia was saddled with the largest foreign-owned debt

of all the great powers. Its dependence on foreign creditors was often embarrassing and occasionally even humiliating.

The years 1907–1913 were marked by a measure of prosperity and a modicum of freedom very modest by Western standards, but considerable when compared with what existed prior to October 1905. The Constitutional Manifesto had granted a bill of rights and thus assured a limited measure of freedom of press, speech, and association. The insurance law of 1912 was rather insufficient: it provided for payment by the plant of from two-thirds to three-quarters of the normal wage in case of sickness or accident. Yet it covered a majority of the industrial workers employed in large enterprises. While workers' unions were strictly supervised and treated with sullen suspicion, they were at least tolerated. On the other hand, it is important to realize that the Russian trade-union movement was rather small and weak. In 1907 there were only about 652 unions with about 200,000 members, or 5.5 percent of all industrial labor. Most unions were small, and only 22 of them numbered over 1,000 members. The largest and strongest of them was the Union of Metal Workers in Petrograd. In case of a labor conflict, the Tsarist government was always on the side of the entrepreneurial class, which increased the alienation of the workers from the regime.

During the last decade of the nineteenth century and the beginning of the twentieth, the Tsarist Empire was undergoing rapid economic expansion. Using an array of measures, starting with high customs barriers, tax reductions, national defense contracts, state orders, and profit guarantees, the Government tried to protect heavy industry. All this encouraged the formation of numerous trusts and cartels. The metallurgical cartel (*Prodameta*) and the coal syndicate (*Prodogul*) were the largest and most influential. These cartels accentuated the already marked trend toward a concentration of industrial production. The percentage of enterprises employing more than

1,000 workers was as large in prerevolutionary Russia as in Germany. Some mighty tycoons, like Sava Morozov, who controlled large textile plants, and Alexis Putilov, owner of numerous metallurgical enterprises, banks, and railroads, exercised considerable influence on the affairs of state through their contacts with cabinet officials and members of the Imperial family.

It is obvious that the antiquated political system, largely based on a huge, rusty, and unwieldy bureaucratic machine, was hardly suitable to the needs of a modern economy. The Empire's real income per capita was lower than Italy's. A whole range of vital industries was either lacking (the automotive industry, for instance) or in their infancy (the electric and chemical industries). Most of the more complicated industrial equipment had to be imported. While Russia's rate of growth was spectacular, it was starting from a very low base, and in 1913–1914 Russia was far behind Western countries in per capita production. For instance, Russian steel production at that time amounted to some 4.5 million tons, while Germany, with half the population of the Tsarist Empire, produced about 17 million tons in the same period. Although Russia had a population four times larger than that of France, both produced approximately the same amount of steel. In 1913, in terms of per capita gross national product, Russia ranked fifteenth out of the world's twenty-three industrial nations.

Russia's economic progress was impressive; its growth averaged about 6 percent per year between 1886 and 1917, which was faster than in most Western countries except Germany, the United States, and Japan. Yet, on the eve of World War I, despite seven-league strides, Russia was a strange mixture of inherited backwardness and rapid, yet highly uneven progress. It was still a largely rural, pastoral society in which modernization based on the latest technology coexisted with semifeudal backwardness. It was this half-modern, half-medieval Russia, with half-suppressed, gradually reviving revolutionary ferment, that was to clash on the battlefields of World War I with a formidable coalition centering around Germany and Austro-Hungary.

SUGGESTED READING

BLACK, CYRIL E., *Dynamics of Modernization*. New York: Harper and Row, 1966.

BUNT, CYRIL G. E., *Russian Art from Scyths to Soviets*. New York: Philosophical Library, 1948.

CALVOCORESSI, MICHEL D., AND GERALD ABRAHAM *Masters of Russian Music*. London: Gerald Duckworth, 1936.

CHMIELINSKI, EDWARD, *The Polish Question in the Russian State Duma*. Knoxville, Tenn.: University of Tennessee Press, 1970.

FAINSOD, MERLE, *International Socialism and World War*. Cambridge, Mass.: Harvard University Press, 1935.

GRAY, CAMILLA, *The Great Experiment: Russian Art, 1863–1922*. London: Thames & Hudson; New York: Abrams, 1962.

HAIMSON, LEOPOLD H., ed., *The Politics of Rural Russia, 1905–1914*. Studies of the Russian Institute, Columbia University. New York: Columbia University Press, 1979.

JOHNSON, WILLIAM H. E., *Russia's Educational Heritage*. Pittsburgh: Carnegie Press, 1950.

KOKOVTSOV, VLADIMIR N., *Out of My Past: The Memoirs of Count Kokovtsov, Russian Minister of Finance, 1904–1914, Chariman of the Council of Ministers, 1911–1914*. Stanford, Calif.: Stanford University Press, 1935.

LEVINE, ALFRED, *The Second Duma*. New Haven, Conn.: Yale University Press, 1940 and 1966.

LIASHCHENKO, P. I., *History of the Russian Economy to the 1917 Revolution*. New York: Macmillan, 1949.

MASLENIKOV, OLEG, *The Frenzied Poets: Andrey Bely and the Russian Symbolists*. Berkeley: University of California Press, 1952.

MILIUKOV, PAUL, *Memoirs, 1905–1917*. Ann Arbor: University of Michigan Press, 1967.

MILLER, MARGARET S., *The Economic Development of Russia, 1905–1914*. London: P. S. King, 1926.

RICE, TAMARA TALBOT, *A Concise History of Russian Art*. New York: Praeger, 1963.

RIHA, THOMAS, *A Russian European: Paul Miliukov*

in Russian Politics. Notre Dame, Ind.: University of Notre Dame Press, 1969.

ROGERS, HANS, *Jewish Policies and Right-Wing Politics in Imperial Russia*. Berkeley and Los Angeles: University of California Press, 1986.

ROGGER, HANS, "Russia," in *the European Right*. ed. Hans Rogger and Eugene Weber. Berkeley and Los Angeles: University of California Press, 1965.

ROSENTHAL, BERNICE G., *Dmitri Sergeevich Merezhkovsky and the Silver Age: The Development*

of a Revolutionary Mentality. The Hague: Martinus Nijhoff, 1975.

SLONIM, MARC, *Modern Russian Literature: From Chekhov to the Present*. New York: Oxford University Press, 1953.

SMITH, JAY C., JR., *The Russian Struggle for Power, 1914–1917*. New York: Philosophical Library, 1956.

WOROSZYLSKI, WIKTOR, *The Life of Mayakovsky*. New York: Orion Press, 1970.

CHAPTER 6

World War I and the Revolutions of 1917

On June 28, 1914, Archduke Francis Ferdinand, heir to the throne of Austria and Hungary, was assassinated by a Serbian terrorist in the Austrian-controlled town of Sarajevo in Bosnia. Although at the time there was no irrefutable evidence of the Serbian government's complicity in the crime, Vienna and Budapest presented Belgrade with a stiff ultimatum that included demands considered humiliating by the Serbians. The acceptance of most of the demands by Serbia, an ally of Russia, did not satisfy either the Austro-Hungarians or the Germans. The military leaders of both countries assumed that this would be the right moment to launch a war that would establish their sphere of influence in the Near and Middle East and give them a steppingstone toward broader, worldwide ambitions.

St. Petersburg correctly anticipated that Austro-Hungary, encouraged by Germany, would want to use the assassination as a pretext for crushing Serbia. Since this would undermine the Russian position in the Balkans, the preservation of Serbian independence was considered by Tsarist diplomats to be vital not only to Russia's position in the area, but also to the balance of power in Europe. Russia's leaders believed that because they had twice urged the Serbian leaders to give way to the Austro-Hungarian demands (in 1909 and in 1913), they could not do it a third time. If the Russians again insisted upon surrender, ran the argument, they would have served notice that they were abdicating their Great Power status and that they were not to be trusted as allies. The establishment of an Austro-German sphere of influence in the Balkans would be a vital step forward in the realization of their ambitious scheme to control the markets, bases, and energy resources of the Middle East.[1] The disaster of 1905 had severely undermined Russia's image as a Great Power. Could it allow a further erosion of its position?

RUSSIA AND WORLD WAR I

Seeing the Russians determined to stand up to the Teutonic powers, the French promised to support their main ally and to fulfill their obligations deriving from the alliance of 1893–1894. Great Britain, although united with France by an informal agreement, refused to commit itself to the French side until the Germans had violated Belgian neutrality. In this way, Europe drifted into a war that proved to be one of the turning points of human history.

Russian propaganda represented the war as one of liberation that would rescue the Slavic peoples from the Teutonic and Magyar yokes. Many Czechs, Slovaks, Serbs, and even some Poles, like the National Democrats, responded to these appeals. The Bulgarians, however, ignored St. Petersburg's urgings, and after some hesitation, joined the Central Powers in 1915. Italy, a formal member of the Triple Alliance, deserted it in the same year and eventually entered the war on the side of Russia, France, Great Britain, and Serbia.

To keep the Russians in the war, in September 1914, the Western allies offered them all the Polish lands then in the hands of Germany and Austria, and promised the Czech throne to a Russian grand duke. The signatories pledged themselves not to sign a separate peace. In March 1915, after the entry of the Ottoman Empire into the war, Great Britain accepted Russian demands concerning the Black Sea Straits and Constantinople. A month later the French acknowledged Russian claims to Turkish Armenia, as well as to a part of Turkish Kurdistan. In return for these promises, the Russians agreed to support various British and French claims to certain parts of the Ottoman Empire, as well as French plans concerning the Rhineland. Moreover, St. Petersburg agreed to the transformation of the central, neutral zone of Persia into a British sphere of influence. The texts of these agreements were kept secret, but soon various details leaked out and became public knowledge.

Imperial Russia entered the war as a cooperative ally of France and Britain and repeatedly proved its loyalty to the common cause. To relieve German pressure on Paris, the Russian armies launched an offensive in East Prussia and Galicia. While most of Eastern Galicia was occupied by Russian troops for nearly a year, the East Prussian offensive proved to be a disaster. Two Russian armies, badly commanded, were surrounded and annihilated in the Masurian lake district.[2]

In the summer of 1915, the Russians had to evacuate their Polish provinces and withdraw far to the east, abandoning most of Lithuania and large stretches of Belorussia and the Ukraine to the Central Powers. Serbia could not be reached by the Russians and was overrun by the enemy. By the end of 1916, Russian casualties (killed, wounded, prisoners of war, and missing) amounted to about 7 million men, or nearly half of the entire force originally mobilized in 1914. Despite Russia's temporary occupation of Eastern Galicia and its successful 1916 offensive on the southern front, the balance sheet of the war for Russia was negative. At the same time, France and Britain were fighting a life-and-death struggle, the outcome of which hung in the

---

[1] Hitherto unknown, Franz Fischer has demonstrated how Germany's expansionist ambitions were not limited only to Europe and Africa. He also pointed out that these ambitions could only succeed through a war that would smash the great power positions of all its principal opponents, Great Britain, France, and Russia; Franz Fischer, *Germany's Aims in the First World War* (New York, W. W. Norton, 1967).

[2] The Russian army's route at Tannenberg and the Masurian lakes in East Prussia has been brilliantly chronicled by Alexander Solzhenitsyn in his epic novel *August, 1914.*

balance until the summer of 1918, when the massive entry of American troops finally tipped the scales and forced the Germans to capitulate on November 11, 1918.

EFFECTS OF THE WAR ON THE TSARIST EMPIRE

In Russia, from the beginning, the war produced a deep crisis that worsened as the murderous conflict progressed. The protracted struggle imposed an unbearable strain on the resources of a fast developing but still emerging country and exposed the very fabric of Russian society to a gruesome ordeal. The mobilization of 15 million men dislocated and unbalanced the Russian economy. Withdrawal of these young men from the country's economy was a heavy burden, especially on industry, which chronically suffered from a shortage of skilled workers. Agriculture, always plagued by surplus manpower, was much less affected. The situation was relieved to some extent, but never completely remedied, by the employment of nearly 400,000 prisoners of war. The armed forces created new demands, not only for military equipment, but also for foodstuffs, leather, and

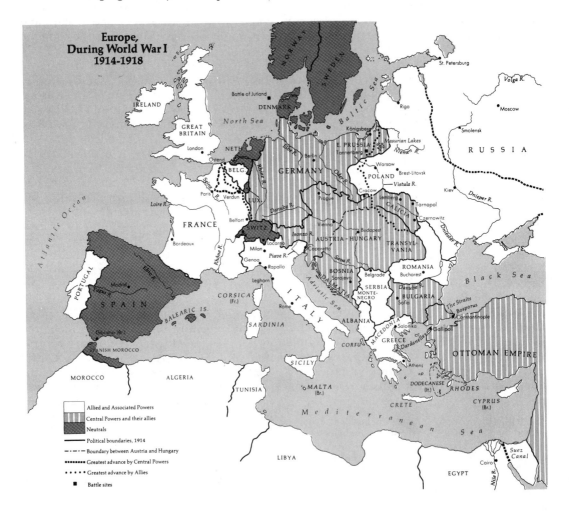

Europe, During World War I 1914-1918

Allied and Associated Powers
Central Powers and their allies
Neutrals
Political boundaries, 1914
Boundary between Austria and Hungary
Greatest advance by Central Powers
Greatest advance by Allies
Battle sites

textiles, which the Russian economy could not satisfy without large imports and assistance from its Western allies.

By 1915, Russian exports had sunk to half of their 1913 level. On the other hand, imports had risen considerably, since the country needed not only large quantities of military equipment and munitions but also machinery for the reorganization of its armament industry. Another debilitating factor was the almost complete isolation of Russia from the outside world. Closing of the major trade routes through the Baltic Sea and the Black Sea resulted in a blockade of Russia by the Central Powers. This situation necessitated a fundamental change in Russia's commercial routes and in the volume and nature of its exports and imports. All supplies from the outside had to be transported through two extended lines, via the more than 5,000-mile-long, one-track Siberian Railroad or through a 1,200-mile-long line built especially for this purpose between the capital (which was now given a Russian name, Petrograd) and the Arctic port of Murmansk. The shift of Russian industry to war production resulted in a shortage of consumer goods. This in turn unleashed inflationary pressures.

To the problem of inflation was added the dislocations that resulted from the withdrawal of Russian forces from the most economically advanced western part of the Empire. The scorched earth policy, the evacuation of a large part of the population, the overburdening of transport, all caused grave problems to military and civilian authorities. Moreover, the administration had to feed and house millions of refugees who were only partially absorbed into the economy. The maldistribution of food, inflation, and worsening living conditions caused serious disaffection among the workers. There was no general shortage of food, but high prices, communication difficulties, and faulty distribution often tended to create that impression locally. This was especially true in the case of Petrograd, located in the Empire's exposed northwestern corner. By

1916, this unrest had assumed menacing proportions. Industrial strikes, so prominent during the first half of 1914 and temporarily silenced by the mood of patriotic elation, were more and more frequent by the end of 1915 and in 1916. The left-socialist movement, initially embarrassed by the nationalistic fervor, began to reassert itself and caused considerable trouble for the security apparatus.

Widespread military incompetence (the East Prussian venture was merely one striking example) and corruption in the civil and military administrations affected the morale of the Russian people. Many of the setbacks suffered by the Russians were due to lack of equipment and supplies, ammunition, and artillery shells. Even ordinary rifles were in short supply. The provisioning of the troops, as well as of the civilian population, was often inadequate.

Responding to the challenge, the public offered its help to the Government by forming a series of "Voluntary Organizations," like the Union of Zemstvos, the Union of Municipalities, and the War Industry Committees. The committees helped to mobilize industries serving the war machine. Chairman of the Central War Industry Committee was the leader of the Octobrist Party, A. I. Guchkov, in cooperation with Prince George Y. Lvov, a veteran among the Zemstvo notables. As praiseworthy as the initiative of the "Voluntary Organization" was, it could not replace lagging governmental leadership.

The defeats of the crucial summer of 1915 dramatically exposed the inadequacy of Russian leadership. In August of that year, the Tsar, at the suggestion of Rasputin, dismissed the Commander-in-Chief, Grand Duke Nicholas Nikolayevich, and assumed supreme command himself. This was a fatal step, since from that time on the Emperor assumed personal responsibility for the conduct of the war. Leaving the capital for his front headquarters in Mogilev on the upper Dnieper, the Emperor delegated his power to the Empress. Surrounded by a clique of courtiers, she decided the most important State issues. She would regularly receive from the Prime Minister—first Goremykin, and then B. V. Stuermer—reports on the work of the Government. She interfered with the upper bureaucracy's appointments and dismissed cabinet ministers and other high dignitaries. Between the middle of 1915 and the February–March revolution of 1917, the Empire had no less than four premiers, five ministers of the interior, three foreign ministers, and three ministers of war. The Empress bombarded the Emperor daily with letters and telegrams and even interfered with the conduct of military operations. This often resulted from the influence of Rasputin, whose role had increased since 1914. Exaggerated rumors about Rasputin's role at the Court filtered down to the front and undermined the soldiers' morale.

The military disasters of 1915, the inefficiency of the leadership, and the growing strain on the economy revealed a deep split in Russian public opinion. The liberals, the radicals, and the right wing of the socialist movement were generally pro-Entente; they hoped that Russia's struggle shoulder to shoulder with the Western democracies would contribute to the eventual liberalization of its domestic system after the war. On the other hand, many Russian conservatives regretted that their country was compelled to fight alongside the liberal democracies against its traditional former allies, with whom the Tsarist Empire had been connected by so many ties, including profitable trade relations. In addition to problems caused by this split, the public was flooded with rumors about alleged treason at the top, negotiations for a separate peace, and scandals in court circles, many of them involving Rasputin. There was no foundation to the rumors then circulating in various circles that the Emperor, under the influence of his German wife and Rasputin, was planning a separate peace with the Central Powers. Yet the rumors persisted. Since the disasters of the summer of 1915, doubts were more and more often ex-

pressed, not only in private conversations but even in governmental circles, as to whether the struggle could be brought to a "victorious conclusion," as the government had repeatedly proclaimed.

ACTIVITIES OF THE OPPOSITION

The mounting crisis alarmed the Duma opposition parties, and in August 1915 they organized themselves into a coalition known as the *Progressive Bloc*. This parliamentary grouping included deputies from three moderate parties: the Cadets, the Octobrists, and the Progressive Nationalists. These parties, composed of moderate patriots, constituted about three-quarters of the fourth Duma. The Bloc, led by Professor Miliukov, called for elimination of "the distrust of public initiative" and enforcement of the rule of law, and urged the Monarch to remove the incompetent bureaucratic government and appoint a new cabinet that was representative of public opinion. The Bloc insisted on repeal of the worst of those measures inspired by racial, religious, and class discrimination (including anti-Jewish legislation). When the Tsar rejected their demands, the Bloc parties, which earlier in a show of patriotic enthusiasm had supported the Government, now became outspokenly critical of the strikingly inefficient and allegedly criminal and treasonous misconduct of the war. Disappointed with the Tsar and his administration and doubting whether things could be improved by legal means, some members of the Bloc became involved in conspiratorial activities. They planned a palace revolution that would place on the throne one of the grand dukes, who would pursue the war with more vigor and prove more amenable to the Bloc's demands.[3]

---

[3] For a conspiratorial interpretation of the overthrow of the Tsarist regime, with an emphasis on the role of the masonic lodges, see George Katkov, *Russia 1917* (New York: Oxford University Press, 1957). Katkov intimates that there might have been some connection between the Freemasons and the German intelligence activities in Russia.

In December 1916 in the midst of these mounting political and economic crises, a conspiratorial group killed Rasputin, considered by many to be a German agent. The Tsar returned from the front to attend Rasputin's funeral and banished those who participated in the plot. Then he returned to the front and sank back into apathy. He remained in this state for several weeks, unmindful of all the warnings of the gathering storm. By the beginning of 1917, the Tsar had practically ceased to be of any importance. By that time rumors of an impending upheaval were circulating in political and diplomatic circles. The problem that preoccupied the patriotic opposition was how to remove him without creating a catastrophe and with whom to replace him. The prospect of rule by the heir-apparent, Alexis, then only twelve years old and an incurable hemophiliac, seemed an insuperable problem.

On the whole, the Russian people started the war in a mood of patriotic euphoria. With the exception of the Bolsheviks and a few minor leftist groups, most socialists followed the example of the veteran socialist Plekhanov and took a pro-war stand. Even the spokesman of the Populist Labor Party, Alexander Kerensky, the future Prime Minister of the Provisional Government, urged the working people first "to defend our country and then set it free." Such an attitude was motivated by the conviction that a Central Powers victory would mean a triumph of reaction and militarism and would spell control of Europe by Germany.

Soon, however, when initial indignation toward the Central Powers had cooled down and the first major setbacks had occurred, the war was carefully scrutinized. People formed many different opinions, and the diverse leftist groups embraced a variety of attitudes toward the war. They stretched from the "defensism" or Social Patriotism of Plekhanov, Kerensky, and most Social Revolutionaries, through the pacifism of many Mensheviks, to Lenin's outright defeatism, with its insistence on "turning the imperialistic war into a civil war."

Lenin presented this program at two international conferences of the socialist left in Switzerland, the first at Zimmerwald in 1915 and the second at Kienthal in 1916. Lenin's extreme defeatist views were, however, rejected even by these radical leftist gatherings. Only a small minority supported his stand that it was impossible to attain social revolution without wishing for the defeat of one's government and actively working for such a defeat. Undisturbed even by the opposition in the ranks of the leftist socialists, Lenin continued to work for the realization of his ideas with his characteristic stubbornness.

Meanwhile, both Berlin and Vienna were eagerly following the domestic situation in Russia, especially the defeatist stand of the Bolsheviks. They were hoping to eliminate Russia by negotiating a separate peace with Petrograd and then dealing a mortal blow to the Western allies. Consequently, the German and Austrian authorities readily allowed the Bolsheviks to circulate their leaflets and pamphlets among Russian prisoners of war. Worsening economic conditions and the mood of dejection that had been spreading throughout the Tsarist Empire since the summer of 1915 helped the defeatist propaganda to gain momentum. From the beginning of 1916 the country experienced a wave of industrial strikes that inhibited the war effort and threatened the stability of the Tsarist regime.

DOWNFALL OF THE TSARIST REGIME

While the liberal circles, determined to continue the war, were debating the domestic choices facing the country, a series of strikes broke out in Petrograd at the end of February. They were the result of a dramatic rise in the prices of necessities, particularly of food. As a result of faulty distribution, there were acute bread shortages in the capital. Faced with rising prices, the workers at the Putilov locomotive and machine factory demanded a 50 percent wage increase; the management turned them down. To this refusal the workers responded with a sit-down strike. On February 22 (March 5) the management retaliated by declaring a lock-out, which left about 40,000 workers jobless. The Putilov men appealed to their fellow workers in Petrograd to help them out of their plight. As a consequence, a wave of sympathy strikes swept the capital. By February 23–26 (March 6–9), some 200,000 workers left their factories in the capital.

On February 23 (March 8), housewives staged mass protests against food shortages. They were joined by the locked out Putilov factory workers; the police fired on the crowds. By Saturday evening February 25 (March 10), Petrograd was in a state of general strike and turmoil. On Sunday, February 26 (March 11), huge crowds protesting the shortage of bread again marched with flags and slogans through the main thoroughfares of Petrograd. In some cases the soldiers, when ordered to shoot, executed their orders; but in other instances they refused to obey and even joined the marchers. The next day, Monday, February 27 (March 12), the whole Volhynian Guard Regiment, largely composed of Ukrainian recruits, joined the demonstrators. Soon most of the Petrograd garrison had followed the example of the Volhynians.

In the meanwhile, the Tsar, who was still at the front, postponed the meeting of the Duma. The deputies, who were afraid that this meant a disguised dissolution, were determined to resist and met on February 27 (March 12), in defiance of the monarch to review the situation. Until that time the revolt had been largely spontaneous and leaderless. It consisted mostly of anonymous workers, soldiers, and students fired by revulsion against military and bureaucratic inefficiency and angry at the indifference of Tsarist authorities to the lot of the common people. Only by February 27 (March 12), when the people learned about the defiant attitude of the Duma, now deliberating against the explicit wish of the Tsar, did delegations of various regiments and civilian institutions begin to arrive at the Tau-ride Palace, the seat of the Duma, to offer their support and cooperation. Emboldened by this popular support, the Duma appointed a Provisional Committee under the Octobrist Speaker of the House, M. V. Rodzianko.

When he was informed about the mutinies and manifestations, the Emperor called them a stab in the backs of the fighting men and ordered their immediate suppression. Meanwhile, however, the revolt spread. The demonstrators captured depots of weapons and began to distribute arms to the mob. Prisons were opened and inmates released. Police headquarters were set on fire. On March 1 (March 14), the Provisional Committee of the Duma proclaimed itself the Provisional Government. A moderate Cadet politician, Prince George Y. Lvov, president of the Union of Zemstvos and a man with a long record of public work, was selected as its Prime Minister, while the leader of the Progressive Bloc, the Cadet politician Professor Miliukov, assumed the portfolio of Foreign Affairs.

THE PROVISIONAL REGIME VERSUS THE PETROGRAD SOVIET

The setting up of the Provisional Government was a challenge to the socialists, who were very imperfectly represented in the fourth Duma. Hasty elections were arranged in various factories and barracks, and by seven o'clock on the evening of February 27 (March 12), a rival proletarian body, the Petrograd Soviet of Workers, Peasants, and Soldiers, gathered to question the legality and credentials of the bourgeois Provisional Government. Symbolically enough, the Soviet met in the left wing of the Tauride Palace, while the Provisional Government deliberated in the right wing. Most members of the Soviet were Mensheviks and Social Revolutionaries, with the Bolsheviks numbering some 10 percent of the delegates.

Although the two rivals for authority and power were linked by their criticism of the fallen regime, they operated from different theoretical premises, used different methods, and aimed at different objectives. Considering the Provisional Government to be an unrepresentative, bourgeois body, the Soviet forbade any of its members to participate in the Government's work. An exception was made in the case of the previously mentioned Labor Party deputy Alexander Kerensky, an able young lawyer of thirty-five and a gifted orator. He alone among the leftist politicians was allowed to accept a ministerial post, the Minister of Justice, to watch over the bourgeois rival on behalf of the Soviet. Since he was at the same time vice-chairman of the Petrograd Soviet, he was the only personal link between the two rival groups.

Throughout the eight months that separated the downfall of Tsardom from the Bolshevik coup d'état, the relationship between the two bodies competing for power was of crucial importance. After some hesitation, on March 2 (March 15) the Soviet agreed to give conditional support to the Provisional Government. The Government was to summon, as soon as possible, a Constituent Assembly to be elected on the basis of universal suffrage; the Government was to allow all local governing bodies to be elected on the same franchise; all civil rights were to be shared by soldiers, while discipline was to be maintained at the front; finally, the garrison of Petrograd was not to be removed from the capital. The conditional support granted the Provisional Government by the Petrograd Soviet was in accordance with the classic Marxist theory of a two-stage revolution. The Menshevik and Social Revolutionary leaders of the Soviet were convinced that the semifeudal country was not ready for socialism and needed a transition period between the bourgeois and the proletarian stages of the revolution to allow the working class to prepare for the future socialist phase.

Meanwhile, however, contrary to the agreement which left the executive power with the Provisional Government, the Soviet, anxious to win over the armed forces to its side, began to circulate a set of instructions addressed to the soldiers. These instructions, which came to be known as *Order Number One*, freed the soldiers from the old fetters of discipline. The death penalty was abolished; political commissars were to be instituted in each unit from the company level on; problems of a nonmilitary nature were to be settled by majority vote; committees in which officers had the same vote as privates were to be elected in each unit; and the saluting of officers was dropped. Order Number One removed actual control of the troops from the hands of the officers and dealt a fatal blow to the cohesion of Russia's armed forces. Order Number One was motivated by the Soviet's fear of the armed forces, commanded largely by conservative-minded generals and admirals. The Soviet suspected that they would sooner or later stage a counterrevolutionary coup and restore the old order in one guise or another. Consequently, decomposition of the old fighting force was considered as a major and worthy objective of the Soviet.

Most military commanders tried to evade the strict application of the Order to their units and restrict the powers of the Soldiers' Committees to strictly nonmilitary matters (education, provisioning the canteens, and the like), but the Committees tended more and more to encroach on all fields of activity. Soon they even insisted that their sanction was necessary to order soldiers to the front line. For the Russian army, composed largely of semi-illiterate peasants, the Order, which went well beyond what the most liberal mind could regard as compatible with military efficiency, had disastrous consequences. It gradually crippled its fighting capacity beyond repair.

THE ABDICATION OF NICHOLAS II IN HISTORIC PERSPECTIVE

As these events were taking place in Petrograd, Tsar Nicholas was at his General Headquarters near Pskov, trying to mount some countermeasures. Meanwhile, the Provisional Government telegraphed principal army commanders asking for support. Practically all of them sided with the Provisional Government, hoping that it would pursue the war with more vigor and determination. Only when he had failed to muster enough troops to suppress the revolt in the capital, had been deserted by his supporters, and was helpless did the Tsar decide to abdicate in favor of his younger brother, Grand Duke Michael. The drama of abdication took place on the night of March 2 (15) at a little railroad station that, symbolically enough, bore the name Dno (which in Russian means bottom). Before giving up his Imperial powers in his own name and that of his adolescent, hemophiliac son, Alexis, the Tsar confirmed the Provisional Government and asked the people to support it in order to carry the war to a victorious conclusion. Immediately after the abdication, Nicholas was put under house arrest.

In the Provisional Government there were two ministers who had monarchist inclinations: Miliukov, Minister of Foreign Affairs, and Guchkov, Minister of War. They wanted to offer the vacant throne to Grand Duke Michael, brother of Nicholas. But when the Grand Duke asked for a guarantee of his personal safety and the Government was unable to grant it, he declined the offer. Thus, after 304 years, the Romanov dynasty fell without much resistance. One could easily argue that the Tsarist regime was not actually overthrown, but tumbled like a house of cards because of the apathy of its leading members and the weakness of its fundamental structure exposed by the strains of war.

In a historic sense, the collapse of the Romanov dynasty in Russia is an important turning point not only in Russian but in world history and is comparable to the downfall of the French monarchy at the end of the eighteenth century. The struggle caught the Tsarist Empire in the middle of a process of transformation (agrarian, educa-

tional, and military), at a point when most of the reforms undertaken during the constitutional period were beginning to produce their first results. Among the principal reasons for the fall of the Tsarist government is its failure to overcome Russia's backwardness by modernizing the antiquated government structure rapidly enough to adapt to fast-changing social and economic conditions. Although the Tsarist Empire was developing rapidly, its socioeconomic progress was more quick than its political evolution. Industrialization was suffering from many drawbacks. First, it was undertaken too late and was handicapped by heavy dependence on foreign capital. Foreign investors required high interest rates and drained much of the country's resources. The Tsarist regime's age-long neglect of the peasant problem and the consequent alienation of the rural masses (which comprised some 80 percent of the population) also played a role. The Stolypin reform, as beneficial as it was, also came late and was interrupted by the war. The same was true for the educational reform of 1908 that was to be completed only in 1921–1922.

Alienation of the politically enlightened members of the society was another cause of the crisis that crippled Imperial Russia. Lack of a representative institution at the Imperial level deprived the educated strata of a chance to develop a sense of political responsibility and coparticipation in the affairs of state. In due time, this might even have filtered down to other social groups. By the middle of the nineteenth century, there was a striking need for an institutional framework that would allow the educated and increasingly articulate intelligentsia, landowners, and professionals to express legally their grievances and aspirations. Such institutions would have gradually associated them with the undertakings of the regime, given them a sense of participation, and thus constituted a school of civic activities. The failure to gradually transform the absolutist regime into a consultative and, later, participatory one was a grave mistake. In the absence of such a system, a large mass of educated, progressive people was pushed into the ranks of the revolutionary movement. The Imperial Duma, granted under pressure in 1905–1906, came too late. What would have been sufficient a generation before seemed not enough to the Miliukovs or the Rodziankos.

To the socioeconomic and political causes of the collapse, one should add the mediocrity of leadership. The last generation of Imperial politicians was perhaps the weakest and least talented in modern Russian history. There is no doubt that at the time of World War I the Russian ruling team, including the Emperor, showed striking ineptitude and passivity. The last phase of the Imperial regime could boast of only three strong men: Pobedonostsev, Witte, and Stolypin. It is characteristic that the first, whose influence was on the whole pernicious, was allowed to linger for two generations and advise both Alexander III and Nicholas II. Witte was twice dismissed and died an embittered man, while Stolypin was assassinated under mysterious circumstances.

It was this Russia, led by confused and hesitant mediocrities, that for the second time in a generation stumbled into a murderous war against much more powerful adversaries. For such a war, Russia was insufficiently prepared—militarily, economically, and politically. Karpovich summarized the supreme crisis of Imperial Russia by stressing the lack of leadership:

A heroic and concerted effort of the whole nation was needed if the imperial structure was to weather the storm. To such an indispensable effort, the political crisis of 1915–1917 was an insurmountable obstacle. The war made the Revolution probable, but human folly made it inevitable.[4]

---

[4] M. M. Karpovich, *Imperial Russia* (New York: Henry Holt & Co. 1932), p. 95.

CONSEQUENCES OF THE ABDICATION

The triumph of the Revolution, evident in Petrograd by the middle of March, had speedy repercussions throughout the Empire. By the close of the month the new revolutionary order had triumphed at the cost of some 2,000 lives. The bureaucracy, the army, and the navy quickly accepted the Provisional Government. The police and the extreme right-wing parties either vanished or went underground.

The fall of Tsardom caused a profound anxiety among the Western allies, who were still desperately struggling for survival. They had made plans for a great concerted offensive on both fronts in the spring of 1917. As soon as the Provisional Government reaffirmed its loyalty to the Alliance, the Allied Powers recognized the Government. In the United States the overthrow of the autocracy in Russia was greeted enthusiastically. President Woodrow Wilson hailed the new liberal government with the words, "Does not every American feel that assurance has been added to our hope for the future peace of the world by the wonderful and heartening things that have been happening in Russia? Here is a fit partner for the league of honor."

While Paris, London, and Washington viewed the Russian upheaval mainly in terms of their own military objectives, for the peoples of Russia the Revolution was a far greater event than the war, and they were increasingly preoccupied with domestic issues. What kind of government should be installed? Should the country be a constitutional monarchy or a democratic republic—or perhaps a federation of her component ethnic parts? What social and economic reforms ought to be introduced? Here the issue of land distribution loomed largest. And above all, could the exhausted country afford to continue the struggle while postponing the solution of its vital and urgent internal problems?

Here one should stress that the Provisional Government, from the beginning, revealed an amazing lack of leadership. The old Tsarist administration had collapsed with the abdication of the Tsar, from whom they had claimed all authority. Now Prince Lvov had the extraordinary idea of inviting local self-governing bodies to organize themselves as they chose. The police had been swept away by a tidal wave of anger and replaced by a voluntary militia incapable of coping with the mounting problems generated by the new situation. The commissars sent by the new Government to replace the old provincial governors were largely inexperienced as administrators and never acquired any real authority. Consequently, the country witnessed a rapid breakdown of the existing obsolete but functioning structure. The Provisional Government selected by the highly conservative and unrepresentative fourth Duma was aware of its weakness and inclined to procrastinate. Lacking in self-confidence and without a clear mandate, the cabinet softpedaled the issue of fundamental domestic reform and repeatedly shifted the burden of decision to the future Constituent Assembly, which was expected to be a panacea for all ills. Under the circumstances, the Provisional Government was merely drifting from one crisis to another and barely deserved the name.

The Petrograd Soviet, rival body of the Provisional Government, also suffered from many handicaps. It was a loose, fluctuating body of between 1,000 and 3,000 deputies who had been hastily elected, primarily by acclamation, in the factories and barracks of the capital. The Soviet claimed to represent not the narrow stratum of the bourgeoisie, like the Duma, but the broad masses of working people, and styled itself an organ of "revolutionary democracy." Although its deputies were elected only by the workers and soldiers of the capital, the Petrograd Soviet arrogated to itself the right to make decisions affecting the whole country. As a rule, no agenda was prepared for deliberations of the Soviet in advance for its meetings; interminable debates were often interrupted by the arrival of delegates or telephone messages. Decisions were often made on the spur of the moment, without a clear understanding of their implications. Actual policy making was in the hands of the Executive Committee, a body of fifty to sixty delegates elected by the Soviet. Under these circumstances, a small, well-organized group of people could easily sway the Soviet one way or another. Unlike the Mensheviks and the SRs, the Bolsheviks, until Lenin's return from Switzerland, played a minor role in the first Petrograd Soviet and tended to follow its "social-patriotic" majority, which, on the whole, supported the Government. The Petrograd Soviet was a model for about nine hundred similar provincial bodies that mushroomed throughout the country in the spring of 1917.

The Provisional Government repeatedly submitted to the Soviet's pressures for fear that the latter would withdraw its precarious conditional support. The shaky cooperation with the Soviet symbolized, in the eyes of the Government, the backing of the broad masses of the population, with whom the amiable, well-intentioned, but politically inexperienced and socially isolated members of the Provisional Government had little contact. Thus from February (March) to October (November), Russia, with no head of state, had two governing bodies: one enjoyed formal authority without power, and the other power without authority.

LENIN RETURNS TO RUSSIA

Events in Russia were watched closely by the Central Powers. In the spring of 1917, with the declaration of war against Germany by the United States, the situation of the Central Powers was becoming increasingly critical, in view of the shortage of food, mounting casualties, and growing political tensions. Under the circumstances, the Germans decided to help the chief Russian defeatist Lenin, then living in Switzerland, to return home. Brockdorff-Rantzau argued that Germany should seek "to create the greatest possible chaos in Russia" so that "internal weakness would compel Russia to withdraw from the war." Berlin agreed and offered free passage through Germany to Sweden to Lenin and twenty of his close co-workers, including such prominent Bolsheviks as G. Y. Zinoviev, L. B. Kamenev, Karl Radek, and A. V. Lunacharsky.

After crossing through Germany, Sweden, and Finland, the Bolshevik team disembarked at the Finland station in Petrograd on April 3 (16). Lenin was greeted with suspicion not only by the Provisional Government, which suspected him of being a German agent, but also by the Petrograd Soviet, which was dominated by his opponents, the Mensheviks and SRs, and was afraid of him as its fierce critic and competitor. When Lenin returned to Petrograd, he was forty-eight years old and at the peak of his powers. He immediately embarked upon feverish, relentless activity on three fronts. His first aim was to win over the Bolshevik party to the defeatist stand. His second was to capture the Petrograd Soviet and turn it into a tool of his party. Third, with the support of the Soviet, he wanted to overthrow the Provisional Government and establish the Bolsheviks in power.

Under Lenin's influence the Bolshevik Party, whose platform had hitherto been only slightly more radical than that of the Mensheviks or the Social Revolutionaries, was thoroughly reshaped. On April 7 (20), Lenin published his program of action known as "The April Theses." Lenin's platform rejected the classic Marxist concept of a two-stage revolution and insisted on the immediate seizure of power by his Party so as to implement his slogan, "Peace, land, bread, and all power to the Soviets." "Land" meant not the agrarian reform to be voted in due time by the future Constituent Assembly, but the immediate radical distribution of state and landowners' land among the peasants. "Bread" was a blanket term for a variety of socioeconomic reforms in a socialist spirit. The first step was to be achieved by immediate seizure of the factories and establishment of workers' control

over them. "Peace" meant not the negotiated, or "white," peace "without annexations or indemnities" advocated by most of the moderate socialists. Lenin advocated an immediate end to the war, which he condemned as imperialist on both sides, in order to overthrow the bourgeoisie first in Russia, and then throughout all of Europe. "Turn the imperialist war into a civil war" was Lenin's battle cry. To foster revolutionary activities on a worldwide scale, the old "social-patriotic," defensist Social-Democratic Second International, discredited by its passivity toward the war, should be scrapped, Lenin said, and thrown into the garbage can of history. A new communist international organization should be established. The Bolshevik Party should shed its old name and assume the adjective "Communist." Behind Lenin's ambitious peace program was an optimistic concept of the potentialities of the revolutionary forces in Europe, especially of the Spartacist groups in Germany, who were determined to seize power in Berlin and act hand in hand with their Russian comrades.

The Provisional Government denounced Lenin's program as "destructive" and "anarchistic" and branded its author as a German agent and spy paid by secret funds of the enemy intelligence.[5] Despite these accusations, Lenin was not arrested, which is another indication of the Government's impotence. Meanwhile, in May, Trotsky returned to Russia from the United States and soon sided with Lenin. Consequently, that spring was a major turning point of the first

---

[5] The problem of the extent of German aid to the Bolsheviks is still a controversial question. According to Soviet sources, the Bolshevik Party published some eighty periodicals in 1917. The Party had between 20,000 and 30,000 members, and no large native resources, while the Germans did spend considerable sums of money for psychological warfare in Russia. For a discussion of the problem see Katkov, *Russia* and Z. Zeman, ed., *Germany and Revolution in Russia 1915–1918* (New York: Oxford University Press, 1958); also W. B. Scharlau and Zbynek A. B. Zeman, *Merchant of Revolution: A Life of Alexander Helphand (Parvus)* (New York: Oxford University Press, 1965).

phase of the Revolution. Until then, both the Provisional Government and the Soviet had lacked strong leaders. No political party had either a clear-cut program of action or the will to act vigorously. With the return of Lenin, one small group, with about 20,000 members that controlled only about 10 percent of the Soviet deputies and thus far had not been particularly active or outspoken in its opposition to the Government, underwent a radical change. It was now headed by a determined and able leader who was bent on achieving a definite program.

THE JULY CRISIS
AND THE KORNILOV AFFAIR

While in domestic affairs the Provisional Government constantly displayed lamentable weakness, it was initially more assertive in foreign and military matters. Despite the dwindling discipline and morale of an army profoundly affected by war weariness and undermined by Order Number One, the Government decided to reaffirm its intention and willingness to continue the war "to a victorious conclusion." In the spring of 1917 the Western allies were hard-pressed by the Germans. Kerensky, since May the Minister of War, and representatives of the Mensheviks and SRs in the cabinet resolved to launch a large-scale offensive on the Galician front, where the Russians were facing weaker Austro-Hungarian forces. In June and July the Russian offensive scored some spectacular initial successes, but it was soon turned into a retreat and eventually became a rout. The failure of the offensive was promptly followed by a governmental crisis over the issue of autonomy for the Ukraine and by a Bolshevik attempt to seize power. At the beginning of July some units of the Petrograd garrison, afraid of being sent to the front to support the sagging offensive, revolted. The Bolsheviks decided to take advantage of the mutiny to seize power. On July 3–5 (16–18), large-scale violent battles took place between the rebels and the units loyal to the Government.

Several hundred people were killed. Order was finally restored by troops brought in from the vicinity of Petrograd. The rebellion was put down and the Government ordered the arrest of other Bolshevik leaders. Lenin managed, however, to escape to Finland, where he was to write his booklet *State and Revolution,* which laid down his blueprint for a future Communist Russia.

The suppression of the July Bolshevik riots in Petrograd gave the Provisional Government a new lease on life, but it was not utilized properly. Soon another crisis followed. On July 7 (20), Prince Lvov resigned his premiership because his cabinet could not agree on three vital issues: whether to proclaim Russia a republic; whether to sanction the spontaneous seizure of land by the peasants, who were impatiently waiting for the promised land reform; and what to do about the Ukraine. When the Cadet ministers resigned as a protest against granting autonomy to that vital part of the former Empire, a new coalition government was formed by Kerensky, with the Mensheviks and the Social Revolutionaries dominating the cabinet but unable to coordinate properly the activities of the Government with those of the Soviets.

By far the most crucial problem was the civilian–military tension that precipitated another crisis. The failure of the July offensive was followed by recriminations and bickering in military quarters. A scapegoat was found in the person of the Commander-in-Chief, General Alexis A. Brusilov, who was dismissed and replaced by Kerensky's nominee, General Lavr G. Kornilov, then commander of the southwestern front. Kornilov was a man of great energy and courage, but he had little understanding of political issues. His former Chief of Staff, General M. V. Alexeyev, called him a "man with a lion's heart and the brain of a sheep." Kornilov believed that the country was drifting toward catastrophe. He insisted on the necessity of restoring order at home and on strict military discipline at the front if the Russian forces were to resume their fighting capacity. He was inclined toward immediate dissolution of the Soviets and banishment of the Bolshevik Party. These requests were rejected, however, by the Socialists, who were suspicious of him as a potential military dictator. Also, they were loath to apply stern measures against fellow Socialists and former co-victims of Tsarist reprisals, however misguided they might appear to outsiders. The Socialists insisted on more rapid "democratization" in domestic and foreign policies. Nevertheless, Kerensky did make some gestures to placate Kornilov; for instance, freedom of the press was somewhat curtailed. The death penalty for desertion and treason was reintroduced at the front.

These measures corresponded to the slowly changing mood of a considerable segment of the Russian population. By the summer of 1917 a large part of moderate public opinion, in agreement with Kornilov, came to the conclusion that no strictly democratic measures could arrest the drift toward catastrophe. Kerensky himself was increasingly inclined toward sterner measures but was too shy and unskillful in their application. Afraid of the growing Bolshevik threat, he secretly ordered Kornilov to keep crack troops in readiness for a march on Petrograd to smash another possible Bolshevik revolt. While both wished to check the Bolsheviks, each visualized the outcome differently. Kornilov understood that Kerensky had agreed to accept him as the future dictator. Acting under this assumption and without clarifying the issue, Kornilov decided to act on his own. On August 25 (September 7), he ordered his troops to march on Petrograd.

Threatened, the shocked Kerensky reversed his stand. He denounced "the Bonapartist threat" of a self-styled dictator, allegedly bent on restoring Tsardom and summoned all supporters of "revolutionary democracy" to fight against him. The Government virtually suspended the ban on the Bolshevik Party, released its leaders on bail, and distributed some 40,000 rifles to the workers, mostly to the Bolshevik-controlled Red Guards. The Petrograd Soviet, facing the immediate menace of an occupation of the capital by Kornilov's troops, was quick to forget the memories of the July Days. A Committee for Struggle with Counter-revolution, which included the Bolsheviks, was set up. The Bolshevik tactics for this important turn of events were summed up by Lenin's dictum: "We shall support the Provisional Government as a rope supports the hanged man." The emergency created by Kornilov's attempted coup allowed the Bolsheviks to re-create their own fighting squads, now armed with weapons supplied by the Government. The arms were never to be returned.

As a result of these measures, the advance of Kornilov's troops was checked. Meanwhile, the morale of his soldiers was undermined by agitators, mainly Bolsheviks, dispatched for this purpose by the Soviet. Moreover, the advance of the troops was sabotaged by the railroad workers, and soon the offensive collapsed. Kornilov and most of his top assistants were arrested. The coup further eroded the prestige of the Government and strengthened the Bolsheviks, who could from now on invoke with some credibility the specter of a "Bonapartist" dictatorship. By September the Bolsheviks had gained control of the Petrograd and Moscow soviets and achieved success in various local soviets throughout the country. At the end of September, Trotsky was elected Chairman of the Petrograd Soviet, which he skillfully manipulated to enhance the Bolshevik position.

In the wake of the aborted coup, disorder and anarchy assumed ever larger proportions. Army deserters, who by October numbered 2 million, were returning home, often committing acts of violence and robbery on their way. The peasants, who had lost patience with the Provisional Government's procrastinating tactics, continued to seize large estates. The land, together with cattle and implements, was divided, the manor houses burned, and the landowners often murdered. In the cities the ignorant wantonness of the the mob was rampant. Shops were looted; hundreds of attacks on officers, officials, and private individuals were recorded every day; and many factory owners and managers were being lynched by the workers. The entire communication system was threatened with breakdown. Famine in the cities was spreading. At the same time, German forces were pushing relentlessly eastward. In September they occupied most of Latvia, including Riga. Evacuation of Petrograd and shifting of the capital to the more secure Moscow were seriously contemplated.

THE BOLSHEVIK COUP D'ÉTAT

Lenin quickly grasped the meaning of the Kornilov coup and concluded that the moment for decisive action was at hand. In October he returned in disguise to Petrograd and began to prepare the ground for the planned Bolshevik armed insurrection. It was on his insistence that the Bolshevik military organization intensified its training and its infiltration of various military and naval units of the Petrograd garrison, especially the Kronstadt naval base. Yet despite Lenin's exhortations, the majority of the Bolshevik leaders initially took a pessimistic view toward Lenin's slogan, "All power to the Soviets through armed insurrection." Mindful of the disastrous July Days, most of the Bolsheviks overestimated the strength and resolution of the Government. Moreover, they were still bothered by vestigial democratic scruples and wanted to be sure of a majority in the All-Russian Congress of Soviets, to assemble at the end of October in Petrograd. Finally, as a result of his stubborn persuasion and support by Trotsky, Lenin managed to galvanize his party into action by October 21–22 (November 3–4).

The Provisional Government, although vaguely aware of the Bolshevik preparations, remained passive. Only on October 24 (November 6) was an order issued to ban the Bolshevik Party and arrest its leaders. Loyal troops were to be brought from the vicinity of the capital to deal with the imminent coup. But these measures came too late. On October 25 (November 7) the Bolsheviks began their operation. Meanwhile, the cabinet was in permanent session but was unable to act effectively in time to cope with the mounting Bolshevik menace. With little resistance, the Kronstadt sailors, the Lettish Sharpshooters, and the Red Guards occupied key points of the capital one by one, starting with the crucial central telephone and telegraph building. Then came the offices of the general staff, various ministries, and banks.

The Provisional Government—barricaded in the Winter Palace and protected by a few companies of officer cadets, a battalion of women volunteers, and forty or fifty veteran cavaliers of the order of St. George—was dictating measures to be undertaken and drafting and redrafting a proclamation to the people of Petrograd, summoning them to oppose the Bolshevik threat. By midday of October 25 (November 7), most of the city was already under Bolshevik control. The Winter Palace was the last citadel of the Government; therefore, it was psychologically vital for Lenin to announce its capture at the Second Congress of the Soviets then gathering in the capital and to get its stamp of approval for the seizure of power by his party.

Most Soviet historians, including Trotsky, give a highly romanticized version of the final assault on the Winter Palace. They stress the alleged grandeur of the master plan and the mastery of its execution. In reality, the capture of the huge Palace was an almost bloodless series of scattered skirmishes interspersed with chaotic negotiations with its confused defenders. Finally, the defenders were convinced of the uselessness of further resistance and surrendered. The whole operation involved only six casualties. As Lenin said, "We found the power lying in the streets, and we picked it up."

The seizure of the Winter Palace and the arrest of thirteen members of the Provisional Government (Kerensky had escaped the siege to seek the help of loyal troops) consummated the Bolshevik triumph in Petrograd. The capture of the Palace was followed by Lenin's proclamation of the Bolshevik victory and the formation of the Council, or Soviet, of People's Commissars, which was the first Soviet Government. The term "Minister" had been discarded as a reactionary, bourgeois title. The composition of the Council was as follows: Chairman of the Council was Lenin himself; Commissariat of the Interior was entrusted to A. E. Rykov; that of Labor went to A. G. Shliapnikov, one of the few genuine proletarians among the Bolshevik leaders; Military and Naval Affairs were directed by a triumvirate of A. Antonov-Ovseenko, N. V. Krylenko, and F. M. Dybenko; Popular Education went to A. V. Lunacharsky; and Foreign Affairs to L. D. Trotsky. As Chairman for Nationalities, a relatively little known Georgian Bolshevik by the name of Iosif V. Djugashvili, better known to us as Stalin, was appointed. Having given its approval to

Iosif V. Djugashvili, known as Stalin, as Commissar for Nationalities, 1917–1923

the Bolshevik coup, the Second Congress of Soviets was immediately sent home.

While the Bolshevik victory in Petrograd was almost bloodless, Lenin's supporters in Moscow encountered much stronger resistance. There the bitter fighting lasted for three days; about five hundred people were killed on the Bolshevik side alone. The triumph in Moscow was followed promptly by similar but much easier victories in most of the Great Russian provincial centers. In the non-Russian periphery of the former Tsarist Empire, the resistance to Bolshevik encroachments was considerably stiffer, and some three years of civil war would be needed to overcome it.

THE BOLSHEVIK VICTORY IN HISTORIC PERSPECTIVE

The victory of the Bolsheviks in Russia has proved to be one of the decisive events of the twentieth century. According to Soviet historiography, the October Revolution was the product of a clearly discernible, irresistible trend in Russian history. Official Soviet history has maintained that the capture of power had been meticulously planned by the Party, acting under the guidance of the omniscient, infallible Lenin. Party historians have insisted that the Bolshevik triumph was the inevitable consequence of Russian domestic conditions and at the same time an integral segment of the international struggle of the proletariat against the bourgeoisie, with the Russian comrades acting as a vanguard of the world proletarian forces. The Communists were victorious in Russia because, under the leadership of the Bolshevik Party, they dealt a timely blow to the weakest link in the "chain of capitalism."

Non-Communist historians, on the other hand, are inclined to see the coup as a result of circumstances; the weak Provisional Government, the victim of its own errors, was overthrown by the cold-blooded determination of a small group of conspirators. Whatever the shortcomings of the Government, argue the non-Communist writers, it represented the only democratic interlude in Russian history. The Government ended racial and religious discrimination, adopted progressive social legislation, including the establishment of factory committees and an eight-hour working day, and introduced basic freedoms, including as large a scope for self-expression as ever existed anywhere in the world. Never did the peoples of Russia enjoy greater political liberty than between February–March and October–November of 1917. Lenin himself admitted that in the spring of 1917 Russia was "the freest country in the world." Non-Soviet historians regard the Bolshevik coup as both a surprisingly successful gamble and a deliberate and rather unfortunate reversal of what is presumed to be Russia's painfully slow evolution toward constitutional democracy. According to them, Lenin was carried to power by a wave of anarchy that he exploited masterfully.

The weakest point in the reasoning of many non-Communist historians is their ambivalent attitude toward the Provisional Government. One must admit that from the very beginning the Provisional Government was deeply divided, hesitant, lacking in self-confidence, and unable to cope not only with the long-range issues but even with everyday problems. The downfall of Tsardom brought no relief to the working masses as inflation continued to spiral. While food prices increased by 500 to 600 percent after the war, wages went up only by 300 to 400 percent. In all three critical periods—in May, July, and September—the Provisional Government revealed astonishing indolence. Actually, the Government was in a permanent crisis, whatever its changing composition.

The abdication of political leadership on the part of the educated, civilized forces revealed the shallow roots of Russian liberal democracy. Courageous, vociferous, and often brilliant in criticizing the abuses of Tsarist autocracy, they were unable to act positively and decisively when exercising political power. Kerensky, "the Hamlet of the Russian Revolution," "the conjurer-in-chief," was perhaps the best exemplar of these shortcomings of the Russian intelligentsia. An able and dedicated lawyer, he was in love with his own flowery oratory but was unable to grasp the practical issues and cope with them resolutely. His faith in the miraculous power of revolutionary phraseology was disastrous.

There were two phases of the revolution: the liberal one that overthrew the Tsarist regime and the Bolshevik coup that destroyed the weak and hesitant, yet basically liberal and democratically inclined Provisional Government. The first upheaval was a revolt of the people against the inefficient, corrupt, and discredited government of Nicholas II. Most testimonies agree that the revolt was a popular one, a largely spontaneous and bloodless uprising from below, greeted with joy by a great majority of politically articulate people. The role of the Bolsheviks in the first phase of the revolution was marginal. Most contemporary observers as well as latter-day historians agree that the Bolshevik seizure of power, on the other hand, was a conspiratorial coup d'état. It was launched by a small but determined, well-organized minority that took advantage of the war-weariness and demoralization of the masses and the helplessness of the Provisional Government.

The crisis of 1917 propelled onto the political stage millions of war-weary, uprooted soldiers, most of them semiarticulate peasants in uniform, desperately looking for effective leadership amidst the monumental confusion caused by the erosion and sudden downfall of traditional institutions. The unexpected, complete, and truly unparalleled freedom suddenly bestowed upon the masses turned their heads and pushed them toward anarchy and license. The Bolsheviks were the only party able to channel this discontent for their purposes. This phenomenon dramatically widened the dangerous rift between the two societies hitherto uneasily coexisting behind the facade of the Tsarist autocracy. The Westernized, civilized, and often liberally inclined thin crust of the Russian polity was profoundly alienated from the largely illiterate, primitive, overwhelmingly peasant masses. These masses were unable to comprehend the lavish freedom granted to them by the benevolent, broadminded, yet highly unrealistic Provisional Government. In a few days, Russia seemed to quickly pass through several stages of political evolution—from age-old submission and apathy to modern democracy, with all the intricate trappings of mass politics. This was obviously too much for the Russian masses to assimilate overnight.

While the leaders of other parties, mostly prisoners of democratic scruples, were busy arguing with each other about fine points of theory, the Bolsheviks were catering to the instincts and hatreds of the masses. In the complex situation, the Bolsheviks were the only group that grasped the true meaning of what was going on and were able to harness those longings for their own objectives. Here they proved master organizers, skillful manipulators of modern mass politics, and imaginative leaders. The Bolsheviks' vigorous organizational effort and grass-roots work were unique. For instance, they were the first to form fighting squads—the Red Guards, Army and Navy committees, factory committees, and so forth. Realizing how elemental was the desire for peace, they put that slogan at the head of their program. They published a special paper for the front soldiers, *Pravda of the Trenches,* that encouraged the soldiers to fraternize with the enemy and to "vote with their feet." They encouraged the spontaneous division of large estates that had been taking place in the countryside since the summer of 1917. To gain the support of ethnic minorities, the Bolsheviks, although at heart rigid centralists, loudly proclaimed the slogan of national self-determination, including the right to secession.

The Provisional Government had failed on all counts as an effective executive power. It was unable either to extricate Russia from the war or to continue the struggle to victory. It proved incapable of convincing the masses that it was going to offer them the fundamental reforms desired by the people, especially radical land reform. On the other hand, one must admit that the task of the Provisional Government was exceedingly difficult. Russia had more than three years of war behind it and had suffered some 7 million casualties. The new government could neither continue the war, because of the growing disintegration of the armed forces, nor sign a separate peace for fear of mortally endangering its Western Allies and helping Germany to establish a hegemonial position in Europe, with all that it would imply for Russia's political position in the future. The land issue was equally difficult. Besides the legal scruples the Government felt concerning the peasants' spontaneous seizure of the land, the anarchic, often violent redistribution was all too quickly diminishing dwindling food supplies. The situation in the factories, with their ineffective workers' committees, was similar.

The failure of the Provisional Government spelled the historic failure of the infant liberal democracy in Russia. The withdrawal of Russia from active association with the West and the militant proclamation by its new leaders of universalistic slogans radically opposed to everything the liberal West stood for were bound to have far-reaching global repercussions. Consequently, the triumph of the Bolsheviks over one-sixth of the earth opened a new epoch in the history of humanity.

SUGGESTING READING

CARR, EDWARD H., *The Bolshevik Revolution, 1917–1923.* New York: Macmillan, 1951–1953, 3 vols.

CHAMBERLIN, WILLIAM H., *The Russian Revolution.* Vol. 1. New York: Macmillan, 1935.

CHERNOV, VICTOR, *The Great Russian Revolution.* New Haven, Conn.: Yale University Press, 1936.

DANIELS, ROBERT V., *Red October.* New York: Scribners, 1967.

DZIEWANOWSKI, M. K., ed., *The Russian Revolu-*

tion: An Anthology. New York: T. Y. Crowell, 1970.

FITZPATRICK, SHEILA, *The Russian Revolution*. New York: Oxford University Press, 1982.

FLORINSKY, MICHAEL T., *The End of the Russian Empire*. New Haven, Conn.: Yale University Press, 1931.

FRANCIS, DAVID R., *Russia from the American Embassy*. New York: Scribners, 1922.

FULLER, JR., WILLIAM C., *Civil–Military Conflict in Imperial Russia, 1881–1914*. Princeton, N.J: Princeton University Press, 1985.

HOSKINS, GEOFFREY, *The Russian Constitutional Experiment, Government and the Duma, 1907–1919*. New York: Cambridge University Press, 1973.

KATKOV, GEORGE, *Russia 1917*. New York: Oxford University Press, 1967.

KEEP, JOHN L. H., *The Russian Revolution: A Study in Mass Mobilization*. New York: Norton, 1976.

KENEZ, PETER, *The Birth of the Propaganda State: Soviet Methods of Mobilization, 1917–1929*. New York: Cambridge University Press, 1985.

KERENSKY, ALEXANDER, *Russia and History's Turning Point*. New York: Duell, Sloan and Pierce, 1965.

LIEVEN, O.C.B., *Russia and the Origins of the First World War*. New York: St. Martin's, 1983.

MANDEL, DAVID, *The Petrograd Workers and the Fall of the Old Regime and the the Petrograd Workers and the Soviet Seizure of Power*. New York: St. Martin's, 1984.

MAYZEL, MATITISHU. *An Army in Transition: The Russian High Command, October 1917–May 1918*. Tel-Aviv: Russian and East European Research Center, Tel-Aviv University, 1976.

MEDLIN, V. D., AND S. L. PARSONS, *V. D. Nabokov and the Russian Provisional Government, 1917*. New Haven, Conn.: Yale University Press, 1976.

MELGUNOV, S. P., *The Bolshevik Seizure of Power*, ed. and abridged by Sergei G. Pushkarev in collaboration with Boris S. Pushkarev. Santa Barbara, Calif., and Oxford, England: ABC Clio, 1972.

MORENSHIELDT, DMITRI VON, ed., *The Russian Revolution: Contemporary Accounts*. New York: Oxford University Press, 1971.

PALEOLOGUE, MAURICE, *An Ambassador's Memoirs*. London: Hutchinson, 1923–1935. 3 vols.

PARES, BERNARD. *The Fall of the Russian Monarchy*. New York: Knopf, 1939.

PERRIE, MAUREEN, *The Agrarian Policy of the Russian Socialist-Revolutionary Party*. New York: Cambridge University Press, 1976.

PIPES, RICHARD, ed., *Revolutionary Russia*. Cambridge, Mass.: Harvard University Press, 1968.

RABINOVITCH, ALEXANDER, *The Bolsheviks Come to Power*. New York: Norton, 1977.

REED, JOHN, *Ten Days That Shook the World*. New York: International Publishers, 1919.

SUKHANOV, N. N. (N. N. HIMMER), *The Russian Revolution, 1917: A Personal Record*. New York: Oxford University Press, 1955.

TROTSKY, LEON, *The History of the Russian Revolution*. New York: Simon and Schuster, 1932, 3 vols.

ZEMAN, Z. A. B., ed., *Germany and the Revolution in Russia, 1915–1918*. New York: Oxford University Press, 1958.

CHAPTER 7

The Brave New World at the Creation

One of the first steps of the Soviet Government was to publish the Peace Decree of November 8, 1917. The decree was actually an appeal to all belligerent powers to start immediate negotiations for ending the hostilities and concluding a peace without annexations or indemnities. The Entente, encouraged by the United States' entry into the war, was reluctant to talk about an end to the struggle, but the Central Powers agreed to the Soviet suggestions. On December 5, an armistice was concluded between the Soviets and the Germans, and between Austro-Hungary and the Ottoman Empire. Soon peace talks were opened at Brest-Litovsk.

Anxious as it was to secure peace, the Soviet Government never forgot during its negotiations with the Central Powers that fomenting social revolution was its primary task. Immediately after publishing their Peace Decree, the Bolsheviks started sending out fiery radio appeals addressed "to all, all Peoples of the World," urging them to struggle for peace through every available means. At that time the expectation of a social revolution in Germany and Austro-Hungary was Lenin's main hope for the survival of the weak, infant Soviet regime. Consequently, the Bolsheviks sent agitators among the soldiers of the Central Powers urging them to desert and/or revolt. The German soldiers were told to throw down their arms and go home or, better yet, to turn their weapons on the exploiters and oppressors and change the "imperialistic war" into a civil war.

DOMESTIC REFORMS OF THE BOLSHEVIKS

One day after the publication of the Peace Decree, the Soviet regime took its next important step, publication of the Land Decree. This decree ordered immediate partition of large estates—whether belonging to private individuals, members of the former imperial family, or the church—and their distribution to the peasants. All their livestock and implements were also to be seized and shared by the rural populace. The land was to be the property of the State, and only those willing to cultivate it themselves were to be permitted to use it. In this way the Bolshevik leaders gave their legal blessing to splitting up the land into some 25 million small holdings. They acquiesced to this for tactical reasons, but they did not abandon their ultimate goal of the collectivization of agriculture. When and how it was to be collectivized would depend on later circumstances. Thus the Land Decree was a stopgap measure; another agrarian revolution would follow when circumstances warranted.

On the heels of these two momentous decrees came the establishment of an eight-hour working day, followed by a series of measures that reasserted Communist egalitarian principles and reshaped the privilege-ridden social structure of Tsarist Russia. All titles were abolished. Individuals were to be addressed as "citizen" or, if a member of the party, as "comrade." A similar principle was introduced into the militia, which was to replace the old armed forces. The militia was to be composed of citizen volunteers; again, all titles and ranks were to be eliminated, and commanders were to be elected by the rank and file.

The struggle against religion, considered by Marx to be "the opiate of the people," was not forgotten. For a long time the church has been subservient to the state; since 1721, when Peter the Great abolished the office of Moscow Patriarch, it had been administered as a government department. This subservience had had a crippling effect upon its spiritual life and had made the church bureaucratic, ossified, and entirely dependent on secular authorities. In fact, the hierarchy became completely identified with bureaucratic authorities, thereby rendering Orthodoxy useless as an instrument of social and political reform. As a tool of the autocracy, the church had automatically become a target in the struggle against the Tsarist state.

As early as February 15, 1918, a decree of the Council of People's Commissars declared the separation of the State from the Orthodox Church. The same decree proclaimed freedom of worship insofar as it did not "violate public order." At the same time, all church property was confiscated and all religious instruction in the schools abolished. Only civil marriages were recognized by the state. Divorce could be obtained at once by a simple declaration of agreement; when one side objected, the procedure would be longer. Many traditional cultural patterns were also altered. The old Cyrillic alphabet was simplified, and on February 14, 1918 (February 1, old style), the Julian calendar was abandoned and the West's Gregorian calendar introduced. Arrests, deportations and executions of the clergy multiplied. These measures brought the party into bitter conflict with all churches and religious groups, but especially with the Orthodox Church. The Patriarch of Moscow denounced the Bolshevik regime and its leaders as "monsters of the human race" and "madmen." These anathemas made the Bolsheviks redouble their reprisals. According to estimates at least 28 bishops and some 1,000 priests of the Orthodox Church had perished by 1923.

The antireligious campaign did not mean that the Bolsheviks were rejecting all ethical and moral standards. In practice, the Bolsheviks' attitude was stricter in some ways than the traditional one and rather similar to Puritan morality. The Bolsheviks initially prohibited the national drink, vodka, and took ruthless steps against gambling and prostitution. Hard, honest, systematic work for the state was proclaimed the supreme virtue. During the early stages of their rule, some Bolshevik leaders, starting with Lenin himself, set a personal example by leading the austere, comfortless, dedicated life of a secular monk.

The new rulers of Russia were determined to implement as quickly as possible the socialist organization of the country and to institute a centrally planned economy. It was the state that was to fix priorities, allocate resources, and determine prices and wages. Thus, from the beginning, the Soviet economy was a "command economy," one based on instructions issued from above and not the law of supply and demand. These hasty, radical reforms precipitated chaotic conditions that resulted in shortages of basic necessities; consequently factory workers began leaving the cities in search of food, while rampant inflation threatened to paralyze the economy. The remaining workers continued to seize factories, mines, and other enterprises and to administer them through spontaneously elected factory committees, which were to be the chief instrument of "workers' control." Their often genuine enthusiasm, however, was no match for the expert knowledge of their former managers and engineers, and industrial production sank lower and lower.

The factory committees finally proved not only ineffective, but harmful to production, and were suppressed. The workers were ordered to join the new government trade unions, and all strikes were outlawed. As a result, the Bolshevik Party's authoritarianism became firmly entrenched also in the economy.

All banks, insurance companies, and means of communication were taken over by Soviet authorities immediately after the Bolshevik seizure of power. On June 28, 1918, the Bolsheviks went one step further and nationalized most of Russia's large industries (some 1,100 joint stock companies). For the time being, all former administrative personnel were ordered to remain at their jobs or face prosecution for "sabotage." Private trade was gradually extinguished, and the State undertook to distribute food and other available commodities. Consequently, by the summer of 1918, "the commanding heights of the economy," as Lenin put it, were in the hands of the state (see Chapter 9).

Neither the nationalization decree nor the other regulations that kept pouring from the government presses—along with paper money—could stem the rising tide of chaos or provide the cities with food. The spreading famine increasingly caused a great many people of all classes to abandon the cities and search for food in rural areas. Many workers who had maintained ties with their native villages returned home. The result of this mass migration from the urban areas was an acute shortage of manpower. The new regime tried to counter the situation by establishing a system of compulsory labor and by introducing a strict system of rationing in which workers were given priority. One of the Communist slogans was "Those who do not work, should not eat."

THE CHEKA AND THE DISSOLUTION OF THE CONSTITUENT ASSEMBLY

The Bolshevik triumph in the two capitals was far from ending the struggle for power. Even before the outbreak of the civil war in the Winter and Spring of 1918, the Mensheviks and most of the SRs tried to oust the Bolsheviks from power by regaining majorities in the city soviets, and the new rulers of Petrograd and Moscow often suffered resounding defeats in the local elections. On December 20, therefore, in a move to protect the new regime from its actual and potential enemies, the government set up the Extraordinary Commission to Combat Counterrevolution—colloquially called the *Cheka*, which is its Russian acronym. The organization was given complete autonomy and could carry out searches, arrests, and death sentences. The Cheka was described by one of its prominent members as "the eyes, ears, and the mailed fist" of the proletariat and as "the naked avenging sword of the Revolution." At the beginning of 1918, when the capital was shifted from Petrograd to Moscow, the headquarters of the dreaded Cheka were established in the Lubianka, home of a respectable insurance company.

Leon Trotsky as Commissar for War, 1918–1925

An old co-worker of Lenin's and a former member of the Social Democratic Party of Poland and Lithuania, Felix Dzerzhinsky, was placed at its head. With fanatic zeal, Dzerzhinsky dedicated himself to the task of eradicating all enemies of the new regime.[1]

When the Constituent Assembly was dispersed in January 1918 and the Brest-Litovsk Treaty signed in March of that year, opposition intensified, and so did the terror.

The convocation of a democratically elected assembly had been awaited for so long that its sudden dismissal came as some-

thing of a shock. And the terms of the treaty were so unfavorable that it was immediately denounced, especially by the military, as an abomination, a humiliation, and a national catastrophe. To view the issue of the Assembly in its proper perspective, it is necessary to recall the action taken in the late summer of 1917 by the Provisional Government. At that time the Kerensky regime finally fixed November 25 as the date for elections to the assembly. The date itself was a factor in precipitating the Bolshevik coup, as Lenin's apprehension that the voting might go against the Bolshevik Party helped him to persuade his comrades to act without further delay. Once in power, however, the Bolsheviks decided that it would be too risky for the new regime to ignore public opinion by abrogating the election. Consequently, despite serious misgivings about the final outcome, Lenin decided that the elections should be allowed to take place without further postponement or hindrance. Consequently, with the exception of some meddling with the results of a few districts, peaceful elections took place without gross interference on the part of the Bolsheviks.

The voting represented the first—and thus far the only—basically free, unfettered, and democratic elections in Russian history. And as Lenin had presaged, the results proved highly unsatisfactory from the Bolshevik point of view. Out of the total 703 deputies, only 168 were Bolsheviks, while 380 were Social Revolutionaries. The Party made the strongest showing in big cities, where the working class was relatively large; but the masses of the peasantry supported the Social Revolutionaries. Even if the Left SRs had joined in a government coalition as allies of the Bolsheviks, together

---

[1] The Tsarist secret police, known as *Okhrana*, relied on the Special Corps of Gendarmes, a force of some 15,000 men. By mid-1921, the *Cheka* amounted to some 250,000 (seventeen times larger than *Okhrana*). While the *Okhrana* exercised virtually no extrajudicial powers and the number of executions carried out during the last fifty years of the Tsarist regime amounted to some 14,000, those affected during the first six years of the Soviet rule, according to Lenin's estimate, were no less

than 200,000. George Leggett, *The Cheka: Lenin's Political Police* (New York: Oxford University Press, Clarendon Press, 1981), pp. 56–57 and Epilogue. As Lenin put it on April 3, 1920, "A good Communist is at the same time a good Chekist." In October 1918, he declared, "The revolutionary dictatorship of the proletariat is power secured and sustained through coercion of the bourgeoisie by the proletariat, a power unrestricted by any laws."

they would have constituted less than one-third of the deputies.[2]

Once having allowed the elections to take place, the Bolsheviks found it difficult to prevent the assembly from convening. On January 5 (18), 1918, the vicinity of the Tauride Palace, where the inaugural session of Russia's first full-scale parliament was taking place, resembled an armed camp. The Bolsheviks had taken the precaution of distributing admission tickets to the public by the Soviet secret police (the Cheka). Baltic sailors and Latvian sharpshooters crowded the corridors and galleries of the former Imperial residence and threatened the non-Bolsheviks with lynching.

Despite these threats, the Social Revolutionaries and the Mensheviks, who together dominated the assembly, managed quickly to adopt four measures. They elected the moderate Socialist Revolutionary Victor Chernov, former Minister of Agriculture in the Provisional Government, as Speaker. They proclaimed Russia a democratic federal republic; they disregarded the negotiations at Brest for a separate peace and issued an appeal for an international socialist conference that would achieve a "general democratic peace;" and, ignoring measures already passed by the Soviets, they proclaimed the basic principles of a Land Law that would affect land reform in accordance with Socialist Revolutionary agrarian programs. Though the land would be nationalized, it would be equally accessible to all who wished to till it.

All these measures were regarded by Lenin as a challenge to the authority of the Soviet regime. When it became apparent

that the assembly would persist in its deliberations and that it refused to legitimize the Bolshevik rule, it was more than Lenin could tolerate. At five o'clock on the morning of January 19, Lenin ordered the sailors to clear the hall. "The interests of the Revolution," he explained, "stand over the formal rights of the Constituent Assembly."

Thus ended in less than twenty-four hours the only democratically elected parliament in Russian history.

PEACE NEGOTIATIONS

Meanwhile, the Bolsheviks had to confront the hard facts of international life. The armistice of December 5 was followed by protracted peace negotiations at Brest-Litovsk. The Soviet delegation, led first by Adolf Joffe and then by Trotsky himself, and the Central Powers' delegation could not agree on the basic premises of the settlement. The Soviet side insisted on peace "without annexations or indemnities," whereas the Central Powers demanded territorial concessions and reparations in cash as well as large supplies of food produce. The upshot was that at the end of December the Soviet delegation broke off the talks and left Brest-Litovsk. But not for long, for with their army in shambles and facing the formidable war machine of Germany and Austro-Hungary, the defenseless Bolsheviks were in a desperate situation. Semiofficial contacts were established with Western representatives in Petrograd to try to induce the Allies to join the Soviet Government at the peace table. There was some loose talk that the Allies would lend the Soviets military assistance. Mutual distrust, however, prevented any agreement, and the Soviet Government was left to its own resources, face to face with Germany, Austro-Hungary, Bulgaria, and Turkey.

In the annals of diplomatic history the negotiations of Brest-Litovsk represent the beginning of a new diplomatic style, one that no doubt contributed to the mistrust between the Bolsheviks and the Allies.

---

[2] According to an American scholar, of the total 41 million votes cast, the Social Revolutionaries (Russian as well as Ukrainian) polled 17 million; the Bolsheviks, 9.8 million; the Cadets, 2 million; the Mensheviks, less than 1.4 million. Of the 703 deputies, 380 were Social Revolutionaries; 39, Left Social Revolutionaries; 168, Bolsheviks; 18, Mensheviks; 17, Cadets; 4, Popular Socialists; and 77 represented various ethnic minorities. Oliver H. Radkey, Jr., *The Election to the Russian Constituent Assembly of 1917* (Cambridge, Mass.: Harvard University Press, 1950), pp. 15–16.

When he broke off the talks on December 29, Trotsky issued an appeal urging the workers of the West to rise. The working classes of Europe, however, remained by and large loyal to their leaders, while the armies of the Central Powers resumed their slow but relentless eastward march, hampered only by the heavy snows of winter.

Within days of breaking off the talks, the helplessness and full gravity of their situation was brought home to the Bolshevik leaders. On January 9, 1918, they returned to Brest. As soon as the Soviet delegation reappeared, Trotsky was faced with new, stiffer demands by the Central Powers. The Germans brushed aside Trotsky's verbosity and insisted on a prompt settlement in which the Russians would provide indemnities and agree to territorial concessions. To break Soviet resistance to these stiff demands and obtain grain supplements from the Ukraine, the Germans ingeniously bypassed the Bolshevik representatives and invited a delegation of the Ukrainian Central National Council of Kiev, or the Central Rada, to Brest, an offer the anti-Bolshevik Ukrainians eagerly accepted.

The Bolsheviks, driven into a corner, were split. A large segment of the Party, led by Nicholas I. Bukharin, continued to favor defiance. Remembering the French Revolution and still hoping for a social upheaval throughout Europe, Bukharin preached a revolutionary war against the Central Powers. However, the minority, headed by Lenin and supported by Zinoviev, Kameniev, and Stalin, were for immediate peace, whatever the conditions imposed by the victors. Between those two factions stood Trotsky, who wanted to adhere to the terms of the armistice but sign no formal peace treaty.

The Bolsheviks' revolutionary oratory failed to frighten the Central Powers, and on February 18 their troops resumed their eastward march. First the Germans occupied unresisting Latvia and Estonia; then they threatened Petrograd. This grim reality (which forced the removal of the capital to Moscow), combined with Lenin's

determination, made the Soviets declare, six days later, their readiness to sign the peace agreement. Meanwhile, the Turks had put forward new demands for restitution of the regions lost to Russia at the Congress of Berlin of 1878—the Armenian cities of Kars, Batum, and Ardahan. The helpless Bolsheviks had to capitulate.

THE TREATY OF BREST-LITOVSK

The day the Soviet delegation arrived at Brest-Litovsk (February 28, 1918), a strange scene took place at the railroad station. On the platform stood a knot of officials: diplomats in top hats and swallowtail coats and officers impressively dressed in their gold-braided, bemedaled uniforms. When the Soviet representatives detrained, the self-assured bureacrats of the Central Powers found to their astonishment that they were facing a motley gang of shabby, long-haired bohemians, cheap cigarettes in their mouths, their pockets full of revolutionary leaflets. As they formally greeted the Soviet delegates, Karl Radek drifted over to the amazed onlookers and began to distribute pamphlets urging the violent overthrow of the very governments with which the Soviets were about to start peaceful relations.

The scene marked a transition in international behavior. Heretofore, discussions between nations had been conducted in secret by professional, old-school diplomats. In the past, the function of diplomacy had been to influence restricted political circles. Brest-Litovsk initiated a new era in which diplomatic intercourse would be carried on largely in the open in an effort to influence masses of people through propaganda. This new approach to diplomacy was made easier with the advent of mass journalism and radio.

By the terms of the Brest-Litovsk Treaty, the Soviet Government agreed to recognize the independence of the Ukraine, Finland, and Georgia. Moreover, the Soviets agreed to accept the status that the Central Powers had bestowed on Poland, Lithuania, Latvia, and Estonia in the name of national self-determination. These countries would be vassal states ruled by German princes. The Russians also lost a strip of Transcaucasia to the Ottoman Empire. The treaty reduced Soviet territory by 1,267,000 square miles and its population by 62 million. Furthermore, the peace cost the Russians 32 percent of their arable lands, 26 percent of their railroads, 33 percent of their factories, and up to 75 percent of their coal mines. The Soviet Government also had to accept a commercial treaty that committed it to supply the victors with large quantities of food. The German and Austrian press greeted Brest as "bread peace."

The *diktat* of Brest was the final act of Russia's withdrawal from World War I; it was the most humiliating treaty in modern Russian history. It took away the acquisitions of more than two centuries of territorial expansion. As a result, European Russia was reduced to about the size of the old Grand Duchy of Muscovy as it existed before Peter the Great. If the human losses suffered during the war (2 million men killed, 4 million wounded, and 2.5 million prisoners of war) are added to the territorial concessions, the price the Russians paid for their participation in the struggle was staggering.

The signing of the treaty ended the most precarious period in the history of Russia's Bolshevik regime. At that time the Soviet state was practically defenseless. In early 1918 the forces of the Central Powers could easily have reached Petrograd and Moscow. They could have set up whatever government they wished. Even the Romanians, who had been crushed by the Central Powers, could afford to annex the province of Bessarabia. Thus, from the point of view of the regime's survival, Lenin's decision was farsighted and statesmanlike; any other policy would have brought disaster. The position Lenin took on the issue further enhanced his prestige. It helped to make him the uncontested leader and arbiter of the Communist Party. After Brest-Litovsk, he came to be recognized not only as the founder of the Soviet state, but also as its savior in an hour of mortal danger.

Trotsky and Bukharin, on the other hand, the chief opponents of Lenin's decision to sign the treaty, lost in stature. Almost immediately after the passions aroused by the February–March 1918 intraparty debates had subsided, it became obvious to everyone that the two had advocated an adventurous and potentially catastrophic line of conduct. Their opposition was to have far-reaching consequences for both in the struggle for power that was to follow Lenin's death.

The Brest-Litovsk negotiations represented for the Bolsheviks their first major confrontation with the harsh realities of international life. They had started the discussions in a high-spirited, idealistic mood, persuaded that the proletarian revolution was just around the corner and that it would be possible to bluff their way to diplomatic success with slogans. They ended by signing the treaty in a sober mood, aware of their impotence and of the value of material and military power.

The treaty lasted no more than a few months (March–November 1918), for it was soon invalidated by the November 11, 1918, armistice. Moreover, the Brest agreement was never fully implemented. The Bolsheviks signed it with a firm determination to evade it, and the Central Powers, temporarily masters of Eastern Europe, interpreted it in such a way as to make a mockery of it. While it lasted, however, the Brest-Litovsk Treaty represented the most brutal attempt by a foreign power to intervene in the domestic affairs of postrevolutionary Russia. The treaty was even more significant than the later Allied intervention. The German–Austrian occupation covered an incomparably larger segment of the former Tsarist empire than the much publicized intervention of the Entente. The troops of the Central Powers, totaling some 100 divisions, stretched from Estonia in the north to the Caucasus in the south. The Central Powers managed to set up in these lands a series of vassal states. The most important was the Ukrainian *Hetmanate*, with Pavlo P. Skoropadsky, a conservative former Tsarist general, serving as Hetman or Head of State. Short-lived though the occupation by the Central Powers was, it was marked by intense exploitation of the natural resources of Eastern Europe. The spectacular success of Germany's armchair diplomacy seemed to open dazzling vistas for Berlin in Eastern Europe. The chief of the German general staff, Erich Ludendorff, even toyed with the idea of a large-scale deportation of the native populations of Poland and Ukraine to Siberia in order to make living space (*Lebensraum*) for German war veterans and other settlers from Germany.

THE AFTERMATH OF BREST-LITOVSK

Not surprisingly, the surrender at Brest-Litovsk precipitated an acute crisis, domestic as well as international, that contributed to the outbreak of civil war and to Western Allied intervention. The Entente powers, hitherto opposed to the idea of armed intervention in Russia, used the treaty as further proof of Soviet–German collusion and conspiracy that should justify open involvement on the side of the anti-Soviet opposition. At home Lenin was accused—not only by the opposition but also by many of his followers—of selling Russia's birthright to the enemy. The Left Social Revolutionaries withdrew their support from the Bolsheviks and recalled their representatives from the Council of People's Commissars. From then on the SRs were in the forefront of the opposition to Russia's Communist regime. Hoping to provoke a renewal of hostilities, one member of the Social Revolutionary Party assassinated the German ambassador in Moscow, Count von Mirbach. Another, Dora (Fanny) Kaplan, shot Lenin on August 30, 1918, wounding him in the neck and shoulder. The injury would contribute to shortening his life.

Despite mounting reaction against the Brest-Litovsk settlement, Lenin remained firm. On March 6, he made his report to the Seventh Party Congress and underlined the fact that the treaty offered the infant Soviet regime a breathing spell indispensable for its consolidation and survival. He was still hoping for a proletarian upheaval in Germany. But, as he put it: "Germany is only pregnant with revolution; in our country we already have a healthy baby—the Socialist Republic—which we will murder by resuming war." This reasoning prompted him to urge his comrades to accept the peace and to abandon their ideological antimilitarism and devote more attention to the issue of forging a new instrument of action, the Red Army. Lenin warned that the Soviets might soon find themselves fighting either alongside a communist Germany or against an imperial Germany, and, in either case, against the remaining bourgeois powers. The Seventh Congress approved the motion to accept the peace treaty.

The Seventh Congress moved the Party one step further along the path of authoritarianism by asserting that "there can be no question of freedom for the bourgeoisie. . . . The Party must mercilessly suppress all attempts of the bourgeoisie to return to power. And this is what is meant by a dictatorship of the proletariat." The Congress renamed the Russian Social Democratic Workers' Party (Bolshevik) the Communist Party.

THE BIRTH OF THE RED ARMY

The aftermath of the Brest-Litovsk Treaty, then, marked a turning point in the evolution of the Communist regime in Russia. The Party reluctantly shed its utopian pacifist illusions and antimilitarist notions; it also became more intolerant of opposition. Slowly the Bolsheviks began to rescue from the chaos the few surviving organized units of the army and navy—the regiments of the Lettish Sharpshooters, for instance. Even so, these units were helpless against the massive, disciplined legions of the Central Powers. The Bolsheviks' dire military situation vis-à-vis the Germans was made even worse by the armed resistance of the White Forces, which began to appear at various scattered points in Russia in the spring of 1918. White Russian resistance further contributed to the crystallization and expansion of regular Bolshevik fighting units.

In April 1918, Trotsky, who had left the Commissariat for Foreign Affairs and was now Commissar for War, set out to reorganize the existing militia into a more tightly organized and disciplined conscripted force. Compulsory military training was ordered for all able-bodied workers and for those peasants who did not hire labor and were considered poor or medium peasants. Rich peasants (*kulaks*) and members of the bourgeoisie, mistrusted as class enemies, were denied the privilege of bearing arms in defense of the Revolution; instead, they were to serve in the auxiliary labor battalions. Officers were no longer elected. The old bonds of authority and discipline were not immediately reintroduced, for it was believed that strict, systematic ideological indoctrination would suffice. Nevertheless, the death penalty was restored for military crimes. Because trained officers of communist persuasion were in rather short supply, Trotsky ordered the conscription of officers from the old Imperial army, provided they would conform politically and do their professional duty conscientiously. Some 50,000 of them obeyed that order. To guarantee their good behavior, they and their families were treated as hostages. To make sure they were loyal and to carry out the political indoctrination of all military personnel, Trotsky appointed political commissars to the armed forces.

In its organization, motivation, and objectives, the Red Army was a new type of armed force. Its regulations stressed the principle of equality at every step, a principle reflected in simple, Spartan uniforms, in the attitude of the commanders toward their rank and file, and in the everyday behavior of the officers. Hierarchy was determined solely by function. The title of officer was replaced by that of commander (*komandir*). To this single acceptable title was added a definition of the officer's function, like company commander, regimental commander, divisional commander, and so on, up to the top. The hated Tsarist badges of rank, especially the gold and silver braided shoulder straps, were done away with altogether and superseded by simple, austere symbols—a few red squares, stripes, or triangles. Another distinctive feature of the Red Army was the duality of its command; to the authority of the regular field commanders was added that of the political commissars, the party's eyes and ears within the armed forces. The commissars' tasks were manifold and complex, and included bolstering discipline, supervising the political reliability of the field commander, carrying out educational functions, and watching over the ideological indoctrination of the soldiers. They combined the functions formerly performed by educational officers and chaplains with their unprecedented duties as the eyes and ears of the ruling Communist Party within the armed forces.

The new Red Army was to be motivated not by traditional patriotism, semireligious and seminationalistic in nature, but by "proletarian internationalism"—the solidarity of workers in all lands united through their hatred of the capitalist system and fired by devotion to the revolutionary cause. Nor were the objectives of the Red Army similar to those of its Tsarist predecessor. Besides being "the sword of the first Socialist State," as well as of the Bolshevik Party, the Red Army was to be an instrument of the world proletarian revolution. It was to be ready to defend its bulwark, the Soviet State, and to intervene, when necessary, on behalf of other revolutionary movements all over the world. The models for Red Army soldiers were not the old marshals Suvorov, Kutuzov, or Alexander Nevsky, but Spartacus, Marat, and the heroes of the Paris Commune. The cosmopolitan mood of the early Soviet state was also reflected in the adoption of the "Internationale" as its first anthem.

The Moscow Kremlin after the Bolshevik Revolution. An old monument erected for the Tsar is boxed and draped with red cloth.

THE FIRST SOVIET CONSTITUTION

The Bolsheviks did not hide their profound contempt for "bourgeois legality," as they demonstrated by their dismissal of the Constituent Assembly. Yet the necessity for some sort of legal framework could not be entirely disregarded. On July 19, 1918, therefore, the first Soviet Constitution for the Russian Socialist Federated Soviet Republic was promulgated by the Fifth Congress of the Soviet. According to its ambitious preamble, the chief goal of the Communist regime in Russia was "the pitiless suppression of the exploiters, the socialist organization of society, and the victory of socialism in all countries." The constitution repudiated all secret treaties and colonial policies; it granted independence to Finland and the right of self-determination to Armenia. The Declaration of Rights of Toiling and Exploited People, which had been one of the initial acts of the new regime, was now included in the charter. The Declaration guaranteed, but only to the working class, freedom of speech, press, and association, as well as free access to education. Members of the former ruling groups and the bourgeoisie in general were disenfranchised. The constitution gave only workers and peasants the right to bear arms in defense of "the first Socialist State." The church was to be separated from the state and the schools, and freedom of both religious and antireligious propaganda was proclaimed. The Constitution confirmed the repudiation of all debts contracted by the Imperial regime and reaffirmed the nationalization of the means of production, trade, banking, and communication.

The first Soviet Constitution guaranteed to urban residents a five-to-one preponderance in suffrage over those who lived in the countryside; in addition, deputies from rural constituencies were to be elected indirectly. The pyramid of local and regional councils, or soviets, was to be the basis of the whole political hierarchy, at the apex of which would be the All-Russian Congress of Soviets. The Congress was to have supreme authority. Between meetings of the Congress, supreme power was to be exercised by the Central Executive Committee, a large, unwieldy body elected by the Congress and composed of more than two hundred members. The Central Executive Committee was to appoint the Cabinet, or Council of People's Commissars. The principle of the dictatorship of the proletariat, so firmly expressed in the resolution of the Seventh Party Congress of March 1918, was written into the charter. Strangely enough, the first Constitution failed to mention the driving force that stood behind, directed, and energized the whole complicated machinery— the Communist Party.

While the first Soviet Constitution was being promulgated and the new regime was being challenged by Russians and foreigners alike, the living symbols of the old regime were destroyed. In the summer of 1917, Nicholas II and his family were deported to Tobolsk, and then to Ekaterinburg (now Sverdlovsk) in the Urals. In July 1918, with the Civil War developing in Siberia, the local soviet resolved that the Imperial family should not be allowed to fall into the hands of opponents of the Communist regime, to become a symbol of anti-Communist resistance. During the night of July 16–17, 1918, Nicholas II, his family, his doctor, and servants were taken to the cellar of the house where they lived under arrest and shot to death. Their bodies were sprayed with chemicals and burned in a nearby mine and the ashes scattered in a swamp.

The annihilation of the former Tsar and his family coincided with the intensification of the Civil War. In the summer of 1918, the war entered its crucial phase.

SUGGESTED READING

Bailey, Thomas A., *America Faces Russia*. Ithaca, N.Y.: Cornell University Press, 1950.

Bunyan, John, and Harold H. Fisher, eds., *The

Bolshevik Revolution, 1917–1918: Documents and Materials. Stanford, Calif.: Stanford University Press, 1934.

CHAMBERLIN, WILLIAM H., *The Russian Revolution*, Vol. 1. New York: Macmillan, 1935.

CLEMENTS, BARBARA EVANS, *Bolshevik Feminist: The Life of Aleksandra Kollontai*. Bloomington: Indiana University Press, 1979.

DEGRAS, JANE T., ed., *Soviet Documents on Foreign Policy, 1917–1941*. New York: Oxford University Press, 1951–1953, 3 vols.

EUDIN, XENIA J., and HAROLD H. FISCHER, eds., *Soviet Russia and the West, 1920–1927: A Documentary Survey*. Stanford, Calif.: Stanford University Press, 1957.

EUDIN, XENIA J., and ROBERT C. NORTH, eds., *Soviet Russia and the East, 1920–1927: A Documentary Survey*. Stanford, Calif.: Stanford University Press, 1957.

FARNSWORTH, BEATRICE, *Aleksandra Kollontai. Socialism, Feminism, and the Bolshevik Revolution*. Stanford, Calif.: Stanford University Press, 1980.

GARDER, MICHEL, *History of the Soviet Army*. New York: Praeger, 1966.

GEONG, SOW-THONG, *Sino-Soviet Diplomatic Relations, 1917–1926*. Honolulu: University of Hawaii, 1976.

GERSON, LEONARD D., *The Secret Police in Lenin's Russia*. Philadelphia: Temple University Press, 1976.

GOODMAN, ELLIOT R., *The Soviet Design for a World State*. New York: Columbia University Press, 1960.

KEEP, JOHN L. H., *The Russian Revolution: A Study in Mass Mobilization*. London: Weidenfeld and Nicholson, 1976.

KENNAN, GEORGE F., *The Decision to Intervene*. Princeton, N.J.: Princeton University Press, 1958.

———, *Soviet–American Relations, 1917–1920*, Vol. 1, *Russia Leaves the War*. Princeton, N.J.: Princeton University Press, 1956.

LEGGETT, GEORGE, *The Cheka: Lenin's Political Police*. New York: Oxford University Press, 1981.

NOVE, ALEC, *An Economic History of the U.S.S.R.* London: Allen Lane, Penguin Press, 1969.

RADKEY, OLIVER H., *The Elections to the Russian Constituent Assembly of 1917*. Cambridge, Mass.: Harvard University Press, 1950.

SAUL, E. NORMAN, *Sailors in Revolt: The Russian Baltic Fleet in 1917*. Lawrence: Regents Press of Kansas, 1978.

SHAPIRO, LEONARD, *The Origins of the Communist Autocracy, 1917–1922*. Cambridge, Mass.: Harvard University Press, 1955.

TROTSKY, LEON, *From October to Brest Litovsk*. New York: Socialist Publication Society, 1919.

———, *Lenin: Notes for a Biographer*. New York: Capricorn Books, 1971.

VOLIN, SIMON, and ROBERT M. SLUSSER, eds., *The Soviet Secret Police*. New York: Praeger, 1957.

WHEELER-BENNETT, JOHN W., *The Forgotten Peace: Brest Litovsk, March 1918*. New York: Macmillan, 1939.

WHITE, D. FEDOTOFF, *The Growth of the Red Army*. Princeton, N.J.: Princeton University Press, 1944.

CHAPTER 8

The Ordeal
of the Civil War, 1918–1921

Initially, the Bolshevik coup d'état was accepted by the great majority of the Russian people without much active opposition. Absorbed in the routine of making a living amidst mounting chaos and threatening starvation, exhausted by everyday cares and chores, they did not at first grasp all the implications of the upheaval. Only after the doors of the Constituent Assembly had slammed shut and the Bolsheviks bowed to the humiliating terms of the Treaty of Brest-Litovsk, while the harshness of Bolshevik rule became increasingly apparent, was the opposition galvanized into action.

During the first weeks of Bolshevik rule, in December 1917, General Lavr Kornilov and several other senior officers who had been involved in his attempted coup escaped from house arrest. Most of them went to the Don Cossack territory, an area where Communist rule had not yet been estab-

lished. There they contacted former chief of staff General Mikhail Alexeyev and began to organize the first armed groups to fight openly against the Bolsheviks. To the military was soon added a handful of politicians such as Cadet leaders Miliukov and Rodzianko. Around this nucleus was organized the Anti-Soviet Volunteer Army, at first composed almost exlusively of officers and numbering only 3,000 men.

In one of the early skirmishes in March 1918, General Kornilov was killed, and a month later General Alexeyev died. As a result, the leadership of the army fell to its highest ranking officer, Anton I. Denikin. Denikin was at the start of the war a divisional commander; later on, he became commander of the southern and southwestern fronts. A man of peasant stock, he was a fairly moderate republican. What he lacked was the skill and experience necessary to lead a group of people that was not only a fighting unit but also represented a politically motivated movement. Despite his shortcomings, however, he was able to shape the small group under his command into a force that became the most effective of all the White Russian fighting units.

THE ALLIED INTERVENTION

Although Denikin's army eventually became the greatest threat to Bolshevik rule, it was not destined to deal the first serious blow. That came almost by accident from a group of Czech and Slovak prisoners of war who had either surrendered earlier to the Tsarist armies or had simply deserted their Austro-Hungarian units. These prisoners, most of them seething with anti-Hapsburg sentiment, were organized into a Czecho-Slovak brigade stationed in the Ukraine. By the close of the war, they numbered approximately 30,000 men. After the Treaty of Brest-Litovsk and the collapse of active Russian resistance to the Germans, the Czecho-Slovak National Committee of Paris, headed by Tomaš G. Masaryk, decided to transfer the POWs from Russia to France. The Soviets, trying to prove that despite their abject surrender at Brest they were not "German agents," gave their consent to the plan.

In March 1918, the Czecho-Slovak Legion left its camps, located mostly in the Ukraine, for Vladivostok. Their long journey along the Trans-Siberian Railway was often slowed by clashes with local Red authorities and partisan units. Rumors spread among the POWs that the Soviets were constantly delaying the convoys in order to incorporate the Legion into the Red Army or to deliver it to the Central Powers. In this tense atmostphere, a minor skirmish triggered a major crisis. On May 14 at Chelyabinsk, a fight between the soldiers of the Legion and some Hungarian pro-Communist POWs ended in a Czecho-Slovak victory. Trotsky, then Commissar for War, declared the Legion a counterrev-olutionary force, and ordered its soldiers to be disarmed or, if they resisted, shot.

The Legion almost unanimously decided to continue on to Vladivostok, even if it meant shooting their way there. Their decision resulted in a series of armed clashes and pitched battles between the Legion and Red units as the convoy advanced toward the Pacific. The well-organized and disciplined Legion, commanded by French officers, proceeded to inflict one defeat after another on the Reds. In the process the convoy, often acting in tactical alliance with local anti-Bolshevik forces, captured a whole string of Siberian towns and cities. On June 29, the Legion triumphantly reached Vladivostok.

Thus it was a body of foreign soldiers that dealt the first major, spectacular armed blow to the Soviet regime. The long series of victories compiled by a small group of POWs over the Red units had an electrifying effect on Paris and London. To the leaders of the Entente, the establishment in Russia of a "dictatorship of the proletariat" dedicated to opposing practically everything the West believed in was totally abhorrent. That this regime immediately repudiated all financial obligations of the Tsarist government only served to aggravate further the situation. Finally, the signing of the Brest-Litovsk Treaty, construed by Western diplomats as an unconditional surrender, if not an alliance with the Central Powers, was more than the statesmen of Paris and London could take. Their reaction to the situation in Russia was no doubt partially colored by the fact that these were the crucial moments of the war; German troops were closer to Paris than ever before, and the transfer to the west of more troops by the Central Powers, now that the Eastern Front was quiet, seemed likely to tip the scale. Furthermore, the Bolshevik regime, regarded in the West as barbarous and treacherous, now proved to be weak as well. It looked as if it needed merely a push to be toppled. The temptation to push, therefore, was overwhelming. On July 2, 1918, the

Allied Supreme War Council decided to give active, armed support to the forces of resistance against the Bolshevik regime.

This declaration notwithstanding, the Allies were still locked in a life-and-death struggle on the Western Front and could not do anything significant about Russia until the armistice was signed on the Western Front on November 11, 1918. What the West did in the meantime was to move to secure vast stores of war materiel that had previously been dispatched to the Tsarist authorities to bolster Russian resistance. The main locations of these stores were the ports of Murmansk, Archangel, and Vladivostok. After the Brest-Litovsk Treaty was signed, wild rumors circulated that these depots were falling to Germans. In March 1918 a small detachment of British troops, followed by French and American ones, landed first in Murmansk and Vladivostok and then in Archangel solely to protect the military stores there.

Soon the Japanese, who had their own interests in mind, joined the Allied intervention. The presence of a considerable body of Japanese soldiers at that strategic point made President Wilson suspicious, and soon an American Expeditionary Corps was dispatched to Vladivostok. Within a year some 7,000 American soldiers had been dispatched to counterbalance, at least partially, the 72,000 Japanese already in the Maritime Territory around Vladivostok. The small garrisons at Murmansk and Archangel were, meanwhile, also reinforced by the Western Allies. In addition, the British sent a squadron of the Royal Navy to the Baltic soon after the armistice and supplied some aid to the small White Army operating from Estonia under the command of General N. N. Yudenich. At the end of November, the British and French cooperated in dispatching a ship to Novorossisk in the Black Sea, loaded with arms and munitions for General Denikin and his Volunteer Army. Also during this flurry of activity, in April 1919 a French infantry division landed in Odessa, and the British transferred some of their troops from their sphere of influence in Persia to the Caucasus, to Batum, and to Baku. By 1919, the Allied intervention was in full swing.

THE EMERGENCE OF KOLCHAK

When the various Western attempts at mediation between the Whites and the Reds failed, the Entente powers decided to press on with their efforts to bolster the anti-Communist forces. These forces were centered in four principal areas: (1) in the south, where Denikin's Volunteer Army was deployed; (2) in Estonia, where General Nikolay Yudenich operated; (3) in the far north at Murmansk and Archangel, where some small White units were organized with the support of the Allied detachments; and (4) east of the Volga River and in Siberia, where numerous White groups were operating independently, at least initially. On September 8, 1918, the White groups around Samara on the Volga combined resources with those of various Siberian centers of anti-Communist resistance and formed an executive body known as the *Directorate*. The Directorate, based in the city of Ufa in the Bashkir region of Eastern Russia, was the result of a shaky political compromise; the body was composed of two SRs and three Liberals. The Directorate was intended to be the successor to the overthrown Provisional Government and it was to coordinate the struggle against the Bolsheviks throughout the entire former Tsarist empire.

However, a compromise over the Directorate contrived under foreign pressure satisfied no one. Quarrels erupted frequently, and for all practical purposes the Directorate resembled Krylov's fable in which a chariot is drawn by a swan, a crab, and a pike, with each pulling in a different direction. Especially indignant were some of the Tsarist officers who unjustly suspected the Socialist Revolutionary members of the coalition of secretly sympathizing and even conspiring with their former socialist comrades, the Bolsheviks. The absurd situation could not last long. And indeed, by mid-November a group of officers had overthrown the Directorate and proclaimed Admiral Alexander V. Kolchak Supreme Ruler and Commander-in-Chief of all Russia.

Kolchak was a competent naval officer and a former commander of the Black Sea Squadron. A scholarly person, he had little interest in politics and none of the qualities necessary for leadership in the midst of a very tricky and complex civil war. Hesitating, procrastinating, and lacking good judgment of character, he was unable to either choose the proper co-workers to whom he could delegate authority (he had no less than ten war ministers in fifteen months) or act as a true dictator himself. Yet, with British support, Kolchak soon established his authority in Siberia west of Lake Baikal. (The region east of Baikal was in the hands of a Japanese puppet.)

For a time—at the close of 1918 and the beginning of 1919—the Entente believed that Kolchak might become the head of the future government of Russia. As a consequence, Allied support was given mainly to him, although other White groups were not totally neglected. Kolchak's forces by the winter of 1918–1919 numbered about 120,000 well-trained and well-equipped soldiers. Pressed by the Allies, the other White leaders accepted Kolchak's leadership and started preparing a combined offensive for the spring of 1919. They hoped to overthrow the Bolsheviks, who controlled most of the heartland of the old empire.

The offensive was to be a three-pronged drive by White forces with Allied assistance. Kolchak's units were to strike from their Siberian bases against Moscow. At the same time, Denikin's army was to attack from the south, while Yudenich, operating from Estonia, was to execute a diversionary attack on Petrograd in order to pull Bolshevik forces away from the defense of the Red capital. Paris and London were confident that by the end of the year the Bolsheviks would be swept into the garbage bin of history.

THE KOLCHAK OFFENSIVE

The offensive was opened by Kolchak, who by April had reached the Volga cities of Samara and Kazan. Despite these successes, he had not been able to establish contact with Denikin, who was operating far to the south. Kolchak's weaknesses soon came to the fore. The peasants did not trust a pretender to power who refused to confirm by word and deed their possession of the land. Behind his rapidly advancing troops, riots and mutinies broke out constantly. Most of his own soldiers were "peasants in uniform," and not too reliable. Red partisans were also active in sabotaging the advance of his army. By June Kolchak's victorious march was stopped dead in its tracks and reversed by an able Red Army commander of Kirgiz origin, Mikhail V. Frunze.

Kolchak's retreat was even more spectacular than his advance. Leaving supplies behind, he abandoned Ufa in June, and in July was already east of the Urals and had to evacuate the Siberian city of Omsk. From then on, his forces disintegrated with astonishing rapidity. Not only was Kolchak incapable of controlling his own soldiers; he also quarreled with the leaders of the Czecho-Slovak Legion. In January 1920 he fled further eastward, resigned his post as Supreme Ruler and Commander, and appointed Denikin his successor. Arms and food provided Kolchak by the West became a windfall for the Bolsheviks. At Ufa alone they captured some 230,000 rifles, over 100,000 sets of uniforms, 96,000 tons of wheat, and 64,000 tons of oats. Forsaken by his followers, Kolchak was soon handed over by the Czechs to the Bolsheviks. In February 1920 he was tried and executed by the Soviets. Now all of Siberia west of Lake Baikal was under Communist hegemony,

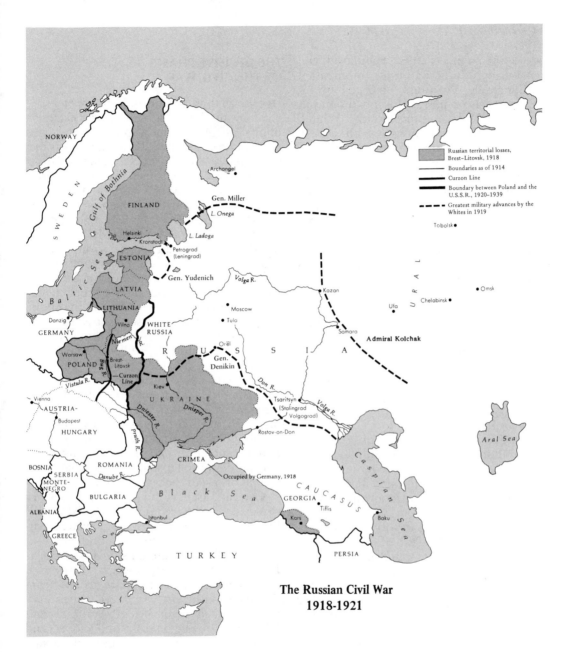

The Russian Civil War
1918-1921

although there were still some White groups, as well as some American and Japanese detachments, east of Baikal.

The victory over Kolchak was only one aspect of a civil war that was not so much a succession of separate campaigns as a conglomeration of them. Many events took place simultaneously, and the complex situation changed kaleidoscopically. In May and June 1919, while Kolchak was still fighting, Deniken's Volunteer Army launched a vigorous drive from its southern bases. One of the major objectives of the White offensive was to secure a junction of their two most important armies, Kolchak's and Deniken's. This was never achieved because at Tsaritsyn (subsequently named Stalingrad and then Volgograd) the Red units commanded by Kliment E. Voroshilov (assisted by his chief political commissar, Joseph Stalin) put up a successful resistance to the Whites' attacks. In the west, however, the small, self-confident Volunteer Army, together with the local Ukrainian nationalist forces and irregular local bands, took Kharkov and went on to capture Kiev on August 30. Unfortunately for the Whites, their initial victories came too late to save Kolchak from being routed beyond the Urals.

Deniken's forces soon encountered the same difficulties that had plagued Kolchak's troops: their base of operations and rear flank were not secure. One of the main reasons for this insecurity can be traced to the inscription on all the White generals' banners—"Russia: one, great, and indivisible." This slogan made Denikin an anathema to the Ukrainian nationalists, who were dreaming of independence. To Denikin, the Ukrainians were simply a branch of the Russian nation. Even the very name "Ukraine" was rejected by the Whites, who used the terms "Little Russia" or "Southern Russia." Some of the Ukrainian nationalists might have considered a federation with Russia, but any return to the old centralism preached by Denikin was totally unacceptable to most of them.

Because the Ukrainian forces were fragmented and independent of one another, their mutual jealousies could be exploited. In addition to Simon V. Petlyura, who commanded the army of the Ukrainian Directorate, there were dozens of smaller guerrilla chieftains fighting the Bolsheviks, the most colorful of whom was Nestor I. Makhno. Makhno was an anarchist who was not above changing sides. For the most part, though, he collaborated with the Bolsheviks, who skillfully took advantage of his political idiosyncracies and personal vanity. The result was that Makhno's and other bands harassed the Volunteer Army, sapping its strength and diverting it from its main objective.

THE DECISIVE PHASES OF THE CIVIL WAR

Despite all these obstacles, Denikin, emboldened by his initial successes, was eager to plunge northward and capture Moscow. By the middle of October, his advanced cavalry units were in Orël, some 250 miles south of the capital. The Bolshevik leaders prepared to go underground once again, and Lenin ordered false passports to be manufactured for them. But Denikin was fighting too many enemies simultaneously. He had failed to make satisfactory compromises with the Ukrainians, and he was not able to reach a workable agreement with the Poles, who insisted on a guarantee of their newly won independence as a precondition for their cooperation. Consequently, Denikin, who had spread his forces too thinly, had to face the Bolsheviks while isolated and threatened on all sides. His rear was soon penetrated by Red cavalry detachments led by Semën M. Budënny, the able former sergeant major of a Tsarist dragoon regiment. By autumn, Denikin's lines of communication and supply were impossible to defend, and at the end of October his offensive suddenly collapsed. Like Kolchak's, his retreat also soon became a rout.

Certain aspects of Yudenich's story closely parallel Kolchak's and Denikin's, but his stupidity is more striking. During Denikin's offensive on Moscow, Yudenich—at the head of 20,000 men, Estonians as well as Russians—advanced toward Petrograd. The Soviets, unable to spare troops from the main southern sector, were contemplating the evacuation of the city. At the gates of Petrograd by the middle of October and convinced that the city might fall at any minute, Yudenich declared: "There is no Estonia. It is a piece of Russian soil, a Russian province. The Estonian government is a gang of criminals." The shocked Estonians withdrew their detachments and, understandably, returned home. Yudenich, no longer strong enough to attack Petrograd, had to halt his offensive. This crisis gave the Bolsheviks a much needed breathing spell. Trotsky managed to rally the local Red Guard, arm some workers, and stop Yudenich's attempts to advance further. Meanwhile, events in the south–the defeat of Denikin–took away the significance of Yudenich's diversionary attack. By mid-November, Yudenich had to fall back to his base in Estonia. Denikin's rout and Yudenich's retreat marked the turning point of the armed struggle for power in Russia.

By the end of 1919, the battered remnants of the Volunteer Army were being forced to seek shelter in the Don Cossack region, where they regrouped, re-equipped themselves, and prepared for a 1920 spring offensive. Denikin, however, split with the Don Cossacks over the question of autonomy for their region, and at the end of March 1920, 35,000 of his soldiers had to be evacuated by the Royal Navy from the Don region to the Crimea. To compound his troubles, Denikin lost the confidence of his subordinates, resigned his command, and left for the West.

The new commander of the Volunteer Army, General Baron Piotr N. Wrangel, was probably the most capable and energetic of the White military leaders, but he came to power too late in the day. In addition to lowered morale, he had to contend with the relative consolidation and stiffening of Bolshevik rule over the Great Russian hinterland and hesitation in the Entente capitals over whether to continue supporting the anti-Bolshevik cause.

The interventions that had started with such high hopes suffered one setback and disappointment after another. In April 1919, for instance, there was a mutiny in the French Black Sea squadron. Furthermore, France was exasperated with the political and military ineffectiveness of the Whites, who were obviously unable to use to their advantage the large sums of money, weapons, and equipment supplied by the British and French. Displeased, the French decided to withdraw most of their forces from Rus-

sia. Meanwhile, the British had become anxious to lift the Allied blockade and to resume trading with the area that traditionally had been one of their sources for grain and lumber supplies. As Lloyd George bluntly put it in replying to criticism by one of his opponents, "One can trade even with cannibals. . . ." The British outposts in Transcaucasia and Central Asia were abandoned. In September and October 1919, most of the Allied detachments were withdrawn from the Far East. In January 1920, the Supreme Command of the Entente decided to end its economic blockade of the Soviet Union. By that spring, all Allied forces except the Japanese were out of Russia.

With the Allies gone, the situation of the remaining White detachments operating in the south became critical. The Polish victories over the Red Army in the spring of 1920 and the occupation of the right bank of the Dnieper Ukraine seemed to augur well for Wrangel's cause, yet there was no effective cooperation with the Poles. By the autumn of 1920, victorious but exhausted, the Poles decided to quit; in October, Soviet–Polish peace negotiations opened in the Latvian capital of Riga. This event finally convinced Wrangel that his situation was hopeless. His soldiers and their families, some 135,000 people, were evacuated from the Crimea to Constantinople. From there they dispersed throughout the world and merged with the large mass of Russian émigrés. The Civil War was now practically over. Only in the Caucasus, Central Asia, and the Far East did some spotty resistance to Soviet rule persist.

THE WESTERN BORDERLANDS

The effects of the Russian Civil War were not limited to Russia. In a sense they were a cyclone whose forces could be felt indirectly in many parts of the world. The struggle directly affected neighboring countries, but its impact was greatest on the multiethnic fringes of the former Tsarist empire. Anti-

Bolshevik elements were strongest in the western and southern borderlands where the tendency toward autonomy and even independence had been stimulated by the fear of the Bolshevik regime. In some cases the events taking place on the periphery had considerable effect on the contest for power between the Reds and the Whites. But to understand this aspect of the Civil War, it is necessary to ask what impact the downfall of the Tsarist regime had on the non-Russian nationalities and what response they had to the Soviet challenge of Communism.

To many ethnic leaders of the Tsarist empire, the February–March Liberal Revolution in Petrograd had seemed like a turning point in human history, another "Spring of Nations." Some were convinced that a new era of liberty and justice was dawning for all. For a full six months, it had seemed as if the empire of Nicholas II might be transformed into a democratic federation, but the triumph of the Bolsheviks in Petrograd and Moscow altered the situation overnight. Many of the nationalities, including Ukrainians, Lithuanians, Latvians, Estonians, and Caucasians, might have been willing to have autonomous regions within a democratic, federal Russian republic. But most of the ethnic groups were suspicious of the Bolsheviks. It was not so much class struggle as it was national liberation that preoccupied the majority of the leaders of the smaller nationalities on the western and southern fringes of the old empire. In the liberal phase of the upheaval, the ethnic groups saw a chance to escape from the domination of the Great Russians. The authoritarian and universalist strivings of the Bolshevik revolution, however, argued nothing but danger to the diverse cultures on the edges of the empire.

Indeed, following Germany's capitulation in the west, the pressure of revolutionary forces could be felt all along the empire's outer reaches. As the Germans withdrew from the territories they had occupied in Eastern Europe after the Brest-Litovsk Treaty, the Bolsheviks promptly recaptured them—repudiating the treaty—and with a mixture of military pressure and political warfare, extended their rule to the west. The westward movement of the Red Army began on November 17, 1918, less than a week after the armistice had been signed on the Western Front. By the end of the year Soviet troops, supported by local Communists, had occupied a large part of Belorussia and Lithuania, plus portions of Latvia and Estonia.

The latter two were invaded on November 29 by local Communist detachments supported by Moscow. An Estonian Workers' Council was set up in Communist-occupied territory and claimed authority over the entire country. By December 10, more than half of it was in Red hands. On December 25, *Izvestia*, the official newspaper of the Soviet Government, wrote: "Estonia, Latvia, and Lithuania are directly on the road from Russia to Western Europe, and are a hindrance to our revolution because they separate Soviet Russia from revolutionary Germany." It was only through a valiant effort by the Estonian people, aided by the Allies (mainly the Royal Navy), that the immediate danger to the very existence of their tiny country was staved off.

In Latvia, things were quite different. There, because of an unbalanced social structure that was a result of the survival of a number of large estates and an abundance of rural proletarians, the Communists could command substantially more popular support. In January 1919, Latvia's capital, Riga, was captured by the Red Army. Further to the south, the Lithuanian capital of Vilnius (Wilno), previously evacuated by the Germans, was taken by the Bolsheviks on January 5. By the middle of January, three-fourths of Latvia and a large slice of historic Lithuania were under Communist rule. These successes gave the Bolshevik regime a precious foot-hold on the Baltic Sea and the only access to it south of Petrograd.

Communist successes in the Baltic area must be viewed as part of the revolutionary upsurge throughout Central and Eastern Europe. In March 1919, communists seized power in a prostrate Hungary, set up a Soviet regime in Bavaria, and attempted a coup d'état in Berlin. The Soviet Government, conveying its congratulations to the two newly established Communist republics of Hungary and Bavaria, expressed the hope that "the proletariat of the whole world, having before its eyes the striking examples of the victorious uprisings of the workers in three countries of Europe, will follow them with complete faith in victory." Spartacist ferment mounted in Westphalia and Württemberg, and unrest spread in Austria. So in 1919, as the First Congress of the Communist International was gathering in Moscow, the situation in Eastern Europe was fluid, and Communism was on the offensive.

THE SOVIET–POLISH CLASH

The revolutionary turmoil in Russia, together with the chiliastic aspirations of its new rulers, elicited various responses from the Soviet Republic's neighbors, including active opposition from Poland. To the leaders of Poland, which had been re-created in 1918, after the more than a century of being partitioned, the apparent weakening of central authority in Russia seemed like a splendid opportunity to reverse the wheel of history, recapture the initiative from Moscow, and reassert Poland's former position in Eastern Europe. During the sixteenth and seventeenth centuries, the area between ethnographic Poland and Russia proper—Lithuania, Belorussia, and the Ukraine—had been an object of contention. Now, with the old empire disintegrating, the Poles felt they had an excellent chance to regain at least some of their historic patrimony. The main proponent of the idea that Poland should establish a belt of buffer states between itself and Russia was the old socialist fighter Piłsudski. A man of Lithuanian stock, Piłsudski was a firm believer in the modern-day restoration of the old Polish–Lithuanian federation. He considered the Dnieper Ukraine to be the key to the balance of power in Eastern Europe; he argued that whoever controlled this crucial area and its resources would be able to organize Eastern Europe. Piłsudski found a partner in Simon Petlyura, the Ukrainian Socialist military leader. Petlyura, as commander-in-chief and leader of the Ukrainian Directorate, was the most serious antagonist of Bolshevik rule on the Dnieper. In the autumn of 1919, after the defeat of the Ukrainian nationalist forces, Petlyura made a deal with Piłsudski regarding a cooperative effort against Soviet Russia to establish an independent Ukrainian Republic on the Dnieper.

The campaign launched by Polish–Ukrainian forces on April 25, 1920, scored impressive successes. In May the Polish troops captured Kiev and most of the lands on the right bank of the Dnieper. There Petlyura started to reconstruct his Ukrainian state. But in June the Red Army launched a long-prepared counteroffensive, and the Poles and Petlyura's forces had to retreat.

The battle for Kiev, which took place at the beginning of June 1920, could be called the second battle of Poltava. The first was in 1709, when Charles XII of Sweden, supported by the Ukrainians, was defeated by Peter the Great. Both battles decided the fate of the Ukraine for a long time to come. The victory opened new vistas for communism in East Central Europe. When the Red Army launched its counterattack that June, Stalin, who was not only the Soviet Peoples' Commissar for Nationalities but also the Chief Political Commissar of Budënny's First Cavalry Army, was already exchanging letters with Lenin on national and colonial questions. With Stalin at the army's headquarters were groups of Serbian and Hungarian Communists who dreamed of returning to their own countries in the event of a Soviet victory over Poland. However, the battle of Warsaw in August 1920 made

Soviet plans for East Central Europe irrelevant. The Red Army, commanded by M. N. Tukhachevsky, was defeated. Realization of the Soviets' plans was delayed a quarter of a century, until the end of World War II.

Poland won the war militarily, but it was not strong enough to exploit its victory politically. The compromise Treaty of Riga in March 1921 divided both the Ukraine and Belorussia into two segments, Western (Polish) and Eastern (Soviet). Like present-day Germans and Koreans, the Ukrainians and Belorussians were to live as two distinct, separate entities. One part would be within the framework of the Polish state, and the other a Soviet Ukrainian or Soviet Belorussian Republic.

THE CAUCASUS AND CENTRAL ASIA

The Soviet–Polish contest, a crucial aspect of the vast panorama of the Civil War, was only one component of the gigantic sociopolitical struggle in a nation that covered one-sixth of the earth. Another was the battle fought almost simultaneously in the south, on the border between Europe and Asia. Shortly after the Communist takeover in Petrograd and Moscow, the Caucasians—Georgians, Armenians, and Azerbaijanis—broke away from Russian rule. Like the Ukrainians, these peoples, with their strong, native movements—mostly of the Menshevik variety—were motivated by a mixture of national sentiment and revolutionary zeal against the spirit and practice of Bolshevism. On April 22, 1918, the three groups set up a TransCaucasian Federal Republic with a Georgian Menshevik as its president. The endemic ethnic, political, and personal rivalries among the main partners, however, were difficult to control. After only a month, the federation fell apart. From then on each nationality tried to fend for itself and follow an independent path in search of outside aid and protection against powerful neighbors.

Georgia, with its Menshevik Party in power and afraid of the Bolsheviks whom it had outlawed, turned to Germany for support. The Germans were willing to extend their protectorate over Georgia, but were loath to do the same for the Armenians because of Berlin's alliance with the Turks, the traditional enemies of Armenians. After the Central Powers surrendered in November 1918, the Georgians tried to seek British protection. Once Azerbaijan—Muslim, Turkish-speaking, and rich in oil—declared its independence, the British found themselves competing fiercely in that region with the Bolsheviks and the Turks. After the November 11 armistice, the British were able to establish their protectorate over Azerbaijan. Because of the devastation and chaos created by the Civil War, however, the Western oil firms found it difficult to exploit the deposits, and the British Government soon lost its enthusiasm for Azerbaijan's independence.

The Armenian Republic, ruled by a party of radical nationalists, was initially successful in defending its sovereignty against the Turks. But unable to rid themselves of the fear of their perennial persecutors and exterminators, the Armenians threw their support behind the then seemingly triumphant General Denikin. In so doing, they trusted that a strong Russia would not allow their absorption into the Ottoman Empire, for the earlier massacres of their conationals did not betoken a bright future there. After the collapse of the White Army, the desperate Armenians sought help from the United States and appealed for protection to the newly established League of Nations.

The Entente Powers were willing to grant de facto recognition to all three Transcaucasian republics but, absorbed in their own postwar problems, they did little to help them defend themselves against the Bolsheviks. In the spring of 1920, after Denikin's defeat, the Bolsheviks turned their attention farther south, to the Georgians, Armenians, and Azerbaijanis. In April the Red Army conquered Azerbaijan and began to make military and political preparations for an offensive against Georgia and Armenia. The Polish–Ukrainian offensive of April–

May 1920 temporarily upset their timetable. Meanwhile, the overconfident Armenians became imprudently involved in a war with the Turks over an Armenian-speaking region in eastern Anatolia. Taking advantage of this, Moscow issued an ultimatum on December 2, 1920, and the Armenians capitulated. In February and March of 1920 the Bolsheviks, again matching military force with political subversion, finally conquered the Republic of Georgia. Thus by the spring of 1921, Transcaucasia was under Communist control. In December 1922, the region was declared the Transcaucasian Soviet Socialist Republic.

Conquest of the vast Moslem areas of southeast and central Asia took the Bolsheviks somewhat longer. Stalin's Commissariat of Nationalities, taking into account the seriousness of local racial and religious problems in this region, paid considerable attention to the sentiments of the Muslim peoples. Moscow used not only political subversion and infiltration to neutralize the pan-Islamic and local nationalist groups, but also made generous promises in matters of religion, culture, and economics. For instance, Stalin set up a Central Muslim Commissariat, recognized the existence of an independent Muslim Communist Party, and even allowed, for a time, the organization of the Muslim Military College directed by the Tatar, Sultan Galiev. At one time a large segment of Red Army units facing Kolchak were Muslim. It was Sultan Galiev who applied Lenin's concept that imperialism was the highest stage of capitalism to the Muslim world and proclaimed that all classes of the colonial nations, being oppressed by their Western masters, should cooperate with the Bolsheviks by forming "national liberation movements." This initially Soviet thesis was, later on, developed by Mao Tsetung and Ho Chi Ming and other Third World Marxist leaders. After Kolchak's defeat, the largest Muslim area, Turkestan, was gradually subdued. Local partisan units, known as *Bahmachi*, operated sporadically until the middle of 1920, but by 1923 Turkestan was for all practical pur-

poses a part of the Soviet Union. The two former Tsarist central Asian protectorates, the Khanates of Khiva and Bukhara, along with other minor central Asian territories, were also reconquered and incorporated into the expanding Soviet state. Once the Bolsheviks were securely in power, the separate Muslim Communist Party was suppressed, and Sultan Galiev was arrested and in 1928 sent to a concentration camp in Solovki.

REASONS FOR THE BOLSHEVIK TRIUMPH

By the beginning of 1921 the Bolsheviks had won the Civil War. After more than two years of fighting, with luck, pluck and cunning, they had emerged as masters over most of the old Romanov empire. The reasons for this Bolshevik triumph are varied and complex.

The first reason for their victory was their unity of purpose. All their enemies were hopelessly divided among themselves by political and ethnic differences. The Bolsheviks, on the other hand, formed a single, highly centralized, strongly motivated force. Their rivals were a loose, heterogeneous, and precarious coalition of political groups. The White coalition included reactionary military circles at one end of the political spectrum, and some SRs and the Mensheviks at the other. These differences were perhaps best reflected in the attitude of these groups toward Russia's number one problem—land. The reactionaries advocated an outright return to its former owners of the land the peasants had seized, whereas the socialists were in favor of recognizing the legitimacy of the seizure. The middle-of-the-road Cadets insisted upon relegating all fundamental reforms—including those involving land, nationalities, and constitutional issues—to the Constitutent Assembly, which would be reconvened after the victory over the Bolsheviks. The SRs and Mensheviks were ready to accept the division of the land among the peasants, but were too weak to make their point of view prevail.

Next in importance to the land question was the ethnic problem. Most of the armed attempts to overthrow Bolshevik rule originated in the non-Russian areas of the old empire. Yet, ironically, all the leaders of the White armies were Great Russian nationalists. The ethnic minorities made repeated attempts to strike a bargain that would reshape the old centralized structure of the Russian state, but their efforts were in vain. The Whites would listen only to their own battle cry, "Russia: one, great and indivisible." The Whites assumed an especially scornful attitude toward the largest, and hence potentially most helpful, of the ethnic groups, the Ukrainians.

In their ethnic policies, the Bolsheviks were much more subtle than the Whites. As early as November 15, 1917, the Council of People's Commissars solemnly proclaimed the right of national self-determination, including the right of secession. But the Bolsheviks did not equate the *right* of self-determination with a demand for actual separation and insisted that the principle be interpreted dialectically, according to the interests of the proletarian revolution. Prior to the revolution, the Bolsheviks had opposed any attempt by a Tsarist government to retain by force any national group that wanted to secede from the empire. Once they seized power, however, they reversed their stand. They argued that because economic exploitation and ethnic oppression did not exist in the Soviet Republic, all reasons for secession had been eliminated. Yet throughout the civil war the Soviet Government loudly proclaimed the lofty principle of self-determination, all the while trying by both persuasion and coercion to keep all the former empire's ethnic groups within the Soviet Republic.

The Bolshevik treatment of the Ukrainian problem is a good example of their approach to the nationality issue. A few weeks after the March revolution, the Ukrainians demanded home rule and set up a Central National Council, or Central *Rada*, in Kiev. Insisting upon broad local autonomy and planning for federation with the All-Russian Democratic Republic, the Rada shunned secession. Complete independence was proclaimed only after the Bolsheviks had triumphed in Petrograd and Moscow. On December 17, 1917, the Council of People's Commissars formally and unconditionally recognized the Ukraine's independence from Russia. At the same time, the Soviets sent Kiev an ultimatum demanding free passage over Ukrainian territory for Red troops marching south to fight the Volunteer Army. Also simultaneously, a rival prefabricated Communist government was set up in Kharkov—the eastern, more industrial, and hence more proletarian and Russianized, segment of the Ukraine. Through subversion and military action, this Soviet Ukraine government was soon planted in Kiev. Ousted from the Dnieper Ukraine by Denikin in August 1919, the Reds returned at the end of that year. Chased from Kiev by the Piłsudski–Petlyura offensive of April–May 1920, the Bolsheviks again conquered the Dnieper valley in June and re-established their rule, initially under the guise of a Russian–Ukrainian federation.

As previously noted, similar attempts by the Soviet Union to intervene in the affairs of its neighbors were made in Finland, Estonia, Latvia, Lithuania, and Belorussia. With the exception of Belorussia, they all failed because of the resistance of local anti-Communist forces, who were often assisted by the West. There is no doubt that Soviet "revolutionary intervention" in neighboring countries was far more systematic, extensive, and forceful than Western intervention in Russia.

Paradoxically, the party that had so vociferously condemned both the old Imperial regime and the Whites for centralistic and chauvinistic policies was the one that managed to triumph over most of the irredentist strivings that in 1919 and 1920 were corroding the old empire. Against extraordinary odds, they managed to keep not only all of the historic Great Russian lands but also most of the Ukraine, the entirety of Transcaucasia and Siberia, including the Pacific Maritime Territory, and the Central Asian regions of the old empire. In historic perspective, the Bolsheviks appear as the watchful guardians of the heartland of the Russian Empire. If they were unable to reconquer Finland, Estonia, Latvia, Lithuania, Poland, Bessarabia, and the western fringes of Belorussia and the Ukraine, it was not for lack of effort.

There was yet another aspect of the Bolshevik victory: the scope and nature of Allied intervention. Slow in arriving, it was badly planned and clumsily executed. Allied intelligence was often misinformed about Soviet strength and objectives; on the whole it underestimated what it initially called "the Bolshevik bands." The Entente Powers also underestimated the xenophobic and anti-interventionist sentiments of the Russian masses and the pacifistic mood of their own people, who were eager to end all fighting. The rivalries between France and Great Britain in Europe, and Japan and the United States in the Far East, were also a factor in undermining the Allied venture. Each nation had its own reasons for intervening and different methods for carrying it out. Different policies were advocated at various times and at different theaters of operation by the same power. In the oil-rich Caucasus near the British sphere of influence in Persia, for example, London was far more willing to support irredentist tendencies than in the Ukraine, where French interest predominated.

The intervention also constituted a negative psychological factor; the Whites depended so heavily on foreign aid that they failed to pay attention to generating enough domestic support. The Bolsheviks, who relied mainly on native support, avoided this mistake. In some ways, the intervention helped rather than hindered the Bolshevik cause, by arousing popular xenophobia and turning the Reds into unwitting champions of Great Russian nationalism.

From a military point of view, the Bolsheviks had a great advantage in that they controlled the Great Russian heartland with its internal lines of communication and its industrial centers at Petrograd and Moscow. True, the industries of these centers were dislocated by the revolutionary upheaval. But under the rigid discipline of "war communism," they still supplied the Reds far more adequately than the erratic Entente Powers did the Whites. Its internal lines of communication, coupled with its enemies' lack of coordination, allowed the Red Army to carry out strategic redeployments from one front to another; some divisions were transferred from one sector to another four and five times, according to the demands of the military situation. Another secret of the Bolshevik victory was a wiser, more economic use of their always scarce and often primitive resources. The Bolsheviks were frequently innovative in their use of the materiel they did have. They mounted machine guns on horse-drawn carriages, for example, which made the machine guns highly mobile and always ready for use. This simple device allowed Budënny's Cavalry Army to break the White's resistance several times.

The Bolsheviks were also imaginative in their use of propaganda and political warfare. Here they were infinitely superior to the Whites, whose propagandistic efforts were almost invariably crude, clumsy, and often counterproductive. Most White leaders were inept at the art of persuasion and ignorant of the elementary principles of political tactics. The Bolsheviks, on the other hand, were experts when it came to propaganda and agitation. They made use of secret presses and numerous radio stations, and they published several thousand newspapers and bulletins. The Civil War posters of the Bolsheviks—simple, suggestive, exhortative—are an excellent example of their demagogic brilliance.

Another crucial and controversial aspect of the struggle was the use of naked violence and terror. There is no doubt that both rivals for power acted ruthlessly and committed any number of atrocities. The vindictive hatred on both sides made the maxim

"Two eyes for one eye, all teeth for one tooth" the prevailing rule of the Russian Civil War. If those of the Bolsheviks were more cruel and perpetrated on a more massive scale, they were also better calculated to exact political benefit. By and large they were not acts of blind fury, as were most anti-Jewish pogroms and other acts of reprisal perpetrated by some of the Whites.

The last though not least element of importance in the Civil War was the quality of the leading elites. On the whole the Bolsheviks demonstrated far greater energy, enthusiasm, and political skill than their opponents. And in evidencing these qualities, the Communist Party was an essential factor. While the Whites represented a plethora of political groups, the Bolsheviks were directed by one closely knit, utterly ruthless team. While on the White side there was a dire shortage of political talents, the Reds had one highly gifted leader who enjoyed unquestioned authority—Lenin. Around him was a band of able and dedicated people, many of them, particularly Trotsky, distinguished by their organizational as well as political skills. On both sides, the Civil War was decided by a relative handful of people. The masses, exhausted by the trials of the previous grim half decade, were neutral and often apathetic. In such a monumental struggle, it was a small but highly integrated and centrally directed team that played the crucial role. The opponents of Communist rule had little to match the Bolshevik elite. Their political ineptitude surpassed even that of the last phases of the Imperial regime. Some anti-Bolshevik leaders were benevolent prophets of the past, some could be classified as anachronisms, and others were merely narrow-minded, brutal reactionaries. People like Wrangel or Savinkov were exceptions to the rule. Numerous acts of individual heroism could not counterbalance the more systematic efforts by the Reds.

The Civil War devastated Russia. It turned it into a swamp of misery and human degradation, and it was an unforgettable, horrifying experience for all who lived through it. It not only left the homeland in blood and ruins, it also profoundly altered future Soviet relations with the outside world. The Civil War, in which France, Britain, and the United States intervened on the side of the Whites, contributed to the further deterioration of relations between the Soviet Union and the Western World.

SUGGESTED READING

ADAMS, ARTHUR, *The Second Ukrainian Campaign of the Bolsheviks.* New Haven, Conn.: Yale University Press, 1963.

BRADLEY, JOHN, F. N., *Civil War in Russia, 1917–1920.* New York: St. Martins, 1975.

———, *Allied Intervention in Russia, 1917–1920.* Lanham, Md.: University Press of America, 1984.

BRINKLEY, GEORGE, *The Volunteer Army and the Allied Intervention in South Russia, 1917–1921.* Notre Dame, Ind.: University of Notre Dame Press, 1966.

BUNYAN, J., AND FISHER, H. H., EDS., *Intervention, Civil War and Communism in Russia, April–December 1918: Documents and Materials.* Baltimore, Md.: Johns Hopkins Press, 1936.

CARR, EDWARD H., *A History of Soviet Russia, 1917–1923*, Vol. 2. New York: Macmillan, 1952.

CHAMBERLIN, WILLIAM H., *The Russian Revolution, 1917–1921*, Vol. 2. New York: Macmillan, 1935.

DANIELS, ROBERT V., *Russia. The Roots of Confrontation.* Cambridge, Mass.: Harvard University Press, 1985, Ch. 6.

DENIKIN, ANTON, *The Russian Turmoil.* London: Hutchinson, 1922.

———, *The White Army.* London: Johnston Gate, 1930.

DZIEWANOWSKI, M. K., *A European Federalist: Joseph Pilsudski, 1918–1922.* Stanford, Calif.: Stanford University Press, 1969.

FOOTMAN, DAVID, *Civil War in Russia.* New York: Faber, 1962.

KAZEMZADEH, FIRUZ, *The Struggle for Transcaucasia, 1917–1921.* New York: Philosophical Library, 1951.

KENEZ, PETER, *Civil War in South Russia, 1919–1920: The Defeat of the Whites.* Berkeley: University of California Press, 1977.

KENNAN, GEORGE F., *The Decision to Intervene.* Princeton, N.J.: Princeton University Press, 1956.

LOCKHART, R. H. BRUCE, *British Agent.* New York: Putnam's Sons, 1933.

MORLEY, JAMES W., *The Japanese Thrust into Siberia, 1918–1920.* New York: Columbia University Press, 1957.

PIPES, RICHARD, *The Formation of the Soviet Union: Communism and Nationalism.* Cambridge, Mass.: Harvard University Press, 1964.

RESHETAR, JOHN S., JR., *The Ukrainian Revolution, 1917–1920.* Princeton, N.J.: Princeton University Press, 1952.

RODKEY, OLIVER, H., *The Unknown Civil War in Russia.* Stanford, Calif.: Hoover, 1976.

ROSENBERG, WILLIAM, G., *Liberals in the Russian Revolution: The Constitutional Democratic Party, 1917–1921.* Princeton, N.J.: Princeton University Press, 1974.

STRAKHOVSKY, LEONID I., *The Origins of American Intervention in North Russia.* Princeton, N.J.: Princeton University Press, 1937.

ULMAN, RICHARD H., *Anglo-Soviet Relations, 1917–1920,* Vol. 1. Princeton, N.J.: Princeton University Press, 1961.

UNTERBERGER, BETTY M., *America's Siberian Expedition, 1918–1920.* Durham, N.C.: Duke University Press, 1956.

VERNECK, ELENA, *The Testimony of Kolchak and Other Siberian Material.* Stanford, Calif.: Stanford University Press, 1935.

WHITE, JOHN A., *The Siberian Intervention.* Princeton, N.J.: Princeton University Press, 1950.

WRANGEL, PIOTR N., *The Memoirs of General Wrangel.* London: Williams and Norgate, 1929.

CHAPTER 9

From War Communism to the New Economic Policy

The Bolsheviks inherited from the Provisional Government an economy in shambles. The Government was able to stem neither the rebelliousness of the peasantry, the restlessness of the workers, nor the suspicion of business establishment. Wartime inflation amounted to nearly 600 percent, with wages trailing far behind prices. Production was falling rapidly, and by the autumn of 1917 had sunk to between 30 and 40 percent of the 1913 level. Transport was disorganized, and as early as the summer of 1917, shortages of food and fuel were critical.

The Bolshevik leaders had no concrete program for the rehabilitation of the country. The platform of the RSDWP adopted by its second congress in London in 1903 had made general reference to "replacing private property in the means of production and exchange by social property and introducing planned organization of the social-productive forces." Now the Soviet Communists had to experiment by applying this broad formula to the nearly catastrophic economic situation. They had to act quickly and decisively, lest they themselves be engulfed by the same tide of discontent that had swept away the Provisional Government.

WAR COMMUNISM

To cope with the chaos, the new rulers were forced to resort to a variety of Draconian measures collectively called War Communism. War Communism had three main characteristics. The first was the nationalization of banking, transport, foreign trade, and large-scale industry; this meant that economic power was concentrated in the hands of the State, which administered all four of these through its highly centralized bureaucratic system. The second aspect of War Communism was a shift away from commercial and monetary forms of exchange and distribution and toward the rationing of basic goods and services. The third feature was the widespread application of coercion whenever exhortation and persuasion failed to supplant the usual economic stimuli.

War Communism had two principal aims: to prevent the total collapse of the economy and to mobilize the existing resources for the struggle against domestic and foreign enemies of the new regime. To most of the Party leaders, however, War Communism was not only expedient, but it also represented a daring attempt to reshape radically the socioeconomic structure of the country through a rapid transformation from capitalist to communist patterns. The economic policies of War Communism were implicit in the doctrine of revolutionary Marxism and were largely an expression of the doctrinaire zeal of Russia's new rulers. A market economy, in which production was carried out essentially by independent, autonomous producers for exchange on the open market, was to be replaced by a centrally planned, state-controlled economy organized "on the lines of the postal service . . . all under the control and leadership of the armed proletariat," as Lenin put it in his 1917 *State and Revolution*. In June 1918, about half a year after the take-over of all banks, other credit institutions, and insurance companies, the Soviets nationalized most large industrial enterprises. Despite the survival of small and medium-size enterprises and of individual control of land by the peasantry, the Government had obtained a firm grip on what Lenin called "the commanding heights" of the Soviet economy. By the close of 1920, most of Russian industry was run by the State.

To manage this, a vast bureaucratic machinery, with the Council of the National Economy at the top, was set up in December 1917 and endowed with vast powers. It was empowered to confiscate, reorganize, and run all industries, and also to coordinate and plan the country's future economic expansion. The central Council of the National Economy in Moscow had its pro-

vincial and local counterparts, which were to control individual enterprises and plan for the future. The turbulent conditions of the Civil War, however, were not conducive to long-range planning. Yet planning was such a Marxist axiom that in 1920 the first steps in that direction were taken under the guise of the State Commission for Electrification. Lenin's hopes regarding the Commission were reflected in his statement, "Electrification plus Soviets equals Communism." Hydroelectric stations were to provide power for industry and transport, as well as for the villages. In 1921, the task of long-term planning was transferred to a specialized institution, the State Planning Commission, or *Gosplan.*

Marx considered buying and selling as parasitic. The Government's prohibition of free trade, however, placed on it the burden of rationing food to the urban population and supplying the peasants with industrial goods. This theoretically rendered money unnecessary. During War Communism, the Soviets constantly toyed with the idea of abolishing money, and the period was crowded with fantastic ideas concerning a moneyless economy. However, the concept failed completely; it merely contributed to the chaos and rampant inflation which made the ruble practically worthless.

Meanwhile, in view of the general economic breakdown, the Soviet government was faced with certain urgent objectives in fighting the Civil War. One of them was to make the industrial workers—many of whom had fled to their villages in search of food—return to the factories and increase productivity. Unable to cope with these tasks because of the failure of food rationing, the Bolsheviks resorted to state impressment and, in 1920, introduced a system of labor conscription. The ineffective workers' councils were abolished. The old functions of the trade unions were declared superfluous, since private capitalists had been wiped out by the Revolution, and the factories now belonged to the workers. Membership in trade unions was obligatory, and the unions were turned into government-controlled organizations whose purpose was no longer to defend the workers' rights and organize strikes, but to prevent them; not to defend workers' rights, but to bolster production. This caused bitter criticism from a Party faction called the Workers' Opposition. Strikes, though not specifically forbidden, were condemned as "sabotage" by official propaganda. The right to strike was not included in the Soviet Constitution of 1918.

At the same time, wage incentives and bonuses (mainly in the form of food as well as in money) were gradually reintroduced. While imposing iron discipline, the Government made efforts to kindle a new kind of enthusiasm by propagating a "Socialist competition of labor," as well as by means of various honorific titles and awards. For instance, individuals able to produce more than the norm were granted such titles as "shock worker" and were given other honorary awards. To obtain extra unpaid labor, the Party and the Soviet mass media exercised pressure upon laborers to "volunteer" an extra day of work for the sake of "building Socialism."

Nowhere was compulsion more visible than in the countryside. It should be made clear that the spontaneous seizure of the large landed estates that had taken place in the summer and autumn of 1917 did not end rural inequalities. Again, "the sober and the strong" usually acted more quickly than the rest of the peasants. Consequently, the *kulak* segment of the peasantry was strengthened. This frightened the Bolsheviks. Committees of poor peasants were organized by them to promote "class struggle in the countryside," of which the *kulaks* were the main target. These most industrious and productive farmers were now often deprived of their surplus produce for the benefit of the poorer peasants and the urban workers. The term *kulak* was applied very broadly; theoretically, anybody who hired labor was automatically denounced as an exploiter—a *kulak*. Yet often the disparaging label was applied to any peasant who

did not submit willingly to the confiscatory measures of the new regime.

To remedy the growing shortage of food in the cities, it was decreed that all peasants had to supply to the State all their produce above the specified subsistence minimum. The regulation assumed that the peasants, in turn, would be supplied by State enterprises with what they needed. This proved unachievable because of the low productivity of the workers and the needs of the Red Army fighting the Civil War. In view of the peasants' passive resistance, in May 1918 the so-called "grain dictatorship" was set up. To make the peasants "disgorge" their alleged surpluses and deliver the compulsory food levy to the cities' semimilitary detachments, known as the "Food Army," were organized. By 1919, they numbered some 45,000 armed workers.

FAILURE OF WAR COMMUNISM

The procurement of food was not only a critical emergency measure required to forestall urban starvation and promote the survival of the Soviet regime; the principle of confiscation of surplus was also an essential point of the War Communism's program. The theoretical justification of requisitioning was that it was in accordance with the socialist tenet of the equal distribution of basic resources. There was still another long-range goal behind the forced seizure of food: to compel individual peasants to abandon their homesteads and join the collective farms the Soviets were either setting up or planning to organize. For this purpose the Soviet authorities had preserved some of the more advanced large estates to establish model agricultural collectives, or Soviet State farms.

To encourage at least a segment of the peasantry to give up their private allotments, pool their equipment, and accept collective forms of land exploitation, the peasants were given various incentives; they were promised loans, cattle, and agricultural implements. Yet the first drive toward collectivization fell flat because the overwhelming majority of Russian peasants were reluctant to join either the collective farms (*kolkhozy*) or the State farms (*sovkhozy*). The term *kolkhoz* is an abbreviation of the words *kolektyvnoe khoziaistvo*, which means collective farm. Theoretically, a *kolkhoz* is an agricultural cooperative controlled and operated by its members, who have pooled their land, cattle, and equipment in order to work together. Each member of the cooperative shares in its output proportionate to the number of labor days contributed.[1] Some of the annual output is delivered to the State, while the rest is either divided among the members or sold for the benefit of all the members of the collective farm. The term *sovkhoz* is an abbreviation for *Sovietskoe khoziaistvo*, or Soviet farm; this is a State-owned and -operated agricultural enterprise. In such an enterprise, everything—the land, equipment, and cattle—belong to the State, while the peasants are employed as mere field workers and paid a fixed wage.

In an overwhelmingly agrarian country where some 80 percent of the population was still living in the countryside and responsible for more than 50 percent of the national income, the attitude of the countryside was of decisive importance for War Communism. Widespread resistance, expressed in innumerable peasant uprisings, served as a warning to the Government. by the beginning of 1921, peasant resistance was overwhelming.

Another major difficulty facing the Soviet regime was the continuous flight of starved workers to the villages in search of food. The workers, together with speculators known as "bagmen," wandered from village to village trying to buy and/or beg for food. By August 1920, Moscow had lost about half of its population and Petrograd nearly two-thirds. Even those who remained could

hardly be fed in view of the peasants' reluctance to deliver food to cities that had virtually nothing of value to offer them in return.

Other difficulties facing the government included the state of the railways, which were largely in ruin. As a result most factories, deprived of raw materials, could operate only part time; some establishments had to close down completely. By the end of 1920 total industrial production had dropped to about one-fifth of the 1913 level. The output of consumer goods, especially shoes and clothing, was actually lower than that. Labor productivity sank to less than half of its prewar level. By the beginning of 1921, many factories had to close down altogether for lack of fuel, which was as scarce as food. On January 22, 1921, the meager bread ration in large population centers was cut by one-third. By February, fuel shortages in the large cities had become catastrophic, and that month workers of sixty-four large factories in Petrograd, including the Putilov metal works, went on strike. Their employees not only demanded larger food rations, but also wanted to restore the workers' councils and the trade unions as their true representatives.

However, starvation was not limited to the cities. To the ruinous effects of War Communism were added natural disasters: drought, dust, and locusts. The peasants also suffered from the confiscatory measures outlined above; very often even grain seed had been taken away from them. As a consequence, in 1920–1921, there were large-scale peasant uprisings in western Siberia, in the Ukraine (where Makhno was still active), and in Central Russia, mainly in the province of Tambov, where an able guerrilla leader, Antonov, waged a successful partisan war against the Soviet authorities. During February 1921 alone, there were 118 major peasant risings in various parts of the country. There were also numerous strikes and riots in the various urban centers.

---

[1] The labor day unit does not correspond to a day's work, but to a particular amount of work, with different yardsticks for different kinds of work.

THE KRONSTADT REVOLT

Dissatisfaction also penetrated the ranks of sailors and soldiers, most of them recruited from the countryside. Of these outbursts of discontent, the most important and dramatic was the uprising at the naval base of Kronstadt. Situated in the Gulf of Finland on the long, narrow, and rocky island of Kotlin some twenty miles west of Petrograd, Kronstadt had originally been built by Peter the Great to protect the capital from the open sea. With its garrison of 15,000 sailors and soldiers, Kronstadt had a long revolutionary tradition dating back to 1905. The rowdy "blue jackets" played a prominent part both during the ferment of those days and in the overthrow of the Tsarist regime. Throughout the Civil War, the Baltic sailors were in the forefront of the struggle against the Whites and suffered heavy losses.

The end of the Civil War, however, brought about a change of mood even among the "pride and glory of the Revolution," as Trotsky called the Kronstadt fighters. For three years they had been struggling, hoping to abolish the hateful rigors of War Communism. The sailors resented that nothing of the sort had happened. The iron discipline Trotsky had reimposed on them (abolition of ship's committees, appointment of political commissars from outside) was compounded by the continuation of old privations: poor rations, inadequate clothing, cold, unheated barracks. At the end of 1920 there was an epidemic of scurvy in the Baltic fleet.

With the end of the Civil War, home leaves, previously practically nonexistent, were now granted more liberally. This was an eye-opener to the "peasants and workers in uniform," for it acquainted the sailors and soldiers first-hand with the often desperate conditions of the country. Their rate of desertion increased. By the middle of February 1921, tensions in the Baltic squadron, stimulated by the wave of strikes sweeping the factories of Petrograd, reached the boiling point. The garrison of Kronstadt elected a Provisional Revolution-

ary Committee and voted a resolution. While expressing sympathy for the strikers' demands, it declared a lack of confidence in "the present Soviet" because it did "not express the will of the workers and peasants." The resolution insisted on immediate free elections open to all left socialist parties and that the peasants be granted "full freedom of action in regard to the land" as long as they did not use hired labor. The resolution did not ask for the overthrow of the regime, but rather for its democratization. The Kronstadt sailors acted as the conscience of the Bolsheviks: they appealed to them to live up to their old slogans and grant political power to the freely elected Soviets. The resolution turned the Kronstadt sailors into spokesmen for the sentiments of the broad popular masses smarting under the coercive policies of War Communism.

The Soviet government promptly denounced the Provisional Revolutionary Committee and its acts of defiance as "counterrevolutionary" and asked for the unconditional surrender of the rebels. When this was rejected, an attack was ordered by war commissar Trotsky; the rebels who would not surrender were to be "shot like ducks." The military drive against the heavily fortified island opened on March 7 during a heavy blizzard and lasted for over ten days. On March 18 the attackers crushed the last centers of resistance. Many defenders, including some of the principal leaders, managed to flee across the solid ice to Finland. In violation of the conditions of capitulation, all the captured leaders and many other rebels were shot. Those who remained were sent to distant forced labor camps.

The Kronstadt uprising was one of the most dramatic episodes in early Soviet history. It was neither inspired nor engineered by any political party or conspiracy. The participants belonged to various leftist radical groups—the SRs, the Mensheviks, and the Anarchists—as well as to a plethora of splinter factions. The revolt represented an attempt to reshape the Bolshevik dictatorship by appealing to the Soviet masses in the name of a return to the original but by then discarded battle cry, "All power to the Soviets." Most of the rebels understood this to mean local committees, freely elected by leftist parties only, that would operate autonomously, under the supervision but without the blatant interference of central Party authorities. To the rebels the soviets represented the spirit of the old village communes in revolutionary garb. The Bolsheviks had very skillfully manipulated this essentially Populist myth and used the soviets as an instrument for the destruction of the old order. In Lenin's scheme, however, the soviets were always to be controlled by the Party, which was to remain the sole locus of power. Soviets independent of the Party represented to the Bolsheviks a spontaneous, uncontrollable, and hence dangerous, force. That is why, immediately after the Revolution, the Bolsheviks reduced the soviets' role to a purely symbolic one, and they operated under firm Party control.

The impact of the uprising was considerable, both at home and abroad. Abroad, the revolt delayed international recognition of the Soviet regime. At home, the uprising touched off several mutinies and local disturbances, and compelled the Bolsheviks to replace the bankrupt War Communism by a new set of policies. The failure of War Communism had been obvious for months to all sober-minded Bolshevik leaders. On February 24—five days before the beginning of the rebellion—Lenin had already presented a draft of new economic directives to the Central Committee of the Communist Party for inclusion on the agenda of its Tenth Congress, which was to gather in Moscow on March 8. There is no doubt, however, that the Kronstadt affair, by dramatizing the desperate plight of the masses, helped Lenin overcome the resistance of the left wing of the Party still bent on enforcing radical measures despite the opposition of the masses.

When one analyzes the end result of War Communism, one must admit that it con-

tributed a great deal to breaking down the old capitalist system, but little positive to building a new, stable socioeconomic order. In the nationalized industries, a slow beginning had been made toward the establishment of self-government in the form of workers' councils, but the lack of proper personnel and adequate know-how pushed the Bolsheviks toward a policy of strict control of the trade unions and sui generis state capitalism with pronounced militaristic features. The peasantry, temporarily neutralized by the redistribution of the landed estates, was soon driven into sullen hostility toward the regime by the indiscriminate requisitioning of their produce. In the field of procurement, little was achieved beyond the extension of the grain monopoly (which had been established by the Provisional Government) and the introduction of rationing. Both institutions functioned in as spotty and perfunctory a manner as the chaotic circumstances of the Civil War and famine dictated.

Thus War Communism was a highly experimental period that saw a violent but rather futile attempt to drive the country at full speed toward socialism–communism, despite its unreadiness and unwillingness of the masses to submit. As we have seen, the experiments of War Communism greatly contributed to deepening the chaos and famine into which Russia had been plunged by World War I, the Revolution, and the Civil War.

THE NEW ECONOMIC POLICY (NEP)

By 1921, most of the Soviet leaders realized that they had overreached themselves and must embark on a new policy. They understood that the transition from a capitalist to a socialist economic order could not be achieved overnight, in one great leap forward. The task had to be faced in a more realistic manner, stretched over long years, and performed by different methods. This was the rationale behind the steps Lenin took in March 1921 at the Tenth Congress of the Communist Party, which was one of the most dramatic gatherings of this type thus far in the annals of communism.

Lenin's report to the Congress did not hide the extreme gravity of the situation. Arguing against the opponents of the new course with a frankness that often shocked his comrades, he admitted that the danger of peasant revolt constituted a far greater menace to the Soviet regime than the White armies had ever been. Consequently, he urged a radical departure from the principles and practices of War Communism and the adoption of a set of new economic policies. While insisting on holding on to "the commanding heights," that is banking, transport, large industry, and foreign trade, Lenin urged that positions of secondary importance be left in private hands, and that the peasants be placated by means of a series of concessions. Instead of the food levy, which forcibly wrested from the peasants all their surplus produce and often their means of livelihood, a definite tax was introduced. Initially levied in kind (mostly in food produce), the tax was later converted into cash. The decree specified that the tax should not exceed half of the former requisition. It was calculated progressively, and was to fall more heavily on the *kulaks* than on the poor or middle-income peasants. The rest of the surplus the peasant could sell on the open market. The decree spelled the end of arbitrary requisitioning, the peasants' nightmare during the preceding three years.

The launching of the new economic policy, usually referred to as NEP, came too late and did not prevent a large-scale famine. While the NEP was unfolding, the famine was spreading during 1921 and part of 1922. Large stretches of the countryside had been ravished and abused for years. The famine hit especially hard in the Volga region and the Ukraine, and millions there were on the verge of starvation. Extreme and urgent measures were needed to remedy the situation, yet the Moscow government, desperately short of resources, was unable to undertake them. In July 1921, the

writer Maxim Gorky wrote a plea addressed "To All Honest People" of the world imploring them to help Russia in its predicament. One of the first to respond was the United States. For twenty-two months (August 1921–June 1923), about 180 foreign, mostly American, relief workers operated in Soviet territory, feeding some 22 million people. The Vatican and the Quakers, as well as many other organizations, folllowed with their relief missions.[2]

The NEP did not develop in accordance with a preconceived plan; it evolved spontaneously in accord with its own internal logic. One of the consequences of the freedom to sell food produce was the reestablishment of freedom of trade in general. Initially, the government hoped to organize, and thus control, the entire system of distribution; however, lack of financial resources as well as qualified personnel made it impossible. Consequently, the peasants themselves proceeded to sell the surplus of the bumper harvest of 1922 to the buyers who offered them the best price. This resulted in a rapid revival of small traders and of thousands of marketplaces, bazaars, and traditional fairs. The middlemen, who under War Communism had a precarious existence as black marketeers, or "enemies of the people," now reappeared and started openly to apply the skills hitherto used in shadowy operations.

CONSEQUENCES OF THE NEP

One step led to another; from trade the new economic system expanded to industry and then affected property relations. If the peasant was to produce more food, he had to be granted a measure of security in the form of reasonably long land tenure. This

---

[2] The resolution of the Council of People's Commissars of July 10, 1923, paid tribute to "an enormous and entirely disinterested effort of the American Relief Administration," that "rescued from death . . . millions of people of all ages." It is estimated that between 5 and 6 million people died of starvation before the foreign relief measures were applied.

was done via a series of concessions to the peasants, which in 1922 were embodied in the Land Code. While the principle of land nationalization was reaffirmed, the peasant was declared a long-term tenant. Leasing of the land was allowed; later, even the hiring of additional labor (previously condemned as an evil capitalistic practice) was permitted under certain conditions.

Moreover, the NEP could not be limited only to the countryside and small trade. Once the countryside returned to the market economy, industry was bound to be affected. If the peasants were to sell their surpluses to the cities, the industries had to have something to offer in return. This would inevitably influence the entire economic system. And indeed, licenses soon had to be granted for private enterprise. Development of consumer industries, commercial enterprises, and service shops was soon tolerated, and even encouraged. Many small industrial enterprises, previously nationalized, were now returned to their previous owners or leased on certain strictly defined conditions to these "Nepmen." With astonishing rapidity, the industries revived. Small-scale, light industries, especially leather and textiles, mushroomed in response to the enormous demand for shoes, clothing, harnesses, and the like, products that had hardly been manufactured for years.

The confusion of the NEP created opportunities for quick and easy profit. Soon large fortunes were made by some of the Nepmen. The speed with which small private companies and speculators reestablished themselves and prospered was shocking to diehard, orthodox Communists of a puritanical mold. But the people at large, after having been deprived not only of the small amenities of life but even of its bare necessities, were now enjoying them to the utmost without being in the least ashamed.

Simultaneous with the limited and selective toleration of private initiative, significant changes were introduced into the management of socialized enterprises. The State industries were reorganized into approximately five hundred trusts; each enterprise was to be run on a commercial basis and submit its plans and accounts to the Supreme Economic Council for approval and supervision of their expenditures and revenues. Other than that, managers of individual factories were allowed considerable scope for initiative. The huge, unwieldy bureaucratic machinery that was to manage them was decentralized, somewhat streamlined and provided with individual managers who replaced the previously predominant but usually cumbersome committees. Strict cost accounting was reintroduced. At the same time, wage incentives (piece rates and bonuses) replaced "socialist competition." The Labor Code of 1922, which included compulsory work, was abolished; it was to be applied only in cases of national emergency or as a punishment for offenses against the State. Trade unions, although still controlled by the State, regained some of their autonomy and were now called the spokesmen of "true, proletarian democracy." Strikes were allowed—and even encouraged—when they were directed against private entrepreneurs.

The rapid increase in the food supply permitted the abolition of food rationing. The NEP also affected the country's foreign relations. The end of foreign intervention was followed by the lifting of the Allied blockade and a gradual resumption of international trade. Soon concessions were granted to foreign capitalists on the basis of partnership with the Soviet Government. The promulgation of NEP coincided with the signing of the first Anglo–Soviet trade agreement. By the German–Soviet agreement of Rapallo (April 1922), the Weimar Republic followed Great Britain's example and had soon overtaken it and established itself as Soviet Russia's best customer. (See Chapter 10 on early Soviet foreign policy.)

The growth of a money economy increased the demand for credit. From 1922 on, a network of State banks for financing commercial as well as industrial enterprises was organized. Soon the banks were followed by State insurance agencies. A vodka monopoly was reintroduced together with a variety of old indirect taxes and excises. All of these steps required a stable currency. The first Soviet ruble had become worthless as a result of the spiraling inflation and therefore had to be replaced by a currency that would command confidence. Meanwhile, the Soviet State Bank was reorganized in 1922 and empowered to issue a new ruble based partially on gold. In 1925, the old, worthless currency was withdrawn and exchanged for a new ruble. This in itself was a major reversal of the original tenets of Bolshevism. Before the seizure of power, Lenin had treated gold with the utmost contempt; he said it was to be used in making fixtures in public lavatories. Now his attitude changed and he declared, "When we conquer power on a world scale, we shall use gold to build lavatories. Meanwhile we must save gold . . . sell it at the highest price. When living among wolves, let's howl like wolves."

CONTRADICTIONS OF THE NEP

From a historic perspective, there seems to be no doubt that the abandonment of War Communism was a necessity if the Communist Party wanted to preserve its power. The hopes for a "great leap forward," for a quick transition from capitalism to a full-scale socialist system, had proved illusory. The introduction of the NEP was a tactical, temporary retreat from positions the Soviets found impossible to defend at that moment, but which they were determined to recapture later on. In the meantime, the paramount need was to embark upon the long-run task of rehabilitating the starved and ruined country and of creating a workable economy.

The NEP represented a painful rethinking by the Bolsheviks of the practical consequences of their seizure of power in a backward, agrarian country. By 1921–1922 the millennial, maximalist mentality had had to give way to a more evolutionary-reformist mood. In the mixed economy established by the NEP, the state sector included the central banking system, large industrial enterprises, foreign trade, and communication. The private sector comprised most agriculture, most of the retail and part of the wholesale trade, and all the handicraft. The predominance of the state sector was overwhelming. While private business accounted for 88.5 percent of the total number of enterprises, it employed only 12.4 percent of the industrial labor force. On the other hand, state-controlled companies employed 84.1 percent of the nonagricultural labor force.

The 24 million peasant households were the main beneficiaries of the NEP. The peasantry gained three things: security of land tenure, freedom from requisitioning, and a free hand in selling agricultural surpluses. By making these concessions, Lenin admitted that, in the long run, the Soviet regime could ill afford to disregard the interests of some 80 percent of the population and had to win their cooperation. This also meant the return, under duress, to his original concept of the alliance of workers and peasants (*smychka* in Russian). The decision "to retreat in order to jump higher" in the future was essentially a political one. It represented a temporary capitulation by the Soviet Government to the peasantry, "a peasant Brest-Litovsk," as a leftist opponent put it.

The NEP, based on a precarious balance of two sectors, private and public, represented a shaky compromise between communism and capitalism, between collectivism and individualism, between private initiative and state control. From the very beginning, the NEP's mixed structure suffered from a variety of contradictions and paradoxes. The Communists were to coexist competitively with the small capitalists, learn from them how to be efficient and productive, and eventually demonstrate the superiority of the socialist system. In everyday practice, however, the capitalists proved their superior efficiency and flexibility. They were producing and distributing better goods more quickly and cheaply, despite being hampered at every step by high taxes, an intricate net of regulations, and a variety of discriminatory administrative practices. The state-controlled industries, on the other hand, were lagging behind both in volume of production and in quality. The fact that the private initiative represented by the Nepmen was doing relatively better than the nationalized sector was insufferable in the long run, because it disproved, by daily practice, the basic tenet of the doctrines on which the Bolsheviks based their claim to power. It was obvious that either the forces inherent in the NEP would corrode the Soviet system or the system would have to destroy them in order to survive.

The preparation for a showdown was visible in a variety of political measures undertaken by the Party. While retaining control of the "commanding heights" of the economy, which is to say, banking, large-scale industry, transportation, and the monopoly of foreign trade, the Party kept the reins of political power tightly in its hands. Despite the pressure of a group of Party members headed by Alexander D. Shliapnikov and Alexandra Kolontai, a faction known as the Workers' Opposition, Lenin rejected the idea of granting freedom of speech and press to other Socialist parties like the Mensheviks and the SRs. On the contrary, it was during the NEP that the surviving representatives of these groups were either imprisoned or driven abroad, and the remainder compelled to join the ruling party or abstain completely from any political activity. By 1922, most of the surviving leaders of the former opposition, including Martov and Chernov, had to emigrate. Step by step, Communist authoritarianism was assuming increasingly rigid features.

The Tenth Party Congress reemphasized the ban on all factionalism and reinforced inner Party discipline. In the midst of general confusion, Party members were to rekindle their "revolutionary vigilance" and to remain the bulwark of the system. In the summer of 1921 the Party went through its first mass purge, which reduced its membership by one-third. In 1922, the Cheka, or the Extraordinary Commission for Fighting Counter-Revolution and Sabotage, was reorganized and given a new, more innocuous name, that of *GPU* (*Gosudarstvennoe Politicheskoe Upravlenie*, or State Political Administration). Thus from an *extraordinary* institution it became an *ordinary*, standing institution of Soviet reality. Moreover, its jurisdiction was expanded; it was now granted the right to arrest Party members, a privilege not enjoyed by the Cheka.

The period of the NEP coincided with the emergence of Stalin as the most influential factor of the regime. In May 1922, he was entrusted with the post of Secretary General of the Central Committee. Initially, few Party people attached much importance to this appointment and his activities, and Stalin was known as "Comrade Card Index."

Meanwhile, the Party directed more measures against religious freedom. In 1921, religious instruction to the young was forbidden and all parochial schools closed; Church lands and treasures were confiscated. The Criminal Code of 1926 prescribed forced labor as the punishment for any religious teaching. All religiously oriented writings were banned, and seminaries and monasteries closed. Any resistance to these measures was regarded as "sabotage" and "counterrevolution." Well over a thousand bishops, monks, and priests were executed, and many surviving ones, including the Patriarch of Moscow, arrested. Atheistic propaganda was intensified.

THE NEP AND CULTURE

The first socioeconomic changes brought about by the Communist victory were reflected in the fields of education and culture. As we have previously discussed, the war was preceded by a period of great vitality and intellectual experimentation. The Bolsheviks seized power determined to reshape the country's cultural and educational patterns to serve their goals.

Popular education was the first target of the new regime. It was to be treated as an instrument of class struggle, a transmission belt from the Communist Party to the masses. The struggle against illiteracy was declared objective number one. As Lenin so bluntly put it, "an illiterate person is outside politics"; this meant that he could not be effectively reached by the Party. At the end of the Civil War, all schools were placed under State control. A large-scale campaign to teach reading and writing to the masses was effectively organized. At the same time, the old high schools, or *Gymnasia,* were eliminated. The new Soviet secondary school, Lenin asserted, was to be a composite of "basic scientific knowledge of both nature and society, the world outlook of scientific materialism, Communist morality, physical exercise for good health." Moreover, close links were to be established between study and productive labor. This concept of "polytechnization" meant two things: first, pupils were to combine general education with practical vocational training; this in turn implied an emphasis not on the humanities, but on the natural sciences. Simultaneous with "polytechnization," the new regime embraced certain ideas of progressive education, and during the 1920s most Soviet schools abolished textbooks, examinations, and grading systems.

Institutions of higher learning also suffered bitterly from Soviet Russia's cultural revolution. It was during the Civil War that academic instruction received its heaviest blows; most professors of "bourgeois" origin who did not emigrate were dismissed. While such scholars as Nicholas Berdiaev, Mikhail I. Rostovtsev, Pitirum Sorokin, and George Vernadsky had to leave the country, the Marxist historian Michael Pokrovsky became virtual dictator of the "academic sector" and ran it with an iron fist. The traditional university ceased to function. To repopulate technical schools with working class students, new institutions known as Workers' Faculties were created. The Workers' Faculties, loosely affiliated with the old polytechnical institutions and universities, hastily furnished college preparatory instruction at times and places convenient to working people.

Parallel with the transformation of the educational system, the new regime nationalized all publishing houses and organized a central state publishing and coordinating agency. Gradually, strict censorship of all printed material was enforced. Nevertheless, during the NEP era, Soviet literature continued to be characterized by a variety of attitudes and modes of expression. All this was tolerated for the time being, provided it did not openly contradict the basic principles of the regime.

The Bolsheviks realized that the education of society does not take place exclusively in school and soon made provisions for youth organizations dedicated to Communist goals—the "All-Union Leninist–Communist Children's Organization" known as the Young Pioneers, and the "All-Union Leninist–Communist Youth Organization," better known as *Komsomol*. The Young Pioneers included children from the ages of ten to fourteen; the *Komsomol* included young people up to their early thirties. Both organizations have since been under the close ideological supervision and guidance of the Communist Party, which regards them as nurseries for its future members. Membership in the Komsomol facilitates, but does not guarantee, acceptance into the ranks of the Party.

FINE ARTS AND LITERATURE

While focusing their attention on education, publishing, and other mass media, the Bolsheviks were less strict with regard to fine arts and literature. Their initial leniency toward the arts was partly due to the cultivated and sensitive personality of the first Commissar for Education, Anatoli V. Lunacharsky, a prominent Marxist critic and an old Bolshevik who enjoyed Lenin's confidence. After the Bolshevik coup, Lenin put him in charge of education and intervened only sporadically, when he suspected that Lunacharsky's tolerance might threaten the guiding role of the Party in the field of culture. Lunacharsky, supported by some moderate leaders like Bukharin, pursued a somewhat permissive policy toward artists, including those of the avant garde.

Many leading Russian writers emigrated. Those who did remain, such as Akhmatova, Blok, Biely, Briusov, Mandelshtam, Mayakovsky, and Pasternak, continued to write, trying to adapt to the new regime. Some of them, like Blok and Mayakovsky, lent their support to the new rulers. Blok even greeted the Bolshevik coup with an ecstatic poem, "The Twelve" (1919). This poem is a symbolic vision of Christ crowned with a wreath of white roses leading twelve Red Guardsmen who shoot their way to victory. Blok survived the Revolution by three more years, but his progressive disillusionment and despair made him artistically sterile. He died of starvation in 1921. Another writer who had started his career before the war as a Futurist, Boris Pasternak, soon developed a personal style both in prose and poetry. In addition to producing several volumes of original and often brilliant verse, he translated into Russian many works of Shakespeare, Goethe, and Verlaine, as well as some of the leading Georgian poets.

But perhaps the most significant Bolshevik writer of the period was Mayakovsky. Besides writing poetry and prose, drama, and political satire attacking the opponents of Communism and eulogizing the new regime, he also designed posters for Party propaganda campaigns. His poem "The Left March" was an enthusiastic welcome to the dawn of the new Communist era. Initially, Mayakovsky persuaded Soviet authorities to lend official support to the Futurists as pioneers of a new "revolutionary" style, not only in literature but also in painting, graphic art, and architecture. This short-lived decision proved beneficial to Soviet art and literature, particularly to the plastic and graphic arts. As a result, for the first time in their national history, Russian architects created during the postrevolutionary decade a school of design

and urban planning equal to the best Western models. The graphic artists, especially poster designers, also profited from the stimulus given them by Futurism and Cubism, as well as the German movement known under the name of *Bauhaus*, led by Walter Gropius.

Soon, however, Futurism fell from official favor, and hesitant government support was temporarily shifted to the "Proletarian Cultural and Educational Organization" known as *Proletkult*. The Proletkult united a large body of two thousand to three thousand artists and writers, brought together by the desire to educate the workers in the arts as well as in Marxist ideology. These artists were organized in a number of clubs spread throughout the Soviet Union. The main theorist of the Proletkult was Alexandr A. Bogdanov (Malinovsky), a philosopher and economist as well as a physician. A man of original and independent mind, he argued that the new art and literature that were to express the proletarian revolution would be created not solely by people of proletarian stock. He insisted that the treasures of the old culture be preserved and passed on to the coming generations as a foundation for new achievements. Lenin soon came to suspect that the Proletkult harbored too many ideologically alien elements that might constitute a threat to the Soviet regime. He insisted that no organization be independent of the Party and ordered the group to be subordinated to it. By 1928, an organization of Communist writers known as RAPP (the Russian abbreviation for "Russian Association of Proletarian Writers") assumed a quasi-dictatorial position in the literary field. Shortly thereafter, although not without official prodding, similar organizations were established by other groups of independent artists and writers.

Meanwhile, however, they still enjoyed limited and precarious freedom. To them belonged the talented, lyrical peasant poet, a sentimental Slavophile, Sergei A. Yessenin, author of melodious verses idealizing the old Russian countryside and its folklore. Yessenin's verses soon came to reflect the mood of despair and resignation that led him to suicide in 1925. Another writer, Yevgeny I. Zamyatin, in a surrealistic novel entitled *We* published in 1924, described a small clique of ruthless people establishing a state that controls all aspects of human activity. Zamyatin's vision anticipated George Orwell's nightmarish society of the future by more than a generation. Soon, Zamyatin had to emigrate. The NEP era saw also the debut of the most widely read of Soviet novelists, Mikhail A. Sholokhov. By the late 1920s, he had achieved great renown with the appearance of his great novel *And Quiet Flows the Don.* This panoramic epic describes the life of the Don Cossacks on the eve of World War I and during the revolutionary period. It has been translated into many foreign languages, and it won the Nobel Prize for Literature in 1965.

The 1920s also saw the emergence of a number of brilliant new writers, among them Isaac E. Babel, a former political commissar of Budyonny's Cavalry Army. Babel described with savage realism his impressions of the Civil War and of the Soviet–Polish campaign of 1920 in a series of stories published under the title *Red Cavalry* (1926). Babel also wrote novels and theater plays, the best of which is probably *Benya Krik* (1928), the story of a Jewish gangster in the author's native Odessa.

PERFORMING ARTS

The NEP also witnessed remarkable innovations in the field of performing art. With the exception of the ballet, which was largely left alone, the Bolshevik regime tried to manipulate the performing arts, especially theater and cinema, to serve their objectives. While Stanislavsky continued to direct more or less as before, his two pupils Yevgeny B. Vakhtangov and Vsevolod E. Meyerhold tried to make the old plays more understandable to the now largely proletarian audiences, and even tended to subordinate esthetic considerations to the dictates of ideology. Using teams of young, enthusiastic actors, Vakhtangov successfully integrated often highly stylized folklore with grotesque buffoonery and even acrobatics. The activities of Vakhtangov and Meyerhold gave a powerful stimulus to a number of similar but more modest local enterprises organized by various trade unions, cultural clubs, schools, and ethnic groups. During the 1920s there were numerous people's theaters functioning in various Soviet republics, including the newly established Central Asian Republic, but especially in the Ukraine, which was then witnessing an outburst of creativity, a veritable national cultural renaissance. One of the most original people's theaters was the Jewish Theater of Moscow. The cultural Russification of ethnic groups was discouraged and anti-Semitism officially condemned.

The most remarkable progress during the 1920s, however, was made in the cinema. To Lenin, movies were "the most important of all arts" because of their far-reaching propagandistic potential and especially their influence on the still largely illiterate masses. And, indeed, immediately after the Civil War the Soviet Government rapidly expanded the seven movie studios and approximately one thousand theaters inherited from the old regime. Within a decade they had covered the country with a network of movie theaters supplied with films produced by numerous State-controlled production centers. Two early Soviet directors reached high artistic levels, Sergei M. Eisenstein and Vsevolod I. Pudovkin. Both scored their greatest successes in the late 1920s and the 1930s. Both Eisenstein and Pudovkin are best remembered as cinematic iconographers of the historic revolutionary era. The middle of the 1920s brought Eisenstein's film "Battleship Potiomkin," which dramatized to the Soviet spectator the story of the revolt of the Black Sea sailors in the summer of 1905. The tenth anniversary of the Bolshevik revolution was celebrated by two major films, Pudovkin's "Last Days of Petersburg" and Eisenstein's "Ten Days that Shook the

Dmitri D. Shostakovich before a concert in New York City in 1923

World" (an adaptation of John Reed's well-known book).

THE NEP: A BALANCE SHEET

The NEP represented a baffling, paradoxical panorama crowded with experiments in many fields. During the years 1921–1928, the Party, as well as artists and economists, was groping for new solutions in the quickly changing society emerging from the turmoil. Despite the losses that Russian culture had suffered during the preceding traumatic period, and despite its increasing regimentation, the first decade after the Revolution represents the freest, richest, and most creative period of the Soviet era. While the last traces of political pluralism were gradually disappearing, they were still precariously surviving in the field of culture, which showed remarkable vitality. Economic recovery was speedy, and by 1925–1926 the standard of living of an average worker probably exceeded the prerevolutionary level, while an average peasant also lived better than ever. The authoritarian features of the Soviet system, already quite pronounced, were not yet as rigid and oppressive as they were to become during the 1930s. Consequently, in historic perspective, the NEP represents a period pregnant with possibilities. During the mid-1920s it was not quite clear in which direction the Soviet system would develop—toward greater freedom, more private enterprise, and the development of what was later termed "socialism with a human face," or toward more state control and repression.

SUGGESTED READING

AVRICH, PAUL, *Kronstadt 1921.* Princeton, N.J.: Princeton University Press, 1970.

BAYKOV, ALEXANDER, *The Development of the Soviet*

Economic System. New York: Cambridge University Press, 1946.

CARR, E. H., *The Bolshevik Revolution, 1917–1923,* Vol. II, *The Interregnum.* New York: Macmillan, 1954.

DOBB, MAURICE, *Soviet Economic Development Since 1917.* London: Rutledge & Kegan, 1948.

EASTMAN, MAX, *Artists in Uniform: A Study of Literature and Bureaucracy.* New York: Knopf, 1934.

FARNSWORTH, BEATRICE, *Aleksandra Kollontai. Socialism, Feminism, and the Bolshevik Revolution.* Stanford, Calif.: Stanford University Press, 1980.

FISCHER, HAROLD H., *The Famine in Soviet Russia, 1919–1923: The Operations of the American Relief Administration.* New York: Oxford University Press, 1927.

FITZPATRICK, SHEILA, *The Commissariat for Enlightenment . . . 1917–1921.* New York: Cambridge University Press, 1970.

GETZLER, ISRAEL, *Kronstadt 1917–1921, the Fate of a Soviet Democracy.* New York: Cambridge University Press, 1983.

HOSKING, GEOFFREY, *A History of the Soviet Union.* London: Fontana Press-Collins, 1985, Ch. 5.

KINGSTON-MANN, ESTHER, *Lenin and the Problem of Marxist Peasant Revolution.* New York: Oxford University Press, 1983.

KOLLONTAI, ALEXANDRA, *The Workers' Opposition in Russia.* Chicago: Industrial Workers of the World, 1921.

KOPP, ARISTOTLE, *Soviet Architecture and City Planning, 1917–1935.* New York: George Braziller, 1970.

LONDON, KURT, *The Seven Soviet Arts.* New Haven, Conn.: Yale University Press, 1938.

MIRSKY, D. S., *A History of Russian Literature.* New York: Alfred Knopf, 1949.

NOVE, ALEC, *An Economic History of the USSR.* London: Allen Lane, 1969.

POGGIOLI, RENATO, *The Poets of Russia, 1890–1930.* Cambridge, Mass.: Harvard University Press, 1960.

SCHWARTZ, HARRY, *Russia's Soviet Economy.* Englewood Cliffs, N.J.: Prentice-Hall, 1954.

SERGE, VICTOR, *Memoirs of a Revolutionary, 1901–1941.* New York: Oxford University Press, 1963.

SPINKA, MATTHEW, *The Church in Soviet Russia.* New York: Oxford University Press, 1956.

CHAPTER 10

Between the Comintern and the Narkomindel: Early Soviet Foreign Policy

As Marxists, the Bolsheviks had based their ideas about relations among states on two assumptions. The first was that international conflicts are merely an outward manifestation of the inner contradictions of capitalism and are therefore bound to disappear with its downfall. Second, Soviet leaders took it for granted that since "workers have no country," international solidarity would replace the proletarians' loyalty to their respective nation-states.

The latter assumption suffered its first heavy blow from 1914 to 1918. Most of the socialist parties of Europe, starting with the Social Democrats in Germany, basically supported the war efforts of their respective governments. Throughout the war, moreover, the proletarians of the belligerent countries slaughtered each other like everybody else. Finally, at the end of the war the workers failed to turn "the imperialistic war into a civil war," and thus aid the Bolsheviks. All this made Lenin condemn the Social

Democratic party members as "social traitors," "renegades" and "Judases" to the proletarian cause. Consequently, he resolved that the Second International, which united the socialist parties, should be scrapped, and that all truly revolutionary proletarian parties should be modeled on the Bolshevik example and grouped into a new, more militant, international organization.

THE COMMUNIST INTERNATIONAL

When Lenin was still an émigré he could do little. His chance came only after November 1917, when he became undisputed head of the Soviet Government. As a result of the Bolshevik triumph, most working-class movements began to split and their extreme left wings, one by one, began to form "parties of the new type," modeled on the Bolshevik party and calling themselves Communists. Initially, however, there were

139

only sporadic contacts between them. The decision to set up a Communist International was precipitated early in 1919 by the news that the Social Democratic (or Second) International, shaken by the events of 1914–1918, had decided to revive its structure. There was no time to lose, argued Lenin. Early in March some thirty representatives of leftist parties sympathetic to the Bolshevik point of view gathered in Moscow.

It was a strange gathering, and many among the motley crowd of delegates had dubious credentials. For instance, the fledgling American Communist movement was represented by John Reed. Christian Rakovsky, a French-educated Bulgarian, former Romanian citizen, and at that time head of the new Soviet Ukrainian government, claimed to represent the fictitious Balkan Revolutionary Federation. Most other delegates were members not of political movements but of tiny leftist splinters of the existing Social Democratic movements. The only sizable Communist Party, besides that of Soviet Russia, was the German. Yet its leadership, inspired by Rosa Luxemburg, was afraid that a Communist International set up at that time in Moscow would be nothing but a *Russian* International.

Despite German objections, and at Lenin's insistence, on March 4, 1919, the conference proclaimed itself the First Congress of the Communist International and promptly elected an Executive Committee. Lenin's close co-worker, Grigori Zinoviev, became its chairman, while Karl Radek was selected as its Secretary. The *Comintern*, as the new organization came to be called, immediately issued an appeal "To the Workers of All Countries," urging them to follow the Bolshevik example, overthrow their bourgeois governments, and establish the dictatorship of the proletariat. The rebels were promised aid from the "first Socialist Government" of the world.

Soon after its foundation, the *Comintern* suffered a severe setback. Although in De-

cember 1918 the left wing of the German Social Democratic Party, the Spartacists, had succeeded in setting up the Communist Workers' Party of Germany, the party was too weak to stem that country's drift to the right. When in January 1919 the Communists staged an uprising in Berlin, the revolt was ruthlessly suppressed by the German Army. The two leaders of the Spartacists, Rosa Luxemburg and Karl Liebknecht, were shot, and the party banned. In May 1919, the Communist regime in Bavaria collapsed, while the government of Bela Kun in Hungary went down in August of that year, undermined by its own ineffectiveness and swept away by the rightist forces led by Admiral Nicholas Horthy. At the same time in Russia the White Armies of Denikin and Yudenich were converging on Moscow. Only at the close of 1919, with the destruction of Denikin's army, did the Bolsheviks' self-confidence revive.

Watching the changing European scene, Lenin decided in 1919 that while the Bolsheviks should persist in their revolutionary attempts, other approaches should not be neglected. Abandoning his previous diatribes against the democratic process and trade unionism, he wrote his pamphlet *Left Communism—Infantile Disease of Communism.* The booklet took to task those foreign comrades who were reluctant to exploit the opportunities provided them by existing trade unions and parliamentary institutions in their own countries. This attitude was mistaken, naive, and childish, he admonished. By participating in parliamentary or trade union activities, a revolutionary proletarian party would not necessarily become a parliamentary reformist party. Tactical alliances with non-Communist groups were permitted, provided the Communists retained their organizational as well as ideological identity. Flexible tactics adapted to changing local conditions were to be used by all foreign Communist parties. But above all, the politics of foreign comrades ought to be guided by one objective, that of helping the infant Soviet State.

THE SECOND CONGRESS
OF THE COMINTERN

The slow rate of the postwar European economic recovery led to mounting restlessness of the masses and the spread of social ferment. This was reflected in the mushrooming of Communist parties. Consequently, when the Second Congress of the Comintern gathered in Moscow in July 1920, it was a much more impressive affair than the first; this time some two hundred delegates represented forty-one Communist parties. They stressed not only defending the Soviet State, but also carrying the revolution abroad through Poland to Germany. The Congress exhorted the Red Army, then fighting the Poles, to capture Warsaw and not to lay down its arms until Poland had become a member of a world federation of Soviet republics.

While deliberating about the future "International Soviet Republic," the Congress laid down the organizational foundations of the world Communist movement in the form of twenty-one conditions for admission to the Comintern. They were molded by the Leninist assumption that a small, doctrinally pure, hierarchically structured party would be preferable to a broad, loosely organized mass movement. To be admitted to the Comintern as a section, each party had to have its platform approved by the Comintern. Each platform had to denounce colonial exploitation and actively work for the destruction of colonial empires. Each party had to carry out periodic purges and expel from its ranks all reformists and gradualists and introduce the Bolshevik principles of "democratic centralism" in its functioning. This meant, first, election to all leading party organs from lower to higher bodies, from primary cells to top executive committees; second, periodic reports of the elected party organizations; third, complete subordination of the minority to the majority; fourth, the absolutely binding character of decisions of higher bodies upon lower bodies. Out-

wardly, the formula was to strike a balance between authority and autonomy, central control and local initiative. In actuality, however, democratic centralism as practiced by people brought up in the Bolshevik tradition of centralism meant stressing authority over democracy, and resulted in the strict subordination of the lower bodies to the will of the self-perpetuating, increasingly co-opted, and nonelected leadership.

By imposing their own specifically interpreted principles of democratic centralism upon the national sections of the Comintern, the Soviet leaders had started the process of eliminating from the newly formed Communist parties the still lingering Social Democratic spirit and gradually assimilating the member parties to the Soviet patterns. This conscious and systematic "Bolshevization" soon resulted in a far-reaching unification of the international Communist movement. As a consequence, the Comintern soon became not a federation of autonomous parties, but an integrated organization spreading its branches to each and every country. This was reflected in the terminology used by the Comintern. Each member party was to bear the uniform title "The Communist Party of . . ." (a given country), followed by the words, "Section of the Communist International."

In addition to these integrative, Bolshevizing measures undertaken by the Soviet leadership, further control over the Comintern was to be exercised through the establishment of its General Headquarters in Moscow. This advantage was further enhanced by the composition of the Executive Committee of the Comintern. Of the twenty-one seats, five were reserved for "the country in which the Executive Committee is located," while no other national section was to be represented by more than one delegate. Thus by 1920 the infant Soviet State had already managed to erect an institution which for over twenty years would function parallel with the Commissariat for Foreign Affairs, or *Narkomindel*. Although initially the Comintern seemed to be a rival of the Commissariat, soon the center of gravity began to shift to the Commissariat for Foreign Affairs.

DUALITY OF SOVIET FOREIGN POLICY

When the Red Army offensive was smashed at the Battle of Warsaw (August 14–18, 1920), the Comintern's original mood of jubilation gave way to one of frustration. The capitalist Jericho had failed to collapse before the trumpet blasts of Soviet propaganda, and the Comintern now had to settle down and face reality. The frontal offensive had to cede its place to a long series of shifting skirmishes, which Lenin characterized in *Left Communism* as "a war for the overthrow of the international bourgeoisie, a war which is a hundred times more difficult and complicated than the most stubborn of ordinary wars between states."

This strategy of indirect approach was reflected in the Third Congress of the Comintern, which again took place in Moscow, in June and July 1921. Following the proclamation of the NEP, Soviet Russia badly needed technical and financial aid from the West and could hardly afford to unduly offend the capitalist powers, especially Great Britain. This was one of the reasons the Third Congress played down the colonial problem. The main slogan of the Third Congress was "To the masses." Since the industrial working masses were largely controlled by the Social Democrats, a rival "Red International of Trade Unions" was set up. Its purpose was to split up the existing International Federation of Trade Unions run by the Second or Social Democratic International, and assure to the Communists direct access to the workers over the heads of their leaders. Later a Moscow-controlled international peasant organization was established to carry out a similar mission.

With the founding of the Comintern and its subsidiaries, the Soviet State assumed a dual character in world affairs. On the one hand, despite its largely novel socioeconomic and political structure, it was a state like any other. Through the People's Commissariat of Foreign Affairs (*Narkomindel*), it tried to conduct more or less conventional relations with other nations. On the other hand, Moscow was the general headquarters of a supranational, universalistic, militant movement (the Comintern) devoted to subverting all other non-Communist states. Both organizations were masterminded by the same center of disposition, the Bolshevik Party, and both operated out of Moscow. This was, however, repeatedly denied by Soviet state leaders, who pretended to be unaware of the activities and objectives of the Comintern, which was allegedly a private organization. This bifurcation of Soviet foreign policy was an unprecedented phenomenon in international relations. Sporadic mutual encouragement of internal subversion among rival nation-states was not a novel phenomenon in history. What was without precedent, however, was the open, institutionalized character of the Comintern's challenge to all existing states, as well as the worldwide scope of the Comintern's activity in the fields of propaganda, subversion, and intelligence gathering.

CONVENTIONAL DIPLOMATIC RELATIONS

Initially, Soviet leaders regarded their more traditional and largely improvised diplomatic activities as transient. Trotsky, the first Foreign Commissar, was convinced that after issuing a few revolutionary declarations, he would "close the shop" and shift his energies to more important matters. Following the Brest-Litovsk Treaty, however, and faced with the harsh realities of the international arena, the Bolsheviks had to revise their views. Gradually, the *Narkomindel* had to develop more systematic activities and establish outwardly conventional diplomatic, consular, and trade relations.

From the very beginning, Germany represented to Soviet Russia the most important country in Europe. Since the time of Peter the Great, the Russians had been fascinated with things German, as if to illustrate the maxim about the attraction of opposites. This fascination was inherited by the Russian Marxists for a variety of reasons. Both Marx and Engels were German. The strongest and most prestigious Marxist party in the early twentieth century was that of the German Social Democrats. Germany was the most advanced industrial state on the European continent. In addition, it was Berlin that had sent Lenin back to Russia in 1917 and initially lent him considerable support. It was on the German proletariat that Lenin focused his hopes during the early moments of the Bolshevik regime. And it was with the Germans and their allies that the first formal diplomatic agreement was signed at Brest-Litovsk by the Bolsheviks in March 1918. Not surprisingly, therefore, the German language became the first *lingua franca* of the Comintern.

As Lenin has anticipated, however, the Brest-Litovsk Treaty was soon swept away by the revolutionary event that took place in Germany in November 1918. The overthrow of the German Imperial regime brought to power a provisional government composed largely of Social Democrats. The reformist and gradualist German Social Democrats, however, refused to resume diplomatic relations with Moscow. Relations had been broken off the same year when the first Soviet envoy, Adolf Joffe, was ordered out of Berlin soon after his arrival shortly before the end of the war for having indulged in secret, subversive propaganda. In January 1919, as mentioned earlier, the attempted Communist uprising in Berlin had been ruthlessly crushed, and a number of Communist leaders executed.

Soviet relations with the sponsors of the Treaty of Versailles, France, Great Britain, and the United States, were still worse. The Civil War in Russia and the role played in it by the British, French, and American troops had not exactly endeared these powers to the Bolsheviks. According to the Bolsheviks, the British and French had won the "imperialistic" and "predatory" war and were busy dividing the spoils: markets and mandates, military bases and economic concessions. The newly created League of Nations was immediately denounced by Moscow as the "League of Robbers," an instrument of the Entente powers for the preservation of the post-Versailles system and the stabilization of capitalism, a "capitalist International."

Nevertheless, the Bolsheviks had to negotiate more or less conventional agreements with various components of the "capitalistic encirclement." During 1920 and 1921, having failed to subvert and conquer its western neighbors, Soviet Russia signed, one by one, peace treaties with Estonia, Latvia, Lithuania, Finland, and Poland. Romania was an exception because Moscow never recognized the incorporation of Bessarabia by Bucharest. Then came a trade agreement with Britain, followed by similar arrangements with Norway, Austria, and Italy.

The May 1921 trade agreement with London was of particular significance for the new rulers of Russia. To the Bolsheviks of the early 1920s, Britain still appeared as the great world power, the impressive center of a vast colonial empire, the main bastion of capitalism, and therefore the ultimate enemy of Communism. At that time the City of London, and not Wall Street, was the symbol of international capitalism. The trade pact was only a small break in the wall of isolation, since it was not immediately followed by *de jure* recognition of Russia's new regime and the resumption of full-scale diplomatic relations. However, the modest trade agreement with Great Britain was a significant step in the direction of normalizing relations with the capitalist world. The pact was signed largely on Soviet terms. Moscow did not reverse its repudiation of the pre-1917 debts and did not indemnify British investors. It was true that both sides pledged to "refrain from hostile acts and measures against the other party" and that the Soviet Government promised to "refrain from any attempt of incitement . . . of any Asiatic nations to activities hostile to British interests," but Moscow undertook these obligations with firm determination not to honor them. Yet the moral significance of the treaty was unmistakable; it spelled the gradual loss of the revolutionary zeal of the vanguard of world Communism.

Next to Great Britain, France was regarded by Bolshevik leaders as the major enemy of the Soviet state and world Communism. During the Civil War, it was Paris that had been in the vanguard of the intervention. During the 1920s, it was France that managed to construct in Eastern Europe a network of treaties of alliance with Poland, Czechoslovakia, Romania, and Yugoslavia. The purpose of these alliances was twofold: the French clients were not only to watch over a defeated, but restless and still potentially dangerous, Germany by serving as a *barrière de l'est,* but also to contain Communist Russia by forming a *cordon sanitaire,* or quarantine line, against Bolshevism. The hostility and suspicion of the French and British toward these two outcasts of the Versailles system gradually tended to push them toward each other.

THE RAPALLO TREATY

The first step toward breaking through the wall of isolation surrounding Soviet Russia was the international conference of April 1922 in Genoa. The conference was an attempt by the European countries to deal collectively with their postwar economic problems. The two outcasts, the Russians and the Germans, were invited because it was widely believed that their cooperation would be indispensable to Europe's economic rehabilitation.

The Genoa Conference was a memorable event in Soviet history; it could be compared to the first appearance of Communist Chinese delegates at the United Nations (UN) in 1972. For the first time since the Revolution a large Soviet diplomatic delegation appeared outside its native land at an important international gathering. The delegation was led by the second Soviet Commissar for Foreign Affairs, Grigori Chicherin, dressed—surprisingly—like all the other delegates, in top hat and cutaway. Of aristocratic origin, he displayed impeccable manners and spoke fluent French. The attitude of the Russians toward the Genoa Conference was mixed. On the one hand, they saw an opportunity to secure Western economic aid for their country; on the other, they suspected that their capitalist creditors might form a united front and again raise the issue of the old Tsarist debts. While participating in the official activities of the conference, Chicherin never lost sight of his main aim, that of inducing Germany to collaborate with Soviet Russia, thereby permitting Russia to reenter the diplomatic arena hand in hand with a potentially powerful partner. Chicherin's cause was helped by Allied claims for German war reparations, amounting to approximately 132 billion gold marks. The Germans had anticipated the stiffening of the Western powers' attitude in this matter. Since the Russians were also afraid of the renewal of Western pressure concerning the Tsarist debts, this—combined with the existing social boycott of the two pariahs of Europe—automatically created a strong community of interests between the Russians and the Germans. Almost immediately after the opening of the conference, secret negotiations between the two delegations began at a nearby resort town, Rapallo.

From the Soviet point of view, Germany was a large reservoir of unemployed military personnel and a source of the technical knowhow so badly needed for the reconstruction of the Soviet armed forces and their devastated war industry. The Soviet economy also needed German civilian engineers to speed its rehabilitation. Berlin's goal, on the other hand, was to evade the disarmament clauses of the Treaty of Versailles, which limited the German Army to 100,000 men, deprived it of its general staff, and forbade the manufacturing as well as the maintaining of tanks, planes, and poison gas. These could be done on Soviet soil.

Chicherin's policy of rapprochement with Germany had been pursued methodically. The first step in that direction was the agreement signed in April 1920 providing for the return of POWs and civilian internees. A year later, on May 6, 1921, a regular trade agreement was concluded between the two countries. At approximately the same time, the Red Army command began secret talks concerning clandestine military collaboration with the skeleton German Army.

The events that eventually pushed Germany into the Soviets' arms were precipitated by their fear of Western demands for strict execution of the reparation clauses of the peace treaty. (One should remember that the French had inserted Article 116 into the Treaty of Versailles, signed in June 1919, at a time when the Entente Powers were anticipating a speedy White victory in Russia.) Article 116 reserved for Russia, which did not attend the Paris Peace Conference, the right to obtain reparations from Germany. The clause was inserted with the expectation that the reconstruction of Russia, and hence the repayment of prewar French investments, would be greatly facilitated by German war indemnities. However, the article boomeranged, for it frightened the Germans and made them more susceptible to Chicherin's offer. He suggested the cancellation of mutual debts and a loose cooperation in defiance of the Western powers.

On April 16, 1922, at Rapallo, Chicherin and his German counterpart, Walter Rathenau, signed a Treaty of Friendship and Cooperation. The agreement provided for resumption of normal diplomatic relations between the two countries; both sides renounced all war reparations and granted each other preferential treatment in trade relations. The pact also provided for mutual

Gregory Chicherin, People's Commissar for Foreign Affairs, 1918–1930

consultation prior to all important international agreements. The Treaty of Rapallo, despite its modest title and outwardly innocuous content, covered a variety of cooperative Soviet–German ventures, including secret military arrangements. It was an important turning point in the diplomatic annals of Soviet Russia and a significant factor in European diplomacy for well over a decade. The treaty formed the foundation for a partnership between the two great losers of World War I, who were now bent on sharing their isolation in order to defy the Versailles system and jointly overcome their temporary weaknesses. For Soviet Russia, Rapallo was a great diplomatic victory; it represented Moscow's return to an active role in the diplomatic arena on terms of equality.

For the Western powers, Rapallo came as a shock. In London it brought about the fall of Lloyd George's cabinet. In Paris, Rapallo caused alarm lest it be followed by the evasion of the disarmament clauses of the

Versailles Treaty by Germany and threaten France's East European allies from the east, thus effectively neutralizing their role as anti-German instruments.[1]

THE AFTERMATH OF RAPALLO

The consequences of the Soviet–German agreement of 1922 were far-reaching. German experts began to build on Russian soil war planes and submarines as well as to manufacture poison gas. Such firms as Krupp, Daimler, and Rheinmetal established branches in Russia and began to produce tanks in cooperation with Soviet technicians. These collaborative ventures in manufacturing war material were paralleled by the exchange of military but not naval, personnel. German officers were sent to Russia to attend military training courses; Soviet officers, including such aces as Tukhachevsky, were dispatched for the same purpose to Germany. Three secret German military training grounds were established in Russia: one for tanks, another for chemical warfare, and a third for aviation. The foundations of German rearmament were laid down on Soviet soil, thanks to Rapallo. Military collaboration was accompanied by economic cooperation between the two partners. From 1926 on, Berlin gave guarantees to German firms that sold goods to the Russians on credit. Soon Germany regained its position as Russia's major economic partner. The close collaboration between the two countries continued until 1934, after Hitler's seizure of power.

Despite the pact's mutual benefits, Soviet–German relations were characterized by a strange ambivalence. On the one hand, the *Narkomindel* considered Berlin its main partner in the field of international relations. On the other hand, highly industrialized Germany, with its vast masses of class-conscious proletarians and the largest Communist movement outside Soviet Russia, was still considered the key target of the Comintern's revolutionary strategy. Here the Soviet quest for security through an alliance with a strong, stable partner clashed with its hope of subverting this very partner in order to gain a jumping-off point for further Communist expansion in Europe—indeed, in the whole world.

The best example of this schizophrenia occurred in 1923. At that time Germany was suffering from a disastrous economic depression, acute social unrest, and chronic political instability; inflation had spiraled to an unprecedented extent. Only a wheelbarrow full of money would suffice for the daily shopping. The situation was aggravated by the problems of war reparations and the feverish agitation for a revision of the Treaty of Versailles. In January 1923, the German Government refused to pay the current installment on its reparations. Paris replied by militarily occupying the Ruhr Basin, a vital industrial area on the Rhine. This in turn precipitated a wave of passive resistance, sabotage, and acts of terror, not only in the Ruhr but throughout the entire Rhineland, then still under inter-Allied military control. Moscow believed that occupation of the Ruhr might be the first step toward French domination of the Continent, and with luck, the beginning of a European general war. The "revolutionary situation" created by the Ruhr crisis was a temptation to Comintern strategists, convinced that the hour of the proletarian revolution in Germany was at hand. Karl Radek, a close co-worker of the head of the Comintern, Zinoviev, advocated a "united front," that is, cooperation between Communists and Socialists, and even a "popular front," or an alliance of all elements opposing the status quo, including even German nationalists. He urged the German Communists to work hand-in-hand with all political elements in fighting the French and to make the national cause their own.

---

[1] For an introduction to Soviet–German dealings during the Weimar republic, see Gerald Freund, *Unholy Alliance: Russo-German Relations from the Treaty of Brest-Litovsk to the Treaty of Berlin* (New York: Harcourt Brace Jovanovich, 1957); see also F. L. Carsten, "The Reichswehr and the Red Army," *Survey* (London; October 1962).

The ferment continued in Germany, and Zinoviev resolved to take advantage of the apparent opportunity to spread Communism to the West. There was, however, sharp disagreement on the timing and the methods to be used. Trotsky and Radek supported Zinoviev's optimistic estimate of the situation, while Stalin took a negative view of it. The German Communist leader Heinrich Brandler came to Moscow for consultation and returned to Berlin with a set of instructions that encouraged him to seize power in Germany. The first step in this direction was to be the entry of the Communists into a coalition with the socialists of Saxony. There the elections had given an absolute majority in the local parliament, or *Landtag,* to the unified Social Democrats and Communists. Since a similar situation also existed in Thuringia, things looked hopeful to the Comintern strategists. The Berlin Government and the German Army, however, had been forewarned about the Communist designs. Brandler's appeal for a general strike issued on October 21 met with little response from the German working masses. Meanwhile, on October 22, another Communist leader, Ernst Thaelman, started a revolt in Hamburg at Moscow's insistence. The small but efficient *Reichswehr* ruthlessly put down both centers of revolt.

Almost simultaneously, another radical but right-wing and nationalistic leader, Adlof Hitler, seized on the prevailing confusion and staged his rightist revolt in Munich. The suppression of his *putsch* cost him an imprisonment in the fortress of Landsberg. There he wrote his main work, *Mein Kampf* (or *My Struggle*), the bible of his National Socialist movement. One of the book's main themes was the author's deep hatred for the non-Aryan, "inferior races," not only for Jews, but also for Slavs, and his vision of a vaster living space (*Lebensraum*) for the Germans to be found on the plains of the Soviet Union, mainly in the Ukraine.[2]

The failure of the Comintern's German

stratagem had its repercussions in the incipient struggle for power then beginning in Russia. (This is discussed in the next chapter). The defeat of the German Communists diminished the role of the Comintern and adversely affected the prestige of its head, Zinoviev. The failure also undermined the position of Trotsky, whose theory of "permanent revolution" was discredited by the events of 1923 in Germany.

SOVIET RUSSIA AND THE ORIENT

Next to Germany, the most important foreign policy item on the agenda of the Soviet leadership in the 1920s was the problem of the colonial and semicolonial countries of the Orient, especially China. Russo-Chinese relations go as far back as Peter the Great, who by the Treaty of Nerchensk of 1689 expanded the Muscovite boundary in southern Siberia at China's expense. This expansion, slowed down under his successors, was resumed around the middle of the nineteenth century, when the antiquated Chinese Empire was weakened by the Opium War of the 1840s and by various European encroachments. In the chaotic situation of the 1860s, Russian pioneers, frontiersmen, and eventually statesmen wrested three large territories from Peking by various means. The first of these, then called Turkestan, stretched from the present Chinese province of Sinkiang all the way westward to the Aral and Caspian seas. The second was Outer Mongolia, and the third included the present-day Soviet maritime provinces on the Pacific Ocean. These enormous stretches of land covered all the area east of the Ussuri and north of the Amur rivers and amounted to some 580,000 square miles, a region as big as Alaska. Tsarist control of Outer Mongolia—which in 1911 declared itself an "autonomous republic" but was actually a protectorate of St. Petersburg—pushed the Russian holdings within approximately 400 miles of Peking.

The revolution of 1905 was closely watched by Sun Yat-sen, head of the

---

[2] Norman Rich, *Hitler's War Aims, Vol. I* (New York: W. W. Norton and Company, 1974).

Chinese nationalists. The downfall of the Manchu dynasty in 1911 plunged China into anarchy. Sun Yat-sen was unable to control it and consolidate his hold on the country torn by a civil war. Greatly impressed by the Bolshevik Party and its techniques for the seizure of power, he resolved to follow in their footsteps and apply some of Lenin's methods, if not his ideology, to his own party, the *Kuomintang*. Sun Yat-sen considered the Bolshevik Party to be both an ally and an organizational model, but he rejected Communist doctrine, with the exception of its anticolonialism and its antiimperialism. Moreover, he welcomed whatever technical and military help Moscow would send him to free China from foreign overlordship and to modernize his country.

From the Soviet point of view, cooperation with the *Kuomintang*, the strongest political movement in Asia and a staunch opponent of "Western imperialism," was of considerable value. To Lenin, the Western colonies were the weakest link in the capitalist chain. Anticolonialism was a fundamental principle of the Comintern. One of its early proclamations appealed to the "colonial slaves of Africa and Asia," and promised them that "the hour of proletarian dictatorship in Europe will also be the day of your own liberation." The chief purpose of this propaganda for national liberation was to undermine the hold the Western powers Great Britain and France had on their overseas possessions, and thereby weaken their economic and consequent military potential. The British, whom Bolshevik leaders still considered as their main enemies both in Europe and in Asia, were singled out by Comintern propaganda as the chief oppressors and exploiters of the colonial lands. As Bukharin frankly admitted, the Communists were willing to support the slogan of independence even for "Hottentots, Bushmen, Negroes, Hindus, etc.," precisely because their struggle for national liberation hurt Soviet Russia's main enemy, the British. If the colonial tentacles of the British and the French could be cut in Asia, Africa would follow, and the West, deprived

of its sources of raw material and markets, would then become easy prey for domestic proletarian revolution.

The Second Congress of the Comintern repeated the anticolonialist slogans of the First and went a step further; it organized the Congress of Peoples of the East in Baku in September 1920. There the Comintern proclaimed itself the champion of the struggle against colonialism. Zinoviev summoned the Muslims to a "holy war" against the Western exploiters and oppressors. He stressed the role of Communism as a natural protector of the suppressed and exploited colonial peoples of the world, especially of Asia. The Comintern propaganda did not hesitate to compare the trip to Baku with the yearly pilgrimage every pious Muslim is expected to make to the holy places of Mecca and Medina. Through the Middle East, Zinoviev said, Communist-inspired agitation would penetrate to India and China.

Lenin realized the crucial importance of China in the anti-Western strategy. Aware that the Tsarist expansionist and imperialist heritage there was a hindrance to the Bolshevik plans, he proceeded to sweep away its remains immediately after the Revolution. During 1919 and 1920, Moscow repeatedly denounced the "unequal treaties" imposed by the Tsarist Government upon Peking and gave up most of the Tsarist privileges, including the extraterritorial rights that had been extracted by St. Petersburg from the Chinese Government. Initially, Soviet diplomacy carefully dissociated itself from the customary, and often discriminatory, practices of the Western powers in the Orient, such as separate law courts, extraterritorial rights, and exclusive clubs. The Russians even promised to restore to Peking the Chinese Eastern Railway, the branch of the Trans-Siberian Railroad. This, however, never materialized. After the initial period of anti-imperialist euphoria, the Bolsheviks sobered up and proceeded to act as spokesmen for perceived Russian national interests. They kept the Chinese Eastern Railway and even reasserted the protectorate over Outer Mongolia first extended by Nicholas II in 1912.

In 1921, a tiny Communist Party of China was organized. Following the Comintern's instructions, it soon accepted the idea of a "united front." Sun Yat-sen, who needed Russian assistance and every bit of domestic help he could muster, promptly accepted the hand extended to him by the then minuscule Communist Party. Soon a team of Soviet advisers was sent to China under the leadership of the versatile Michael Borodin. The *Kuomintang* was accepted as an "associate member" of the Comintern, and the Chinese Communists were allowed to join the *Kuomintang* without giving up their original party affiliation. All this time the country was ravaged by civil war; numerous centers of power and local warlords were fighting with each other for control over a country vaster than Europe. The domestic struggle for power was complicated by the competition between the Western powers and Japan for control of Asian markets and bases. In Europe, Moscow's major preoccupation at that time was the fear of a possible rapprochement between Great Britain and Germany. Soviet leaders were apprehensive lest London, bent on restoring the European balance of power and allegedly upset by the French preponderance in Eastern Europe, offer an alliance to Weimar Germany and thus lure Berlin from the Rapallo partnership. In Asia, the possibility of London's returning to an alliance with Japan was never completely absent from the calculations of the Soviet leaders, mindful of the 1902–1905 precedent.

AFGHANISTAN, PERSIA, AND TURKEY

In both Europe and Asia the common denominator of a possible anti-Soviet coalition was Great Britain. Consequently, the entire Soviet policy throughout the Orient, not only in the Far East but also in the Near and Middle East, should be viewed as a struggle against British influence. To create as many

difficulties as possible for the British was Moscow's chief objective. It is in this light that one should examine the subsequent Soviet policies along the Oriental semicircle that stretches from China to Afghanistan, Persia (Iran), and Turkey.

As in the case of China, soon after the seizure of power the Bolsheviks renounced the special position of Imperial Russia in Afghanistan, Persia, now known as Iran, and Turkey, and signed a series of agreements with these countries. The 1921 treaty with Persia was of particular significance. The Soviets renounced all claims to the railways and military highways the Tsarist authorities had built in northern Persia, then treated as a Russian sphere of influence. Moscow also gave up its rights to all the lands belonging to the Russo-Persian Bank. This contrasted with the attitude of the British, who strictly maintained all the rights and privileges deriving from the treaty of 1907 that had made southern Persia a British sphere of influence. But even at this early idealistic and utopian stage of Soviet policy, Lenin insisted on a quid pro quo in the form of fishing concessions for Russia in the Persian-controlled southern segment of the Caspian Sea (a major source of sturgeon and hence of caviar), and for a voice in determining Persian tariffs. The latter concession soon began to pay handsome dividends and catapulted Soviet exports to Persia into second place in Soviet trade, just behind Great Britain.

Another interesting aspect of the Soviet-Persian Treaty of 1921 was the right granted to Moscow to send their troops into Persia, should the government in Teheran be unable to prevent a third power from using Persian territory as a base of operation against Soviet Russia.

In 1921, Soviet Russia also concluded a treaty of "Peace and Friendship" with another country nurturing numerous grudges against the British after World War I, the defeated Turkey. In the treaty, the Soviet Government agreed to give up the Armenian cities of Kars and Ardahan, which Tsar Alexander II had acquired at the end of the

Russo-Turkish war of 1877–1878. This dramatic reversal of Moscow's policies toward Turkey was especially noteworthy in view of the implacable and almost continuous hostility that had characterized the relations between the two countries for over two hundred years. In addition to the renunciation of past privileges and territorial concessions, the Bolshevik leadership now offered the Turks their assistance in their efforts to recover from the catastrophe of the Great War. Reversing the traditional and relentlessly pursued policy of the Tsars, the Bolsheviks insisted that the Turks alone be left as guardians of the strategic Black Sea Straits, the Bosphorus and the Dardanelles. Moscow declared that they were no longer needed for Russia's safety and insisted that Soviet security could be safeguarded as long as free commercial passage from the Black Sea to the Mediterranean would be assured. The new Russia, it was argued, no longer needed the Straits to be open to their Black Sea fleet in order to enter the Mediterranean. On the other hand, Moscow urged the closing of the Bosphorus and the Dardanelles to warships of foreign powers wishing to penetrate the Black Sea. The fact that Turkey was dictatorially ruled with an iron fist by Kemal Atatürk and pursued a policy of repression of its native Communists was not an obstacle.

From the beginning, Moscow's attitude to the revolution in the Orient was different from that in the West. In the West the struggle was primarily that of the industrial proletariat against the bourgeoisie, with the peasants acting as a sporadic auxiliary force. In the East, there were very few industrial workers. Consequently, the Comintern was resolved to support temporarily the "local national liberation" movements, represented mostly by "progressive" bourgeoisie in its opposition to both "Western imperialism" and native feudalism. In the long run, it was calculated in Moscow, the backing lent to the native bourgeoisie by the Comintern would not hinder the eventual destruction of capitalism, but would merely postpone it.

SUMMARY

During its first decade, Soviet diplomacy was characterized by a pronounced duality; it often made idealistic gestures, but never entirely forgot Russian national interests, which were simply expressed in the Marxist verbiage and in the light of "proletarian internationalism." Soon, however, "proletarian internationalism" was subject to a reexamination that gradually changed its meaning entirely. When the great revolutionary expectations and euphoria of 1917–1920 faded away, the Bolsheviks, while still paying lip service to the old slogans, gradually reconciled themselves to existing realities. They accepted the "temporary stabilization" of capitalism and tried to adjust themselves to the facts of international life. The Baku Congress was not reconvened.

Initially, Soviet diplomats were distinguished by a demonstrative "proletarian" and "revolutionary" style; for instance, they used different titles, refused to wear the customary dress uniforms, and so on. Soviet diplomacy, however, little by little, conformed to the alien environment in which it had to function. The outward bifurcation of the Soviet foreign policy expressed in the symbiosis of the *Narkomindel* and the *Comintern* persisted until the late 1930s, but the center of gravity was dramatically shifting already during the early 1920s toward the conventional style of diplomacy.

Although the Comintern's activities occasionally caused a great deal of embarrassment to the *Narkomindel,* they also paid handsome dividends, for they provided Moscow with excellent sources of intelligence, as well as with an instrument of pressure on other governments. It was largely owing to the Comintern that the Soviet Union, despite its limited military and economic capabilities, did play the role of a de facto world power by the late 1920s. In every country of the globe, local Communist parties not only voiced the grievances of their own proletarian masses, but also defended the interests of "the Rome of the Proletariat."

SUGGESTED READING

ANGRESS, WERNER T., *Stillborn Revolution: the Communist Bid for Power in Germany, 1921–1923*. Princeton, N.J.: Princeton University Press, 1963.

BORKENAU, FRANZ, *World Communism: A History of the Communist International*. New York: Norton, 1939.

CARR, E. H., *German-Soviet Relations between the Two World Wars, 1919–1929*. Baltimore, Md.: Johns Hopkins Press, 1951.

DALLIN, DAVID J., *The Rise of Russia in Asia*. New Haven, Conn.: Yale University Press, 1949.

DEGRAS, JANE, ed., *Calendar of Soviet Documents on Foreign Policy, 1917–1941*. New York: Royal Institute of International Affairs, 1948.

———, *Soviet Documents on Foreign Policy*. New York: Oxford University Press, 1951–1953, 3 vols.

———, *The Communist International, 1919–1943*. London: L. Cass, 1971.

FISCHER, LOUIS, *The Soviets in World Affairs, 1917–1929* (2nd ed.). Princeton, N.J.: Princeton University Press, 1951, 2 vols.

FISCHER, RUTH, *Stalin and German Communism*. Cambridge, Mass.: Harvard University Press, 1948.

FREUND, GERALD, *Unholy Alliance: Russo-German Relations from the Treaty of Brest-Litovsk to the Treaty of Berlin*. New York: Harcourt Brace Jovanovich, 1957.

HILGER, GUSTAV, and ALFRED G. MEYER, *The Incompatible Allies: A Memoir-History of German-Soviet Relations, 1918–1941*. New York: Macmillan, 1953.

HULSE, JAMES W., *The Forming of the Communist International*. Stanford, Calif.: Hoover, 1964.

ISAACS, HAROLD R., *The Tragedy of the Chinese Revolution* (rev. ed.). Stanford, Calif.: Stanford University Press, 1951.

KENNAN, GEORGE F., *Russia and the West under Lenin and Stalin*. Boston: Little, Brown, 1961.

TANG, PETER S. H., *Russia and the Soviet Policy in Manchuria, 1911–1931*. Durham, N.C.: Duke University Press, 1959.

ULAM, ADAM B., *Expansion and Coexistence: The History of Soviet Foreign Policy, 1917–1967*, Chaps. 1–4. New York: Praeger, 1968.

ULLMAN, RICHARD H., *Anglo-Soviet Relations, 1917–1921*. Princeton, N.J.: Princeton University Press, 1961–1973, 3 vols.

WHITING, ALLEN S., *Soviet Policy in China, 1917–1924*. Cambridge, Mass.: Harvard University Press, 1954.

ZENKOVSKY, SERGE A., *Pan-Turkism and Islam in Russia*. Cambridge, Mass.: Harvard University Press, 1960.

CHAPTER 11

The Formation of the USSR and Lenin's Death

While reorganizing their economy and groping for a new international bearing, Soviet leaders were also reshaping the structure of their state as it emerged from the ravages of the Civil War. At the time, Lenin was ailing, and the prospect of his death triggered the first jockeying for position of advantage by potential successors. The constitutional issue and the problem of succession were closely interconnected.

As discussed earlier, the Civil War resulted in the eventual reconquest of the Dnieper Ukraine, Belorussia, and the three Caucasian republics–Georgia, Armenia, and Azerbaijan–by what was then called the Russian Socialist Federal Soviet Republic (RSFSR). Through an agreement with Tokyo, the Far Eastern Province, temporarily a Japanese protectorate, also rejoined the RSFSR in 1922. Meanwhile, at Stalin's insistence and despite the fierce opposition of many Georgian Communists, Georgia, Armenia, and Azerbaijan were merged into a single Trans-caucasian Re-

public. Thus, although a large segment of the multinational western fringe was lost, the remaining core of about 140 million people was about 48 percent non-Russian (64 million people). They represented a bewildering variety of ethnic groups at various stages of cultural and socioeconomic development. While the Great Russian heartland, especially its major cities, was fairly Westernized, most of the seminomadic inhabitants of Central Asia, the Muslim tribes of the Northern Caucasus, and the inhabitants of Siberia were backward, illiterate, and lacked a conscious feeling of nationality.

FEDERALISM VERSUS CENTRALISM

How to weld these areas and peoples together again was the subject of lively and often embittered discussion in the Party and in government circles in the early 1920s. The 1918 Constitution had already provided for a federal structure, which was favored by Lenin himself. Once again, as with the peasant question, he followed the SR program. On the other hand, people like Trotsky, Stalin, and Dzerzhinsky opposed federalism as making undue concessions to local nationalism and thus being fraught with danger. Instead, they favored central-ism, combined with limited autonomy if local conditions warranted. Yet the emerg-ing Soviet Republic was very similar to the former Imperial Russia, at least in one re-spect: it was decidedly a multinational state.

Both Lenin and Stalin had observed how shallow and ineffective had been the Tsarist policy of Russification, and how difficult it had been to impose Russian-Communist rule on the borderlands during the Civil War. In view of this, federalism seemed a better solution. Federalism was in accord-ance with the Bolshevik slogan of national self-determination so loudly proclaimed during the Civil War; it tended, moreover, to soften the impact of the reconquest of non-Russian areas by permitting the contin-ued coexistence of various peculiarities in an ethnically heterogeneous republic, while the existence of an ethnic mosaic of peoples, some of them without developed national sentiments, provided an opportunity for Communist social engineering. In addition to these not inconsiderable advantages, fed-eralism, if shrewdly manipulated, would make the Soviet State a structure open to others who might wish to join it in the future.

All these assets were eventually recog-nized even by the opponents of federalism. On December 27, 1922, the Tenth All-Russian Congress of Soviets accepted Sta-lin's motion to establish the Union of Soviet Socialist Republics, or USSR. It was origi-nally composed of four member-republics: Russia, the Ukraine, Belorussia, and Trans-caucasus. In October 1924, the Russian Re-public split and gave birth to two Central Asian Republics: Uzbek and Turkmen. In 1929 these six republics were joined by the Tajik Soviet Republic. In 1936 the Trans-caucasian Republic broke into three

segments—Georgia, Armenia, and Azer-baijan—thereby transforming the USSR at that time into a union of nine federated segments. Within most Soviet republics, es-pecially within the RSFSR, settlements of smaller ethnic groups were consolidated into autonomous areas in accordance with their stage of development. The RSFSR, for instance, contained a Volga German auton-omous republic and the autonomous terri-tory of the Kalmucks.

By 1923, the USSR had framed a new constitution. Ratified in 1924, it remained in force until 1936. The new charter was merely the former constitution of 1918 ad-justed to the new federal structure of the Soviet State. The 1924 basic law differenti-ated between the governmental bodies of the USSR, or the Union, and those of the four previously mentioned individual Union Republics then in existence. The All-Union Congress of Soviets was made bicameral and was to be composed of the Council of the Union and the Council of Nationalities. While the Council of the Union was to be selected on the basis of population, the Council of Nationalities was to be composed of five delegates from each Union Republic and each autonomous re-public, and one delegate from each autono-mous district (*oblast*).

The Constitution provided for three kinds of ministries, then still called commis-sariats. There was the All-Union Commis-sariat for the USSR as a whole, and one for each Union-Republic or autonomous re-public. The federal, or All-Union, govern-ment was given authority in questions of armed forces, war and peace, foreign rela-tions, foreign trade, and fiscal matters, as well as for economic planning for the USSR as a whole. The authority of the constituent republics was limited to such powers as were not reserved for the All-Union government, and this was precious little. The new char-ter also provided for the establishment of a Supreme Court for the whole USSR. There was no bill of rights, and no change was made in preunification legal systems.

The supreme power of the USSR theoretically was represented by the All-Union Congress of Soviets. The Congress, consisting of delegates from the soviets, was to be summoned every year by its Central Executive Committee. Only the lowest in the hierarchical pyramid, the village and city soviets, were to be elected by direct vote. All the higher soviets, the county, province, and republican ones, were composed of delegates selected by the soviets immediately below. The franchise was limited to people over eighteen involved in "productive work"; this included officials and soldiers but excluded former members of the bourgeoisie and priests. The Executive Committee was to be elected by the All-Union Congress from among its members and was to act as a governing body between congresses. The actual governmental functions of the Committee were to be performed by its Presidium, the chairman of which was to act as head of state. The first Chairman of the Presidium was Mikhail I. Kalinin, son of a poor peasant from the Tver province, a metal worker until 1917, and a man of flexible disposition. He was ideally suited to perform this purely symbolic function in full harmony with the wishes of the ruling Party, as he was to do for well over twenty years.

Like the Constitution of 1918, the new charter bore only a vague relationship to political realities and power in the USSR and had a strong propagandistic ring. The preamble stated: "The family of brotherly peoples" of the USSR represents a "voluntary union of equal peoples, ready to embrace others who desire such association." The 1924 Constitution went so far as to provide for the right of each republic to secede freely from the USSR. Various semiofficial comments left no doubt, however, that a request for secession would be regarded as a hostile act opposed to the true interests of the proletariat which were best expressed by the Communist Party. The Constitution also made specific provision for the admission of "all Socialist Soviet republics, both those now in existence, and

Mikhail I. Kalinin, Chairman of the Central Executive Committee of the Soviets of the RSSR, 1919–1937, and Chairman of the Presidium of the USSR Supreme Soviet, 1937–1946

those which will arise in the future." Under the new charter, the USSR would thus continue to be the nucleus of an eventual world federation of Communist states. Presenting his report on the new Constitution, Stalin hailed it as a "decisive step on the road toward uniting the toilers of the whole world into a World Soviet Socialist Republic."

CENTRIPETAL FACTORS

The outward decentralization allegedly resulting from the establishment of the federal system was a daring and imaginative feat of political engineering. The operation was made possible by the preservation of the centralized and hierarchically organized Communist Party, which reached from its Moscow GHQ into the remotest provinces. It was the unitary Party that formed the firm infrastructure, the reliable nerve center of the USSR. The existence of this autocratic Party allowed the construction of an alluring and impressive federal facade for the Soviet State, yet simultaneously rendered federalism illusory. Like the 1918 Constitution of the RSFSR, the new charter of the USSR made no reference to the real locus of power.

Another factor that permitted the Bolsheviks to put federalism into practice and implement an outwardly liberal ethnic policy was the overwhelming strength of its Great Russian hard core, the RSFSR. In 1923–1924 it comprised about nine-tenths of the territory of the USSR and over two-thirds of its population. Of some 140 million people inhabiting the USSR at that time, slightly over 76 million were Great Russians, who in turn constituted nearly 80 percent of the membership of the Communist Party. Moreoever, within the territory of the Russian republic were situated three of the four major industrial centers of the USSR: Petrograd, Moscow, and the Southern Ural region. Only the fourth industrial area, the Ukraine, was outside the Russian Republic.

From the Soviet point of view, the establishment of a federal state served several purposes. First, it helped to attract and maintain within the Union those ethnic elements for whom Communism would otherwise have had little appeal, such as the radical yet nationalistic segments of various minority groups. Second, the theoretically generous ethnic policy was a potentially effective instrument of foreign expansion, especially among the states to the west of the Soviet Union like Poland, Romania, Czechoslovakia, or Turkey, where Ukrainian, Belorussian, or Armenian minorities lived without the benefit of an outwardly generous federal structure. In organizing their multinational federal state, the Bolsheviks were helped by their Civil War allies among the national minorities. The belief that national emancipation could be achieved through tactical, temporary cooperation with Communism was strong among leftist socialists, and even the radical democrats in various ethnic groups, especially the Ukrainians, the Belorussians, and some Moslems. Typical of them was the Ukrainian nationalist revolutionary leader Volodymyr K. Vinnychenko. He was convinced that by passing through the inevitable stage of "National Bolshevism" the Ukrainians might, perhaps, eventually achieve national independence. Among many Ukrainians this belief was strengthened by the development of their national culture, previously suppressed by the Tsarist administration and now flourishing under Soviet rule.

In the beginning, many of the pro-Bolshevik nationalists had reason to be optimistic because the Communist revolution, with its principle of expropriation of all the means of production, was definitely advantageous to the ethnic minorities, especially the Ukrainians and Belorussians. The upper classes in both regions were either Russian or Polish, and most of the capital, including the land, belonged to foreigners. During the period of the NEP, there was little collectivization. Many petty traders and small industrialists were natives, and the Communist administration, short of qualified people, had to rely on whatever local talent was available, which often meant overlooking the political views of the people who were not anti-Communists. Economic planning could already boast some achievements. The figures, although often inflated, were outwardly impressive. From 1922 on, Soviet mass media constantly reported the building of new factories, highways, railroads, and canals, like those connecting the Dvina, the Niemen, and the Dnieper with the Volga. Electric light began to appear in the villages.

The NEP was paralleled by the policy of "taking native roots" (*korenizatsiia*). Lenin in particular was determined to make the Communist system penetrate more deeply into the multinational fabric of the USSR. Consequently, national cultures were encouraged, education was fostered, native literatures were developed, often from scratch among some Central Asian tribes, and native tongues were revived. Lenin was in favor of teaching the national language and culture at state schools to every child of each nationality. On the other hand, he opposed separate political organizations (autonomous Communist parties) for each ethnic group.

Among the people who benefited from the Leninist ethnic policy were not only Ukrainians and Belorussians, but also some 3 million Jews, formerly largely restricted to the Pale of Settlement and cramped by its discriminatory legislation. As a result of the liberal revolution, the Jews had already obtained legal equality. The Bolsheviks officially condemned anti-Semitism and made it a punishable offense. Yiddish, the language of most Soviet Jews, was introduced into the Jewish schools. A Jewish press developed rapidly, and as early as the end of 1918, there were eighty-one Yiddish and ten Hebrew newspapers. A first-class Jewish theater was organized in Moscow. At the same time, however, religious Jews suffered from the official atheism of the new regime. Synagogues were being closed and rabbis often had to suffer indignities, not unlike the clergy of other denominations. At the same time, the Soviet regime, with the Jewish section of the Communist Party (or the *Yevsektsiia*) as its willing tool, was trying to assimilate the Jews into the rest of the population.

One method of assimilation was to diversify the hitherto rather one-sided socio-economic structure of the Jewish population by encouraging Jews to leave the urban centers, settle in the countryside, and practice agriculture. And indeed, during the 1920s Jewish villages were set up in the Ukraine and in the Far Eastern segment of Birobijan. The Jewish culture, like the Ukrainian and Belorussian, enjoyed a brief period of expansion and flowering. The internationalist aspects of the Communist doctrine greatly appealed to many cosmopolitan Jews, who sincerely believed that they were undergoing a process of genuine amalgamation. They renounced their Jewishness not in order to become Russians or Ukrainians, but "New Soviet Men," members of a supranational proletarian community to cover, eventually, "the great globe itself."

During the 1920s the Bolsheviks also paid a great deal of attention to the Muslim peoples, who numbered around 25 million. Kazakhs, Uzbeks, Turkmens, Tatars, and others were united by a common religion and the Arabic script. Mirza Sultan-Galiev, a Muslim Volga Tatar and a member of the All-Russian Muslim movement, was largely instrumental in reconquering the Central Asian provinces for the Bolsheviks. Once in control of Central Asia, the Bolsheviks began to pursue a step-by-step policy of integration. They gradually cut off the Muslims of the USSR from their brethren who lived south of its borders by discouraging travel and interpersonal contacts, and by replacing the original Arabic script first with the Latin and finally with the Russian. Secularization and Sovietization were fostered, initially without exaggerated zeal and excesses. "Don't paint nationalism red!" Lenin warned his comrades. Local cultures were to be "national in form but Marxist in content."

The Soviet ethnic policy was especially important in the Soviet Ukraine. As long as Poland, Romania, and Czechoslovakia ruled over the western segments of the Ukrainian people, an outwardly liberal policy could serve as a means of pressure and diversion against these countries. The granting of cultural, if not political, autonomy to the ethnic minorities was also very useful to the Comintern in its propaganda; it could present the USSR as an attractive model for all peoples of the world to join eventually or at least emulate.

LENIN'S ILLNESS

At the time the new Constitution was being formulated, Lenin had been partially paralyzed by his first stroke. His illness generally prevented him from exercising a more vigorous influence on the shape of the charter. For instance, the merger of the three Transcaucasian republics into one was carried out against his wishes, at Stalin's insistence and with Trotsky neglecting to support Lenin.

Lenin's illness had far-reaching consequences for the balance of forces within the ruling Party. He was Chairman of the Council of People's Commissars, or in Western terms, the Prime Minister. His authority as the Founding Father of the Party and the State was enormous. Hitherto, thanks to his exceptional authority, his manipulatory skills, and his powers of persuasion, Lenin exercised an overwhelming influence over Party affairs. With his influence gradually fading away from both government and partisan work, a vital linchpin of the still fluid Soviet system was removed. To fill the gap, the ailing Lenin wanted a resolute and resourceful deputy to carry out his functions as chief executive. Twice, in May and December of 1922, he offered the post of Vice-Chairman of the Council of People's Commissars to Trotsky. Trotsky twice refused the offer, pleading ill health.

During Lenin's illness, Trotsky, then Commissar for War and a member of the Politburo, was also frequently indisposed and absent from Moscow. The situation created a power vacuum and suggested new arrangements. One of them was to create a post that would effectively coordinate the working of the main Party bodies, like the Political and Organizational Bureaus (colloquially known as the Politburo and Orgburo) as well as the Party Control Commissions, with the fast multiplying state institutions. The name given to the new post established for that purpose was Secretary General of the Central Committee. The post seemed innocuous and was meant to be of a purely bureaucratic nature. The title suggested that the main function of the Secretary General would be to keep the Party records and act as the coordinator of various Party bodies in order to serve better what the by-laws termed the most important body of the Party structure: its Central Committee.

In May 1922, after Lenin's first stroke, Stalin was entrusted with this job. The office did not originally convey any political power of prestige and was bound to involve a lot of hard, thankless work. Nobody wanted the job except Stalin, who was reputed to be an efficient, tireless Party wheelhorse. Whether he perceived all the potentialities of the new position is not clear. Whatever his original motives, he did accept the job, and by methodical, patient work began to use it for his purposes. Since the Secretariat administered the personnel files, Stalin utilized this function to gain the vital power of appointment, and hence of patronage. Soon, under the meticulous management of a man with a flair for organization, an immense capacity for work and a lot of patience, the office of Secretary General became a formidable instrument, a reliable base for the expansion of Stalin's power. Systematically, he began his grassroots work. Imperceptibly, step by step, he began to gather around him his Civil War cronies and all those he could make dependent and subservient. At the same time, he was cultivating all who could be useful to him, while ruthlessly undercutting his potential opponents.

STALIN'S ASCENDENCE

The bedridden Lenin had noticed the growing power, intolerance, and arrogance of Stalin. He clearly anticipated the struggle for power that was likely to take place after his death, in view of the lack of rules to regulate this unprecedented situation. To provide some guidance for his comrades in their choice of his successor, Lenin wrote a memorandum, dated December 23, 1922, expressing his views about the Party's leading personalities and their possible future roles. Trotsky and Stalin were the two ablest members of the Central Committee, according to Lenin. Despite his high opinion of Stalin's native ability, he warned his Party comrade, "Comrade Stalin, having become Secretary General, has concentrated enormous power in his hands; I am not sure that he always knows how to use that power with sufficient caution." On January 9, 1923, Lenin added a postscript in which he issued another warning: "Stalin is too rude, and this fault, entirely supportable in relations among us Communists, becomes insupportable in the office of General Secretary." Lenin therefore proposed to find a way to remove Stalin from his position.

Lenin's memorandum, often called his Testament, came too late to have a decisive influence on the succession contest. Other factors had intervened. In October 1922, Lenin had recovered sufficiently to resume his active leadership for three months or so. Then, on December 16, came the third and final stroke, which resulted in his total loss of speech and incapacitated him permanently. From then on Lenin was able to communicate only by means of written messages. It was during his brief return to work that his relations with Stalin worsened. The split was triggered by Stalin's rudeness as well as his ruthless way of handling the nationality problem, especially the purge of Communist leadership in his native Georgia. Alarmed by Stalin's high-handed policies, Lenin wrote his "Letter on the National Question" on December 30–31, 1922, in which he criticized Stalin's "Great-Russian chauvinism," as expressed in his merging of the three newly annexed republics—Georgia, Armenia, and Azerbaijan—into a single Transcaucasian Republic. In addition, a few days before his third stroke, Lenin had learned about Stalin's rudeness to Nadyezhda Krupskaya, Lenin's wife since 1898. He wrote a blunt letter threatening to break off all personal relations with Stalin unless he apologized to Krupskaya.

By that time, however, Stalin, supported by two other Politburo members, Zinoviev and Kameniev, felt strong enough to prevent the publication of Lenin's Testament, or even its wider circulation in Party circles outside the top echelons. Zinoviev and Kameniev, both old Bolsheviks and close co-workers of Lenin, were at the head of the Party organization in Leningrad and Moscow respectively. Both of them, at that time, were more afraid of the brilliant and versatile Trotsky as a potential competitor for Lenin's mantle than of Stalin, whom

they regarded as a junior partner of the emerging triumvirate (or *Troika*).

Acting with a mixture of cunning and caution, Stalin continued to work hard behind the scenes by making himself useful to key Party members, thus improving his position within the only body that really mattered. His spade work produced its results at the Twelfth Party Congress, which deliberated from April 17 to 25, 1923. This was the first Congress from which Lenin was absent. Many delegates knew about Stalin's disagreements with the ailing leader over the nationality issue and personal matters. Yet the Congress was so well prepared and manipulated by Stalin that nobody dared to raise either issue. Trotsky, the only man who could have done so, refrained from exploiting these opportunities. Despite his earlier promises to Lenin, he did not take up the problem of Georgia, an issue on which Stalin was rather vulnerable.

Trotsky's disinclination to take advantage of the golden opportunity to present the two issues to a Party Congress not yet completely dominated by Stalin is an enigma. Later, Trotsky explained that such a step would have been embarrassing to him and beneath his dignity, but such an interpretation carries little conviction. His behavior suggests either lack of judgment or a lapse of will power, or perhaps both. So the course of the succession struggle was largely predetermined before Lenin's death by Trotsky's refusal to challenge Stalin with the authority of the still living Lenin and with Trotsky's supporters still in control of many vital posts. He himself was then still a member of the powerful Politburo, and Commissar for Army and Navy, thus controlling most of the formidable defense establishment.

LENIN'S DEATH

Trotsky's failure to act at the Twelfth Congress was aggravated by his absence from Moscow during the last days before Lenin's death, recovering from another illness.

Lenin died on January 21, 1924. Everyone expected Trotsky to rush back to the capital to attend the funeral. He did not do that, however, for reasons he later tried to explain in various ways; one of them was Stalin's telegram giving him a false, early funeral date and urging him not to interrupt his sick leave. Whatever the real reason, Trotsky was not in Moscow when Lenin's body was buried. The absence of the second most prestigious Bolshevik provided Stalin with an ideal opportunity to present himself as the closest and most loyal lieutenant of the dead leader.

Stalin not only eagerly presided over the funeral ceremonies and exploited the situation to the hilt, but he immediately followed it up with a series of moves to consolidate his new place in the Soviet hierarchy. At the meeting of the All-Union Congress of Soviets that was held on January 26 to commemorate Lenin, Stalin pledged to the

A line of Soviet people waiting to visit Lenin's Mausoleum in the Red Square in Moscow, 1924; Saint Basil's Church in the background

Party to carry out the deceased leader's presumed will. Each segment of his long, litanylike oration was followed by the rhetorical refrain: "We swear to thee, Comrade Lenin, that we will fulfill with honor thy command!" Stalin's funeral oration, often referred to as "the Lenin oath," tried to sum up, in the form of succinct slogans, the essence of the dead leader's teaching, and further enhanced Stalin's image as his loyal lieutenant.

Contrary to Lenin's intentions, an officially sponsored cult of his personality was promptly encouraged, and Petrograd was renamed Leningrad. On the order of a Politburo already largely dominated by the triumvirate and manipulated by Stalin, the dead leader's corpse was embalmed and placed in an impressive red granite mausoleum built next to the Kremlin in Red Square. This resulted in an almost uninterrupted and still ongoing series of pilgrimages by Soviet citizens, who began to come from the remotest parts of the USSR to pay homage to the mummy of the founder of the Soviet State and its ruling Party, a new, secularized version of St. Vladimir.

After the funeral, the Politburo decided to keep Stalin in his post of Secretary General and not to publish Lenin's "Testament." Again Trotsky could have insisted on disclosure, but again he refrained. This gave his rival time to consolidate his hold on the increasingly crucial post of Secretary General, now surrounded with Lenin's reflected glory and identified with his heritage.

LENIN IN PERSPECTIVE

Lenin's death brought to a close the initial, formative period of the Soviet State and its ruling Party. Lenin was the founder, organizer, unquestioned leader, and theoretician of both of them. With the seizure of power by the Bolsheviks, he became the top executive of the Soviet Republic, whose authority, although frequently challenged, was never seriously undermined. His position as founder of the Party, chief architect of its victory in 1917, and father of the Soviet Republic, as well as its savior in times of crisis, gave him a unique place in Soviet history. At least twice his decisions—one to sign the peace treaty with Germany and the other to abandon War Communism—rescued the Soviet regime from catastrophe. Formally, he was merely Chairman of the Council of People's Commissars and one member of the Politburo. Yet his power had a strong individual imprint and was virtually dictatorial. He remained the principal driving force of the State and the Party until his fatal illness in 1922.

Lenin's achievement as a leader of men was impressive. A provincial Russian lawyer, he built a small group of revolutionaries into an effective political organization. Out of the twenty or so original members of the Bolshevik party, he forged an instrument that in fourteen years captured control of the largest country of the world and has kept power for some three generations. The movement he created soon spread over the entire globe. In its various modified forms, the ideology fathered by him today controls over one-third of the earth. Although his movement has split into various sects and factions in the interim, one of the few things that still unites all of them is the cult of Lenin.

Lenin's personality was multifaceted and complex. Despite his preoccupation with action and organization, he wrote prolifically, with zest and vigor, and produced several books as well as innumerable articles and speeches. His collected writings number some fifty volumes. While Lenin's skills as a practical politician and statesman are generally accepted even by his fiercest opponents, his caliber as a philosopher and theoretical political writer is a more controversial point. Some of his more pragmatic works, such as *What Is To Be Done?*, are seminal political tracts written with polemical verve and the force of conviction. His *Development of Capitalism in Russia* (1899) is a work of factual socioeconomic research. *Imperialism, the Highest Stage of Capitalism* (1916), although not based on an original concept, is an important book because of the influence it has had not only on Soviet and Chinese policy but also on the Third World. On the other hand, his philosophical works, such as *Materialism and Empiro-criticism* (1909), are amateurish attempts at poaching in an unfamiliar field.

Despite numerous attempts at theory, Lenin was primarily a practical politician, endowed with an impressive sense of reality and a flexibility possessed by few men. These qualities were revealed many times during his career. The first was when he deemphasized the orthodox Marxist idea that the urban proletariat should be the main carrier of the revolution in predominantly rural Russia, and advocated an "alliance of workers and peasants." The second was when he adopted the agrarian and nationality programs of the Social Revolutionary Party. Third, he accepted the harsh Brest-Litovsk peace as a precondition of survival of the Soviet rule in Russia; and fourth, he launched the New Economic Policy. In each case his decision largely determined the fate of the Bolshevik party and the Soviet state.

As there are few purely theoretical considerations in Lenin's writings, so is there little Marxist orthodoxy in his practice.[1] While constantly paying lip service to the Word, Lenin reversed most basic assumptions of the Prophet. Whereas Marx stressed the paramount importance of "objective" socioeconomic conditions, the value of spontaneity, and the crucial role of the masses, Lenin emphasized the organized, willful effort of a small group consciously shaping events to fit their goals. While Marx hardly ever dealt with organizational matters and tended to dwell in the realm of lofty speculations, the down-to-earth Lenin stressed the role of organization and as-

signed crucial importance to it. In Lenin's teachings, the hierarchically structured elitist party was to play the decisive role; it was to overcome the impracticality of the intellectuals, the amorphous, anarchic spontaneity of the masses, and, as "the vanguard of the proletariat," it was to lead that class to victory. It was the Party that was to be the repository of power in the new type of state. The concept of a tightly woven, elitist, and militant Party represents the essence of what is called Leninism. This concept is probably the single most significant contribution of Lenin to Marxist political theory and practice.

Lenin's second major contribution to modern political theory was the adaptation of Marxist doctrine to conditions of a multinational, backward, agrarian country. In Russia this meant acceptance of the peasantry and the ethnic minorities as the main partners in the struggle against Tsarism. Recognizing the power of the peasantry, Lenin agreed to the highly non-Marxist distribution of the land, and in 1922 legalized it, at least temporarily, by promulgating the Land Code.

The third revision of Marxism was Lenin's rejection of a two-stage revolution in a developing country. He was impatient with the deterministic approach to history and was eager to give it a push. He advocated, therefore, an immediate seizure of power by the proletariat—irrespective of its political maturity—by means of an armed insurrection. His saying, "Let's grab political power and then we shall see . . ." is very characteristic of him.

Another revision of Marxist doctrine was Lenin's nationality policy. By his shrewd and flexible ethnic policy, wittingly or unwittingly, Lenin rescued the bulk of the old Tsarist empire from final disintegration. It was he who was primarily responsible for the acceptance of federalism as a basic theoretical principle underlying the Soviet state structure, again a rather un-Marxist yet politically effective device.

Thus, Lenin made a series of bold departures from the original Marxist theories.

---

[1] One of Lenin's faithful followers, the Soviet historian Pokrovsky, said, "You will not find in Lenin a single purely theoretical work; each has a propaganda aspect." *Molodaia Gvardiia (The Young Guard),* February–March 1924, p. 248.

Despite his rigid insistence on orthodox Marxist terminology, the departures are so numerous and so far-reaching as to make Lenin a major revisionist of Marxism. What is usually called Leninism is less an integrated doctrine and more a set of flexible rules on the seizure and control of power in an underdeveloped, multinational state. So great was Lenin's authority in the Party and the State he founded that anyone who wanted to compete for his place had to identify himself with this heritage, or at least to pay lip service to this legacy.

SUGGESTED READING

DEUTSCHER, ISAAC, *The Prophet Armed: Trotsky, 1879–1921*. New York: Oxford University Press, 1954.

———, *The Prophet Unarmed: Trotsky, 1921–1929*. New York: Oxford University Press, 1959.

DMYTRYSHYN, BASIL, *Moscow and Ukraine, 1918–1953: A Study of Russian Bolshevik Nationality Policy*. New York: Bookman Associates, 1956.

FAINSOD, MERLE, *How Russia Is Ruled* (rev. ed.). Cambridge, Mass.: Harvard University Press, 1963.

FISCHER, LOUIS, *The Life of Lenin*. New York: Harper & Row, 1964.

KOLARZ, WALTER, *Russia and Her Colonies*. New York: Praeger, 1954.

KUCHEROV, SAMUEL, *The Organs of the Soviet Administration of Justice: Their History and Operation*. Leiden: Brill, 1970.

LENIN, V. I., *Selected Works* . . . . Moscow: Progress Publishers, 1970, 3 vols.

MEYER, ALFRED, *Leninism*. Cambridge, Mass.: Harvard University Press, 1957.

NORTON, H. K., *The Far Eastern Republic of Siberia*. London: Allen and Unwin, 1923.

PAGE, S. W., *Lenin and World Revolution*. New York: New York University Press, 1959.

PIPES, RICHARD, *The Formation of the Soviet Union: Communism and Nationalism, 1917–1923*. Cambridge, Mass.: Harvard University Press, 1954.

SCHAPIRO, LEONARD, and PETER REDDAWAY (eds.), *Lenin. The Man, the Theorist, the Leader— A Reappraisal*. Boulder, Colo.: Praeger, 1987.

SCHWARTZ, SOLOMON M., *The Jews in the Soviet Union*. Syracuse, N.Y.: Syracuse University Press, 1956.

SULLIVAN, ROBERT S., *Soviet Politics and the Ukraine, 1917–1957*. New York: Columbia University Press, 1962.

TUMARKIN, NINA, *Lenin Lives! The Lenin Cult in Soviet Russia*. Cambridge, Mass.: Harvard University Press, 1983.

ULAM, ADAM, *The Bolsheviks*. New York: Macmillan, 1965.

VAKAR, NICHOLAS, *Belorussia*. Cambridge, Mass.: Harvard University Press, 1956.

ZENKOVSKY, SERGE A., *Pan-Turkism and Islam in Russia*. Cambridge, Mass.: Harvard University Press, 1960.

CHAPTER 12

The Struggle for Lenin's Mantle: The Stalin–Trotsky Controversy

The Bolshevik Party, despite Lenin's stress on discipline and unity, was far from being homogeneous. Actually, in-group fighting was constantly going on. The first postrevolutionary faction, formed in 1918 by Bukharin and known as the "Left Communist Opposition," criticized Lenin for his readiness to sign the Brest-Litovsk treaty. In 1920, a number of prominent Communists, mostly trade union leaders, headed by A. G. Shlyapnikov, Commissar for Labor, and Alexandra Kollontai, Commissar for Social Security, formed the so-called "Workers' Opposition." This group criticized the bureaucratic control of industry and favored a syndicalist solution; they urged the establishment of an All-Russian Congress of Producers to run the economy. The Tenth Party Congress of March 1921 censured the "Workers' Opposition" and condemned all "factionalism" as incompatible with the principles of democratic centralism. During the years 1919–1922, a group of upper-level Party functionaries called "democratic centralists" favored less censorship and a freer intra-Party regime by urging that democratic centralism be more democratic and less centralist. They too were defeated by Lenin.

As his illness progressed, factional tendencies again surfaced. During the last two years of Lenin's life, an intense feud smoldered between the two personalities designated by the ailing leader as the most able in the Party leadership—Trotsky and Stalin. Since the feud was as much a conflict of ideas and methods of operation as a clash of personalities, a brief examination of the rivals' backgrounds is in order.

TROTSKY'S CREDENTIALS

Leon Trotsky was born Lev Davidovich Bronstein in 1879. He came from the Kherson region of the Ukraine, from a family of prosperous Jewish farmers. He became a revolutionary at the age of nineteen; he was soon arrested and exiled to Siberia, but escaped abroad. It was at that time that he assumed the name of Trotsky. In 1902 in London he met Lenin. Impressed with the vivacity of his mind as well as his enthusiasm, Lenin invited Trotsky to collaborate on the editorial board of *Iskra*, to which he contributed articles signed with the pseudonym *Pero* (Pen). Despite this early and fairly close association with Lenin, Trotsky was to be critical of him for a long time. He oscillated between the Bolsheviks and the Mensheviks for a decade and a half. In 1904 he went so far as to denounce bitterly Lenin's authoritarian tendencies. One day, argued Trotsky, these tendencies would lead to a state of affairs in which "the organization of the party takes the place of the party itself; the Central Committee takes the place of the organization; and finally the dictator takes the place of the Central Committee."

Trotsky first became prominent during the revolution of 1905 as Vice-Chairman and then Chairman of the St. Petersburg Soviet. Arrested and exiled once more to Siberia, he again escaped abroad and lived mostly in Austria, France, and finally the United States. After the fall of Tsarism, Trotsky returned to Russia from the United States and only then, in the summer of 1917, formally joined the Bolshevik Party and was soon elected to its Central Committee. After Kornilov's attempted coup, in September 1917, the Bolsheviks won the majority of the Petrograd Soviet and Trotsky was elected its chairman. In October 1917, he also became Chairman of the Military Revolutionary Committee, which prepared the Bolshevik seizure of power in the capital. In the first Soviet Government, Trotsky was Commissar for Foreign Affairs. Opposed to the signing of the Brest-Litovsk peace treaty, he argued for "neither peace nor war," but in the end voted with Lenin. From 1918 until 1925, Trotsky was Commissar for War, chief organizer of the Red Army, and one of its leaders during the Civil War.

Trotsky's position was unique. He was a major leader of the Bolshevik Party, second in importance only to Lenin. In addition, he was intellectually brilliant. He was a magnetic speaker, bursting with exuberant vitality and wit, as well as the prolific author of articles, pamphlets, and books. But these qualities were coupled with glaring weaknesses; he was vain, self-centered, and self-confident to the point of arrogance, which made him widely disliked and distrusted by many of his comrades. He loved theatrical gestures, tended to be haughty, hated routine work, and lacked consistency and singleness of purpose.

STALIN'S CREDENTIALS

Trotsky's main rival, Joseph Stalin, born in 1879 as Josip Djugashvili in the village of Gori near Tiflis, was as complete a contrast to Trotsky as one could imagine. Stalin was the son of an obscure Georgian cobbler who was a drunkard and an adventurer and a pious, devoted mother. He was sent, at her insistence, to the Orthodox Theological Seminary in Tiflis. In 1898, he was expelled from the seminary for his revolutionary outlook and activity. In 1903, Djugashvili joined the Bolshevik faction of the RSDWP and later assumed the pseudonym Stalin, or "man of steel."

Until 1913, Stalin worked as an active follower, mainly in the revolutionary underground of Transcaucasia. In 1907 he organized several raids (or "expropriations") on banks to provide funds for the treasury of the Bolshevik Party. After the Prague Conference of 1912, Stalin was coopted to the Party's Central Committee by Lenin and Zinoview, both of whom desperately needed an energetic and systematic co-worker of non-Russian ethnic stock; Stalin fitted this description perfectly. In November 1912, he visited Lenin in Cracow and spent several months in Vienna. It was during this first trip that Stalin, with Bukharin's assistance, wrote his early theoretical work, *Marxism and the National Question*.

According to N. N. Sukhanov, author of *Notes on the Revolution* and its faithful chronicler, when Stalin returned from his Siberian exile to Petrograd in the spring of 1917, he was still merely "a gray blur, which glimmered dimly and left no trace."

From 1917 to 1923, Stalin was Commissar for Nationalities, and from 1919 to 1923, Commissar for State Control. The purpose of the second position was to guard the administrative apparatus against bureaucratization. The combination of these two posts gave Stalin a great deal of political and administrative experience. He became a close co-worker of Lenin's only after the crisis precipitated by the Brest-Litovsk treaty; unlike Trotsky, Stalin formly supported Lenin's stand, thus winning his confidence and gratitude. Both Trotsky and Stalin were members of the Politburo from its inception on the eve of the Bolshevik coup d'état.

During the Civil War Stalin, like many other leading Bolsheviks, was a high-ranking political commissar and in this capacity a subordinate of War Commissar Trotsky. In 1919 Stalin was attached to the Red Army group commanded by Voroshilov that successfully defended Tsaritsyn on the Volga (later renamed Stalingrad, and now called Volgograd). It was at that time that the first bitter disagreements arose between Stalin and Trotsky. During the Soviet-Polish campaign of 1920, Stalin was with Budënny's First Cavalry Army, again as its chief political commissar. During those crucial August days, Stalin advised Budënny to march on Lvov and not on Warsaw, where Trotsky as Commissar for War had wanted to deal the decisive blow to the Poles. Stalin's responsibility for the catastrophe that befell the Red army at the Battle of Warsaw became a touchy, controversial problem in Soviet politics and historiography.

STALIN VERSUS TROTSKY: A STUDY IN CONTRASTS

It is hard to imagine two more contrasting personalities. Trotsky was well read and widely traveled, cosmopolitan, flamboyant, extroverted, exuberant, and brilliant. Stalin, on the other hand, seemed provincial, introverted, secretive, dull, and, to a superficial observer, might have appeared devoid of outstanding abilities. Trotsky was a scintillating writer, a dramatic as well as a witty orator; Stalin's literary and speaking performances were rather crude and pedestrian. Trotsky's physique was striking: he had a broad chest, high forehead, black fiery eyes, and a mane of black hair. Stalin looked rather insignificant: small with a pock-marked face, a crooked arm, black teeth, yellow eyes, and a half-shy, half-sinister smile under a cockroach mustache. He had a heavy Georgian accent and, unlike Trotsky, spoke no foreign language. Trotsky was a mercurial and neurotic intellectual, an inspirational man who tended to react spontaneously, on the spur of the moment, and who experienced frequent emotional ups and downs. Stalin, on the other hand, was nerveless, steady, systematic, capable of cool judgement, patient planning, and meticulous execution.

By 1922–1923, these two men had emerged as the main rivals for the leadership of Soviet Russia. Each had strong and weak points in his respective claim to be Lenin's heir. Trotsky, despite his role during the Revolution and the Civil War, was a latecomer to the Bolshevik Party. Prior to July 1917 he had repeatedly quarreled with Lenin and attacked him on various issues, including that of his arbitrary leadership. Trotsky split with Lenin at the time of the Brest-Litovsk negotiations. He failed to heed Lenin's advice to raise the Georgian question and thus attack Stalin's "Great Russian" chauvinism at the Twelfth Party Congress. Finally, Trotsky twice refused to be Lenin's deputy as Chairman of the Council of People's Commissars. Stalin, on the other hand, while he had never openly embroiled himself in a controversy with Lenin until his illness, was strongly disavowed in Lenin's Testament.

"TROIKA" VERSUS TROTSKY

During the crucial years of 1922–1924, Trotsky, who initially appeared to be

Lenin's natural successor, was, as has been noted, often ill and absent from Moscow. Supremely self-centered, self-confident, and arrogant, he had few intimate friends. Moreover, after the end of the Civil War, he tended to neglect public relations. On the other hand, Stalin devoted much effort to cultivating political allies and meticulously manipulating the party machine. While his rival was a loner, Stalin worked hand-in-hand with two leading Politburo members, Zinoviev and Kameniev. This automatically gave them a strong position in the seven-member top policy-making body, for only five members regularly attended the meetings; Lenin was ill and Trotsky often absent.

Zinoviev, a man of middle-class Jewish origin, was Chairman of the Communist International, and as such enjoyed considerable prestige in world revolutionary circles. As head of the Petrograd Soviet, he also had an important power base at home. He was an adroit journalist and a fiery speaker of a rather demagogic brand who lacked both the capacity for systematic work and perseverance in his undertakings. Zinoviev's bosom friend, L. V. Kameniev, had a similar background. Under Lenin, Kameniev was Deputy Chairman of the Council of People's Commissars and Chairman of the Moscow Soviet. He excelled in routine administrative work, which was Zinoviev's weak point, but he had little talent for writing and speaking. In a way, Zinoviev and Kameniev complemented each other and they soon became the Castor and Pollux of Soviet politics. Both of them, however, lacked Trotsky's rich intellectual endowment. The Troika members—Stalin, Zinoviev, and Kameniev—had been in Lenin's faction since 1903, while Trotsky was a relative newcomer. All three could boast of considerable achievements during the preceding heroic period, yet all were overshadowed by Trotsky. It seems likely that it was feelings of inferiority that made the Troika form a tactical alliance against the man they feared and of whom they were jealous; they ac-

Grigori Y. Zinoviev, a member of the "Troika" and chairman of the Executive Committee of the Comintern, 1921–1926

cused him of harboring "Bonapartist" ambitions. All four contenders probably dreamed of being Lenin's successor, yet none of them would ever publicly admit to harboring such an ambition. They pretended to foster not their own claims to Lenin's mantle but the Great Leader's version of Marxism applied to the current situation of Soviet Russia.

THE PERMANENT REVOLUTION

The ideological differences between Trotsky and Stalin can be epitomized in two battle cries: "permanent revolution" versus "socialism in one country." The term *permanent revoluton* was first used casually by Marx and Engels in their *Communist Manifesto* to describe revolutionary ferment spreading from one country to another. This concept was first elaborated upon by a leftist German Social Democrat, Alexander Helphand, while writing (under the pseudonym of Parvus) an introduction to Trotsky's pamphlet on the domestic situation in Russia at the beginning of 1905. According to Parvus, the Russian proletariat begins to make a revolution which, while it may initially be bourgeois, does not stop there and continues "in permanence" until it changes into a world proletarian revolution. In his biography of Stalin, Trotsky admitted that the concept had captured his imagination.

Inspired by Parvus, he expanded upon his ideas in a collection of essays entitled *Our Revolution*, published in 1905, and in a book, *Results and Prospects*, published in 1906. At that time most Russian Socialists, following Marxist doctrine, were convinced that the forthcoming upheaval in their backward country would be confined for a considerable time to its bourgeois stage. Trotsky, on the other hand, considered this school of thinking to be a too literal and formal interpretation of Marxism. As a result of his observation of the events of 1904–1905, Trotsky came to the conclusion that the Russian bourgeoisie was too weak to keep political power for any appreciable period of time. Although the initial phase of the coming revolution might indeed be bourgeois in a historic sense, it would have to be carried out by the working class, and the dynamics of the revolutonary process would push it beyond its first stage. Once in power, the Russian working class would be forced, by the weakness of the native bourgeoisie, to carry the process to the next, socialist, phase. Thus, argued Trotsky, Russia would jump from the lower to the higher stage of the process even before the proletarian revolution had begun in the West.

The reason Russia was predestined to become the pioneer of Socialism–Communism was to be found in the peculiarities of Russian history: in the endemic indolence of its middle class, its conservatism, timidity, and its dependence on the all-powerful state and upon foreign capital. In view of the lethargic passivity of the Russian bourgeoisie and its political proponents, the Liberals, the tough, young, dynamic Russian proletairat was the only force capable of seizing and holding power. Yet because Russia was still an underdeveloped peasant society with a proletariat that amounted to 3 million people out of a population of 150 million, a workers' government could not survive for long; it would soon be overthrown by a domestic counterrevolution, toppled by foreign intervention, or both. Consequently, the proletarian revolution in Russia could be saved only by extending it to other, more advanced, industrialized countries. Trotsky defined his "permanent revolution" as a process "of which every next stage is anchored in the preceding one and which can end only with the total liquidation of the class society." In this way, the revolutionary spark in Russia would eventually initiate a worldwide conflagration. To succeed, the national Russian revolution must eventually become a world revoluton. Russia's primitive economy, argued Trotsky, was not ripe for socialism, but that of Western Europe was. That is why the Bolsheviks, immediately after the seizure of power in their native country, should spread their gospel to the West, especially to Germany. This would assure Russia of adequate resources for the continuing development of socialism in its own country.

Trotsky's theory appeared to be an accurate forecast of events in the fateful years 1917–1919, as revolutionary upheavals occured in Russia, Germany, and Hungary. But when in mid-August 1920 the Red Army's westward offensive was smashed at the gates of Warsaw, the chain reaction was broken. For Trotsky, however, the recovery of Western capitalism was merely a temporary phenomenon, a "rotten stabilization." Despite mounting evidence to the contrary, despite the proclamation of the NEP, he continued to preach his pet idea with his characteristic zeal and brilliance, arguing that his concept was in accordance with Lenin's teaching and practice. Yet it was increasingly obvious that Trotsky's theory was rather alien to most of the party leadership, let alone the masses of the Soviet people exhausted by seven years of war, exertion, and starvation, and eager for normalcy.

SOCIALISM IN ONE COUNTRY

In his desire to succeed Lenin, Stalin welcomed an opportunity to argue in public about fundamental issues affecting Soviet domestic and foreign policies. As has already been mentioned, after Lenin's death each contender for power took special care to establish his credentials as a "good Leninist" and to stress his special devotion to the deceased founder of the Bolshevik party and the Soviet state. Here was an opportunity for Stalin to prove that he was a theoretician comparable to Trotsky, and that he would perpetuate Lenin's teachings. A careful search of Lenin's papers resulted in the unearthing of one of his essays of 1915 vintage in which Lenin had anticipated that, in view of the unequal development of capitalism, the proletarian revolution might initially break out in only one country—which one Lenin did not specify—and might not immediately assume an international character. Stalin seized upon this idea of Lenin's and elevated it into a fundamental stance, a beacon for Soviet Russia to follow in the immediate future.

In April 1924, three months after Lenin's death, Stalin gave a series of lectures at the Sverdlov Party University in Moscow in which he skillfully summarized what he claimed to be the essence of Lenin's teaching, and bluntly opposed it to his rival's teaching.

According to Lenin the revolution draws its forces above all from among the workers and peasants of Russia itself. According to Trotsky we have it that the indispensable forces can be found only in the arena of world-wide proletarian revolution. And what if the world revolution is fated to come late? Is there a hope for ours? Comrade Trotsky gives us no hope at all. . . . According to him, our revolution has one prospect: to vegetate in its own contradictions and have its roots rot, while awaiting for the world-wide revolution.

Stalin insisted that it was not only possible but even necessary to construct and consolidate the already existing socialist system in the USSR before starting a series of similar upheavals in the West. To try spreading the proletarian revolution to other countries would be a gamble, because it would invite new foreign intervention and thus jeopardize the very existence of the infant Soviet state. Stalin concluded his argument by saying that the only sensible goal the Bolsheviks could pursue was:

to consolidate the dictatorship of the proletariat in one country, using it as a base for the overthrow of imperialism in all countries. . . . He who denies the possibility of inaugurating Socialism in one country alone, must, if he be logical, likewise deny the expediency of the October Revolution.

In March 1925, the Fourteenth Party Conference proclaimed Stalin's theory the official Party line. By this means he had won another round in the struggle for supreme authority and had not only further identified himself with Lenin, but also established himself as a Party theoretician to be reckoned with. The decision of the Fourteenth Conference was an important turning point in the evolution of Soviet Communism from its originally lofty, yet rather utopian international goals toward its present-day national Communist orientation.

SOCIALISM IN ONE COUNTRY VERSUS THE PERMANENT REVOLUTION

In opposing Trotsky's theory of permanent revolution, Stalin gauged the mood of the Party leaders more perceptively than his opponent. Many who were basically sympathetic to Trotsky's stand on the continuation of the heroic period of Bolshevism were asking themselves whether the young Soviet state, ruined, starved, and exhausted, would be courting disaster in undertaking such an adventurous course. The policy of permanent revolution was, moreover, contrary to the NEP's attempts to rehabilitate the country, attract foreign investments, expand trade with the outside world, and obtain diplomatic recognition for the Soviet Union. To these arguments, based on objective considerations, one should add those rooted in psychology. To whom could such an intellectually brilliant, yet rather subtle and highly speculative theory appeal? Certainly neither to the Soviet workers and peasants, nor to the members of the bureaucracy, many of whom were of a parochial background. Just emerging from a protracted and cruel seven-year period of trial and tribulation, all were preoccupied with consolidating their gains: the eight-hour working day, the land, or in the case of the Soviet establishment, their newly acquired position of power and prestige. A complex theory of this type could appeal only to internationally-minded intellectuals, a small group in a fast-expanding Party composed largely of workers, peasants, and their children. To them Stalin's ideas appeared more in accordance with their immediate interests; most of them were eager to consolidate their newly acquired hold on Soviet Russia.

Moreover, by placing Russia's destiny in the hands of foreigners, even if they were Communists, Trotsky's stand implied that the Russian people were dependent on the outside world, incapable of "going it alone." By saying that Socialism could not be built in Russia without outside aid, Trotsky took a psychologically disadvantageous stand. This allowed his rival to represent him as an adventurer, prepared to squander Russia's resources for the sake of spreading Communism abroad while neglecting the country's rehabilitation, then successfully proceeding as a result of the NEP. Stalin, asserting that Socialism could be built even in one-sixth of the earth isolated from the outside world, assumed a psychologically advantageous position. By 1924, even the most evangelical Party activists had grown weary of Communist adventurism, of waiting for the long-proclaimed world revolution. Stalin's theory of socialism in one country, therefore, was more attuned to their sentiments; it tended to restore their pride

and confidence in their own achievement, the survival of which was not necessarily dependent on outside events, but only on their own strength and resources. To Trotsky's argument that his rival lacked revolutionary zeal, Stalin would answer that Trotsky lacked faith in the future of the Russian revolution by making its ultimate fate dependent on outside assistance.

The Bolshevik revolution had been achieved in the name of universalistic principles, or "proletarian internationalism." Yet very early on, the nationalistic undercurrent began to reassert itself. Stalin, although a Russified Georgian, sensed this trend better than any other Bolshevik leader and became its spokesman. By proposing "Socialism in one country," he was urging his countrymen not to depend on the world proletarian revolution. Even if it should be delayed, he argued, Russia should be capable of developing its own brand of Socialism—Communism. This preaching of self-reliance had a deep meaning for the Russians because it bolstered their latent yet powerful national ego.

In retrospect, the actual differences between the two rivals, as reflected in their public pronouncements, were not as great as they then appeared. Trotsky did not advocate slacking the tempo of "socialist construction" in the USSR to channel all Soviet resources into promoting the revolution abroad. Quite the contrary; his domestic program at that time was more ambitious than that of his opponent and critical of the gradualist NEP. Neither did Stalin argue for abandoning the idea of proletarian revolution outside of the USSR. He merely argued that Soviet Russia must first be made into the solid, secure base of the world Communist movement. Thus their differences were actually small and could be reduced to timing, wording, and emphasis. Consequently they could be reconciled—provided a modicum of mutual trust and good will existed. What made reconciliation impossible was not so much conceptual differences but rather temperamental incompatibility. Coveting the same prize, they despised each other. They were two stars belonging to different constellations, two lions who could not share the same den. One had to destroy the other.

STALIN'S POWER BASE

Historians, often fascinated with dramatic, colorful events, have a tendency to imbue political duels between powerful personalities with a romantic aura. This has largely been the case in the feud between Stalin and Trotsky. Aside from the intellectually fascinating theoretical debates, aside from the clash of two irreconcilable personalities, there was often sordid and brutal jockeying for positions of power and behind-the-scene maneuvering and intrigue. While Trotsky believed in the power of the word, either spoken or written, Stalin relied primarily on tangible levers of power: the control of the Party apparatus. Much earlier than his rival he realized that this was the main locus of power, that it was the Party that ultimately controlled the State bureaucracy, the armed forces, and last but not least, the secret police. Beginning in the spring of 1922, when he became Secretary General, Stalin worked very hard to undermine Trotsky's position in the two places where the latter had power: first in the Politburo, and then in the Commissariat for Military and Naval Affairs.

In the Politburo of seven members, as we have seen, this was achieved by the formation of the triumvirate. The two members who have not yet been accounted for here were Rykov and Tomsky. They tended to be more sympathetic to the moderate line embodied in the NEP, and hence to the slogan "Socialism in one country." Consequently, Trotsky was increasingly isolated in the chief policy-making body. Had Trotsky accepted the post of Vice-Chairman twice offered to him by Lenin, he would have been, it is safe to say, Lenin's natural successor as chief executive of the Soviet Union. This would have strengthened his power and prestige and somewhat counterbalanced

Stalin's growing influence. But Trotsky's fear of new administrative responsibility allowed Stalin to place Alexey I. Rykov, then Deputy Chairman of the Council of People's Commissars, as Lenin's successor in the crucial post. By this means Stalin made Rykov into his ally in the crucial Politburo, and further weakened and isolated Trotsky.[1]

By the winter of 1924, Stalin had further consolidated his already formidable position. No longer was Lenin there to watch him and criticize his arbitrariness, arrogance, and chauvinism. As Secretary General, Stalin increasingly controlled Party work through patronage; and through Rykov, he also had a powerful influence over governmental affairs and the everyday functioning of the State apparatus, which the Party ultimately supervised anyway.

LENIN'S TESTAMENT

One of the decisive moments in the struggle for power came in May 1924, when Lenin's Testament was read aloud to the Central Committee members. Stalin sat silent and embarrassed by Lenin's request that he be removed from his influential post as Secretary General; he actually tendered his resignation. But again Trotsky failed to act, thus missing his last chance to oust Stalin. It was Zinoviev who rescued his ally by making a statement that sounded as if he were representing the opinion of the entire Politburo. Referring both to the Testament and to Stalin's funeral oration, known by then as "the Lenin oath," Zinoviev said, "We are happy to say that in one point Lenin's fears have proved baseless. I have in mind the point about our General Secretary. You all have witnessed our harmonious cooperation in the last few months. . . ." The Central

---

[1] Kameniev, who had presided over the Council during Lenin's illness, was denied the job, at Stalin's suggestion, because of his Jewish origin. As Stalin put it, early revealing his xenophobic and anti-Semitic bias, "We must consider the peasant character of Russia." Rykov was a Russian with a strong peasant background.

Committee decided not to publish the Testament and to keep Stalin in his post.[2]

Soon after Lenin's death, on Stalin's initiative the Politburo decided to launch a recruiting drive. It resulted in the admission of over 200,000 new members; the Party expanded by about one-third. Outwardly, the campaign was conducted to bolster the working class element in the Party ranks. Actually, the Secretariat that controlled the recruitment process made sure that only Stalin's supporters were admitted. Consequently, his control of the Party increased even more.

Gradually it dawned on his two main allies, Zinoviev and Kameniev, that Stalin was making constant progress and that rather than using him, they were being used by him as pawns in his game. Just when Stalin's two chief allies were starting to reconsider the value of their association with the increasingly omnipotent and arrogant Secretary General and beginning to grope toward a rapprochement with their alleged enemy, Trotsky committed another crucial mistake. In the autumn of 1924, he published a book entitled *The Lessons of October*. With his usual biting brilliance he attacked Zinoviev and Kameniev as the most reluctant supporters of Lenin's plan of armed insurrection and hence as "defeatists." Stalin grasped the opportunity and came out in support of his allies. He spoke of Trotsky's record both before and after 1917, and especially of his disagreements with Lenin. Thus, instead of winning Zinoviev and Kameniev over to his side by splitting Stalin's majority in the Politburo, Trotsky pushed his potential allies back into the arms of his mortal enemy. To take revenge on the man who had tried to denigrate them, both Zinoviev and Kameniev lent their support to a renewed anti-Trotsky drive aimed at discrediting him for having conspired to corrupt the Leninist purity of the party doctrine with the "petty-bourgeois," "Menshevik" doctrine of permanent revolution, which was again condemned as "dynamite under the foundation of the Party," and a threat to its "general line" as embodied in the NEP.

At the peak of the campaign directed against him in September 1925, Trotsky committed another tactical mistake. He tried to conciliate Stalin by repudiating Lenin's Testament. Writing in the September 1 issue of *Bolshevik,* Trotsky said:

Vladimir Ilich left no "testament." . . . Under the guise of "testament," the émigré, foreign bourgeois and Menshevik press habitually refers . . . to one of the letters of Vladimir Ilich which contains advice of an organizational sort. . . . All talk about the concealment or violation of the "Testament" is evil fantasy.

Despite, or perhaps because of this gesture, Stalin pressed his advantage to its logical end. All this time Trotsky, isolated in the Politburo, still controlled an important power base, the Commissariat for Military and Naval Affairs; as such, he was also Chairman of the Revolutionary Military Council. Trotsky's absenteeism and his neglect of routine work greatly facilitated Stalin's task. In January 1925, on Stalin's initiative, Mikhail Frunze, victor over Kolchak and Wrangel and Chief of Staff of the Red Army, replaced Trotsky in these crucial posts. However, the ambitious and independent Frunze proved less subservient to his promoter than had been expected; he died in October of that same year under mysterious circumstances as a result of a mishandled and essentially unnecessary stomach operation in which an excessive amount of chloroform had been used. The convenient vacancy was filled, again at the insistence of the Secretary General, by Stalin's Civil War companion, Klement Voroshilov. Through the Political Administration of the Army and the Navy, he made sure that they were loyal to the Party. Now Stalin could sleep more comfortably, for the Soviet armed forces were under the watchful eye of a subservient man with limited abilities and with no Bonapartist ambitions.

---

[2] The Testament was not published in the Soviet Union until 1956.

Stalin's power was eventually concentrated in two bodies: the Secretariat and the Politburo. As Secretary General he could steer the working of the entire Party apparatus. By manipulating the majority of the Politburo he could pass almost any measure he wanted. Through Rykov he influenced the everyday running of the bureaucratic machine of the State. Moreover, the chief of the Secret Police, Dzerzhinsky, was his friend; so was Voroshilov, the Commissar for Army and Navy. Through Tomsky, he could manipulate the trade unions as well. Thus the decision-making, administrative, and enforcement organs were all ultimately controlled by Stalin.

From the close of 1925, Stalin's struggle against Trotsky proceeded from one success to another. His rival was not only deprived of his power base, but increasingly isolated from his supporters by Stalin's control of all official mass media. Trotsky, a fierce and resourceful fighter, could do little against a systematic campaign of vilification openly waged against him; his pronouncements were suppressed or ignored by the press; he was a voice crying in the wilderness.

THE NEP'S FUTURE

One of the important issues in the struggle was the domestic program. The main question was, should the NEP, which favored the peasants, be continued, or should it be replaced by a more vigorous industrialization drive? Here Stalin—supported by Zinoviev, Kameniev, Rykov, and Bukharin—defended the NEP as the only way of preserving the Leninist alliance of workers and peasants. Trotsky, on the other hand, argued for a more energetic collectivization drive to alter the overwhelmingly individual structure of Soviet agriculture, allegedly dominated by the prosperous kulaks. He criticized his opponents as being "pro-kulak and pro-Nepman," giving too much support not only to the peasants but also to light industry, while he believed that a vigorous modernization drive should be

based on the quick expansion of heavy industry. But by now Trotsky and the gradually shrinking group of his supporters were denounced as "deviationists" or "Left Opposition" to the only truly Leninist line of policy, that of consolidating the NEP.

The swiftness and smoothness of the Secretary General's victory over Trotsky surprised both Stalin's opponents and allies. Zinoviev and Kameniev now launched a belated attack on the policies they had supported in concert with Stalin. After Trotsky's dismissal, in the same crucial autumn of 1925, Zinoviev published a book entitled *Leninism* in which he condemned the NEP as a "continuous retreat from the original goals set by Marx and Lenin." He insisted on resumption of the socialist offensive, especially in the countryside, to destroy the growing power of the kulak. As Chairman of the powerful Leningrad Soviet, Zinoviev managed to mobilize his local Party organization against the NEP. His close friend Kameniev, the Moscow Party boss, was also uneasy about Stalin's growing power; he backed Zinoviev. Since their theoretical premises were close to Trotsky's, a gradual rapprochement took place among the three. Thus, after having refused an alliance with the powerful Commissar for the Army and the Navy, the disgruntled Zinoviev and Kameniev belatedly sided with the now powerless Trotsky and fought a hopeless rearguard action as the leaders of the shrinking joint Left Opposition.

In December 1925, at the Fourteenth Party Congress, Zinoviev and Kameniev launched a frontal attack on Stalin. Since the Congress had been carefully packed by him, the attack miscarried. At the Congress Bukharin, Rykov, and Tomsky gave public expression of their full acceptance of "socialism in one country," and consequently became Stalin's allies. The NEP, argued Bukharin, was a slow but sure way for socialist construction, while the policy of the Left Opposition represented adventurism, and threatened with ruin what had been already achieved, the nearly complete restoration of the economy above the 1913 level.

This implied continuation of the mixed economy, a distinct characteristic of the NEP. In this way the NEP, originally conceived as a temporary tactical retreat, became a long-range policy. Stalin supported Bukharin, Rykov, and Tomsky, and the Fourteenth Congress ended in another victory for him.

Strengthened by his new triumph, Stalin proceeded to deal with the Left Opposition. The reaffirmation of his slogan "socialism in one country" meant not only continuation of the NEP at home, but also a cautious policy abroad. This in turn had far-reaching implications for the Comintern, still headed by the restless and rebellious Zinoviev. His aggressive policy as Chairman of the Executive Committee of the Comintern was now increasingly out of tune with the Party's general pro-NEP line. In October 1926, Zinoviev was removed from his post and replaced by Stalin's new chief supporter and ideological spokesman, Bukharin. At the same time, Zinoviev and Trotsky lost their Politburo posts. The Politburo was reconstructed by the addition of three new members, Kalinin, Molotov, and Voroshilov, all of them devoted to the Secretary General, body and soul.

FOREIGN POLITICAL FACTORS

The struggle for power was closely intertwined with foreign policy. The German fiasco of 1923, which finally shattered Soviet hopes for an early European revolution, gave additional support to Stalin's concept of building socialism in isolation with exclusively native resources. To the failure in Germany were soon added setbacks in Great Britain and Poland, and finally, the debacle suffered by the Chinese Communists. These three fiascoes came as much greater shocks because they had been preceded by a series of apparent Soviet successes.

There were two countries where the united front policy had achieved some success: Great Britain and China. In 1924, the first Labor Government in British history,

headed by former trade union leader Ramsay MacDonald, granted *de jure* recognition to the USSR. This, together with the establishment of diplomatic relations with France, considerably enhanced Moscow's international prestige. In 1925 an Anglo-Soviet trade union committee was established. However, a letter allegedly written by Zinoviev as head of the Comintern was published in the British press. It urged British comrades to spread subversive propaganda in the British armed forces in order to prepare for the forcible overthrow of the London government. The Conservative opposition exploited the letter to the full and managed to oust the Labor Government. The newly established diplomatic relations between Moscow and London were broken off.

In May 1926, the outbreak of a general strike in Britain seemed to create a propitious atmosphere for revolutionary agitation. However, the strike soon collapsed and revealed the lack of revolutionary enthusiasm of the partially Communist-infiltrated coal miners' union, as well as the impotence of the Communist Party of Britain. This failure was paralleled by Pilsudski's *coup d'état* in Warsaw, where the seizure of power by an old antagonist of Soviet Russia had been actively supported by the Polish Communists, who had hoped to be able to use him for their purposes.

This double, almost simultaneous blow was followed by a full-blown catastrophe in China. As was mentioned earlier, the Comintern favored a fairly intimate collaboration between the tiny Communist Party of China and the Kuomintang in order to overthrow the warlords and the weak central government of Peking. They were to be aided by an able and resourceful diplomatic agent, Michael Borodin, who was sent to China in September 1923 as head of a team of Soviet military and economic experts. In exchange, the Kuomintang dispatched to Moscow a group of its officers and officials to study Soviet methods. One of them was a close co-worker of Sun Yat-sen, Chiang

Kai-shek. He was soon made an honorary member of the Comintern.

Stalin's objective in China was to establish the "hegemony of the proletariat" within the "bloc of four classes" in the struggle against imperialism. His argument was that China was on the eve of a "bourgeois-democratic" revolution intertwined with a mounting nationalistic revolution against encroachments by foreign imperialists. Soviet Russia, argued Stalin, should use these forces for its purposes and in alliance with the local bourgeoisie, chase the imperialists out of the Chinese subcontinent, thus weakening their hold on the Orient as a whole. Trotsky, on the other hand, denounced any alliance with class enemies as "Menshevism" and urged an immediate offensive by the Communist Party of China to seize power.

STALIN'S FAILURE IN CHINA

By 1925 the revolutionary tide in China seemed to be mounting. The Kuomintang army, reorganized with the assistance of the Soviet experts headed by General Vasily K. Bluecher (known in China as Galen), was ready to march north and seize power in Peking. In March 1926, however, Chiang Kai-shek, who had returned to Canton from Moscow with an extensive knowledge of Soviet methods of infiltration and subversion, decided to regain full control of the Kuomintang's forces before proceeding any further that summer. On March 20, 1926, Chiang arrested the political commissars in his army and placed the Soviet advisers under house arrest. After his successful coup, Chiang insisted on absolute subordination of the Chinese Communist Party to the Kuomintang. This was accepted by the chief of the Soviet advisers, Borodin, with Stalin's approval. The uneasy alliance was now maintained at this price, and soon the military campaign to unite China under Kuomintang rule, the "Northern Expedition," was launched. By April 1927, the combined forces of the Communists and the Kuomintang had reached as far north as

Shanghai. There, alarmed by the growing strength and popularity of the Communists, Chiang put a bloody end to the alliance, executing thousands of Communists and their supporters in a reign of terror known as the "Shanghai massacre."

After the Shanghai massacre, the Comintern at first denied its failure, but when the defeat was too obvious to conceal, its mass media tried to minimize the scope and consequences of the debacle in China. Still, the failure of Stalin's policy was striking. By 1928, having also suppressed a Communist uprising in Canton the previous December, Chiang had united most of China under his leadership. Moscow had overlooked the Kuomintang's many sins because it was anti-Western—primarily anti-British—only to have its policy backfire, thereby delaying the Chinese revolution for a full generation. Virtually silent on foreign policy before the China catastrophe, the Left, inspired by Trotsky, now charged Stalin and his allies with having betrayed the international revolution. From then on, the split between the leadership and the Left opposition was unbridgeable. Comintern failures were compounded by Soviet diplomatic setbacks. The breaking of diplomatic relations by the Conservative British government in May 1927 and the June assassination of the Soviet ambassador to Warsaw, Piotr L. Voykov, by a White Russian émigré created an acute sense of Soviet isolation that helped Stalin propagate a siege mentally conducive to strengthening his control over all the branches of Party and State activities.

The failure of Soviet foreign policy in Great Britain, Poland, and China made Stalin vulnerable to the attacks by the left Opposition. The Chinese disaster in particular lent itself to a critical reappraisal of his concepts and operational methods. Stalin blamed that defeat on the wrong correlation of class forces and the sabotage of Comintern directives by the leaders of the Chinese Party. In a speech on April 6, 1927, less than a week before the Shanghai massacre, he had defended his policy in China by saying: "Chiang Kai-shek has perhaps no sympathy for the revolution, but he is leading the army and cannot do otherwise than lead it against the imperialists. . . . So [the Rightists] can be utilized to the end, squeezed out like a lemon and then flung away." Trotsky soon pointed out that "a few days later, the squeezed-out lemon seized power and the army."

Despite the temporary defeat in China, the original Soviet aim of loosening the grip of the imperial powers on China was eventually accomplished. But it was in spite of Stalin's policies during the 1920s that the groundwork was laid for the eventual triumph of the Communist cause with all its short-range, deceptively positive, and long-range, negative consequences for Soviet Russia.

TROTSKY'S EXPULSION AND EXILE

The alleged threat in 1927 of a new foreign invasion of Russia led by the British allowed Stalin to pounce on the Left Opposition with his full fury. Trotsky and Zinoviev, who had voiced bitter criticisms of both his domestic and foreign policies, were denounced by the Secretary General, supported by Bukharin, as a bunch of "petty bourgeois intellectuals, divorced from life, from the Revolution, from the Party and from the working class." The political division between the bulk of the Party and the Left Opposition reflected a deep-seated class division, argued Stalin. Any opposition to the vanguard of the proletariat must be bourgeois-inspired. Trotsky defended himself with vigor, pointing out the series of blunders and failures of his opponent, but he was helpless against Stalin's organizational power.

Stalin could have tolerated a meek Trotsky vegetating silently on the fringe of Soviet society. He could not tolerate a triumphant Trotsky constantly engineering acts of defiance and shouting, "I told you so." In October 1927, on the eve of the tenth anniversary of the Bolshevik revolution, the leaders of the Left Opposition, driven to

desperation by the denial of access to mass media and their expulsion from the Central Committee, staged a series of public demonstrations in the streets of Moscow and Leningrad. Trotsky led the demonstration in the capital in person. All these processions were dispersed by the police. Finally, on November 15, 1927, Trotsky, Zinoviev, and Kameniev were expelled from the Party.

Trotsky refused to accept the decision and loudly protested against it. As a reprisal he was exiled to Alma Ata in Central Asia. Zinoviev and Kameniev, on the other hand, retracted their criticisms of Stalin and submitted to him; they were pardoned and readmitted. As the triumphant Stalin contemptuously put it, "They crawled back into the Party." When from his exile in Alma Ata, Trotsky tried to maintain secret links with his remaining scattered supporters and continued to criticize the Secretary General's policies, he was banished from the USSR to Turkey in 1929.

Abroad in Western Europe and eventually in Mexico, the exiled prophet published his *Bulletin of the Opposition* and tried to mount a Fourth International, but in vain.[3]

REASONS FOR TROTSKY'S DEFEAT

Stalin's victory over the opposition was a perfect example of political teamwork and timing skillfully manipulated from behind the scenes. At the beginning of 1925, Bukharin, who had joined the Politboro after Lenin's death, coalesced with Stalin to form a new Party leadership. Their coalition originated in the dissolution of the anti-Trotsky triumvirate, which began to disintegrate in late 1924 and collapsed in 1925, when Zinoviev and Kameniev challenged Stalin's leadership of the Party. At that time seven full members sat on the Politburo:

[3] On August 20, 1940, a Spanish Communist, Ramon Mercader, who served as Trotsky's secretary, murdered him in Mexico with an ice pick. He was sentenced to twenty years by a Mexican court, but was decorated *in absentia* by Stalin.

Stalin, Bukharin, Trotsky, Zinoviev, Kameniev, Rykov, and Tomsky. The new duumvirate was able to manage the Politburo because it acted resolutely, supported mostly by Rykov and Tomsky; and because the irresolute Left Opposition had failed to unite effectively until the spring of 1926, when it was too late. The Left Opposition's sense of timing was disastrous, while Stalin's was masterful.

Most of the time Trotsky was the soul of the Left Opposition and its driving force. From the perspective of sixty years, the reason for his debacle emerges more clearly than before. He was essentially more a man of intellect than a man of action. After a prodigious yet meteoric outburst of activity during the Revolution, the Civil War, and in the early 1920s—which is to say, in the decisive opening phases of the struggle for power—he relapsed into intellectual pursuits that were probably more congenial to his temperament than routine peace-time, largely administrative, duties.

Following Lenin's death, when the fight for leadership was going on, Trotsky was an absentee pretender who believed that Lenin's mantle would automatically fall on his shoulders because of his intellectual superiority. He relied too much on his brilliant intellect and not enough on well-planned, consistent, and resolute action. He underestimated his opponent and openly called him "the most eminent mediocrity of his Party," thus mistakenly identifying intellectual caliber with political skill. While the proud Trotsky held himself aloof from the menial, humdrum tasks inherent in everyday organizational routine, the initially self-effacing, humble, methodical, and indefatigable Stalin was always willing to assume arduous albeit unglamorous administrative Party duties. Gathering strength step by step, Stalin built for himself an impregnable position of power in the Party, and indirectly in the State apparatus, armed forces, and secret police. This formidable position no fancy rhetoric of his opponents could destroy.

Besides his outstanding organizational gifts, Stalin, no original thinker, displayed a remarkable talent for propaganda and popularization that none of his opponents could match. Stalin's opponents were misled by his speeches that seemed to them pedestrian, repetitious, and dull. Yet his pronouncements invariably presented the essentials of his point of view in a clear and simple way that was accessible and acceptable to the Party rank and file, most of whom were newly promoted, simple people without much education. In addition to all this, Stalin was endowed with an exceptional gift for behind-the-scenes Machiavellian manipulation and cunning intrigue which neither Trotsky, nor any other of Stalin's rivals could match. Moreover, unlike their opponent, Trotsky and his comrades from the Left Opposition lacked resolution and a clear vision of what they wanted to achieve, and a realistic appraisal of the nature of the system they had built and within whose framework they now had to operate. After having trampled on incipient democracy in 1917, they began to invoke democratic principles only when they themselves were oppressed by the system of their own making.

The leaders of the Opposition were, moreover, victims of the Leninist fetish of "Party unity" as the overriding goal. The accepted principles, "Everything for the Party and through the Party," and "The Party is always right," inhibited their struggle against the man who at that time still carefully veiled his personal goals, always acting as a legitimate spokesman for their common, collective hero. While nothing Stalin said, wrote, or did was divorced from some practical purpose, Trotsky often hesitated or indulged in empty phrases and spectacular but inane gestures. To Trotsky himself, after 1921, one may apply his own criticism of Martov: "his thought lacked the mainspring of will." Stalin, on the other hand, exhibited a remarkable tenacity of purpose and an acute alertness to changes in the popular mood. He usually exercised caution and avoided unnecessary tactical risks until his enemies were ripe for a well-timed blow.

Trotsky's resounding defeat was skillfully camouflaged by his witty aphorisms and catchy slogans. His literary brilliance has created around his catastrophe a lasting legend which is still with us.

SUGGESTED READING

BRANDT, CONRAD, *Stalin's Failure in China.* Cambridge, Mass.: Harvard University Press, 1958.

CARR, E. H., *The Bolshevik Revolution: The Interregnum, 1923–1924.* New York: Macmillan, 1954.

————, *The Bolshevik Revolution: Socialism in One Country, 1924–1926.* New York: Macmillan, 1958–1964, 3 vols. in 4 parts.

CHESTER, LEWIS, STEPHEN FAY, and HUGO YOUNG, *The Zinoviev Letter.* Philadelphia: Lippincott, 1968.

DALLIN, DAVID, *The Rise of Russia in Asia.* New Haven, Conn.: Yale University Press, 1949.

DANIELS, ROBERT V., *The Conscience of the Revolution: The Communist Opposition in Soviet Russia.* Cambridge, Mass.: Harvard University Press, 1960.

DAY, RICHARD B., *Leon Trotsky and the Politics of Economic Isolation.* New York: Cambridge University Press, 1973.

DEGRAS, JANE, ed., *Soviet Documents on Foreign Policy.* New York: Oxford University Press, 1951–1953, 3 vols.

DEUTSCHER, ISAAC, *The Prophet Unarmed: Trotsky, 1921–1929.* New York: Oxford University Press, 1959.

————, *The Prophet Outcast: Trotsky, 1929–1940.* New York: Oxford University Press, 1963.

————, *Stalin: A Political Biography* (2nd ed.). New York: Oxford University Press, 1967.

FAINSOD, MERLE, *How Russia Is Ruled* (2nd ed.). Cambridge, Mass.: Harvard University Press, 1963.

GORODETSKY, GABRIEL, *The Precarious Truce. Anglo-Soviet Relations, 1924–27.* New York: Cambridge University Press, 1977.

HAZARD, JOHN, *The Soviet System of Government* (3rd rev. ed.). Chicago: Chicago University Press. 1964.

ISAACS, HAROLD R., *The Tragedy of the Chinese Revolution: A Narrative History from 1925 to 1938.* London: Secker and Warburg, 1938.

RESHETAR, JOHN, *A Concise History of the Communist Party of the Soviet Union.* New York: Praeger, 1960.

RUBINSTEIN, ALVIN, ed., *The Foreign Policy of the Soviet Union.* New York: Random House, 1960, Ch. III.

SHAPIRO, LEONARD, *The Communist Party of the Soviet Union.* New York: Random House, 1959.

TROTSKY, LEON, *The Real Situation in Russia.* New York: Harcourt Brace Jovanovich, 1928.

————, *The Revolution Betrayed.* Garden City, N.Y.: Doubleday, 1937.

ULAM, ADAM, *Stalin: The Man and His Era.* New York: Viking Press, 1973.

WHITING, ALLEN S., *Soviet Policies in China, 1917–1924.* New York: Columbia University Press, 1954.

WILBUR, MARTIN D., and JULIE HOW, eds. *Documents on Communism, Nationalism and Soviet Advisers in China, 1918–1927.* New York: Columbia University Press, 1956.

CHAPTER 13

The Industrialization Debate and the Five-Year Plans

Stalin's decisive victory over Trotsky and the Left Opposition was made possible by his coalition with Trotsky's opponents, Bukharin, Rykov, and Tomsky. Like the previous *Troika*, and like the Left Opposition, Stalin's new partnership with the right wing of the Party was held together as much by a fear of common foes as by shared ideas. Yet the partnership survived such bitter factional controversies as the foreign policy crisis of 1926–1927. What scuttled this successful coalition was Stalin's sudden and quite unexpected decision to precipitate a grandiose industrialization scheme.

As early as 1923–1924, when the NEP achieved its first breakthrough, the question arose as to whether it should be regarded as a short-range maneuver, "a tactical retreat," or a long-term guide for Russia's economic future. The problem was not easy to solve. Although the NEP scored many successes, even its supporters could not deny that it suffered from many contradictions. One of the most crucial was the disparity between

the development of agriculture and that of industry, which resulted in the glaring difference between the prices of foodstuffs and industrial goods.

The gap between rising industrial and low agricultural prices was compared by Trotsky to two blades opening on a pair of scissors. The term "price scissors" was a graphic metaphor for the growing disparity between the two categories of prices; this was one of the basic contradictions of the NEP. The government's policy was at the root of the crisis, for the State was buying cheaply from the peasants and selling them the often inferior, expensive products of its industry. The difference was pocketed by the treasury and it went to finance further expansion, mostly of heavy industry, which was of no immediate tangible benefit to the average peasant.

Agriculture had recovered much more rapidly and for a simple reason: its basic capital stock was still there, and the essential skills needed for farming were relatively few. It was different, however, with industry, where retooling the ruined factories and training a skilled labor force were a protracted and costly process. A large part of the machinery was of foreign origin, and by the mid-1920s was either used up or obsolete and had to be imported with hard currency, which was not readily available. Moreover, plants were not always used to their full capacity; planning, still in its experimental stages, seldom worked in practice. Finally, overhead expenses were high, and the huge Soviet bureaucracy unwieldly, expensive, and inefficient. As a result of these factors, industrial products were scarce and inferior in quality.

THE CRISIS OF THE NEP

The "goods famine" was especially true of the basic products most needed in the countryside: farm machinery, domestic utensils, hardware, shoes, clothing, and so on. As a consequence of the goods famine, the peasants were not interested in selling their produce in the cities and tended to consume it themselves. This amounted to a spontaneous boycott of the cities by the peasantry. The revival of the countryside had reinforced the traditional self-sufficiency of the peasantry, while the abolition of the peasants' arrears had given them greater freedom in deciding how much and what to sell. Thus the Soviet regime was kept at bay by the defiant peasants.

By 1927 food production had risen to the 1913 level, yet the marketed surplus grain available for urban consumption and export was less than a third of its pre-war volume. The easiest means of increasing the supply of agricultural produce was to end the goods famine by offering the peasantry a quid pro quo in the form of suitably priced and properly manufactured cheap consumer goods. However, suspicious as always of "creeping capitalism" and the growing peasant power in a country where nearly 80 percent of the population lived in the countryside, the Government refused to do so.

As a result, in 1927, State acquisition of grain fell short of the expected minimum by some 2 million tons. The cities were threatened with near starvation.

The Left Opposition reacted to the situation with the slogan, "The kulaks grasped the worker by the throat." The term *kulak* literally means fist; it denotes the tough, hard-working, stingy farmers who were often also tight-fisted local money lenders. By the 1927 census, only 5 percent of the Soviet peasants were in that category because they owned more land than they could cultivate and consequently had to hire labor. Soviet propaganda pictured the kulak as a fat-bellied usurer, a blood-sucking monster eager to exploit his less fortunate fellow villagers. Actually, most kulaks were hard-working, industrious farmers. They used most of the available farming machinery, and most of the market grain came from them.

THE INDUSTRIALIZATION DEBATE: BUKHARIN'S STAND

The question of what was to be done, of whither the Russian economy, became a subject of protracted, passionate debate among the two rival wings of the Party. "The industrialization debate," as the polemics of the middle 1920s were called, was closely connected with the previously described struggle for power, with the coming launching of the First Five-Year Plan, and even with issues of foreign policy. Both the right and the left wings were committed to modernization; their differences were methodological. They argued about the rate of industrialization and the sources of its financing. Both the Right and the Left recognized that further economic progress depended largely on expanding and retooling the existing plants, and on the construction of new ones. While the Left insisted on a more rapid and ambitious investment program in heavy industry, Bukharin advised a more evolutionary and cautious development. He hoped that the steady growth of the State's consumer goods plants combined with the output of the private sector, including handicraft, would alleviate the growing goods famine.

Bukharin's concept envisaged the continuation of two parallel sectors: the public, embracing "the commanding heights" of the economy, and the private, composed of small industry, handicraft, and individual peasant farming. Bukharin insisted on a more balanced development. He suggested a variety of practical measures for economizing on capital while still making significant investments in heavy industry. Bukharin also hoped for "painless" accumulation by encouraging peasants to increase production, make profits, and deposit those profits in State-run banks, which meant putting their savings at the disposal of the State. State intervention through credit investment and control of the "commanding heights," he argued, was more than enough to preserve the balance and the "leading role of the Party." Soviet power's firmest support would be assured by the continuation of the worker–peasant alliance, the Leninist *smychka*, with the workers in the vanguard. Like all other Bolsheviks, Bukharin was far from being a liberal or a democrat. What he wanted was to make the Soviet power more stable by humanizing it somewhat and thus making it acceptable to the bulk of the population—the peasant masses.

The only way out of the scissor crisis, argued the Right, was to cut industrial prices and thus encourage the demand for manufactured goods. This in turn would allow State industry to produce more cheaply. The accumulated industrial profits could enhance industrial growth all along the line. The State monopolistic practices advocated by the Left, such as enforced low prices for food, were decried by Bukharin as a continuation of "War Communism." Such practices would simply stifle incentives for food producers, while at the same time crippling industrial growth for the sake of temporary profit. Given the opportunity to purchase goods they needed, argued the

Construction of a dam on the Volga

Right, the peasants would increase their supply of food to the urban population. Moreover, the surplus harvest could be used as barter to import the capital goods so badly needed for the expansion of industry. Consequently, the Right argued for more stability of land tenure, for State credits and tax relief for the peasants, for supplying the countryside better with the goods the peasants needed most at a suitable price. Bukharin's stand implied an almost indefinite continuation of the mixed economy, the essence of the NEP.

THE LEFT OPPOSITION'S STAND

This economic program was regarded as reactionary by the Left. According to Trotsky and his chief economic supporter, Yevgenii A. Preobrazhensky, all of this meant the appeasement of the petty bourgeois forces represented by the bulk of the peasantry. The Left was unwilling to make concessions to the peasants and insisted upon speedy industrialization above all else, at the same time paying lip service to non-coercive methods. Because there had been little new capital construction since the war, argued Preobrazhensky, the level of technology was relatively low. The size of the capital stock might even diminish as the patched-up machinery started to fall apart. Soviet Russia would therefore be falling further and further behind the advanced, capitalist countries. For these reasons, the Left insisted that immediate, rapid industrial investment was a vital necessity.

Since investment must take place at the expense of consumption, the Left felt that the necessary belt-tightening should be applied first by the peasants, who were living better than ever and consuming most of the surpluses. Collectivization would make the prosperous peasants "disgorge" their surpluses and thus solve the urgent problem of procuring food for the cities. The supervision of some 25 million individual households was impossible; and collectivization would not only solve that problem but would also allow for mechanization, so that modern technology would be introduced into the backward countryside. In the long run, ran the argument of the Left opposition, collectivization would be the best way to ensure that the recalcitrant peasants would supply food regularly and cheaply to the State. The Government could then resell the produce to the urban population. The profit that they would pocket would provide the treasury with the capital necessary for the further development of heavy industry.

"Taxation by price," one of the Left Opposition's formulas, allowed for continued high prices for manufactured goods combined with low prices for produce. The Left also argued that economic growth would be, in the long run, faster and more solid if investment were directed largely to heavy industry. Investment in light industry could only very slowly and indirectly lead to overall economic progress, and at a higher cost. This the Soviet Union, surrounded by capitalist enemies eager to invade it under any pretext, could not afford. It had to modernize at a faster rate than the more advanced bourgeois countries in order to catch up with them. Trotsky maintained that Soviet

Russia without a solid base of heavy industry would be unable to fulfill its revolutionary task as a leader of the world proletariat. It would be "a clawless kitten trying to climb an oak tree."

Besides these economic aspects, the industrialization debate also had ideological implications connected with the clash between Trotsky's "permanent revolution" and Stalin's "socialism in one country." The theoretical controversy was urgently felt because of the growing isolation of the worker's Party in a still overwhelmingly agrarian and partly capitalist country. As Trotsky, paraphrasing Lenin, put it, "A proletarian government cannot function in a country where an overwhelming majority is composed of peasants." It was feared that "creeping capitalist" elements would eventually link up with foreign imperialists and together overthrow the Soviet regime. Thus the growing kulak and Nepman power was regarded by the Left as a threat to Soviet power.

On the other hand, Bukharin hoped that fair prices and an abundance of consumer goods would entice the peasants to increase steadily the amount of surplus food they brought to market, but the prospect was constantly jeopardized by the goods famine. In 1925 when, despite a good harvest, grain collection fell considerably below official expectations, his warning proved judicious. Yet it was not heeded and a similar crisis occurred in 1927.

Without reserves, unable to provide the villages with enough industrial goods to obtain enough food, yet unwilling to disrupt industrial investment plans by raising grain prices sufficiently, Stalin resorted in January 1928 to "extraordinary measures." They involved massive reprisals against the prosperous peasantry, confiscation of the available food produce, and arrest of the owners as "saboteurs" and "speculators." This momentous decision led to the launching of the original inflated version of the five-year plan, which included a scheme of collectivizing 20 percent of the individual farms. This finally precipitated an open break between the Politburo Right and Stalin. It also spelled the end of the NEP era.

SOVIET PLANNING

Before analyzing the first two five-year plans, let us examine briefly the role of planning in Soviet theory and practice. State planning has always been an integral part of Marxist thinking; it is inherent in the public ownership of the means of production, which is the essence of Marxist socialism. "Anarchy of production" was, according to Marx and Engels, the inevitable result of an economic and political organization based on the private ownership of capital, the mainspring of which is not satisfaction of human social needs but blind greed. Reliance on the market mechanism as the sole means of equating supply and demand of goods and services was bound to be subject to the violent fluctuations so characteristic of the capitalistic system. To remedy this, an element of rationality ought to be injected in the form of central planning.

Consequently, planning had been introduced into the Soviet economy almost simultaneously with the nationalization of what Lenin called "the commanding heights": banks, transport, communication, foreign trade, and eventually also most of the industry. Since the early 1920s, centralized planning has been described as a major coordinating mechanism in the Soviet economy. To charter and coordinate economic planning in 1921, the State Planning Commission (Gosplan) was established, directly subordinate to the Council of People's Commissars. The task of the Gosplan was to supervise the allocation of resources and to produce both annual and long-term plans, including the quintessence of Soviet economic thinking: the five-year plans.

A Soviet five-year plan is more than just a purely technical document; it reflects a certain all-embracing vision of the future. It describes in general terms what lies ahead in the planned period in all fields of human activity—not only in the economy, but also in education, science, culture, and internationally. Widely publicized in abbreviated forms and slogans, it is also an instrument of propaganda that aims at mobilizing energy and enthusiasm for the realization of certain overall goals, political as well as economic.

As we know, between 1925 and 1928 Stalin supported Bukharin. The fact that Bukharin's moderate theories momentarily fitted better the policy of "socialism in one country" misled the leaders of the Right. Stalin often denounced the leftist program as "irresponsible adventurism" that would undermine the Leninist principle of worker–peasant alliance. Stalin needed Bukharin's support in the struggle against Trotsky. It is worth remembering that on the surface, the power of the Right was impressive. At that time, they controlled many levers of power: the premiership (Rykov), the Party theoretical organs and the Comintern (Bukharin), the trade unions (Tomsky). In addition, many experts of the Gosplan were also close to the Right, and this enhanced their false sense of security. Like Trotsky, in whose final destruction they had acquiesced, the Right forgot where the real locus of power resided.

THE FIRST FIVE-YEAR PLAN

With the smashing of the Left Opposition, however, Stalin's line underwent a rapid change. In November 1928, in the First Five-Year Plan, he forced a huge increase in investment in heavy industry. Disregarding his former condemnation of the Left Opposition's program as "irresponsible adventurism," he imposed on the reluctant experts of the State Planning Commission capital investment goals far higher than Trotsky and Preobrazhensky had ever dared to advocate. The five-year plan adopted by the Sixteenth Party Congress in April 1929 provided for an increase in total industrial output of 250 percent and in heavy industry of 330 percent. Coal production was to be doubled, pig iron tripled, and electric energy quadrupled. In an agrarian country, diverting such a hugh share of resources to investment in industry could be accomplished only by primitive accumulation at the expense of the peasantry. Here was the great contradiction of the plan: on paper it envisaged collectivization of only 25 percent of the land while providing for an increase in food production of 150 percent. How this paradox was to be resolved was a mystery.

Thus in 1929, overriding the vocal opposition of the Right, Stalin embarked on a superindustrialization program, his "great leap forward." The rapid tempo of industrialization was predicated on the collectivization of agriculture, which squeezed both capital and additional manpower for industrial equipment from the lifeblood of the peasantry by means of "primitive socialist accumulation."

The First Five-Year Plan, which was to go from August 1928 to August 1933, was forced through over the protests of the Right Opposition. According to Bukharin, the October Revolution was a mixture of proletarian upheaval and peasant mutiny. The Bolshevik victory was a result of an alliance, a *smychka*, between these two classes. To assure the continuation of Soviet power, the alliance should be strengthened and not weakened; this was, he argued, the essence of Lenin's phrase, "democratic dictatorship of workers and peasants." Launching a forcible collectivization drive would endanger the foundations of Bolshevik power and plunge the country into another civil war. These arguments were brushed aside by Stalin, who accused the Right not only of dragging their feet on industrialization, but of attempting to "put the brake on the Revolution" and "surrendering the position to the capitalist elements"—the Nepmen and the kulaks.

In November 1929, Bukharin, Rykov, and Tomsky were removed from the Politburo, and Stalin pushed forward with his overoptimistic objective of "putting Soviet Russia in a motor car and the peasant upon a tractor." In his words, "steps were to be taken to restrict the development of capitalism in the countryside and guide peasant farming toward socialism." The statement was misleading and hypocritical. The previous decade had demonstrated that no amount of friendly persuasion would "guide" the peasants, fiercely attached to their land, into collective or state farms. Only massive coercion could achieve that target. Since administrative pressure, vigorous propaganda, and administrative prodding failed again, by the autumn of 1929 an embittered struggle was unleashed in the countryside to press the reluctant and hostile peasantry into the collective farms (*kolkhozy*). The struggle focused on the kulaks. As Stalin put it, the kulaks were to be "liquidated as a class." The term "liquidation" was now assuming an increasingly sinister meaning in the Soviet vocabulary.

In his study of the development of capitalism in prerevolutionary Russia, Lenin defined the poor peasant as one with very little or no land and no horse; the middle peasant as the owner of enough land to support his family and keep one or two horses; those who had more land and more horses, and hired labor to help them cultivate their plots were denounced as kulaks. Even this far from scholarly, rather elastic definition was now brushed aside. Anybody opposed to collectivization, or even to the Soviet regime in general, was accused of being a kulak, hence a member of the exploiting class, and as such declared a "saboteur" or "wrecker." The term kulak, as Soviet officials often admitted quite openly, came to denote not an economic status, or even a social class, but a state of mind.[1]

---

[1] As a British scholar not entirely unsympathetic to the Soviet objectives, if not their methods, admitted, "It was not the class analysis that determined policy. It was policy that determined what form of class analysis was appropriate to a given situation." E. H. Carr, *A History of Soviet Russia: Socialism in One Country* (London: Macmillan Press, Ltd., 1953), p. 47 © 1953 by Macmillan Press, Ltd.

The first measures applied in the process of *dekulakization* were fiscal. In addition to already high taxes, a special household tax was levied on those classified as "exploiters and profiteers," hence "enemies of the people." The high household tax was to be paid in cash and/or food produce, usually within twenty-four hours after its assessment. After the expiration of the time limit, the delinquent's farm was usually raided by members of the "Committee of Poor Peasants" and the Komsomol squads, often backed by the local militia. The farm would be confiscated, the owner arrested and deported. Meanwhile, poorer peasants were allowed to grab the *kulak's* possessions and pool them on the collective farms then painfully taking shape.

Opposition to collectivization was by no means limited to real and alleged *kulaks*. It was so widespread and so fierce that often even the local militia and the Komsomol were unable to cope with it, and Red Army units had to be dispatched. In some cases pitched battles were fought between army detachments and the local resisters. This was, in some localities, like a new civil war. Altogether, some 5 million people were deported to Siberia and other distant parts of the Soviet empire, mostly to the far north. Where the opposition was only passive, peasant hostility was expressed in acts of sabotage and the application of go-slow methods; many refused to sow and reap and perform other duties on the newly founded collective farms. In many instances wholesale slaughter of cattle and horses, or the destruction of implements, or even the burning of farm buildings would take place. At the peak of collectivization, the desperate destructive rage assumed massive proportions and thus crippled the productivity

Harvesting on collective farm (*kolkhoz*)

of Soviet agriculture for at least two decades.

BALANCE SHEET OF COLLECTIVIZATION

Collectivization uprooted and destroyed millions of peasants. The exact figures were still a subject of scholarly dispute. This was modernization achieved through "primitive socialist accumulation by the methods of Tamerlane," to use a phrase of Soviet economist N. Valentinov. Those who were spared either had to join the kolkhozy immediately or flee to the large cities where, behind a veil of anonymity, they would seek employment in the mushrooming industries. Consequently, collectivization achieved several objectives at one blow: it destroyed a fairly large stratum of prosperous farmers and hence relatively independent people who, through their industry and self-sufficiency, were a challenge to the system. In addition to that, the dispossessed peasants, either as forced labor or as fugitives in the cities, increased the manpower available to the State to achieve its ever-ambitious plans. The millions deported to labor camps and compulsory settlements created a sprawling network of concentration camps, or what Alexander Solzhenitsyn would later on term the *Gulag Archipelago.*[2]

Resistance to collectivization was fiercest in those regions of the USSR that had a strong traditon of individual farming, like the Ukraine and the northern regions of the Caucasus. It was there, especially in the Ukrainian provinces, that the aftermath of the dekulakization resulted in a widespread famine that reached its peak in 1932–1933. The famine was only partly a result of an actual food shortage. Since throughout the first and second five-year plans the Soviet Union exported considerable quantities of food, some of it could have been diverted to

feed the millions of starving people. The decision at the top, however, was to punish the widespread resistance to the Kremlin's decrees rather than to diminish the amount of hard currency that food export provided. While some regions experienced actual starvation, all of the Soviet Union was affected by the dramatic drop in food production during collectivization. The scarcity of food and of consumer goods in general was experienced by everyone, except a small group at the top. Food rationing had to be introduced, and it lasted until 1933.

By the end of January 1930, there were slightly over 4 million peasant families on collective farms. By March 1 of the same year the number had increased to 14 million. This amounted to about 45 percent of all peasant families, more than twice what the plan had anticipated. The terrible tensions generated by forcible collectivization, bordering on open civil war, must have been threatening to the stability of the regime. By that time it was obvious that things had gotten out of hand, and Stalin intervened personally. On March 2, 1930, Stalin published an article in *Pravda* entitled "Dizzy With Success." He stressed that nearly 50 percent of all farms had been collectivized; this exceeded by 100 percent the goal envisaged in the five-year plan. In his typically repetitious manner, he stressed that "People are often intoxicated by such successes, they become dizzy with success, they lose all sense of proportion, they lose the faculty of understanding realities."

Stalin's article meant that he was now trying to shift the blame for the ruthlessness with which his instructions had been executed onto the shoulders of his allegedly overzealous agents, who were then punished for their loyalty to him. Meanwhile, collectivization was to proceed at a slower pace so as not to wreck Soviet agriculture altogether. Soon a series of arrests of the most zealous officials of the Ministry of Agriculture took place. These officials were accused of sabotaging the process and persecuting innocent people.

Nevertheless, at the Sixteenth Party Con-

---

[2] The term *Gulag* is an abbreviation of the Soviet official term denoting "General Administration of Labor Camps."

gress in June 1930, Stalin triumphantly proclaimed it "the Congress of the sweeping offensive of socialism along the whole front, of the elimination of kulaks as a class. . . ." In 1928, there had been more than 25 million individually owned farms with an average sown area of 11 acres. By the close of 1930, the land was redivided into some 250,000 collective farms (kolkhozy) with an average sown area of 1,200 acres. In addition, some 4,000 State farms (sovkhozy) cultivated an average of 7,500 acres each. While in 1928 nearly 96 percent of the land was in private hands, by 1938 over 94 percent was, in one form or another, controlled by the State.

The collectivization, completed by 1937–1938, exacted a terrible price. Besides the 5 million people who perished, one way or another, in the collectivization process and the famine of 1932–1933 that parallelled its middle stages, material losses were staggering. While in 1928 the USSR had 32 million horses, by 1934 only 15 million survived; of 60 million cows, only 33 million remained by 1934; similar figures for sheep are 97 million and 37 million. The overall per capita agricultural production of 1928 was not reached again until 1938, if we are to believe official Soviet statistics.

THE SOVIET AGRARIAN SYSTEM

After having crushed peasant resistance by administrative and fiscal inquisition, starvation, and force of arms, Stalin proceeded to reorganize Soviet agriculture to fulfill his goals. While State farms were considerably expanded in number and size, it was the collective farm sector that absorbed the bulk of the land and manpower. While sovkhozy were directly operated by the Ministry of State Farms with hired labor, kolkhozy were supposed to be self-governing cooperatives. They were allegedly voluntarily established agricultural enterprises run by their peasant members. Initially, four types of collective farms were organized; they differed as to the degree of pooling of land and the

amount of livestock and implements. In the strictest type of kolkhoz, everything was owned and operated in common. The loosest type, on the other hand, was reminiscent of the Western agricultural cooperative: each peasant family kept title to its own land, livestock, and implements, while joining with other families to cultivate land, purchase seeds and machinery, and market the surplus produce. In the middle was the arrangement called by the traditional name of *artel* (or craftsmen association) but different from it in nature. In the agricultural artel of the Soviet type, peasants retained possession of their own cottage and livestock, as well as a small garden plot that they were free to cultivate as they saw fit; the remaining resources were to be merged.

While originally the authorities favored the first, tightest type of collective farm, the peasants preferred mostly the loosest form. The violent resistance to the process eventually compelled Stalin to accept the middle-of-the-road type, the agricultural collective. Currently, about 90 percent of the kolkhozy are of this type. The peasantry thereby scored at least a partial victory and preserved the vestigial features of their farms in the form of miniature household plots.

Although legally the kolkhoz is a free, self-governing agricultural cooperative, in reality it has been strictly controlled by the State and the Party. The first instrument of control has been the chairmanship of the farm. Theoretically, the kolkhoz chairmen were elected by their members. In reality, they have mostly been appointed from above and most are Party members. Through them, the authorities communicate their economic plans and political instructions.

The second instrument of control on the farms was, until March 1958, the Motor Tractor Station (or MTS). Owned by the State, the MTS was to furnish to the collective farms the machinery necessary to sow and harvest the crops prescribed by the plan. For these services the kolkhoz had to pay a fixed price, most of it in crops. The remaining annual output of the kolkhoz was as a rule divided in the following way. Under Stalin, priority number one was the compulsory quota of grain to be delivered to the State at a price drastically below its market value. When the prescribed allotments had been made for capital and reserve stock, for seeds, fodder, and insurance, the remainder was distributed in accordance with the number of labor days involved in its production. Consequently, the collective farmers were reduced to the level of sharecroppers or even residual claimants to the fruits of their labor. Obligations to the State were always to be met first, regardless of the size of the crop. Stalin himself bluntly called compulsory deliveries "something of a tribute" imposed on the newly subdued masses of peasantry to force them to finance industrialization.

In calculating labor days, almost all emphasis has been on the quantity of work performed. As a consequence, by and large, the work on collective and State farms is performed carelessly, as it was in times of serfdom. This is especially true of animal husbandry, where individual care and attention are preconditions of success. On the other hand, the peasants tend to lavish their labor on the minute patches of land left to them in the form of household plots. Constantly threatened by the State encroachments and restrictive regulations, the household plot, cultivated with love and care by their owners, has remained an important source of livelihood, not only for collective farmers but also for the rest of the country. So far, no amount of moral or material incentives have been able to persuade the sullen peasantry to provide enough labor for the collective enterprises to function efficiently. In contrast, privately owned plots, amounting to some three percent of all cultivated land, produce nearly half of all Soviet meat, milk, and green vegetables.

The purpose of collectivization was threefold. First, it was to assure steady procurement of cheap food without taxing industry too much. Second, collectivization, to be followed by mechanization of the agricultural processes, was to free a considerable

number of superfluous workers who would then be pumped into the urban labor market. Third, collectivization would make it possible to tighten politico-economic controls over a countryside hitherto relatively free from party intervention. These controls were to assure that the peasant masses would remain politically obedient to the regime's fiat, and that they would deliver the prescribed quotas of produce to the State at fixed, nominal prices. The produce was then to be sold and the difference pocketed by the State to be used for its purposes, largely for further industrialization. Thus the burden of the "second revolution" was overwhelmingly shifted onto the shoulders of the peasantry, now reduced, in many ways, to a status similar to that existing prior to its emancipation in the 1860s. Individual landlords were now replaced by the collective master—the State. Clearly, the quintessence of collectivization was to wrest from the farmer a large share of agricultural output in the form of compulsory deliveries, without providing an adequate quid pro quo.

Forced collectivization, completed at a stupendous human and material cost, produced immediate benefits to the regime by assuring an adequate supply of food to the expanding city population during the crucial states of industrialization. But the long-run effects have been negative. Soviet agriculture was crippled for a decade or more. Even today, over seventy years after the Bolshevik revolution and over fifty years after the end of collectivization, Soviet farms are unable to produce sufficient food for the Soviet population and constant import of food from abroad is a painful drain on Soviet resources.

INDUSTRIALIZATION

Parallel to collectivization, the main lines of the industrialization scheme were unfolding. The first two five-year plans had three main industrial objectives: first, to expand and modernize the already functioning industries; second, to construct entirely new branches of industry to complement the existing plants; and third, to alter the USSR's economic geography by relocating those plants that were too close to the exposed western or southern frontiers of the country and placing them further away in more secure places.

The plan was launched in August 1929 in an atmosphere of officially sponsored optimism. The first apparent successes pushed the leaders even further. The Sixteenth Party Congress, held in June–July 1930, went so far as to adopt the slogan, "The five-year plan in four years." But soon numerous difficulties began to develop. Industrialization was embarked upon too hastily, with insufficient resources, and with a limited pool of skilled labor. Moreover, overcentralized planning did not always work in practice. Often the untrained workers could not operate the complicated machinery, which was frequently put in unsuitable locations. There were cases of factories provided with the wrong type of equipment, or of machinery sent to enterprises unable to house it. Following Stalin's battle cry, "There are no fortresses that Bolsheviks could not conquer," shock tactics were applied. Specially mobilized "brigades" of workers and engineers, some of them volunteers from the Komsomol, were dispatched to perform emergency tasks. "Socialist competition of labor" was encouraged, to be rewarded not only with honorific titles, medals, and citations, but also with bonuses and other material benefits. At the end of 1932, it was officially announced that the overall objectives of the First Five-Year Plan had been achieved ahead of time.

Even now, after more than five decades, it is difficult to judge to what extent the triumphant declaration corresponded to reality. According to official Soviet figures, which have been questioned by many Western economists, the output of machinery and electric equipment expanded by 157 percent over the 1929 level, which would represent overfulfillment of the plan. On the other hand, iron and steel production rose only to 6.2 million (instead of 10 million) tons. The output of coal was only 65,000,000 tons instead of 75 million, while consumer goods production increased by only 73 percent. Whatever the veracity of the Soviet statistics, in the industrial field the overall achievements of the plan were impressive. Two new important industrial centers were established, one in the Urals (Magnitogorsk) and the other in southern Siberia (Kuznetsk). Entirely new branches of industry were developed, such as aviation, plastics, and synthetic rubber. Consequently, the plan constituted an important milestone in the process of the socioeconomic transformation of Russia.

While the quantitative achievements, although undoubtedly exaggerated by Soviet propaganda, were impressive enough, the quality of goods produced left a great deal to be desired. In the case of some consumer goods, rejects amounted to 40 percent or more. In view of this, the fundamental task of the Second Five-Year Plan, launched in 1933, was "the completion of the technical construction in the whole of the national economy," and the improvement of the quality of goods produced. The number of failures and nonfulfillments of the first plan compelled Soviet economists to lower some targets of the second. Nevertheless, the second plan also gave priority to heavy industry. The machine tool industry again expanded considerably, and the output of nonferrous metals (especially copper, lead, zinc, aluminum, nickel and magnesium) was increased dramatically.

One of the weaknesses revealed during the first Five-Year Plan was that of the Soviet infrastructure, especially roads, railroads, and canals. Consequently, the second plan also provided for reconstruction and double-tracking of the principal lines, starting with the Trans-Siberian Railroad. The Japanese occupation of Chinese Manchuria in 1931 made it of strategically paramount importance. By 1933, the altered international position of the USSR resulting from

The dam of Dnieprostroi in construction

Hitler's seizure of power was reflected in an expansion of armament production. The widening of old canals and the construction of new ones (like the Moscow-Volga canal) was another vital task assigned to the new plan.

During the Second Five-Year Plan the Soviet armament industry was reorganized to enhance its centralized structure and to be readier for the quick mobilization of resources in case of a war emergency. The armed forces that had emerged from the Civil War were being gradually reshaped into an increasingly professional, modern fighting machine, comparable to those of other great powers. Between 1933 and 1936, the size of the Red Army trebled; from 562,000 it grew to 1.3 million, which exceeded in size the 1913 Imperial army. The Soviet armed forces were increasingly mechanized, and a powerful air force was developed. The Red Army was the first to organize large parachutist units.

As with the First Five-Year Plan, the second was also officially declared completed ahead of time in 1937. Again, however, not all its goals were achieved. Among the items that surpassed their estimated targets were steel (17.6 million tons instead of the projected 17 million) and the automotive industry, created practically from scratch, which could now boast of an eightfold increase. The most striking failures of the second plan were oil (30.5 million instead of 46.8 million tons), coal (128 million instead of 152 million tons), and consumer goods in general. Cotton in particular fell far behind its relatively modest target.

THE RESULTS

Despite many failures, the first two five-year plans increased the industrial capacity of the USSR dramatically in all major fields—steel, coal, electric power—and created new branches indispensable to any great modern power (automobiles, aviation, chemicals, plastics). Consequently, the first two five-year plans laid the foundation of the present-day industrial might of the Soviet Union.

The first major objective of the plans, expansion and modernization of industry, was largely achieved. In 1928, the share of industry in the total production of the USSR was 58.7 percent, while heavy industry accounted for only 39.7 percent. In 1940, on the brink of World War II, the share of industry in total production had advanced to 84.7 percent, and that of heavy industry to 61.2 percent. Further expression was merely a matter of time and improving the quality of production techniques.

As for the third goal, the relocation of industrial centers, here the successes were also impressive. While in 1929 the USSR had four major industrial centers— Leningrad (metallurgical and machine industry), Moscow (chiefly consumer goods, headed by textiles), the Ukraine (mining, metallurgy, food processing), and the Urals (mining and metallurgy)—by 1937–1938 three new ones were created in Central Asia, Siberia, and the Far East, far away from the vulnerable Western frontiers of the USSR.

Industrial expansion and relocation involved a massive shift of sometimes unwilling citizens, mostly from the countryside to the cities. One of the traditional Marxist goals, the elimination of differences between town and country, was brought closer to realization. Soviet urbanization policy has assumed that the industrial city is the modern sector of socialist society and that urban patterns should triumph over "the idiocy of rural life," as Karl Marx once put it. Here too the progress was striking. While in 1926, out of a total population of 147 million, there were 26 million urban dwellers; in 1939, out of 171 million people, 56 million already lived in urban centers. The more than doubling of the urban population within thirteen years represented in itself a major aspect of the Stalin revolution. Industrialization spelled urbanization and the ex-

pansion of a new style of life more in tune with the Marxist-Leninist ethos.

As in the case of collectivization, the overambitious industrial objectives were also achieved at the cost of great privations and sacrifices. The standard of living of the Soviet population, which by 1928 had reached about the 1913 level, dropped dramatically during the early 1930s. This was Soviet Russia's "iron age." The goods famine was acute, much worse than the over-publicized crisis of 1925–1926. This was reflected in a number of popular stories that people usually whispered in secret. One of them is so characteristic of popular mood that it is worth recording: "How do we know that Adam and Eve were Soviet citizens?" "It is obvious. They had nothing to wear, an apple to share, yet they were told they lived in paradise."

THE SHORTCOMINGS

Breakneck expansion created confusion and an acute shortage of industrial resources and skilled manpower that resulted in fierce scrambling to obtain them at any cost—since fulfillment of the Plan (with a capital P) was often a matter not only of advancement, but even of life and death. Under Stalin, failure was not tolerated; nonfulfillment of the prescribed norm was considered sabotage, and saboteurs were treated as "enemies of the people." One day of unjustified absenteeism was cause for dismissal from work, which meant loss of a ration card and housing, with all the grim consequences for individuals now entirely at the mercy of an increasingly totalitarian regime.

"Socialist competition of labor" led to the establishment of various devices that would assure recognition and reward. For instance, in 1935 a coal miner in the Don basin by the name of Alexey G. Stakhanov organized a team of workers in his mine who apparently achieved spectacular successes by coordinating and directing their efforts toward a common goal. This resulted in their overfulfilling the standard norm many times over. For this Stakhanov received not only a special bonus, but a number of honorific awards, including the Order of Lenin and the Red Labor Banner. He was declared a "hero of socialist labor," withdrawn from actual physical work, and used as a propagandist of the highly competitive Soviet labor system known as Stakhanovism. The example he set was used to justify an increase in production targets for all workers. This in turn resulted in a considerable revulsion against what came to be regarded as a return to the old capitalist sweatshop system in a new guise. In the early 1930s, it was decreed that a worker must go where ordered and carry out tasks prescribed by the authorities at a wage fixed by them. Since collective bargaining had been abolished in 1933, by the middle 1930s Soviet workers found themselves at the mercy of the State.

Stalin's industrialization was hastily undertaken by crude, cruel methods, without adequate know-how or skilled labor. Capital was forcibly squeezed out of the reluctant population, mainly the peasantry, by the process of primitive accumulation.

The arbitrary price system in effect ever since has been politically motivated. Prices for heavy industrial goods were held down by providing subsidies in the form of operational loans granted without interest. Prices of consumer articles were dramatically increased through the imposition of a turnover tax, a sales tax levied on all goods sold by the state to the people. This served a double purpose: on the one hand, high prices of consumer goods curtailed demand; on the other, the exorbitant turnover tax provided a major source of revenue to the Soviet Treasury. By the exercise of ruthless dictatorial power, Stalin succeeded in diverting a huge percentage of the national income to investment and defense purposes.

The first two five-year plans hinged on four fundamental assumptions: first, that

collectivization would bolster Soviet agrarian production; second, that the Soviet Union would have ever-increasing trade surpluses with foreign countries; third, that the Soviet cost of production would decrease and individual labor productivity would increase; and fourth, that the percentage of expenditure for national defense would drop. All these predictions proved false, partly because of Soviet mistakes in executing the collectivization and industrialization and partly because of the rapidly deteriorating international situation.

The Great Depression which began in 1929 resulted in a dramatic decline in world trade. The Japanese invasion of Manchuria in 1931 and Hitler's rise in Germany almost simultaneously created a double menace to the USSR. Both these dangers necessitated reshaping of the five-year plans, especially the second one, and increasing military expenditures. Crop failures, high cost of production, and lagging productivity of labor were the result of domestic mistakes and shortcomings of the rigid, highly centralized planning, of poor management, and not infrequently, of Stalin's love of gigantic projects, as well as his callous indifference to the human cost of achieving his objective.

The program of industrialization was launched by Stalin under the slogan of "catching up with and overtaking the West." Although Soviet modernization was carried out without outside financial aid, it was achieved by importing considerable Western machinery and know-how, as well as by bringing in personnel from Europe and America. The machinery was freely copied by Soviet engineers not hampered by international patent laws. The period of the first five-year plans paralleled the period of the Great Depression. Consequently, Western companies welcomed Soviet orders, while many unemployed American as well as West European engineers, especially Germans, flocked to the Soviet Union in search of work. As Stalin was to admit to the United States wartime ambassador in Moscow, Averell Harriman, more than two-thirds of all foreign companies that were involved in building Soviet industrial projects were American. Stalin and other Soviet leaders often praised American efficiency, and set it as an example to be emulated by Soviet workers and engineers. This quite naive and uncritical admiration for the "American tempo" often led to blind imitation and gigantomania. What was good for the United States was often assumed to be even better for Soviet Russia. An example of this was Stalin's decision on the level of output of the Magnitogorsk Steel Works. According to his close co-worker G. K. Ordzhonikidze, Stalin scrapped the elaborate calculations made by his expert, Professor Ginzburg, as "too defeatist." Then he asked him what was the size of American plants of this type. When he was answered that large pig iron works in the United States produced some 2.5 million tons a year, Stalin bluntly ordered a similar plant built in Magnitogorsk. Later on, he insisted, its output must be increased to 4 million tons. At the same time he ordered Ginzburg to be jailed as a saboteur. Neither order had beneficial results. At that time even a plant producing 2.5 million tons was actually beyond the capacity of Soviet engineers and managers.

SUMMARY

The Stalin revolution of the 1930s created an upheaval far more profound than the Bolshevik revolution of 1917–1921. Besides greatly expanding and restructuring the Soviet economy, the Stalin arbitrary policies profoundly affected practically every aspect of the life of every individual. Internal passports, abolished in 1905, were reintroduced, to remain a standing feature of the Soviet system ever since. Stalin's will was enforced by ruthless mass reprisals and unbridled terror. This resulted in an unprecedented degree of State control over nearly all fields of human activity. The system was characterized by a tight, regimented, centrally planned economy, and rigid thought control, all of which was enforced by an all-pervading terror. Within the framework of the command economy, the Party, manipulated by an increasingly omnipotent dictator, combined its monopoly of political power with tight control over practically the entire economy. In a way, this second revolution represented a return to War Communism, with strong features of Asiatic despotism.

Stalin's grand design stemmed from two things: a totalitarian imperative nourished by inordinate ambition, and a proclivity to treat men in a manipulative way as means to his ends. To him human beings were no more than Pavlov's dogs, to be drilled by conditioned reflexes to perform the desired tricks. Most historians generally agree that, if there ever was a command economy and a totalitarian system, it existed in Soviet Russia for more than a quater of a century under Stalin.

The final judgment about the Stalin revolution is yet to be made by history. Both the results and the price were gigantic. A satisfactory comparison between the rate of Soviet economic progress and that of other countries should be based on adequate, reliable statistics regarding overall input and output. Such data are either lacking or are still so controversial that a final, fair estimate is very difficult. It is perhaps fair to conclude that, whatever the cost involved, Stalin laid down the foundations of the USSR as the second greatest industrial power of the world. From a historic perspective, his "great leap forward" represented a continuation of the work of his two predecessors, Peter the Great and Witte.

SUGGESTED READING

ATKINSON, DOROTHY, *The End of the Russian Land Commune, 1905–1930*. Stanford, Calif.: Stanford University Press, 1983, part V.

BELOV, FËDOR, *A History of a Soviet Collective Farm.* New York: Praeger, 1955.

BERGSON, ABRAM, *The Real National Income of Soviet Russia Since 1928*. Cambridge, Mass.: Harvard University Press, 1961.

BERLINER, JOSEPH S., *Factory and Manager in the USSR*. Cambridge, Mass.: Harvard University Press, 1957.

CHAMBERLIN, WILLIAM H., *Russia's Iron Age*. New York: Arno, 1970.

COHEN, STEPHEN F., *Bukharin and the Bolshevik Revolution: A Political Biography 1888–1938*. New York: Knopf, 1973.

CONQUEST, ROBERT, *The Harvest of Sorrow: Soviet Collectivization and the Terror-Famine*. New York: Oxford University Press, 1986.

DAVIES, R. W., *The Industrialization of Soviet Russia*, 2 vols. Cambridge, Mass.: Harvard University Press, 1980.

HODGEMAN, DONALD R., *Soviet Industrial Production, 1938–1951*. Cambridge, Mass.: Harvard University Press, 1954.

HOLZMAN, FRANKLYN D., *Soviet Taxation*. Cambridge, Mass.: Harvard University Press, 1955.

JASNY, NAUM, *The Socialized Agriculture of the USSR*. Stanford, Calif.: Stanford University Press, 1949.

———, *Soviet Industrialization, 1928–1952*. Chicago: University of Chicago Press, 1961.

———, *The Socialized Agriculture of the USSR*. Stanford, Calif.: Stanford University Press, 1949.

LAIRD, ROY D., ed., *Soviet Agriculture and Peasant Affairs*. Lawrence: University of Kansas Press, 1963.

LEWIN, MOSHE, *Russian Peasants and Soviet Power*, trans. Irene Nove and John Biggart. Evanston, Ill.: Northwestern University Press, 1968.

NOVE, ALEC, *An Economic History of the USSR*. London: Allen Lane, 1969.

———, *The Soviet Economy*. New York: Praeger, 1961.

NUTTER, G. WARREN ET AL., *The Growth of Production in the Soviet Union*. Princeton, N.J.: Princeton University Press, 1962.

PREOBRAZHENSKY, EVGENI, *The New Economics*, trans. B. Pearce. New York: Oxford University Press, 1965.

SCHWARTZ, HARRY, *Russia's Soviet Economy* (2nd ed.), Englewood Cliffs, N.J.: Prentice-Hall, Inc., 1954.

SCOTT, JOHN, *Behind the Urals: An American Worker in Russia's City of Steel*. New York: Arno, 1971.

SHAPIRO, LEONARD, *The Origin of the Communist Autocracy: The First Phase, 1917–1922*. Cambridge, Mass.: Harvard University Press, 1977.

ZALESKI, EUGENE, *Stalinist Planning for Growth 1933–1952*, edited and translated by Marie-Christine MacAndrew and John H. Moore. Chapel Hill: University of North Carolina Press, 1980.

CHAPTER 14

The Purges

In 1944, Stalin told General Charles de Gaulle that the best way to make men achieve things was by instilling fear in them. This axiom he practiced throughout most of his rule. The second revolution was so profound and extensive that it could be enforced only by inhumanly harsh measures. The full fury of the terror did not come at once, however, it was rather a product of the evolution of the Soviet system from one in which coercion existed on a large scale but was selective and controlled, to a regime where terror became its central feature.

Stalin, of course, did not invent mass reprisals. From the beginning, the Bolsheviks considered human life expendable, subordinate to the process of history, and the ultimate goal as sanctifying the means. The Cheka always acted not in accordance with strict legality but by following its "revolutionary conscience." In 1922 the Cheka (the full name of which was "The Extraordinary Committee for Fighting Counter-Revolution and Sabotage") was renamed the GPU, or the Chief Political Administration. Thus the "extraordinary" institution became an ordinary one, an integral part of Soviet life even during the NEP. Its increasingly ubiquitous activity initially affected not so much Party members as actual or suspected enemies of the Soviet regime. Until 1934 the Bolsheviks seldom punished their high-ranking comrades with death; this was reserved for the "enemies of the people." At first, the idea of exterminating one's political opponents within the Party was regarded as unacceptable, and until the mid-1930s there existed an unwritten law that Bolsheviks do not kill Bolsheviks. Even Stalin's archenemy Trotsky, despite the vitriolic attacks and wild accusations hurled against him, was merely expelled from the Party and exiled in 1929.

But, paradoxically enough, as the Stalin regime grew in strength, so did the intensity and the scope of its repression. The launching of the First Five-Year Plan saw the first trials of economic experts as "wreckers" and "saboteurs," allegedly responsible for the shortcomings that were revealed in the execution of Stalin's various grandiose undertakings. This signaled the beginning of a lengthy process of displacing the old professional cadres trained under the Tsarist regime, and replacing them with the new Soviet intelligentsia.

THE PATTERNS OF THE EARLY PURGES

Soon a pattern developed according to which, after each political failure or breakdown of production, the "guilty" ones had to be "discovered," charged with their crimes, made to confess, and purged. Soon specific purge institutions developed and a purge ritual was established. According to this ritual, on an appointed day a purging commission would visit a given enterprise, institution, or Party cell. In an open meeting, frequently attended by hundreds of onlookers, the commission would question each employee or Party member. The questions were based on information derived from their autobiographies, from secret police files, from denunciations by their Party comrades, or even from outsiders. During the 1920s a mechanism known as self-criticism was developed. Its function, according to an official Soviet definition, consisted in

exposing the deficiencies and errors in the work of particular persons, organizations and institutions, on the basis of free, businesslike discussion by the toilers of all the problems of economic-political work . . . and developing the ability to see, to uncover and to acknowledge one's mistakes. . . .

Such self-criticism should be practiced regularly by all Soviet citizens, but especially by Party members.

During the Stalin revolution, under pressure from the security organs and often supported by mass media, self-criticism was practiced on a large scale. Of course, self-criticism was subject to the limitations inherent in the totalitarian nature of the Soviet system: it could only deal with mistakes committed by individuals, usually at a lower or middle level, but could never extend to official policies of the regime. While policy itself was taboo, its execution was not, so that subordinate officials were the usual targets of self-criticism and public denunciation, and could be charged with slackness, inefficiency, corruption, or "lack of revolutionary vigilance." This helped the regime to divorce itself from the less popular aspects of its own policies, or to shift the blame for their failures onto the shoulders of a few carefully selected "slackers," "wreckers," and "saboteurs." It became Stalin's habit not to let any of his mistakes go unpunished.

After completing the investigation, the purge commission would announce its verdict. In the case of Party members, the sentence would follow one of three patterns: cleared, cleared with a reprimand, or found guilty. Party members who were found guilty not only were expelled from the Party, but lost their jobs as well. In either case, even if the actual sentence was light, being purged was tantamount to losing's one's ration card and very often one's lodging. Since by the early 1930s practically the entire economy was already controlled by the State, even the lighter punishment left the victim of the purge and his family homeless and destitute.

The purging of "slackers" and "saboteurs" was soon followed by mopping-up operations aimed at the elimination of both wings of the opposition, ex-Trotskyites and ex-Bukharinites. Throughout 1932–1933, stricter attention was also paid to intellectual and scientific workers, especially those belonging to minority groups. In 1934, the GPU was expanded into the People's Commissariat for Internal Affairs (NKVD). This meant that the secret police was to remain not only a permanent, central feature of the regime, but was also to be integrated with one of the key governmental institutions that controlled much of the country's internal life. Moreover, the NKVD was now placed in charge of all existing labor camps. These were increasingly swollen by former kulaks and other "enemies of the people," including selected members of the Party who had become, according to Stalin, "dizzy with success" while carrying out the dictator's orders.

THE KIROV AFFAIR

The year 1934 was a turning point of the purge. In June of that year the Soviet regime broke with the Western principles of individual responsibility and the presumption that any accused person is innocent until proven guilty. The question of guilt or innocence was usually predetermined by a preliminary inquiry, as a rule conducted by the police. In the same year, a decree on "counterrevolution and high treason" provided for collective family responsibility in cases of flight by military personnel abroad. Severe penalties were established for failing to inform the authorities about an act of treason, whether actually committed or merely contemplated. A decree of April 7, 1935 extended capital punishment down to twelve-year-olds.

A line of reasoning alien to the legal concepts common to the entire civilized world called "legal analogy" was incorporated into Soviet criminal laws. For example, if a workman bungled a job he could be severely punished for sabotage, the analogy being that the damage he had done to the State was equal to what would have been done had he consciously engaged in an act of wrecking "socialist property." Since the standard penalty for sabotage was death, a workman who merely permitted a faulty truck transmission to pass through the inspection line could be executed. During the 1930s, this sort of thing occurred frequently. The denunciation of others was increasingly encouraged by rewards; those who refrained from it for whatever reason were publicly condemned. Reporting on one's fellow citizens or even on family members was pronounced a civic and patriotic duty. One of the heroes of Soviet youth was a small boy, Pavlik Morozov, who did not hesitate to denounce his family as counterrevolutionaries.

Until the close of 1934, the purge, as widespread and severe as it appeared, was still selective, directed mainly against actual or potential opposition. As far as the top Party members were concerned, it was on the whole bloodless. What changed the situation entirely was the December 1934 Kirov affair and its aftermath. Since the personality and activities of Kirov played a central role here, a few words about him are in order. Born Sergei M. Kostrikov, a graduate of a two-year technical school in Kazan, he joined the Leninist faction of the RSDWP in 1905 at the age of nineteen. After the Bolshevik triumph, Kirov took part in the establishment of Soviet power in the Caucasus, where he was a firm supporter of Stalin's stern methods. On the strength of this record, he replaced the demoted Zinoviev in 1926 in the second most important Party district, Leningrad. His purge of the supporters of Zinoviev and Trotsky was as stern as his struggle against "the bourgeois nationalists" in the Caucasus. As a reward, Kirov was promoted to membership in the Politburo in 1930.

Soon, however, the excesses of Stalin's tyranny began to alienate even as tough a man as Kirov. At the Seventeenth Party Congress of 1934, Kirov was already critical of Stalin's personal dictatorship. During the Congress he argued for reconciliation, saying that the class enemies had been routed and the Soviet system was secure and needed all those who were not against it. His speech was applauded. If we are to believe Roy Medvedev's book *Let History Judge* (based on secret police archives temporarily opened to Soviet historians by Khrushchev during the late 1950s), the Seventeenth Party Congress witnessed a major crisis of the regime. In the election to the Central

Committee, Stalin received fewer votes than any other candidate, while Kirov was at the top of the list. Stalin was elected only because there were as many candidates as seats in the Central Committee.

Meanwhile, through the secret police, Stalin had learned that many Party members favored his removal from the post of Secretary General and his replacement by the popular Kirov. The latter, when approached in private, secret conversations, repeatedly rejected the suggestion. What Stalin thought about the matter he never revealed. In any case, on December 1, 1934, Kirov was assassinated in his office in Leningrad under circumstances that pointed at least to criminal negligence on the part of the security organs. In the light of Khrushchev's speech at the Twentieth Party Congress in February 1956, as well as of other evidence subsequently revealed, it is quite clear that Kirov was killed by the secret police in order to remove him from Stalin's path.

Whatever the final verdict, Kirov's assassination stands as one of the most important landmarks in the history of Soviet Russia. Immediately, and without even a summary investigation, the assassin and forty-nine of his alleged accomplices were shot. Soon after that the available former leaders of the Left Opposition, Zinoviev and Kameniev, were charged with complicity. Although they refused to confess, they were immediately sentenced to prison. Soon the hitherto selective purge assumed unprecedented mass proportions, and the country descended into a horrible bloody pit. Numberless "Kirov's assassins" were arrested and deported without trial to distant parts of the Soviet Union under such inhuman conditions that countless casualties occurred even during the journey to labor and concentration camps. No exact data are available, but the number of deported "Kirov's assassins" must have amounted to around half a million. Thus the end of 1934 ushered in the period that was to last for four years, known as the *Great Purge*.

THE GREAT PURGE

The Great Purge was characterized by unbridled mass terror and punctuated by a series of dramatic public "show trials" that differed markedly from previous affairs of a similar type. The political trials of the late 1920s and early 1930s were directed mainly against the survivors of the old technical intelligentsia, tainted with prerevolutionary spirit and counterrevolutionary in mood. Also hard hit by those trials were members of the historic political parties—the Cadets, the SRs, and the Mensheviks—who had not emigrated when the opportunity was still available. Through this means, by the mid-1930s all former opposition groups had already been broken. Whatever dissatisfaction with Stalin's policies still existed was centered around certain restricted Party circles, as the Seventeenth Party Congress served to prove.

By 1935, with the liquidation of some half a million "Kirov assassins," the Stalinist system could look back at the completion of its grimly successful mass purging operation. Resistance, even potential resistance, to its policies had been broken. Yet it was only then that the mass purge, having been unleashed, began to acquire a momentum of its own and to turn against the Party itself. In 1935, in a symbolic move signifying the end of one era and the beginning of another, a number of old Communist societies and associations were abolished on Stalin's order. The first to be dissolved was the Society of Old Bolsheviks, composed of those who had joined the Party prior to 1917; next came the Association of Political Prisoners and the renowned Communist Academy. At the same time, in 1936, a new constitution was promulgated by Stalin, who called it "the most democratic in the world." It contained what appeared on paper as a fairly comprehensive and liberal bill of rights. Yet Article 112 of this constitution subordinated the judiciary to the Supreme Soviet. Since the Soviet is elected under the watchful eye of the Party from a single list of candidates submitted by the Party, the Constitution thereby rejected the principle of separation of powers and did not reintroduce an independent judiciary; so even the outwardly quasi-liberal facade of the 1936 Constitution was a far cry from generally accepted Western standards.

At this time the first national anthem of the USSR, the old battle song of the European revolutionary movement, "The Internationale," was replaced by a new song. The new anthem extolled the Soviet Union as the freest and happiest of all countries. The first stanza of the new anthem ended with the words, "I don't know any other country where man can breathe so freely."

All the time Stalin kept assuring his subjects at home and his followers abroad that he and his Party were devoted to human welfare and to humanistic values above everything else. As he put it in one of his speeches at that time, "People must be tended carefully and lovingly, as a gardener tends a favorite fruit tree." But while paying lip service to loving care, he was increasingly practicing brutal pruning, wood-chopping, and even timber-felling on an increasingly massive scale. It was puzzling that the terror of the years 1936–1938 increased in inverse ratio to the existence of internal opposition.

THE MOSCOW TRIALS

There were three major public show trials in the 1930s. In all of them the main actors were former leading members of the Party and State administration. All the trials were held in Moscow; hence they are often referred to as the Moscow trials. The first was held in August 1936 and involved Zinoviev, Kameniev, and fourteen other leading Communists, all former members of the opposition. All were accused of being part of a "Trotskyite-Zinovievite terrorist center." Within four days the trial was over. The sixteen death sentences were carried out immediately.

Four months later, on November 30, the second show trial took place; it involved

seventeen defendants headed by Karl Radek, one of the most brilliant publicists of the regime and its former semiofficial spokesman. All of the defendants, despite their initial sympathies with the Trotskyite opposition, had recanted and finally sided with Stalin. Of the seventeen, thirteen were sentenced to death. Radek miraculously escaped execution by conveniently disclosing facts implicating some of the top Red Army commanders allegedly haboring "Bonapartist" ambitions.

Having finished with the Bolshevik Left, Stalin now brought the Right to the courtroom in the third and the last great public show trial, in March 1938. The trial involved twenty-one of the surviving former members of the Right Opposition, including such masterminds of Soviet Communism as Rykov and Bukharin. The third group also contained a number of Communist leaders from various national republics. Paradoxically, the trial included as well the previous purger-in-chief, former head to the NKVD Genrikh G. Yagoda. To the standard accusations of sabotage, spying, and treason was now added a new one: Yagoda was accused of having organized a regular murder laboratory for the purpose of exterminating top Soviet leaders, including the writer Maxim Gorky, who had died in somewhat mysteri-

Karl Radek, editor of *Pravda* and one of the victims of the Great Purge

ous circumstances. One of the most grotesque allegations was that Bukharin had plotted the assassination of Lenin and Stalin as early as 1918. The real disagreements between Stalin and Bukharin over the NEP and the collectivization were not even mentioned.

The Moscow show trials were not the only blows dealt by Stalin to his political opponents—past, present, and potential. In June 1937, a sudden trial and immediate execution of top leaders of the Red Army also took place. As a result of secret and summary proceedings, three out of five marshals of the Soviet Union were accused of various crimes, including Trotskyism and conspiracy with Germany and Japan. Among the three marshals was one of the heroes of the Civil War and the actual Chief of the Soviet General Staff, Michael N. Tukhachevsky; Alexander I. Yegorov and Vasily K. Bluecher were also tried.

Following the execution of Tukhachevsky, Yegorov, and Bluecher, the purge of military and naval personnel descended to the lower echelons of the Soviet armed forces. Parallel with the reimposition of stricter controls by the Political Commissars, some 40 to 50 percent of the senior officers were arrested and either shot or deported to various concentration and labor camps run by the NKVD. The Soviet Navy was especially hard hit. Among the lower personnel the purge was less extensive and affected only 20 to 30 percent of the junior officers. The damage the purge inflicted on the Red Army was devastating and came dangerously close to giving Hitler victory in his 1941 onslaught on Russia.

Although the decapitation of the Red Army was not the last dramatic act of what became known as the "Great Purge," in many ways it represented its climactic novelty, and may have been the most original contribution of the Stalinist totalitarian system to the evolution of State-sponsored terror. In the past all dictatorships based themselves to a greater or lesser extent on the armed forces and operated in partnership with their leaders. Stalin was the first to

prove that his regime was capable of relying on other factors like the Party apparatus and the secret police. By using the Party Political Administration and operating through the network of Political Commissars present in every unit, and through an extensive counterintelligence organization, Stalin was able to neutralize any possible reaction of the military personnel to such humiliating blows as the surprising, sudden, and absurd execution of popular and even idolized Army leaders.

The crippling of the Red Army also represented another noteworthy variation in the pattern of the purge. Whereas during the show trials Stalin dealt with already defeated, completely isolated, helpless individuals, here he struck at men in full command of the Soviet armed forces. Both the swiftness and the decisiveness of the blow were revealing. So were the utter helplessness and passivity of the victims and their potential followers. None of the destroyed Army leaders tried to resist, and their executions did not produce even a ripple in the smooth functioning of the Soviet military machine. The stunned Red Army and Navy personnel meekly followed official instructions to maintain strict discipline and "Bolshevik vigilance." The June 12 edition of *Pravda* that carried the news of the trial and execution of the three former idols of the Soviet armed forces also included some interesting items about the reaction of aroused military personnel and factory workers: they promptly passed a series of resolutions justifying the allegedly prophylactic measures undertaken against "the mad dogs." "For the dogs—dogs' death" ran a resolution of one of the night shifts of a Moscow factory.

THE NKVD'S MISTAKES

The charges against most victims of the purges were often hastily prepared. In some cases their absurdity was apparent almost immediately. For instance, on August 24, 1936, six days after the execution of "the

Zinoviev-Kameniev-Trotskyite gang," the Danish paper *Socialdemokraten* pointed out that the Bristol Hotel in Copenhagen, where a representative of the conspirators allegedly met Trotsky's son Sedov in 1932, had been demolished long before the meeting was alleged to have taken place. Moreover, Sedov could not have been in Copenhagen at that time because on that particular day he was undergoing a written examination at the Berlin Technical College, a fact testified to by the College in a legal affidavit. This example, one of many, revealed the inefficiency of the NKVD and could not go unpunished. And indeed, on September 28, 1936, its head Yagoda, was dismissed and replaced by Nikolai I. Yezhov.

From German documents captured by the victors in 1945, it is possible to reconstruct the story of Tukhachevsky and his two comrades. The deputy head of the Gestapo, Reinhardt Heydrich, was familiar with Stalin's morbidly suspicious mind and with Tukhachevsky's outstanding abilities. He decided to create confusion in the ranks of a former ally who was, after 1934, a possible wartime enemy. In 1937, Heydrich forged a letter in Tukhachevsky's name to a former fellow student at a military academy in Berlin. The letter informed his colleague, now a German general, about the mounting opposition to Stalin's personal dictatorship and about Tukhachevsky's plans to overthrow him and reestablish cordial relations with Germany. The forged letter was conveniently sold by the Gestapo to an agent of the Czechoslovak intelligence service in Berlin. Czechoslovak Foreign Minister Beneš —later its President after signing the 1935 alliance with the USSR—was only too eager to pass on this piece of vital intelligence to Stalin without first verifying its authenticity. One should not, however, think that Stalin was tricked by Heydrich and Beneš. Although he received the incriminating letter in January 1937, he did not act upon it until June. Moreover, the letter did not figure in the trial of the marshal and his colleagues; it was added to the file for good measure only after he had been shot. Clearly, Stalin had been determined to get rid of the popular and potentially dangerous military leader by hook or by crook, whatever the evidence. Any serious examination of the Gestapo-manufactured letter probably would have exposed it as a forgery; its political naiveté was obvious because no Soviet military leader would inform a foreigner living in a capitalist country about a planned *coup d'état* against a well-established, formidable ruler controlling the best and most extensive intelligence network in the world.

STALIN'S MOTIVES

Stalin's motives in slaughtering such a vast number of Soviet leaders have been a subject of controversy. One possible explanation for his behavior was given by Isaac Deutscher in his biography of Stalin. In case of a German and/or Japanese-Soviet war— which Stalin as a realistic leader must have envisaged—the Russian opposition leaders might be driven to take action against him, should the course of such a war turn against Soviet Russia. To exclude any such possibility, Stalin decided to accuse them of having already entered into a treasonous alliance with the two potential enemies. Thus, according to Deutscher's imaginative reconstruction, Stalin's move was actually more rational than it appeared; it was an act of prophylactic political surgery aiming at the elimination of all possible alternatives to his rule. Justice was seldom more blindfold than during the Great Purge, for it was made to serve strictly political purposes having nothing to do with legal order.

Another Machiavellian explanation, advanced by the former head of Stalin's bodyguard, Colonel Alexander Orlov, is that the Soviet dictator was a secret admirer of Hitler and believed in the possibility, nay necessity, of a new close agreement with the man whom he considered as the only leader in Europe worthy of such a name. Consequently, from 1934 onwards, he set out to destroy all those who would have opposed such an accommodation with an "Arch Fascist." Still another explanation ascribes the purges to the necessity of diverting the restless population's attention from economic hardships, the shortages of food, fuel, and other basic necessities, by the tales of sabotage, wreckage, and terroristic attempts perpetrated by a selected group of Stalin's real or potential opponents. Every failure or mishap could be conveniently blamed on these scape goats as "enemies of the people."

In some ways, the "Great Purge" represented the last phase of the power struggle precipitated by Lenin's demise. Except for the military leaders, the main victims had all been either politically destroyed or at least neutralized. One of the main purposes of the trials was to dramatize their downfall to the masses and to destroy their image as good Communists, thereby completing their destruction. Thus the trials represented theatrical performances or morality plays. The educational side of the show trials was underscored by the insistence of the chief prosecutor, Andrei Vyshinsky, that the accused confess to the charges against them. Most defendants obliged Vyshinsky and confessed to what were often the most absurd and contradictory crimes. The reasons why they agreed to this final humiliation varied. Kameniev, for instance, did it for a guarantee that his family and those of other accused victims would not be persecuted. Bukharin confessed to spare his young wife and their child a similar fate. Radek admitted his alleged guilt to save his own skin. None of Stalin's promises were kept.

The vilification and moral destruction of the victims of the purge trials was as important as their eventual physical liquidation. Yet many of them had had their pictures displayed in public places, in offices, schools, and barracks. Streets and squares had been named after them; this was especially true of Marshal Tukhachevsky. Now all this had to be erased, places renamed, textbooks withdrawn from circulation and reprinted, and portraits removed and replaced, usually with those of Stalin. During 1936–1938, public adulation of Stalin's personality and achievements reached its peak. There was, moreover, nobody to compete with him in popularity.

THE SCOPE OF THE PURGE

The Great Purge affected not only the Party leaders; it filtered down, spread, and assumed unprecedented mass proportions. The arrest and deportation and/or execution of one member of a family often resulted in the apprehension of other family members. Accusations ranged from acts of sabotage and disloyalty to telling unacceptable political jokes. Dissenters who managed to escape to the West to tell the story often mention in their testimonies that even trivial incidents could cause arrest and severe punishment. A sentence of five years of forced labor camp was considered light. There is a story, that a former inmate of a camp near Novosibirsk was asked by his commander, "What's your sentence?" The prisoner answered, "Twenty-five years." "What for?" "For nothing," answered the prisoner. "You are lying! In our country, for nothing they give you only five years!"

Another authentic report says that one day an old seamstress had been cutting a dress pattern and needed some extra paper for the collar. She reached for a newspaper and, as she was cutting, the tip of her scissors happened to pierce a photograph of Stalin in the paper. Someone saw that and ran off to report to the police. Soon the old lady was hauled off to a camp. It was said that the huge Baltic-White Sea Canal was built by those punished for telling political jokes.

By 1938 the orgy of denunciations, deportations, and executions had reached tidal proportions. In his speech denouncing Stalin in February 1956 at the Twentieth Party Congress, Khrushchev reported that during the time some 8 million people were crowding the prisons and labor camps of the Soviet Union. The power of the secret police had become so extensive as to frighten

Andrei Vyshinsky, the Chief Prosecutor of the Moscow trials and Minister of Foreign Affairs, 1940–1949 and 1953–1955

Stalin himself. Meanwhile, he must have decided that the purge had gotten out of hand. Had Yezhov been allowed to carry it on at the same rate, he would have brought down the very framework of the Soviet state. Consequently, Stalin decided to call a halt. At the Eighteenth Party Congress in March 1939, he admitted numerous excesses and promised Party members to protect their security. In an effort to divorce himself from the disastrous consequences of the repressions, he declared that it was the NKVD, treacherously infiltrated by enemies of the people, that was responsible for the deplorable excesses that had crippled the Party. Moreover, he pledged never to allow another mass purge. But the disaster that had befallen the Soviet people could not be undone: between 7 and 8 million people arrested, about 1 million executed, some 8 million in slave labor camps. Many victims were children. Again, as in the past, selected

scapegoats had to pay for Stalin's mistakes. In December 1938, the dreaded Yezhov was arrested and soon liquidated, like his predecessor, Yagoda. Yezhov's place was taken by Lavrentii Beria, charged with the task of purging the former purgers and resubordinating the secret police to the Party.

Thus by the close of 1938, Stalin weathered another crisis. Although in 1937 he had employed the NKVD to crush the Army, in 1938 he combined the forces of the Party, supported this time by aroused public opinion, against the hated secret police. A campaign against the "opportunists," "careerists," "slanderers," and "liars" in the ranks of the NKVD was unleashed, and numerous arrests were made among its ranks. "The purge of the purgers" resulted in numerous former police agents joining their erstwhile victims in prison cells and camps. Several interrogators committed suicide from fear of arrest. On the other hand, numerous survivors who had been apprehended during the Great Purge were released and rehabilitated.

Once again, as in the case of the "Dizzy with Success" article, the mass media began to picture Stalin as a sincerely magnanimous person concerned with the welfare of each individual member of the Party. For instance, the Soviet press and radio gave wide publicity to the story of a student at the Frunze Military Academy who had been expelled from the Academy because his father was of "bourgeois origin" and hence the son was considered a "socially dangerous individual." When the student appealed to Stalin for help, he was not disappointed. Stalin at once telephoned the Academy's commander and, as the media reported, in a lengthy telephone conversation managed to persuade him to readmit the distressed student.

The intensity of the campaign, punctuated with several similar incidents, indicated the dictator's determination to dissociate himself from the vast scope and fierce intensity of the purge. Meanwhile, Stalin continued to make pronouncements condemning the nefarious activities of his unruly insubordinates who dared to exceed their orders and assured the people that, "Of all the treasures a State can possess, the human lives of its citizens are for us the most precious."

Perhaps the most characteristic feature of the Great Purge (*Yezhovshchina*) was its unprecedented scope and depth. Between 1936 and 1938, nine out of eleven cabinet ministers were executed. So were twenty-seven top political and legal experts who had drafted the Constitution of 1936 with its generous bill of rights. The armed forces were hit harder than any other group. According to the most recent Western estimates not only did 3 out of the 5 Marshals of the Soviet Union perish in the purge, but also 14 of the 16 Army Commanders, all 8 Admirals, 60 of the 67 Corps Commanders, 136 of the 199 Divisional Commanders, and 221 of the 397 Brigade Commanders. All 11 of the Vice-Commissars of Defense and 75 out of 80 members of the Supreme Military Council were also liquidated. Altogether 35,000 officers, about 50 percent of the officers' corps, were affected one way or another by the purge. Not all were shot or perished in the labor camps. Many of them would survive the predicament and be rehabilitated in the emergency of World War II. Some of them would become national heroes, like Marshal of the Soviet Union Konstantine Rokossovsky. Although the purges did not cripple the Red Army completely, they weakened it considerably on the eve of a great international storm.

THE UNIQUENESS OF THE GREAT PURGE

The Great Purge was distinct from the preceding phases of Stalinist repression in many respects. Its most striking feature was its unprecedented scope which affected, one way or another, millions of people. Second, the Great Purge either introduced or intensified extraordinary methods for extracting confessions from selected victims at spectacular, carefully rehearsed show trials. These devices combined subtle psychological pressures with the use of naked force. The "conveyor," or continual interrogation in relays by police officers for hours and even days on end, was a classic example. Third, apart from the public show trials, immense, unpublicized operations were conducted through the country to identify, apprehend, and punish millions of human beings who were considered potentially harmful or inconvenient to the regime or were simply, for one reason or another, disliked by its security organs.

Stalin's terror differed from the reprisals of other authoritarian or totalitarian regimes by two additional features. First, most of the Soviet latter-day purges were directed not against an outside group but against their own people, largely Party members. Second, the purges gave their victims no opportunity to exonerate themselves. Guilt and innocence became completely irrelevant. Individuals were killed or deported not for what they did or said, but for being what they were (for instance, kulaks), or for supposedly thinking disloyal or subversive thoughts.

Many students of Soviet history and politics regard the institution of the violent purge as an integral part of the system. In a society where other ways of change do not exist, they believe, the system must become rigidly static and increasingly bureaucratized. Under the circumstances, the preventive "permanent purge" is the only form of governmental self-renewal. Rapid mobility creates inherent insecurity and thus prevents bureaucratic complacency and political and social arthritis. Thus the purge exemplifies Vilfredo Pareto's theory of circulation of elites as a vital factor in revitalizing political leaderships, applied to the peculiar Soviet conditions of the Stalinist era.

The Great Purge was for the Soviet people a traumatic experience comparable to World War II. Boris Pasternak put these words in the mouth of one of the characters in his novel *Dr. Zhivago*:

And when the war broke out, its real horrors, its real dangers, its menace of real death were a blessing compared with the inhuman reign of the lie, and they brought relief because they broke the spell of the dead letter.[1]

Terror has always been a by-product of revolutionary upheaval. But mass, unbridled terror of the Stalinist type, indiscriminate and deliberately haphazard, with people arrested even when they were known to be perfectly innocent and harmless, was a novelty. It seems that Stalin purposely tried to create an atmosphere in which no one could feel secure and everybody was vulnerable and at the mercy of the omnipotent dictator, the complete master of everyone's destiny. Many historians and political scientists have tried to rationalize the Stalinist purges, but all their explanations are lame if they do not take into consideration the irrational element of Stalin's psyche—his morbid, vindictive mind, warped by suspicion and permeated by paranoiac fears. During a drinking bout Stalin told his intimates that the greatest joy he could imagine was "to choose one's victim, to prepare one's plans minutely, to slake the implacable vengeance, and then go to bed. . . . There is nothing sweeter in the world." Indeed the saying of the French moralist La Rochefoucauld that "we are seldom able to pardon those we have injured" is more applicable to Stalin than to any other modern political personality.

THE PURGE AND THE RESHAPING OF THE PARTY

The Great Purge, which destroyed many, opened unexpected avenues of advance for others. For instance, a minor director of a textile factory named Alexei N. Kosygin climbed to the rank of a Deputy Premier of the Russian Federal Republic. A minor engineer in a metallurgical factory named Leonid I. Brezhnev advanced in a few years only to become Party boss of a key industrial district, Dnepropetrovsk. A little known regional commander, Gregory K. Zhukov, advanced within three years to the post of Chief of the Soviet General Staff, while Nicholas G. Kuznetsov within the same period was promoted from commander of a cruiser to the Chief of the Soviet Navy.

Besides the speeding up of social mobility, another aspect of the purges of the late 1930s was their impact on the country's economy. They were not the sole or even the main cause of the first serious decline in the rate of growth of the Soviet GNP since the launching of the First Five-Year Plan. Yet it seems beyond doubt that the dislocations they caused in the industrial cadres significantly contributed to the economic slowdown and the decline in labor productivity. In 1939, for instance, pig iron and steel output fell below the 1938 level and did not recover until the beginning of 1941. Production of tractors and automobiles also declined during this period. All this was largely the result of the destruction of the cream of Soviet industrial management.

As has been already mentioned, the Party as a whole was proportionately more affected by the purges than the population at large. By the time Yezhov was dismissed by Stalin in December 1938, Lenin's Bolshevik party of the 1920s had been reshaped so that it was now a different body. Of the 140 members of the Party's Central Committee, 98 were purged; altogether some 70 percent of the Party leadership was affected by the Stalinist reprisals. While in 1935 the Party numbered 2,358,000 people, in 1938 it shrank to 1,920,000 or 445,000 fewer members, this despite constant recruitment of new members.

Besides its numerical contraction, the quality of Party membership had been dramatically altered. Although the organizational framework remained the same, its human and ideological content underwent a radical transformation. The extent of the discontinuity becomes striking when one

---

[1] Boris Pasternak, *Dr. Zhivago* (New York: Pantheon Books, a division of Random House, Inc., 1958), p 507; trans. by Max Hayward and Manya Harari.

analyzes the composition of the Seventeenth Congress of 1934 and the Eighteenth Congress of 1939. The latter included less than 2 percent of the rank-and-file delegates of the former. Meanwhile, not only had delegates opposed to Stalin been eliminated, but even those hesitant or potentially mistrustful of him had disappeared from the scene. The delegates to the 1939 Congress were a soulless crowd of automatons hand-picked by the regional bosses. The delegates voted unanimously for the motions presented by the Leader, irrespective of their convictions—if they had any at all. This had been exactly Stalin's goal. Men of conviction were good enough in a revolutionary period, but not in the state of totalitarian normalcy. Total subordination to Number One, and not the revolutionary, innovative, and restless spirit of the earlier evangelical period, became the supreme criterion for survival and promotion. Consequently, the Party became bureaucratized and ossified. After 1938, as life gravitated toward totalitarian stability, there was an increasing need for comfort and material advantages. Stalin cunningly harnessed these desires. The survivors of the purges were rewarded for their servility with a variety of privileges, including special shops, apartments, cars, country villas, and educational advantages for the children of "the new class" or the Party elite.

Another change in the Party was of an ideological character. The old Bolshevik "proletarian internationalism" with its universalist supranational outlook had been discarded in the late 1920s and replaced by a sort of proleterian nationalism that, while paying lip service to the old concept of the international proletarian revolution, increasingly emphasized the domestic interests of the Soviet Union. As a result, during the 1930s, Stalin consummated the marriage of Soviet Communism with traditional Russian nationalism, thus stressing the legitimacy of his rule. While the old Bolshevik party had been dominated by a mixed lot of internationally minded and rather cosmopolitan intellectuals of Russian, Georgian, Jewish, Baltic, and Polish extraction, the Stalinist Party "of a new type" was increasingly dominated by Russian members largely of peasant origin and relatively much less interested in the affairs of the outside world. During the 1930s, Stalin's Party started its evolution from proletarian internationalism toward Russian nationalism. These changes in Party composition and motivation were paralleled by Stalin's new attitude toward the Comintern and foreign affairs.

SUGGESTED READING

ARMSTRONG, JOHN A., *The Politics of Totalitarianism: The Communist Party of the Soviet Union from 1934 to the Present.* New York: Random House, 1961.

BAUER, RAYMOND A., ALEX INKELES, and CLYDE KLUCKHOHN, eds., *How the Soviet System Works.* Washington, D.C.: National Science Foundation, 1961.

CILIGA, ANTON, *The Russian Enigma.* London: Routledge, 1940.

BERMAN, HAROLD J., *Justice in the USSR.* New York: Random House, 1963.

BRZEZINSKI, ZBIGNIEW K., *The Permanent Purge: Politics in Soviet Totalitarianism.* Cambridge, Mass.: Harvard University Press, 1956.

CARMICHAEL, JOEL, *Stalin's Masterpiece: The Show Trials and Purges of the Thirties—The Consolidation of the Bolshevik Dictatorship.* New York: St. Martin's, 1976.

CONQUEST, ROBERT, *The Great Terror.* New York: Macmillan, 1968.

DALLIN, DAVID J., and BORIS I. NICHOLAYEVSKY, *Forced Labor in Soviet Russia.* New Haven, Conn.: Yale University Press, 1947.

DEUTSCHER, ISAAC, *Stalin: A Political Biography* (2nd ed.). New York: Oxford University Press, 1967.

DJILAS, MILOVAN, *The New Class.* New York: Praeger, 1957.

FAINSOD, MERLE, *Smolensk under Soviet Rule.* Cambridge, Mass.: Harvard University Press, 1958.

FRIEDRICH, CARL J., and ZBIGNIEW K. BRZEZINSKI, *Totalitarian Dictatorship and Autocracy*

(2nd ed.). Rev. by Carl J. Friedrich. New York: Praeger, 1966.

GETTY, J. ARCH, *Origins of the Great Purges. The Soviet Communist Party Reconsidered, 1933–1938*. Cambridge, England: University of Cambridge, 1986.

GRAHAM, LOREN, *Soviet Academy of Science and the Communist Party, 1927–1932*. Princeton, N.J.: Princeton University Press, 1967.

KATKOV, GEORGE, *The Trial of Bukharin*. New York: Stein and Day, 1969.

KULSKI, WLADYSLAW W., *The Soviet Regime: Communism in Practice*. Syracuse, N.Y.: Syracuse University Press, 1956.

MOORE, BARRINGTON, JR., *Soviet Politics: The Dilemma of Power*. Cambridge, Mass.: Harvard University Press, 1957.

ORLOV, ALEXANDER, *The Secret History of Stalin's Crimes*. New York: Random House, 1953.

SERGE, VICTOR, *Memoirs of a Revolutionary, 1901–1941*. New York: Oxford University Press, 1963.

SOLZHENITSYN, ALEXANDER, *The Gulag Archipelago*. New York: Harper and Row, 1974, 1975, and 1977, 3 vols.

SOUVARINE, BORIS, *Stalin: A Critical Survey of Bolshevism*. New York: Alliance Book Company, 1939.

VYSHINSKY, ANDREI Y., *The Law of the Soviet State*. New York: Macmillan, 1948.

WEISSBERG, ALEX, *The Accused*. New York: Simon and Schuster, 1951.

CHAPTER 15

A New Nationality Policy
and the
Soviet Cultural Revolution

One of the results of the Stalin revolution was such close integration of economic management with the Party–State bureaucracy that the two became practically indistinguishable. After the 1930s the Party, supported by the iron hand of the ubiquitous security apparatus, became virtually omnipotent. This naturally had profound repercussions on all aspects of social life, including nationality policy, culture, and science.

As a matter of fact, Stalin's views had manifested themselves in the field of nationality policy long before the integrative forces generated by the five-year plans brought about the further welding together of the USSR's multiethnic segments. The creation of ostensibly sovereign federal republics was largely due to Lenin. This was always resented by a considerable segment of the Party leaders, including the then Commissar for Nationalities, Stalin. He and many others, including the first Chief of the Secret Police, Dzerzhinsky and Trotsky

were not satisfied even that in practice an impressive measure of economic control was maintained through unified Party supervision and centralization. Although after 1924 the constituent republics of the Soviet Union preserved their elaborate government and party structures, the tightening of Party controls, already begun durng the NEP, reduced them to ideological window dressing.

Although Stalin was not an ethnic Russian, he was thoroughly Russified. His daughter did not hesitate to say about her father, "I know no other Georgian who had so completely sloughed off his qualities as a Georgian and loved everything Russian."[1] He was always suspicious of local nationalism as a potentially centrifugal force. It was

[1] Svetlana Alliluyeva, *Twenty Letters to a Friend,* trans. by Priscilla Johnson McMillan (New York: Harper & Row, 1967), pp. 119–120. By permission of Harper & Row.

he who ruthlessly repressed all traces of local patriotism, which was condemned as "bourgeois nationalism." It was chiefly at Stalin's instigation that his native Georgia was merged into the Transcaucasian Regional Republic in 1922–1923. Mirza Sultan-Galiev, a founding father of the Tatar autonomous republic, was condemned for advocating the formation of a separate Muslim Communist party.

The horrors of the collectivization and industrialization carried out by storm methods turned the western and southern provinces of the Soviet Union into areas seething with resentment and potential revolt. During this period Stalin could not fail to notice that the opposition to collectivization and other measures was stronger in the multiethnic borderlands than in the Great Russian heartland of the USSR. He obliquely acknowledged it at the Sixteenth Party Congress in 1930: "The survival of capitalism in men's consciousness is much more tenacious in the sphere of national problems than in any other sphere." This observation, combined with his congenital suspicion of ethnic nationalism, made him equate all manifestations of local defiance with irredenta and treason.

RESISTANCE IN THE BORDERLANDS

Nowhere did the resistance to these measures manifest itself more strongly than in Ukraine, Belorussia, and the Caucasus, which includes Stalin's native Georgia. Consequently, the purges of the 1930s hit these border regions with special ferocity. The heaviest blows fell during the mid-1930s on the second most important and populous federal republic, Ukraine. The great famine, which had affected the Ukrainians most severely, tried the loyalty even of local Communist zealots. Their policies, which tried to combine Marxist ideology with Bolshevik methods and local radical traditions, were increasingly attacked and overruled by Moscow. Two men who emboided this peculiar combination of Communism and national-

ism were Alexander Shumsky and Mykola Skrypnik. Both of them had been instrumental in establishing Soviet rule in the Ukraine. As successive Commissars for Education, each tried to apply a hybrid policy that combined Communism and local patriotism to their native republic. Their policy greatly stimulated the flowering of Ukrainian literature and arts during the 1920s and early 1930s. Many Ukrainian intellectuals—for instance, Mykola Khvylovy—took advantage of the apparently relaxed atmostphere that had prevailed on the Dnieper since 1926 to voice their nationalistic aspirations. In 1925, Khvylovy established a weekly in which he assailed the Muscovite centralism now hiding behind the Communist facade, and urged his countrymen to draw closer to the main source of progressive ideas, the West. Other writers denounced the continuing Muscovite policy of economically exploiting the rich Ukrainian natural resources for the benefit of the Great Russian heartland. Although these voices were promptly silenced, the fairly permissive ethnic policy was continued essentially unchanged under Skrypnik until the early 1930s.

Collectivization was more sharply resisted by the Ukrainian peasants, freer of the Russian communal tradition than anywhere else and more attached to their individual farms.[2] Besides fierce active opposition and passive sabotage, the resistance expressed itself in a series of secret societies, the most important of which was the Union for the Liberation of the Ukraine. The trial of forty-five members of the Union in 1930 spelled the beginning of the end of the policy of "Ukrainization," and hence of the Ukrainian cultural renaissance. In June 1933, Skrypnik's policy was sharply attacked by Stalin's henchmen, Pavel P. Postyshev—

---

[2] Collectivization as a political and economic instrument in the struggle against the Ukrainians has been discussed by Robert Conquest in his *The Harvest of Sorrow: Soviet Collectivization and the Terror–Famine* (New York: Oxford University Press, 1986), Part III, "Terror–Famine."

who since 1931 had been Secretary of the Communist Party in the Ukraine—and his associate, Stanisław Kossior. Skrypnik was denounced for allegedly coddling Ukrainian nationalist deviation and "bourgeois nationalistic conspirators." Seeing his policy in ruin, threatened with demotion, and a purge that had meanwhile struck many of his close friends and co-workers, Skrypnik committed suicide. Khvylovy had already done so two months earlier.

The purge of his associates and co-workers, who were being denounced as "deviationists" and "traitors," reached a crescendo under Stalin's new proconsul for the Ukraine, Lazar Kaganovich. In 1937, another of the dictator's close allies, Nikita Khrushchev, became a member of a "purge troika" composed also of Vyacheslav Molotov and Nikolay Yezhov, head of the secret police. By 1937–1938, the "liquidation of the enemies of the people" in the Ukraine had reached its peak. Most members of the Ukrainian government, the Ukrainian Central Committee, and the Ukrainian Supreme Soviet were summarily executed. The purge was not limited to the Party and State apparatus and to military personnel; it fell heavily on the intellectuals as well. Between 1937 and 1938, all thirteen secretaries of the Ukrainian Academy of Science were arrested. The Ukrainian cultural renaissance was thus aborted. Of the seven rectors (presidents) of Kiev university during the same period, six were liquidated; only one died a natural death. This was paralleled by mass deportations of Ukrainians to various distant parts of the USSR, mainly Siberia and the Maritime Provinces.

In the Belorussian Soviet Republic, "bourgeois nationalistic tendencies" were also "unmasked" during the 1930s, and their exponents purged. There too the composition of the local top Party and government leadership was changed several times over. By 1938–1939, the former protagonists of the "national Bolshevik" trend in most of the border republics had disappeared almost completely. The vacated jobs were gradually handed over to younger people trained entirely in the new school, and new members of the *apparat*[3] loyal to the Stalinist way of interpreting the principle of "proletarian internationalism" in the spirit of Russian nationalism.

OTHER VICTIMS

Even more far-reaching changes were meanwhile taking place in the Central Asian Republics. Until 1928–1929, this region had been only slightly affected by the Soviet system, except for the replacement of the old Arabic script by the Latin in 1925. Otherwise, under the new rubric of Communism the old tribal life went on unchanged. This situation began to alter drastically soon after the launching of the five-year plans. Settlers from Russia were sent in increasing numbers, while local nomadic tribes were forced to settle down and compelled to engage in unfamiliar agricultural pursuits. A campaign was launched to uproot Islam and the traditional way of life based on the Koran. Both the Arabic and the Latin scripts were forbidden, and the Russian alphabet made obligatory. These policies caused a great deal of resistance, which was ruthlessly repressed, and resulted in a heavy loss of life. According to Soviet statistics, during the 1930s the Kazakh population decreased by almost a million and became outnumbered by the Russian colonists. The Kazan Tatars fiercely opposed the "alphabetic revolution" and their leader, Sultan Galiev, who had been arrested in 1928, was tried, condemned for his "bourgeois nationalistic deviation," and sent to a concentration camp where he perished.

The Jews also suffered from the new ethnic policy. By 1926, the Jewish Section of the Communist Party (*Yevsektsia*) had already ceased to meet and soon was disbanded. Under the pretext that Jews had no large, compact, rural settlements and no

---

[3] By *apparat*, one understands the body of paid Party officials employed full time in running the Party machine.

agricultural population, both Lenin and Stalin had denied the existence of Jews as a separate national group. Then, in 1928, apparently reversing his previous position, Stalin designated the forbidding Far Eastern region of Birobijan, part of the Khabarovsk province, as a place for Jewish colonization. In 1934, when a considerable number of Jewish settlers had moved in, the region was triumphantly proclaimed the Jewish Autonomous Province. The Jewish population never outnumbered the local settlers and remained essentially urban. Soon Birobijan, initially proclaimed as a success in the Soviet ethnic policy, disappeared as a subject of official propaganda. This was another trick in Stalin's arsenal of "social engineering" that failed miserably. In 1937, Semyon Dimanstein, the secretary of the Communist Party in Birobijan, was purged. Similar fates befell many other prominent Jewish Communists, most of them victims of the Great Purge. The 1930s saw the first manifestations of official anti-Semitism in the form of discrimination against Jews in education and especially in sensitive positions in the Soviet Armed Forces or institutions maintaining contact with foreign countries.

THE MAKING OF THE SOVIET "NATION"

While pursuing Draconian nationality policies, Stalin launched the new concept of "the Soviet nation" that would supersede existing ethnic ties and loyalies. He believed that maximum centralized control required a unified national culture. The original Leninist formula that culture must be "national in form and socialist in content" was now reinterpreted dialectically. National cultures, it was argued, must be allowed to develop and unfold, to reveal all their potentialities, in order to create the necessary conditions for eventually merging them into one common "Soviet culture" with one common language. Given the numerical and historical predominance of Great Rus-

sians within the USSR, Soviet national culture must be essentially a Russian one merely adapted to local conditions.

Consequently, during the middle and late 1930s, new directives were issued to educational and cultural institutions. Anything that bore traces of "bourgeois nationalism" was to be suppressed. Museums, State archives, libraries, and reading rooms were searched in order to remove everything that contradicted the new Russifying trend. New textbooks were printed to de-emphasize the role of local cultures and languages and stress the "leading role" of the Muscovite-Russian civilization. National histories were rewritten to emphasize the common destiny of the family of nations now forming the Soviet Union.

During the early 1930s, a new linguistic policy was launched in the two largest Slavic republics, Ukraine and Belorussia. In 1934, Stalin speeded up the process of bringing the Ukrainian and Belorussian idioms closer to the Russian language. Dictionaries were revised, localisms eliminated, and recent borrowings from Western languages replaced with corresponding loan-words from Russian. The use of local vernaculars in literature was discouraged.

A decisive step was taken on March 13, 1938, when a decree made "the study of the Russian language obligatory in schools of all national republics and [autonomous] regions." The local Commissars of Education were instructed "to compile and publish, before the beginning of the next school year, Russian primers, readers and grammars. . . ." The order meant that by September 1, within about five months, textbooks and equipment had to be made ready and teachers of Russian trained for over 60,000 schools. Because there were not enough teachers at hand, in many cases the Russian language, literature, and history had to be temporarily taught by Red Army officers from the local garrisons. Since replacement of the old textbooks was an intricate process, schools were often to go without them for months and even years.

Behind the constitutional facade of federalism, and while paying lip service to local cultural autonomy, Stalin pursued further his new nationality policy. While a sort of "folklore nationalism" was cultivated and even strongly encouraged, an effort was made to eradicate all manifestations of attachment to genuine local patriotism, and to bully ethnic groups into one Soviet mold. The terms "Soviet nationality" and "Soviet patriotism" took on increasingly strong Russian overtones, although the words "Russia" and "Russian" were avoided whenever possible. Despite this camouflage, it was already obvious during the 1930s that the old, traditional Russia was far from being dissolved in the new Soviet society, which had failed to come to life despite the loud fanfare triumphantly announcing its birth.

To vindicate the new line as the only effective and "progressive" one, Stalin declared that the USSR offered "a system of State organization in which ethnic problems and the problem of cooperation among nations have been solved more perfectly than in any other multinational state." Yet from the point of view of the ethnic minorities, Stalin's policy spelled the return of the old Muscovite colonialism in a new Communist garb.

THE RESHAPING OF LITERATURE

Just as the Marxist concept of economics had a limited effect on Soviet life during the NEP, so the idea of proletarian culture had little actual effect on Soviet art and literature at large. In the 1930s, soon after launching the First Five-year Plan, and upon encountering obstacles to it, the Party resolved to give short shrift to the relatively relaxed intellectual atmosphere of the NEP and undertake a concerted, resolute effort to mobilize all forces and resources to overcome the mounting difficulties. Literature and the arts were to be auxiliary tools in maximizing the modernization drive. In 1928, with official support, the Russian Union of Proletarian Writers had been established to act as the chief spokesman of the profession. In principle, this association recognized the rights of non-Communist writers, but in practice it used all sorts of methods to force them to comply with the new official cultural policy line. Because the Union enjoyed government support, it soon achieved a near dictatorial position over Soviet literature. This it repaid with unquestioned support for Party polices.

The philosophy professed by the leaders of the Union was simple. New socioeconomic conditions and the emergence of the proletarians as mass consumers of culture had created what the leaders of the Association termed a "social command." Writers of the new era should be "engineers of the soul," "craftsmen of words" who ought to satisfy the cultural needs of their new consumers, "the builders of socialism," and help them in their primary task. "Cultural output," like any other type of production, should be planned and carried out according to a plan chartered by the Party. The system of payment to authors was differentiated so as to provide greater rewards to authors who quicker and better fulfilled their assigned tasks.

On February 10, 1930, the main Party organ, *Pravda*, began to publish a special literary page devoted to propagandizing the achievements of collectivization and industrialization. The paper launched the slogan, "Proletarian writers should stand shoulder to shoulder with shock workers" (those who consistently exceeded the prescribed work norm), because they were the new heroes of the "epoch of socialism." Soon "production conferences" of Soviet writers and journalists were organized to "plan literary output," which was to be delivered by a given date, and to participate in various campaigns for the "liquidation of illiteracy," "against alcoholism," or "for speeded-up spring sowing." It was decided that the task of "building socialism" would be assisted not by writing poetry and fiction, but with biographies of shock workers and heroes of socialist labor, travelogues describing, for instance, collectivization campaigns in Uzbekistan or Siberia, and documentaries reflecting the "objective reality" of "building socialism" as a smooth, spontaneous process enthusiastically supported by the people, led by "the great genius of humanity."

Despite all its efforts, the Union did not quite satisfy the expectations of the Party. As a *Pravda* editorial put it, "No Magnitogorsk of literature was created," and intellectual dissent still lingered in many quarters. Consequently, on April 23, 1932, the Union of Proletarian Writers was dissolved. The Party decided that in the future there would be no separate literary groups, even if they called themselves "proletarian." From now on all writers and artists would belong to a single centralized organization under the direct supervision of the Party. That year all existing associations were dissolved; the Union of Russian Proletarian Writers was replaced by the Soviet Writers' Union. Similar unions were established for other branches of artistic activity. Artists, writers, and other professional people were compelled to join centralized unions, one for each branch, and each one supervised by a Party delegate. Only union membership could confer the status without which no artist could exist or produce, no writer publish, and no musician perform. The unions would meet several times a year to plan their "production targets."

SOCIALIST REALISM

1934 was in many ways a turning point in the Soviet cultural revolution. That year *socialist realism* was officially proclaimed as the only prescribed mode of artistic expression. The most authoritative definition of socialist realism can be found in a statute of the Union of Soviet Writers:

Socialist realism is the basic method of Soviet literature and literary criticism. It demands of the artist the truthful, historically concrete representation of reality in its revolutionary development. Moreover, the truthfulness and historical concreteness of the artistic representation of reality must be linked with the task of ideological transformation and education of workers in the spirit of Socialism.

Realism as the term is understood in the non-Communist world has little connection with the realism that is preceded by the word "socialist." The qualification that the presentation of reality must serve prescribed ideological and didactic purposes makes socialist realism a way of presenting life "in the process of becoming the ideal," as another official definition of the term has it. The desirable, the postulated, could hardly be distinguished from the real. What Stalin wanted was an art that would reflect reality as it was seen through the Party's selective eyes and as the Party hoped it would become. The embellishment (or "varnishing") of reality became a standard feature of Soviet literature, as well as of the other arts, during the remainder of the Stalin era.[4]

As another official commentary explained, socialist realism was required to depict "the heroic struggle of the world proletariat . . . the grandeur of the victory of socialism, and the great wisdom and heroism of the Communist Party." Thus loyalty to the Party and willingness to serve as its handmaiden were to be the first hallmark of this concept. In addition, socialist realist art had to be simple and obvious enough to be easily understood by all, even the least educated. The third obligatory principle that gradually came to be accepted in practice by most Soviet writers was the

---

[4] The attitude of most independently minded Soviet intellectuals toward socialist realism was reflected in the following anecdote circulated among them. "Once upon time there was a mighty ruler of a powerful country who had no right arm and no right eye and wanter to have his picture painted for official display. One of the artists submitted to him his portrait as he was, without one arm and one eye. He was immediately hanged for "bourgeois formalism." Another painter presented his picture of the Dictator with both arms and eyes. He was executed for "bourgeois idealism." Finally, the third artist submitted his portrait depicting the tyrant with the left arm and the left eye to the viewer's side. This one was duly awarded the prize for 'socialist realism.' "

presence of one central "positive" figure in each story, novel, or poem. This figure, "the positive hero," has usually been a person of impeccable personal, professional, and ideological credentials, always the first to appear at work in the morning and at the local Party cell meeting in the evening. As a rule he not only fulfilled but even exceeded his norm of nuts and bolts, never lied or cheated, and conducted an exemplary personal life. Fiction of the Stalinist period was Puritanical, even Victorian, in its treatment of the sentimental life of its heroes and heroines. Their sex drive was, as a rule, channeled essentially to reproductive purposes, and reproduction took second place to production. Finally, the "positive hero" of Soviet literature has always been victorious in the struggle against the lesser "negative" characters representing either survivals of the eerie past, "enemies of the people," "saboteurs," or "foreign spies."

The few works that are worth mentioning as documents of the epoch, despite the application of these rigid rules, are all novels. One of them is Mikhail Sholokhov's *Virgin Soil Upturned,* which glorifies collectivization but makes no attempt to hide its accompanying horrors. Another is a broad panorama that provides fictional background to the five-year plans, Boris Pilnyak's *The Volga Flows to the Caspian Sea.* Fyodor Gladkov's two novels *Cement* and *Energy,* focus on the all-pervading theme of the country's modernization under Communism.

THE SOVIET CULTURAL REVOLUTION

The enforcement of socialist realism as the only tolerated artistic form resulted in the stifling and near-extinction of spontaneous, meaningful creativity. State-approved literature consisted mainly of slogans and ideological declarations recited by abstract wooden characters. Lyrical poetry was pushed into the background and replaced by eulogies of Stalin and his accomplishments. More independent Soviet writers increasingly sought shelter in such safe pursuits as editing the approved Russian and foreign classics or translating from foreign languages. This was, for instance, Boris Pasternak's main preoccupation during the later phases of the Stalinist era. While glorifying conspicuous production of steel and kilowatts, Soviet writers were increasingly losing sight of human beings. Painting also came to serve the regime. The canvases and sculptures were naturalistic in rendering and simplistic in their message. They portrayed cheerful, well-fed collective farmers and their families, workers overfulfilling their norms, rosy-cheeked women shock workers singing and smiling as they drove huge tractors on collective (preferably State) farms. Most painters and sculptors were becoming increasingly nationalistic and the Red Army man became, next to the Stakhanovite hero of labor, their favorite theme. Most of the pictures of those days were actually posters designed for the purpose of teaching, preaching, and propagandizing.

As the Soviet cultural revolution unfolded, it stressed more and more the integrating values of Russian nationalism mixed with Communist ideology. For instance, Stalin's early pet writer, Demian Bedny, had been committed since the 1920s to lampooning the idealized Russia's past. Overlooking the new trend, in 1933–1934 he wrote a dramatic poem entitled "Heroes of Antiquity." Produced as a libretto for a comic opera that ridiculed the ancient Muscovite heroes, the poem did not take account of the changing mood of his master. When the operetta was staged at a Moscow theater, it was immediately canceled, while Bedny paid for his mistake with disgrace and downfall. The death in 1936 of Gorky, who had often protected other writers and artists, was another blow to Soviet culture.

From 1936 on, the cultural-ideological campaign was steered by Stalin himself. Taking revenge on the Soviet intellectual elite that had hardly noticed him before, he now kept them under his thumb. Not satisfied with imposing his will on the Party and

Stalin and Maxim Gorky, spiritual father of "socialist realism"

State bureaucracy, he aspired to dictate to the artists' minds and souls. In July 1937, he personally forbade the Moscow Art Theater to go to Paris to perform Pushkin's "Boris Godunov." Stalin explained his decision quite bluntly: "Dmitri [the Pretender] is not presented by Pushkin for what he really was—an agent of foreign [Polish] intervention." During the 1936–1937 season, ten out of nineteen new plays in major Moscow theaters were taken off the stage for being "ideologically unsatisfactory."

A similarly arbitrary course was followed regarding other branches of arts. In 1935, thirty-four movies were stopped in production, thirty-five the next year, and thirteen in 1937. At the same time, on Stalin's instructions the Soviet movie industry undertook the production of a series of historical films about great figures of the Muscovite and Russian past: Alexander Nevsky, Ivan the Terrible, Peter the Great, and Alexander Suvorov. Some of them, for instance Ivan the Terrible, were idealized beyond recognition. The central theme of these movies was the struggle against foreign imperialistic encroachments and the necessary strengthening of autocratic power as the best guarantee of the country's unity and might.

Social sciences and humanities, including history, were subject to a thorough reexamination. Mikhail Pokrovsky's Marxist school was soon discarded and a new interpretation fostered after his disgrace in 1932. The entire history of mankind, Soviet historians were told, should be rewritten to demonstrate that all past events were merely a prologue to the Bolshevik revolution, steppingstones to the eventual triumph of Communism under the leadership of the only legitimate heir of Lenin. Stalin himself revised the history of the Party. Under his supervision, a one-volume compendium known as *The Short Course* was produced. Contrary to the Marxist theory, which claims that not individuals but socioeconomic forces play the decisive role in determining history, Stalin's glorification was now the major objective of historical teaching and research.

EDUCATION AND SCIENCES

The 1930s also saw the extension of new, strict disciplinary methods of thought control in education. Soon after the launching of the First Five-Year Plan, a retreat was sounded from the old permissive ways of "progressive education." From being an experimental educational community, the school returned to being an institution of strict formal learning, with a hearty admixture of Communist indoctrination. School administrators and teachers were ordered to reintroduce the old grading system and militarylike discipline, including uniforms and medals. The old quasi-liberal Anatoly Lunacharsky was replaced at the Commissariat of Education by Andrei Babunov, a former head of the Political Academy of the Red Army. The authority of the teacher was made as great as, if not greater than, during Tsarist times.

The initial broad dissemination of education and enlightenment that characterized the first decade of Soviet rule was accompanied by the Party's insistence on intervenng in all phases of the educational process. Eventually, the Party control also included scientific theory and reseach, which was to be conducted in the spirit of Marxist materialism. While initially, during the years of 1918–1928, Soviet natural scientists enjoyed considerable freedom of scholarly investigation, during the 1930s the Party's grip on them was tightened dramatically. One of its first victims was biology. Biology was especially important because of its direct bearing on man's relation to the natural environment, which, according to

Marx, is more important than heredity. Biology also bears directly on the control and cultivation of nature for man's sake, especially in the realm of genetics and breeding.

In 1930, an agronomist and biologist of Ukrainian origin, Trofim Lysenko, propounded a theory that claimed that environmentally acquired characteristics of animals and plants could be transmitted genetically to the next generation. Lysenko took over the ideas of a Russian plant-breeder, Ivan V. Michurin, who through skillful cross-breeding managed to create a variety of fruit trees suitable for the harsh climate of central Russia. Lysenko managed to convince Stalin that the application of his theory of the early subjection of seeds to low temperatures in order to hasten their development, or vernalization, could greatly increase crop yields. Lysenko's ideas, although contrary to the scientifically proved Mendelian theory, were couched in Marxist language and fitted Stalin's personal conviction that everything, including human beings, can be manipulated. By cleverly shifting from one nostrum to another—seed preparation, planting methods, use of fertilizer, animal breeding—and by flattering the Party bosses, Lysenko was able to survive in the face of a succession of failures. Most of these failures were not even known, since his methods were not objectively tested until the 1960s.

Since Lysenko's supporters struggled for the cause of collectivized agriculture, they won increasing favor from the regime to which they pandered. In 1938, Lysenko became President of the Academy of Agriculture and virtual dictator in the fields of biology and genetics. He survived Stalin and retained a great deal of influence until 1962. "Lysenkism" was made the officially imposed, obligatory theory to be taught in all educational establishments of the USSR, to the exclusion of all other theories. Competing biological theories were banned, and Lysenko's opponents, especially the founder of the Agricultural Academy, N. I. Vavilov, were persecuted, arrested, and deported. There was also a tendency to condemn the relativity theory in physics through arguments based on dialectical materialism. Only clever maneuvering on the part of a small group of Soviet physicists saved this branch of science from the total disaster that had befallen genetics. A lucky exception was the behavioral psychologist Professor Ivan Pavlov, who was allowed to continue his research undisturbed. In 1926 he published his seminal book, *Conditioned Reflexes.* His work was supported by the Soviet Government because his theory apparently supported the Marxist doctrine of the decisive influence of environment on behavior. Stalin especially liked Pavlov's experiments with dogs because he hoped that, by manipulating proper external stimuli, he could eventually control human beings.

Nothing illustrates better the evolution of Soviet scholarship under Stalin than its attitude toward the Norman thesis of the origin of the Kievan State. This was the theory that the Eastern Slavs had to call on the Norman Vikings to organize them into a viable State. During the 1930s, with the gradual rebirth of Russian nationalism, the old eighteenth-century thesis dear to the Westernizers could not be tolerated any more. If the Eastern Slavs had to bring in the Germanic Normans to establish the foundations of statehood, they were obviously incapable of doing it themselves. This would support Hitler's thesis of the superiority of the Nordic race over the Slavs. On the Party's instructions, the thesis was discarded and its teaching in Soviet schools forbidden as harmful to the national pride of the Soviet people. The fate of the Norman theory and the acceptance not only of Pavlov's concept but even of Lysenko's theory are striking examples of Stalin's attitude toward knowledge as an instrument for achieving his ends.

RELIGION

The Stalinist cultural revolution also affected the regime's attitude toward religion, especially the Russian Eastern Orthodox Church. Although fiercely opposed not only to all organized churches but to religion as such, Lenin was wary of its hold on the masses. Consequently, as long as he lived, he tried to avoid a frontal attack on religion. Instead, he pursued a double strategy. While harassing organized churches by all sorts of harsh reprisals, arrests, confiscations, and deportations, he also encouraged the struggle against religious beliefs by propaganda that tried to disgrace and ridicule religion as a fraud, "an opiate for the people."

At the same time, he approved of the attempts to split the Orthodox Church and of tactical compromises with what was regarded as its "progressive wing." This encouraged a group of lower clergy seeking a *modus vivendi* with the new regime to denounce the church hierarchy for its refusal to liberalize church regulations and liturgy and for its reluctance to make religion an instrument of social change. In 1922, these dissenters formed a splinter church called the *Living Church.* It proclaimed the abolition of the Patriarchate and declared its willingness to reform the old structure and compromise with the Soviet regime. The Living Church was immediately recognized by the Government. The splinter faction was soon utilized by the secret police, who had infiltrated its leadership in attempts to take over the remaining, more conservative, segment of the Orthodox Church. These machinations, as well as internal squabbles among the ambitious and mostly unscrupulous leaders of the Living Church, discredited it, however, in the eyes of believers. The final blow to the faction was dealt in 1927 by the recognition of the Soviet regime by Patriarch Sergei, who summoned the clergy and the faithful to accept it as an unchangeable, practical, political necessity, while retaining their doctrinal beliefs and traditional practices. This caused the Soviet regime to withdraw its support from the quarreling splinter group, which soon fell apart.

This step by Patriarch Sergei had profound consequences for the whole Russian

Orthodox Church. Some people obeyed the call and rendered allegiance to Soviet power as being a lesser evil than the possible total destruction of what still remained of the old Church. Some clergymen and faithful believers, on the other hand, protested that the move was an abject surrender by the weak Patriarch to a militant atheistic state bent on a slow but sure destruction of all religion. The intransigent faction has gained the support of a considerable segment of Orthodox communicants living abroad, as well as of a die-hard faction of the faithful within the Soviet Union. Both those inside and outside the country have pointed out the progressive penetration of the Russian hierarchy by agents of the secret police, and the inevitable corruption of the officially tolerated hierarchy which has become a pliant tool of the Communists.

Despite these internal upheavals and splits, despite intensive state-supported propaganda by the League of the Militant Godless and its vitriolic newspaper, *Bezbozhnik* (the Godless), the Orthodox Church (as well as Islam) retained a considerable hold on the minds of the people. This was regarded as highly unsatisfactory by the former seminarian from Tiflis, Stalin. Consequently, the First Five-Year Plan was accompanied by a renewed atheistic campaign. The introduction of a continuous work week abolished Sunday as a day of rest and relaxation. A large number of churches, monasteries, and nunneries were closed and their property was confiscated. The Kazan cathedral in Leningrad was turned into an antireligious museum. The recruitment of members to the League of the Militant Godless was bolstered; in 1932, at the peak of its activity, the League boasted of over 5 million members and of 3,200 "Godless shock brigades." By that time, the number of Eastern Orthodox parishes had sunk from 50,000 to under 30,000. Many members of the hierarchy, despite their previous declarations of loyalty, fell victim to the Great Purge.

Thus the surrender of Patriarch Sergei did not save the Greek Orthodox Church of Russia from the fury of the new anti-religious campaign. His policy, while mitigating only very slightly the attacks on the Church, eroded the credibility of the officially recognized hierarchy as an authentic champion of the surviving religious beliefs of broad masses of people. Nevertheless, religious sentiments survived even the shrill propaganda of the thirties.[5]

SUMMARY

During the Stalin revolution, the majority of Soviet creative individuals, artists and scholars, were caught between the fearful demands made upon them by the Party and the dictates of their conscience. Under attack for a variety of "ideological errors," most submitted with scarcely a murmur. Some, however, tried to pursue an independent line in defiance of the tyrant's will. Among the writers who took such a stand, one must mention, people like Isaac Babel, Anna Akhmatova, Marina Tsvetayeva, and Osip Mandelshtam, who suffered from the Stalinist persecution. A few, like Sergei Bulgakov and Yevgenii Zamyatin, rejected any compromise and emigrated to continue their work abroad. A few broke down under the burden imposed on them by the demonic forces they had worshipped and helped to triumph. To these belonged one hailed by Stalin himself as "the best, most talented poet of the Soviet epoch," Vladimir Mayakovsky. In 1930, he admitted that the Party had "stepped on the throat of his song" and, like Sergei Yessenin before him, he committed suicide.

In his efforts to establish total control in all fields of human activity, Stalin needed artists and scholars as instruments of his "social engineering." Reduced to the level of Pavlov's dogs, they were to serve as tools in the grandiose and grim process of the country's fundamental transformation in accordance with Stalin's design. The increasing

---

[5] The 1937 Census revealed that some 40 percent of the population declared themselves believers. The results of the census were never published.

adulation of the man who allegedly embodied the best features of human nature, the omnipotent and infallible Leader, was the apex of the cult of the "positive hero." This adulation of Stalin, after 1956 euphemistically renamed "personality cult," had already reached obsessive mass proportions in 1929, when he celebrated his fiftieth birthday. The cult of personality crescendoed until his death in 1953. Panegyrics extolling him as "the Father of the People," "wisest of leaders," "people's leader of genius," "great helmsman," "reformer of the world," "forger of world peace," and "the brightest sun of mankind" were commonplace. The following verse, taken from a fourth-grade school reader, is typical of the personality cult in its mature stage:

Thou, our teacher, like the shining sun
Dost open my eyes on heaven and earth;
Light up, my sun, shine in my window,
I see in thee the staff of life.

It is not unusual for the captive and indoctrinated subjects to attribute superhuman qualities to their dictator. But Stalin's cult of personality was unique because of its scope, its intensity, and its all-pervasive character. It penetrated not only political life and the arts but also scholarship, including such branches as for instance, linguistics, which would have been considered immune to these encroachments. The Soviet Union was the first country fully to consider science a vital national resource, to plan systematically the progress of scientific development, and to formulate science policies. The gains of the 1920s, however, were curtailed by Stalin early in the 1930s, thus considerably slowing down the country's progress.

Strangled by the boa constrictor of totalitarianism, the country's intellectuals became servile, sterile, and inbred. Social sciences became primarily propagandistic, with their main purpose the exaltation of the invincible Party led by its infallible Leader marching from one victory to another.

SUGGESTED READING

ANTONOV-OVSEYENKO, ANTON, *The Time of Stalin: Portrait of a Tyranny,* trans. George Saunders. New York: Harper & Row, 1982.

BENNIGSEN, ALEXANDER, AND CHANTAL LEMERCHIER-QUELQUE JAY, *Islam in the Soviet Union.* New York: Praeger, 1967.

BEREDAY, GEORGE F., et al., eds., *The Changing Soviet School.* Boston: Houghton Mifflin, 1960.

BROWN, EDWARD, *A Proletarian Chapter in Russian Literary History, 1928–1932.* New York: Columbia University Press, 1953.

CONQUEST, ROBERT, *The Nation Killers.* New York: Macmillan, 1970.

COUNTS, GEORGE S., *The Challenge of Soviet Education.* New York: McGraw-Hill, 1957.

DE WITT, NICHOLAS, *Education and Professional Employment in the USSR.* Washington, D.C.: National Science Foundation, 1961.

DMYTRYSHYN, BASIL, *Moscow and the Ukraine, 1918–1953.* New York: Bookman Associates, 1956.

ELLIS, JANE, *The Russian Orthodox Church. A Contemporary History.* Bloomington: Indiana University Press, 1986.

GRAHAM, LOREN R., *Science and Philosophy in the Soviet Union.* New York: Knopf, 1970.

HUXLEY, JULIAN S., *Heredity, East and West: Lysenko and World Science.* Millwood, N.Y.: Kraus, 1969.

JORAVSKY, DAVID, *The Lysenko Affair.* Cambridge, Mass.: Harvard University Press, 1970.

KOCHAN, LIONEL, ed., *The Jews in Soviet Russia Since 1917.* New York: Oxford University Press, 1970.

KOLARZ, WALTER, *Russia and Her Colonies.* London: George Philip & Son, 1952.

KOSTIUK, HRYHORY, *Stalinist Rule in the Ukraine . . . 1929–1939.* Munich: Institute for the Study of the USSR, 1960.

LAND, DAVID MARSHAL, *A Modern History of Soviet Georgia.* New York: Grove Press, 1962.

LUCKYI, GEORGE N. S., *Literary Politics in the Soviet Union, 1917–1934.* New York: Columbia University Press, 1956.

MATOSSIAN, MARY, *The Impact of Soviet Politics on Armenia.* Leiden: Brill, 1962.

MEDVEDEV, ZHORES A., *The Rise and Fall of T. D. Lysenko,* trans. I. Michael Lerner. Garden City, N.Y.: Doubleday, 1971.

SCHWARTZ, SOLOMON M., *The Jews in the Soviet Union.* Syracuse, N.Y.: Syracuse University Press, 1951.

SIMMONS, ERNEST J., *Russian Fiction and Soviet Ideology.* New York: Columbia University Press, 1958.

SULLIVAN, ROBERT S., *Soviet Politics and the Ukraine, 1917–1957.* New York: Columbia University Press, 1962.

TOLSTOY, NIKOLAI, *Stalin's Secret War.* New York: Holt, Rinehart & Winston, 1983.

VAKAR, NICHOLAS, *Belorussia.* Cambridge, Mass.: Harvard University Press, 1955.

WHEELER, GEOFFREY, *The Modern History of Soviet Central Asia.* New York: Praeger, 1964.

CHAPTER 16

From Isolation to Collective Security

During the 1920s the Soviet Union, although gradually and reluctantly recognized by most great powers (except the United States), lived in relative isolation from the international community. The USSR did not enter the League of Nations and its network of auxiliary international organizations. Quite the contrary; the League was denounced by the Soviet leaders as a capitalist "League of Robbers," a "Holy Alliance of the bourgeoisie for the suppression of the proletarian revolution." It was regarded by the Kremlin leaders as a conspiracy concocted to petrify the post-Versailles status quo and plot another intervention against "the first Socialist State." On the other hand, the Western powers continued to regard with profound misgivings the godless state that had abolished private property, refused to pay foreign debts, indulged in violent suppression of all political dissent, and sponsored the Comintern with its anticolonialist and subversive propaganda.

Although England's first Labor Government, headed by Ramsay MacDonald, granted *de jure* recognition of the Soviet Union on February 2, 1924, and was followed by Paris and Rome a few days later, the relations between the Western powers and Moscow remained tense and uneasy and mutual recriminations were similar to those of the "cold war" of our days. Revolutionary agitation in Ireland, India, and Egypt was frowned on even by the British Laborites. The cynical remarks of some Comintern leaders—like Zinoviev's, "We shall support MacDonald as the rope supports the hanged"—did not improve Soviet-British relations either. Memories of the past, especially of the Allied intervention, still lingered and poisoned the atmosphere. The first Soviet ambassador at the Court of St. James was systematically ignored by King George V at all social functions, for he was considered the representative of a regime that had murdered his cousin Nicholas II and his family. No agreements were

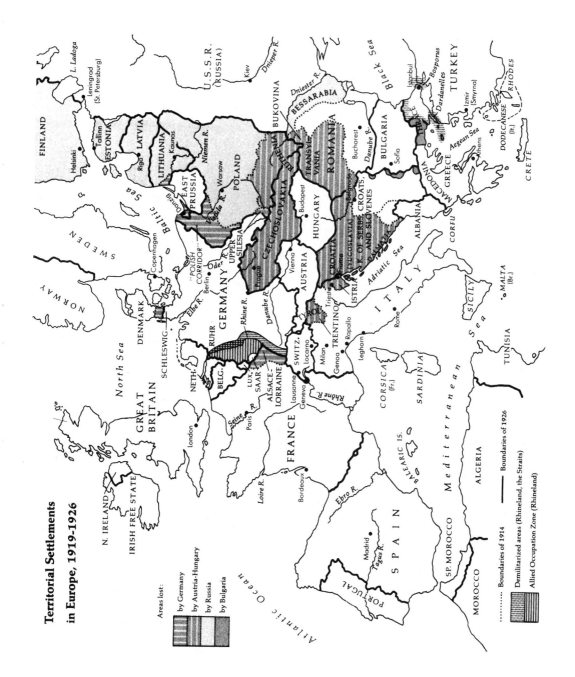

Territorial Settlements in Europe, 1919-1926

Areas lost:
- by Germany
- by Austria-Hungary
- by Russia
- by Bulgaria

········· Boundaries of 1914 ——— Boundaries of 1926

Demilitarized areas (Rhineland, the Straits)

Allied Occupation Zone (Rhineland)

FINLAND

L. Ladoga

Leningrad (St. Petersburg)

Helsinki

U.S.S.R. (RUSSIA)

Kiev

Dnieper R.

ESTONIA

Tallinn

LATVIA

Riga

LITHUANIA

Kaunas

Niemen R.

Dniester R.

BESSARABIA

BUKOVINA

EAST PRUSSIA

Danzig

Warsaw

Vistula R.

POLAND

TRANSYL-VANIA

ROMANIA

Black Sea

Istanbul

Bosporus

Dardanelles

TURKEY

Izmir (Smyrna)

RHODES

DODECANESE (It.)

CRETE

Bucharest

Danube R.

BULGARIA

Sofia

Aegean Sea

Athens

MACEDONIA

GREECE

CORFU

ALBANIA

Adriatic Sea

UPPER SILESIA

Oder R.

POLISH CORRIDOR

CZECHOSLOVAKIA

Prague

Budapest

HUNGARY

Vienna

AUSTRIA

Belgrade

Fiume

ISTRIA

Trieste

CROATIA

YUGOSLAVIA (KINGDOM OF SERBS, CROATS, AND SLOVENES)

Baltic Sea

SWEDEN

NORWAY

Copenhagen

DENMARK

SCHLESWIG

Berlin

Elbe R.

GERMANY

Rhine R.

RUHR

NETH.

BELG.

LUX.

SAAR

ALSACE-LORRAINE

Danube R.

TYROL

TRENTINO

Rapallo

SWITZ.

Locarno

Lausanne

Geneva

Milan

Genoa

Leghorn

Rome

ITALY

Rhône R.

Seine R.

Paris

Loire R.

Bordeaux

FRANCE

GREAT BRITAIN

London

North Sea

N. IRELAND

IRISH FREE STATE

Atlantic Ocean

Ebro R.

SPAIN

Madrid

Tagus R.

PORTUGAL

SP. MOROCCO

MOROCCO

ALGERIA

TUNISIA

Mediterranean Sea

CORSICA (Fr.)

SARDINIA

BALEARIC IS.

SICILY

MALTA (Br.)

CRETE

221

reached with either Paris or London concerning the prerevolutionary debts, or about compensation for French and British property nationalized by the Soviet regime.

The incident of the "Zinoviev letter" contributed to the downfall of the Labor Government, which was defeated in the election of October 1924. Soviet interference with the British coal strike of 1926, frequent Soviet attacks on British statesmen, especially on Winston Churchill as a proponent of a new Western intervention in Russia, all continued to poison relations between Moscow and London. Their low point was reached on May 21, 1927, when British police raided the London premises of the Soviet-British trade company "Arcos." The search resulted in the confiscation of substantial incriminating material which indicated that the company's officials, about a thousand people altogether, engaged in espionage and subversive propaganda in Britain and its overseas domains. Among the confiscated documents were copies of some of the most confidential talks between the British and French general staffs intercepted by the Soviet agents. Despite subsequent vocal Soviet protests, on May 27 London broke off diplomatic relations with Moscow. Soon Canada followed suit. These moves were denounced by the Soviet and Comintern leaders as a first step toward an "international capitalist crusade" against "the first proletarian government in the world." Moscow groundlessly suspected that France's East European allies, especially Poland and Romania, would be used as jumping off grounds for such an intervention.

THREATS IN ASIA AND EUROPE

Although it repeatedly cried wolf, the Soviet regime carried out its momentous, massive experiment in rapid, forcible socioeconomic engineering in relative security until the late 1920s. The situation began to change during the early 1930s both in Asia and in Europe, and by the middle of the decade

Moscow was faced with the specter of potential armed conflict on two distant fronts. The first threat of war appeared in the Far East as a result of the Japanese occupation of Manchuria in 1931; the second potential menace to Soviet security came as a consequence of Hitler's triumph in Germany in 1933.

Initially, the Japanese danger appeared more real and immediate. Tokyo had not recognized the Soviet regime until 1925, largely because of three points of friction that survived the downfall of the Tsarist regime: (1) the issue of the fishing rights of the Japanese in Russian waters; (2) Japanese concessions on the island of Sakhalin, the southern segment of which they had annexed in 1905; and (3) Japan's growing interest in China, especially in Manchuria. While the first two issues were of limited significance and were satisfactorily settled between 1925 and 1928, the third was of considerable importance for both powers competing for influence in Manchuria, the most industrialized and vital province of China. Japanese investments were considerable and on the rise. Moreover, the civil war in China was a temptation for the restless Japanese proponents of imperial expansion on the Asian mainland. Taking advantage of the intensifying Chinese Civil War, the Japanese gave increasing moral and material support to the irredentist tendencies that soon manifested itself among some segments of Manchuria's population, demoralized by years of civil war and encouraged by the activities of local warlords. Unrest spilled over from Central China to Manchuria and gave Tokyo a pretext for dispatching troops, allegedly to protect Japanese nationals and their investments. At the end of 1931 the Japanese went so far as to send troops into Manchuria; on February 5, 1932, they occupied Harbin. On March 9 they proclaimed the establishment of an independent Manchurian state called Manchukuo. The League of Nations debated the problem of the Japanese aggression for a long time but did nothing concrete. Moscow limited itself to verbal protests. Yet Tokyo, angered by the League's eventual censure of its policy, left the organization.

The new strategic situation in the Far East necessitated a reorientation of Soviet Russia's policy in that area. Since the USSR had no diplomatic relations with the United States, steps were undertaken to reestablish such relations. Meanwhile, the aid of another countervailing force closer at hand had to be found. Forgetting the bitter past, in the spring of 1932 Moscow resumed diplomatic relations with Chiang Kai-shek's Chinese nationalist government in Nanking, broken off in 1927. On June 29, Moscow signed a nonaggression pact with Nanking, and a new chapter in the relations between the two countries was opened. While normalizing relations with the government at Nanking, Stalin did not care to safeguard the interests of the Chinese Communist Party. So Chiang continued to fight the Chinese Communists who had proclaimed their government in the province of Kiangsi in December 1931. To destroy it, Chiang Kai-shek launched a series of mopping-up operations. Although officially considered successful, these never resulted in suppressing the spread of the *sui generis* agrarian Communism that had deep roots in China's anomalous, feudal conditions. Despite bitter losses, the Communist forces continued to expand. By 1933, the Chinese Red Army already numbered over 300,000 regular troops and was supported by at least 600,000 men, ably organized by the emerging leader Mao Tse-tung in partisan units scattered throughout the countryside.

In the meantime, the consolidation of Japanese influence on the Asian mainland proceeded apace, and the USSR had to face the new situation realistically. In March 1933, Tokyo offered to buy from the Russians the northern branch of the Manchurian, or Chinese Eastern, railroad. The negotiations dragged on for almost two years. Eventually, on March 23, 1935, the line was ceded to the government of Manchukuo for 170 million yen, far below the actual worth

of the railway. Meanwhile, in August 1932, new agreements concerning oil concessions and Japanese fishing rights had been concluded, all of them advantageous to Tokyo. These conciliatory gestures, which momentarily relaxed the tension between the two rivals, could not safeguard Soviet security in the Far East. They did not mean definite Russian withdrawal from an area vital to the position of the USSR in the Far East.

MOSCOW REACTS TO THE JAPANESE MENACE

A considerable strengthening of the Soviet posture was needed to face Japan's growing appetite. Consequently, while normalizing somewhat its relations with Nanking, Moscow took two steps to cope with the mounting Japanese danger. First, a powerful Far Eastern army was deployed along the Manchurian and Mongolian frontiers and gradually reinforced and equipped with the best weapons the Second Five-Year Plan could supply. This army was established as a semi-autonomous unit because at that time the Trans-Siberian Railroad still had only one track; supplying the Far Eastern army in case of emergency would have constituted a serious logistical problem. Second, Moscow speeded up its negotiations with Japan's most serious countervailing force, the United States. Stalin well remembered the American intervention in the Russian Civil War, but he was also aware that it was Washington that had prevented the Japanese from establishing themselves permanently on Siberian soil after the War. Although the Japanese were supporting the White forces, with which Washington was in basic sympathy, the Americans had insisted on the evacuation of the Japanese troops. Despite the fact that Presidents Wilson and Harding refused to recognize the Bolshevik regime on the grounds that it advocated subversion and atheism, trade relations were soon resumed. In 1926, American companies obtained gold prospecting concessions on the Amur River and the next year Standard Oil signed advantageous contracts with Moscow. Soon General Electric followed suit. By the late 1920s Soviet-American trade was twice what it had been before the war. The USSR of the five-year plans was a fair hunting ground for American engineers and economic experts eager to escape the Great Depression.

The Democratic Party, which came to power in Washington in 1933, was under increased pressure from business circles to resume diplomatic relations with a country that represented a potential market for American goods. This, combined with Washington's suspicion of Tokyo's designs in the Far East, pushed both countries toward a compromise. In November 1933, the United States recognized the Soviet Union *de jure,* in exchange for Soviet promises to refrain from subversive propaganda and to resume talks about indemnifying American citizens whose assets had been confiscated after the Bolshevik revolution. A friend of President Roosevelt, William Bullitt, who had led an exploratory diplomatic mission to Russia in 1919, became the first American ambassador in Moscow. Yet trade between the two countries increased only slightly, while Stalin's expectations of American support against Japan were soon to be disappointed. The Soviet pledges concerning Comintern propaganda and the repayments of both private and public debts remained a dead letter.

THE SPIRIT OF RAPALLO

The ominous changes taking place along the eastern approaches to the USSR were paralleled by equally menacing developments in Central Europe. The latent instability of the Weimar Republic was intensified by the Great Depression, with its crippling social consequences. During the early 1930s, unemployment in Germany was spreading rapidly. Soon nearly 6 million jobless became easy prey for extremist

agitation, including the mushrooming Communist Party of Germany and all sorts of paramilitary fighting squads of the Right. Slogans calling for the destruction of the Versailles Treaty and a return to the 1913 frontiers were propounded by numerous spokesmen. The most ruthless, vitriolic, and dynamic of them was a former lance corporal of the Imperial German army, an Austrian by birth—Adolf Hitler. As head of the National Socialist Workers (Nazi) Party, he preached racism, revenge, and the establishment of a millennial Teutonic empire reaching far to the East, including the Soviet Ukraine. After the elections of July 1932, the Nazis became the largest party in the Parliament.

Beneath the Soviet-German military and economic collaboration, there were numerous misgivings in Berlin. Western-oriented statesmen, including Gustav Stresemann, Foreign Minister from 1923 to 1929 who favored the policy of conciliation with France and Great Britain and brought Germany into the League of Nations, guaranteed that Germany would respect the status quo, but only in the west. Chancellors Heinrich Brünning and Franz von Papen, both Roman Catholics, could not hide their aversion to cooperation with the Communists who, despite their professed friendship, encouraged subversive activities and supported Germany's fast-spreading Communist movement. But all these voices were silenced because of the double pressure from military and industrial circles, which stressed the profits to be derived from Germany's special relationship with the USSR, including the value of burgeoning trade during the Depression.

Overall, the spirit of Rapallo seemed unimpaired during the early 1930s. Trade relations, guaranteed by so-called "Russian credits" as security to German exporters were developing satisfactorily; cultural exchanges were flourishing; collaboration between the Red Army and the small German forces went on undisturbed. Throughout this period high Soviet officers attended secret and not so secret military courses in

Germany, while German pilots and tank crews were being trained in the USSR. The peak of this military intimacy was reached in 1931 when a large German military delegation was allowed to attend Soviet maneuvers near Kiev. Observers witnessed a massive display by Red Army paratroopers, which strongly impressed the envious German guests.[1]

LITVINOV'S NEW COURSE

While the entire strategic situation of the Soviet Union was gradually undergoing change, the management of Soviet foreign relations was handed over to a new team of younger people. In 1930 the main architect of Soviet-German rapprochment, Chicherin, had to resign because of prolonged illness, and his place was taken by his deputy, Maxim Litvinov. Born in Bialystok in Russian Poland in 1876, the son of a Jewish bourgeois family, Litvinov had joined the RSDWP in 1903 and thus, unlike Chicherin was an old Bolshevik. Married to an Englishwoman, the niece of newspaper publisher Sir Sidney Low, Litvinov spoke English fluently and was at home in Britain, whose culture he admired. To erase the old image of the Soviet Union as opposed to the post-Versailles system and to overcome British and French fears of the "Red menace" became the task of the smiling, smooth-operating new Commissar for Foreign Affairs. He tackled the task tactfully, with great skill and remarkable persistence.

With the rise of the Japanese menace in the Far East and the mounting revanchist, militaristic, and racial agitation in Germany, Soviet foreign policy began to undergo a gradual yet quite definite reorientation. Step by step, taking advantage of existing geopolitical realities, Litvinov proceeded with his task of securing the Western approaches to the Soviet Union. The USSR was separated from Germany by a belt of smaller states stretching from Finland to Romania and including the three Baltic Republics and Poland. Since Germany might again become a threat to Soviet security, it was deemed essential to normalize relations with these border states so as to prevent them from being used as bases of an attack against Russia. To turn these Western neighbors into a buffer zone protecting the USSR through a series of diplomatic arrangements now became a major objective of Soviet diplomacy. It was Litvinov's task to negotiate and sign in 1931 and 1932 a series of nonaggression pacts with all of Soviet Russia's western neighbors, with the exception of Romania. The Soviet-Romanian negotiations broke down because of Moscow's reluctance to accept the incorporation of Bessarabia into Romania.

The most important of these nonaggression treaties was with France's chief ally, Poland. The Soviet-Polish nonaggression pact signed on July 25, 1932 was a stepping stone toward a similar agreement with Paris, which was concluded on November 29, 1932. Meanwhile, nonaggression pacts had

---

[1]In October 1918, during World War I, General William "Billy" Mitchell proposed to capture Metz by using parachutists, but the war ended before his scheme could be put into practice. During the 1930s, the Red Army tried several experiments with airborne troops. In 1936, for instance, they parachuted two battalions, light field guns, and some 150 machine guns during the maneuvers near Kiev, and the airborne team swiftly occupied the city. The German military attaché was impressed by the operation and urged Hitler to emulate the Soviet performance and develop such airborne detachments on a large scale.

Maxim Litvinov, Foreign Affairs Commissar Minister, 1930–1939

been also signed with the three Baltic republics of Lithuania, Latvia, and Estonia. In view of the increasingly menacing situation in the Far East Litvinov tried to protect the Soviet rear by diminishing the chances of Russia's western neighbors' participating in any hostile combination against it.

STALIN AND THE RISE OF HITLER

To understand Stalin's attitude toward the rise of Hitler and his Nazi party, one has to go back to the Sixth Congress of the Comintern, which took place from July to September of 1928. Although the Congress deliberated under the chairmanship of Bukharin, its spirit and temper were already thoroughly Stalinist. At the Congress, Stalin declared, "He is a revolutionary who, without reservation, unconditionally and openly . . . is ready to defend the USSR. He who thinks to defend the world revolutionary movement apart from and against the USSR is going against the revolution." The emphasis of the Congress was on thorough "Bolshevization" of all national sections of the Comintern; this implied strict discipline, ideological intransigence, subordination to Moscow and rejection of cooperation with other "anti-Fascist" forces. All previous attempts at forming "united fronts of the working class" together with Social Democrats were to be abandoned. They were too "soft," too "reformist." The only permissible united front, therefore, was to be made from below by wooing away the proletarian masses from "the social-traitors" of the working class—the socialists who had to be "unmasked" as "Judases" and "social fascists." This reflected Stalin's contemptuous attitude towards Western social democrats who, despite occasional and rather ambivalent sympathy toward the huge Soviet socioeconomic experiment, were still critical of the way it was being conducted. In 1927, while discussing the possibility of collaborating with them and other leftist elements against the bourgeois parties, Stalin said,

"Rather let them go to hell, all these liberal-pacifist philosophers with their 'sympathy' for the USSR."

Thus, after the Sixth Congress of the Comintern, the socialists emerged as the main enemy of the Communists, their chief competitors for control of the working masses. The Great Depression, which played havoc with most Western institutions by breeding mass unemployment and ruining world trade, did not much alter the extreme, uncompromising course of the Comintern. If anything, it sharpened it by stressing the Communist parties' intolerance and exclusivism. According to Moscow theoreticians, the final crisis of capitalism was opening marvelous new vistas for hard, determined parties that would use methods similar to those applied by the Bolsheviks in 1917. This meant going it alone, adopting the most radical positions on practically every issue, and seizing every opportunity to implement them by the most militant methods.

The application of the 1917 analogy to the situation created by the Great Depression in the West had especially momentous consequences in Germany. With the expected final and inevitable disintegration of the capitalist system, the Social Democrats, who still controlled a large segment of the trade unions and other working-class organizations, loomed as the last serious obstacle to the Communist objectives. They were, as Molotov put it, "the last resource of the bourgeoisie among the workers."

In view of this attitude, any idea of cooperation between the German Communists and the German Social Democrats against the rising specter of Hitlerism was condemned by the Kremlin as unnecessary. In a way, the mushrooming of the Nazi movement after 1930 was welcomed by Stalin. The Nazis, he calculated at that time, were after all merely the tools of bankers, large landowners, and capitalists. Hitler's triumph was bound to be ephemeral, while the consequences of his inevitable doom would be beneficial. By depriving the German masses of their democratic and parliamentary illusions and by finally running the capitalist economy of the country, Hitler (whom Stalin regarded as a combination of Kerensky and Kornilov) would merely prepare the ground for the Communists. That is why Stalin explicitly forbade the leader of the Communist Party of Germany, Ernst Thaelmann, to cooperate with the socialists against Hitler.

TOWARD THE BREAK
WITH GERMANY

When on January 30, 1933, Hitler was appointed Chancellor, Stalin was hardly disturbed. He tried to ignore the event and continue his good relations with Berlin. The subsequent massacre of the German Communist Party was not particularly bemoaned by the Soviet dictator. Although he issued a series of vitriolic condemnations of the Nazi actions, he did not allow them to upset the smooth functioning of the two countries' economic and military collaboration. Besides, Stalin took a dim view of foreign comrades and considered them expendable; he cared about them only insofar as they could be useful to his purposes. As he said once, "One Soviet tractor is worth ten thousand foreign Communists."

Meanwhile, as Hitler consolidated his power and watched the passivity of France and Britain he disregarded more and more openly the disarmament clauses of the Versailles treaty and embarked on open massive rearmament, Soviet airfields were no longer indispensable. In addition, continuing German-Soviet collaboration was difficult to justify in view of Nazi attacks on Communism as the main threat to Germany.

Stalin was meanwhile increasingly impressed with the German dictator's skill and boldness and persisted in his efforts to maintain at least a modicum of good relations with Berlin. Speaking at the Seventeenth Party Congress in January 1934, Stalin, who had abandoned his early views of Hitler as a fly-by-night phenomenon,

more than hinted at the possibility of continuing close relations with Nazi Germany:

Some German politicians say that the USSR has now taken an orientation toward France and Poland . . . and that this change is to be explained by the establishment of the Fascist regime in Germany. This is not true. Of course we are far from enthusiastic about the Fascist regime in Germany. But Fascism is beside the point, if only because Fascism in Italy, for example, has not kept the USSR from establishing the best of relations with that country.

Stressing the primacy of Soviet security over ideological issues, Stalin concluded that the Soviet Union would be willing to consider rapprochment with any country "which is not interested in disturbing peace." As late as May 1933, a high-ranking German military delegation visited Moscow and held exchanges with representatives of the Soviet General Staff. The delegation was warmly received by distinguished representatives of the Red Army. At the banquet given in honor of the German guests, the Commissar for War, Klement Voroshilov, expressed the desire to maintain friendly links between the two countries. Hitler, however, took a different view. A few weeks later, the Rapallo Treaty was formally denounced by Hitler. Thus ended a twelve-year period of steady Soviet-German collaboration.[2]

The balance sheet of the period is difficult to assess, for both partners derived significant profit from the partnership. While Hitler's rapid rearmament in the 1930s would have been impossible without the spade work by German experts working in the privileged sancturay of Russia, the Red Army learned a great deal from the Germans. Without the Reichswehr's blueprints for tanks, planes, and guns, speedy and extensive modernization of the Soviet armed forces would have been very difficult.

---

[2]For a collection of documents illustrating the evolution of the Soviet diplomatic posture; see Jane Degras (ed.), *Soviet Documents on Foreign Policy, 1917–1941* (New York: Oxford University Press, 1951–1953).

STALIN'S SEARCH FOR SECURITY

Left out in the cold, the disappointed Stalin had to play the lone wolf. By that time his contempt for the German dictator had already turned into a mixture of fear and grudging admiration for efficiency. The skill, speed, and ruthlessness with which Hitler liquidated Major Röhm and his radical wing of the Nazi movement impressed Stalin immensely. Stalin had read the German dictator's work *Mein Kampf (My Struggle)* in which Hitler openly declared: "If we talk about new soil and territory . . . we can think primarily of Russia and its vassal border states." How to discourage Nazi Germany from carrying out this threat became now Stalin's major task. Isolated and still largely ostracized in the international arena and increasingly menaced both in Asia and Europe, Stalin began to probe for a reorientation of Soviet strategy. Overcoming this isolation now became an urgent task of Soviet diplomacy.

Some of the preparatory agreements aimed at normalizing relations with the USSR's western relations had been achieved between 1930 and 1932 by Litvinov's skillful diplomacy. But the various nonaggression pacts were merely general, largely negative, arrangements designed to make more difficult any future attack by a rearmed Germany and/or prevent the formation of another *cordon sanitaire* that would turn the border states into a jumping-off point for another "capitalist intervention." In view of Hitler's menacing pronouncements and the tempo of the German rearmament, Litvinov continued his attempts to elaborate upon the already existing nonaggression pacts. The result was Soviet participation in the "definition of aggression agreement." This agreement specified more concretely who would be regarded as an aggressor in case the Kellogg–Briand Pact was violated. The agreement, signed in London on July 3, 1933, was also adhered to by Russia's Western neighbors, including Romania.

In view of the steady growth of German militancy, these regional pacts had to be bolstered by more solid security arrangements with the Great Powers against any violation of the status quo. What was needed now was a system of alliances, primarily with Paris and London, that would provide the USSR with military assistance against the two restless and expansionist powers in Asia and Europe—Japan and Germany. This quest for security through alliances with German's opponents was obviously incompatible with the line of policy hitherto pursued by the Comintern. The policy that treated all non-Communist forces as equally evil, to be fought against in the same way as the Fascists, became an anachronism. As has been already stressed, besides actively dispensing subversive propaganda inside both France and England and their overseas possessions, the USSR had also opposed the concept of collective security sponsored by these two powers in the League of Nations. To achieve a rapprochement with Paris and London, Moscow had to overcome the fears generated by the Comintern's explosive revolutionary propaganda and its denunciations of the League as an imperialist instrument of the status quo powers. The virulent anti-democratic and anti-Western campaign the Comintern had conducted during the previous six years (from 1928) had to be dropped. All of this required radical reorientation of the work of various Communist parties, including soft pedaling anti-League propaganda and shifting the policy of the Comintern to work even more closely with the Narkomindel. If the USSR was to cooperate with the Western democracies against Nazi Germany, the intransigent Left course of the Comintern pursued since 1928 had to be abandoned.

THE GREAT SHIFT OF SOVIET POLICY

There was no time to lose. The shift came abruptly in 1934, soon after the denunciation of the Rapallo Treaty by Hitler. All national sections of the Comintern were ordered to approach the Social Democratic leaders with proposals of cooperation against the common "Fascist menace." The first to obey was the Communist Party of France, weathervane of the Comintern. Despite his previous emphatic declarations that "a marriage between Communists and Socialists is fundamentally alien to the spirit of Bolshevism," the French party boss, Maurice Thorez, after his visit to Moscow, opened negotiations with the French Socialist Party for mutual abjuration of criticism and the eventual establishment of a workingclass united front to struggle against the common danger.

In May 1934, Litvinov met in Geneva with French Foreign Minister Louis Barthou. They discussed closer cooperation between the two countries, Soviet Russia's possible entrance into the League of Nations, and a potential Soviet-French alliance providing for mutual aid and assistance in case of unprovoked attack by a third power. Overnight Litvinov became one of the most eloquent defenders of the League and an ardent supporter of the principle of collective security. According to him this concept was the main hope of the "peace-loving people" of the world, irrespective of class origin.

The autumn 1934 session of the League of Nations witnessed the Soviet Union's entrance as a full-fledged member with a prominent seat on the Council. This step underscored the end both of Moscow's denunciations of the League and its sabotage of the policy of collective security based on the League's Covenant. Russia was once again recognized as a great power interested in preserving the status quo. Entrance into the League permitted more intimate association with the Western powers, especially France and Great Britain, who were also frightened by Germany's rearmament and Hitler's growing ambitions. The USSR's decision acknowledged the Soviet hope that the League, weakened by the absence of the United States and the desertion of Japan

and Germany, could still be a useful international forum and a potential instrument in the struggle against the aggressive designs of its enemies in Asia and Europe.

On May 2, 1935, the USSR and France signed a treaty of alliance which pledged both partners to come to each other's assistance "in case of an unprovoked attack on the part of a European state." Meanwhile, instructions had been issued to the Communist Party of France to drop its antimilitaristic propaganda and its policy of sabotaging the French rearmament effort. On May 16, 1935, the world was surprised to read in the French press a French journalist's interview with Stalin, who declared his support of "the policy of national defense followed by France so as to maintain her armed forces on the level necessary to maintain national security."

SOVIET ALLIANCES WITH FRANCE AND CZECHOSLOVAKIA

To appreciate how momentous a step this was, one has to recall the history of bitter mutual hostility that had divided the two countries ever since the Communist revolution. Let down by its former ally as a result of the Brest-Litovsk separate peace and despoiled of its huge investments in Russia, France had become the main sponsor of Allied intervention against the Bolsheviks. In Soviet eyes France was, next to Britain, the embodiment of imperialist, predatory capitalism and the chief symbol of the Versailles peace, which was not only directed against Germany but also designed to surround Soviet Russia with an East European *cordon sanitaire.* In June 1933, with Hitler already a clear menace, Stalin did not hesitate to call France "the most aggressive and militaristic country of all aggressive and militaristic countries of the world." Nothing but fear of Hitler's boundless greed could have brought Paris and Moscow together.

The new Franco-Soviet alliance was much more restrictive than that of 1894. The treaty of May 1935 not only was limited to Europe and did not provide for French assistance against Japan, but unlike its nineteenth-century predecessor, it did not envisage the automatic use of force in case of aggression by a third power against one of the contracting parties. The treaty of 1935 spoke only about "mutual consultations" in case of an act of aggression. Moreover, the fact of aggression had to be recognized as such by the League of Nations under Article 16 of its Covenant. Furthermore, the new pact was signed under different geopolitical conditions. Unlike the situation prior to World War I, Russia and Germany were no longer immediate neighbors. They were now separated by a chain of independent states: Romania, Poland, Lithuania, Latvia, and Estonia. The lack of a common border between the USSR and Germany made it necessary to assure the adherence of the intermediary states, or at least Rumania and Poland, to the new security arrangements. For the Red Army to render effective assistance to France in case of an attack by Germany, Soviet units would need to have a right of passage through some of these states to reach German soil. The key country was Poland, the largest segment of the area. The problem of putting Soviet bases on Polish territory proved to be a deadly obstacle to effective coordination of Soviet and French preparations. Although allied with the French since 1921 and committed to the Polish-Soviet Nonaggression Pact since 1932, the Poles steadfastly refused to allow the Red Army to be stationed on their territory in peace time. To French pleas, the Warsaw diplomats would always give a stubborn refusal, one that was grounded in the long history of Russo-Polish relations. As Vice Minister of Foreign Affairs Jan Szembek retorted to a French ambassador in Warsaw, "That's just the way the partitions of Poland began in the eighteenth century."

Any effective military cooperation in wartime presupposes close peacetime exchanges and detailed planning of future moves. Although some preliminary general staff exchanges were conducted between the two allies immediately after the signing of the pact, they were soon interrupted (partly because of the purge of the top Soviet military personnel and partly because of their endemic futility). They were to be resumed only in the spring of 1939 when it was too late and Soviet foreign policy was again about to shift radically. Consequently, the French-Soviet alliance was only a pale shadow of its 1894 predecessor. All this time mutual suspicion lingered; French inhibitions were reflected in the fact that the French Parliament dragged its feet on ratification of the treaty until February 1936.

A few days after the signing of the Franco-Soviet Treaty, France's ally, Czechoslovakia, followed the example of its western protector and signed a similar treaty. The Soviet-Czechoslovak pact, however, included an additional clause worth remembering in view of the Soviet behavior during the Munich crisis of 1938: any Soviet aid to Czechoslovakia, in case of war, hinged on a previous French entry into the conflict.

Thus, without a specific, detailed, military convention to provide the alliance with some substance, the pact of 1935 was more a declaration of intention than an effective instrument of defense. What was lacking was not only mutual trust, but also a sense of mutual purpose and the determination to pursue it together.

THE COMINTERN FOLLOWS SUIT

The dramatic reversal of Soviet policy had immediate consequences for the national standing of French Communism. Hitherto it had been regarded as an alien, antipatriotic force, and the Communists had therefore been ostracized by most of the French, including a large section of the working class that owed its allegiance to the Socialists. This now began to change while the French Communists became increasingly jingoistic. The 1935 spring local elections registered considerable gains by the Communists, who were now working hand-in-hand with the

Socialists, who only shortly before they had denounced as "Social Fascists."

The success of the United Front of the French working class emboldened Thorez to extend it toward the center to include the Socialist Radical Party which, despite its name, represented mostly middle and lower-middle class people. Thus the united front was to be turned into a broader coalition of "all democratic forces," a "popular front." Despite some opposition from the left wing of the Socialist Party, negotiations to this effect were initiated in the name of joint resistance to the mounting wave of domestic right-wing menace and to the threat represented by Nazi Germany.

To appreciate fully the psychological significance of the abrupt about-face of Soviet policy for foreign Communists, one also has to view it against the background of Comintern policy in effect since 1928. Between 1924 and 1928, Stalin turned the Comintern into a pliable tool of his policy of socialism in one country; that is, of consolidating and defending Soviet national interests as he interpreted them. Without even so much as consulting its World Congress, he promoted or demoted the chairman and members of the Comintern's executive committees. In 1926, for instance, Stalin removed Zinoviev and appointed Bukharin Comintern Chairman, then used him and the prestige of this office in the domestic struggle against Trotsky. He often referred to the Comintern as "my little shop" (*moia lavochka*). The Comintern, he repeatedly stressed, "represents nothing and exists only thanks to our support." This downgrading and bureaucratization of the Comintern's role was described by Isaac Deutscher, at one time a prominent member of the Communist Party of Poland, as resulting in growing financial dependence on Moscow of the foreign Communist leaders.[3]

By the mid-1930s, Stalin's control over the Comintern was nearly complete. Consequently, it was a matter of just a few instructions and stepped-up propaganda among the rank and file to alter the leftist course of the Comintern, first to a pro-united front line. While the most obedient of all Communist Parties, the French, acted as a harbinger of the new policy, most other parties needed some pressing, but finally all of them submitted to Moscow's newest line. The official proclamation of the new strategy was staged at the Seventh (and last) Comintern Congress, again held in Moscow, in July and August 1935. The dominant figure of the Congress was the Bulgarian leader Georgy Dimitrov, who was elected the Comintern's secretary general. Dimitrov was at that time basking in the glory of the courageous and eloquent stand he had taken at the 1933 Reichstag fire trial in Leipzig. During the trial he had assumed an attitude of defiance toward the judges and made many Nazi leaders, including Prussian Minister of the Interior Hermann Goering, a laughingstock by exposing their complicity in the fire, which had been engineered by the Nazis to look like it had been set by the Communists. The imprisoned Ernst Thaelmann, leader of the Communist Party of Germany, which had been decimated and bled white by Hitler soon after the fire, was proclaimed Honorary President of the Seventh Congress of the Comintern.

Most speakers at the Congress were seething with hatred and contempt for German and Japanese militarists and imperialists. They stretched out their hands to "all sincere opponents of Fascism" and "imperialist aggression." Yet despite all these rhetorical exercises the Congress, manipulated by its real master, failed to commit the Communist movement to an irrevocable struggle against Germany. One of the Congress's resolutions went so far as to declare, "The main contradiction in the camp of imperialists is the Anglo-American antagonism." The national sections of the Comintern were still instructed to "fight against military expenditures," although not in

---

[3] For details of Stalin's intentional demoralization of the Comintern *aparat*, see Isaac Deutscher, *Stalin: A Political Biography*, 2nd ed. (New York: Oxford University Press, 1967), p. 397–398.

those "weak states" that could be attacked by "one or more big imperialist powers." Actually, the stand against Japan seemed to be stiffer than against Germany. While the Chinese Communists were instructed to "extend the front of the struggle for their national liberation," the German Communists were ordered to enter such organizations as the Nazi Labor Front and to work there for higher wages and better labor conditions. Thus, even at the peak of its "anti-Fascist" offensive, the Comintern's policy was highly differentiated, and it never completely closed the door to a renewed understanding with one or both of the increasingly aggressive states of Asia and Europe.

The popular front phase of Soviet foreign policy marked the final downgrading of the Comintern and the ultimate exposing of its role as a mere tool of Moscow's will.

The downgrading of the Comintern was also reflected in its calendar. During Lenin's era, the Comintern met five times: once every year from 1919 to 1923. Under Stalin it met only three times in nineteen years: in 1924, 1928, and 1935. To placate his Western allies, Stalin dissolved it altogether in 1943. But meanwhile, especially during the 1930s, it had had to follow the twists and turns of the General Secretary's tortuous "general line," while hailing his capricious infallibility. The Comintern's messianic, evangelical urge became weaker, as foreign Communists became only a means toward strengthening the Soviet State and solidifying the position of its ruling group. By the late 1930s, by corruption and terror, Stalin had imposed the principle that loyal Communists were to have no opinions of their own; they were simply to obey his orders.

In view of this growing corruption of the world Communist movement and its slavish subordination to the whim of the General Secretary of the CPSU, the indignant Trotsky declared in a letter to his American supporter Max Eastman, "Stalinism is the syphilis of socialism."

SUGGESTED READING

BAER, GEORGE W. ed., *A Question of Trust: The Origin of U.S.–Soviet Relations: The Memoirs of Loy W. Henderson*. Stanford, Calif.: Hoover Institution Press, Stanford University, 1987.

BELOFF, MAX, *The Foreign Policy of the Soviet Union, 1929–1941*. New York: Oxford University Press, 1947–1949, 2 vols.

BORKENAU, FRANZ, *World Communism: A History of the Communist International*. Ann Arbor: University of Michigan Press, 1962.

BROWDER, ROBERT P., *The Origins of Soviet-American Diplomacy*. Princeton, N.J.: Princeton University Press, 1953.

BUDUROWYCZ, BOHDAN, *Polish-Soviet Relations, 1932–1933*. New York: Columbia University Press, 1963.

CARR, E.H., *Twilight of the Comintern, 1930–1935*. New York: Pantheon Books, 1983.

CRAIG, GORDON, and FELIX GILBERT, eds., *The Diplomats, 1919–1939*. Princeton, N.J.: Princeton University Press, 1953. Especially important are the chapters on Soviet diplomacy, Chicherin, and Litvinov.

DEGRAS, JANE, *Calendar of Soviet Documents on Foreign Policy, 1917–1941*. New York: The Royal Institute of International Affairs, 1948.

———, ed., *The Communist International, 1919–1943, Documents*. New York: Oxford University Press, 1956. In 3 vols., with vol. 2 the most useful.

———, *Soviet Documents on Foreign Policy, 1917–1941*. New York: Oxford University Press, 1951–1953, 3 vols.; vol. 2 is the most valuable.

DEUTSCHER, ISAAC, *The Prophet Unarmed: Trotsky, 1919–1929*. New York: Oxford University Press, 1959.

———, *The Prophet Outcast, 1929–1940*. New York: Oxford University Press, 1963.

DRAPER, THEODORE, *American Communism and Soviet Russia*. New York: Viking, 1960.

EUDIN, XENIA J., and ROBERT M. SLUSSER, eds., *Soviet Foreign Policy, 1928–1941: Documented Materials*, vol. 1. University Park: Pennsylvania State University Press, 1966.

FILENE, PETER G., *Americans and the Soviet Experiment, 1917–1933*. Cambridge, Mass.: Harvard University Press, 1967.

FISCHER, RUTH, *Stalin and German Communism*. Cambridge, Mass.: Harvard University Press, 1948.

KENNAN, GEORGE F., *Russia and the West under Lenin and Stalin*. Boston: Little, Brown, 1961.

McKENZIE, KERMIT E., *Comintern and the World Revolution, 1928–1943; The Shaping of a Doctrine.* New York: Columbia University Press, 1964.

McLANE, CHARLES B., *Soviet Policy and Chinese Communists, 1913–1946.* New York: Columbia University Press, 1958.

RUBINSTEIN, ALVIN Z., ed., *The Foreign Policy of the Soviet Union.* New York: Random House, 1960.

ULAM, ADAM, *Expansion and Coexistence* . . . . New York: Praeger, 1968 (mainly Chs. 4 and 5).

CHAPTER 17

Prelude to World War II

The new line of Soviet foreign policy was soon challenged by one crisis after another. On February 26, 1936, after long hesitation, the French Chamber of Deputies finally ratified the Franco-Soviet alliance. Hitler immediately denounced the treaty as an attempt at encirclement of Germany and ordered his troops into the hitherto demilitarized left bank of the Rhine (March 7), in blatant violation of the Treaty of Versailles as well as the Locarno agreements. Despite the suggestion of its Polish ally that they jointly oppose Hitler's move, the centrist French government of Prime Minister Pierre Flandin hesitated to act without prior consultation with London. The Conservative cabinet of Stanley Baldwin, however, refused to support the French. From captured German documents and from the Nuremberg trial, we know that German troops had been provided with blank ammunition only and ordered to withdraw if the Western powers resisted the German move. Thus France and Great Britain lost the last chance of calling Hitler's bluff before he completed his rearmament plans.

The Soviet attitude toward the crisis was diplomatically correct. An official Tass communique declared that "Help would be given to France in accordance with the 1935 Treaty and with the political situation as a whole." Since the USSR had neither a common frontier with Germany nor a right of passage over the intervening territories of Russia's western neighbors, the gesture was safe and purely platonic. The last thing Hitler had in mind at that time was to attack France.

Whatever his cynicism, Stalin must have taken a rather dim view of the passive attitude of the two Western powers. If the French would not stand up to the Germans in defense of their own back yard, how would they behave in case of an attack on the distant allies like Czechoslovakia, Poland, or Soviet Russia? His doubts as to the real value of his French alliance must have deepened considerably. On the other hand, he must have been impressed by Hitler, who again behaved like a true statesman and leader.

Immediately after the occupation of the Rhineland, Hitler ordered a chain of strong fortifications built all along the Franco-German frontier. This crash program, combined with further expansion of the German air force and armored divisions, all executed with great speed and efficiency, soon altered the balance of forces in Europe. In the future, the French army, even if it were willing to intervene on behalf of its Eastern European allies to fulfill its obligations toward the USSR, Czechoslovakia, or Poland, would be unable to do so effectively because access to the heart of Germany would be denied by the rapidly expanding *Wehrmacht*.

FAILURE OF A POPULAR FRONT IN FRANCE

Whatever Stalin's suspicions concerning the West, for the time being he persisted in keeping his Western option open and persevered in his policy of collective security combined with the popular front tactic of moderate politics pursued through broad coalitions of the Left and Center. As we mentioned in the previous chapter, the tactic was tried almost immediately in France and Spain. In May 1936, the French parliamentary elections resulted in an impressive victory for the coalition of Communists, Socialists, and Socialist Radicals. Five out of nine million voters cast their ballots for this popular front coalition. The number of votes cast for the CP of France, made respectable by its tricolor flag-waving, was impressive. For the first time in history, the Party garnered more than a million votes, while their Socialist partners made no progress. Nevertheless the French Communist leader, Maurice Thorez, on Moscow's order, kept a low profile and decided not to enter

the new cabinet headed by the moderate Socialist Leon Blum. The Communists were to support the new administration, however, on the condition that it would implement the original, rather moderate, popular front program, which included a forty-hour work week, collective bargaining, paid vacations for workers, and the like. Soon Socialist and Communist trade unions merged to form the General Confederation of Labor (*Confédération Général du Travail*, or *CGT* in French). The French popular front government assumed power on July 5, 1936, just two weeks before the outbreak of the Spanish Civil War, which was to usher in a more daring experiment in collaboration between the rivals for control of the working masses.

The honeymoon between the French Communists and Socialists did not last long; lingering suspicions and latent animosities, combined with the acute economic crisis that had crippled the French economy, soon upset it. One of the paradoxes that frustrated the coalition was the fact that the top Communist leaders, again instructed by the Comintern to make a show of moderation, were much less eager to foster strikes than their Socialist partners or the Communist rank-and-file workers. Maurice Thorez's attempts to overcompensate for his antimilitaristic stands in the past by now backing rearmament ran counter to the desire of the masses to force on the reluctant French capitalists the social advantages promised the workers by the popular front agreement. Consequently, while trying to help the government in its effort to catch up with the breakneck German remilitarization, the French Communist leaders ran into a conflict with their own supporters, who were bewildered by the sudden advocacy of what they had regarded as French jingoism. These contradictions resulted in a most confusing situation. The French rearmament program was bogged down in a flood of wildcat strikes. The mounting conservative backlash resulted in the downfall of the popular front government. After two years in power, it was replaced in 1938 by a more moderate coalition headed by the Radical Socialist politician Edouard Daladier.

CIVIL WAR IN SPAIN

While the French popular front coalition was taking its first steps, a civil war broke out in Spain in July 1936. The war represented the delayed aftermath of the 1931 downfall of the Spanish monarchy. From its inception, the Spanish Republic suffered from the antiliberal, antidemocratic heritage of the past, as well as from Spain's age-old socioeconomic backwardness. Taking advantage of the chaos, two vigorous autonomist movements in the north and in the east—in the Basque provinces and in Catalonia—immediately reasserted themselves against Madrid's past centralist polices. Because of the confusion resulting from the first two years of the republican regime, the parliamentary elections of November 1933 produced a rightist reaction. The new government proclaimed a law-and-order policy and often used the army to suppress a series of strikes, mutinies, and uprisings, the most significant of which were the revolt of the Asturian miners and an insurrection in Catalonia.

The iron-fist policies of the government and the spread of a native variety of protofascist groups, the most important of which was the Falange movement headed by José Antonio Primo de Rivera, created among the leftist elements fears for the fate of the Spanish Republic. In January 1936, they decided to confront the Fascist menace collectively and signed a popular front agreement. The main partners of the coalition were the Republican Left led by Manuel Azaña, the Spanish Socialists, the small but very active Communist Party of Spain, the Workers' Party of Marxist Unity (representing the anti-Stalinist and pro-Trotsky wing of the Communist movement), and the Catalan Left. The less organized but still numerous Anarchists, who were especially strong in Catalonia, did not join the coalition but lent their support to the popular front government, thus making its victory possible. In the February 1936 parliamentary elections, this heterogeneous coalition won a large parliamentary majority, but by a very narrow margin; the leftist victory was largely due to electoral geography.

The unexpected triumph of the popular front alarmed the conservative forces of the country, which was soon flooded by a wave of strikes, riots, and assassinations. The rightist opposition was especially strong among the officers stationed in Spanish Morocco. In July 1936, several colonial detachment, led by General Francisco Franco, revolted against the leftist government in Madrid. Military uprisings soon occurred throughout Spain. Consequently Spain was torn between the supporters of the government (or Loyalists) and the rebels (or Nationalists).

THE GREAT POWERS AND THE SPANISH CIVIL WAR

The bloody and protracted Civil War in Spain soon became an event of considerable international significance. Separated from France only by the Pyrenees, controlling most of the Iberian peninsula and thus a large segment of the western Mediterranean, Spain was also an important source of such vital strategic raw materials as copper, zinc, iron ore, and lead. Traditionally, what was happening south of the Pyrenees was of great significance to the French and also to their British allies; both countries had considerable investments in Spanish industry and agriculture, especially the vineyards. Germany and Italy, on the other hand, were eager, for strategic and ideological reasons, to see their fascist kinsmen, the Falangists, win the fight against Madrid's leftist government, which Berlin and Rome declared to be infected by Marxism and Communism. Italy in particular immediately lent direct military support to the rebels. The Spanish tinderbox threatened to turn into a European war. To prevent this, Paris and London tried to localize the conflict by forming the Nonintervention Committee, which was to isolate the war and keep the conflict strictly a Spanish domestic affair.

Moscow's attitude was quite different. There were powerful international factors that argued for quick and active Soviet intervention. Spain was the scene of the second experiment in popular front governments; therefore, it was difficult for the Kremlin, as well as for the leftist forces of the world, to allow such a government to be destroyed by the rightists, increasingly dominated by the fascist Falange and brazenly supported by Germany and Italy.

Here one should add that the CP of Spain, a small sect with about 1,000 active members in 1931, counted over 100,000 members by 1936, and mushroomed in the course of the war to reach 1,000,000 in June 1937.[1] Through the united front the Party exercised powerful influence on the larger but much more sluggish Socialist movement, especially on its youth organization, which soon merged with its Communist counterpart. To add to the bewildering complexity of the Spanish vortex, almost from the beginning one segment of the Spanish popular front, the "Trotskyite" Workers' Party of Marxist Unity (*POUM* in Spanish)[2] was in opposition to the Fabian tactics of delay and avoidance of too drastic revolutionary changes pressed by Moscow on Spain's pro-Stalin CP. Moreover, in Catalonia the POUM was numerically stronger and by far more dynamic than the orthodox Communist movement; often supported by the Anarchists, it successfully pursued its own line: it desired an unbridled revolutionary war. The official line of the CP of Spain—to win the war first and only

then restructure the country in a Communist spirit—was decried by the POUM as a Stalinist trick to sabotage the cause of the proletarian revolution.

If only to counteract Trotsky's accusation about "the betrayal of the Revolution" and to prevent Germany and Italy from scoring a rapid victory, Stalin had to act. On the other hand, to intervene too openly risked alienating France and Great Britain by raising the "Red Specter" in Western Europe. Since the Spanish Civil War could become the first practical test of collective security, Stalin could not afford to boycott the Nonintervention Committee so strongly supported by his main prospective partners. While reluctantly agreeing to participate in the Committee's work, Moscow tried to preserve its revolutionary integrity and minimize its participation in this bourgeois body through a series of militant pronouncements by the Comintern. For both ideological and strategic reasons Stalin was duty-bound to help the Republic, but power–political considerations dictated moderation. A Communist-influenced, let alone dominated, Spanish government would be likely to drive France and Great Britain into the Hitler-sponsored anti-Comintern coalition.

Another consideration that emerged after the first stages of the fighting was of a logistic nature: both Axis powers were obviously using the Spanish Civil War as a testing ground for their newly produced war equipment, especially tanks and planes. The Russians could hardly afford to miss such an opportunity to match their hardware against that of their potential opponents. As a result, Stalin's interest was in a protracted war. Italy's and Germany's military assistance to the rebels in violation of the principle of nonintervention was leading toward an early victory. (Madrid almost fell in November—December 1936.) This was what Stalin hoped to prevent, so as to keep the expansionist Axis powers looking westward and to persuade Britain and France of the need for collective security. After three months of hesitation, the Soviet

---

[1] Pierre Broué and Emile Temime, *The Revolution and the Civil War in Spain* (Cambridge, Mass.: MIT Press, 1970), p. 229.

[2] The POUM was led by former members of the Communist Party who had sided with Trotsky and Zinoviev in the late twenties. They had subsequently broken with Trotsky over political differences, but this did not prevent the Communists from conveniently labeling the POUM Trotskyite.

Union decided in October to lend military support to the Spanish Republic.

SOVIET INTERVENTION IN THE SPANISH CIVIL WAR

Soviet aid to the Loyalists was granted on four main conditions. First, Spain's pro-Moscow CP was to be given a greater role in the Madrid government. Second, Soviet experts were to have a strong say in the use of Soviet material without being compelled to participate in the actual fighting; they were instructed to "keep out of the range of artillery." Third, political commissars would be introduced to all units above the company level. Fourth, the deliveries were to be paid for in gold from the Spanish National Bank. All these conditions were complied with, and in September 1936 two Spanish Communists entered the popular front government headed by a Socialist, Francisco Largo Caballero. In Catalonia the local Communists merged with the Catalan Socialist Party and formed the United Catalan Socialist Party, which the Communists soon managed to dominate completely. Meanwhile, the USSR helped the Loyalists with arms, munitions, and other equipment under the supervision of a team of Soviet military advisers.

At the same time, via the Comintern, foreign Communists were encouraged to enlist in several *International Brigades.* With Soviet aid, these volunteers were trained, equipped, and transported to Spain, where they came to play a vital role in bolstering the Loyalist resistance. One of those brigades was composed of American volunteers and bore the name of Abraham Lincoln. The International Brigades attracted many prominent foreign Communists who were destined to play an important role during and after World War II; among them were Joseph Broz (Tito) of Yugoslavia, "Ercoli" (Palmiro Togliatti) of Italy, Laszlo Rajk of Hungary, and many others. They were soon backed by numerous radically minded non-Communists like Ernest Hemingway, George Orwell, and André Malraux, all eager to participate in, or at least support, a "crusade against Fascism."[3] Altogether the International Brigades numbered between thirty and forty thousand people. And indeed the brigades, together with direct Soviet aid, considerably bolstered the Republican forces; without them Madrid would most probably have been captured by the Nationalist troops of General Francisco Franco in November 1936.

As has been previously mentioned, the official Soviet policy of moderation and of sharing power with other nonsocialist members of the popular front alliance was opposed by the Spanish, but especially by the Catalan Trotskyists, Poumists, and Anarchists, who believed that the Civil War in Spain provided an excellent opportunity for an immediate seizure of power by the working class. The establishment of a Communist republic at the other extremity of the European continent would constitute an ideal launching pad for the further spread of a revolution whose favorable outcome seemed likely in the Western world as a result of the persistent Great Depression. This, however, was one more reason why Stalin was determined to be cautious in aiding the Republican forces. Their triumph, he was more and more afraid, might spell the strenghtening not of his brand of national Bolshevism but of the revolutionary, evangelical Communism preached by his archenemy, Trotsky. At the same time, it would destroy the incipient common front that he was trying to build with France and Britain based on the status quo.

Stalin realized that Spain had become a focal point for Trotskyist and anarcho-syndicalist sentiments throughout the world and that the Loyalist camp was crowded with rivals for control of the world revolutionary movement. While pursuing his other objectives he therefore took the opportunity to destroy his ideological enemies

---

[3] Each of the writers mentioned produced a major work based on his experience in Spain; respectively these were *For Whom the Bell Tolls, Homage to Catalonia,* and *L'Espoir (Hope).*

among the Communists. Together with Soviet tanks, planes, munitions, and Soviet advisers came a team of NKVD security officers. Their task was to hunt not so much the native pro-Franco elements (this was left largely to the Spanish republican militia), but to destroy the heterodox Communists and real and suspected Trotskyists. Thus the Spanish Civil War paralleled the Great Purge in Russia.

Soviet assistance, given belatedly and in limited quantity, could not counterbalance the massive systematic aid extended to the rebels by the Axis from the very beginning of the war to its end. Italy had sent to Spain several fully equipped army divisions under the guise of volunteers, while the Germans, in addition to the crack "Condor" air force squadron, dispatched a considerable amount of first-class, newly manufactured equipment, tanks, planes, and ammunition. Thus the Civil War in Spain, like the later wars in Korea and Vietnam, represented a trial conflict by proxy: the Great Powers not only tested their hardware, but used smaller countries as pawns in their intricate imperial game.

THE SPANISH CIVIL WAR ENDS

Supported more consistently by their sponsors, the rebels were gaining the upper hand step by step. The more precarious the situation of the Loyalists grew, the greater became their dependence on their only source of supply, the USSR, and the firmer the hold of Russia's instrument and mouthpiece, the local pro-Moscow Communist Party. By the spring of 1937 it had come to dominate most of the governmental apparatus and through the Political Commissars, the Loyalist armed forces. All this, however, was not sufficient to stem the rebel tide, which advanced slowly but relentlessly northeastward.

Meanwhile, in March 1938, having already subverted his native country through its local Nazi movement, Hitler occupied and annexed Austria. France and Britain meekly accepted it. As a result of the *Anschluss*, the Third Reich increased its population by about 8 million, gained considerable industrial resources and reserves of timber, oil, iron ore, and water power, and came to dominate the middle Danube. With the annexation of Austria the frontiers of the Reich moved considerably to the east toward the USSR, whose ally Czechoslovakia became surrounded from the south and increasingly menaced by Hitler's expansionist drive. By that time the Spanish Loyalists' defeat was in sight.

As the Czech crisis was mounting in July and August 1938, tension in Asia escalated as the Japanese intervened more and more openly in the affairs of China, established themselves in Manchuria, and thereby threatened southern Siberia as well as Vladivostok. There were several serious incidents on the Soviet-Manchurian borders which necessitated further reinforcing the Red Army in the Far East, thus making more tangible the connection between Soviet Asian and European defenses. Bitter hostilities between the USSR and Japan required more extensive deployment of Soviet forces in the Far East. While Hitler was exploiting the momentary Soviet weakness as well as the passivity of the West, the Japanese were the first to probe Soviet defenses in Mongolia and Siberia. In view of this, the limited Soviet resources were urgently needed in Asia as well as in Central Europe. In November 1938, soon after the partition of Czechoslovakia at the conference of Munich, the International Brigades were recalled from Spain and direct Soviet aid stopped. This was the kiss of death to the tottering Republican regime. In February 1939, the forces of General Franco captured Barcelona, the capital of Catalonia, and in March, after a prolonged siege, Madrid fell into his hands.

CONSEQUENCES OF THE SPANISH CIVIL WAR

In the spring of 1939 the Spanish Civil War was over. It lasted nearly three years, caused untold suffering, and left over one million dead, while compelling at least that many supporters of the Loyalist cause to seek shelter abroad. Some of them went to the USSR and some settled in Western Europe, mainly in France. Soviet assistance to the Loyalists was just enough to keep the Republicans fighting, but not sufficient to let them win the war. The Italian, but especially the German, planes, tanks, and artillery proved superior to the Soviet models. Soviet experts and advisers did help but on Moscow's orders, they were generally more eager to fight their ideological rivals (mainly the Trotskyists) than to cope with strictly military matters.

This setback in Spain was a painful blow to Soviet prestige, but it had its silver lining. Stalin had also the opportunity to test his hardware, for which he was handsomely paid with $500 million in Spanish gold which on his insistence was shipped to Moscow; he also had an opportunity to test the willingness of his Western allies to cooperate against common enemies on his conditions. While apparently manifesting his revolutionary zeal, he had destroyed a large number of his Trotskyite rivals. The main Soviet representative in Spain, a former supporter of Trotsky, Vladimir Antonov-Ovseyenko, was arrested and liquidated soon after the end of this mission, as were most of the Soviet advisers who served in Spain, including some who had advocated a radical modernization and reorganization of Soviet mechanized troops to integrate them into powerful armored divisions.

Soviet intervention in the Spanish Civil War represented Stalin's last effort to exploit the antifascist cause in Western Europe for his purposes. The effort failed only partly because of France and Britain's hesitation and passivity; it foundered also because Moscow's objectives in Spain were unlike those of the Western Powers and had as much to do with domestic politics as with Russia's international objectives. Moscow's experience in the Nonintervention Committee had made it increasingly suspicious of the Western powers, and was a major factor in the diplomatic about-face that was soon to

follow. As a result of his attempted cooperation with France and Britain, Stalin came to be convinced of the bankruptcy of collective security; he even came to believe that certain groups among the British Conservatives hoped the Soviet Union and the Axis powers might clash sooner or later, leaving the Western democracies free.

On the other hand, the persistence of revolutionary phraseology and terrorist practices applied by Soviet security organs in Spain made many European statesmen doubt the sincerity of Stalin's policy, despite Litvinov's diplomatic skills and eloquence. What damaged the Soviet image still further were the massive domestic purges, deportations, and show trials that paralleled most of the Spanish Civil War. The purge of the Red Army leaders dealt a particularly powerful blow to confidence in the USSR as a stable and reliable partner in any coalition. Most Western military experts reached the conclusion that the Soviet armed forces would be unable, for the time being, to fulfill their numerous obligations in both Eastern Europe and the Far East and that one cannot count on them as serious, reliable allies.

THE ANTI-COMINTERN PACT AND THE CZECHOSLOVAK CRISIS

While the Spanish Civil War was going on, the international position of the USSR deteriorated further. On October 25, 1936, Italy and Germany signed an agreement that provided for close cooperation in foreign affairs, especially as far as the "Communist menace" was concerned. In November of that year, Japan, by now master of Manchuria, signed a five-year pact with Germany. The document declared Communism to be their greatest common danger and bound its signatories to unite their forces to fight "Communist subversive activities." In November 1937, on the first anniversary of the German-Japanese pact, Italy joined what became known as the Berlin—Tokyo Axis or the Anti-Comintern Pact. Japan recognized the Italian conquest of Ethiopia, while Rome recognized the state of Manchukuo (Manchuria). Thus came into being the triangular alliance among the three authoritarian and aggressive powers, each of them opposed to Soviet Russia.

At that time, Stalin must have been wondering what would the Japanese do after their conquest of China? Would they turn toward the Soviet protectorate of Outer Mongolia and to Soviet southern Siberia, both of them former segments of the Middle Kingdom? This need for military vigilance in the Far East, for maintaining a powerful, well-equipped, and well-supplied army there that was involved in not only intermittent skirmishes but occasional pitched battles with the Japanese, affected Stalin's posture in Europe.

The bloodless occupation of Austria seemed to be fulfilling Hitler's last major avowed territorial demands. The remaining ones appeared less important: the Czechoslovak Sudetenland, Danzig and the Polish Pomerania (often called by German propaganda the Polish Corridor), and the Lithuanian harbor-city of Memel (Klajpeda). Whichever way Hitler advanced would bring him uncomfortably close to the Soviet borders.

By May 1938, it became quite clear that Czechoslovakia would be Hitler's next target. After Austria's annexation extended the frontiers of the Greater German Reich 400 miles to the east, Czechoslovakia's strategic situation became critical. The republic built by Thomas G. Masaryk and his successor Edward Beneš, like the prewar Hapsburg Empire, contained numerous national minorities, including over 3 million Germans. They lived in compact areas and were concentrated mostly along its western frontiers, adjacent to Hitler's Reich. After a vitriolic preparatory subversive campaign which lasted throughout the spring and summer of 1938, Hitler vigorously pressed his demand that the Sudeten Germans be given the right of self-determination. Should their right to secede be denied, he threatened war. This was the gist of the militant speech he delivered at the Nazi congress in Nuremberg on September 12, 1938. To dramatize his demands, Hitler openly began to make war preparations.

THE MUNICH APPEASEMENT

The rest of the month was marked by acute international tension. Prague, while offering concessions that bordered on granting complete autonomy to its German citizens, ordered the mobilization of its armed forces. France followed suit, promising to fulfill the alliance treaty of 1924. Great Britain ordered the partial mobilization of its navy. Europe was brought to the brink of war.

As we discussed earlier, Czechoslovakia was bound by an alliance not only to France but also to the USSR. The Soviet alliance hinged, however, on the prior fulfillment by the French of their obligations. After having publicly renewed their pledges to defend the Czechs in case of a German attack, in May 1938 the French, along with the British, privately began to press Prague to surrender to the ever-growing German demands. Consequently, from a strictly legal point of view, the Russians were freed from their obligations toward the Czechs. Nevertheless, Litvinov kept on repeating that the USSR was ready to discharge all its duties toward Czechoslovakia "in accordance with the treaty of May 16, 1935," and with the League of Nations Covenant. Despite French refusal to aid them, the Czechs could have invoked Soviet aid, but they never did, either out of fear of provoking Hitler, or perhaps out of doubt that it would be effective. Would the Soviet armed forces, decimated by the purges, be able to protect Czechoslovakia against the Germans? How would the Red Army reach Czechoslovak territory? Polish territory lay between the two countries, and the Poles, who were making their own demands on Czechoslovakia, refused to let the Russians cross. Even the Romanians, Prague's partners in the Little Entente, were reluctant to let the Red

Army pass. As King Carol II declared to the German ambassador in Bucharest, "I would prefer to see the Germans in Romania as enemies, than the Russians as allies." Nevertheless, Moscow emerged from the Munich crisis with the image of being the only power willing to stand up to Hitler and defend Czech liberty.

After being strongly urged by President Franklin Delano Roosevelt, Mussolini, and British Prime Minister Neville Chamberlain, Hitler finally agreed to attend an international conference to settle the Czech issue peacefully. The conference, which took place at Munich, was attended by the representatives of only four powers: Germany (Hitler), Italy (Mussolini), Great Britain (Neville Chamberlain), and France (Daladier); the USSR and Czechoslovakia itself were excluded.

At Munich, under the concerted pressure of all the Big Four powers, including its formal ally France, Prague was forced "in the interest of peace" to cede immediately to Germany the Sudeten borderlands whose inhabitants were more than 50 percent German; this area included most of the country's frontier fortifications and most of its industry. All four powers agreed to guarantee the integrity and sovereignty of the remaining rump Czechoslovakia, which was neither economically viable nor militarily defensible. The Sudeten resources, especially its armament industries, strengthened Hitler's arsenal and prestige dramatically. This led to a political landslide in Eastern and Central Europe that resulted in establishing the Greater German Reich as the predominant military force, not only in that area but on the European continent as a whole.[4] Hitler's next prospective victim, Poland, was now outflanked from the south. Belying his repeated solemn promises not to seek new territorial gains, a few days after Munich Hitler asked Warsaw for Danzig and the establishment of an extraterritorial highway to connect Berlin with the East Prussian enclave. The Poles flatly refused. Then Hitler immediately began preparations for war against them.

MOSCOW AND THE MUNICH PACT

The four-power Munich conference was a public, provocative humiliation of Moscow which spelled its exclusion from the European concert and thus its diplomatic isolation. Neither were the Russians consulted by their allies, the French, in vital matters pertaining to their mutual ally, Czechoslovakia. The sacrifice of Czechoslovakia to Hitler's appetites and the conciliatory attitude of the Western powers toward him gave rise to further Soviet suspicions that France and Britain plotted to channel the German expansionist drive eastward toward the Soviet borders. In view of this, Stalin had to reappraise once more his participation in what

Vyacheslav M. Molotov, Soviet Foreign Minister, 1939–1946 and 1953–1957

---

[4] For a description and perceptive analysis of the Munich Conference, see John Wheller-Bennett, *Munich—Prologue to Tragedy* (New York: Duell, Sloan and Pearce, 1963).

had originally been intended as a system of collective security. Faced by growing Nazi pressure on the lands immediately adjacent to his domains like the Baltic states, Poland, and Romania, he had to consider two options. He could either bolster the zone separating him from Nazi Germany in alliance with France and Britain, or he could make a deal with the potential agressor. Unable to make a reasonable choice, he kept both irons in the fire.

The autumn of 1938 marked the peak of France and Britain's appeasement policy, which was based on the delusion that peace could be bought with concessions. One of the premises of the Munich settlement had been that, once having united all ethnic Germans, Hitler would be satiated and hence would no longer seek new conquests. He finally destroyed this delusion in March 1939. On March 15, German troops occupied Prague and the western remnants of Bohemia and Moravia, which Hitler declared a German protectorate. Meanwhile, encouraged by Berlin, Slovakia established itself as a separate state, also under German tutelage. Thus Hitler was caught in a flagrant breach of promise; he disregarded the declarations he had made when he said that he merely wanted to unite the German people. The second Czechoslovak crisis was still more ominous from the Soviet point of view. Paris and London, surprised and unprepared to act in fulfillment of their Munich guarantees, again merely issued diplomatic protests.

Their policy of appeasement in ruins, Paris and London finally decided to switch to a policy of containing Hitler. While they were busy consulting with each other and with Poland, the next prospective victim of Hitler's aggression, Lithuania, was compelled to cede to Germany the port of Memel (Klaipeda) on March 27. This brought the Third Reich a few miles closer to Soviet territory.

Moscow's apparent aloofness in the spring of 1939 could only camouflage its profound mistrust not only of Hitler's intentions but also of the Western powers' impo-

tence. The establishment of the German protectorates of Bohemia and Moravia and the separation of Slovakia, which now became a German military base, all moved German influence beyond the middle Danube. Hungary had already been penetrated by the Nazis, while the Balkan countries, from Romania to Greece, had been under increasing economic and political pressure from Berlin since Austria's annexation in March 1938. The German pincers were crawling inexorably eastward toward the Soviet frontiers, both along the Danube and the Baltic. The snowballing German might and the whetting of the Nazi appetite for conquest made the German threat a clear and present danger not only to the Soviet Union's interests, but to its very existence. Should the Soviet Union's largest western neighbor, Poland be conquered, the situation of the USSR, in the middle of its great socioeconomic experiment and still recovering from the collectivization and the Great Purge, would become critical overnight. This necessitated an urgent reappraisal of the Soviet Foreign policy. Should Moscow establish closer military ties with Paris and London and bolster Warsaw's determination to oppose Hitler's expansionist drive? Or should the Soviets seek other ways to protect their security?

MOLOTOV REPLACES LITVINOV

While Hitler was preparing his final annexation of Bohemia and Moravia, the Eighteenth Party Congress (the first in more than five years) was gathering in Moscow on March 10, 1939. A posture of watchful waiting and diplomatic flexibility permeated the speeches of its main orators, who were as much anti-German as anti-Western. In his general report Stalin restated his pet thesis that Britain and France, by sacrificing Czechoslovakia, wanted to divert Hitler's attention from the West and encourage his eastward expansion toward the USSR. Although warning that the Soviets were ready to defend themselves, Stalin offered the

Germans the benefits of expanded trade. He admonished France and Britain that the Soviet Union would not "pull the chestnuts out of the fire for them," and that it stood "for peace and the strengthening of business relations with all countries." The accent was on *all*.

While the Eighteenth Congress was still in session, Hitler occupied Prague on March 15 and forced the Lithuanians to cede Memel a few days later. At the end of March, the British replied by extending guarantees of Poland's sovereignty and integrity in case they should be threatened. Soon London and Paris made a similar pledge to Romania. France associated itself with these guarantees. Poland and Romania now became a sort of buffer: any German attack on the USSR would involve a violation of these guarantees and hence a war with Britain and France.

Hitler obviously had expected a Polish Munich and was looking for another pushover. Furious at Poland's refusal to surrender, on April 28 he denounced the German-Polish nonaggression pact of 1934, claiming that it had been violated by Warsaw's acceptance of London's "provocative" guarantees. In this speech there were none of his customary unfavorable remarks about the Soviet Union. Stalin understood the hint.

An impending shift of the Kremlin's policy was foreshadowed by a change of its pilot. On May 2, Litvinov, whom the Germans had ostracized as a Jew, was replaced as Commissar for Foreign Affairs by an ethnic Russian and Stalin's close co-worker, Molotov. For the first time since Trotsky's resignation from that post on the eve of the Brest-Litovsk treaty, Soviet foreign policy was in the hands of a full member of the Politburo as well as Prime Minister of the Soviet Government. The change of the Soviet Foreign Commissar had a beneficial effect on the intermittent secret talks that Soviet diplomats had been conducting with their German counterparts since the eve of Munich in order to tone down the polemics between the media of the two countries.[5]

While pursuing these negotiations, the Kremlin tried to prove the exact extent of the unprecedented British commitment to Eastern Europe. Did the British really intend to go to war in defense of Poland and Romania? The apparently serious nature of this inquiry seems to indicate that the British involvement was a welcome novelty. On April 18, Litvinov had suggested to the British ambassador in Moscow that France should join in these pledges. The three powers, he urged, should guarantee militarily all the "East European states situated between the Baltic and Black seas and bordering on the USSR." The three powers were to hold staff talks as to the details of such help and pledge not to conclude a separate peace in case of war. To negotiate the details of the proposed cooperation, British and French military missions were dispatched to Moscow in May.

During the talks the Russians objected to the low caliber of the Western representatives. Neither side seemed to be in a hurry to conclude the talks. Two serious barriers seemed to impede them at every step: the right of passage of Soviet troops through Poland and Romania, and the Baltic question. All three Baltic republics—Lithuania, Latvia, and Estonia—unequivocally refused to accept the extensive Soviet guarantees to be forced upon them even in the case of threat of aggression. They interpreted it as blanket Western consent for the Russians to do as they wished in the eastern Baltic area. The Western powers were hesitant as to whether they could impose such a drastic solution on sovereign pro-Western states. On the other hand, when the French and British delegates promised to press Poland, Romania, and the Baltic states to be more flexible, the Russians immediately put forward another issue, that of establishing

---

[5] For a background of the German-Soviet rapprochment, see Gerhard L. Weinberg, *Germany and the Soviet Union, 1939–1941* (Leiden: E. J. Brill, 1954).

their foothold on Finnish soil. Consequently, the frustrating negotiations dragged on throughout the hot and tense summer of 1939 until the end of August. Meanwhile the secret German-Soviet talks that had been going on in Berlin under the guise of trade negotiations soon revealed that Hitler was indeed willing to share Poland and the Baltic states with Stalin and would even add the Rumanian province of Bessarabia for good measure.

THE STALIN–HITLER PACT

Stalin, with both sides competing for his favors and with plenty of time to choose the highest bidder, was in a more advantageous position than the Germans, and hence in no hurry. Hitler, on the other hand, eager to pounce on Poland before the autumn rains would make his tanks useless, was getting restless. On August 2, German Foreign Minister von Ribbentrop held out as bait a new partitioning of Poland and the offer of German intervention in Tokyo in regard to the Soviet-Japanese clashes then going on along the Manchurian and Mongolian borders. The Russians, however, were still hesitant; the legacy of years of mutual recriminations and suspicions was hard to overcome, and the Russians suspected a trap. Since Stalin did not react to his previous overtures, on August 3 Hitler ordered the German ambassador in Moscow, Count von Schulenburg, to assure Molotov that Berlin was also resolved to respect fully the vital Soviet interests in the Baltic region. Stalin was still reluctant to commit himself in view of the obvious risks involved in a decision that would amount to giving a green light to a German attack on Poland and thus demolish the territorial buffer zone separating Germany from the USSR. Now Hitler became angry. On August 20, he insisted that von Ribbentrop be invited to Moscow within twenty-four hours; otherwise the whole planned deal of sharing Eastern Europe would be off.

This was a virtual ultimatum and Stalin gave in.

On August 23, von Ribbentrop flew to Moscow for a brief but momentous visit. The same day at the Kremlin, in an atmosphere of cordiality, he and Molotov, with Stalin supervising, signed three documents: a trade agreement; an open declaration of nonaggression, friendship, and cooperation; and a secret protocol. This protocol, the most important of the three documents, divided Eastern Europe into two spheres of influence: Estonia, Latvia, Poland east of the Vistula, and Bessarabia were originally to be left to the Soviet Union; Lithuania and Poland west of the Vistula were to remain within the German sphere. Each side was given a free hand in its respective sphere. The nonaggression pact provided that both parties would refrain from attacking one another in case one of the signatories should be attacked by a third party. Both promised to refrain from any activity aimed directly or indirectly at the other party.

The signing of this triple agreement, which was to enter into force immediately, was followed by a banquet at the Kremlin. Both sides were elated. Ribbentrop slapped Molotov on the back and said he felt as if he

Stalin at the Kremlin raises his glass of champagne to Hitler

were among "old revolutionary comrades" now struggling together against a common enemy, the "Western capitalists." Von Ribbentrop was in an especially exuberant mood and told Stalin a German joke: soon the Soviet Union would join the Anti-Comintern Pact. Stalin refused to laugh, but gave his "word of honor" that the Soviet Union would not betray Germany. He raised his glass of champagne and drank a toast to Hitler: "I know how much the German people love their Führer."

THE OUTBREAK OF WORLD WAR II

The Stalin–Hitler Pact hit the world like a dynamite blast. The Soviet diplomatic about-face had been suspected by only a few Western observers whose warnings had met with the skepticism of all those who had reasoned in purely ideological terms that the Communist-Nazi hostility was unbridgeable. Hardly had the outside world had time to analyze the full implications of the pact when, on September 1 at 4:00 A.M., German troops attacked Poland. On September 3, Britain and France declared war on Germany without, however, undertaking any major military operations. World War II was on.[6]

The German troops made rapid progress and soon occupied large stretches of land originally assigned by the secret protocol to the Soviet partner. Despite repeated urgings, Stalin refused to openly enter the fray. All the time he was anxiously watching the situation in western Europe and in the Far East. During the first stages of the Polish campaign, in fact, the Red Army was still engaged in a series of savage encounters along the Manchurian border. Finally, in

August its commander, General Georgi K. Zhukov, launched a crushing blow against the Japanese that knocked the shattered Japanese Sixth Army back into Manchuria. The military and psychological effect of the Soviet victory on the Japanese was so severe that the Tokyo General Staff had to rethink its original plan of expanding on the Asian mainland, mainly at the expense of Soviet Southern Siberia. This gave the upper hand to the Japanese Navy eager to spread the "Asian Co-prosperity Sphere" in Southeast Asia instead.

September 15, the same day that the Soviet-Japanese armistice in the Far East was signed, the Red Army was ordered to march into Eastern Poland. On September 17, six Soviet armies crossed the Riga frontier to "liberate Russia's Ukrainian and Belorussian brethren." The Soviet invasion met with hesitant resistance since the Polish forces, fighting without the promised assistance of their Western allies, had been badly mauled by the Germans. By the beginning of October, the Red Army took some 200,000 POWs, of whom 15,000 were officers. The fate of these officers would constitute a grave problem with weighty political consequences for Soviet-Polish relations.

By the end of September, German troops had occupied large stretches of Central Poland originally allotted to the USSR and refused to withdraw. This necessitated a revision of the deal of August 23. By a supplementary agreement of September 28, the Germans gave up Lithuania in exchange for the lands west of the rivers Narev, Bug, and San. This redistribution still left the Soviets 48 percent of Poland's territory, with nearly 13 million inhabitants.

Throughout this period the Soviet media followed a rigidly pro-German line. The Soviet anti-Western campaign was supported by the whole apparatus of the Comintern. On September 29, a joint Soviet-German declaration held London and Paris responsible for the continuation of the "imperialistic" war. When the last traces of Polish resistance collapsed at the beginning

---

[6] For full documentation, see R. J. Sontag and J. S. Beddie (eds.), *Nazi-Soviet Relations, 1939–1941.* For an analysis of Stalin's motivations, *see Adam Ulam, Expansion and Coexistence* . . . , pp. 275–279. For the Soviet view, see Jane Degras (ed.), *Soviet Documents on Foreign Policy,* Vol. III (New York: Oxford University Press, 1963), pp. 315–381.

of October, Stalin sent Hitler personal congratulations which ended with the words, "Our alliance has been sealed in blood."

THE WINTER WAR WITH FINLAND

In October 1939, while the Russians were establishing military bases in Lithuania, Latvia, and Estonia, and stern political controls in Eastern Poland, negotiations were opened with Finland. Unlike the three small republics which had submitted to the Soviet ultimatums without firing a shot, the stronger and strategically better-situated Finns squarely opposed most of the Soviet demands that focused around the Karelian isthmus, including the Finnish fortifications (the "Mannerheim line"), Western Karelia, Petsamo (the ice-free Finnish port on the Arctic Sea), the several islands controlling the approaches to Leningrad, and leasing of the Hangoe peninsula. The Soviet argument was that the Mannerheim line was only twenty miles north of the outskirts of Leningrad and Kronstadt, while the strategically vital railroad connecting Leningrad with the Soviet ice-free port of Murmansk had to be protected by a wider belt of Karelian territory. The Finns offered considerable territorial readjustment in favor of the Soviet Union, including four islands, and moving their frontier thirteen miles further north of Leningrad; but they refused cession, demilitarization of their system of fortifications protecting their southern approaches, and disarming their armed forces. Neither would they permit the establishment of Soviet military bases on their territory. The long-drawn-out negotiations broke down on November 13. On November 28, after a provoked border incident in which a Soviet frontier guard was killed under mysterious circumstances, some thirty Soviet divisions attacked the Finns in eight places simultaneously. At the same time, in the border village of Terijoki, the "Karelo-Finnish Soviet Socialist Republic" was established, headed by Otto Kuusinen, a veteran Finnish Communist, and acceded to Soviet demands.

The war between the Finnish David and the Soviet Goliath raged in snows five to six feet deep, with temperatures often dropping to thirty and forty degrees below zero. The Finns defended themselves with skill and tenacity. At the same time the Helsinki Government appealed to the League of Nations which, on December 14, declared the USSR the aggressor and expelled it from the League. The sympathy of the whole civilized world was overwhelmingly on the Finnish side. In the course of murderous fighting that lasted through January 1940, the Red Army managed to advance between fifteen and forty miles, depending on the sector. Only on February 21, after ten days of storming by twenty-seven Soviet divisions and after having suffered some 200,000 casualties, did the Russians break the Finnish resistance. The peace treaty was concluded in Moscow in March 1940; the treaty compelled Finland to cede the Karelian isthmus, including the town of Viborg, a naval base at Hangoe, the region north of Lake Ladoga, a peninsula in the north of Murmansk, and a group of several islands controlling the Gulf of Finland, altogether over 16,000 square miles, and containing a population of 450,000. Nursing their wounds, the Finns contemplated reconquest of their lost lands, alongside Germany if need be.

The "Winter War" considerably strengthened the Soviet strategic position in the Eastern Baltic and made Leningrad more defensible. But the price, moral and material, was very steep. The USSR eventually committed to the Finnish campaign about 1 million men, 3,000 planes, and almost as many tanks. Yet this huge mass was for three months bogged down by a tiny Finnish force. The bitter experience of the Finnish campaign dramatized to the Soviet leadership the necessity of military reforms.

The "Winter War" compelled the Red Army to modernize. First, unified command was reintroduced and political commissars were subordinated to field commanders;

The Soviet-Finnish Treaty of Moscow, March 1940

ATLANTIC OCEAN

ARCTIC OCEAN

Rybachi Peninsula

NORWAY

Petsamo

Nautsi

Narvik

Ivalo

Kiruna

I O

Kandalaksha

Gaellivare

Arctic Highway

SOVIET UNION

Rovaniemi

WHITE SEA

SWEDEN

Torneo

Lulea

Oulu

Suomussalmi

Kajaani

FINLAND

Nurmes

GULF OF BOTHNIA

Tampere

Pori

Aaland Is.

Aabo

Viborg

LAKE LAGODA

HELSINKI

GULF OF FINLAND

Hangoe

LENINGRAD

Tallinn

BALTIC SEA

ESTONIA

| 0 | 50 | 100 | 150 |

MILES

KEY:

	Soviet Union
	Territories Ceded to the Soviet Union
	Swedish & Norwegian Territories
I O	Swedish Iron Ore Mines of Kiruna & Galivare
⚓	Soviet Navel Base at Hangoe
┿┿┿	Narvik-Lulea Railroad
▭▭	Mannerheim Line

field officers were made solely and unquestionably responsible for all military decisions. Second, cooperation among different branches and the services of the armed forces were improved. Third, training of troops under various conditions was perfected, and field regulations were revised to make them correspond to the demands of modern warfare. The most important improvement was a vigorous effort at resupplying the Red Army and Air Force with modernized weapons, often through crash programs. While adopting some of the Finnish innovations, like the "Molotov cocktails" and the wooden boxes to hide land mines, Red Army researchers promptly developed an array of new weapons, including massed rockets.[7] Another improvement was application of newly developed lubricants that allowed their weapons, tanks, artillery, and aircraft to function in frigid temperatures. In Marshal Zhukov's words, 1940 was for the Red Army the year of "the great transformation."

The Soviet strategic and economic gains in the Baltic region were counterbalanced, however, by political and moral liabilities. The spectacle of Soviet incompetence greatly encouraged Hitler to plan his future attack on Russia. In his opinion, it would be a walk-over.

THE STALIN–HITLER PACT: AN APPRAISAL

Many factors contributed to Stalin's deal with Hitler. One of them was the menacing situation in the Far East and the fear of being involved in a two-front war. Another was Stalin's growing disillusionment with the prospects for making the French and British cooperate with him against Germany. The tardiness with which the British, and especially the French, entered the war, their lack of effective help to Poland, all reinforced Stalin's conviction that the West was weak and lacked the will to fight.

From the Soviet point of view, the pact with Hitler must have appeared to be the least dangerous alternative. Stalin's tactic was to keep his country out of the war as long as possible, even at the price of destroying the belt of buffer states, Poland and the Baltic Republics, which hitherto separated the USSR from the aggressive Third Reich. While the two brands of almost equally contemptible capitalists were to massacre each other, the Russians were to remain on the sidelines as vigilant observers, ready to enter the fray at the last, decisive stage, calculated the Soviet dictator. The Stalin–Hitler deal was not the determining cause of the war, yet it considerably enhanced Germany's ability to wage the war. By securing Germany's eastern flank, Stalin removed the last obstacle to Hitler's attack on Poland, which started World War II.

Was Stalin's decision a rejection of the ideological premises of Communism and a definite shift to the traditional Russian nationalist position? There were certainly some such elements in his policy visible in 1939. The loss of the broad belt of territory in the west to Russia's western neighbors after 1917 was painfully felt by all Great Russian nationalists, with whom Stalin gradually came to identify himself. These losses, a humiliating reminder of Russia's defeat in World War I and its aftermath, also made the Soviet strategic situation precarious. In 1939, three of the USSR's major ports were virtually frontier cities: Leningrad was only twelve miles from the Finnish border, Odessa was about twenty miles from the Romanian boundary, and Murmansk was separated by fifty miles of tundra from Finland.

To the strategic and political factors must

---

[7] For the Soviet evaluation of the Soviet-Finnish War and its outcome, see Nikita Krushchev, *Krushchev Remembers* (Boston: Little, Brown & Co., 1970), 152 ff. The Finns, who had only a few antitank guns, perfected the weapon improvised in Spain in 1936–1939, gasoline, alcohol, and tar-filled bottles wrapped in rags. Thrown at air intakes or open hatches of enemy tanks, such bottles would instantly set them ablaze. These successful "Molotov Cocktails," as they were called, were to be also produced by the Red Army in 1941–1942.

be added economic considerations. Stalin believed that the acquisition of better warm water ports—Tallin, Riga, or Liepaja— would improve Soviet access to the world's sea routes, as well as allow him to eventually control the Baltic sea, so vital also for Soviet security. He remembered that a hostile power could reach Archangel, located in the desolate and sparsely populated Sub-Arctic region, several months a year via the open sea. These political, strategic, and economic motifs were closely intertwined with another of Stalin's paramount considerations, the achievement by his Russia of a leading position among world powers. Here, as in domestic matters, Stalin was also in a way a continuator of Peter the Great.

All these geopolitical considerations, however, do not necessarily prove that nationalism was Stalin's main motivating force, and that he definitely rejected the ideological premises of Communism. His appetite for old Tsarist lands and international prestige, it can be argued, did not affect his basically Marxist analysis of the world situation. For Stalin a war between the two brands of capitalist and hence necessarily imperialist powers would speed up the ongoing disintegration of the Western world and thus enhance the chances for further Soviet gains. That is why Soviet Russia, Stalin believed, should not be reluctant to fan the conflagration and intervene only at the last stage in order to impose Soviet peace on the exhausted foes.

SUGGESTED READING

BROUÉ, P., and E. TEMINE, *The Revolution and the Civil War In Spain.* Cambridge, Mass.: MIT Press, 1970.

CATTELL, DAVID T., *Communism and the Spanish Civil War.* Berkeley: University of California Press, 1955.

———, *Soviet Diplomacy and the Spanish Civil War.* Berkeley: University of California Press, 1957.

CZAPSKI, JOZEF, *The Inhuman Land.* New York: Sheed and Ward, 1952.

EHRENBURG, ILYA, *Eve of War, 1933–1941.* London: MacGibbon and Kee 1963.

ERICKSON, JOHN, *The Soviet High Command.* New York: St. Martin's, 1962.

FEDOTOFF-WHITE, DIMITRI, *The Growth of the Red Army.* Princeton, N.J.: Princeton University Press, 1944.

GARLIŃSKI, JÓZEF. *The Enigma War.* New York: Charles Scribner's Sons, 1979.

HERLING, GUSTAV, *A World Apart.* London: Heinemann, 1957.

HILGER, GUSTAV, and ALFRED G. MEYER, *The Incompatible Allies.* New York: Macmillan, 1953.

JAKOBSON, MAX, *The Diplomacy of the Winter War: An Account of the Russo-Finnish War, 1939–1940.* Cambridge, Mass.: Harvard University Press, 1961.

KAHN, DAVID, *The Codebreakers.* New York: Macmillan, 1967.

———, *Hitler's Spies.* London: Hodder and Stoughton, 1978.

KENNAN, GEORGE F., *Russia and the West under Lenin and Stalin.* Boston: Little, Brown, 1961.

LACQUER, WALTER, *Russia and Germany.* Boston: Little, Brown, 1965.

NAMIER, LOUIS, *The Diplomatic Prelude.* New York: Macmillan, 1948.

ORWELL, GEORGE, *Homage to Catalonia.* New York: Harcourt Brace Jovanovich, 1952.

PAANEN, LAURI, *The Winter War, The Russo-Finnish Conflict, 1939–1940.* New York: Scribner's, 1973.

SONTAG, RAYMOND J. and JAMES S. BEDDIC, eds., *Nazi-Soviet Relations, 1938–1941: Documents from the Archives of the German Foreign Office,* Washington, D.C.: Department of State, 1948.

TANNER, VAINO, *The Winter War, Finland against Russia, 1939–1940.* Stanford, Calif.: Stanford University Press, 1950.

TARULIS, ALBERT, *Soviet Policy toward the Baltic States, 1918–1940.* Notre Dame, Ind.: University of Notre Dame Press, 1959.

ULAM, ADAM, *Expansion and Coexistence: The History of Soviet Foreign Policy, 1917–1967.* New York: Praeger, 1968. Chapters 5 and 6 in particular.

WEINBERG, GERHARD, *Germany and the Soviet Union, 1939–1941*. Leiden: Brill, 1954.

ZAWODNY, J. K., *Death in the Forest: The Story of the Katyn Forest Massacre*. Notre Dame, Ind.: University of Notre Dame Press, 1962.

ZHUKOV, GEORGI K. *Marshal Zhukov's Greatest Battles*. New York: Harper & Row, 1969.

———. *The Memoirs of Marshal Zhukov*. New York: Delacorte Press, 1971.

CHAPTER 18

"The Great Patriotic War"

The bolstering of the Russian position in the Baltic that resulted from the Winter War and the establishment of Soviet bases in the three Baltic States was no source of comfort to Hitler. Nevertheless, he had to accept it as the price of Stalin's benevolent neutrality, since Hitler was too busy putting out peace feelers while preparing his Western drive. Germany, now under the Allied blockade, badly required supplies of Soviet raw materials such as oil and iron ore. Meanwhile, the Reich profited from the help of Soviet intelligence, as well as from the cessation of Communist subversion, which Stalin imposed on the Moscow-controlled parties of the German-occupied territories throughout the period of the Soviet-Nazi entente. Communist propaganda blamed the Anglo-French alliance for the continuance of "the senseless, imperialistic war," which was "nothing else but a crusade of the Western capitalists" against Germany. Moreover, the Hitler–Stalin Pact of 1939 had permitted the Germans to withdraw most of their troops from the East in order to use them successively against Denmark, Norway, Holland, Belgium, France, and Britain.

The news of the German offensive in Denmark, Norway, Holland, Belgium, and France in the spring of 1940 was received at the Kremlin with relief. It was considered the beginning of a long and exhausting war that would be conducted far away from Soviet frontiers. While the capitalists were tearing each other to shreds, the Red Army would watch them and wait for the moment to enter the contest at its decisive stage to share in the loot. The softness of the Western resistance and the speedy collapse of France in June shocked Stalin profoundly. Britain's decision to continue the war alone was regarded by him with reluctant admiration. Altogether the sudden shift in the European balance of power could augur no good for Russia.

INCOMPATIBLE ALLIES

Meanwhile, taking advantage of Hitler's temporary involvement in the West, Stalin tried to make up for Germany's gains by consolidating the Soviet position on the Baltic-Black Sea isthmus. In June 1940, Soviet intelligence had conveniently discovered a secret plot allegedly hatched by the governments of Lithuania, Latvia, and Estonia, directed against their eastern protector. The plots gave the Red Army the excuse they needed to occupy militarily all three Baltic states. Soviet troops brought in their baggage trains teams of Communist agents who, together with the local supporters, established new governments "friendly to the USSR." Soon, as a face-saving device, hastily prepared plebiscites ratified these governments. In July, the three Baltic states were incorporated into the USSR as its fourteenth, fifteenth, and sixteenth republics.[1]

At the same time, Stalin took advantage of the 1939 pact with Hitler concerning Romania. In a note to Bucharest on June 26, 1940, Moscow insisted that "in the interest of justice" the provinces of Bessarabia and Northern Bukovina be ceded to the USSR. The latter demand was stretching the secret protocol, for while Bessarabia had been a part of the deal, Northern Bukovina had never been mentioned. The Soviet demands made King Carol II appeal to Berlin for help, but Hitler, still busy in France and contemplating an invasion of Britain, advised compliance with both requests. With the occupation of Northern Bukovina, Stalin for the second time pushed beyond the old boundaries of the Tsarist Empire. Eastern Galicia, which, like Northern Bukovina, had belonged to the Hapsburg Empire until 1918. When Bessarabia was declared the Moldavian Soviet Socialist Republic, North-

ern Bukovina was incorporated into the Soviet Ukraine. The annexation of these two former Romanian provinces extended the Soviet frontiers to the crest of the Carpathian Mountains to face now the Danubian valley.

Hitler, angered by the Soviet violation of the secret protocol, reasserted German hegemony in the Danube region by rewarding his Hungarian and Bulgarian allies. On August 30, 1940, in Vienna, he compelled the Romanians to cede Northern Transylvania to Hungary and later on Southern Dobrudja to Bulgaria. Moreover, the Soviet Union was not invited to the reconstituted Danube Commission.

Simultaneously, on September 27, 1940, Germany, Italy, and Japan issued a solemn declaration in Berlin dividing the world into three "natural spheres of interest." Europe was to be Germany's sphere and Africa Italy's, while Southeast Asia was allotted to Japan. The three anti-Comintern powers undertook "to assist one another with all political, economic and military means" should one of the contracting powers be attacked by a country "not at present involved in the European war, or in the Sino-Japanese war."

The aggressive restlessness of the Axis, the repeated exclusion of the Russians from decisions concerning the Balkan and Danubian regions, and a deal concerning the stationing of German troops in such countries like Slovakia, Finland and Romania created a great deal of tension between Moscow and Berlin and precipitated a series of sharp Soviet protests. To cope with the mounting tension and to explain to Moscow the meaning of the tripartite declaration, Hitler invited Molotov to visit Berlin on November 12 and 13.

Molotov's visit was the first official call by a Soviet statesman on the Nazi capital. There Hitler and Ribbentrop made an offer to the Soviet Union to participate in the repartitioning of the world, foreshadowed by the Tripartite Pact. They suggested that Russia redirect its interests away from the Balkan-Baltic area and toward the Middle

---

[1] For a background, see Albert Tarulis, *Soviet Policy toward the Baltic States, 1918–1940* (Notre Dame, Ind.: University of Notre Dame Press, 1959) and George von Rauch, *The Baltic States: The Years of Independence, 1917–1940* (Berkeley: University of California Press, 1974).

East, Iran, Afganistan, and the Indian Ocean, which was the British sphere of influence. While accepting German recognition of Soviet interests in the Persian Gulf and the Middle East, Molotov repeatedly stressed the primacy of Russia's European security perimeter stretching from Finland to Turkey, and asked a series of embarrassing questions. How to explain the presence of the German military instructors in Rumania? Against whom were the Romanian borders guaranteed? And what about the Soviet security zone in the Balkans, Bulgaria, and Turkey, where the Soviets wanted to have their bases? During Ribbentrop's speech, in which he proposed jointly partitioning the British Empire and asserted that the war against England was really over, an air alarm was sounded because of a massive British air raid over Berlin. Molotov asked, "If Britain is finished, whose bombs are falling on us?" There was no answer, and the negotiations broke down. They merely revealed the widening gap separating two partners.

Molotov's stubbornness finally convinced Hitler that he would have to prepare for a military showdown with Russia. On December 18, 1940, he issued directives for an operation to be called "Barbarossa." It was to be a short, swift campaign against Russia, to open in May 1941 and end in September or October. The spring of 1941, however, brought two surprising events that, at least indirectly, upset Hitler's calculations; one resulted from Japan's growing disillusionment with Germany's increasingly independent policy; the other took place in the Balkans.

ON THE EVE OF THE INVASION

The fall of France was followed by a diplomatic landslide. The small states of Eastern Europe, formerly pro-Western, one by one, starting with Romania, sought protection of the now-dominant Germany. Yugoslavia, a former ally of France, was no exception. With the dispatch of German troops to Bulgaria on March 2, 1941, the government of Prince Paul, regent for the sixteen-year-old King Peter, succumbed to Axis pressure and in April adhered to the Tripartite Pact. This shocked many traditionally pro-Western Serb patriots. During the night of March 26–27, a *coup d'état* overthrew the Regency and established the youthful King Peter on the throne in Belgrade. On April 4, the new government while outwardly adhering to the Pact, reestablished close relations with Britain, and even concluded a friendship pact with the USSR. Two days later the furious Hitler ordered twelve German divisions "to punish the Yugoslavs" for their "breach of faith." The order was executed with ruthless efficiency. Within a fortnight, Yugoslavia was overrun by the Wehrmacht, supported by its allies: Italy, Hungary, and Bulgaria.

Meanwhile, the steady growth of Hitler's power in the Danubian basin had alarmed not only the Russians, but Mussolini as well. On October 28, 1940, using their Albanian bases, the Italians suddenly attacked Greece. After a few initial successes, the Italian forces were bogged down and had to beg their German allies for help. Hitler decided to oblige and divert considerable forces to subdue the Greeks. The Yugoslav campaign, however, together with the German intervention in Greece on behalf of the indolent Italian allies, resulted in some twenty German divisions being tied down in the Balkan peninsula, thus weakening his armies deployed against the Soviets.

Another factor that intervened on behalf of the USSR was the shifting attitude of Japan; offended by the unilateral and quite unexpected signing of the Hitler–Stalin Pact while Japanese troops were fighting the Red Army in the Far East, the Japanese were sulking. The fact that Tokyo was not consulted, as well as the impressive performance of the Red Army in the Far East in the summer of 1939, determined the subsequent decision in Tokyo to channel its drive away from Soviet Siberia toward Southeast Asia. As a consequence of this decision, despite gestures of outward solidarity with the Anti-Comintern Pact, the Japanese began to pursue their own independent policy, which was to be directed eventually against the Western powers, including the United States. The result of this policy was the nonaggression pact which Japanese Foreign Minister Matsuoka signed with the USSR during his visit to Moscow on April 13, 1941. In case of an attack by a third power against one of the signatories, the other was to remain neutral. The Soviet-Japanese neutrality agreement was a blessing to Stalin and freed him of the risk of a two-front war in case of a possible conflict with Germany.

Meanwhile, relations between Germany and the Soviet Union were becoming strained. The steady concentration of German and satellite troops (Finnish, Romanian, Hungarian, and Slovak) along the western approaches of the USSR from Bulgaria to Finland was no secret to anyone. Not only Soviet intelligence but many outside sources (including President Roosevelt and British Prime Minister Winston Churchill) kept sending Stalin warnings about the impending German attack on Russia. Stalin nevertheless leaned over backwards to oblige Hitler and fulfill his part of the bargain. As a rule, Soviet deliveries of large amounts of raw materials were made in better order and more punctually than those coming from Germany. The Soviet supplies were delivered up until the last moment, despite constant delays from the German partner. Whatever partial Soviet mobilization measures were undertaken, they were carried out as discreetly as possible in order "not to provoke the Germans." Most of the surviving German Communists who had found shelter on Soviet soil were handed over to the Nazis. Referring to the constant Western warnings about the impending German invasion, Stalin said to the then-General (later on Marshal) Zhukov: "You see, *they* are trying to frighten us with the German menace, while the Germans are being scared with the Soviet menace. *They* want to pit us against each other."

One of the few visible signs of Stalin's concern was the fact that on May 6 he took over from Molotov the premiership of the USSR while remaining the Party's Secretary General. Thus the two supreme offices of the country were officially united in the hands of its actual ruler.

THE FIRST BLOW

The German attack had already started on the night of June 21, 1941, before the German ambassador in Moscow, Count von Schulenburg, handed Molotov the official declaration of war. Molotov's reaction was most revealing: "Can it really be that we have deserved all that?" Berlin's note justified the invasion with the pretext that the Russians "were about to attack Germany from the rear" while Germany was getting ready for its final blow at Great Britain. The unpreparedness of the Soviet forces at the time of the invasion and Stalin's obsequious helpfulness toward Hitler were the best refutation of the German claims.

The battle of Russia was the largest, bitterest, and bloodiest campaign of World War II. Hitler's objective was to crush Soviet Russia in one swift blow before the close of 1941 and then, with the resources of the USSR at his disposal, return to the West for a showdown with Britain. Consequently the success of his plan hinged on the speed of the advance of the 154 German and satellite divisions he had deployed along the more than 1,200-mile front from the Baltic to the Black Sea. They were facing some 170 Soviet divisions.[2]

The Soviet forces, like the invaders', were organized into three army groups (in Russian terminology, "fronts")—Northern, Central, and Southern. They were commanded

---

[2] John Erickson, *The Soviet High Command* (New York: St. Martin's, 1962), p. 584. Although not members of the Axis, the Finns joined the offensive on June 25; they declared that they regarded their participation as a continuation of the war of 1939–1940 to regain the territories lost at that time. Italy, Hungary, and Romania declared war on the same day as Germany; Slovakia, on the following day.

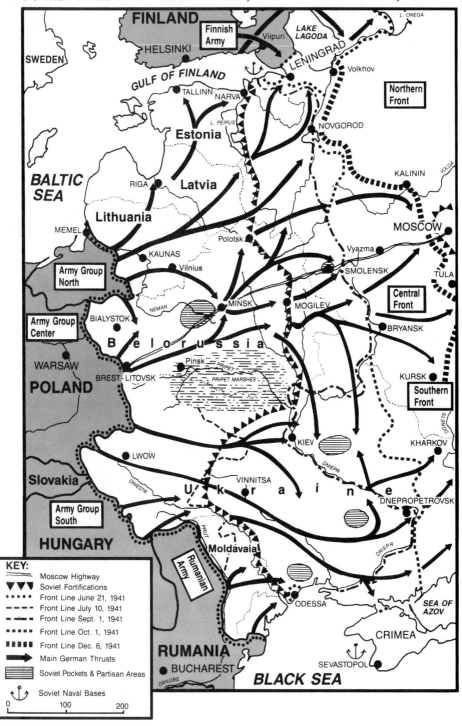

German Invasion of Soviet Russia, June 22-December 6, 1941

FINLAND

SWEDEN

Finnish Army

HELSINKI

Viipuri

LAKE LAGODA

L. ONEGA

LENINGRAD

Volkhov

GULF OF FINLAND

TALLINN NARVA

Estonia

L. PEIPUS

NOVGOROD

Northern Front

KALININ

VOLGA

BALTIC SEA

RIGA

Latvia

MOSCOW

Lithuania

Polotsk

Vyazma

MEMEL

KAUNAS

SMOLENSK

TULA

Army Group North

Vilnius

NEMAN

MINSK

MOGILEV

Central Front

Army Group Center

BIALYSTOK

B e l o r u s s i a

BRYANSK

WARSAW

Pinsk

PRIPET

KURSK

POLAND

BREST-LITOVSK

PRIPET MARSHES

Southern Front

LWOW

KIEV

KHARKOV

DNIEPR

DONETS

Slovakia

DNIESTR

U k r a i n e

VINNITSA

DNEPROPETROVSK

Army Group South

PRUT

HUNGARY

Moldávaia

DNIEPR

Rumanian Army

SEA OF AZOV

ODESSA

CRIMEA

RUMANIA

SEVASTOPOL

BUCHAREST

BLACK SEA

DANUBE

KEY:

~~~~~ Moscow Highway

▼▼▼ Soviet Fortifications

••••• Front Line June 21, 1941

– – – Front Line July 10, 1941

–·–·– Front Line Sept. 1, 1941

▪▪▪▪▪ Front Line Oct. 1, 1941

▮▮▮▮▮ Front Line Dec. 6, 1941

➤ Main German Thrusts

▦ Soviet Pockets & Partisan Areas

⚓ Soviet Naval Bases

0   100   200

by Voroshilov, Timoshenko, and Budënny, respectively. Although the Red Army had numerical superiority not only in men but also in guns, tanks, and planes, it was stretched in linear formation along the borders; moreover the attackers enjoyed an undoubted technical superiority compounded by the advantage of strategic initiative. The crash rearmament program, started after the Finnish campaign, had hardly begun to produce its first fruits.

Stalin himself had little to do with the first few weeks of the Soviet war effort. The first official announcement and war appeal was made by Molotov. When Stalin awakened on the morning of June 22, he refused to take seriously the report of the enemy attack and called it a "rumor spread by *agents provocateurs.*" By midday, when the news was confirmed by innumerable Soviet sources, he lost his nerve. For several days he plunged into a drunken orgy, punctuated by violent outbursts of anger and self-pity. Only on July 3 did he address the Soviet people in a broadcast speech, making an effort to justify the pact with Hitler as having provided both the time and space necessary "for preparing our forces to repulse Fascist Germany." Stalin deemphasized Marxist ideology and appealed to traditional Russian sentiments, calling on the population to "fight our patriotic war of liberation against the Fascist enslavers," even using scorched earth tactics if necessary.

From then on the Soviet war effort was directed by a State Defense Council presided over by Stalin himself, assisted by Voroshilov for military problems, Molotov for diplomatic issues, Beria for security matters, and a younger member of the Politburo, Gregory M. Malenkov, for technical equipment of the armed forces as well as various party matters. By the time Stalin resumed leadership, the three German army groups had broken through the surprised Soviet forces and made deep inroads on all three sectors, but especially in the south. There the mostly Ukrainian units, commanded by the old, incompetent

Marshal Budënny, were either surrendering in large masses or retreating in confusion. The Germans again applied the methods of the "lightning war" (*Blitzkrieg*), which they had perfected during the Polish and French as well as Balkan campaigns; this combined the use of armored and mechanized units capable of deep penetration into enemy territory with devastating air raids, not only against military targets but also against the civilian population, thus causing panic and disorganizing troop and supply movements. What undermined Soviet resistance the most were these combined strikes where least expected. The German tactics were facilitated by the fact that the Red Army divisions were, as a rule, strung out along the new, still largely unfortified, western frontiers. The Soviet troops had been moved as much as 250 miles to the west in 1939 and 1940. Mostly indifferently commanded by survivors of the purges, the Red Army suffered from extended communication lines stretching back to their old supply bases. This strategic disposition made them especially vulnerable to concentrated German thrusts. Once through the largely linear Soviet defenses, the Wehrmacht would encircle the Soviet units and then destroy them or make them capitulate. To slow down their onslaught, the desperate Stalin ordered the Soviet troops to engage the enemy piecemeal, in increments of brigades and divisions. When Soviet units were surrounded by the enemy, they were ordered to stand fast. The mostly young and inexperienced commanders, who still remembered what had happened to their predecessors during the Great Purge, obeyed orders from Moscow under the watchful eye of the Political Commissars, whose full powers had been reinstated just a few weeks before the attack.[3]

The rapidity of the German advance all

---

[3] The problem of responsibility for the Soviet lack of preparedness has been discussed in the book by Vladimir Petrov and A. M. Nekrich, *June 22, 1941: Soviet Historians and the German Invasion* (Columbia, S.C.: University of South Carolina Press, 1968).

Soviet artillery at the outskirts of Leningrad

along the front was disconcerting. Their Army of the North, after having captured all naval bases valiantly defended by the Soviet navy, and having destroyed the Soviet units in the Baltic area, besieged Leningrad by the beginning of September. The city could then communicate with the rest of the country only through Lake Ladoga, which mercifully froze earlier than usual. The German Army of the South swept like a tornado through the Western Ukraine, took masses of POWs, and pushed irresistibly toward Kiev, and then beyond the Dnieper, thus achieving by far the greatest territorial advances, and taking the most prisoners. Kiev was lost on September 19, together with 600,000 Soviet soldiers captured by the Germans. The Soviet southern front almost collapsed; Odessa and Sevastopol held out heroically. The Army of the Center, which had the strongest concentration of tanks, took about 300,000 POWs and pushed through Minsk and Smolensk toward Moscow. It seemed that the Soviet capital would be conquered by September or October.

THE BATTLE OF MOSCOW

The unprecedented advances along all three sectors made Hitler overconfident. He took it for granted that he could have Moscow any time he wished. In August his Propaganda Minister, Joseph Goebbels, ecstatically announced to the world, "We have smashed the Red Army to splinters. Russia lies like a limp virgin in the arms of the German Mars." In the meantime, the huge Nazi war machine operating largely on costly synthetic gasoline and limited European oil supplies, was getting dangerously low on fuel. Consequently, to reach the oil of the Caucasus seemed to Hitler a more vital target than capturing Moscow.

On August 3, despite the urging of his military advisers, Hitler ordered one segment of the best armor dispatched to the south to get him the Caucasian oil; at the same time, some units were to be diverted to the north to seize Leningrad before it could be resupplied through the frozen Lake Ladoga. This momentous decision caused a major crisis. Utterly bewildered and frustrated by Hitler's order, many senior officers sabotaged his order, considering it senseless; some of them resigned in protest. As a result, while the northern and southern sectors of the German front were not reinforced in time to reach the oil fields, the central group was weakened enough to slow down its advance on Moscow.

As the same time the weather worsened dramatically; the October mists and rain, mixed with wet snow, turned the Russian plain into a sea of mud. Tanks, artillery, and transport vehicles sank deep into the boggy ground. By November heavy snows were falling throughout the area and the temperature sank below zero. The German soldiers, prepared only for a short, swift summer campaign, were frequently victims of frostbite and other winter ailments. On December 2, when Hitler ordered an all-out assault on Moscow, the mercury stood at 40 degrees below zero. The breechblocks of rifles froze solid, oil in the tanks and trucks had the consistency of tar, the drag on dynamos made it impossible to start their engines, cylinder blocks were split open, and axles refused to turn. The forest around Moscow limited the mobility of the German tanks while increasing the effectiveness of Soviet cavalry and the increasing number of partisans. In these circumstances bayonets and grenades were the only effective weapons, and in the hand-to-hand fighting the Red Army's mostly peasant boys proved superior. Moreover, the frozen and exhausted Wehrmacht now had to face the first large units of the Soviet Siberian army which Stalin had begun to withdraw from the Far East soon after signing the nonaggression pact with Japan in April.

By December, when the battle for Moscow was at its peak, about twenty Siberian divisions, all in fine condition, and equipped for winter warfare with 1,700 tanks and 1,500 aircraft, were already at the crucial Moscow sector. By December 1941, every third defender of Moscow came from the Siberian units. Whereas the German motorized communications were often paralyzed because of deep snow, the Red Army kept their communication lines opened thanks to the small, tough, shaggy Siberian horses, which were used to such conditions. Moreover, their phenomenal capacity of survival, even when they were given nothing to eat except conifer twigs or root-straw, allowed such cavalry units to penetrate deep behind enemy lines, causing havoc among the unsuspecting German rear echelons. In peak condition, dressed in white, quilted uniforms, with felt boots and fur caps, the units withdrawn from the Far East now faced the shivering, exhausted German soldiers of von Bock's Central Army Group. During the battle of Moscow, instances of individual heroism were especially striking and frequent. For instance, on December 6, 80 miles to the east on the highway connecting Volkolamsk with Moscow, 28 soldiers of the Panfilov division held up the enemy advance on the capital for a whole day. Only three of the 28 warriors survived, but they had destroyed 18 out of 50 German tanks before being overwhelmed.

Meanwhile, the Soviet troops, under the experienced eye of the veteran commander of the Far Eastern Army, General Zhukov, were learning how to use effectively and in large numbers a few weapons of theirs which from the beginning of the campaign proved superior to their German counterparts: the Soviet T-34 tank and their batteries of rockets, endearingly called "Katiushas," or "Kathies." The Soviet air force, decimated mostly on the ground by the early German surprise attacks, was resupplied and reorganized. After repeated, bitter attempts to break through the Moscow front, on December 8 the German Army Command announced suspension of military operations "because of the severe conditions." Moscow was saved.

FAILURE OF THE LIGHTNING CAMPAIGN

To the military factors responsible for the German failure to score a quick victory, one must also add the changing political climate inside the Soviet Union. Hitler had entered the USSR with the slogan of abolishing its Communist system and liberating its oppressed national minorities, especially the Ukrainians, Belorussians, and the Baltic peoples. That is why, at the beginning of the invasion, very often the German soldiers were greeted by the population of the western borderlands with the traditional welcoming gestures of bread, salt, and flowers, while many Soviet units composed of recruits of these nationalities were surrendering in large masses. Yet none of the original German promises were carried out. Brushing aside the various national committees he himself had helped create, Hitler promptly established his own centralized administration in the conquered areas and ran them with an iron fist in accordance with racist Nazi doctrine and for the sole benefit of the German Reich. The primarily Slavic inhabitants of these lands were treated as inferior creatures, almost like colonial slaves. In addition, some of the most hated Soviet institutions, like the collective and State farms, were preserved; they were now to be used by the German authorities to exploit the resources of the occupied areas. Some 3 million workers were forcibly conscripted to slave in German factories and mines while being treated like subhuman creatures. Finally, Soviet POWs were mistreated in blatant disregard of the Geneva Convention. Well over 2 million of them were surrounded by barbed wire and either allowed to starve or otherwise destroyed. Soon it became obvious to the people of the German-occupied areas that Hitler had nothing to offer to the Soviet people but a still worse form of oppression and exploitation. By the autumn of 1941 instances of terror, sabotage, and even organized armed resistance to the invaders became more and more frequent.

As the German occupation continued, a full-scale partisan movement developed. The first bands were formed by Communist Party activists and by Red Army soldiers caught behind the lines by the German advance. The partisan units could communicate with the unoccupied areas of the country by radio and air, and so could coordinate their activities with the regular army. While the partisans lived off the land, they were often supplied with arms and munitions by air drops. They were able to harass the Germans, sometimes seriously disrupting Nazi lines of communication.

When the news about Nazi policies in the conquered territories filtered back behind the Soviet lines, resistance to the invaders began to stiffen dramatically, especially in the Great Russian areas. This was reflected in the attitude of both the Soviet front-line soldiers and the populations of the occupied areas. Also, Stalin had aroused the patriotic feelings of the Russian people. In this he was aided by the Russian Orthodox Church. From the day of the German attack, the leaders of the Church urged the faithful to support the regime in its efforts to repel the invaders. The head of the Russian Church was even to acclaim Stalin as "the divinely anointed leader of the nation." The population of the occupied areas was threatened with excommunication if it collaborated with the Nazis. At the same time, the Communist Party and state put an end to the persecution of the Church. The Orthodox church and the atheistic state worked together throughout the war to whip up patriotic fervor.

Meanwhile, Stalin salvaged some of the surviving victims of his purges from the concentration camps and had them rehabilitated and put into a number of key jobs, civilian as well as military. Several of them, like Konstantin Rokossovsky, became "heroes of the Soviet Union." On top of this, the first months of the terrible ordeal proved to be a good school, particularly for many Soviet commanders, who were quickly learning on the job the tricks of modern warfare. This was already evident by late autumn of 1941, during the battle of Moscow, when instances of growing military sophistication, as well as of individual heroism were especially numerous and striking.

By the end of 1941, the desperate and often chaotic retreat had turned into a patriotic war of increasing ferocity.

FORMATION
OF THE GRAND COALITION

The checking of the German onslaught on Moscow coincided almost to the day with another major turning point of World War II—the Japanese attack on Pearl Harbor. The attack was greeted in Moscow with a sigh of relief. Now pushed into the war, the United States became a partner of the USSR in the war against the Axis powers. Immediately after the German invasion of Russia, Great Britain, disregarding Stalin's previous collaboration with Hitler, had offered its unconditional aid to the Soviet Union. In a radio speech on June 22, Winston Churchill declared, "Any man or state who fights against Nazidom will have our aid." The generous but limited help of Britain, under German air attacks, fighting a desperate battle in the Atlantic, and itself dependent on the United States, could not be substantial. But the entry of the United States into the war multiplied the resources of the anti-Axis coalition dramatically. By extending "lend-lease" assistance to both Britain and Russia, the United States soon became the arsenal of the anti-Axis coalition.

Even before the Japanese attack on Pearl Harbor, on August 14, 1941, President Roosevelt had met with Winston Churchill aboard a battleship in mid-Atlantic, where they issued a joint declaration of basic principles and underlying their approach to the war. The Atlantic Charter, as the declaration was to be called, promised "a better future for the world . . . after the final destruction of Nazi tyranny," and that "sovereign rights and self-government" would be "restored to those who had been forcibly deprived of them." Both countries "hoped to see established a peace which will afford to all nations the means of dwelling in safety within their own boundaries, and which will afford assurance that all the men in all the lands may live out their lives in freedom from fear and want."

Soviet Russia's position within the grand coalition was ambivalent from the very beginning. Stalin did not join the partnership against the Axis as a willing ally but rather as a betrayed accomplice of Hitler. Having committed numerous acts of aggression in collaboration with him, the Soviet dictator had been guilty of many violations of those very human rights extolled by the Atlantic Charter. Soviet entry into the anti-Axis coalition posed questions: How would it affect the Atlantic Charter and the moral posture of the anti-Axis coalition in general? Would Stalin subscribe to the Charter? And if so, would he respect its principles in practice? Even after the West had welcomed the USSR into the Allied camp, Stalin was unwilling to put aside his congenital suspicion of his capitalist partners; he feared that their antagonism toward Communist Russia would revive immediately after Hitler's defeat. Consequently, he was determined to pursue an independent line of policy camouflaged by the deceptive slogan of "Allied unity," which he would exploit for his benefit.

Britain and the United States, delighted to see the Soviet soldiers bearing the brunt of Hitler's onslaught, did not put any conditions on their aid. Unable to match Russia's massive contribution to the land war or satisfy Stalin's urgent requests for the immediate establishment of a "second front" on the continent of Europe, the Western allies were happy to buy Stalin's cooperation with military and economic aid, as well as with initially vague but momentous political promises, mostly at the expense of their weaker allies like Poland and China.

THE BLACK SUMMER OF 1942

During 1941 the Germans had captured large stretches of land and inflicted tremendous losses on Russia, but they were unable to win the war quickly. Many factories and some rolling stock had been successfully evacuated beyond the Volga to the Urals and even to Central Asia. Thanks to this gigantic operation, often paralleled by the superhuman sacrifices of numerous individuals, by the spring of 1942 most of these factories had started production on their new sites. Together with British and American aid, which was increasing as time went by, they began resupplying the Red Army with new equipment. Once Hitler had lost his chance of winning a quick war by the autumn of 1941, the superior Soviet and overall Allied manpower and resources, gradually reinforced by those of the United States, slowly began to shift the balance against him.

Still, the battle of Moscow was only the first major German defeat on land since the beginning of the war. Soviet Russia was momentarily saved from defeat but not yet out of danger. The badly battered Wehrmacht was still a formidable fighting machine that was getting ready for another try in the spring of 1942.

Disregarding the advice of his main military expert, Stalin ordered a spring counteroffensive in May 1942. Its main objective was to free the industrial district of Kharkov from enemy occupation. The badly planned and poorly executed offensive ended in one of the worst disasters of the war. Again the Red Army suffered its heaviest losses in the Ukrainian sectors. In July the Germans captured Sevastopol and the entire Crimea. Pressing his gains, Field Marshal Manstein reoccupied Rostov-on-the-Don, which had been momentarily recovered by the Red Army, and continued his spectacular sweep toward the key area of the lower Volga and the Caucasus. By the end of August the German troops were on the northern slopes of the Caucasus, near the oil fields of Grozny. The industrial and communications center, Stalingrad, was Hitler's next target. The Germans also made impressive gains during July and August in the northern and central sectors. Again the surrender and rout of entire units assumed

epidemic proportions. The specter of a total collapse again appeared on the horizon. That is why the period of July to August was called the Red Army's "Black Summer."

In this desperate situation, Stalin resorted to a series of Draconian reprisals. Special NKVD detachments were to follow front-line units and shoot on sight all those retreating and hesitating. Summary executions for disobeying orders or for cowardice now became a standard procedure, and several generals were among those shot. A special antiespionage organization was created under the code name, "Death to the Spies" (*Smersh*.) The hate-the-Germans campaign was stepped up and reached unprecedented intensity. At the same time patriotic propaganda further replaced the old Communist slogans. The military oath pledging the soldier to struggle for the emancipation of workers was replaced by a new one making it his primary duty to fight for the Motherland. The dual command, reinstated on the eve of the German invasion, was abolished definitively; the political commissars were now turned into officers in charge of political education, propaganda, and welfare, and forbidden to interfere with military decisions of the field commander. Former distinctions of rank (military titles) were reintroduced; they included the gold and silver braided shoulder straps abolished by the Bolshevik revolution. In January 1942, a magazine, *Slavyanye* (Slavs), was established in Moscow to present the war as a pro-Slavic crusade against Hitler's Teutonic invasion. This was followed by a series of Slavic congresses and conferences. Concessions were made to the religious sentiments of the mostly peasant soldiers, and atheistic propaganda was soft-pedaled, if not entirely forgotten.

THE BATTLE OF STALINGRAD AND ITS CONSEQUENCES

Through the summer of 1942, the German juggernaut continued its seemingly irresistible sweep toward the mother of the Russian rivers, the Volga. By September 4 the offensive of the crack Sixth Army of Marshal Friedrich Paulus had reached the outskirts of Stalingrad. On August 25 Hitler issued a personal order to capture it and to cut the oil supply line to Moscow. The period from mid-September to mid-November was the peak of the battle for Stalingrad, which the bitter street fighting soon turned into a heap of ruins. Although several times the Germans were half a step from capturing the headquarters of the Soviet commander, General Ivan V. Chuykov, each time they were frustrated by the dogged, desperate resistance of the Red Army men. By November 19, the exhausted Sixth Army had to give up because of intolerable losses and the onset of winter. At the same time, Paulus's supply lines had been cut by a broad encircling movement of three Soviet reserve armies, assembled by Zhukov, totaling 1 million men. Paulus wanted to retreat, but was forbidden to do so by Hitler, who ordered him to fight to the bitter end. Meanwhile, several German attempts at cutting the Soviet ring failed.

While the Sixth Army stuck to the smoking debris of Stalingrad, the Red Army prepared a mighty counteroffensive. Ably assisted by Deputy Supreme Commander Zhukov, Stalin planned his counterstroke, involving three army groups (or fronts) amounting to some eighty divisions of nearly one million men, supported by 13,500 guns and mortars and 1,100 aircraft. The Soviet counterattack started on November 19. First, the army group of General Nicholas Vatutin hit the poorly armed Rumanian troops on the Don covering the northwestern approaches to Stalingrad. Overnight, the flimsy Rumanian contingents collapsed and their divisions surrendered. At the same time, from those Don bridgeheads that still remained in Soviet hands, Red Army tanks pounded on the remnants of the German Sixth Army. Simultaneously, the mechanized forces of General Fedor Tolbukhin carried out a broad enveloping movement from the

south. The Soviets then moved swiftly from north and south through the breach to exploit their gains. Within four days, the German Sixth Army with its 200,000 men was cut off by this brilliant envelopment. With the outflanking of the Sixth Army by November 23, the German position in the northern Caucasus became untenable. The agony of the Sixth Army grew so severe that finally on February 3, 1943, Paulus felt compelled to surrender. Some 91,000 frost-bitten and half-starved survivors of the once-elite Sixth Army trudged into Soviet POW camps. The captured included Field Marshal Paulus himself, 23 generals, and 2,500 other officers. Some 140,000 German and satellite soldiers had died fighting and from hunger and disease. More than a decade later in 1955–1956, only about 6,000 of these survivors finally returned to their homeland.

The Soviet booty was impressive. It included 750 planes, 1,550 tanks, 480 armored cars, 8,000 guns and mortars, 61,000 trucks, 235 ammunition dumps, and a vast quantity of other equipment and the remaining reserves of food, including large quantities of champagne that the farsighted German command had shipped to celebrate its victory. Experts have long pondered the significance of the battle of Stalingrad. Was Stalingrad worth the price Hitler was willing to pay for it? The city was an important communication center and posed a considerable danger to German forces protecting the left flank of the Caucasus drive. Yet, strategically, Stalingrad was no more important to the Germans than Voronezh, for example, which they decided to leave in Russian hands. Stalingrad did not control use of the Volga waterway, on which oil as well as Anglo-American war aid were shipped northward.[4] Through stubborn sacri-

---

[4] From June 1941 to April 1944, the Red Army was sent 4,292 British tanks, 3,734 American tanks, and 1,400 tanks from Canada. Yet for most of their battle equipment the Red Army relied mainly on their own factories. Food and petroleum products were delivered in bulk. By mid-1943 the Americans had shipped in over 900,000 tons of steel, 1.5 million tons of food,

Street fighting in Stalingrad, November 1942

fice, the Red Army successfully drew the vast bulk of German resources on the southern front into the Stalingrad meatgrinder. Psychologically, Stalingrad spelled an end to the myth of the Third Reich's invincibility and a start for another myth, that of Stalin's military genius.

The vigorous Soviet drive that followed the Stalingrad victory soon resulted in the recovery of Kharkov and the German withdrawal from the Northern Caucasus. The situation changed all along the front. In the northern sector the Russians relieved the siege of Leningrad by cutting a gap seven miles wide between Lake Ladoga and the German lines. This made the life of the

remaining 600,000 inhabitants easier. The siege of Leningrad, which lasted for almost 900 days, has a unique place in the history of modern warfare. During the American Civil War, Vicksburg endured a siege from May 18 to July 4, 1863. The siege of Paris during the Franco-Prussian War lasted only four months, from September 19, 1870 to mid-January 1871. In neither case was there a population comparable to the two and a half million Leningraders, nor was it exposed to constant air raids, nor did the temperature ever drop to twenty or thirty degrees below zero. Food supplies were extremely scarce. Every inch of ground within the city, including some public squares and cemeteries, were turned into "victory gardens." Yet despite constant bombardment and extreme exhaustion, the determined people stubbornly continued their resistance. The relief of the siege of Leningrad made the central sector of the front more secure.

The climax of the battle of Stalingrad was preceded by the halting of the Japanese advance in the Pacific by the American Navy in the summer of 1942 and the victory of the British Eighth Army at El Alamein in

---

138,000 trucks and jeeps, boots, industrial equipment, raw materials—in all a highly variegated military-industrial shipping list that included 12,000 tons of butter sent for Soviet troops convalescing in hospitals. However, it was not for the tanks or the aircraft that Stalin pressed; it was mostly for the food and industrial supplies, metals, chemicals, and machine tools, and lorries. The two-and-a-half ton American lorries allowed infantry to keep up with armored assaults and were fundamental for offensive operations and logistic support. Erickson, *The Road to Berlin*, pp. 83–4. Some of the lorries delivered during the war would serve the Soviet armed forces well into the 1950s.

North Arica, which stopped the advance of Marshal Rommel's Africa Corps on Cairo at the end of October 1942. That November the landing of British and American forces in the then-French protectorate of Morocco and Algeria established a firm Allied base for an invasion of southern Europe. In May 1943, the German and Italian forces in Tunisia capitulated. These events, which succeeded each other kaleidoscopically, marked a decisive turning point in World War II. While the battle of Moscow indicated that Hitler could not knock down the Russians instantly, the battle of Stalingrad and the Allied successes in North Africa raised the question of whether he could win the war at all.

THE BATTLE OF KURSK

The issue of the Russian campaign was settled during the summer of 1943. Faced with disaster, Hitler ordered total mobilization of all the resources at the command of all his satrapies, then covering most of Europe from the Dnieper to the Pyrenees and from Norway to Greece. This extraordinary effort produced a panoply of new weapons by the summer. They were to be used in an unprecedented concentration in the central Russian sector around the city of Kursk, an important point welding the central and southern sectors of the front. The Russians, forewarned about Hitler's plans by their intelligence network inside Germany, had fortified the area around Kursk for about sixty-five miles in depth, and had massed still larger quantities of tanks and approximately 20,000 guns of all calibers. In sectors where the attack was expected an average of 4,000 antitank and antipersonnel mines were laid per mile. The battle of Stalingrad had not only lifted the Red Army's morale but had also given it invaluable battle experience, which was fully applied at Kursk. Fresh divisions had also been trained. By the spring of 1943 large quantities of lend-lease supplies, especially trucks, had reached the Soviet front line and made the Red Army more mobile and much better equipped than it had been at the beginning of the war.

To split the Soviet front and capture Moscow was Hitler's order to his crack force of seventeen armored divisions. They were

Soviet artillery in the battle of Kursk, July 1943

provided with over 2,000 of the most modern tanks and nearly 2,000 of the newest planes. The Battle of Kursk was the greatest tank battle of all time. The Germans launched their formidable offensive on the night of July 4. Fighting with great skill and determination, they penetrated the Soviet defenses to a depth of between ten and thirty miles.

At that critical moment, as if to prove that nothing fails like failure, Hitler's grand coalition began to crumble. After Stalingrad, practically all his allies (the Italians, the Romanians, the Hungarians, the Slovaks, and the Finns) began to negotiate secretly with his enemies about leaving the leaky ship. As the Battle of Kursk was reaching its climax on July 10, the Western Allies landed their forces on Sicily. Moreover, on July 12 the Russians launched a diversionary counteroffensive toward Orël and cut the rear of the German Ninth Army, the backbone of the Kursk drive. The Italians had meanwhile failed to stop the Allied advance. To prevent a complete collapse of the Axis southern front, Hitler had to stop the Kursk offensive and send several of his elite divisions south of the Alps.

Thus ended Germany's supreme effort in Russia. In the process of this greatest and fiercest tank battle of World War II, the Nazis had suffered crippling losses in their elite troops and newest war material that could never be made up by the Reich's already shrinking resources. Kursk put an end to Hitler's hopes of winning the war in the east. From now on the Germans could wage only a defensive war, and the strategic initiative fell into the Russians' hands. Advancing steadily despite stubborn German delaying tactics, the Red Army gradually reconquered the area around Leningrad and the Ukraine. By June 1944, the pre-1939 frontiers of the USSR had been crossed and the conquest of East Central Europe began.

In 1943, Stalin assumed the title of "Generalissimo," donned a Marshal's uniform, and began to stress more and more his role as the mastermind behind the victorious

Soviet strategy. Several of the most successful field commanders, including Zhukov, Rokossovsky, Rodion V. Malinovsky, and Vasily D. Sokolovsky, were granted the title Marshal of the Soviet Union. New military decorations to be awarded to officers only were now created, among them the orders of Suvorov, Kutuzov, and Alexander Nevsky. A new parade uniform was introduced for the Red Army and Navy.[5] In October 1943, the restored Patriarchate of Moscow was recognized as the sole legal representative of all Orthodox Christians of the USSR and was granted the right to own property. On August 22, a reconstruction program for the reconquered territory was proclaimed by Stalin.

WARTIME DIPLOMACY

Entry of the Red Army onto the pre-war Polish territory in January 1944 raised a series of highly sensitive political problems. As long as the Russians were fighting a life-and-death struggle, military issues overshadowed everything else. But with the military climax behind them and with the Germans retreating from Soviet lands and the Red Army approaching the contested areas of East Central Europe, political problems

---

[5] The British authorities were astonished when they received from Moscow an urgent request for a large quantity of silver and gold braid as a high-priority military supply, apparently more important than food, blankets, or cloth for soldiers' uniforms. The British termed this request as "absurdly frivolous" but complied with it "for the sake of Allied unity." The introduction of the gold braid was to emphasize the professionalism of the Red Army: it was to abandon its revolutionary roots and become a regular, national army; its officers were ordered to look smart; they were assigned orderlies and were to travel in first-class carriages only. Stalin also ordered establishment of officer cadet schools, where the surviving Tsarist instructors were to teach their pupils not only the basics of military science and drill, but also good manners, ballroom dancing and French; Werth's book, *Russia at War,* (pp. 415–416 and 426–428), contains not only a vivid description of the Stalingrad battle, but also the dramatic changes that transformed the old revolutionary Red Army into what it is now.

began to loom larger and larger. One of them was the Soviet-Polish controversy. In July 1941, under British pressure, the Polish Government in London reestablished diplomatic relations with Moscow. A Polish Army was to be organized from among the Polish POWs in the USSR and the deportees from the Soviet-occupied eastern provinces of old Poland, who were now released from various camps. However, the army desperately needed the 15,000 officers captured in 1939, and Soviet authorities were unable to explain their absence. "Maybe they have fled to Manchuria," Stalin once tried to explain. The problems of the former Polish eastern provinces, the future of the Polish government-in-exile, and the issue of the missing officers constantly plagued Polish-Soviet relations.

In April 1943, the Germans had discovered graves of several thousand Polish officers in the Katyn forest near Smolensk. They had apparently been executed in the spring of 1940, a year or so before Hitler's attack. When the Polish Government in London asked the International Red Cross to investigate the issue, Moscow broke off diplomatic relations with the "London Poles," accusing them of slandering the Soviet Union. At the same time Stalin began to gather the surviving veterans of the old, once-dissolved Communist Party of Poland and other pro-Soviet elements from all over East Central Europe and coach them for their future role. These issues, as well as the problem of the second front, necessitated top-level consultation.

In May 1943, Stalin dissolved the Comintern and declared that it was no longer needed. By appearing to abandon the worldwide ambitions of militant Communism, he hoped the West would be more trusting of his future intentions. By 1943, Moscow had achieved such far-reaching control over other Communist parties that the old, rusty, cumbersome machinery of the Comintern seemed unnecessary. In June the old battle song of the international revolutionary movement, "The Internationale," was discarded as the Soviet national anthem and replaced by a new one, more in tune with the new, patriotic mood. Leaders of the Communist underground movements in all Axis-occupied lands were instructed to achieve rapprochements with the local forces of "anti-Fascist resistance" in order to form a "broad national front." In June 1943, a "Union of Polish Patriots in Russia" was created to rival the London Poles. In July 1943, a "Free Germany Committee" was organized from among the captured German POWs. Working hand-in-hand with veterans of the old Comintern like Walter Ulbricht, the Committee began to act not only as an instrument of propaganda and political diversion, but also as the nucleus of a future pro-Soviet German government. To assuage the suspicions of the Western allies, both Committees soft-pedaled Marxist slogans while emphasizing patriotism and the old popular-front line of uniting all anti-Fascist forces.

These skillful moves and the almost uninterrupted series of Soviet victories that had carried the Red Army from Stalingrad to Kiev and almost to the old boundaries formed the background of the first summit conference at Teheran, close to the Soviet border and then under Allied occupation. With a record of spectacular Soviet successes that the Western Allies could not match—even with Italy's capitulation in September and their further victories in the North Atlantic, and the Pacific—Stalin could negotiate from a position of strength. By that time the Western Allies were already preparing to launch their invasion of Hitler's "Fortress Europe" in the spring of 1944, but no one could guarantee its success. The lack of a second front imbued both Roosevelt and Churchill with a sui generis guilt complex, and Stalin seldom missed an opportunity to exploit it. Stalin was determined to exact political quid pro quos for the human hecatomb his people were undergoing. Supported by American Chief of Staff General George C. Marshall, he vigorously opposed the idea of the Allies attacking the Axis's "soft underbelly," the Balkans, which would probably have resulted in the arrival of British and American troops in Sofia, Belgrade, Bucharest, Budapest, and Vienna before the Red Army. Stalin insisted instead on the scheduled cross-channel invasion of the European continent (*Operation Overlord*). And indeed, at Teheran the Western Allies agreed to jettison the Balkan landing and firmly promised to carry out the Overlord operation in May 1944. Stalin reciprocated with a pledge that the Western invasion would be supported by a concerted Soviet drive from the east.

At the conference the Big Three recognized the partisans of Joseph Broz-Tito as the most effective resistance group in Yugoslavia and therefore most deserving of Allied support. Roosevelt and Churchill also agreed to discuss with Stalin the highly explosive Polish problem. This was done without consulting their ally, the Polish Government in London, which was firmly supported by a strong underground resistance movement in Poland. Stalin, claiming the principle of self-determination, insisted that Poland's eastern provinces should be allotted to the USSR as they were mostly composed of Belorussians and Ukrainians. Churchill and Roosevelt agreed "in principle" to Stalin's demands, but Roosevelt wanted his acquiescence kept secret until after the 1944 presidential election so as not to lose the Polish vote in the United States. Since the Poles had been the first to fight Hitler in September 1939, had suffered enormous losses, and had remained loyal allies of the West, Churchill agreed to the idea that Poland be compensated at the expense of Germany's former Slavic eastern provinces—East Prussia, Pomerania, and Silesia—to resettle the Polish population of the former eastern marches.

Assuming a posture of moderation, Stalin did not seek at Teheran formal and final recognition of all his territorial claims in Eastern Europe. By frustrating the Balkan landing and obtaining firm assurances of an invasion of Western Europe, he merely created a situation in which his country's ambitions would be safeguarded. And through his promise to help the United States against Japan and to support Roosevelt's idea of a new international security organization to replace the old League of Nations, Stalin won the American President's gratitude. The way in which the Americans and the British treated their Polish ally strengthened Stalin's opinion that Eastern Europe was of marginal importance to Washington and London and that they were more interested in the facades of the future Eastern European governments than in their real contents.

THE CRUCIAL YEAR OF 1944

With this conviction in mind, Stalin was driving his battered but reinvigorated troops through the Baltic states—Poland, Romania, and Hungary. Throughout 1944 the by-now crippled *Wehrmacht* was unable to stage anything but a series of desperate delaying actions at the eastern front. In the west, however, Hitler's position was still strong; protected by formidable fortifications, he confidently awaited an Allied invasion.

On June 6, 1944, came the long-delayed Allied landing in Normandy, France. The successful invasion was greeted by Moscow with great relief. The supporting Soviet summer offensive was launched, symbolically enough, on June 23—one day after the third anniversary of Hitler's attack. The result was a series of strongly contested but almost uninterrupted Russian victories. From then on, in every offensive the Red Army had a decisive superiority not only in men, but also in tanks, artillery, and aircraft. While in the west the Allies occupied most of Italy, France, and the Low Countries up to the Rhine, the Red Army reached the Vistula and the heart of Romania. When an uprising occurred in Warsaw on August 1, 1944, that attempted to liberate the Polish capital ahead of the advancing Russians, the commander of the Soviet First Belorussian Front, Marshal Konstantin Rokossovsky, stopped the advance on Stalin's order. For sixty-three days while the uprising went on, the Red Army remained almost inactive, passively watching as the flower of the Polish resistance movement was crushed and the city utterly ruined. Consequently, the bulk of the non-Communist forces was destroyed. This allowed the Communist-dominated "Polish Committee of National Liberation" to be proclaimed the Provisional Government of Poland on January 1, 1945.

During the crucial summer of 1944, while delaying its offensive on the Polish front and postponing its advance on Berlin, the Red Army advanced rapidly in the Danubian valley and in the Balkans. The first country to be occupied was Romania, where the pro-Nazi, police regime of Marshal Antonescu had been overthrown. King Michael not only surrendered his country to the Russians on August 23, but also declared war on Germany. The traditionally pro-Russian Bulgarians, who had never been in a state of war with the USSR, were now anxious to capitulate to the Western Allies. To prevent the possibility of the appearance of British or American troops in the Balkans, Moscow declared war on Bulgaria on September 5. The reluctant Bulgarians therefore had to surrender to the Russians. Pushing rapidly forward, the Red Army linked up with Marshal Tito's Yugoslav partisans, who had meanwhile liberated most of their country themselves. On October 20 the Soviet and Yugoslav troops jointly entered Belgrade and, ignoring the royal government of King Peter, established a Communist-dominated administration.

In Hungary, however, Soviet progress was much slower. There on October 15, the Regent Admiral Nicholas Horthy tried to emulate the Romanian example and surrender his country first to the Western Allies and then to the Soviets. His attempts were frustrated, however, by the local fascist movement called the "Arrow Cross" which collaborated with the Germans. Horthy was imprisoned. During the late autumn and winter of 1944, the Red Army advanced to

the heart of Hungary and besieged Budapest. Meanwhile, a pro-Soviet coalition government was set up in Debreczen; on January 20, 1945, it signed an armistice with Moscow and declared war on Germany. On February 15, Budapest capitulated and the Debreczen government was installed in the Hungarian capital. In the autumn of 1944 there was also an uprising in Slovakia, directed not only against the Germans but also against the local Fascist regime. Like the Warsaw insurrection, the Slovak upsurge too was let down by the Russians, eager to see the non-Communist resistance forces exterminated by German hands.

Hence by the close of 1944 Hitler had lost all his satellites, while his forces, outnumbered and outweaponed, were fighting a desperate delaying struggle as they fell back to their bombed and exhausted homeland. Reversing his earlier policies, in September 1944 Hitler allowed the formation of a "Russian Liberation Army" under a Soviet POW, General Andrei A. Vlasov. The Army was to fight for the "creation of a new People's political system without Bolsheviks and exploiters." Hitler's desperate move came too late to affect the course of the war. Similar Ukrainian, Belorussian, and Baltic units had been formed earlier.

Hitler's last effort to wrest the initiative from the Western Allies and compel them to begin separate negotiations with him took place in December 1944, when he launched a sudden counteroffensive in the Ardennes and forced British and American troops to retreat. On January 10, while the Battle of the Bulge was hanging in the balance. Winston Churchill sent an urgent personal message to Stalin requesting "a major Russian offensive on the Vistula" during January to relieve the German pressure in the West. Stalin, although invoking inclement weather as a deterrent, promised to oblige. And indeed, on January 12, 1945 the Soviet drive was resumed and the ruined Warsaw captured by Marshal Rokossovsky's First Belorussian Front, which included units of the Soviet-sponsored Polish army.

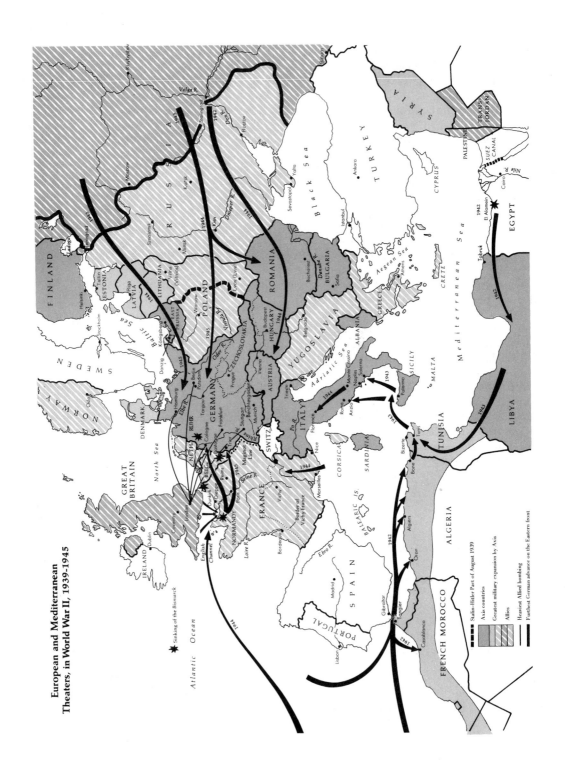

European and Mediterranean
Theaters, in World War II, 1939-1945

THE YALTA CONFERENCE

On January 29, on the eve of the twelfth anniversary of Hitler's seizure of power, the massive Soviet juggernaut crossed the pre-1939 Polish-German boundaries and penetrated into the German province of Brandenburg. Berlin lay beyond the last natural obstacle, the Oder. At the same time that the Red Army was pushing toward Bratislava and Vienna, the Western Allies were bogged down in the Italian Apennines and on the Rhine. It was against this background of practically uninterrupted Soviet triumphs that the second summit conference gathered at Yalta in the Crimea at the beginning of February 1945.

In October 1944, between the Teheran and the Yalta conferences, Winston Churchill visited Moscow. On the night of October 9, after a long wrangle about the respective spheres of influence, the British Prime Minister, a co-author of the Atlantic Charter, scribbled on a scrap of paper the following suggestions for dividing the spheres of influence in Eastern Europe:

Romania: Russia 90 percent, the others 10 percent

Greece: Great Britain and the United States 90 percent, Russia 10 percent

Yugoslavia: 50–50

Hungary: 50–50

Bulgaria: 75 percent Russia, the others 25 percent

Then Churchill pushed the sheet across the table toward Stalin, who examined it, put a check mark on it, and passed it back. The matter was settled. Later, in view of the rapid advance of the Red Army, the Hungarian formula was revised, at Molotov's insistence, to 75–25 and the Bulgarian to 80–20, both in the Soviet favor.[6]

While the Russians were ready to negotiate at Yalta from a position of strength, the Western powers were inhibited not only by

the temporary stalemate in Europe, but also by uncertainties in the Far Eastern theater of war. On the way to the Crimea, President Roosevelt had been informed by the Pentagon that an invasion of the Japanese home islands "might be expected to cost over a million casualties to American forces alone." When Roosevelt met Churchill on the island of Malta en route to Yalta, the President expressed his fear that the war against Japan "might continue until 1947." The Yalta decisions pertaining to both Poland and China were largely influenced by these grossly exaggerated apprehensions.

The Yalta Conference took place in two palaces that had formerly belonged to Tsar Nicholas II and his cousin Prince Yusupov, Rasputin's assassin. The Yalta Conference acknowledged the Churchill–Stalin deal of October 1944 and resulted in a common understanding for enforcing the unconditional surrender of Germany and its occupation by the three Great Powers—the Soviet Union, the United States, and Great Britain. (France was allowed to share in the allied occupation regime only after the war.) Germany was to be disarmed, its war industries dismantled, and its general staff abolished. German society was to be de-Nazified. Those responsible for war crimes were to be tried and punished. The Germans were to pay reparations to the victorious powers. For ceding nearly half of its pre-war territory to the Soviet Union, Poland was to be compensated with the southwestern slice of East Prussia and with territories east of the Oder-Neisse line.

The Yalta agreement also contained a provision concerning the terms under which the USSR would enter the war against Japan. The entry was to be carried out no later than three months after the end of the war in Europe. In exchange Stalin was assured of generous benefits. The status quo in Outer Mongolia, formerly a segment of China but by then a full-scale satellite of the USSR, was to be maintained. Southern Sakhalin, lost to Japan in 1905, was to be restored to Russia; the Kurile Islands, never a Russian possession, were added for good

---

[6] Winston S. Churchill, *Triumph and Tragedy* (Boston: Houghton Mifflin Company, 1962), p. 197.

Generalissimo Stalin and Prime Minister Churchill at the Yalta Conference

measure. The Chinese port of Dairen (Dalny) was to be internationalized, and Soviet interests there were to be recognized as preeminent. China was also to be persuaded to lease to the USSR a naval base in Port Arthur, and the Chinese-Eastern and Southern Manchurian railroads were to be jointly operated by a Soviet-Chinese company.

At Yalta the Russians were ready to pursue a coordinated Big Three policy in China; they forgot all about their Chinese comrades and were ready to accept the regime of their erstwhile mortal foe, Generalissimo Chiang Kai-shek. Molotov went so far as to declare that the Soviet Union was disinterested in the fate of the party led by Mao Tse-tung, who was not a Communist anyway, but an "agrarian reformer." At Yalta the Chinese allies, whether Communist or not, were treated like the Poles—

without their consultation, behind their backs, a bargain benefiting Russia was struck at their expense.

From Yalta the Big Three issued the "Declaration on Liberated Europe." Invoking the Atlantic Charter, the declaration announced that in any country "where in their judgment conditions require," the Soviet Union, the United States, and Great Britain would "jointly assist" the people concerned to establish domestic peace, to set up "interim governmental authorities broadly representative of all democratic elements," and to hold free elections. The declaration made no distinction between the allied countries—Poland, Czechoslovakia, Yugoslavia, and Greece—and the enemies—Germany, Italy, and their satellites, Hungary, Romania, and Bulgaria. Since the October 1944 deal between Churchill and Stalin made Western influence in Eastern

Europe vestigial in nature, the declaration was merely a face-saving device that resulted in handing over East Central Europe to Soviet hegemonial power. What was outlined at Teheran was more specifically spelled out and confirmed at Yalta.

GERMAN CAPITULATION AND THE POTSDAM CONFERENCE

The last great battle of World War II in Europe, the storming of Berlin, started on April 16, 1945, from the bridgehead on the River Oder. It was forced by the armies of Marshal Zhukov. At the same time Marshal Ivan Koniev's troops, after capturing Vienna and Prague, swept toward the German capital from the south. The Western Allies were also pushing toward Berlin from the west. On April 25, a United States patrol from the 96th Division met a Soviet horseman at the river Elbe. Later on the same day another American patrol made its way across the damaged bridge over the Elbe at Torgau. There the GIs met and briefly fraternized and drank toasts with a group of Red Army men. On May 2 came the capture of Berlin by Soviet troops. The Germans capitulated on May 8. Hitler had committed suicide in his underground bunker on April 30.

While preparing for another top-level interallied conference and yet another campaign in the Far East, Stalin staged a great victory parade in Moscow's Red Square at which over two hundred captured German banners were thrown at the feet of the triumphant Generalissimo. From then on he was to be honored as a great, progressive statesman and mankind's most brilliant military leader. It was at the lavish reception at the Kremlin following the parade that Stalin drank his toast to "the leading nation" of the USSR, the Great Russian people, whom he feted as "remarkable for its clear mind, its patience and its firm character." This singling out of one out of over one hundred Soviet ethnic groups by the leader of a Party dedicated to the "Leninist principle of proletarian internationalism" and equality marked another step along the line that had been initiated during the 1930s and was to be continued after the war.

Moscow, June 24, 1945. The Victory Parade on the Red Square. Standards and banners of the German Army thrown at the feet of Stalin

The end of the hostilities in Europe was followed by the last summit meeting of World War II. Potsdam, a small garrison town in the Soviet sector and a symbol of Prussian militarism, was decided on because no suitable premises could be found in the vast, once proud, but now devastated German capital. The most logical choice, Hitler's Chancellery, was no more; the triumphant Russians had razed it to the ground. The area was covered with sod, leaving a grassy mount where rats and rabbits roamed over the symbol of the Nazi Reich that was to have lasted for a thousand years.

The Potsdam Conference (July 17–August 2, 1945) revealed once more the brittleness of the wartime alliance. Mutual distrust resulting from different philosophies and postwar objectives was surfacing more and more. Aware of this, Stalin, always a meticulous planner, tried to arrange every detail so as to preserve the partnership that had contributed to his weathering the storm. He still hoped to persuade his allies to resume lend-lease supplies to his war-ravaged country and finance its reconstruction with Western credit. After inspecting the hall in which the deliberations of the Big Three were to take place, he immediately ordered that the ceiling, which depicted a sailing ship surmounted by a dark cloud, be redecorated. Sensing an ill omen, the Soviet host ordered a star, a symbol common to the heraldry of both the Soviet Union and the United States, to be painted shining over the ship.

Despite these efforts, the divergent interests of Soviet Russia and the Western powers cropped up at every step. President Roosevelt had died in the interim, and Winston Churchill was at Potsdam only until his defeat in the British parliamentary election of July 28. This left Stalin as the only veteran. Faced by two novices in international affairs—President Harry Truman and the head of the new Labor government, Clement Attlee—Stalin proved more than ever that he was the most clearsighted, consistent, and determined of all the wartime Allied leaders.

The main task of the Potsdam Conference was to establish the frontiers and the occupation regime of the defeated Germany. The country was split: the Elbe valley, Upper Saxony, and all of Thuringia were to be occupied by Soviet troops; the area to the west was to be shared by the United States, Britain, and later on France. Berlin was to be jointly occupied by the four powers, and the economic policy to be applied to all zones of the Allied occupation was to be collectively determined. After having made the gesture of consulting with the representative of the new, Communist-dominated Warsaw regime, the Big Three decided that lands east of the Oder–Western Neisse rivers were to be put "under the administration of the Polish State" "pending final delimitation" at the future peace conference. The two million Germans remaining in this area were to be transferred to the Soviet and Western occupation zones. The Allies put at Polish disposal enough transport facilities to carry out this operation as quickly as possible.

By this time, after the withdrawal of Hitler's troops from Czechoslovakia, the Czechs had expelled practically all the Germans, numbering some 3 million people, from the Sudetenland. Since, at the same time, numerous although more limited deportations of Germans had taken place in Romania, Yugoslavia, and Hungary, the ethnic map of Eastern Europe, now under Soviet hegemony, had undergone a further radical change. To Hitler's extermination of the Jews was now added the expulsion of most Germans. By sponsoring the transfer of the Germans as well as by encouraging their Polish allies to push their boundaries as far to the west as possible, the Russians achieved three interlocked objectives: first, they reduced the territorial base of their potential future enemy, Germany; second, they denied as much land and as many resources as possible to the Western powers; third, they supported their control over the heart of the former Reich by a broad belt of buffer states that depended on Soviet Russia in various ways. All this was backed by stationing a powerful army between the Elbe and the Oder.

JAPAN'S SURRENDER
AND THE END OF WORLD WAR II

Before the Big Three finished with the German problem, they had to deal with another partner in the Axis triangle. In the summer of 1945, Japan was still fighting a bloody delaying action both on the Asian mainland and on the Pacific islands. On July 26 the Big Three issued a declaration threatening Japan with annihilation unless Tokyo surrendered unconditionally and immediately. On July 27 the Tokyo government rejected the Potsdam declaration and reaffirmed its resolution to continue the war to the bitter end. As a consequence, President Truman ordered the first atom bomb to be dropped on the naval and military base of Hiroshima on August 6. This resulted in 135,000 casualties (66,000 killed and 69,000 wounded) and the utter destruction of three-fifths of the city. When the Japanese continued to fight, another bomb was dropped a few days later on another city, Nagasaki.

On August 9, meanwhile, the USSR had launched its land offensive, fulfilling its earlier promises. Within ten days the Soviet Far Eastern force, about one and a half million men, smashed the Japanese Kwantung army in Manchuria. Pursuing the retreating forces, the Red Army entered northern China and Korea. The devastating results of the first military application of nuclear weapons had shattered Japanese morale. On August 14, Tokyo accepted the Potsdam declaration and asked for peace. On September 2, 1945, General Douglas MacArthur, accompanied by Soviet representatives, accepted Japan's capitulation on the deck of the *Missouri*, which was anchored in Tokyo Bay. World War II was over.

At the time of the armistice the Soviet troops pursuing the Japanese in Korea had reached, roughly speaking, the 38th parallel; it was then designated as the demarcation line between the American and Russian occupation zones. While Korea, like Germany, was split between its Communist-dominated and American-controlled parts along the 38th parallel, another great prize of World War II, Japan, avoided division because of Washington's stubborn opposition. As in the case of another Axis partner, Italy, no Soviet soldiers were admitted on Japanese soil. Despite Soviet protests, Japan remained a United States preserve. This became another bone of contention between the two superpowers and contributed to the mounting tensions. Without the integrating pressures of wartime necessity, the facade of Allied unity was disintegrating very fast. Nevertheless, despite its short and largely superfluous contribution to the Far Eastern war, the USSR obtained practically everything it had been promised at Yalta and Potsdam, which more than reversed the 1905 settlement at Portsmouth.

There was no peace treaty at the end of World War II. To negotiate one was impossible because of the divergent objectives of the Big Three powers. Germany and Japan were the great prizes of World War II, and the problem of who would control their territories and resources began to overshadow most other issues.

SUGGESTED READING

ANDERS, WLADYSLAW, *Hitler's Defeat in Russia.* Chicago: Regnery, 1953.

ARMSTRONG, JOHN A., *Ukrainian Nationalism, 1939–1945.* New York: Columbia University Press, 1955.

———, ed., *The Soviet Partisans in World War II.* Madison: University of Wisconsin Press, 1964.

BIALER, SEWERYN, ed., *Stalin and His Generals: Soviet Military Memoirs of World War II.* New York: Praeger, 1969.

CHUIKOV, VASILI I., *The Battle for Stalingrad.* New York: Holt, Rinehart and Winston, 1964.

————, *The End of the Third Reich.* London: Macgibbon & Kee, 1967.

CIECHANOWSKI, JAN, *The Warsaw Rising of 1944.* New York: Cambridge University Press, 1974.

CLARK, ALAN, *Barbarossa: The Russian-German Conflict, 1941–1945.* New York: Morrow, 1965.

CLEMENS, DIANE SHAVER, *Yalta.* New York: Oxford University Press, 1970.

CONQUEST, ROBERT, *The Nation Killers: Soviet Deportation of Nationalities.* New York: Macmillan, 1970.

COOPER, MATTHEW, *The Nazi War against Soviet Partisans, 1941–1944.* New York: Stein and Day, 1979.

CURTISS, JOHN S., *The Russian Church and the Soviet State, 1917–1950.* Boston: Little, Brown, 1953.

DALLIN, ALEXANDER, *German Rule in Russia, 1941–1945.* New York: Macmillan, 1957.

DEANE, JOHN R., *The Strange Alliance.* New York: Viking, 1947.

DJILAS, MILOVAN, *Conversations with Stalin.* New York: Harcourt Brace Jovanovich, 1956.

DMYTRYSHYN, BASIL, *Moscow and the Ukraine, 1918–1953.* New York: Bookman, 1956.

DZIEWANOWSKI, M. K., *The Communist Party of Poland* (2nd ed.). Cambridge, Mass.: Harvard University Press, 1976.

ERICKSON, JOHN, *The Road to Stalingrad.* London: Weidenfeld and Nicolson, 1975. New York: Harper & Row, 1975.

————, *The Road to Berlin.* Boulder, Colo.: Westview Press, 1983.

————, *The Soviet High Command.* New York: St. Martin's Press, 1962.

FEIS, HERBERT, *Between War and Peace: The Potsdam Conference.* Princeton, N.J.: Princeton University Press, 1960.

————, *Churchill, Roosevelt and Stalin: The War They Waged and the Peace They Sought.* Princeton, N.J.: Princeton University Press, 1957.

FISCHER, GEORGE, *Soviet Opposition to Stalin.* Westport, Conn.: Greenwood, 1952.

GOURÉ, LEON, *The Siege of Leningrad.* Stanford, Calif.: Stanford University Press, 1962.

HERRING, GEORGE, C., JR., *Aid to Russia, 1941–1946.* New York: Columbia University Press, 1973.

KOLARZ, WALTER, *Russia and Her Colonies.* Hamden, Conn.: Shoe String, 1967.

KORIAKOV, MIKHAIL, *I'll Never Go Back, A Red Army Officer Talks,* trans. Nicholas Wreden. New York: Dutton, 1948.

LIDDELL-HART, BASIL H., *The Soviet Army 1946 to the Present.* Gloucester, Mass.: Peter Smith, 1956.

————, *History of the Second World War.* New York: Putnam, 1971.

NEKRICH, ALEXANDER M., *June 22, 1941: Soviet Historians and the German Invasion.* Columbia: University of South Carolina Press, 1968.

————, *The Punished Peoples: The Deportation and Fate of Soviet Minorities at the End of the Second World War,* tran. George Saunders. New York: Norton, 1978.

PAVLOV, DMITRI V., *Leningrad, Nineteen Hundred Forty One: The Blockade,* trans. John C. Adams. Chicago: University of Chicago Press, 1965.

ROZEK, EDWARD J., *Allied Wartime Diplomacy: A Pattern in Poland.* New York: Wiley, 1958.

SALISBURY, HARRISON E., *The 900 Days: The Siege of Leningrad.* New York: Harper & Row, 1969.

SEATON, ALBERT, *The Russo-German War, 1941–1945.* New York: Praeger, 1970.

VARDYS, STANLEY, ed., *Lithuania under the Soviets.* New York: Praeger, 1965.

WERTH, ALEXANDER, *Russia at War, 1941–1945* (4th ed.). New York: Dutton, 1964.

ZAWODNY, J. K., *Nothing But Honour: The Story of the Warsaw Uprising, 1944.* Stanford, Cal.: Hoover Institution, 1978.

ZHUKOV, GEORGI K., *Marshal Zhukov's Greatest Battles,* edited with an Introduction and Explanatory Comments by Harrison E. Salisbury; trans. Theodore Shabad. New York: Harper & Row, 1969.

CHAPTER 19

The Aftermath of the War: Rehabilitation and Retrenchment

The outcome of the war revolutionized the geopolitical situation of the world. Because of the USSR's paramount military and naval might, the Baltic Sea became almost a Soviet lake. In East Central Europe and in the Balkans, the Soviet Union was now the dominant force; in the Far East, because of Japan's crushing defeat and the continuing civil war in China, Moscow's position was also paramount. With the exception of Finland and Central Poland, the USSR had directly incorporated all the land that had ever belonged to the Tsarist Empire. In the cases of the northern segment of former East Prussia, Galicia, Northern Bukovina, and Carpathian Ruthenia (which Czechoslovakia had been compelled to relinquish), Stalin went beyond the old imperial borders. The incorporation of the last three provinces finally gathered all the Ukrainian-speaking people under Soviet rule. The grand total of Soviet territorial acquisitions amounted to 265,850 square miles with a population of 23,477,000. In addition to these direct gains, Moscow extended its writ over a large slice of Germany, plus Poland, Czechoslovakia, Hungary, Romania, Yugoslavia, Bulgaria, and Albania in Europe; and Northern Korea and Outer Mongolia in Asia. All these states, numbering some 120,000,000 inhabitants, were now clients of the Kremlin.

In terms of the sheer increment of material power and prestige, the outcome of World War II brought to the Soviet Union gains without parallel in modern history and made the USSR into one of the two global superpowers. Yet even this unprecedented triumph did not satisfy Stalin. When Averell Harriman, then the United States Ambassador in Berlin, asked him whether he was happy now that his soldiers were in Berlin, the Soviet dictator answered wistfully, "Yes, but those of Alexander I were also in Paris."

REHABILITATION
AND RECOMPRESSION

Despite these unprecedented gains the USSR, while it had achieved great prestige, was economically exhausted by the autumn of 1945. Its war damages were staggering. The population losses, if one counts the decline in the birth rate caused by the hostilities, may be estimated at from twenty-five to thirty million. The USSR accounted for more than half the direct loss of life in the European theater of war. The Soviets lost nearly one hundred times as many lives as did the Americans, who lost 292,100. Most of the western and southwestern provinces of the USSR were in ruins. Some 1,700 towns and cities and 70,000 villages were either razed to the ground or severely damaged. So were about 35,000 plants and factories and over 6,000,000 buildings of all sorts, while nearly 25,000,000 people were left homeless. By 1945, about a quarter of the capital assets of Soviet industry had been destroyed, and industrial production had dropped by about 30 percent as compared with 1940. Starvation was rampant and cases of cannibalism not infrequent. Yet the spirit of the people was unbroken; they set out to rebuild their war-ravaged country, their numerous disappointments notwithstanding.

The reconstruction plan was based on the theory that the Communist institutions had passed the grim test of the war with flying colors and should now be consolidated. All vestigial, whispered criticism of the regime was therefore once again silenced and regarded as treason. Any notion of economic reform was rejected by Stalin. At the close of the war he emerged not only in his restored glory as the wise teacher and most far-sighted statesman, but also as the Generalissimo, the organizer of victory, and the greatest military leader of all time. The cult of personality was revived and even intensified. A monumental, multivolume history of the "Great Patriotic War" commissioned by Stalin attributed to him a masterful plan of luring the invaders deep into the territory of the USSR to destroy them more thoroughly. The chief hero of the "Great Patriotic War," the man responsible for the victories of Moscow, Stalingrad, Kursk, and Berlin, Marshal Zhukov, was soon relegated to a provincial command and then compelled to retire. The triumph was to be attributed solely to the Communist system, masterfully orchestrated by the greatest statesman and leader of all time.

Immediately after the war Stalin proceeded to reassert the shaken political controls. Security measures were always his first priority. As a historically minded man, Stalin remembered that political agitation had almost invariably followed foreign wars. The Decembrist revolt of 1825 was a distant echo of the Napoleonic campaigns and the wide-ranging presence of Russian soldiers in Europe. The Great Reforms of the 1860s were largely a result of the Crimean War. The 'revolutionary populism of the 1880s was attributable to some extent to the Russo-Turkish War of 1877–1878. The connection between the revolutions of 1905 and 1917 and the two wars that had preceded them was a part of Stalin's own life experience. He was aware of how much the dislocations resulting from the German invasion had contributed to the relaxation of political control over the fluid, shifting, and hence unmanageable population. He was also aware of the ferment generated by the soldiers, forced laborers, and former POWs now returning from the West. To prevent this, to reimpose the old controls over those that had strayed, now became Stalin's paramount task. The returning POWs and Soviet laborers from the West had to go through reindoctrination camps, and many of them did not escape deportation either. The former soldiers of the Russian Liberation Army of General Vlasov were punished with the usual severity; Vlasov himself was hanged.

During the war some ethnic and social groups that were suspected of potential disloyalty had already been deprived of their meager autonomy and moved to distant locations. Of these the most important group was the Volga Germans, who were deported in the summer of 1941 to Central Asia, and dispersed there. Between October 1943 and May 1944, six other ethnic groups were driven out of their original locations as punishment for alleged wholesale collaboration with the Germans. Among these groups were the Crimean Tatars, the Kalmyks of the lower Volga, and four North Caucasian peoples: Chechens, Ingush, Karachay, and Balkars. These hasty deportations, which affected 1,250,000 men, women, and children, were extremely costly in human lives.

After the war the restless Ukrainians were next on Stalin's list, but as he admitted frankly to his then close co-worker, Secretary of the Ukrainian Communist Party Nikita S. Khrushchev, there were not

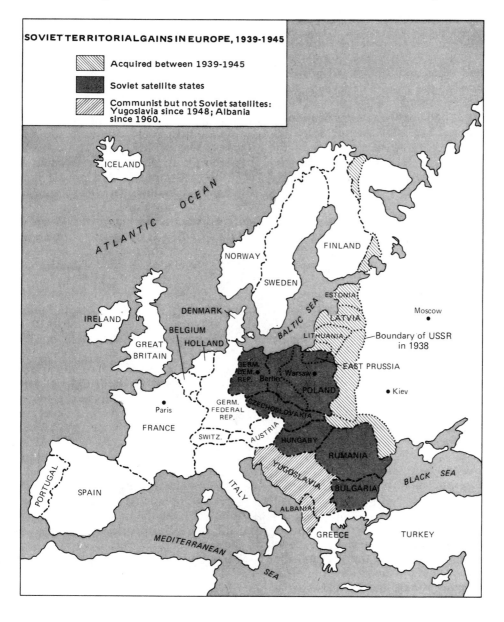

SOVIET TERRITORIAL GAINS IN EUROPE, 1939-1945

Acquired between 1939-1945

Soviet satellite states

Communist but not Soviet satellites: Yugoslavia since 1948; Albania since 1960.

enough trains in the whole USSR to deport 40 million people from their homeland to the wastes of Central Asia and Siberia. Nevertheless, the reprisals against Ukrainian collaborators and anti-Soviet partisans were massive and extraordinarily harsh. Eastern Galicia, Northern Bukovina, and Carpathian Ruthenia, which formerly belonged to Poland, Romania, and Czechoslovakia respectively, had been the mainstay of the Greek Catholic (Uniate) Church that united fidelity to the Greek Orthodox liturgy with allegiance to the Pope. Fearing this foreign connection, Stalin ordered an enforced merger of the Uniate Church with the Orthodox Church of the USSR. Surprisingly enough, the outwardly atheistic Soviet State threw all of its authority behind the proselytizing activities of the Orthodox clergy, which was mostly Great Russian. The largely recalcitrant Greek Catholic, or Uniate hierarchy, was arrested and deported, while church property was confiscated or handed over to the Orthodox clergy. At the same time the familiar Soviet institutions, including land collectivization, were promptly extended to all the newly incorporated territories. Although the terrible terror of the Great Purge period never returned in its full fury, the cumulative effect of all the retrenchment measures amounted to the reimposition of the old iron corset on the entire, vast, and now greatly expanded USSR.

ECONOMIC REFORMS AND THE FOURTH FIVE-YEAR PLAN

Soviet Russia's postwar economic situation was in shambles and called for radical rehabilitation measures. The war had been largely financed by printing paper rubles, great quantities of which found their way into the countryside in payment for extremely scarce produce. The money was usually kept by the peasants not in the form of savings accounts but in their coffers and mattresses. Stalin was determined to cut down the supply of money while increasing the supply of labor. In 1947 the people were

ordered to exchange ten old rubles against one new ruble. This 1,000 percent devaluation had a double effect: it at once wiped out wartime cash savings and encouraged persons who were idle to re-enter the labor market. Both consequences affected mostly the rural population. The extensive process of illegal land seizure by the peasants, who during the wartime relaxation of controls in the countryside had tended to enlarge their private plots at the expense of the collective land, was stopped and then reversed. In the summer of 1946 the authorities enforced severe measures to combat the wartime laxity that prevailed in many factories and on collective and State farms. "Labor discipline" was strictly enforced again. Absenteeism and similar offenses were to be severely punished as of old. To tighten political controls and increase administrative efficiency, many collective farms were merged; two, three, or four of them were pooled and reorganized around what became known as "agrarian towns" (*agrogoroda* in Russian). These operations were carried out under

Nikita S. Khrushchev

the supervision of rising Politburo member Nikita S. Khrushchev.

The magnitude of the war damage was such that it soon became obvious that some form of outside aid had to be considered, even by the autarkic-minded Stalin. The lend-lease deliveries had been discontinued in the spring of 1945 and the Marshall Plan was rejected by Stalin as politically too dangerous; moreover, any hope for foreign loans was fast fading because of the cold war. Consequently, war booty, reparations, tribute in cash, and forced delivery of goods from the satellite countries, plus ruthless mobilization of all native resources remainded the immediate instruments of the country's rehabilitation. Combined with patriotic exhortations, extremely severe measures proved on the whole successful, and the rehabilitation of the ravaged country proceeded at a faster pace than had been expected by Western economists. Later, a series of highly advantageous trade agreements and other economic arrangements (such as joint stock companies) between Moscow and its client states of East Central Europe were to augment the reparations and help to make Soviet reconstruction a success. Its symbol was the Fourth Five-Year Plan, launched in 1946 and expected to end in 1950. Its purpose was to make up for the losses suffered during the hostilities, and to exceed the 1940 economic level. The Fourth Five-Year Plan followed the well-established tradition of focusing on heavy industry, while again grossly neglecting agriculture and consumer goods. The highly centralized prewar command economy was soon restored and even reinforced. The emphasis was again on quantity and not on quality, on more rather than better. During the late 1940s, many Soviet people, hoping for a brighter future, worked with a dogged determination reminiscent of their wartime exertions. The industrial targets were achieved, and in 1950 the output of heavy industry doubled. At the same time, agriculture, saddled with compulsory deliveries, lagged behind; it did not exceed the 1940 level until 1959, and then only by 7 percent.

THE ANTI-WESTERN CAMPAIGN

By 1945, after one of the great victories of all time, the veterans of Stalingrad, Kursk, and Berlin were longing for a respite from their exertions. Their lingering hopes for a fuller, freer, and more prosperous life were shattered by Stalin's radio address of February 9, 1946. In this speech, Stalin extolled the virtues of the Soviet system and proclaimed a program of austerity, hard work, and discipline. He attributed World War II to the political and socioeconomic forces behind Western monopoly capitalism. Quoting Leninist doctrine, Stalin pointed out that "the capitalistic system of world economy conceals elements of crisis and war" and that "the development of world capitalism does not follow a steady and even course forward, but proceeds through crises and catastrophes." Stalin stressed that "so long as capitalism existed, the world would not be free from the threat of war." His conclusion was that while the war against Fascism was over, the danger of a clash with the Western capitalists and imperialists was ever-present. Therefore, the Soviet people should be ready to make more sacrifices and face new dangers.

Stalin's appeal for vigilance was put into practice immediately. Soon there began a full-blown campaign against cultural and intellectual "rootless cosmopolitans." The term was broadly used to describe those who tended to glorify Western ideas and ways. Slogans like "toadying to the West" often appeared in newspaper headlines. The Museum of Modern Western Art was closed to the public. Books by contemporary Western authors were denounced as "seditious" and "subversive," while jazz was banned. Many intellectuals were arrested and the more independent professors were removed from their chairs, often on the basis of student denunciations that had been officially encouraged. "Socialist realism" was reimposed as the prescribed norm of artistic creativity.

The anti-Western drive was conducted under another close co-worker of Stalin's, Andrei A. Zhdanov, a man who in 1934 had

Andrei A. Zhdanov

replaced Kirov as head of the Leningrad Party district and now emerged as the dictator's heir apparent. In the sphere of culture he ruled supreme. He sharply criticized three of the best Soviet composers—Sergei Prokofiev, Dmitri Shostakovich, and Aram Khatchaturian—for "formalistic deformations" and "encouraging antidemocratic tendencies in contemporary Soviet music." Their work, thundered Zhdanov, reflected "too closely the spirit of the modern bourgeois music of Europe and America." In such an atmosphere, original creativity was stifled. When an American journalist was told by a leading Soviet poet and novelist, Boris Pasternak, that he was engaged exclusively in translating foreign writers—mainly Shakespeare—the American asked him, "Aren't you writing anything original?" Pasternak replied, "Writing original works *these days?* One would have to be crazy . . . !"

ANTI-ZIONIST DRIVE

Under Zhdanov's supervision the Soviet authorities radically switched their previously benevolent attitude toward the surviving Jewish population of some 2 million people. This was officially justified by many considerations. One was that there had been a large number of defections to the West by Red Army soldiers of Jewish extraction stationed in the Soviet zone of occupation. Also, Stalin came to believe that many of those who had been active on behalf of the USSR in organizing the Jewish international assistance during the war in the West, especially in the United States, had established secret links abroad. Stalin's suspicion of foreign espionage and subversion was thus further aroused. Consequently, he ordered the removal of Jews from most positions of power, especially from jobs involving security matters. Another reason for official encouragement of anti-Semitism, camouflaged by the less offensive term "anti-Zionism," was the regime's desire to divert away from itself the growing popular resentment against the austerity measures and the tightening of political controls.

The factor that finally made Stalin launch an open, massive "anti-Zionist" campaign was the establishment of the State of Israel in the spring of 1948. Initially, nothing seemed to forecast such a negative attitude on the part of the Soviet dictator. In 1946–1947, Stalin supported the Jewish struggle against the British mandate, which he saw as a form of colonialism or imperialism, hence the generous Soviet supply of weapons to the Israelis as long as they were fighting the British rule in Palestine. When the State of Israel was established, the USSR was the first to recognize it *de jure*. Moreover, hoping that Israel, largely founded by Russian Jews of radical socialist proclivities, would turn to Moscow for guidance, Stalin continued his material and diplomatic assistance for a time. However, he was soon disappointed by the Israeli government, which leaned more and more heavily on the West, especially on the United States.

The final blow was the enthusiastic greeting extended to the first Israeli ambassador in Moscow, Golda Meir. The sight of Soviet Jews openly manifesting their devotion to a foreign envoy angered Stalin and made him launch a thorough and often vicious purge of the Jewish cultural institutions and other organizations still tolerated by the State. From then on, Jews were purged from most responsible posts in the Party and governmental apparatus. Jewish cultural life suffered cruel losses because of the widespread arrests of leading intellectuals and professional people. Altogether the purge affected several hundred people; many of them were executed and others deported to various concentration and labor camps. In August 1948, Zhdanov, then at the peak of his prestige and power, died suddenly. Nevertheless the anti-Western, anti-Semitic, and essentially anti-intellectual campaign continued.

START OF THE COLD WAR

Theoretically, the decisions of the Teheran and Yalta summit conferences were reached by Soviet Russia, the United States, and Great Britain unanimously. But at Potsdam it was already obvious that the Soviet Union and the United States were the only survivors of the global conflict that commanded enough manpower and resources to compete in the mid-twentieth-century world. This bipolarity of power, was coupled with sharp ideological antagonism and was one of the contributing causes of a series of diplomatic clashes and military confrontations that soon came to be called the *cold war*.

The main stake of the cold war, as in the hot one, was Europe's geopolitical heartland—Germany, while in Asia it was Japan, the main industrial power of the area, and China, the world's most populous country. The signing of a peace treaty with Germany, which at Potsdam was thought to be an event that would take place in the near future, was postponed indefinitely in view of the growing differences of opinion among the victors. Germany, after satisfying the territorial claims of its neighbors, was divided into four zones of occupation between the Soviet Union, the United States, Britain, and France. Similar arrangements were carried out in Austria. The fourfold military occupation of Germany was initially intended as a temporary solution. From the Soviet point of view the stationing of the Red Army on German soil, especially in Berlin, had a double purpose. First, the USSR wanted to deny at least a segment of the German territory and resources to the West while exploiting them to the hilt for Soviet purposes. Second, it satisfied Soviet pride and prestige since it symbolized the completeness of the Russian victory.

One of the more divisive issues at Yalta was the question of postwar German reparations; it was finally settled by President Roosevelt's agreeing to an overall sum of $20 billion, of which the USSR would be entitled to half. The cessation of lend-lease and the fading hopes for an American loan made Stalin determined to squeeze the maximum in reparations out of Germany. Since the divided and devastated Germany was unable to pay in cash, the Russians immediately set about removing whatever they could in the way of capital equipment from their own zone. They wanted to extend the same policy to the Western zones in order to get their half share. When the Western powers vetoed this idea, Stalin grew increasingly restive. As early as July 1946 at the Paris Council of Foreign Ministers meeting, when American Secretary of State James Byrnes asked Molotov what the Soviet Union wanted, the reply was blunt: the $10 billion promised at Yalta.

By 1946 the Russians had repeatedly violated the Potsdam agreements. They had sealed off their occupation zone (economically as well as politically). In July, Britain and the United States had agreed on a complete economic fusion of their zones. Both the British and the Americans were supplying reparations to the USSR from their zones while also pouring money into

Germany in an attempt to set up a viable economy there. Such a state of affairs was untenable in the long run. Therefore in September 1946, when Secretary of State Byrnes spoke at Stuttgart—one of the main industrial cities of southern Germany—he confirmed the policy of suspending reparations from the American zone and denounced the plan of dismantling German industry or "pastoralizing" the country. Moreover he promised American support for German economic reconstruction. By 1947, "Bizonia"—created from the fusion of the British and American zones—was already a political and economic reality. Looking back, we can see that it was then that the foundations of the present West German state were laid. The only tangible fruit of an interallied policy in Germany was the jointly staged trial of the major Nazi war criminals at Nuremberg. Twelve defendants were sentenced to death by hanging.

The different attitudes of the two main victors of the war toward the defeated Germany were shaped by their different past experiences. During the course of the first half of the twentieth century, the Russians had suffered enormous human and material losses as a result of two German invasions. Not surprisingly, they assumed an intransigent attitude and insisted on reprisals as well as reparations. The Americans, who had not experienced the Nazi cruelties and had considerable investment in German industries, were far less vindictive, despite their revulsion toward Hitlerism.

Both main antagonists were meanwhile preparing to set up their "own" Germany as a steppingstone for the eventual unification of the country, each one hoping it would be under their exclusive guidance and supervision. The integrating steps taken by the Western powers, followed by the currency reform in their zones, were understood by Stalin to be the initial moves toward rebuilding a powerful Western Germany, a future jumping-off point in the inevitable showdown between capitalism and communism. While the Western armies had been demobilized, the Red Army remained partly on war footing and in 1947 still exceeded

its 1941 size. Throughout the years 1945–1948, the political situation in war-ravaged Western Europe was highly unstable. After the war the French and Italian Communist parties, then still fully subservient to Moscow, emerged as powerful political instruments and could be relied upon to support any Soviet move. Although Stalin never used them as such, and they even participated in the French and Italian governments until 1946, the Western fears of Communism persisted.

SOVIETIZATION OF EAST CENTRAL EUROPE

To the east and southeast of the Soviet-German zone, between the Baltic, the Adriatic, and the Black seas, stretched a belt of states which the Red Army had occupied at the closing stages of the war: Poland, Czechoslovakia, Romania, Hungary, Bulgaria, Yugoslavia, and Albania. These countries, containing altogether some 100 million people, commanded important strategic bases as well as natural resources important for the Soviet economy. Stalin regarded this area as a buffer zone that was to cushion any possible attack on the part of any future reborn and remilitarized Germany or a state allied with Germany. Consequently, he was determined to control these countries by means of "friendly" governments that would be allied with the USSR and would put their respective territories at its disposal for "guarding Soviet communication lines" with the Red Army bases in Germany. And indeed, with the baggage trains of the Red Army came teams of native Communists who, together with local politicians either sympathetic to the Soviet point of view or simply submitting to the inevitable, formed a series of popular-front type of governments termed "people's democracies."

While Yugoslavia and Albania had been freed from Axis occupation largely owing to the effort of local Communists, the other aforementioned countries were occupied by the Red Army at the end of the war. Only

Finland escaped Soviet occupation; it has remained ever since an independent country, merely allied to the USSR by a defensive treaty that obliges the Finns to stand by the Soviet Union in case of an attack coming through Finnish territory. While the Communist takeover was practically immediate in Yugoslavia, Albania, and Bulgaria, where the Communist movements had deeper native roots, the traditional monarchy in Romania and the Western-type democracy in Czechoslovakia survived for a while. The Romanian coalition government, however, was from the beginning under the thumb of the local Communists backed by the Soviet garrisons. In June 1947, the National Peasant Party was suppressed and its leader, Iuliu Maniu, sent to prison for life. King Michael was forced to abdicate and leave the country. In Hungary a coalition government of four political parties, including the

Small-holders' Party and the Social Democrats, lasted for about three years. In Poland the process of Sovietization was much shorter; after the rigged elections of February 1947, the leader of the Polish peasant Party, Stanisław Mikołajczyk, had to flee the country, which, by that time, was already a people's democracy, "a transition form between bourgeois democracy and a Soviet type of government."

The last country to succumb to undisguised Communist domination was Czechoslovakia, where the geniunely free elections of May 1946 had resulted in a government in which the Communists held key portfolios but were not in exclusive control of the entire administration and had to share power with the Social Democrats and the National Socialists. In February 1948, the Communists, blackmailing President Beneš by the threat of a Soviet invasion, as well as by using various types of domestic pressures including a general strike, compelled him to appoint a government in which the only genuine non-Communist was Jan Masaryk, son of the founder of the Czechoslovak republic. Soon, however, Masaryk died under strange circumstances, while his death was officially declared a suicide. By early 1948, while the Soviet-Yugoslav dispute was still brewing under the surface, all the countries of East Central Europe were under Moscow's control.

During this time, the process of *Sovietization*—gradual assimilation of local political, socioeconomic, and cultural patterns —was going on throughout the area at various speeds. The dosage of violence was determined by circumstances and local conditions. The general pattern, however, was clear everywhere. First, the remaining large landed estates were divided among the land-hungry peasants. On the whole the Communist agrarian reforms were conducted with an eye to eventual collectivization; the parcels of land were small and the necessary credits, implements, and cattle were not always provided. While this method neutralized the peasant masses during the crucial stages of the Communist takeover, it was also intended to demon-

The Soviet Marshal Konstantin K. Rokossovsky in the uniform of Commander-in-Chief of Poland's Armed Forces

strate the alleged absurdity of individual farming. At the same time, propaganda drives extolled "socialist farming." The collectivization process was speeded up during the 1950s. When Stalin died in March 1953, collective and State farms amounted to approximately 20 percent of all farms in Poland and Romania, 30 percent in Hungary, 43 percent in Czechoslovakia, and 62 percent in Bulgaria. These results were achieved by means of intensive agitation mixed with various degrees of what was euphemistically called "administrative pressure"—a mixture of fiscal harrassment and threats of violence. The pressure, although brutal enough, never approached the horrors of the "dekulakization" experienced by the Soviet peasantry in the early 1930s.

In a second step toward Sovietization, all banks, credit and insurance companies, and large industrial and commercial enterprises were taken over by the State, or "socialized," a euphemistic term for confiscation. Eventually, only the small service and artisan shops were left in private hands as a vestigial, barely tolerated form of private ownership, harassed by high taxes and administrative chicanery. The third part of Sovietization involved the cultural patterns of each country, which underwent intensive reshaping in order to emphasize atheistic education, socialist realism, and folklore elements in art. These last were seen as embodying people's art, as contrasted with the decadent, Westernized art of the former ruling bourgeoisie. Close cultural and trade relations were established by these countries with the USSR. In all of them the local Communist parties, each acting under a different name, were the driving force for the changes that were eventually to make the people's democracies more similar to the superior Soviet model. The Social Democratic movements were compelled to merge with the Communists.

In exchange for "Soviet fraternal aid" in "liberating" and rehabilitating their respective countries, the grateful new regimes granted generous economic concessions to the USSR, either directly or through the intermediary of "joint stock companies," which were run as a rule for the benefit of the Soviet partner. The net of reciprocal military alliances that soon linked the people's democracies with the center allowed for the stationing of Soviet garrisons on the territories of their respective countries; Yugoslavia and Czechoslovakia were so trusted that no Soviet troops were stationed there. Foreign trade was reoriented eastward. At the same time Western contacts were discouraged, if not forbidden outright.

So it was that between 1945 and 1948 the area east of the Elbe and the Adriatic became separated from the rest of Europe, not only by barbed wire fences guarded by armed sentries, but by a less tangible, but nevertheless real, psychological barrier of mistrust and even outright hostility toward things Western. Before the term "Iron Curtain" was coined by Winston Churchill in March 1946, it had already become more than a propaganda slogan.

THE BERLIN BLOCKADE AND THE TWO GERMAN STATES

While this was going on, Stalin observed the differences among the Western powers, especially the British-American and French attitutdes toward Germany, and decided to attack the West's weakest point. This was the Berlin enclave, separated from the Western powers by 110 miles of Soviet-occupied territory. Three years after the end of the war, a peace treaty still had not been signed. The territorial rearrangements in Eastern Europe, therefore, had not been recognized by the Western powers. Stalin hoped to use the vulnerability of the western enclave of Berlin to pressure the West into legitimizing the new boundaries of the Soviet Union, Poland, and East Germany. He must have seen the spring of 1948 as a propitious moment to challenge the Western position in Berlin by means of a series of combined military and political operations that would be effective, yet gradual enough so as not to warrant a nuclear response. On June 24, 1948, after months of intermittent Soviet harassment, all railroad connections to Berlin from the West were cut off by the Soviets on the ground of "technical difficulties."

Washington, while reluctant to resort to its nuclear arsenal, was inferior in conventional weapons. On the other hand, it saw in Stalin's challenge an ominous step toward ousting the Western powers from Berlin, destroying their political and military credibility, and eventually pushing them, step by step, beyond the Rhine, if not further. The Americans feared that, if the technical know-how of a united Germany were ever combined with Soviet manpower and natural resources, Soviet Russia could become a power superior to the United States. West Berlin, besides being a symbol of the victory over Hitler and of Allied rights in Germany, was also a valuable listening post, as well as a gap through which the Germans could flee to the West, thus weakening the Communist economic potential.

To prevent the creation of a dangerous aggregate of military and economic potential, Washington decided to accept the Soviet challenge. Rejecting the option of using American atom bombs, the Western Allies, led by President Truman, decided nevertheless to reassert their right of passage to the former all-German capital. An air lift was organized, chiefly with American resources, to maintain the vital supply lines and defy the Soviet land blockade. At the same time Washington initiated military consultations with most of its wartime allies in the Western hemisphere—the countries of the North Atlantic area—to organize an integrated western defense system. By April 4, 1949, the North Atlantic Treaty Organization (NATO) was established. The military potential of NATO, combined with the success of the airlift, compelled the Russians to lift the Berlin blockade and to open negotiations for new traffic regulations.

Meanwhile, during the blockade, from June 1948 to May 12, 1949, Soviet authorities had converted their zone of occupation, containing 17 million people, or less than half of the West German population, into a separate entity called the German Democratic Republic. Thus, while demonstrating Soviet inability to oust forcibly the Western powers from Germany, the Berlin blockade also contributed to laying the foundations of a separate East German state. The new state was run by a Communist party that used the name Socialist Unity Party (*Sozialistische Einheitspartei Deutschlands,* or *SED*). It was headed by a Comintern veteran, Walter Ulbricht.

PERSIA, GREECE, AND TURKEY

While these events were taking place in Central and Eastern Europe, a critical situation was unfolding in the Near and Middle East, in Iran, Turkey, and Greece. During the war Soviet Russia, Great Britain, and the United States had occupied Iran to assure oil supplies for their war machines. They all agreed to leave the Iranian territory simultaneously soon after the end of hostilities. The two Western powers complied with these conditions, but the Russians did not. They not only stayed beyond the agreed deadline, but they tried to engineer a rebellion against the government of Teheran in Azerbaijan, the northern segment of Iran adjacent to the USSR, and even set up a pro-Soviet Azerbaijani government there. Blackmailing the central Iranian authorities with this instrument of pressure, in 1946 the Russians extracted from the government a series of oil-exploitation rights in Northern Persia. The Iranian government of the 1940s was not that of the 1970s or 1980s. It seemed, therefore, that a Soviet takeover of Iran would soon follow those already accomplished in East Central Europe. Seeing their vital oil supplies threatened, the United States and Great Britain had the Soviet machinations in Iran condemned by the United Nations as an interference in the internal affairs of a member state, and threatened military action. Faced with these determined measures, Stalin backed down and ordered Soviet withdrawal from Northern Persia.

The Persian experience served as a guide for Western behavior in adjacent Turkey and in Greece. During the Italian and German occupation of Greece, the local Communists managed to organize a strong underground movement. In September 1941 a popular-front kind of coalition based on a broad understanding among most anti-Axis political groups had been established by the Communist Party of Greece, which, as the coalition's best organized and most disciplined segment, dominated the front. While fighting the Germans and the Italians, the Communists never lost sight of their ultimate objective of seizing power after the war. And indeed this almost took place in October 1944, before British forces from North Africa could intervene to install a pro-British government.

Meanwhile, Stalin acted correctly. Having conceded Greece as a Western sphere of influence, he refrained from assisting or even encouraging the Greek Communists.[1] But Stalin's Yugoslav, Bulgarian, and Albanian henchmen had no such inhibitions; they eagerly sent instructors and volunteers, weapons, and other supplies to the Greek Communist partisans. With this considerable outside aid and with a fair amount of local support, the Communist camp in Greece was gradually getting the upper hand. The British, who tried to bolster anti-Communist resistance, had been so weakened by their extraordinary war efforts from 1940 to 1945, followed by the crises in Palestine and India, that they were in no position to continue their assistance to the Greek government.

The Communist subversion of Greece was paralleled by an almost equally menacing situation in the formerly nonbelligerent Turkey. Continuing the traditional Russian attempts to obtain a foothold in the Eastern Mediterranean, soon after the war Stalin began to insist on naval and military bases in the Black Sea straits, the Bosphorus, and the Dardanelles. While the nonbelligerent Turkey was in much better shape than the war-exhausted Greece, the scope and persistence of Soviet diplomatic pressure, supported by a massive concentration of Red Army soldiers near the Turkish border, was such that Ankara's resistance to it might have crumbled if it had not been bolstered from outside. The threatening double surrender in Greece and Turkey would overnight have turned the Eastern Mediterranean into a Soviet sphere of influence, threatened the oil supplies of the Middle East, and thus undermined the whole Western position in the area.

This prospect was intolerable to President Harry Truman. In a message to the Congress on March 17, 1947, he announced the American determination to grant moral and material aid to "countries whose political stability was threatened by Communism," and asked for $400,000,000 in military and economic aid to Greece and Turkey. Moreover, he ordered military and naval advisers sent to both countries. Although the Soviet Union was not mentioned by name, the *Truman Doctrine* was obviously directed at its expansion beyond the lines agreed upon during the wartime summit conferences. The principles underlying the doctrine were applied with varying degrees of consistency throughout the period of the cold war.

The proclamation of the Truman Doctrine was merely the first step in the American global strategy of opposing Communist encroachments on the Western sphere of influence agreed upon at Yalta. In June 1947, United States Secretary of State General George C. Marshall proposed a plan of massive economic aid to Europe. The European Recovery Plan (also called the *Marshall Plan*) invited all European countries without distinction to appraise their need for help and their attitude toward

---

[1] In his war memoirs Churchill remarked that, while there was protest within Britain against the invasion of Greece, Stalin adhered faithfully to the October, 1944 agreement; during the long weeks of fighting in Greece, no reproach came from Moscow. Winston Churchill, *Triumph and Tragedy* (Boston: Houghton Mifflin Company, 1962), p. 197.

broad economic cooperation to rehabilitate the war-ravaged continent. Surprisingly enough, on June 27, 1947, Soviet Foreign Minister Molotov, then attending a conference of allied foreign ministers in Paris, expressed the USSR's qualified readiness to participate in the plan. So did the foreign ministers of Czechoslovakia and Poland on behalf of their countries. On July 2, however, Stalin reversed this stand and condemned the Marshall Plan as "an infringement on European state sovereignty." This plan, an American instrument in the global competition with Soviet Russia, constituted a momentous step in bolstering the tottering economies of Western Europe, saved them from collapse, and initiated a process not only of rehabilitation but even of dynamic expansion.

CONTAINMENT AND THE SOVIET REACTION

The Truman Doctrine and the Marshall Plan were complementary moves on the chess board of the cold war. But Western morale was still shaky and the fear of an allegedly impending "Soviet march to the Atlantic" was paralyzing economic reconstruction. To bolster Western resistance and to demonstrate American interest in defending the Western Hemisphere, Washington decided to prove its determination to confront Soviet Communism, arms in hand if necessary. On April 4, 1949, twelve Western European countries and the United States joined together to form NATO, the North Atlantic Treaty Organization. Within days, substantial American air forces were being redeployed to bases in Western Europe.[2]

The launching of the Marshall Plan and the establishment of NATO were two major

turning points of the cold war in Europe. The fact that the standard of living of the Western European workers was steadily rising—it soon exceeded its prewar level—tended to mitigate the militancy of such powerful Communist parties as those of Italy and France, and gradually compelled them to function within the democratic framework of their respective states, with no immediate hope of gaining power. Preconditions for the present-day "Eurocommunism" had been created, although its germination was retarded by the ingrained mental habits of a large part of the Western European Communist leadership, shaped in the Stalinist school of absolute obedience to the Center.

If the Truman Doctrine and the Marshall Plan created the material preconditions for West European recovery, the head of the State Department's planning staff, George Kennan, provided the theoretical framework for the new long-range United States strategy toward Soviet Russia. In a 1947 article in *Foreign Affairs* signed "Mr. X" and entitled "The Sources of Soviet Conduct," Kennan stressed that the basic antagonism between the USSR and the United States would continue, whether in the foreground or the background, until the internal nature of Soviet power is fundamentally altered. In these circumstances, Kennan suggested that the main element of future United States policy toward Soviet Russia must be patient, determined, and vigilant containment of the Soviet expansive drive.

Moscow replied to the policy of containment by two moves. On October 5, 1947, the Party press organ *Pravda* revealed that a conference of delegates of nine Communist parties (the USSR, Poland, Czechoslovakia, Hungary, Romania, Yugoslavia, Bulgaria, France, and Italy) had taken place in September in Poland and established a new coordinating body, the Communist Information Bureau (Cominform), which was to coordinate various activities of the Communist parties. Later on, in January 1949, the Soviet Union initiated the establishment of another coordinating body, the Council of

---

[2] In 1951, Greece and Turkey joined the original twelve nations and in 1955 West Germany (or the Federal Republic of Germany) was also admitted to NATO, originally headed by the General Dwight Eisenhower.

Mutual Economic Assistance (COMECON). The Council included the USSR, Poland, Czechoslovakia, Hungary, Romania, Bulgaria, and Albania. The constituent document reiterated the refusal of "the Socialist countries to submit to the dictates of the Marshall Plan," and announced their commitment to the "exchange of experience in the economic field and mutual assistance in regard to raw materials, foodstuffs, machinery and equipment. . . . " The seat of the COMECON was to be in Moscow. Conspicuous by its absence was Yugoslavia.

TITO'S YUGOSLAVIA

Among the Soviet Eastern European client states, Yugoslavia was in many respects an exception. It had been liberated in 1944, earlier than most other countries of the area, and this was largely due to the native partisan Communist-controlled forces of Marshal Broz-Tito, an old Comintern hand. The Soviet troops that did help withdrew very early, leaving the victorious partisans of Tito to establish a highly regimented Communist regime. Real power was in the hands of the Communist minority, though the fiction of a coalition was maintained. Thus, the Yugoslav people, like all other East Europeans, really had no chance to create the democratic institutions of their choosing provided for in the Yalta Declaration. The Yugoslav Communists, largely Moscow-trained, were among the most pro-Russian of the whole world movement. The cult of Stalin was fanatical and widespread. At one time one of Tito's lieutenants, Edward Kardelj, insisted that the country should become one of the constituent Soviet republics. Yet, in the end, Yugoslavia was the first country to oppose the Soviet designs to turn the country into a meek satrapy of Moscow.

To understand this paradox, one has to examine Yugoslav-Soviet relations during and immediately after the war. In 1942 and 1943, as with China, so with Yugoslavia, Stalin was much more inclined to reach a compromise with the British and Americans. He was willing to support the Yugoslav royalist *Chetniks* of Colonel Drazha Mikhailovich rather than Tito's partisans, who then constituted an unknown force. Tito's successes, against both the Axis and the Chetniks, were thus scored with largely native resources. When it became apparent that Tito, as Churchill put it, was "killing more Germans" than his rival, Mikhailovich, the Western powers were the first to extend to the Communist partisans significant support, which was only then followed by Soviet aid. The fact that Tito had won his local civil war (as Mao would do later on) by his own effort made Stalin suspicious of his independence.

After the war there were numerous clashes in Soviet-Yugoslav relations. The Russian representatives made it clear that they had orders to found such Soviet-Yugoslav joint-stock companies in Yugoslavia as would give the Soviet Union a monopoly in whole branches of industry and mining, especially tin, copper, and bauxite. The handsomely paid Soviet experts were proud and rigid; they wanted to transplant everything as it was in the Soviet Union, making no allowance for specific conditions in Yugoslavia. The camel's back was broken by Stalin's attempts to fill most of the key positions, especially in the army, the security apparatus, and the Party machine, with his agents. Seeing his newly conquered power undermined in his own bailiwick, Tito was reluctantly compelled to fight back for his own political survival and, probably, his neck. He began to cancel ruinous economic contracts and dismiss both Soviet experts and secret agents. In reply, the angry Stalin summoned a meeting of the remaining members of the newly founded Cominform to try the Yugoslav comrades as "deviationists" and "traitors." One June 28, 1948, the Cominform condemned Yugoslavia because of its "un-Marxist line on major domestic as well as foreign issues" and expelled it from that body. At the same time Stalin appealed to the Yugoslav party to overthrow Tito. The armies of the neighboring satellites—Hungary, Romania, Bulgaria, and Albania—had meanwhile been massed along the Yugoslav borders. At the peak of his power and international prestige, he was supremely self-confident and said, "It is enough for me to lift my little finger and Tito will be no more."

The Yugoslav Communists, however, with few exceptions, rallied around Tito and with remarkable tenacity resisted the Soviet political pressure, which was vigorously supported by an economic boycott and military threats. The near-totalitarian controls that Tito had established, combined with an upsurge of patriotic and anti-Soviet sentiments, allowed him to suppress the few native supporters of the Cominform. For the first time, Stalin made a frontal attack on a determined man who knew how to turn his own methods against Soviet blackmail. The skill and toughness of the Yugoslav leaders and the favorable geopolitical situation of the country, which had territorial and maritime contacts with the West, all greatly helped Tito to survive this critical period. Another vital factor was the promptness of American aid. Brushing aside ideological considerations and forgetting Tito's past provocative policies, including his confiscation of American property,

Marshal Broz-Tito

Washington decided to aid the Communist rebel and send him food, fuel, and arms. At the time of its expulsion, Yugoslavia had oil supplies left for only eight days.

Yugoslavia's expulsion from the Cominform, the first major breach in the hitherto monolithic structure of the Stalin empire in Eastern Europe, was a painful blow to Soviet prestige and to its strategic position in the Mediterranean. Communist Albania was isolated from the rest of the bloc. Moreover, Belgrade overnight became a center of attraction for many restless Communists who, despite the long years of Stalinist brainwashing, still preserved a certain independence of mind and favored autonomy of national Communist movements. Soon they began to journey to Yugoslavia in search of shelter, support, and enlightenment. This made Stalin still more angry. One of the consequences of Tito's expulsion was the tightening of police regimes in the satellite countries. All symptoms of sympathy with Tito's "national Bolshevik" views, or "Titoism," were spotted by Soviet intelligence and their local henchmen. Those Communists who were suspected of favoring the type of Communism more attuned to particular native conditions, like Laszlo Rajk in Hungary or Władysław Gomułka in Poland, were arrested. In the case of Rajk, his trial and execution soon followed. Gomułka, on the other hand, owing to a set of favorable circumstances, survived to play a crucial role in the process of political decompression that was to take place in Poland after Stalin's death in 1953.

Another result of Tito's expulsion was the defeat of the Communist guerrillas in Greece and the end of the four-year-old civil war there. Beleaguered and fighting for survival, Yugoslavia was unable to spare any more resources for the Greek partisans. Since the other two major suppliers, Bulgaria and Albania, were now busy blockading and subverting their new ideological enemy on Stalin's orders, they were also incapable of aiding the Greek Communist forces. Deprived of outside assistance, they were crushed by the superior British- and

American-trained troops of the Athens Royalist government. The survival of the rebel Yugoslavia, achieved partly thanks to American aid, constituted a major setback for Moscow in what was now a global cold war.

THE COMMUNIST VICTORY IN CHINA

According to Lenin's theory of imperialism, the last stage of capitalism must be broken in its weakest links—the colonial areas. To achieve this objective, Asian Communists, supported and encouraged by Moscow to varying degrees, played a leading role in a series of "national liberation struggles" that followed on the heels of World War II. While in Europe the cold war between the superpowers was played in conformity with certain ground rules that excluded the overt use of force, in Asia the situation was different. There pent-up socioeconomic forces intermingled with bitter anticolonial hatreds tended to form a high-explosive mixture that even Moscow found difficult to control. The native radical anticolonial forces, often materially aided by the Soviet Union, more often than not resorted to violence. While in Europe Moscow was, on the whole, not effective beyond the boundaries fixed at Teheran, Yalta, and Potsdam (Iran, Turkey, and Greece), the national liberation wars in Asia were by and large much more successful, especially in China and Indochina.

Throughout China's civil war (1946–1949), Stalin was less interested in the Chinese Communist cause than in economic and strategic advances and territorial gains. That disposition was reflected in particular in the bargain that Stalin struck with Chiang Kai-shek on Aug. 14, 1945, which legitimized the arrangements formulated at Yalta. Chiang thereby sanctioned paramount Russian influence both in Manchuria—China's most industrialized, richest province and the strategic center of Northeast Asia—and in Outer Mongolia. In exchange Stalin

agreed to do business in China only with Chiang Kai-shek's government and to facilitate the eventual restoration of Kuomintang authority in Manchuria. During the war, at Stalin's directive the Chinese Communists, led by Mao Tse-tung, had adopted a sort of truce with Chiang Kai-shek, which was to last as long as the hostilities against Japan were going on. While pursuing a policy of limited cooperation with Kuomintang forces in resisting the Japanese invasion, the Communists never abandoned their ultimate objective of expanding their territorial and political base. When the Japanese troops in the Far East surrendered in August 1945, the Big Three arranged that in China they should yield to Chiang's forces with two exceptions. Japanese forces in Manchuria and North Korea north of the 38th parallel were to capitulate to the Red Army.

Stalin repeatedly urged the Chinese Communists to disband their partisans, forget about the revolution, and join Chiang Kai-shek's government. Mao would have none of it since his basic principle was that "the seizure of power by armed force is the central task and the highest form of revolution." Fortunately for him, many Red Army commanders acting on their own did hand to the Chinese Communists much of the weaponry and equipment taken from the Japanese Kwantung Army. During the years 1946–1949, this equipment, together with superior organization, morale, and leadership, greatly helped the Chinese Communists to defeat the Kuomintang forces. They skillfully applied partisan warfare based in the countryside, where they were supported by the land-hungry peasantry. By October 1949 Mao had chased the remnants of the Kuomintang forces to Taiwan (Formosa) and a series of minor offshore islands. Thus, the most populous country in the world, comprising nearly one-fourth of humanity, was now under Communist control. Soon after they had seized power, the Chinese Communists launched a series of revolutionary socioeconomic reforms. To emulate his Soviet comrades, Mao attempted to encapsulate over two decades of Russian history into a few years.

During the first several years the new masters of China, friendless and isolated, desperately needed outside aid for their country, which had been starved and ruined by nearly four decades of civil war. Since help could come only from the USSR, Mao had to adopt a humble posture despite his grudge toward Stalin. During Mao Tse-tung's first long visit to Moscow, which lasted from mid-December 1949 to February 1950, he was treated like a poor cousin. He was given accommodations in a hotel, not in one of the palatial residences usually assigned to foreign dignitaries. He had to wait for several weeks to be received by Stalin. But in the interim he did some very tough bargaining with condescending minor Soviet officials. In exchange for a token loan of $300,000, the Soviets were allowed to retain temporarily their positions in Manchuria and the Kwantung peninsula. Moreover, joint Russian-Chinese companies, with the Russians in control, were established to exploit Sinkiang's oil and mineral resources. These arrangements were not much different from the kinds of deals Standard Oil or Shell Petroleum made with colonial chieftans. Yet the exhausted Chinese had to suffer indignities for the time being.

WARS IN KOREA AND INDOCHINA

Korea was another Asian front in the cold war. In December 1945, some four months after Japan's surrender, a joint Soviet–United States commission tried to establish a provisional government for the whole country, but the plans never materialized. The Soviet military authorities, who controlled the area north of the 38th parallel, never permitted the commission to set foot on their territory. By February 1946 they were sponsoring their own North Korean government, headed by a Moscow-trained Communist, Kim Il Sung. In view of this American authorities in the South decided to establish their own client administration. Thus Korea was divided into two segments along the 38th parallel, and like Germany, each was organized along different, mutually exclusive, and antagonistic principles. By June 1949 both protecting powers, believing that their tasks were finished, withdrew their forces—the Americans to Japan, and the Russians to their Siberian and Manchurian bases.

For a year the situation seemed to be stabilizing. Stalin repeatedly sought to participate in the occupation and postwar control of Japan, no doubt anticipating the role it would eventually play in Asia. Frustrated in this endeavor by Washington, he encouraged Kim Il Sung to absorb South Korea and the Chinese to help him. Stalin most probably calculated that a united Communist Korea would affect the Asian balance of power, but especially the still fluid situation in Japan. And indeed on June 25, 1950, following a speech by United States Secretary of State Dean Acheson, who had failed to mention South Korea as a part of the American defense perimeter in Asia, the Soviet-trained and equipped North Korean forces invaded South Korea without any provocation. Soon most of South Korea was captured.

In reply to this attack, President Truman ordered the American Armed Forces in the Pacific to come to the aid of South Korea. At the same time he submitted the case of the North Korean aggression to the United Nations Security Council. It happened that at that time the Soviet delegate was absent from the Council because he had walked out in protest at the refusal of the United Nations to admit Communist China to the United Nations. Therefore, the USSR could not exercise its absolute veto power to block the Council's resolution condemning North Korea and ordering United Nations members to aid in resisting the aggression. Many countries responded and supported efforts by the United States, whose forces were commanded by General Douglas MacArthur, to check the progress of the invasion.

By the end of the year, the North Koreans had been repulsed as far as the Yalu River, which forms the Korean-Chinese frontier. China responded to the possible security threat by sending in some 200,000 "volunteers." Together with the regrouped North Korean forces, the Communist forces regained most of the land and even re-crossed the 38th parallel. By July 1951, truce negotiations were opened at Panmunjon. For two years the negotiations dragged on because of the controversial problem posed by the Korean and Chinese POWs. While the Western side wanted the voluntary principle to govern their repatriation, the Communist representatives insisted that they be sent back home without asking them about their preferences.

As the events in China and Korea were unfolding, still another cold-war front was taking shape in a former French colony, Indochina. There French rule lasted until May 1945, when the Japanese decided to occupy Indochina militarily, only three months before their own capitulation. This brief overthrow of the French colonial rule brought to the surface the native anti-Japanese, as well as anti-French, resistance movement led by a Paris-educated intellectual, Ho Chi Minh. In accordance with the armistice agreement, Kuomintang Chinese troops took over Northern Indochina, which was a former dependency of Peking. Chiang Kai-shek, who opposed the restoration of French rule, generally cooperated in this task with Ho's partisans. While in Southern Indochina the British forces handed over their administration to the returning French colonial authorities, Chiang's reluctance to let the French officials in allowed Ho to consolidate his hold on the countryside and form a popular-front government. By February 1946, when the Chinese finally did allow the French to return to Northern Indochina, Ho was already well-established, someone to be reckoned with. Soon numerous points of friction between the conservative bureaucracy—which was most interested in protecting the French economic interests and those of the

local landowners—and Ho's revolutionary movement resulted in a series of clashes between the French troops and the local partisans. By the end of 1946, the country was in a state of civil war. The first stage of this conflict was to last for eight years, end with a French withdrawal, and lead to numerous complications affecting the relations between Moscow, Peking, and Washington.

STALIN AND THE AMERICAN NUCLEAR MONOPOLY

The Soviet-sponsored invasion of South Korea that followed the Berlin blockade, the formation of a militarized Marxist East German state, and the spectacular triumph of the Communists in China alarmed the West. Moscow's influence in the world seemed to be at its peak. Washington interpreted the North Korean attack not in the local Asian context, but as an indication of escalated Soviet militancy stimulated by their newly acquired atomic weapons. By the mid-1950s, American leaders came to suspect that the pattern of the Korean "aggression by proxy" might be repeated to unite Germany under Communist rule. The aroused American sense of global insecurity precipitated Washington's decision to rearm the Federal Republic of Germany and strengthen Japanese defenses by the formation of a native territorial army. At the same time, the program of American rearmament at home was speeded up to cope with new prospective tasks and multiplying military commitments. This in turn further intensified the already formidable tension prevailing between the two superpowers and their respective allies and clients. By the early 1950s, the United States had acquired an enormous arsenal of offensive weapons, both nuclear and conventional, which were deployed at home, in Europe, in East Asia, and on the high seas in such a way as to be able to attack and destroy almost any other country on earth. On the basis of capability if not intent, the United States was perceived by Stalin as a threat to the USSR. It was during the 1950s that the cold war entered its most intense phase.

One factor seems particularly responsible for the successful containment of the intermittent Soviet encroachment on the Western sphere of influence in Europe and the Middle East (Berlin, Iran, Turkey). This factor was the initial monopoly of nuclear weapons by the West, especially the United States. Stalin learned about the terrible efficiency of the atom bomb while at the Potsdam Conference. It was no coincidence that ten days after Hiroshima and Nagasaki the Gosplan was instructed to go full speed ahead with incorporating many hydraulic projects that would be helpful in furthering the development of Soviet nuclear weapons. At the same time, Stalin strained his intelligence network to achieve two purposes: first, to detect any symptoms of a forthcoming enemy attack; second, to obtain the secrets of the deadly atomic bomb from the West, and the United States in particular. When his hopes of sharing the nuclear weapons with the United States were frustrated, he decided to combine whatever scientific know-how was available at home with secrets obtained abroad one way or the other and begin a crash program to build his own atom bomb.

For four years or so the United States had a monopoly on the atom bomb, and hence the capacity to obliterate Soviet cities and defense installations, while Moscow, despite its huge military establishment kept on a partial war footing, would not be able to retaliate in kind. Projecting his own way of reasoning, Stalin expected an invasion of the Soviet Union before it could develop its own matching weapons. The system of global alliances so rapidly built up by Washington since 1947 confirmed his suspicion. As Khrushchev reported in his memoirs, Stalin lived in constant terror of an American attack and kept the antiaircraft guns around Moscow on a twenty-four hour alert. Since during the 1940s and 1950s, the main military threat was from manned bombers carrying nuclear weapons, the greatest possible depth for air defense seemed vital.

Hence Stalin's emphasis on vast territorial acquisitions, as well as the consolidation of a buffer zone of Communist-dominated satellite states. The existence of uranium mines in some of them, like Czechoslovakia, made it doubly necessary to keep the area under tight military and political control.

By the early 1950s, however, the global strategic balance began to change for two reasons. When NATO came into being in the spring of 1949, the economic recovery of Western Europe was well under way, and the situation in the West seemed rather stabilized. In Greece the Communist partisans had been crushed, West Berlin had been successfully defended, and Yugoslavia had become independent. No sooner had the North Atlantic Treaty been ratified than, at the end of August 1949, a United States aircraft flying over the Pacific got a radioactive air sample—fallout from a recently exploded Soviet atom bomb. This meant that the Russians had managed to explode it three years ahead of the schedule anticipated by the Pentagon. This momentous event, followed by Mao's triumph over Chiang Kai-shek's forces on the mainland of China, further escalated international tensions.

The rapid development of the Soviet atomic bomb and the eventual completion of hydrogen weapons during the early 1950s took the West by surprise. The USSR's possession of nuclear weapons profoundly affected the rivalry between the superpowers. From then on, what Winston Churchill termed the "balance of terror" became a dominant factor in the global strategic situation.

SUGGESTED READING

Brzezinski, Zbigniew, *The Soviet Bloc: Unity and Conflict* (2nd ed.). Cambridge, Mass.: Harvard University Press, 1961.

Clay, Lucius, *Decision in Germany*. Westport, Conn.: Greenwood, 1950.

Counts, George S., *The Country of the Blind: The Soviet System of Mind Control*. Westport, Conn.: Greenwood, 1959.

DEDIJER, VLADIMIR, *Tito*. New York: Arno, 1972.

DJILAS, MILOVAN, *The New Class: An Analysis of the Communist System*. New York: Praeger, 1957.

DZIEWANOWSKI, M. K., *The Communist Party of Poland: An Outline of History* (2nd ed.). Cambridge, Mass.: Harvard University Press, 1976, Chs. 9–14.

FEIS, HERBERT, *The China Tangle: The American Effort in China from Pearl Harbor to the Marshall Mission*. Princeton, N.J.: Princeton University Press, 1953.

HAHN, WERNER G., *Postwar Soviet Politics: The Fall of Zhdanov and the Defeat of Moderation, 1946–1953*. Ithaca, N.Y.: Cornell University Press, 1982.

HAZARD, JOHN N., *The Soviet System of Government* (4th ed.). Chicago: University of Chicago Press, 1964.

HOFFMAN, GEORGE W., *Yugoslavia and the New Communism*. Millwood, N.Y.: Kraus, 1962.

JORAVSKY, DAVID, *The Lysenko Affair*. Cambridge, Mass.: Harvard University Press, 1970.

LaFEBER, WALTER, *America, Russia, and the Cold War, 1945–1971* (2nd ed.). New York: Wiley, 1972.

LEE, WILLIAM T., AND RICHARD F. STAAR, *Soviet Military Policy Since World War II*. Foreword by William R. Van Cleave. Stanford, Calif.: Hoover Institution, 1986.

LISKA, GEORGE, *Russia and World Order: Strategic Choices and the Laws of Power in History*. Baltimore, Md.: Johns Hopkins University Press, 1980.

LYONS, EUGENE, *Our Secret Allies*. New York: Duell, Sloan and Pearce, 1953.

MASTNY, VOJTECH, *Russia's Road to the Cold War: Diplomacy, Warfare and the Politics of Commu-nism, 1941–1945*. New York: Columbia University Press, 1979.

McLANE, CHARLES B., *Soviet Strategies in South East Asia: An Explanation of Eastern Policy under Lenin and Stalin*. Princeton, N.J.: Princeton University Press, 1966.

MIKOŁAJCZYK, STANISŁAW, *The Pattern of Soviet Domination*. London: Sampson Low, Marston, 1948.

NETTL, J. P., *The Eastern Zone and Soviet Policy in Germany, 1945–1950*. New York: Oxford University Press, 1951.

PARRY, ALBERT, *Russia's Rockets and Missiles*. New York: Doubleday, 1960.

REMEIKIS, THOMAS, *Opposition to Soviet Rule in Luthuania, 1945–1980*. Chicago: Institute of Lithuanian Studies Press, 1980.

SETON-WATSON, HUGH, *The East European Revolution* (3rd ed.). New York: Praeger, 1956.

SHUB, BORIS, *The Choice*. New York: Duell, Sloan and Pearce, 1956.

SHULMAN, MARSHALL D., *Stalin's Foreign Policy Reappraised*. Cambridge, Mass.: Harvard University Press, 1963.

STARR, RICHARD F., *Poland 1944–1962: The Sovietization of a Captive People*. Baton Rouge: Louisiana State University Press, 1962.

TANG, PETER S. H., *Communist China Today* (2nd ed.). Washington, D.C.: Research Institute on the Sino-Soviet Bloc, 1961.

ULAM, ADAM B., *Dangerous Relations*. New York: Oxford University Press, 1983.

———, *Titoism and the Cominform*. Westport, Conn.: Greenwood, 1971.

ZINNER, PAUL E., *Communist Strategy and Tactics in Czechoslovakia, 1918–1948*. New York: Praeger, 1963.

CHAPTER 20

The End of an Epoch: Stalin's Death and the Twentieth Party Congress

During his last, declining years Stalin was more and more preoccupied with his place in history. Would he be considered greater than Peter the Great? What achievements would testify to his superiority? This preoccupation with the future made Stalin launch a series of gigantic projects that were to leave his name permanently engraved on the face of the country and thus testify forever about his might. Officially these projects were aimed at "transforming nature," yet they were to serve as Stalin's memorials. Huge dams, canals, and hydroelectric stations were to be constructed on the Dnieper, the Don, and the Volga. Enormous skyscrapers to rival those of Manhattan were to be erected in Moscow. The fact that the sandy and often marshy soil of the region did not lend itself to this sort of high-rise building was overlooked. Stalin's order to make Moscow "the most modern and beautiful city in the world" had to be obeyed. All these projects were on such a

gigantic scale as to eclipse the most impressive kinds of similar accomplishments in the rest of the world, especially in the United States.

BIOLOGY AND LINGUISTICS

The intensely transformist outlook of Stalin's last years was reflected in the 1948 debate about biology. The debate centered mostly around two individuals and their allegedly scientific theories: Ivan V. Michurin and Trofim D. Lysenko. While "Michurinism" and "Lysenkism" were officially supported even before the war, in 1948 Stalin went so far as to formally outlaw Gregor Mendel's classic theory, which emphasized the decisive importance of hereditary (as opposed to environmental) influence. By 1948, all agricultural and genetic research and all teaching were to conform to Michurinism-Lysenkism, and a fantastic notion of heredity was officially fostered. According to it, heredity was a mysterious property unattached to any material structure, but "permeating" all the "granules" of a living body. The old Lamarckian theories about the possibility of inheriting acquired characteristics and of the sudden transformation of species were enforced.

The Lysenko affair was characteristic of the aging dictator's last phase, and soon this manipulative approach penetrated many areas of Soviet thought. Stalin interpreted the theories of Michurin and Lysenko as containing a doctrine of the transformation of organisms on the biological level. His materialistic view of human beings made him wonder whether these discoveries could also be applied to society. If Michurinism–Lysenkism could produce new species of plants, might it not be used as an instrument of creating a new species of men and women?

This concept, worthy of the science fiction of Aldous Huxley or the fantasies of George Orwell, haunted the Soviet leader more and more. In the process he came to rediscover the teachings of Ivan Pavlov about conditioned reflexes. The Pavlovian theory fitted well Stalin's mentality and his conviction that human beings are nothing but signal-receiving creatures. He decided that the Pavlovian theory should be applied not only in physiology and medicine, but also in education. Here was a formula that seemed ideally suited to the process that would mold human beings in accordance with a set of well-coordinated verbal commands to create a new person—Soviet man. This was connected with Stalin's attitude toward linguistics. The ringing of a bell was sufficient in the case of Pavlov's dogs to make their saliva flow in anticipation of being fed. Human beings, however, needed a more complex set of signals to follow their Master's will, concluded Stalin; so he began to study ways to use language as an instrument of political indoctrination.

As a result of these reflections, in 1950 Stalin initiated a public debate on the relationship between Marxism and the theory of language. Prior to that time the officially accepted theory was that of a Soviet linguist, Nikolai Marr, who considered language part of the superstructure of society. It is a central theorem of Marxism that a society's superstructure is determined by its economic base. Consequently, as society's socioeconomic base was fundamentally reshaped by Socialism—Communism, the linguistic superstructure must also change. When Communism triumphed on a world scale, these changes were bound to be reflected in a new global *lingua franca,* the "language of Socialism." This theory was now rejected by Stalin as too mechanical and cosmopolitan. Stalin declared that language was sui generis; not only was it independent of socioeconomic changes; it was even capable of influencing them profoundly. He rejected the idea of a merger of languages and declared that in a Communist world federation, one of the already existing languages would triumph. You may guess which language he had in mind!

Stalin's verdict was immediately hailed by startled Soviet linguists as illuminating and definitive. The promotion of Russian as the language of Communism was in line with the spreading glorification of all things Russian and the growing emphasis on the universal significance of the Soviet State, led by its most worthy component, the Great Russian stock. Stalin's linguistic pronouncement also had significant implications for his transformist approach to society.

THE NINETEENTH PARTY CONGRESS

Meanwhile, adulation of Stalin continued to grow. It reached its peak during the last major public affair attended by the dictator, the Nineteenth Party Congress.[1] The con-

---

[1] An American correspondent in Moscow, Harrison Salisbury, reported that at the Soviet Art Exhibit of 1949 at the Tretyakov Galleries, nearly 70 of the 600 works entered in the exhibition depicted some aspect of Stalin's life. Salisbury stressed that the Soviet censor removed from his dispatch to New York the words

gress, the first in thirteen years, gathered in Moscow on October 5, 1952. By that time Stalin was seventy-three years old. He was present at the deliberations but took no active part in them; like a silent demigod he remained in the background. On the eve of the Congress Stalin had published an essay entitled "The Economic Problems of Socialism in the USSR." The work presented his reflections on some of the key domestic and foreign issues and set the tone for the Congress. Both by his presence and through his writings he overshadowed its deliberations.

The main theme of Stalin's essay was the problem of the transition from Socialism to Communism. According to the hitherto authoritative Soviet interpretation, the USSR had reached the socialist stage of development with the completion of the Second Five-Year Plan. Since that time the Soviet people had been "marching forward toward Communism" and would reach it in the foreseeable future. Stalin gave no definite date, however, for arrival at the goal. "The Economic Problems of Socialism" also emphasized not only the "contradictions between the camp of socialism and the camp of capitalism," but also pointed out the alleged growth of antagonism between various capitalist countries. Stalin's analysis seemed to indicate that war was more likely to break out between capitalist countries than between the Soviet Union and the United States. The future conflict in the ranks of "the capitalistic encirclement," argued Stalin, should be again, as in 1939, exploited by the Soviet Union for the furtherance of its preordained goals. "Under a certain confluence of circumstances," he continued, "the struggle for peace may possibly develop in one place and another into a struggle for Socialism."

The main report at the congress was delivered by his close collaborator, Gregory M. Malenkov. He was the first person other than Stalin to do so since 1923. The report

faithfully echoed the leader's main ideas. The slogan "struggle for peace" was featured prominently not only in most key speeches, but also in many resolutions. The international "peace offensive" which Moscow had launched immediately after the war was to redouble its efforts. The offensive represented an attempt by the Soviets to blame the Western powers for the cold war. It was intended to foster pro-Soviet, but not necessarily pro-Communist sentiments among leftist and pacifist elements in the West.

The Congress also belatedly sanctioned the Fifth Five-Year Plan (1951–1955) which focused on the final rehabilitation of war damages and the assimilation of the newly incorporated territories, especially those in Eastern Europe. The Fifth Five-Year Plan anticipated the further rapid expansion of heavy industry; it continued to neglect agriculture and the need for consumer goods.

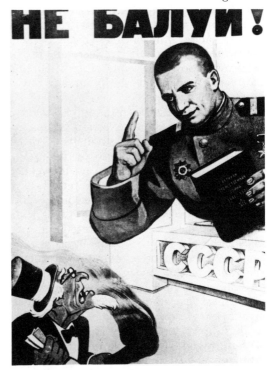

"Don't be a fool!" A Soviet soldier warns Uncle Sam holding an atom bomb. A Soviet Cold War poster

---

"nearly 70 of," thus leaving the impression that all were devoted to Stalin. Harrison Salisbury, *Moscow Journal* (Chicago: University of Chicago Press, 1961), p. 82.

By a show of hands, the delegates unanimously rubber-stamped a radical reshuffling of the Party's top structure. The Politburo and the Orgburo were merged and renamed "Presidium of the Party Central Committee." The presidium was composed of twenty-five members. Another attempt to water down the old top Party apparatus was made by expanding the Central Committee's Secretariat from five to ten members. Prior to the congress, the Secretariat (besides Secretary General Stalin) was composed of five members: Gregory M. Malenkov, Deputy Premier of the USSR; Averky R. Aristov, Secretary of the Chelyabinsk province, or oblast; Nikita S. Khrushchev, first Secretary of the Moscow oblast; Mikhail A. Suslov, editor of *Pravda* and the Soviet delegate to the Cominform; and Pantaleymon K. Ponamarenko, the former premier of Belorussia and since 1950, Soviet Minister of Supplies. To this old team were now added five younger, little-known people. Among them was Leonid I. Brezhnev, a Party member only since 1931, an engineer by profession, First Party Secretary in the Moldavian Soviet Republic since 1950, and not yet a member of the other key Soviet body, the Politburo.

The reorganization of the top Soviet governing bodies was a reflection of Stalin's paranoid mistrust of the small group of his closest co-workers, especially of the eleven-member Politburo. He wanted to weaken their established position by watering down the body's membership with younger bureaucrats entirely drilled in Stalin's school of silence, obedience, and strict discipline. Parallel with these changes in the internal Party machinery were changes in its external appearance, including its name. The term "Bolshevik," which had followed in brackets the words "Communist Party of the Soviet Union," was now dropped. This, together with suppression of the traditional terms Politburo and Orgburo represented further attempts to discard the past and create a new image of the Soviet Union as a status quo power.

Because Stalin had designated Malenkov

to deliver the main report at the Nineteenth Party Congress, and Malenkov, as Deputy Premier, was the dictator's closest co-worker, his eventual assumption of power was taken for granted. After all Malenkov was also a member of both the newly created Presidium and the expanded Secretariat. Only Khrushchev, also a member of both key bodies, could compare with his accumulation of political power.

STALIN'S DEATH

Following the noisy celebration of his seventieth birthday on December 21, 1949, Stalin became more and more sullen, suspicious, and isolated—even from his close co-workers. They were excluded from important decision making, often insulted, and even threatened. Shortly before the Nineteenth Party Congress, Stalin publicly called Molotov and Voroshilov British spies, and Mikoyan (who was an Armenian), a Turkish spy. Molotov lost his ministry of foreign affairs for he had incurred Stalin's displeasure because of his Jewish wife, who was sent, without her husband's protest, to a labor camp. Even Stalin's closest henchmen like Molotov, Mikoyan, Voroshilov, and Beria were not entirely free from danger. Not until Khrushchev's speeches of February 25–26, 1956, did the outside world learn that most of the Leningrad party leadership associated with Zhdanov had been destroyed in the secret purge known as the "Leningrad affair" that followed Zhdanov's disappearance. In 1949, the life of future Soviet prime minister Alexei Kosygin was, as Khrushchev put it, "hanging by a thread." The Leningrad purge apparently had been arranged by Beria and Malenkov to eliminate a group of potential contenders for power. Consequently, the Nineteenth Congress took place in an atmostphere of insecurity and expectations of worse reprisals. Between 1946 and 1953, selective arrests had again become a standard feature of Stalin's regime.

Since 1939, Beria had been the chief of

the security apparatus and hence the main instrument of Stalin's repressive policies. Yet, after the Nineteenth Congress, in November 1952, Beria was mysteriously implicated in a "nationalistic plot in Mingrelia," a province of Georgia and Beria's native region, where he had many intimate ties. The discovery of the "Mingrelian plot"was followed by the arrest of several of Beria's close associates. All of them were carried out on Stalin's orders. Since it was his habit eventually to turn all his past chiefs of police into scapegoats of one sort or another, these arrests could be interpreted by Beria only as ominous signs.

Meanwhile, the anti-Zionist campaign continued. There is some evidence that Stalin intended to begin mass deportations of Jews from the great urban centers of the European USSR to Siberia. On January 3, 1953, nine distinguished doctors, most of them of Jewish extraction, were arrested. They soon confessed that they had murdered Zhdanov and other high Soviet dignitaries at the instigation of the CIA. "The doctors' plot" seemed to be concocted to justify the planned deportations.

Amidst the rumors accompanying these plots, faked accusations, and arrests, it was suddenly announced on the night of March 4, 1953, that Stalin had suffered a massive brain hemorrhage and as a result was losing consciousness and the power of speech. On March 5 came the solemn announcement: "The heart of the comrade-in-arms and brilliant continuor of the work of Lenin, of the wise leader and teacher of the Communist party and the Soviet people—Joseph Vissarionovich STALIN—has ceased to beat." Four days later he was buried with great pomp in the Lenin mausoleum in Red Square. The tomb was immediately renamed the Lenin—Stalin mausoleum. To show that from now on there would be collective leadership, three speakers in succession bade farewell to their former boss: Molotov, Malenkov, and Beria. The latter's well-armed and ubiquitous security forces, massively displayed during the entombment, seemed to control the situation.

Stalin's disappearance from the scene represented an event of the first magnitude. He had become *the* central institution of the Soviet Party–State, linked so closely with the image of the USSR that many outsiders had come to identify the two. After almost three decades of his rule, most people had gotten used to their terrible and unpredictable master and could hardly imagine a world without this father figure. Up until March 1953, everything had been enacted and justified in Stalin's name. Suddenly this seemingly immortal diety vanished, creating a huge power vacuum. The official communiqué of Stalin's death was intended to console the people. It stated: "The immortal name *Stalin* will always live in the hearts of the Soviet people and of all progressive mankind."

THE EMERGENCE OF KHRUSHCHEV

After the war, Stalin had exercised dictatorial power through government channels rather than through the Party apparatus. He had delegated his duties as secretary general of the party to Malenkov, to whom he gave the title first secretary of the Central Committee, while he acted primarily as prime minister of the USSR. This was more convenient for taking international steps in the name of the USSR.

During the transition period following Stalin's death, power was indeed in the hands of the three members of the Presidium who had given his funeral oration: Malenkov, also a deputy premier and the Party's senior secretary; Beria, chief of state security; and Molotov, a one-time foreign minister, who immediately aligned himself with Beria. Forgetting the lesson of nearly three decades, hypnotized by Stalin's recent practice of stressing governmental power rather than party office, his successors focused their attention on what seemed to them the main prize: the premiership of the USSR.

The day after the announcement of Stalin's death, a joint meeting of the Central

Committee, the Council of Ministers, and the Presidium of the Supreme Soviet, at Beria's suggestion, designated Malenkov as prime minister. Malenkov repaid the favor by proposing a merger of the recently split ministries of Internal Affairs (MVD) and State Security (MGB) into one ministry with Beria as its head. Molotov became First Deputy Premier and regained control of the Ministry of Foreign Affairs. Voroshilov became chairman of the Presidium of the Supreme Soviet or official Head of State. Marshal Zhukov, perhaps the most popular man in the country, was made Minister of Defense. At the same time, the Presidium of the Central Committee was reduced from thirty-six members to fourteen members and candidates to resemble the old Politbureau. Full voting members were listed in the following order: Malenkov, Beria, Molotov, Voroshilov, Khrushchev, Bulganin, Kaganovich, Mikoyan, Saburov, and Pervukhin. This meant that Khrushchev, then fifty-nine years old, was only in fifth place.

Yet as early as March 14, 1953, the Central Committee accepted Malenkov's resignation from the position of First Secretary of the Party's Central Committee so that he could devote himself to governmental work as Prime Minister. Khrushchev, the only Party secretary who was also a member of the Presidium, took over his Party post.[2]

Khrushchev was born in 1894, the son of a small farmer from the Kursk province of the Ukraine. He went through only three years of formal schooling and initially eked out a living as a miner and locksmith. In 1918, at the age of twenty-four, he joined the ranks of the Bolshevik Party and fought in the Civil War. Soon he caught the attention of Stalin's proconsul in the Ukraine, Kaganovich, who enlisted him for organizational work. In 1929, Khrushchev was rewarded for his services by being transferred to Moscow to study at the Industrial Academy while doing work in the central Party

apparat. Vigorous, loquacious, sly, and ruthless, Khrushchev rose swiftly. In 1931, he was Party Secretary of the largest and most crucial Moscow city district. In 1934, he was elected a member of the Central Committee and four years later was entrusted with the responsibility for Party work in the entire Moscow province. In 1938, we see him already an alternate member of the Politburo; the next year he was a full-fledged member. After being Stalin's emissary in the Ukraine between 1938 and 1949, while intermittently acting as a high-ranking political commissar during the war, he returned to Moscow. During the period 1947–1949, Khrushchev quarreled with his former protector, Kaganovich, who had accused Khrushchev of "insufficient vigilance" toward Ukrainian nationalism. Stalin's death found Khrushchev occupying three strategic posts: he was not only Party Secretary of the Moscow province, but also a member of the two key bodies, the Presidium and the Secretariat. These provided him with a strong triple power base.

It was this generally underestimated, self-educated peasant-worker who replaced Malenkov as the head of the Secretariat of the Party's Central Committee, the post that had allowed Stalin to rise to the top. During the last years of Stalin's rule, Khrushchev had gained a reputation for being deeply preoccupied with agrarian matters, and not entirely unsympathetic to the peasant point of view at a time when agriculture was in a deplorable state of neglect and the sector of the Soviet economy that was most in need of immediate attention. Khrushchev's promotion had strong symbolic significance. At the head of the Party was a man who could alleviate the feelings of despair that had been spreading throughout a countryside crushed by excessive delivery quotas and taxes. At the same time, the sensitive top Party post went to a man who, it appeared, could never aspire to supreme power because of his simplistic mind, lack of serious theoretical training, and extreme crudeness of manner.

[2] Roy A. Medvedev and Zhores A. Medvedev, *Khrushchev: The Years in Power* (New York: Columbia University Press, 1976), pp. 3–4.

A May Day parade in 1953 in Peking, extolling Stalin

THE THAW AND THE DOWNFALL OF BERIA

While avoiding open criticism of the late dictator, yet wanting to contrast "the new course" with the policies and practices of Stalin, the "collective leadership" step by step initiated a series of small concessions. On April 3, Beria himself declared that the "doctors' plot" had been a hoax, charged one of his assistants, M. D. Riumin, with responsibility for it, and had him arrested. Beria further admitted that "inadmissible" methods had been used by state security agents in interrogating suspects. The doctors, as well as those implicated in the "Mingrelian plot," were released and rehabilitated. This was sensational. For the first time the Soviet security organs were going back on their word. The concessions announced by Beria were soon emulated by a move of Premier Malenkov. He ordered wider distribution of food, especially grain, and promised the Soviet people more consumer goods "in two or three years."

These political and economic concessions and reforms were paralleled by a slight relaxation of censorship and the regulations concerning foreign travel. All of this instantly created a new political and moral climate in the USSR. The mood of hope and the sense of relief felt by many people in the spring and summer of 1953 were captured by a perceptive observer of the Soviet scene, Ilya Ehrenburg, in a novel bearing a significant title, *The Thaw*. This title gave a name to the immediate post-Stalin era.

In this popularity contest, Khrushchev remained, for the time being, a spectator. Yet he was soon to enter the race with a trump card of his own, the post of the First Secretary of the Central Committee. Khrushchev's daring climb to the top of the ladder led him through a series of dramatic adventures, the first of which was the removal of his most dangerous competitor, Beria.

Although in theory the Soviet Union was controlled by the Party, Beria's powerful system of state security, which had pre-viously been subordinate only to Stalin himself, loomed over everybody. After Stalin's death, Beria reorganized his now all-encompassing controls. It soon became obvious to everybody, even to his friend Malenkov, that Beria was determined to use this power to further his own ambitions. At the time of Stalin's burial, Beria ordered several divisions of MVD forces to the city to maintain order. After the funeral these divisions were not sent back to their regular garrisons. Shortly after Stalin's death, a general amnesty had been declared for prisoners serving sentences of less than five years. This did not include most political prisoners, whose minimum term was normally from eight to twenty-five years, but mostly common criminals. Thus thousands of criminals appeared in Moscow and other cities, and the crime rate soared and caused general public indignation. This, in turn, gave Beria an excuse to retain large contingents of MVD forces in the capital.

These and other similar measures alarmed his former allies and precipitated a conspiracy organized by Khrushchev and supported by the military establishment, including Marshals Zhukov and Koniev. The conspirators acted with remarkable secrecy and precision. On June 28, 1953, Beria's MVD guard at the Kremlin and the Central Committee buildings was replaced by regular Army sentries. Meanwhile, Army units under the command of Marshals Zhukov and Koniev surrounded and blockaded the central MVD buildings in Moscow. Trapped in the Kremlin, Beria was arrested by the marshals, summarily tried, and executed. Over a period of several days most regional MVD officials were also arrested, as were MVD ministers in the republics. Practically all the officials of the central MVD administration were arrested right in their offices. Several of the most dangerous of Beria's aides were shot on the spot.

Beria's downfall meant cutting down to size the Secret Police, which was now purged and reorganized to be more fully subordinated to the Party rather than a potential menace to its primacy. Soon after

Beria's execution, some of his domestic henchmen and their trusted men in various Soviet satrapies were removed from their key positions one by one. This resulted in a considerable weakening of the whole Soviet security network, not only in the Soviet Union, but also in Eastern Europe where it had its branches.

The investigation of Beria's activities revealed not only monstrous personal crimes but also the scope of reprisals that surpassed even the imagination of the former conspirators, no strangers to Stalin's system of bloody repression. Meanwhile, the courts were flooded with millions of appeals for review of the cases of people still in prisons and camps. The country's judicial apparatus could not deal with so many requests. Of the twelve to thirteen million people who had been in concentration camps during Stalin's time, only about four thousand were released in 1953, but even this small trickle from the Gulag archipelago was to have a great impact on the climate of public opinion. Those released were mostly people with influential political connections; they generated more pressure for the further release and rehabilitation of the surviving political inmates. This led to the creation of the Special Investigating Committee and a net of extraordinary, temporary judicial commissions to deal with between five and six million cases. For obvious reasons, Khrushchev took a vivid interest in the progress of the investigation.

THE VIRGIN LANDS CAMPAIGN

The removal of the most determined and resourceful competitor in the struggle for power, the Soviet godfather, narrowed the competition to two men; Malenkov and Khrushchev. Since it was Khrushchev who had initiated and engineered Beria's destruction, the former's position was now strengthened. The position of Malenkov, who had been much more closely associated with Stalin, was weakened. While paying lip service to the principle of "collective leader-

ship," Khrushchev tried to bolster his own image by various means. He traveled widely, making dramatic and often quite amusing speeches; his signature appeared more often on public documents than that of his more sedentary and less dramatic competitor. While the problem of the "excesses of the past period" was being investigated, the most immediate issue was that of food shortages caused by the lamentable state of Soviet agriculture. The 1953 harvest was exceptionally poor; the per capita grain output was lower than in 1913. In September 1953, Khrushchev delivered a major public address sharply criticizing the condition of the Soviet countryside. He pointed out its sorry state and admitted that the total number of cattle was now lower than in 1916. Stating that "the agricultural sector" had become a major bottleneck for further development, he promised its reorganization along more functional, efficient lines. Since Malenkov had been, during the postwar years, mainly responsible for the whole economy, including its agrarian sector, the target of Khrushchev's accusations was unmistakable. To provide more incentives to the apathetic collective farmers, Khrushchev decreed three immediate measures. First, prices for compulsory deliveries of food were to be considerably increased; second, the criminal prosecution for nonfulfillment of compulsory norms was now to be replaced by fines; taxes on the output of household plots were dramatically lowered.

In February 1954, Khrushchev announced that to end the chronic grain shortage the available arable land of North Kazakhstan and West Siberia should be plowed. Using various methods mixing encouragement with coercion, he dispatched to those lands thousands of young peasants and Party workers to turn "the virgin lands" into a "new granary of the Soviet Union." The first harvest seemed to justify fully the great drive. By 1956, the tilled land of the USSR had increased by some 87 million acres, nearly 50 percent. In January 1955, Khrushchev launched another drive for the cultivation of more corn, or "the sausage on a stalk," as he put it. The expansion of corn fields from 10 to 70 million acres was to provide the main source of concentrated fodder for Soviet cattle herds. By 1970, argued Khrushchev, the USSR should "overtake the United States in meat and milk production per capita." One of the chief supporters of Khrushchev in his effort to farm the virgin lands was the then First Party Secretary in Kazakhstan, Leonid Brezhnev (see Chapter 21).

Relaxation of the cruel Stalinist rule at home and a series of Soviet concessions abroad had numerous repercussions in the USSR and throughout its satellite empire. In the spring of 1953 there was an uprising of the inmates of the huge Vorkuta and Karagand labor camps and minor riots in various Czechoslovak industrial centers. In June the East Berlin workers rose in revolt against the high labor norms and inhuman working conditions in their factories. All these disturbances were successfully put down. In the case of the East Berlin rebellion, Soviet troops and tanks decisively helped the East German security apparatus. At the same time, symptoms of intellectual ferment could also be observed in Hungary and Poland.

MALENKOV REPLACED BY BULGANIN

In December 1954 and January 1955, the conflict between the Prime Minister, Malenkov, and the First Party Secretary, Khrushchev, surfaced in the form of a press polemic in which *Izvestia,* the government newspaper, and *Pravda,* the Party paper, took opposite points of view for the first time in Soviet history. While *Izvestia* stressed the need for more consumer goods, *Pravda* denounced such tendencies as a "rightist deviation" reminiscent of the despised "Bukharinism." This was a unique event: nothing of this sort had occurred in Soviet Russia for over a quarter of a century, since the Stalin–Trotsky controversy.

It was obvious that the press debate was an outward symptom of a behind-the-scenes struggle for power. (A former United States ambassador in Moscow, Charles Bohlen, once said that in its initial phases a top-echelon struggle for power resembles two people wrestling under a thick carpet: although one realizes that something is going on, it is very difficult to say who has the upper hand.) Any doubts that might have been entertained on the subject were soon cut short by an official communiqué issued on February 8, 1955, announcing Malenkov's resignation as Premier of the USSR. In an unusually frank public self-critique, Malenkov repudiated his former ideas about producing more consumer goods and confessed his "inexperience" in the affairs of state. Malenkov went so far as to assume full responsibility for "the unsatisfactory state of affairs in agriculture." Malenkov, although demoted from premiership, still retained his post in the policy-making Presidium. On Khrushchev's motion, the Supreme Soviet elected Minister of Defense Marshal Nikolai A. Bulganin as Premier.

Bulganin was another classic product of the Stalinist school. One year younger than Khrushchev, he had joined the Bolshevik Party in 1917, a year before Khrushchev, and since 1922 had devoted his energies to secret police work. In 1931, he became chairman of the Moscow City Soviet. In 1934, he became a member of the Central Committee, and in 1948 was selected by Stalin for membership in the Politburo. Simultaneously, from 1937 to 1938, Bulganin was Premier of the Russian Republic. During the war, promoted to the rank of general, Bulganin had acted as a junior member of the top defense council and also, since 1944, as a political commissar on several fronts and as the Deputy People's Commissar for Defense. At the end of the war he was made a marshal. From 1947 to 1949 and from 1953 to 1955, he acted as defense minister and at the same time, between 1947 and 1955, as Deputy Premier of the USSR. Khrushchev had probably selected Bulganin as his partner because of his wide administrative background and varied connections with the bureaucratic machine, the "military-industrial complex," and the security apparatus. He had experience but lacked brilliance, and was familiar with administrative routine without having real political ambition. He could act as Khrushchev's solid alter ego without threatening him or outshining his histrionic and mercurial personality.

Thus the "collective leadership" underwent further transformation: it was now led by Khrushchev and seconded by Bulganin; Malenkov, Molotov, and others were relegated more and more to the background. Despite his downfall, Malenkov suffered no hardships. The fact that he was not imprisoned or killed was a novelty in the hitherto bloody game of Soviet politics.

FOREIGN POLICY OF THE COLLECTIVE LEADERSHIP

Besides making a series of small concessions to their subjects, the "collective leadership" initially also tried to follow a conciliatory foreign policy that would reduce the main points of friction between the USSR and its Western opponents. One of the first such conciliatory steps was its agreement to sign the Korean armistice in July 1953. The conclusion of the armistice, which reconfirmed the 38th parallel as the line dividing South Korea from North Korea, was made possible by the Soviet, North Korean, and Chinese acceptance of Washington's demand that the repatriation of POWs be voluntary. This was a bitter pill to swallow, for some three-quarters of the Chinese "volunteers" who had fought on the side of the North Koreans decided, despite considerable pressure, not to return home but to go to Taiwan.

In January 1954, the Council of Foreign Ministers convened again in Berlin, after years of inactivity, to discuss peace treaties for Germany and Austria. While nothing was accomplished as far as the German treaty was concerned, the council decided to hold a conference in Geneva to deal with

Austria and with the problems created by the French withdrawal from Indochina. The participants agreed to the partitioning of the former French colony near the 17th parallel. It was recognized that Ho Chi Minh's forces controlled the north, but his Communist partisans were to be withdrawn from the south. At Geneva, Soviet Foreign Minister Molotov supported the Chinese, who urged Ho to accept this setback in order to stabilize the area. In September 1954, Khrushchev and Bulganin traveled to Peking, where a second Sino-Soviet treaty returned Manchuria to Chinese sovereignty and promised to do the same to Port Arthur, which they did by May 1955. The scope of Soviet assistance to China was expanded, but Peking still had to pay for it dearly.

Meanwhile, after protracted negotiations, in May 1955 the Russians agreed to withdraw their forces from Austria, provided that the Western powers did likewise; and they agreed to the permanent neutralization of the country. The Austrian treaty considerably relaxed international tensions and resulted in the first meeting of top Soviet representatives with their Western counterparts in neutral Switzerland. In July 1955, Khrushchev and Bulganin traveled to Geneva to meet United States President Dwight Eisenhower and Secretary of State John Foster Dulles, British Prime Minister Anthony Eden, and Premier Edgar Faure of France. Although such crucial questions as disarmament and the reunification of Germany were discussed without success, some improvements in East–West trade and cultural exchanges did result. In view of the previously dismal state of relations between the two rival camps, these meager results, preceded by the signing of the Austrian peace treaty, were hailed as the dawn of a new era of peaceful coexistence. The "spirit of Geneva" became a slogan used to designate the momentary relaxation of the tensions so characteristic of the previous decade.

The summit meeting in Geneva was followed by the abandonment of the Soviet naval base in Porkkala near Helsinki; in September 1955 it was handed back to the Finns. While making these concessions, the Khrushchev–Bulganin team undertook some measures to strengthen the inner structure of the Soviet camp. At a meeting in Warsaw in May 1955, representatives of the USSR, Albania, Bulgaria, Czechoslovakia, the German Democratic Republic, Hungary, Poland, and Romania decided to sign an agreement that would coordinate their defense preparations and place their forces under the command of Marshal Koniev. The *Warsaw Pact* was a response to progressive remilitarization of Germany and the resulting strengthening of NATO. By playing up the issue, Moscow hoped to exploit a measure of popular support in countries like Poland and Czechoslovakia, where the threat of possible German territorial vindications was still a useful instrument of Soviet control. The main advantage of the Warsaw Pact, however, was that it provided an additional contractual basis for the continued stationing of Soviet troops in some of the satellite countries. As a result of the Warsaw Treaty, the USSR gained a convenient lever of control over its East European neighbors. They were now not only economically linked to the USSR by the Council of Mutual Economic Assistance and a net of bilateral military alliances, but also by the multilateral Warsaw Treaty, which was superimposed over the original military arrangements of the immediate postwar period.

The year 1955 also witnessed the first Soviet steps toward extending the geographical range of Soviet foreign policy beyond its traditional continental orientation. Khrushchev made bold attempts at penetrating the Middle East by exploiting the tensions resulting from the Arab-Israeli armistice of 1949. Here the emancipation of Egypt from Western tutelage stood him in good stead. The emergence of Colonel Gamal Nasser as an ambitious and restless leader anxious to modernize the country and regain full sovereignty over the vital Suez Canal was skillfully exploited by Mos-

cow. In the summer of 1955, the new Soviet Foreign Minister, Dmitri T. Shepilov, who had replaced Molotov in the spring, visited Cairo and offered Nasser economic and military assistance which the West was hesitant to provide. Meanwhile, Khrushchev and Bulganin made a triumphant journey through India, Burma, and Afghanistan.

RECONCILIATION WITH TITO

The most dramatic reversal of Stalin's foreign policy, however, concerned Yugoslavia. During the early 1950s, after two or three years of resistance to Moscow, Tito—motivated overwhelmingly by his desire to stay alive and in power—began to change his strategy. Unable to find ideological justification for his disobedience to the Center, and with his protestations of loyalty contemptuously scorned, he reoriented his line, domestic as well as foreign. Suspended between the Soviet and Western camps, like Mohammed between heaven and earth, Tito decided to rationalize his difficult situation by devising the theory of "active neutrality" and by taking a position uncommitted to either side while pursuing his own policy of defending the interests of the Third World. During this time, both camps were often accused by Yugoslav leaders of imperialistic iniquities and injustices, but the main thrust of the Yugoslav attacks was overwhelmingly directed against their former Soviet comrades.

Tito's rage came to a climax at the Sixth Congress of the Yugoslav Party in November 1952. It seemed as if all the participants in the Congress were vying with each other to see who could most violently denounce the old idol, Stalin, and the entire Soviet system. In his report, Tito attacked every aspect of Soviet policies, both foreign and domestic. He accused the Soviet Union of having transformed the "once independent East European states . . . into mere colonies in the heart of Europe." He placed full responsibility upon the USSR for having "pushed Northern Korea into an aggressive war." He bewailed the fact that some of the non-Russian nationalities were "erased from the earth's surface."

These attacks were combined with liberalization of the Yugoslav political and economic system. Economic planning was decentralized. Most of the collectivized land was gradually returned to the peasants, self-government in the form of workers' councils was instituted in the factories, and later some elements of a market economy were introduced and became an integral feature of the country's system. All this had a demoralizing effect on other Eastern European Communists, smarting under Mos-

cow's rigid control, and bound to notice the mostly beneficial effects of the reforms, while envying Tito's freedom. What was worse, Yugoslavia, threatened by its Communist neighbors Albania, Bulgaria, Romania, and Hungary, began to draw nearer to Greece and Turkey, both members of NATO. The last step in this direction was made on August 4, 1954, when a treaty of alliance, political cooperation, and mutual assistance was signed between Yugoslavia, Greece, and Turkey. Perhaps more than anything else, this dramatized the bankruptcy of Stalin's policy toward Tito.

Concluding that Stalin's policy toward

Marshal Broz-Tito triumphant

Yugoslavia was increasingly counterproductive, Khrushchev decided to change it and woo Tito back to the Soviet fold, whatever the price. The price was stiff indeed. The long list of conditions that Belgrade submitted to Moscow included the acceptance of the right of different nations to build socialism in their own way; the rehabilitation of the executed or jailed "Titoists" and the ousting of their jailers and executioners still in power in Eastern Europe; and the dismissal of Soviet Foreign Minister Molotov from office for his part in the expulsion of Yugoslavia from the Comintern. These demands, rather arrogant when one considers that they were made by a small country to a mighty superpower, were nevertheless accepted by Khrushchev, who hoped to have Yugoslavia back in the Soviet camp. With this objective in mind, he went to Belgrade to seal the reconciliation with Tito. The June 1955 journey of the future dictator of one-sixth of the earth to visit the triumphant Balkan chieftain at his capital to seek forgiveness for the admitted errors of Stalin was an almost unparalleled historical event. It was almost as if the Pope of Rome had canceled the excommunication of Martin Luther and gone to Germany to apologize to him and offer him readmission into the Catholic Church.

After having accepted the Soviet recantations and thereby scoring an immense political and propaganda success, Tito refused to return to the Soviet camp. This triumph of the former heretic, the public and solemn Soviet acceptance of his peculiar position toward socialism–communism, was bound to have profound repercussions throughout the entire Communist world. This was especially true of Eastern Europe, still suffering from the years of Stalinist oppression. Moreover the now legitimized principles of separate, national roads to socialism–communism were in the long run bound to affect the Communist parties of the West as well. The Stalinist principle of the universality of the Soviet experience lay in ruins, and the seeds of Eurocommunism were sown.

THE TWENTIETH PARTY CONGRESS

The concessions the collective leadership was granting to the Soviet people and to the outside world during the first three years and the intermittent, rather shy references to "the cult of personality" indicated that the new team was uneasy about the enormity of the crimes then under methodical examination by the Special Investigating Committee. Yet nobody dared to attack openly "the period of mistakes and aberrations." Despite the surface calm, many expert observers of the Soviet scene guessed that something was brewing behind the apparent unanimity studiously displayed by the collective leadership. The pent-up emotions accumulated during the past three decades had to find some outlet eventually, but even the most experienced students of Soviet affiars were unable to foretell when it would surface and what form it would assume.

This was the situation on the eve of the Twentieth Party Congress, which gathered in February 1956 in Moscow. As with all such major public manifestations of the past period, it was a strictly structured and staged performance that contained few surprises. It started with a long tribute to the defunct "Great Leader and Teacher." It was only three years after his death, and he still seemed to overshadow the Soviet scene from his grave. His monuments were visible everywhere, while only 12,000 out of the 5 or 6 million political prisoners had been freed. The congress unanimously approved the changes introduced by Khrushchev into the ranks of the ruling bodies: the Presidium and the Secretariat. Khrushchev's chief supporter in his virgin land drive, Leonid Brezhnev, then first Secretary of the Kazakh party and a member of the Secretariat, was now rewarded with an alternate seat in the Presidium. About one-third of the members of the Central Committee had been replaced. The Congress also rubber-stamped the Sixth Five-Year Plan, which was to last from 1956 to 1961. It promised increased productivity that was to provide more consumer goods and a larger investment in agriculture.

In his report, Khrushchev revised somewhat the Leninsit thesis that war was inevitable "as long as imperialism exists." He ventured to say that imperialism had ceased to be "an all-embracing world system" because one-third of the world now lived under Communism, and the rapid process of decolonization made further expansion of the socialist system very likely in the future. Moreover, the steady strengthening of the "antiwar forces" made the outbreak of a world conflict less likely. This meant that there was a chance for "peaceful coexistence between states of various political and social systems." While the "final triumph of socialism" was inevitable, there were various roads leading to its achievement. He cited the Yugoslav approach as one of the "forms of transition" from capitalism to socialism.

On the last day of the congress, after all the routine work had been accomplished, Khrushchev suddenly convened an extraordinary session on the night of February 23. No foreign observers were admitted. At this session he delivered a long, passionate speech about four and a half hours long, in which he denounced Stalin's personality, methods, and policies in a resolute and often spiteful way seldom encountered even among the most violent Western anti-Communists. Although he did not spare the late tyrant's harmful policies, Khrushchev mainly emphasized his personal shortcomings, his thirst for power, his sadism, and his increasing paranoia. "The negative characteristics of Stalin, which, in Lenin's time, were only incipient, transformed themselves during the last years into a grave abuse of power, which caused untold harm to our Party. . . ."

Among the main targets of Khrushchev's denunciations were the mass purges and show trials of the 1930s and their crippling effect on the functioning and morale of the Party. He said, "When the cases of some of these so-called 'spies' and 'saboteurs' were examined it was found that all their cases were fabricated." Then he went on, "Many thousands of honest and innocent Communists have died as a result of this monstrous falsification of such 'cases.'" He admitted that all the old Bolsheviks' confessions had been false, and that many critical comments made about the Moscow trials abroad were actually true, and often rather understated.

Despite his furious onslaught, Khrushchev did not blame the late dictator's excesses on the Communist system as such, but rather on Stalin's vicious character. The Communist system and the CPSU were not to be blamed for one man's mistakes. While Stalin was bad, Khrushchev said, Communism is good; it should simply be cleansed and consolidated. Stalin, according to Khrushchev, was a man of incredible criminality, a pathological paranoiac who suffered from an acute persecution mania caused both by hereditary predisposition and corruption induced by the unlimited power he had appropriated through flagrant violations of the principles of "socialist legality."

Besides dwelling on Stalin's evil deeds, Khrushchev thoroughly revised some of the theoretical premises on which his predecessor's policies had been based. For instance, he argued that it is not absolutely necessary that the transition from capitalism to socialism involve civil war, since several other alternatives are imaginable. "The application or nonapplication of force in the transition to socialism depends not as much upon the proletariat as upon the resistance of the exploiters. . . ." Khrushchev questioned Stalin's nationality policy. He charged him with responsibility for the break with Tito. Despite these condemnations, Khrushchev closed his "secret speech" by praising some of Stalin's achievements and said that despite his numerous mistakes, he had "performed great services to the Party, to the working class and to the international [Communist] movement." In the name of Lenin, Khrushchev summoned the Party to do away with "the cult of personality" and return to "the Leninist principle of socialist democracy."

One of the most striking features of Khrushchev's speech was its selectiveness. It denounced mainly the crimes directed against certain Party members, not against the people at large. While he exonerated Rykov and Tukhachevsky, he completely omitted Trotsky, Zinoviev, Kamenev, and their followers. They still remained not only "enemies of the people" but "unpersons," to use George Orwell's terminology. Following the Congress, while several million inmates of prisons and labor and concentration camps were gradually freed and rehabilitated, several categories of political prisoners were not rehabilitated, even though they had been released. Finally, neither the rehabilitation commissions nor the procurator nor the Party dared to prosecute those guilty of the monstrous crimes committed under Stalin. Neither were the chiefs of jail and camps tried and punished, nor were the names of slanderers and informers revealed, nor were the interrogators responsible for torturing people prosecuted.

Yet despite these shortcomings, inconsistencies, and even glaring mistakes, the secret speech was an event of the highest significance. By denouncing Stalin as a blood-stained maniac, the violator not only of the Marxist-Leninist principles of "socialist legality" but of common humanity, Khrushchev performed a dramatic operation the consequences of which are still with us. First, he destroyed the myth of Stalin's infallibility as an interpreter of orthodox Marxism-Leninism. By so doing, Khrushchev cast doubt upon the legitimacy of any leader or regime trying to govern in the name of similar principles. As a consequence, Khrushchev seriously undermined the foundations of Soviet rule in the USSR and severely damaged its international image. If a sadistic monster could rule supreme in Soviet Russia for nearly three decades in the name of Marxist-Leninist

legitimacy, how reliable could these principles be? And how trustworthy were the methods by which Stalin's successors have been selected?

WHY THE SECRET SPEECH?

Khrushchev's speech discredited not only Stalin, but also placed a time bomb under the regime's foundations. The Soviet regime is an ideocracy, or a logocracy, where the leader of the Party is the chief theoretician, the keeper of the Word, and its sole interpreter. He is the Emperor as well as the Pope, both the Sultan and the Caliph. Knowing the Truth is the Soviet leader's main claim to total power and the reason for enforcing his subjects' total obedience. The top dog is also the top dogmatist. Once this myth is broken, the system becomes open to challenge. And indeed, the present-day dissent movement is one of the secret speech's foster children.

The question of what moved Khrushchev, a former trusted henchman of the late dictator and an old Stalinist, to the eloquent, although incomplete exposure of his former master's crimes, is complex and controversial. It was certainly not squeamishness about Stalin's bloody record, for as chief of the Moscow party and as Stalin's delegate in the Ukraine during the Great Purge, Khrushchev had stained his own hands with the blood of countless innocent victims. A more convincing explanation would be his conviction that the rule of unmitigated terror was an ineffective, and in the long run dangerous way of ruling the country because of the alienation and sedition it had produced and would continue to produce in the future. The experience of World War II must have been of crucial importance. As Stalin's proconsul in the Ukraine, Khrushchev had witnessed the near-collapse of most of the southern front because of mass desertion by the recruits, who were largely members of various non-Russian minorities. Moreover, Khrushchev was also aware that compulsion was not the best economic incentive. He must have concluded that the Stalinist system of terror was counterproductive, especially for a fast developing industrial society such as the Soviet Union. By making his "secret speech," he was actually defending the stability of a system that urgently required more effective ways of managing and motivating people.

Another reason for the Khrushchev denigration of Stalin was that he realized the necessity of improving the Party's image at home and abroad by dissociating it from the excesses of "the past period of errors and aberrations." By making Stalin the chief villain, Khrushchev hoped to rescue the Party from its low estate. Still another motive to Khrushchev's speech must have been the pressure of the Party apparat. The Stalinist purges had been a traumatic experience that haunted the Soviet people, including the Party oligarchy. By 1955–1956, everyone was yearning for security, stability, and "normalcy," and the cry "Never, never again!" could be heard also in many Party circles. The political balance of forces in the Party must have been such that its leader had no alternative but to expose his predecessor's misdeeds to preserve the vital support of the apparat. If he did not do it, one of his rivals would. On February 16, a prominent member of the Presidium, Anastas Mikoyan, had been the first to criticize openly Stalin, and he had been loudly applauded. To keep power, Khrushchev had to exorcise Stalin's ghost once and forever and promise to the "new class" that the horrors of the purges would never be repeated again.

Thus Khrushchev, who had assumed Stalin's office and ruled for nearly three years as his heir, came to preside over the partial dismantling of Stalinism. This made the Twentieth Congress one of the most momentous events of Soviet history. By his secret speech Khrushchev, without ever planning it that way, opened up for discussion the fundamental premises of Communism and thereby started a crisis perhaps more profound than any previously experienced by the movement.

STALINISM AS A HISTORIC PHENOMENON: FOUR SOVIET VIEWS

Stalin was the most powerful personality of Soviet Russia and the world Communist movement for over twenty-nine years, from Lenin's death in January 1924 to March 1953. Even after Stalin's demise he overshadowed the Soviet political scene for a long time. The significance of this is that the formative period of Soviet history has been shaped by his personality. That is why Stalinism is the central problem of Soviet history, and an explanation of its complexities is in order.

Stalin and his system have been the subjects of numerous controversies, both in the Soviet Union and abroad. Let us now examine three main Western schools of thought and four Soviet approaches to Stalinism as a unique historic phenomenon. The first approach that must be analyzed is the official Soviet one. It is embodied in Stalin's speeches and official declarations; it is encapsulated in one authoritative book entitled *History of the Communist Party of the Soviet Union (Bolsheviks), Short Course,* edited by Stalin himself and published in many editions up to his death, and in various revised versions under his successors. *The Short Course,* as the work is usually called, represents the authentic interpretation of Stalinism from the horse's mouth. If we are to believe this version, the history of the USSR during Stalin's rule was a record of farsighted policies formulated by a wise, benevolent leader and carried out enthusiastically by the Soviet people, with only a few exceptions. Those who did oppose the Great Helmsman's policies were mostly traitors, saboteurs, and foreign agents. They were punished, and rightly so. Most were relegated to corrective labor camps. Some of the more vicious ones had to be removed altogether for the sake of State security. On the whole, however, the political and socioeconomic transformation of the USSR has been conducted smoothly, successfully, and even brilliantly. The correctness of these policies was tested during the "Great Patriotic War," which validated the wisdom of the Leader's policies and consolidated the position of the Soviet Union as "the main progressive and peace-loving force" of humanity and one of the two superpowers.

The official Stalinist version of Stalinism has been challenged not only by most Western scholars, but also by some independent Soviet minds. The earliest major critic of Stalin was, of course, his main rival, Leon Trotsky. Most of Trotsky's writings after his removal from power in 1926 actually focused on criticism of Stalin. Trotsky was a prolific and brilliant writer and his views, which often changed as the situation in the Soviet Union and the international arena fluctuated, can only be telescoped very briefly here. The gist of Trotsky's and his followers' basic analysis may be summarized as follows. Classical, Western European Marxism was a model designed for a developed, industrialized, homogeneous country, whereas what happened in Russia was the triumph of socialism–communism in a backward, multinational empire that happened to constitute the weakest link in the capitalist chain. Therefore, Stalinism was a product of the anomaly that after the failure of the revolution in the West, primitive, unindustrialized Russia had to assume the role of vanguard in the march toward the international proletarian revolution. While Marx had said that the revolution should be preceded by industrialization, in Russia it was the other way around. This unnatural reversal of the sequence was bound to produce Stalinism, a degeneration of the original Marxist idea. The same explanation of Stalinism as essentially a product of Russia's economic retardation has been continued in the works of numerous Trotskyists, including Isaac Deutscher, whose biographies of Stalin and Trotsky, as well as numerous minor writings, expand upon this main idea. As Trotsky put it, "Stalinism is the syphilis of Socialism."

Another interpretation of Stalinism as a spoiler of the Good Thing that is Communism was embodied in the aforementioned

Khrushchev speech and in many of his subsequent pronouncements. His interpretation, however, differed from Trotsky's in its heavy emphasis on Stalin's personality as a quintessential part of the process of corruption of the originally correct theory of Marxism–Leninism. While Trotsky, especially in his biography of Stalin, also emphasized the personality factor, he had never considered Stalin's morbid thirst for power, his vindictiveness, and his sadistic proclivities as decisive factors. It was Khrushchev who analyzed the cult of personality and its consequences for the Party and the country at large in terms of the idiosyncrasies and perversions of "a giddy despot." Besides presenting a rather simplistic and highly un-Marxist interpretation of Stalin, Khrushchev left aside many problems that were often raised not only by Western historians but also by some representatives of Soviet historiography. One of them is that it was perhaps Lenin himself who had prepared the ground for Stalinism by smashing the old administrative and legal system, especially the judiciary, in a country where the notions of law and legality had only recently begun to germinate. Moreover, was it not also Lenin who had created the omnipotent Party and the ubiquitous secret police which he put above the law, thus constructing the mechanism that Stalin only perfected and used for his own ends?

Leaving aside these broad historiographic issues as outside the scope of what is after all merely an outline of Soviet history, let us examine the fourth approach to Stalinism as represented by a Soviet historian, Roy Medvedev. In his book *Let History Judge—The Origins and Consequences of Stalinism*, Medvedev has accused Stalin of corrupting Marxism–Leninism by excessive, unbridled application of terror because of a pathological thirst for personal power and glorification. Here Medvedev leans toward Khrushchev's view that Stalinism was not a cancer in the Soviet body politic but a nonmalignant growth, actually a skin-deep disease on the essentially healthy Leninist system, a disease that should and could have been removed in due time by a cosmetic operation before it spread deeper. Using some of Trotsky's original arguments as well as Khrushchev's reasoning, Medvedev represents a crossbreed between the two schools of thought, while leaning toward the psychohistorical approach. Instead of analyzing in a Marxist fashion the political, social, and economic roots of the Stalinist phenomenon, both Khrushchev and Medvedev preferred to stress the deficiencies of his personality. Both of these professed Marxists, therefore, reduced a complex historic phenomenon to subjective factors. Of course, Stalinism was marked by the personality of the great tyrant more than any other totalitarian movement; hence Stalin's psyche is of considerable importance. Yet to ascribe decisive importance to his heredity and mental makeup obfuscates rather than clarifies the essence of the phenomenon.

STALIN: SOME NON-SOVIET VIEWS

Non-Soviet views of Stalinism can be boiled down to three main currents. The first should be called a histroical school because it stresses the roots of Communism in the Russian past, in the peculiarities of the Muscovite-Russian development that contributed to the triumph of Bolshevism in the former Tsarist Empire. Typical representatives of this school believe that Communism, including its Stalinist variety, is a unique product of peculiarly Russian historic conditions. Such typical representatives of the historical approach as Nicholas Berdiaev (*The Origin of Russian Communism*), Jan Kucharzewski (*From the Whie Tsardom to the Red, The Origins of Modern Russia*), Tibor Szamueli (*The Russian Tradition*) or Robert V. Daniels (*Russia. The Roots of Confrontation*) stress the continuity of the Muscovite-Russian development.[3] They all argue

that a retarded, underdeveloped, amorphous Muscovite-Russian society was bound to produce a despotic government and that when Tsarism went bankrupt only another type of despotism could replace it. Communism, therefore, is nothing but a mutation of the Tsarist autocracy in a new, Marxist garb—a red Tsardom. By extension, Stalinism is a historically conditioned, modernized phase of the system Muscovy–Russia had already experienced under Ivan the Terrible, Peter the Great, and Nicholas I.

On the other hand, the traditional liberal school of thought finds the roots of the Stalinist tyranny in the suppression of political liberty compounded by the deprivation of private property. Private property is the foundation of individual liberty, argue such conservatives as Friederich Hayek (*The Road to Serfdom*). If one replaces private property with State property, this makes everybody a slave of an omnipotent State. By controlling both political power and material resources, the rulers exercise total control over each individual. As long as a measure of private initiative and property was still tolerated under the NEP, Soviet Russia was merely a stern authoritarian police state of a somewhat new type. It became a fully totalitarian structure only as a result of the Stalin revolution, which wiped out the remnants of private property, even in land ownership.

The third non-Soviet approach to Stalinism is represented by the supporters of the "industrialization theory." Its spokesmen find a coherent explanation of the Communist experiment, especially of its Stalinist stage, in Russia's economic retardation. According to them, Stalinism was Russia's response to the challenge of industrialization under the peculiarly trying conditions of political isolation, the constant threat of renewed foreign intervention, and a shortage of native capital, as well as the know-how needed for modern industrial

---

[3] The American historian goes as far as to write, "In terms of the revolutionary process, by extirpating the spirit of revolutionary innovation and liquidating the vast majority of the makers of the Revolution, Stalinism became the functional equivalent of a royal Restora-

tion." Robert V. Daniels, *Russia. The Roots of Confrontation.* (Cambridge, Mass.: Harvard University Press, 1985) p. 21.

progress. Menaced by foreign powers, with no chance for foreign aid, the Communist rulers of Russia decided to pull themselves up by their own bootstraps. Facing both external and internal dangers to the newly established regime, they decided on the desperate, cruel measures covered by the blanket term of Stalinism. The industrialization theory is represented by a plethora of works of which Barrington Moore's *Soviet Politics: The Dilemma of Power* or Walt Rostow's *Dynamics of Soviet Society* are perhaps the most representative. Isaac Deutscher's previously mentioned political biography of Stalin is a link between this school of thought and Trotsky's reasoning.

This typology merely simplifies and telescopes a broad spectrum of views that include various shades of opinion. These theories often overlap and/or supplement each other. No single theory comes near to the full interpretation of the historical phenomenon of Stalinism. Even their combination falls short of adequately explaining the incredible "success" of the sole ruler in history who exterminated more of his own people than did all of their enemies put together. Was Stalin "the greatest reformer of all times," as Isaac Deutscher called him, or was he the greatest criminal of all times?

Without embracing either of these positions, one should try to draw up a balance sheet of Stalin's rule of nearly three decades. On the negative side one should put the establishment of the strictest and harshest police regime on record, the stifling of individual initiative in all fields, including intellectual activity, the ruining of native agriculture, the thorough bureaucratization and militarization of society, and the slaughter of some twenty to thirty million people, including most of his close friends and co-workers. Even if one puts on the positive side the turning of Soviet Russia into the second leading industrial and military power of the world, the winning of World War II, and the expansion of Soviet frontiers even beyond those of the Tsarist Empire—the achievements that have so flattered the Russian national ego—there always remains the problem of the human price paid for these successes. It is worth noting that all the positive or allegedly positive achievements have to do with State power and prestige, while most of the negative ones pertain to the lot of the individual.

SUGGESTED READING

ADAMS, ARTHUR E., *Stalin and His Times*. New York: Holt, Rinehart and Winston, 1972.

ALI, TARIQ ed., *The Stalinist Legacy: Its Impact on Twentieth-Century World Politics*. Boulder, Colo.: Lynne Rienner Publishers, 1984.

ARMSTRONG, JOHN, *The Politics of Totalitarianism*. New York: Random House, 1961.

CRANKSHAW, EDWARD, *Khrushchev: A Career*. New York: Viking, 1966.

DANIELS, ROBERT V., *The Stalin Revolution: Foundations of Soviet Totalitarianism*. Lexington, Mass.: Heath, 1972.

DAVIS, L. E., *Cold War Begins: Soviet-American Conflict over Eastern Europe*. Princeton, N.J.: Princeton University Press, 1974.

FISCHER, LOUIS, *Life and Death of Stalin*. New York: Harper & Row, 1952.

GIBIAN, GEORGE, *Interval of Freedom: Soviet Literature During the Thaw, 1954–1957*. Minneapolis: University of Minnesota Press, 1960.

HALPERIN, ERNST, *The Triumphant Heretic: Tito's Struggle against Stalin*. London: Heinemann, 1958.

HINGLEY, RONALD, *Joseph Stalin: Man and Legend*. New York: McGraw-Hill, 1974.

JORAVSKY, DAVID, *The Lysenko Affair*. Cambridge, Mass.: Harvard University Press, 1970.

KAHIN, GEORGE M., *The Asian-African Conference, Bandung, Indonesia, April 1955*. Ithaca, N.Y.: Cornell University Press, 1956.

KOREY, WILLIAM, *The Soviet Cage: Anti-Semitism in Russia*. New York: Viking, 1973.

KULSKI, WLADYSLAW W., *Peaceful Co-Existence*. Chicago: Regnery, 1959.

LEONHARD, WOLFGANG, *The Kremlin Since Stalin*. New York: Praeger, 1962.

McCARLEY, MARTIN, *Khrushchev and the Development of Soviet Agriculture: The Virgin Land Program*. New York: Holmes and Meier, 1976.

MEDVEDEV, ROY A., and ZHORES A. MEDVEDEV,

Khrushchev: The Years in Power. New York: Columbia University Press, 1976.

MEDVEDEV, ZHORES A., *The Rise and Fall of T. D. Lysenko,* trans. I. Michael Lerner. Garden City, N.Y.: Doubleday, 1971.

MOORE, BARRINGTON, *Soviet Politics: The Dilemma of Power.* Cambridge, Mass.: Harvard University Press, 1951.

NOVE, ALEC, *Stalinism and After.* London: George Allen & Unwin, 1975.

PISTRAK, LAZAR, *The Great Tactician: Khrushchev's Rise to Power.* New York: Praeger, 1961.

RANDALL, FRANCIS, *Stalin's Russia.* New York: Free Press, 1965.

RIGBY, T. H., ed., *Stalin.* Englewood Cliffs, N.J.: Prentice-Hall, 1966.

RUBINSTEIN, ALVIN Z., *Red Star over the Nile.* Princeton, N.J.: Princeton University Press, 1977.

RUSH, MYRON, *The Rise of Khrushchev.* Washington, D.C.: Public Affairs Press, 1957.

SCHWARTZ, HARRY, *The Soviet Economy Since Stalin.* Philadelphia: Lippincott, 1961.

SOUVARINE, BORIS, *Stalin: A Critical Survey of Bolshevism.* New York: Octagon, 1972.

SWAYZE, HAROLD, *Political Control in Literature in the USSR, 1946–1959.* Cambridge, Mass.: Harvard University Press, 1962.

TROTSKY, LEON, *Stalin: An Appraisal of the Man and His Intentions.* New York: Harper & Row, 1941.

TUCKER, ROBERT C., ed., *Stalinism. . . .* New York: Norton, 1977.

URBAN, G. R. ed., *Stalinism: Its Impact on Russia and the World.* New York: St. Martin's, 1982.

WOLFE, BERTRAM D., *Khrushchev and Stalin's Ghost.* New York: Praeger, 1957.

CHAPTER 21

The Khrushchev Years: The Upward Trend

During the last two or three years of Stalin's life, the whole immense machinery of the Soviet State had been in danger of running itself into the ground because of the senile rigidity of its dictator. The fundamental problem faced by Stalin's heirs could be summed up in one sentence: how to thaw out the country's productive and creative forces from the Stalinist ice age without unleashing a torrential flood. Two people, Malenkov and Khrushchev, were determined to implement a reform program. Both of them perceived that the apparatus of power fashioned by Stalin could not indefinitely rely on terror alone. Both understood that the old machine required for its tolerable functioning a reasonably well-fed and well-housed labor force that could put its heart into the tasks at hand without constant threat of arrest and deportation. The open question was who would be able to lead this process of reforming the obsolete system and putting it into operation.

The more intellectual, yet practical and sober-minded Malenkov had run the Party for years on Stalin's behalf. Having packed its top echelons with Stanlin's yes-men, Malenkov obviously acquired a deep contempt for the servile, slovenly *apparatchiki*. On the other hand, as vice-premier in charge of the economy, he came to value some of the more efficient government bureaucrats and technocrats like Nikolai Bulganin or Alexei Kosygin, on whose efficient routine work the country's very existence depended. As a result of this, as well as of Stalin's increasing postwar reliance on State rather than Party organs, Malenkov came to the conclusion that cultivating and supporting these forces, rather than the more corrupt Party apparatchiki, would better guarantee the success of his reform program. Hence his willingness to relinquish the post of senior Party secretary to Khurshchev while keeping the premiership. In so doing, Malenkov disregarded some of the basic facts of Soviet life.

Khrushchev, on the other hand, never forgot where the locus of power resided. At the end of 1953 and the beginning of 1954, the story of Stalin and Trotsky's struggle for power was reenacted in miniature in a bloodless fashion, thus opening a new phase in the saga of Soviet succession struggles. After having first denounced Malenkov's reform program, Khrushchev soon adopted it and began to peddle it with the zeal and exuberance so characteristic of this human dynamo.

But Khrushchev was still far from outwitting his rivals, and for over a year they were to be a constant danger to him. The first major test came at the end of the Twentieth Congress. Khrushchev's speech debunking Stalin was intended as both another blow to his chief enemy, who had been Stalin's closest henchman, and as another steppingstone toward supreme power. Initially, as mentioned earlier, the speech was intended to be secret and only the Party's top officialdom was to have heard it. Soon, however, the gist of Khrushchev's denunciations filtered down to the masses and leaked abroad, where its full text was published in June 1956 by the United States State Department. While the speech may have had a beneficial effect on the Soviet people and on Khrushchev himself, the shattering contents of this pronouncement were bound to produce profound repercussions both in the Soviet Union and in the world at large.

One result of this speech was the release of millions of former political prisoners, who soon began to look for work. Another consequence was the beginning of political and intellectual ferment in the Soviet Union. The great debate on Stalin's crimes inevitably resulted in people's questioning the very foundations of the Soviet regime. This debate was the origin of the dissent movement. Its danger had been anticipated by Khrushchev's hard-line opponents, and the early manifestations of political and intellectual unrest were immediately blamed on him.

While the traditionally subservient Soviet people were relieved by the break with the past and limited their show of discontent to a few mutinies in labor camps—in Vorkuta, for instance—the reaction of the newly subdued peoples of East Central Europe was much deeper, more dramatic, and widespread. There the vestiges of Western liberalism and democracy and the traditions of the national independence these people had enjoyed during the two interwar decades were fairly strong. These traditions, combined with the resentment against Soviet hegemony, created a highly explosive situation in at least three countries: East Germany, Poland, and Hungary. The situation in that area should be viewed against the background of its general evolution during the late 1940s and early 1950s, and of the foreign policy initially followed by the collective Soviet leadership.

THE THAW SPREADS TO THE SATELLITE EMPIRE

The last three or four years of Stalin's rule had been the bleakest in the history of the Soviet hegemonial sphere. Arbitrary arrests and show trials of "Titoists" and "Zionists" were increasingly frequent in Eastern Europe. Gradually the stern, stifling atmosphere of Stalinist dogmatism had enveloped life in the buffer-zone countries. Literature was muzzled and emasculated, and along with all the other arts fell victim to socialist realism. In all writings, at least lip service had to be paid to Soviet achievements.

During this period all people with Western links or sympathies were under suspicion in Eastern Europe. This included Communists of Jewish extraction, who were increasingly regarded as security risks. As in the USSR, the new anti-Semitic line was camouflaged by the euphemisms "the struggle against cosmopolitanism" and "anti-Zionism." Such Jewish Communists as Ana Pauker in Romania or Rudolf Slánský in Czechoslovakia were purged. While Pauker was merely exiled, Slánský was hanged for being a "Zionist" as well as an "agent of the CIA." Hundreds of lesser leaders of similar background were also purged. The struggle against organized religion, especially Roman Catholicism because it had ties beyond the limits of the Soviet sphere, was continued. Numerous members of the Catholic hierarchy were arrested and tried, including Cardinal Mindszenty in Hungary and Archbishop Beran in Czechoslovakia. The religious persecution survived even Stalin's demise; the Primate of Poland, Cardinal Stefan Wyszynski, was arrested in September 1953.

Stalin's death and the struggle for power that followed were bound to have considerable effect on the whole Soviet orbit. The slight domestic thaw that could be observed in the Soviet Union during the years 1953–1955 was reflected almost immediately in the revolt of the East Berlin workers in June 1953. Its suppression was followed, nevertheless, by a measurable decompression in Hungary and Poland. One of the factors that precipitated far-reaching changes in Hungary and Poland was the July 10, 1953, Soviet announcement that Beria had been arrested. Beria's liquidation brought about at least a temporary disorganization of the Soviet security network in Eastern Europe, with which all East European secret police systems had been intimately linked. From then on events in Hungary and Poland, both of which had a long tradition of defiance to foreign domination, snowballed.

In July 1953, the most cruel of all East European dictators, Matyas Rákosi, had to yield the premiership to a representative of a milder variety of Hungarian Communism, Imre Nágy, although Rákosi kept the post of First Secretary of the Party. Nágy, picking up on Malenkov's attempts to placate Soviet consumers, inaugurated a similar "new course" in Hungary. He released a number of political prisoners, permitted peasants to leave collective farms and somewhat relaxed censorship. A number of debating and literary clubs were formed, the most significant of which was the Petöfi

Club, named after the great Hungarian poet of the "Spring of Nations" era of the 1848 revolution. By 1954–1955 Hungary was in a state of feverish ferment. In the spring of 1955 came Khrushchev's visit to Belgrade and his acceptance of the "national" way to Socialism–Communism.

In Poland the event that unleashed a series of incidents was the flight to the West in December 1953 of a high official of the Ministry of Public Security, Joseph Swiatlo. His revelations of the corruption of the "new class" (as Milovan Djilas called the party *apparat*) and the bestiality of its secret police were broadcast by Western radio systems in 1954 and 1955; they increased the existing tensions. Swiatlo's revelations eventually precipitated a purge of numerous discredited security officers and Party dignitaries. At the same time, Imre Nágy's Polish counterpart, Wladyslaw Gomulka, was released from detention and became the object of considerable attention from various party groups. While the Party's Stalinist wing wanted to win him over to bolster their tottering ascendancy, the more "liberal" faction hoped to use him as the standard bearer for a reformed, watered down, "humanized" Communism more attuned to the sentiments of the broad masses.

The crisis at the top was, in Poland as in Hungary, accompanied by growing unrest among the youth and the intellectuals, eager for more freedom of expression. Soon many basic tenets of Marxism were criticized, often quite openly, and the universality of the Soviet experience challenged.

THE "POLISH OCTOBER"

In February of 1956 came the Twentieth Soviet Party Congress and Khrushchev's secret speech. The speech put both the Hungarian and the Polish party bosses, Matyas Rákosi and Bolesław Bierut, on the spot; both of them, but especially Rákosi, had been as guilty of arbitrary rule as Stalin himself.[1] The debunking of Stalin amounted to undermining the Communist grip in the satellite area; for most East Europeans, Stalinism and Communism were indistinguishable from each other.

In Poland the gist of Khrushchev's speech filtered down to the masses and produced an instantaneous reaction. On June 28, during the yearly international fair at Poznań, Polish factory workers staged a demonstration whose slogan was, "We want bread and freedom!" The demonstrators clashed with the police, who were supported by army detachments. According to official figures, 53 people were killed and some 300 wounded.

After the Poznań riots, events in Poland gathered momentum. In August, Gomulka had been readmitted to the United Polish Workers' Party, and on October 19 was chosen as the Party's First Secretary. In his acceptance speech, Gomulka submitted the "past period" to searching and vehement criticism and promised broad reforms that would make the Communist system of Poland more domesticated, more democratic, and less dependent on Moscow. One of his decisions was to send packing Marshal Konstantin Rokossovsky, whom Stalin had made Commander-in-Chief of the Polish armed forces. The same order was given to several hundred Soviet officers who had occupied most of the key positions in the Polish defense establishment. Most collective farms were dissolved. Optional religious teaching was permitted in schools.

Hardly had Gomulka undertaken these steps when Khrushchev, at the head of an impressive military and civilian Soviet delegation, descended upon Warsaw. Despite strong Soviet pressure supported by threats of a full-scale military intervention. Gomulka stood by his decisions. In a stormy interview he managed to persuade Khrushchev that a firmly Communist but semiautonomous Poland loyal to the Warsaw Pact obligations and maintaining its membership in the CMEA would be a more reliable ally of the USSR. The Polish armed forces, now under native command, overwhelmingly supported Gomulka, and the people of Poland, especially its workers and students, manifested their solidarity with his attempts to gain at least a modicum of domestic independence from Russia.

Faced with the grim, resolute resistance of a great majority of Poles and reassured by Gomulka about the preservation of a triple link with the center (the Polish party's leading role, and military and economic ties), Khrushchev accepted the compromise, which was fully in accordance with the principle of separate roads to socialism he had proclaimed in Belgrade in 1955.

Poland had meanwhile been relegated to the background in the Soviet order of global priorities because of the highly explosive situation in the Middle East and the mounting crisis in Hungary. Here again the events of October–November 1956 have to be viewed in the light of the secret speech. In Hungary, Khrushchev's revelations precipitated the downfall of the cruel satrap Rákosi, who had to relinquish his last stronghold, the post of First Secretary, to a less compromised man, Ernö Gerö. Under public pressure Gerö had to rehabilitate Laszlo Rajk, who had been executed as a Titoist in 1949. The solemn reburial of Rajk's body on October 6, 1956, turned into a silent but impressive mass demonstration by the people of Budapest.

THE HUNGARIAN REVOLT

The largely peaceful triumph of Gomulka in Poland triggered a revolutionary situation in Hungary. There the mixture of suppressed patriotic longings and inveterate

---

[1] Bierut died of a heart attack soon after the Twentieth Congress and the secret speech, which was probably too much of a shock for the old Stalinist. Among other things, a special commission established by the congress had rehabilitated the Communist Party of Poland, dissolved and decimated by Stalin in 1938. The role of Bierut during the Great Purge is still controversial.

The Soviet Bloc in 1956

Neutral and Non-Aligned countries

NATO countries

Soviet Bloc countries

SWEDEN

DENMARK

Baltic Sea

Riga

(EAST GERMANY)
Berlin

GERMAN DEMOCRATIC REPUBLIC

Warsaw

POLAND

U.S.S.R.

Prague

CZECHOSLOVAKIA

Kiev

FEDERAL REPUBLIC OF GERMANY (WEST GERMANY)

Vienna

NEUTRAL AUSTRIA

Budapest

HUNGARY

ROMANIA

Belgrade

NON-ALIGNED YUGOSLAVIA

Bucarest

Rome

ITALY

Adriatic Sea

BULGARIA

Sofia

Black Sea

ALBANIA

Tirana

GREECE

Aegean Sea

TURKEY

socioeconomic grievances was even more potent than in Poland. Because of old historic ties between the two countries, the Polish events were closely watched by the Hungarians. On October 23 a demonstration was organized in Budapest mainly by university students in support of the Poles— then already celebrating their limited but enviable success. The next day a similar manifestation occurred in front of the Budapest radio building to press the government to implement the resolutions the demonstrators had voted the day before. Their demands included the reconstruction of the government under Imre Nágy (who had been ousted by Rákosi because of his reforming zeal), free elections, freedom of expression, and last but not least, the immediate withdrawal of Soviet garrisons from Hungary. The peaceful demonstration was fired upon by the secret police supported by Soviet troops. This precipitated large-scale street fighting. Soon a large part of the Hungarian army had joined the rebels and the fighting spread from the capital all over the country.

That same night of October 24, the Hungarian Party leaders, alarmed by the strength of the revolt, accepted one of the rebel's demands and reinstated Nágy as Prime Minister. At the same time the desperately isolated party requested Soviet military assistance under the terms of the Warsaw Pact. On October 25 the helpless Gerö was removed as First Secretary and replaced by the more energetic and resourceful Jánŏs Kádár. Meanwhile, the fighting in Budapest and in the provinces continued, with the rebels victorious more often than not. On October 27, under mounting pressure from the triumphant insurgents, Nágy's government was broadened to include a former leader of the Smallholders' Party, Bela Kovács, and a Social Democrat, Anna Kethly. Lulled into a sense of false security by the conclusion of a cease-fire, the apparent withdrawal of the Soviet troops from Hungary, and the Soviet pronouncement promising the establishment of an ostensibly more democratic "commonwealth of social-

ist states," the exhilarated Nágy undertook two momentous steps: he declared that Hungary would no longer be a one-party state, and that it was withdrawing from the Warsaw Treaty Organization to become a neutral country like Austria or Switzerland.

Here the contrast between Gomułka's Poland and Nágy's Hungary became quite striking. Whereas Gomułka had fought for a limited measure of domestic autonomy and for a slightly reformed party, while willing to preserve all existing links with the USSR, Nágy insisted both on complete independence and neutrality. The severing of all existing political, military, and economic links with the USSR was obviously a serious matter for Moscow. A neutral Hungary would separate Czechoslovakia from Romania and thus split the Soviet satellite empire, setting a dangerous precedent for other nations of the region. While the Hungarians were celebrating their apparent and quite unexpected victory, the reinforced Soviet troops swept back into the country in the early hours of November 4. Despite massive Hungarian resistance, the superior forces of the Red Army crushed the insurgents within a few days. Nágy sought shelter in the Yugoslav Embassy while protesting Soviet violation of Hungary's neutrality and vainly appealing to the United Nations. Meanwhile, the victorious Soviet army installed Jánŏs Kádár as First Party Secretary and Prime Minister.

The Hungarians paid a high price for their attempts at freedom. Some 3,000 people perished during the uprising and its aftermath, while nearly 15,000 were imprisoned. Over 200,000 left the country and settled in the West, about 40,000 of them in the United States. This was a terrible bloodletting for a nation of some 8 million people that was already suffering from a deficient birth rate. All this, however, was soon forgotten by the West, as if to confirm the saying of the French moralist de la Rochefoucauld that "We have always enough strength to bear the misfortunes of others."

In the midst of the Hungarian uprising,

the world's attention was diverted to another crisis. On October 29, Israeli troops, acting in concert with the French and the British, who were smarting over Nasser's nationalization of the Suez Canal, attacked Egypt. The Israeli, French, and British troops were about to capture the canal when the Soviet Union issued a stern protest and demanded immediate international action to stop the invasion of Egypt. Khrushchev's intervention included a threat to use the Soviet atom bomb to enforce the Israeli-French-British withdrawal.

Almost at the same time the United States also took a determined stand against the triple invasion of Egypt. This parallel action of the two superpowers, hitherto bitter opponents in the cold war, brought about an instant armistice and the withdrawal of the Israeli, French, and British forces. The unexpected cooperation of the two global rivals dramatized their role as guardians of the status quo created by World War II. This was underscored by the fact that Washington, despite its often vigorous advocacy of the "liberation of Eastern Europe from the Soviet yoke" and "rolling back the Iron Curtain," now refused to respond to the appeals of the Hungarian rebels for moral and material help. Quite the contrary, the United States reaffirmed its adherence to the status quo created by the wartime diplomatic agreements with the USSR.

The suppression of the Hungarian uprising had numerous consequences for the Soviet domestic situation and for its international prestige. The United Nations, despite angry Soviet protests, denounced Moscow's highhanded action in Hungary as an act of aggression. Among more liberal-minded and humanitarian Communist intellectuals, the Soviet action provoked protests and encouraged desertion from the Party ranks. For instance, such Marxist writers as Jean-Paul Sartre in France and Howard Fast in the United States tore up their Communist Party cards and voiced their strong disapproval of Moscow's brutal behavior.

While the world soon forgot about the fate of Hungary, the 1956 events in Eastern Europe, combined with some Soviet domestic events, seriously threatened Khrushchev's newly established position at the Kremlin. His opponents blamed the ferment in Poland and Hungary on his too rash and unconditional acceptance of Tito's independent line and on Khrushchev's too liberal attitude toward the increasing manifestations of Communist heterodoxy in other dependent countries. To this criticism of his foreign policy, domestic arguments were also added.

KHRUSHCHEV'S TACTICS

To understand Khrushchev's ascent to power, one must consider the events of the first three years of the post-Stalin era. The first in emotional importance was cutting the security apparatus down to size and returning to what was termed socialist legality. Then came the rehabilitation of 7 to 8 million actual or former political prisoners and deportees. These people, their families, and friends automatically became Khrushchev's enthusiastic supporters. From the ashes of Beria's autonomous Ministries of State Security (MGB) and of the Interior (MVD) arose the Committee of State Security (KGB), which was directly subordinate to the Council of Ministers and hence ultimately to the Party. The KGB still ruled with an iron hand, but mass arrests and deportations without trial were things of the past. In comparison with the unbridled reign of terror, this was a great improvement. Censorship was relaxed and books like Vladimir Dudintsev's *Not By Bread Alone*, which was strongly critical of the Soviet bureaucracy, could see the light of day. Poetry and public balladeering began to flourish again, and artists like Yevgenii Yevtushenko or Bulat Okudzhava made public appearances and presented their verses and ballads to thousands of eager listeners. By the spring of 1956, Khrushchev had already become a national hero in the eyes of a sizable majority of the Soviet people, including most of the Party rank and file.

The magnitude of the process and its far-reaching consequences made most people forget how selective and arbitrary these rehabilitations were.

Second in importance among Khrushchev's reforms were numerous improvements in the standard of living. The suppressed, but very extreme popular disenchantment with Stalin's postwar economic policies was rooted in an abysmally low level of consumption that was only partly caused by objective necessities. The austerity of this period had been largely imposed by Stalin's inordinate desire to make the USSR a military power far beyond its means. Enormous resources had been channeled toward atomic research projects, most of them carried out on a crash basis under the supervision of Beria's security apparatus. The Gulag Archipelago expanded like a cancerous growth, penetrating practically every field of human activity.

The main victims of Stalin's economic policies were the Soviet peasants. In rehabilitating the country, Stalin had again turned his back on the villages, and overwhelmingly focused on rebuilding the cities and restoring heavy industry, starting with those primarily serving defense. Consequently, the countryside, ravaged and depopulated, was far behind in regaining even its low prewar productive capacity. Former peasants, discharged from the armed forces, did not want to return to the semiserfdom of the collective or State farms where they were legally tied to the land like serfs. Instead, they rushed to better-paying and more mobile urban jobs that held some prospect of advancement.[2] As this trend brought about a further decline in the young, able-bodied rural population, it also increased the need for greater food production. Yet Soviet agriculture, operating under a system of sui

generis peonage, starved of fertilizers and modern machinery, and harassed by rising taxes and delivery quotas, was stagnating. By 1953 it was on the verge of collapse. The prices paid by the State for the products of collective farms often amounted to only a fraction of their production costs. After 1946, taxes on the household plots began to exceed the point at which it would be worthwhile to increase their cultivation. Fines and criminal charges were again imposed on those who were in arrears. Since for tax purposes the household plots were assessed on their output rather than their size, the peasants not only stopped cultivating them, but often destroyed what they had. Fruit trees were chopped down to avoid the exorbitant taxes on them, and pigs, cows, and poultry were slaughtered. By the early 1950s, potatoes had become the main crop of the household plots because their quota and taxes remained fairly reasonable. As Khrushchev admitted in September 1953, the per capita grain production of that year was lower than in 1913.

Stalin had never cared to visit a collective farm and was blind to the plight of the peasantry. He had no idea whatsoever about farming, and mistrusted peasants as greedy and rebellious "petty bourgeois." Most of his close co-workers, like Zhdanov, Malenkov, and Mikoyan, tended to assume a similar attitude, either because of ignorance or to please Stalin. Among the people around Stalin, Khrushchev was the only one born and bred on a farm and he preserved some sympathy for the downtrodden and exploited villagers.

By the spring of 1953, Khrushchev realized that the rescue must come quickly and that redemption of the country's agriculture was its number one priority. One of his first steps, therefore, was to lower delivery quotas and taxes on household plots, and to increase dramatically the prices to be paid by the State to the peasants. Prices to be paid for meat and poultry were augmented 550 percent, for milk and butter 200 percent, and for vegetables, 40 percent. Old debts of the collective farms were canceled. This

---

[2] People working in a town or city were registered with the police and had internal passports for identification. Peasants had no passports, only identification papers from their respective collective or State farm authorities. These papers did not entitle them either to travel beyond a certain narrow radius or to work anywhere else.

immediately brought some relief of the economic plight of the peasantry and an improvement in their morale. For the first time in a quarter of a century, the squeeze on them had been not only halted, but even somewhat relaxed.

The results of this relaxation, together with the initially successful virgin land campaign, were quick and tangible. While in 1953 almost a quarter of the 20 million peasant families did not have a cow, by 1959 virtually every family had at least one cow. The number of sheep more than doubled, while poultry and pigs also multiplied. Orchards and vegetable gardens revived. The 1956 harvest was the best in Soviet history. All this represented, on balance, a modest progress and did not remedy the nationwide shortage of food, especially of milk, meat, fruit, and vegetables; but in comparison with the near-disastrous situation in the early 1950s, it resulted in an improvement in the people's diet and mood.

Khrushchev was also responsible for the considerable expansion of housing construction. To speed it up, he ordered the application of new methods of prefabrication. Despite the fact that he lacked scientific training and had only a rather rudimentary education, he displayed a keen interest in technology. One of his favorite pastimes was to watch technical documentary films, especially those on American agricultural methods. During his 1959 journey to the United States, Khrushchev was fascinated by the efficiency of American farming. After his trip, Khrushchev was more determined than ever to rescue Soviet agriculture from its slovenly backwardness by using selected capitalist technological methods, including intensive fertilizing. He also began to propagate cafeteria-style mass

A view of Moscow from the top of the new building of the Lomonosov University

feeding establishments, vending machines, and other innovations previously frowned upon as typical of the "decadent, capitalistic West." For Khrushchev, the United States, with its automobiles, refrigerators, and washing machines, was the model to emulate. For the first time since the NEP, the standard of living of the ordinary Soviet citizen became an important consideration of economic policy.

KHRUSHCHEV AT BAY

What delighted the average Soviet citizen and even most Party members, appeared, however, as anathema in the eyes of a small group of *apparatchiki*, who had been Stalin's closest henchmen. These were people who had been intimately connected with his criminal acts and who resented Khrushchev's growing ascendancy and popularity and were determined to oust him. The hard core of this die-hard Stalinist faction centered around Malenkov, Molotov, and Kaganovich. All of them, to a greater or lesser degree, had been coresponsible for Stalin's excesses. Moreover, they resented being eclipsed by the "upstart" Khrushchev, whom they regarded as their inferior. This *troika* was soon joined by a small but influential part of the Party machine as well as by some bureaucrats who had been planted in high State positions by Malenkov. The opposition also included the surviving, and now mostly retired, former members of the old security network. All these people felt threatened by the ongoing process of liberalization and were looking for opportunities to strike back at Khrushchev.

In addition, the Stalinists were psychologically motivated. During his rule of nearly three decades, Stalin had created certain habits and conditioned reflexes difficult to eradicate. Some of them had deep roots in the Muscovite-Russian history, while others were of fresher vintage. The domestic ferment, including the first public political dissent, the unrest in Eastern Europe, the worsening relations with Mao, who disapproved of the secret speech and refused to accept Khrushchev's leadership of the world Communist movement—all this was now blamed on Khrushchev's exuberant pronouncements and rash reforms.

Until the spring of 1957, despite his popularity with the masses, Khrushchev's party position was shaky; he was under constant pressure and unsure as to how quickly he could proceed. The first indications of another bountiful harvest in the virgin lands, however, bolstered his position dramatically by vindicating one of his pet schemes. The apparent successes of the corn-growing campaign also emboldened Khrushchev beyond measure. Now, with exuberance exceptional even for him, he put forward two new schemes. One established a number of regional economic bodies called "People's Economic Councils" (*sovnarkhozy*), which, he argued, would cut through red tape by decentralizing economic planning and thus engage local talent and initiative. The scheme, while offering the promise of promotion to tens of thousands of local Party men, was a heavy blow to the central ministries.

Khrushchev's second scheme was to make the Soviet Union take a "great leap forward" as far as the diet of its citizens was concerned. In May 1957, speaking in Leningrad, he put forth a gigantic plan for greatly expanding the Soviet production of meat, milk, and butter. By 1960–1961, the USSR was to surpass the United States in these three fields. Overtaking the United States in butter production was quite possible, since its consumption of this item was rapidly declining as a result of an increased marketing of vegetable oil and margarine. In meat production, however, the USSR lagged so far behind its competitor that Khrushchev's scheme bordered on lunacy. At that time the United States produced more than twice as much meat as the Soviets. Consequently, Khrushchev's idea was decried as fantastic even by many of his supporters. Yet he stuck to his guns despite the objections of most of the Presidium and many of his economic advisers, whom he had not consulted before his speech anyway.

DEFEAT
OF THE ANTI-PARTY GROUP

The bitter inner-Party clash was precipitated by the two schemes, but especially by the Leningrad speech, was taken advantage of by his opponents. The plot to unseat Khrushchev was hatched in June 1957 while he and Bulganin were on a state visit to Finland. On June 18, the day after his return from Helsinki, Khrushchev had to face a critical majority of the Presidium, which denounced him as an irresponsible adventurer leading to the country to ruin and ridicule. He was outvoted eight to four. His only supporters were Mikhail A. Suslov, Anastas I. Mikoyan, and his own lady friend, Katerina A. Furtseva, Minister of Culture. Malenkov, Molotov, and Kaganovich were joined by Voroshilov; First Deputy Premier and Chairman of the State Planning Committee Mikhail G. Pervukhin; Maxim Z. Saburov, another First Deputy Premier; and Dmitri T. Shepilov, the Foreign Minister. Bulganin also sided with the opposition. Having outvoted Khrushchev by two to one, the conspirators insisted on his instant resignation from the post of First Secretary of the Central Committee. Khrushchev, however, objected. Arguing that the "rules of arithmetic do not always apply in politics," he appealed from the Presidium to a plenary meeting of the Central Committee, whose members, after all, had elected him as their secretary.[3]

At that time Leningrad was celebrating the 250th anniversary of its founding by Peter the Great, and many members of the Central Committee were gathered there. Informed about the situation, Minister of Defense Marshal Zhukov, grateful to Khrushchev for recalling him from retirement, put military jet planes at his disposal. By June 21, over one hundred members of the Committee, more than a third of the entire body, had arrived at the Kremlin to insist on their statutory right to decide the fate of their First Secretary. Most Central Committee members were regional Party functionaries whose power and sense of security were increased by Khrushchev's plans to decentralize authority and by his abandonment of the Stalinist terror. During the June 22–23 session, they outvoted the conspirators. Out of 309 present, 215 voted for Khrushchev and only a few abstained.

The conspirators, henceforth called by their opponents "the anti-Party group," were denounced and accused of applying "anti-Party, factional methods in an attempt to change the composition of the Party's leading bodies." The main ringleaders—Malenkov, Molotov, and Kaganovich—were expelled from the Presidium and the Central Committee. Shepilov was deprived of his alternate Presidium membership and his place at the Party's secretariat as well as in the Ministry of Foreign Affairs, where he was now replaced by his deputy, Andrei Gromyko. For reasons of expediency and decorum, Bulganin's and Voroshilov's punishment was delayed. In March, the former was ousted from his premiership. The latter would be retired from the largely ceremonial post of Chairman of the Presidium of the Supreme Soviet, or head of the Soviet State, in 1960.

Khrushchev's victory was surprising and complete. It was followed by a far-reaching reshuffle of the apex of the power pyramid. The four main leaders of the anti-Party group were not given the punishment that would have been their lot under Stalin. Malenkov, once in charge of the whole of Soviet industry, was appointed manager of a power station in a remote corner of Central Asia. Molotov was made ambassador to Mongolia. Kaganovich, who had once been boss of the Ukraine, was made director of a cement factory in Sverdlovsk. Shepilov, an economist, became a professor in one of the Moscow colleges. By these relatively mild reprisals, Khrushchev was trying to show that terror was no longer needed to run the country.

Meanwhile, the Presidium was packed

---

[3] This was a justified demand: according to the Party bylaws, the First Secretary is elected and/or removed by the plenum of the Central Committee.

Andrei A. Gromyko, Foreign Minister, 1957–1985

than under Stalin, yet pronounced enough, began to develop around him. Despite a resolution by the Twentieth Congress forbidding places to be named after living leaders, several towns and villages were allowed to break the rule. One of them was his native village of Kalinovka, in the Kursk province. Khrushchev's picture began to appear everywhere. His speeches were printed, as a rule, ahead of other pronouncements, and eventually published in book form.

In 1959, Khrushchev made a thirteen-day tour of the United States. He visited farms and factories, universities and film studios, paying special attention to American agricultural techniques, especially corn growing. In Hollywood he raised hell with one of the directors, sternly admonishing him that the can-can was obscene and decadent.

with Khrushchev's supporters. Four candidates were raised to full membership. One of them was Leonid Brezhnev, then First Party Secretary of the Kazakhstan republic and one who was instrumental in launching the virgin land project. Another noteworthy promotion to full membership in the Presidium was that of Marshal Zhukov, who was now rewarded for his support. Zhukov's political role did not last very long, however. His insistence on further downgrading the political commissars' role ran counter to the concept of strict Party control of the armed forces. In October 1957, after his return from a visit to Yugoslavia, Zhukov was dismissed from the post of Minister of Defense. Zhukov was replaced by Marshal Rodion Malinovsky, who had been closely associated with Khrushchev during the Stalingrad campaign.

After smashing the anti-Party group, Khrushchev abandoned the pretense of collective leadership and ruled in a dictatorial way. This became especially true when, in 1958, both the premiership and the post of First Secretary were in his hands. Now a new sort of personality cult, more subdued

KHRUSHCHEV'S APOGEE

The years 1957–1959 were Khrushchev's apogee. He was popular at home and feared abroad. Among the faceless and colorless Soviet chieftains, he stood out as a dramatic and often quite witty personality, an accomplished actor, although frequently one of a somewhat clownish variety. Even his controversial and coarse pronouncements were greeted as a welcome relief from the unbearable boredom and banality of other Soviet bureaucrats. Radiating vitality and exuberance, he traveled throughout the country, mixing with ordinary people as no Soviet leader has done before. His populist-like pronouncements, emphasizing the importance of non-Party elements in building socialism, were greatly appreciated by the people in the street. Khrushchev opened the Kremlin to visitors for the first time since 1930. Ordinary citizens were allowed to enter freely the old fortress, its churches and palaces, and to see their treasures, while only certain government buildings were closed to the public. After Stalin's haughty and unapproachable manner and his isolation behind heavily guarded Kremlin walls, most people liked to see Khrushchev mixing freely with the people, and they enjoyed his trips around the country, his attention-getting journeys abroad, and even his incessant speeches, which initially were a refreshing novelty.

In the scientific field, Khrushchev's liberalizing attitude toward non-Party scholars, especially technicians, paid good dividends. Under Stalin about half of all scientific projects pertaining to nuclear and space research had been conducted by political prisoners who in everyday life had been distinguished specialists in their fields. They worked in closely guarded institutes controlled by the MGB or MVD. Khrushchev freed most of them and showered them with favors. He ordered the construction of an "academic city" at Novosibirsk and allowed the study of cybernetics. A few years of such a policy produced beneficial results. In October 1957, the Soviet space scientists successfully launched the first artificial earth

A Soviet cosmonaut in his space ship

satellite, the *Sputnik,* or Co-traveler; *Sputnik II* followed in November. The West was struck dumb. These achievements, followed by a series of less significant but comparable experiments in space, also had a stunning impact on the morale of the Soviet people. Communism and not capitalism appeared to them as the wave of the future. The international prestige of the Soviet Union now skyrocketed. The USSR seemed to have demonstrated its superiority over its main rival in the field of technical education, especially in the vital sphere of space technology. Peaceful competition among nations would decide the course the world would take.

The launching of the Sputniks was also a great personal victory for Khrushchev. After all, it was he who had given high priority to space research in general and to missiles in particular. The chief designer of the Sputnik, Sergei P. Korolev, had been arrested before the war on Stalin's orders for allegedly sabotaging work on standard aircraft and had spent years in the Kolyma gold mines as punishment. Khrushchev had freed Korolev and made him chief designer of the Soviet space program. The two Sputniks, which ushered in the space age, created in the United States and throughout the West a crisis of confidence. One of the most striking features of the new epoch has been the Soviet-American rivalry in the cosmos.

For the moment Khrushchev's remaining opponents were silenced. His popularity throughout the country was impressive. If he had succeeded so brilliantly against heavy odds against the majority of the Presidium, in the space competition with the United States, and in making wheat grow abundantly on the arid steppes of Kazakhstan, then maybe his other programs would also be beneficial. Maybe even his corn crusade, which advocated the cultivation of this essentially mild-climate plant far in the north, would also be successful.

While Khrushchev was wallowing in his genuine as well as imaginary successes—magnified by his exuberant oratory—his errors were inexorably catching up with him. During 1957 and 1958, when his country had two bumper crops in a row, it was difficult to anticipate all his future mistakes and misfortunes. Yet their seeds had already been sown during his fat years.

SUGGESTED READING

BRANT, STEFAN, *The East German Rising.* New York: Praeger, 1957.

BRZEZINSKI, ZBIGNIEW, *The Soviet Bloc: Unity and Conflict* (2nd ed.). Cambridge, Mass.: Harvard University Press, 1961.

CAMPBELL, JOHN C., *American Policy toward Communist Eastern Europe: The Choices Ahead,* Minneapolis: University of Minnesota Press, 1965.

COHEN, STEPHEN F., ALEXANDER RABINOWITCH, ROBERT SHARLET (eds), *The Soviet Union Since Stalin.* Bloomington: Indiana University Press, 1980.

CRANKSHAW, EDWARD, *Khrushchev: A Career.* New York: Viking, 1966.

DALLIN, ALEXANDER, et al., *The Soviet Union, Arms Control and Disarmament.* New York: Columbia University Press, 1964.

DJILAS, MILOVAN, *The New Class: An Analysis of the Communist System.* New York: Praeger, 1957.

DZIEWANOWSKI, M. K., *The Communist Party of Poland: An Outline of History* (2nd ed.). Cambridge, Mass.: Harvard University Press, 1976, Chs. 12–16.

FIELD, MARK D., *Doctor and Patient in Soviet Russia.* Cambridge, Mass.: Harvard University Press, 1957.

HILDEBRANDT, RAINER. *The Explosion.* New York: Duell, Sloan and Pearce, 1955.

KHRUSHCHEV, NIKITA, *Khrushchev Remembers.* Boston: Little, Brown, 1971.

———, *Khrushchev Remembers: The Last Testament.* Boston: Little, Brown, 1974.

LEONHARD, WOLFGANG, *The Kremlin Since Stalin.* New York: Praeger, 1962.

LEVINE, IRVING R., *Main Street USSR.* Garden City, N.Y.: Doubleday, 1959.

LINDEN, CARL A., *Khrushchev and the Soviet Leadership, 1957–1964.* Baltimore, Md.: Johns Hopkins University Press, 1966.

MACINTOSH, J. M., *Strategy and Tactics of Soviet Foreign Policy.* New York: Oxford University Press, 1963.

MATTHEWS, MERVYN, *Education in the Soviet Union: Policies and Institutions Since Stalin.* Winchester, Mass.: Allen & Unwin, 1982.

REMINGTON, ROBIN, *The Warsaw Pact: Case Studies in Communist Conflict Resolution.* Cambridge, Mass.: MIT Press, 1971.

RUSH, MYRON, *Political Succession in the USSR.* New York: Columbia University Press, 1965.

SCHOLMER, JOSEPH, *Vorkuta.* New York: Holt, Rinehart and Winston, 1955.

SCHWARTZ, HARRY, *The Soviet Economy Since Stalin.* Philadelphia: Lippincott, 1965.

STEHLE, HANS JAKOB, *The Independent Satellite.* New York: Praeger, 1965.

SWEARER, HOWARD R., *The Politics of Succession in the USSR.* Boston: Little, Brown, 1964.

SYROP, KONRAD. *Spring in October: The Polish Revolution of 1956.* New York: Praeger, 1958.

TATU, MICHEL, *Power in the Kremlin: From Khrushchev to Kosygin.* New York: Viking, 1969.

ULAM, ADAM, *New Face of Soviet Totalitarianism.* New York: Praeger, 1965.

VALI, FERENC A., *Rift and Revolt in Hungary.* Cambridge, Mass.: Harvard University Press, 1961.

ZINNER, PAUL E., *Revolution in Hungary.* Plainview, N.Y.: Books for Libraries, 1962.

CHAPTER 22

Khrushchev's Decline and Fall

In October 1964, when Khrushchev was overthrown, a saying was coined in the diplomatic and journalistic quarters of Moscow that he lost power because of three "Cs": China, Cuba, and corn. As with most dicta of this sort, this one reduces a complex problem to a witty alliteration. But if Cuba is meant to cover the totality of Soviet-American relations, and if corn stands as a symbol of Khrushchev's domestic politics, then the saying acquires some real meaning. Applying the formula of the triple "Cs," therefore, let us examine the causes of Khrushchev's decline and fall.

THE CHINESE PROBLEM

The launching of the two Sputniks months before United States' ventures seemed to have opened an era of Soviet ascendancy in space technology. The fact that these achievements took place when Moscow was celebrating the fortieth anniversary of the Bolshevik revolution lent them a symbolic significance. The Chinese were even more impressed by the Soviet space feats than the rest of the world. In November 1957, Mao, forgetting his previous differences with Khrushchev concerning the de-Stalinization campaign, attended the fortieth anniversary conference of the Communist Parties in Moscow to persuade the Soviet leaders to take advantage of this apparent ascendancy over the West. The first step in this direction should be a challenge in the Far East to the United States by supporting, with the Soviet navy and nuclear weapons if necessary, a planned invasion of Taiwan and the off-shore islands of Quemoy and Matsu. The USSR, long master of the hydrogen bomb, now led the Americans in intercontinental missiles. Soon Mao Tse-tung began to argue that the socialist camp headed by the Soviet Union would triumph over the imperialists in every way. He claimed that the United

States was a "paper tiger" and that "the East Wind is prevailing over the West Wind." In a talk with a Yugoslav delegation in Peking, Mao observed that a nuclear war would mean the end of capitalism but not of Communism: even if 300 million Chinese were killed, there would still be 300 million left alive.

Khrushchev was shocked by Mao's arguments. The USSR was building up Socialism, not inviting its destruction, he retorted. His ballistic missiles were instruments of Soviet state power. He had not the slightest intention of placing Soviet nuclear weapons at the disposal of China or even of teaching China how to make them.

This refusal to aid Peking militarily was soon followed by theoretical disputes concerning Soviet Russia's and China's stages of historic development. After his return from the November 1957 Communist rally, Mao launched a new program aimed at demonstrating China's self-reliance. Within a short period of time, Peking announced that some 90 percent of the Chinese peasantry had joined rural communes in which private property and the family were nearly obliterated in favor of a strictly regimented communal life style. This was combined with a new crash program of industrialization epitomized by the "back-yard blast furnaces." As a result of this attempted "great leap forward," by the autumn of 1958 the Chinese countryside was plunged into chaos reminiscent of, if not worse than, the early stages of Stalin's collectivization.

Initially the Soviet leaders had cautiously praised the experimental policy of their Chinese comrades. This changed, however, when Peking proclaimed that it was about to pass the Socialist stage of development and achieve full Communism. Such a proclamation constituted an open challenge to the Soviet leadership of the Communist camp; the Chinese claim that Mao had found a short-cut to the final goal, and thus had overtaken the Soviet Union in its march toward Utopia, was a serious blow to Moscow's title to leadership of the world Communist movement. The title was based not only on Moscow's "revolutionary seniority," but also on the axiom that the Soviet Party headed the most advanced society, one that had already constructed Socialism and was well along the way to Communism, but had not as yet achieved this millennial goal.

Because the Sino-Soviet dispute was initially conducted in strictly Marxist terms, most Western experts interpreted it as an essentially ideological quarrel. The two Communist giants, it was argued, were in basic agreement about revolutionary strategy and the destruction of their Western, capitalist enemies. They were merely quarreling about tactical details. However, by the early 1960s, with the emergence of a bitter territorial conflict, the power–political factors began to loom larger and larger.

THE SINO-SOVIET SPLIT

During the late 1950s, Khrushchev ignored the repeated requests of his Chinese comrades for more military aid against America's protegé Chiang Kai-shek, and for more economic aid to stave off the catastrophic failure of Mao's "second revolution." Khrushchev blatantly disregarded China's warning not to consort with the "capitalist imperialists" and pursued his policy of coexistence. The high-water mark of these efforts was his 1959 trip to the citadel of capitalism, a visit which Khrushchev enjoyed immensely. In October of 1959, after his American trip, Khrushchev flew to Peking to celebrate the tenth anniversary of the Communist triumph in China. At that time the prolonged artillery duel between the Chinese People's Liberation Army and the Nationalist forces defending the offshore islands was still going on.

When Khrushchev landed in Peking, Mao did not even extend his hand to the First Secretary of "the fraternal Soviet Party" and ignored him throughout his brief stay. Khrushchev retorted by leaving the Chinese capital before the conclusion of the anniversary celebration. The snub was followed by the further worsening of Sino-

Soviet relations. After his return, Khrushchev ordered the withdrawal from China of most of the Soviet military, economic and scientific experts who were helping their comrades in a variety of fields. This further damaged the already shaky relations between the two Communist colossi, who, until this point, were still considered by many Western observers as ideological partners and military allies.

Until June 1960 the depth of the Sino-Soviet disagreements was camouflaged as a quasi-theological dispute between the "dogmatist" and "revisionist" wings of the same movement, which were welded forever by common ideology. This illusion was abruptly shattered late in June 1960 at the conference of Communist leaders in Bucharest, where, for the first time, Khrushchev openly leveled bitter criticism of the Chinese behavior. He attacked the absent Mao for his ignorance of modern warfare, especially of the dangers inherent in nuclear weapons; he upbraided him for his domestic politics that were not only "un-Leninist," "ultra-leftist," and "left-revisionist," but were also totally detached from the realities of the modern world.

The head of the Chinese delegation in Bucharest indignantly retorted by accusing Khrushchev of having sabotaged the Chinese economic plans and having conspired with the "American imperialists" against China's vital interests. He charged the Soviet leader with total blindness to the dangers of imperialism. Among the Communist delegates present in Bucharest, only Albania's leader, Enver Hoxha, openly sided with Peking.

Despite attempts at papering over the Sino-Soviet dispute, it went from bad to worse. In August 1960, the remaining Soviet students, scholars, and experts were promptly evacuated from China. Peking reciprocated. While most of their experts were safely released, the departure of the Chinese nuclear specialists studying at various Soviet atomic centers (mainly at Dubna near Moscow) was delayed for a long time. The Soviet authorities refused to accept

Peking's offer of military planes to transport the Chinese experts and insisted on sending them back in their own aircraft. When they were finally dispatched in a Red Army transport plane, it exploded in midair. There were no survivors. The Soviets explained the accident as "engine failure." When the news was communicated to Chou En-lai, he burst into tears. According to Chinese testimony, this was the only time he was seen crying in public.

The outbreak of the Sino-Indian border dispute in September and the Cuban crisis in October of 1962 further complicated the relations between Moscow and Peking. During the Sino-Indian war, the Soviet Union assumed a "neutral" position, which was immediately denounced by the Chinese as tacit support of a "bourgeois" country against a Communist one, and hence a flagrant violation of "proletarian solidarity." From then on, Sino-Soviet relations continued to deteriorate. Charges of mutual "betrayal," "perfidy," and "duplicity" appeared more and more often in constant, acerbic polemics. In March 1963, relations were further embittered by Peking's terrritorial demands. The Russians were reminded that the Soviet Maritime Provinces in the Far East and the whole valley of the Amur River had once belonged to China and that they had been wrested away as a result of the "unequal treaties" imposed on Peking by the Tsars.

Tension along the common frontier mounted and resulted in a series of armed incidents. The signing by the USSR of the partial nuclear test ban treaty in July 1963 brought relations between Moscow and Peking to their lowest point yet. The Chinese heatedly denounced the agreement as "a capitulation to United States imperialism," and a "dirty fraud" calculated to prevent all the threatened peace-loving countries, including China, from increasing their defense capabilities.

The Sino-Soviet cold war gradually spread all over the world. The Chinese, using their Albanian allies as an instrument of propaganda, launched a sharp campaign against the Soviet domination of Eastern Europe. Skillfully, they made numerous attempts at splitting other Communist parties. Soon every party had its pro-Chinese as well as pro-Soviet faction. The Romanians, without openly siding with Peking, tended to assume an increasingly neutral position by publishing official communiqués of the two rivals side by side. In December 1963, Chou En-lai embarked on a two-month journey through African countries to try to win over the allegiance of various black leaders to the side of Peking and to sabotage Soviet efforts to dominate the Afro-Asian Solidarity Conference to be held in Algiers.

It is probable that the Sino-Soviet split was inevitable in the long run. But it is certain that it was precipitated and made more ferocious than it needed to be by Khrushchev's rashness and arrogance. For instance, Khrushchev often referred to Mao as "a subversive splitter," "a racist," "a mixture of petty bourgeois adventurist and a great-power chauvinist," and a "worn-out galosh" that should be discarded. He ridiculed the specific cult of personality that surrounded him. Khrushchev thus unnecessarily embittered the quarrel by adding personal factors to the already potent ideological and power–political differences.

MOSCOW AND THE THIRD WORLD

The second cause of Khrushchev's downfall was the lost Cuban gamble of 1962. The Cuban crisis must be viewed against the broad background of Soviet-United States as well as Soviet-Chinese relations. Khrushchev's inner admiration for American drive and efficiency was enchanced by his 1959 trip to the United States. Good relations with the United States, which still enjoyed definite nuclear superiority, fitted his doctrine of the peaceful but competitive coexistence of states with different socio-political systems, since it made a virtue out of necessity. Khrushchev's quest for better relations with the United States was hampered,

however, by the growing Soviet contention for influence in the third-world countries, especially Latin America, Africa, and Southeast Asia, coupled with repeated challenges to the Western position in Germany. Competitive coexistence suited Soviet objectives because it allowed the still weaker of the two cold war opponents to make peaceful, and often not so peaceful, penetration of the other side's perimeter without the risk of immediate confrontation.

In the aftermath of World War II, the Western powers had granted independence to most of their former colonies. This opened the way for the two superpowers to extend their influence into these newly emerging countries. Khrushchev revised Stalin's doctrine, which was based on the assumption that all nations newly freed from Western bondage, but silll preserving ties with their former colonial masters, were in fact "cryptocolonial" and run by "enemies of the people." Khrushchev came to recognize the existence of a new vast sphere of political neutralism, the *Third World,* where the competitive coexistence was to be tested. He was ready to bid against the West by sending material and diplomatic aid to nationalist anti-Western xenophobic regimes. But whenever he perceived an opening to establish Soviet influence he would act promptly, daringly, and often recklessly. It was this reckless side of his nature that led him into trouble.

Increased Soviet assertiveness in the countries of the Third World found its theoretical expression on December 6, 1960, in the form of a "Declaration of Representatives of the Communist and Workers' Parties" signed in Moscow by representatives of eighty-one Communist parties. The declaration formally announced that the Communist world aimed to step up its offensive "by all means" and to follow a more militant policy in underdeveloped countries in order to eradicate all Western influence—political, military, and economic—in these areas. The Communist parties were to support politically, economically, and even militarily all anti-Western forces in underdeveloped countries and to prevent or decisively rebuff interference by the imperialists in the affairs of the people of any country that had risen in revolution. All these points were incorporated into the new Soviet Party program adopted by the Twenty-second Party Congress in October 1961, which thereby formally endorsed this new Communist militancy that did not stop short even of local "wars of national liberation."

In the early 1960s, the Soviet offensive in the underdeveloped countries of the Third World found its most striking expression in Indonesia, the Congo, and Cuba. Following Khrushchev's extended tour of Indonesia, Moscow granted Djakarta $250 million in credits in February 1960. In addition, the Soviet Union contracted to supply the Indonesians with heavy cruisers, long-range jet bombers, jet fighters, ground-to-air missiles, and other sophisticated weapons, and assumed responsibility for the training of Indonesian economic and military specialists. The Russians agreed to build 410 miles of road, a metallurgical plant in Borneo, an iron and steel plant in West Java, a hydroelectric power station, an aluminum plant in North Sumatra, as well as an atomic reactor. During the early 1960s, it seemed as if Indonesia would definitely fall under the Soviet spell. The sudden Soviet ascendancy in Indonesia was bound to irk the United States and its Southeast Asia Treaty Organization (SEATO) partners, particularly Australia and New Zealand, but also the Philippines, Pakistan, and Thailand. (Established in September 1954 and modeled on NATO, SEATO was a compact for common defense against Communist aggression and "internal subversion.")

The new Soviet militancy in the Third World was soon to manifest itself in the formerly French and Belgian sub-Saharan Africa as well. In Africa it centered around the Congo (now Zaïre), newly emancipated from the Belgian rule. The Soviets were attracted to that country by its strategic location, its vast resources, and its political instability, as well as the amenability of one

of the Congo leaders, Premier Patrice Lumumba, to Soviet persuasion. During the summer of 1960, Moscow made a vigorous but unsuccessful attempt to support Lumumba and the radical forces he led. The attempt backfired, however, because of the timely intervention of the United Nations forces, energetically supported by Washington. By September 1960, anti-Communist forces had expelled the Soviet ambassador from the Congo and chased Lumumba out of office. In February 1961, Lumumba was assassinated by his opponents.

The Soviet government blamed UN Secretary General Dag Hammarskjöld for Lumumba's death, insisted on the withdrawal of United Nations Forces from the Congo, and refused to pay its share of the UN's Congo expedition. Moscow recognized the pro-Soviet regime of Antoine Gizenga in Stanleyville as the legal government of the Congo and threatened to intervene on his behalf.

The Soviet anti-UN offensive continued in the meantime. Late in 1960 the Soviets started a forceful offensive to undermine and discredit that world body. Speaking as the head of the Soviet delegation to the Sixteenth General Assembly of the United Nations in October 1960, Khrushchev argued that a true world organization must reflect the actual distribution of world power, which he believed to consist of the Communist, the Western, and the uncommitted nations. He insisted that the office of Secretary General be replaced by a three-man directorate, a *troika*. At one point in his violent speech, Khrushchev went so far as to remove his shoe to pound his desk. His behavior at the UN created an appalling impression not only on the assembled delegates, but also on the millions of television viewers who watched the debate all over the world.

The Soviet threat to withdraw from the UN never materialized, but the whole campaign tarnished both the Soviet world image and Khrushchev's prestige. All that remained of the Congo adventure was the renaming of a University for the Friendship of Peoples established in Moscow in February 1960 as the Patrice Lumumba University. The school was set up to train 3,000 to 4,000 students from Africa, Asia, and Latin America and thus create a living link between the Soviet-trained intelligentsia of those regions and the USSR.

THE BERLIN CRISIS

The marked deterioration of Soviet relations with the Western powers did not stem exclusively from Moscow's repeated attempts to win over the countries of the Third World, nor from the continuing Communist anti-Western propaganda. In addition, the Soviets stepped up their efforts to dislodge the Western powers from Germany. The relations with Washington got still worse when in May 1960 an American U-2 reconnaissance plane was shot down over Sverdlovsk, deep inside the USSR. The United States government first claimed that the U-2 was an unarmed weather plane.

To the amazement of the entire world, Khrushchev produced the captured pilot, Francis Gary Powers, thereby forcing Washington to admit that the U-2 was not a weather plane but a high-flying craft on an espionage mission. This incident doomed the planned Khrushchev–Eisenhower summit meeting. Khrushchev insisted that the President publicly acknowledge that the United States had committed an act of aggression against the USSR, apologize for it, and punish all those responsible.

The U-2 incident was followed in June by the Soviet shooting down of another American plane, an RB-47, in the Arctic Ocean. Both incidents created frigid Soviet-United States relations, which remained in that state until well after the election of John F. Kennedy in November 1960. Khrushchev

N. S. Khrushchev looks at the United States U2 spy plane shot down over Soviet territory in May 1960

sent the President-elect a congratulatory message and in January 1961, as a gesture of "friendship," ordered the release of the imprisoned fliers of the RB-47 plane. Early in June 1961, the two leaders met in Vienna to examine their respective positions on world problems. From Khrushchev's point of view the meeting was to be exploratory in nature; its results were negative. The new President, scion of a wealthy family and a young man of little international experience, must have appeared to Khrushchev as a playboy with a toothpaste-advertising smile. During the meeting, Khrushchev handed to Kennedy an eight-point memorandum outlining the Soviet view of the German situation and insisting on Western withdrawal from Berlin. On June 17, the Western powers replied with a detailed outline of their negative response to the Soviet proposal, stressed their determination to maintain their position in Berlin, and alerted their garrisons in the isolated and divided city.

On August 13, 1961, the international situation took a turn for the worse. To prevent further massive East German escapes to the West, East German leader Walter Ulbricht ordered the construction of a concrete wall across Berlin and began to tamper with Allied traffic within the city. This challenge, combined with numerous incidents along the border, made Berlin the most explosive spot in the world. Early in September 1961, abandoning his self-imposed moratorium on thermonuclear atmospheric tests since the United States had failed to reciprocate, Khrushchev ordered resumption of nuclear tests. Throughout the rest of 1961 and most of 1962, both sides confronted each other with open preparation for what seemed like an approaching nuclear war.

The Berlin crisis soon became intertwined with another critical situation centering around Cuba and also indirectly related to the Sino-Soviet rivalry. It seems likely that the fury and intransigence displayed by Khrushchev during the Berlin crisis and the U-2 incident may have been prompted by pressure from "hard liners" within the Soviet leadership, but it may also have had a great deal to do with the rapidly deteriorating Sino-Soviet relations. The incident gave him a pretext for cooling off his relations with Washington and thus made him appear no less anti-imperialistic than Mao.

THE CUBAN MISSILE CRISIS

In 1959, the relations between Washington and Havana deteriorated rapidly as a result of the seizure of power in Cuba by a radical leader, Fidel Castro. He not only nationalized the holdings of United States citizens, but insisted on the return to Cuba of the United States naval base at Guantánamo Bay. At the same time, Castro systematically developed a close collaboration with the Soviet Union. In February 1960, he signed a trade agreement with the USSR and was given a loan of $100 million. From that time on, the Soviet influence over the island proceeded apace, to the extent that on December 2, 1961, Castro openly declared himself a "Marxist-Leninist." In June 1960, a new economic agreement provided for the exchange of Soviet iron ore for Cuban sugar. The Cuban army was gradually equipped with Soviet weapons, including tanks and planes. Further help, including rockets, was promised "if the aggressive forces of the Pentagon should dare to start an intervention against Cuba." These steps, paralleled by Castro's vigorous anti-United States propaganda campaign, which found a measure of support in other Latin American countries, resulted in the rupture of diplomatic relations with Washington. In April 1961, the United States backed attempts by some anti-Communist Cuban refugees to overthrow the Castro regime; the attempt, known as the "Bay of Pigs invasion," failed miserably.

While Washington was gradually reconciling itself to the idea of having a Communist island some ninety miles off the Florida coast, the Castro regime proceeded to develop still more intimate military ties with the Soviet Union. In July and August 1962, Fidel's brother, Raúl Castro, who was the Cuban Minister of Armed Forces, and Che Guevara, the Minister of Industries, visited Moscow and concluded an agreement that provided for the dispatching of Soviet personnel and sophisticated offensive equipment, including intermediate ballistic missiles, to Cuba.

United States intelligence promptly spotted these arrangements. On October 22, President Kennedy in a televised speech warned the Cubans and their Soviet allies against the dangers of constructing launching pads for such offensive weapons as intermediate ballistic missiles on an island so close to American shores and declared a quarantine on Cuban waters as of October 24. At the same time, Washington submitted to the UN Security Council proofs of the construction of the Cuban missile bases by Soviet rocketry specialists. The evidence was angrily denied by the Soviet delegates. Meanwhile, on October 23, all military leaves for Soviet defense personnel were canceled, and the supreme commander of the Warsaw Pact countries put their forces on alert. In addition to the Berlin crisis, another highly explosive situation was now created in the Caribbean.

One cannot fully understand Khrushchev's Cuban or German gambles without taking into consideration the rapidly widening Sino-Soviet split. By 1962, Khrushchev was under strong pressure to reassert the prestige of the Soviet Union both as a state and as the headquarters of the world revolution. The reckless Chinese talk about the hollowness of the American threat, about the stupidity of all those Communists who were afraid of a showdown with the craven capitalist "paper tiger," impressed some radical Communists all over the world. In Cuba there seemed to be an excellent opportunity to throw Moscow's generous and determined support to a fledgling Communist regime and thus belie Peking's accusation of Moscow's betrayal of the proletarian revolution in the interests of a doubtful and merely temporary detente with the citadel of capitalism. Khrushchev believed that the price of reasserting the Kremlin's revolutionary role, which at the same time immensely strengthened the Soviet position toward the United States, was worthwhile.

John F. Kennedy, Nikita S. Khrushchev, and Andrei A. Gromyko in Vienna, in June 1961

In the back of his mind he must have mistakenly thought that "the playboy" President, then facing another presidential campaign, would never risk even the theoretical danger of nuclear incineration of millions for the sake of a few missiles on Cuban soil. Should the Cuban missile gamble succeed, for the first time the Soviet Union would have a chance to deliver nuclear salvoes to some parts of America, an advantage enjoyed up to then only by the United States in regard to the Soviet Union.

THE COMPROMISE

At this critical point, by at the end of October 1962, UN Secretary General U Thant offered a suggestion that led to an exchange of letters between the leaders of the rival superpowers, now half a step from a full-scale military showdown. As a result of that exchange, it was revealed that Khrushchev was willing to compromise and dismantle the missile bases in Cuba in exchange for the withdrawal of the American missiles in Turkey as a face-saving measure. President Kennedy rejected this proposal, which was made on October 26. The next day he ordered further military preparations, including the mobilization of United States paratroop reservists. The Cuban missile crisis had reached its peak.

At this point of supreme danger, around noon on October 28, Radio Moscow made public a third letter from Khrushchev to the White House. The letter, without insisting on the previously proposed exchange of bases, offered to dismantle the Soviet missile installations on the Cuban soil. The sudden Soviet surrender was a tacit acknowledgment of American strategic superiority over the Soviet Union, obviously unable to back its Cuban gamble with sufficient naval and air support. Contrary to Mao's allegation, America was not a "paper tiger," or at least, as Khrushchev pointed out later, it was a "paper tiger with nuclear claws."

As a result of the Soviet capitulation, the threat of a thermonuclear holocaust was averted. From a historical perspective, the Cuban missile crisis appears as a major turning point in the global tension generated by the two superpowers. Faulty perceptions and miscalculations among the three nations involved led to a situation that none of the three had either foreseen or desired. Castro saw American-sponsored counterrevolution and the eventual invasion of Cuba as the greatest threat to his revolution. The Soviet Union had a chance to place its missiles within range of the United States for the first time and could thereby partially offset American missile bases overseas, as well as place the first Communist state in the Western Hemisphere under a protective nuclear umbrella. Washington regarded the placement of offensive nuclear missiles only ninety miles away as a mortal threat.

The crisis ended with a compromise imposed on all three sides by the fear of a nuclear war. Khrushchev, who had again miscalculated President Kennedy's reaction, was happy to withdraw from the Cuban adventure without catastrophic consequences for his country, while extracting an American guarantee of respect for Cuba's independence. Washington was relieved to see the missiles withdrawn, its strategic superiority confirmed, and Monroe Doctrine at least partially reasserted. Finally, Castro profited from an agreement that the United States would not again sponsor an invasion of Cuba.

The Cuban confrontation, besides further discrediting Khrushchev and tarnishing Soviet international prestige, had far-reaching consequences. The crisis dramatically revealed the Soviets' naval weakness. After the Suez crisis of 1956, the far-sighted and energetic Admiral Sergei G. Gorshkov had started to expand the Soviet naval forces initially neglected by Khrushchev, but this crash effort was not sufficient to counterbalance the preexisting American naval superiority. It was only as a result of the Cuban crisis that the USSR eventually developed a global presence commensurate with its status as a great power. The Cuban crisis, during which Khrushchev acted without sufficient consultation with his defense leaders, further alienated the military establishment from the leader whose ill-considered moves brought about discredit to the country's armed forces.

The removal of the danger of possible Soviet nuclear blackmail and the gradual relaxation of tension in Berlin that soon followed led to an improvement in the relations between Moscow and Washington. The Cuban crisis dramatized the danger of the hitherto slow conventional diplomatic channels in an age when the fate of the world could be decided in a matter of seconds. As a result of this realization, on June 20, 1963, the two powers agreed to establish a direct communication link between the White House and the Kremlin called "the hot line." Moreover, frightened by the spiraling atomic arms race, on July 25, 1963, the USSR, the United States, and the United Kingdom successfully negotiated a partial nuclear test ban treaty. The three powers pledged to stop test explosions of nuclear weapons in the atmosphere, in outer space, and under water, but not underground. The signatories reserved the right to propose amendments to the treaty, as well as the right to withdraw from its obligations should any one of them feel that its vital interests had been jeopardized. They invited all other powers to join the ban. Many states expressed their readiness to be a party to the treaty, but neither China nor France subscribed to it, and both continued to experiment with all sorts of nuclear weapons.

The Cuban gamble was Khrushchev's last great venture in the field of foreign policy. From then on, discredited as a reckless gambler in world affairs, he had to channel most of his energies toward the increasingly critical domestic situation.

DOMESTIC DIFFICULTIES

During the early 1960s, while Khrushchev was busy with foreign affairs and Soviet astronauts continued to make history in space, the Soviet economy deteriorated. Industrial growth was slowing down, consumer goods were still in short supply and poor in quality. Agriculture was the festering wound of the economic illness. Even the triumphal flight of half a dozen Soviet space ships could not obscure the fact that the Soviet people were shortchanged of those promises that Khrushchev had repeatedly made in the past.[1]

While propagandizing these "new triumphs of Lenin's ideas" as a manifestation of "the might of socialism," Khrushchev had to eat his words and renege on his 1957 boasts of overtaking the United States. The harvests of both 1959 and 1960 were bad; the latter was 20 million tons of grain short of what had been expected. At the same time, the livestock situation also deteriorated: in 1960, according to official statistics, almost 10 million sheep starved and the number of cattle also decreased greatly. In view of these facts, declared Khrushchev at the extraordinary meeting of the Central Committee called to cope with the agricultural crisis in January 1961, the Soviet Union had to postpone surpassing the United States in per capita production of dairy and meat products (promised by him in 1957 for 1961) by at least five years.

This time Khrushchev blamed the failure not so much on climatic conditions as on the poor, obsolete organization of agricultural administration, the backwardness of the So-

---

[1] During the late 1950s and early 1960s Soviet astronauts successfully completed at least six spectacular cosmic feats. A direct landing on the moon was made by a Soviet space ship on September 12, 1959, and pictures of its hidden side were taken. On April 12, 1961, a major in the Soviet Air Force, Yuri A. Gagarin, achieved the first manned orbital flight around the earth aboard the space ship *Vostok I*. Four months later, on August 6, Herman S. Titov, another Soviet Air Force major, successfully completed seventeen orbits in the ship *Vostok II*. In mid-August 1962, Major Andrian G. Nikolaev in *Vostok III* orbited the earth sixty-four times, and his "traveling companion" Colonel Pavel R. Popovich in *Vostok IV* made forty-eight orbits; and in mid-June 1963, Lieutenant Colonel Valeri F. Bykovsky made eighty-two orbits, and his female "traveling companion" Lieutenant Valentina V. Tereshkova completed forty-eight orbits in a space ship dubbed "The Seagull."

viet agrotechnology, and the large-scale pilfering of grain before and during the harvest. To correct this, he pledged to divert a larger share of capital investment to agriculture. At the same time, the death penalty was ordered for several categories of "economic crimes." Between May 1961 and May 1964, several thousand people were reprimanded and jailed for such crimes, and about 200 were sentenced to death by shooting. But despite these reprisals, two personal supervision journeys to the country's most important agricultural regions during the spring and autumn of 1961, and numerous pledges of cooperation from local Party officials for greatly increased food production, the actual results were not satisfactory.

THE TWENTY-SECOND PARTY CONGRESS

Meanwhile, in October 1961, the Twenty-second Party Congress, solidly packed with Khrushchev's supporters, unanimously approved a new Party program, the third in its history.[2] The program anticipated that "the building of the foundations of Communism" in the Soviet Union would be completed by 1980. At that time the principle "from each according to his abilities, to each according to his needs" was to be achieved. This objective was to be reached in two stages: from 1961 to 1970 the country was to create a material and technical base for Communism, improve the living standards of the people, and surpass the United States in per capita production. From 1971 to 1980, the USSR was to achieve "a gradual transition to a single form of public ownership."

For agriculture this Twenty-Year Plan

had a twofold aim: to provide an abundant supply of food and to obliterate "the distinction between town and country." To attain these goals Soviet agriculture was expected to achieve a high degree of mechanization, irrigation, and a "scientific system of land cultivation and animal husbandry." The Plan postulated that the extension of "the luxury of city living" to the countryside would make peasant plots economically "obsolete" and unprofitable and that the peasants would "give them up of their own accord." By 1980, the total volume of production was to increase by 250 percent; grain output was to double, milk to triple, meat to quadruple, and the productivity of agricultural labor was to rise by between 400 and 500 percent.

The Twenty-second Party Congress was notable for its abandonment of the term "dictatorship of the proletariat" in favor of a new characterization of the Soviet regime as "a state of the whole people," a change thought by some scholars to indicate a tendency toward greater openness in Soviet politics and a switch from Communism to Populism.

The Twenty-second Party Congress also sharply denounced once more the entire "anti-Party faction"—Molotov, Voroshilov, Malenkov, Kaganovich, and Bulganin—for their continuous adherence to "factionalism" and their active participation in Stalin's crimes. At the Congress, for the first time in public, Khrushchev called Stalin a murderer, an instigator of mass repression against Communists and army leaders, and a man who had seriously violated Lenin's principles and abused power. Many Congress delegates seconded Khrushchev's charges against Stalin and the "anti-Party" group. On October 30, 1961, the delegates voted unanimously to remove Stalin's body from the Lenin mausoleum in Red Square for reburial alongside the Kremlin wall. Stalin's name was to be erased from the tomb. Shortly after this gesture, the city of Stalingrad was renamed Volgograd. Soon other cities, streets, collective farms, mountains, canals, factories, and the like through-

---

[2] The original program of the movement was adopted at the Second Congress of the Russian Social Democratic Workers' Party in London in 1903. The program called for the overthrow of the Tsarist regime and the establishment of the dictatorship of the proletariat in Russia. The second was adopted at the Eighth Party Congress in March 1919 and called for the building of Socialism in Russia.

out the USSR and its European dependencies—save for Albania, led by staunch Stalinist, Enver Hoxha—followed suit. Khrushchev went so far as to suggest that a monument to Stalin's victims be erected in the heart of Moscow.

THE UPS AND DOWNS OF DESTALINIZATION

The Twenty-second Congress was followed by substantial price increases for food in order to shift some of the cost of intensifying agricultural production to the urban population. On June 1, 1962, the mass media announced that the retail price of meat was to be increased 30 percent and that of butter 25 percent. This staggering price rise coincided with a state-sponsored "economy drive," which had already reduced the take-home pay of the workers by approximately 10 percent. In reply to these measures, widespread riots, sit-down strikes, and mass demonstrations broke out among Soviet workers. In Novocherkask, a city of 100,000 residents, these lasted over a week and cost hundreds of lives. Street protests also flared up in Moscow, Groznyi, Gorkii, Krasnodar, Donetsk, Iaroslavl, and Zhdanov. The disastrous harvest of 1963 resulted in panic buying of food and in serious food shortages. Massive sit-down strikes occurred in Leningrad, Krivoi Rog, Omsk, and several cities in the Urals.

The Twenty-second Party Congress not only resulted in a new wave of rehabilitations of people like Chicherin and Voznesensky, but it was also followed by a partial relaxation of controls over intellectuals. The most outstanding example of this freedom was the publication in the November 1962 issue of *Novyi Mir* of the novel *One Day in the Life of Ivan Denisovich* by Alexander Solzhenitsyn, a former inmate of a labor camp. The work describes the phantasmagoric life of prisoners in a forced labor camp under Stalin—a world apart ruled by its own unwritten laws—which reflected the Soviet reality of those days. The work was published in book form as a result of Khrushchev's personal decision. It is paradoxical that the man who in 1958 had been shocked by Boris Pasternak's fairly mild indictment of the Soviet regime in his epic Nobel Prize-winning novel, *Doctor Zhivago,* now sponsored the incomparably more traumatic story of Ivan Denisovich.

Meanwhile, some Soviet intellectuals, encouraged by the momentary loosening of ideological supervision over published material, began to press for further concessions, including the abolition of censorship. Following the publication of Solzhenitsyn's book, Soviet publishers and editorial offices were flooded with thousands of similar accounts. All of this frightened Khrushchev himself and made him clarify the Party's position in the matter of freedom of expression.

At a series of conferences between Party leaders and intellectuals during the first half of 1963, liberal intellectuals suddenly found themselves face to face with angry Party leaders. As always at such affairs, the principal spokesman was Khrushchev himself. He cautioned "the smiths of the human psyche" that freedom had its limits and that the Party was still bound to delineate them. He warned the artists not to expend their energies on "one-sided" presentations of such aspects of Soviet reality as "lawlessness, arbitrary reprisals and abuse of power" during "the years of the personality cult." The Hungarian uprising, he said, would never have occurred if the Budapest government had had the courage to shoot a few of the rebellious writers in good time. Should a similar situation occur in Moscow, he would know what to do: "My hand would not tremble."

As Khrushchev's domestic and international difficulties increased, he began to softpedal his anti-Stalin campaign and himself resorted to harsh practices usually associated with the late tyrant. The fairly broad application of the death penalty for "economic crimes" is one such example. At a meeting with artists in March 1963, Khrushchev retreated from the anti-Stalin position he had proclaimed at the Twenty-second Party Congress and largely justified Stalin's actions up to 1934. He said that there must be due recognition for "Stalin's contributions to the Party and to the Communist movement. Even now we feel that Stalin was devoted to Communism, he was a Marxist, this cannot and should not be denied."

THE AGRARIAN CRISIS

The showdown with the liberally inclined intellectuals and artists was paralleled by an acute economic crisis. By the spring of 1963 it became evident that the goals set by Khrushchev were beyond the reach of the Soviet economy, whose rate of growth was declining rather than increasing. Moreover, constant "reforms" and "reorganizations" produced nothing but chaos. The 1963 harvest, despite the fact that that year the USSR had the largest sown area in its history (some 350,000,000 acres), was disastrous, so during the summer the Soviet government had to negotiate two huge grain purchases. One was from Canada and involved 6.5 million tons; the other, amounting to 1.6 million tons, was from Australia. Soviet officials also tried to purchase 5 million tons of grain from the United States, but Washington's insistence that at least half of the American grain be transported in United States ships, in addition to difficulties in obtaining long-term credits, brought Soviet-American negotiations to an end. The extent of Soviet grain purchases abroad in 1963 reflected the magnitude of the failure of the Soviet collectivized system and resulted in a catastrophic setback to Khrushchev's prestige. The suppressed opposition raised its head and began to attract people hitherto devoted to Khrushchev. The largest imports of grain in Soviet history, nay, all of Russian history, combined with his mistakes in the field of foreign affairs, his ill-advised reorganization schemes, and his cavalier style of leadership, spelled the beginning of the end of Khrushchev. To understand the full reasons for his over-

throw, we have to examine more closely his erratic economic policies as well as the impact of his restless personality on Soviet politics.

According to Khrushchev, overtaking the West, especially the United States, in per capita production should occur first in the production of food, where Soviet Russia would be less handicapped by technology, and where it would have both a considerable reservoir of rural manpower and large reserves of unutilized land in Southern Siberia and Central Asia, especially Kazakhstan. Hence Khrushchev's two pet projects: the virgin land campaign and the corn campaign.

The initial success of the virgin land campaign, which produced the bountiful harvest of 1956, made him expand its acreage. Everything—manpower, machinery, and fertilizers—was poured into the new agricultural regions, to the neglect of the old, vital grain-producing areas like Ukraine or the Northern Caucasus. Yet throughout the entire Seven-Year Plan of national development (1958–1965), in only one of those years was the government's grain quota for the virgin lands met. This was caused by a variety of factors overlooked by Khrushchev, who was bent on immediate, spectacular success. Soil erosion increased and became an ecological disaster by the early 1960s. Some experts had predicted that this would happen and warned Khrushchev of the folly of plowing millions of hectares of open steppe lands unprotected by forest zones. He had dismissed them, however, as "pessimistic scarecrows." The hasty cultivation of the virgin lands could have been less disastrous if some attempt had been made to apply well-proven agricultural methods (proper crop rotation, animal husbandry, and so forth), and if a permanent work force had been settled there. But with shallow plowing, inadequate fertilizer, and periodic hasty mobilizations of labor and equipment recruited for a month or two during the harvest, this was utterly impossible. Not only were fertile lands plowed, but so were saline areas and large expanses of light sandy loams which were soon blown away by the wind. During the dry summer of 1962, wind erosion struck at several million hectares. But this was only the beginning. In the spring of 1963, a huge ecological disaster occurred. Severe wind storms (with winds up to ninety-five miles an hour) blew away millions of tons of fertile soil.

THE "CORN CAMPAIGN"

Another of Khrushchev's pet projects was his insistence on planting corn, both as a supplement to human diet and as silage or fodder crop for livestock. His vow to overtake the United States in meat, milk, and egg production largely hinged on the latter part of the program. The initial small increase of corn acreage in 1954 did not satisfy Khrushchev. And although the necessary seed, fertilizer, machinery, silos, and experience were lacking, he issued a directive and corn acreage was to be substantially expanded in almost all agricultural areas. This meant a reversal of the newly adopted system of agricultural planning whereby kolkhozes would be permitted to decide for themselves what crops to raise. They were now ordered to plant corn, corn, and more corn. At every possible meeting or conference, Khrushchev arued about the importance of corn, recalling that Catherine II had had to use force to introduce potatoes into Russia in the eighteenth century. As a result of this pressure, the amount of corn planted rose dramatically. Soon everyone jumped on the corn bandwagon. New silos were planned, systems of feeding livestock with corn silage were worked out, special equipment to mechanize planting was made available, and the production of pure strains of corn was expanded everywhere. In 1954, the corn area had increased to 4.3 million hectares (one hectare equals two and a half acres). By 1955, under Khrushchev's relentless pressure, it was expanded to 18 million hectares. Yet he was not satisfied with these advancements and he pressed for further expansion of corn cultivation. By 1960, corn acreage had risen to 28 million hectares and in 1962 it reached 37 million hectares.

Having put forward his program for tripling meat production in 1957, Khrushchev then felt that only corn could guarantee the livestock herds he desired. He failed to consider that corn requires not only great inputs of labor and fertilizer, but also hot weather and rich soil. The obsession with corn and the pouring of vast manpower and technical resources into its cultivation inflicted heavy injury on the entire agricultural sector and consequently retarded the further economic progress of the entire country. Lest the kolkozniks turn back to their hay making, the government halted the manufacture of equipment for improving and maintaining natural meadows. As a consequence, brush and hummocks overgrew the hayfields and pastures. One-third of all meadowland was almost completely abandoned. The average annual production of hay dropped from 64 million tons in 1953 to 47 million tons in 1965.

Perhaps if Khrushchev had proceeded slowly, with the gradual and cautious introduction of corn, proper cultivation, mechanization of all operations, irrigation, and adequate amounts of fertilizer, a "corn belt" like the one in the United States might have been created in the USSR. But in the absence of any cautious restraint, the "corn campaign" was a catastrophe and only added to the nation's agricultural woes, which were serious enough without it. After Khrushchev was overthrown, the corn campaign came to an end. When administrative pressure was lifted from the kolkhozes, corn planting dropped below the 1940 level.

KHRUSHCHEV'S STYLE OF LEADERSHIP

To complete the examination of the reasons for Khrushchev's downfall, we should say a few words about his style of leadership. A typical authoritarian personality, he spontaneously tended toward arbitrary one-man decisions, consulted only those whom he personally trusted, and suffered with difficulty any outside criticism. Moreover, Khrushchev had a tendency to surround himself with advisers who had no official role in Party or government. In many cases he relied on the advice of these personal aides rather than on the recommendations of members of the Presidium and the Politburo, or the cabinet ministers. This bypassing of the Party and government hierarchy made him many additional enemies. Khrushchev traveled about a great deal, both within the Soviet Union and abroad, and frequently made decisions during these travels when only his own coterie was available for consultation. Gradually, there formed around him something like an "inner cabinet," a clique consisting of his closest associates. They tended to operate quite independently of the Council of Ministers or the Presidium. As the "Inner cabinet's" influence increased, Khrushchev's relations with members of the government and of the Party steadily eroded. In his early years of power, the creation of a group of experts was needed to help Khrushchev map out certain programs, and keep them secret from his main rivals, including Malenkov, Molotov, and Kaganovich. But after 1957 this modus operandi was no longer necessary and only swelled the ranks of his secret enemies.

Khrushchev's practice of relying on his own personal assistants extended not only to economics, but also to culture and international affairs. Here A. I. Adzubei, husband of his daughter Rada and editor of *Izvestia*, enjoyed the greatest influence and gradually became his unofficial adviser on international relations. Adzhubei accompanied Khrushchev on almost all of his trips abroad and was often dispatched to carry out various confidential missions, including the secret trip to Bonn in the summer of 1964 to seek accommodation with the Federal Republic of Germany. During the Cuban missile crisis, Adzhubei on several occasions acted as Khrushchev's personal emissary abroad, while neither the actual foreign minister, Gromyko, nor the Soviet ambassadors in the countries involved were informed of the details of these missions.

Khrushchev changed his official expert advisers as he changed his reorganization plans. In ten years he had five ministers of agriculture. By 1957, T. D. Lysenko, who enthusiastically publicized all of Khrushchev's favorite projects, was restored to grace and managed to enter the select inner circle of his advisers. Without any formal education in agronomy himself, Khrushchev quickly fell under Lysenko's spell and in various addresses and reports supported Lysenko in his disputes with his scientific opponents. In 1961, Lysenko was reinstated as President of the Academy of Agricultural Sciences. By this time, Lysenko's theories and programs had already been totally discredited in scholarly circles.

A NEW PERSONALITY CULT

These practices irritated government bureaucrats as well as the party top apparat and greatly contributed to their ganging up against the man who not only overlooked them, but also often treated them with contempt. All this and more they had for a long time suffered on the part of Stalin, but they would not endure it from one of his former henchmen. Moreover, after 1957, a sort of Khrushchev cult had developed. The press was inundated with innumerable, often bombastic reports about his various activities. This served to embitter further Khrushchev's relations with the members of the Soviet elite, who were apprehensive about the possible return to "past times of mistakes and aberrations." As a result Khrushchev's popularity, which had been based on his successes during 1953–1958, plummeted by 1961–1962 in the vital upper strata of the Party apparat.

To the dissatisfaction that permeated the Party network was added Khrushchev's loss of popularity with the military establishment because of his sudden unilateral decision to reduce the size of the Soviet Armed

Forces and cut down the military budget. This resulted in the premature retirement of thousands of career officers, while for reasons of economy Khrushchev also reduced the size of their pensions. His explanations that he needed the manpower and money to develop agriculture and industry were not generally accepted by the Soviet defense establishment. In the opinion of the military leaders, such a reduction had a strong adverse effect on the Soviet defense capability.

Aware that his popularity among Communist hard-liners had been considerably undermined by his de-Stalinization, Khrushchev stepped up three policies likely to endear him to the Stalinists: an antireligious campaign, the curtailment of the growth of household plots, and a drive to turn kolkhozes into State farms. This last policy was congenial to Khrushchev, who was temperamentally fond of the giant and the grandiose. But the second backfired. The resistance of the peasants, fiercely attached to their household plots, cut down food production and increased the provisioning difficulties in the cities. As a result of the renewed antireligious drive, thousands of churches were closed and in many cases turned into garages or, in rural districts where there were not enough buildings suitable for storing agricultural equipment, into warehouses. Religious persecution increased in 1961 as a result of the enactment of the new Criminal Code of the Russian SSR. Article 227 of that Code declared criminal any religious activity that might cause citizens "to reject socialist activity or the performance of their duties as citizens," as well as "the enticement of minors into a [religious] group." This meant that parents were now forbidden to give their children religious instruction, even at home.[3]

---

[3] After years of persecution, the Orthodox Church had been legalized by Stalin in 1943 to enlist its help in mobilizing the Russian masses for the war effort. The Patriarchate had been restored and a considerable number of places of worship and seminaries had been returned to the faithful. Although the religious prac-

KHRUSHCHEV AND THE PARTY

Khrushchev tried to modify Party rules, as well as to recast its program. Under the new rules, which were applicable to governing Party bodies, and even to the Central Committee itself, it became mandatory for one-third of the members of each committee to be replaced by new Party workers at each election. This theoretically applied to the Presidium too, but it did not extend to Khrushchev as the First Secretary, or to certain "experienced Party workers of special merit." The new rules meant that there would be a periodic evaluation of the performance of people in office. While the new rules enabled Khrushchev to shuffle Party personnel and remove those he disliked, they deprived most of the Party apparat of the sense of security they had enjoyed since 1953.

In November 1962, Khrushchev, without consulting the Party Congress, made a move that was to precipitate a deep crisis. He decreed a radical reorganization of both Party and government structures. This reorganization reversed the decentralization measures of 1957 and concentrated all economic planning in the USSR in the Supreme Economic Council (SEC), headed by First Deputy Premier and former Minister of Armaments Dmitri F. Ustinov. Directly below the SEC were two pivotal agencies: the Gosplan, which was responsible for the current plan, and the National Building Agency. The new reform sharply reduced the number of economic regions that had been set up in 1957 and decreed the division of each local party organization into two bureaus, one for agriculture and one for

---

tices were still frowned on by the Party, the influence of the Church spread rapidly, and it was calculated that in the 1950s even in Moscow as many as 50 percent of babies were baptized. For the reasons still unsufficiently explained, Khrushchev ordered stricter control of religious congregations and confiscation and even destruction of several thousand churches, some of them of historic value. For instance, the church of Transfiguration in Moscow's Preobrazhensky square was demolished to make way for a Metro station and the shrine Lavra Pecherska was turned into a museum.

industry and construction. The central Party bodies also split their functions, both for the individual republics and for the Soviet Union as a whole. A Central Committee Bureau for Industry and a Central Committee Bureau for Agriculture were formed. Although at the top the industrial and agricultural Party hierarchies were subordinate to one head, its First Secretary, virtually the entire Party structure was now divided into two independent constituents. The principle of territorial administration had thus been replaced by functional administration as a category of production.

The intended aim of all these changes was twofold: to tighten Party control and to weaken the central State bureaucracy. This measure, however, reduced the authority of the provincial Party secretaries, who comprised the bulk of the Central Committee. By alienating such a substantial portion of the Soviet leadership, Khurshchev gravely weakened his own position. Soon an undercurrent of tension arose between Khrushchev, for whom the Central Committee had been his chief prop, and the secretaries of the oblast committees, who in large measure formed its membership. This tension was skillfully exploited by Khrushchev's rivals in the struggle for control of the Central Committee.

Khrushchev's opponents gathered strength as the unworkability of the reforms became apparent. While industry was less affected, agriculture staggered under new handicaps. For instance, the agricultural sections had no power to recruit urban factory or office workers for seasonal agricultural labor in case of emergency, and emergencies were almost constant. The industrial sections, now free of responsibility for agriculture, were no longer interested in lending thousands of their workers to mow hay, bring in the harvest, or dig potatoes. Without this assistance, agricultural quotas were impossible to fulfill. The shock of the Party split, compounded by the agricultural failures that culminated in the gigantic grain purchases abroad, galvanized Khrushchev's rivals into action.

KHRUSHCHEV'S DOWNFALL AND HIS PLACE IN HISTORY

The splitting of the Party into two sections was the proverbial straw that broke the camel's back. In October 1964, while Khrushchev was vacationing on the Black Sea, all those who opposed his Party restructuring and were alarmed by the economic chaos drew together to bring him down. The opposition enjoyed the support of the dissatisfied marshals and the head of the secret police, Alexander N. Shelepin. Summoned by the Presidium back to Moscow on "urgent business," the surprised Khrushchev had to face a formidable barrage of criticism on the part of a hostile Presidium. This time his old trick of appealing from the Presidium to the Central Committee did not work. By that time, even they had been alienated by his innumerable "hare-brained schemes," his erratic and irresponsible style of leadership, his nepotism, and his recent secret overtures to Bonn made through Adzhubei.

Although the overthrow of Khrushchev was officially described as a "resignation," there was never any doubt that it was more of a palace revolution preceded by a sharp power struggle. The main Party daily, *Pravda*, on October 17, 1964, probably faithfully reflected the debates that led to Khrushchev's fall by accusing him of "wild schemes; half-baked conclusions and hasty decisions and actions divorced from reality; bragging and bluster; attraction to rule by fiat; unwillingness to take into account what science and practical experience have already worked out. . . ." A most striking feature of the crisis was the lethargic passivity of the Soviet masses. They meekly accepted the results of the revolution at the top without even an outward sign of interest in what had happened at the pinnacle of power.

Khrushchev's downfall introduced several elements of novelty into the annals of Soviet history. Khrushchev was the first top Soviet leader without prerevolutionary experience. He was also the first true proletarian Party head. In addition, he was the first ruler in Russia's history to be deposed by being successfully outvoted by a process that at least vaguely resembled Western parliamentary procedure. He lost power, but not his head. He became an un-person, but not a corpse. He was kept under close supervision in his summer home near Moscow until his death in 1971.[4]

Khrushchev's most important historic role was that he presided over the desacralization of the Stalin myth and the partial dismantling of the Great Tyrant's inhuman system. Thanks to Khrushchev, hundreds of thousands, if not millions of survivors of the Gulag Archipelago returned to more or less normal life without being constantly threatened with arbitrary arrest. Despite his denunciation of the past, Khrushchev often relapsed into the old, heavy-handed methods; yet his "administrative methods" of repression could never compare with Stalin's mass terror. They were limited to such measures as expulsion from the Party or dismissal from a job.

Khrushchev suffered from the old Stalinist habit of frequent launching of crash programs (*sturmovshchina*), which amounted to hastily throwing massive human and material resources into one great drive after another with its concomitant inevitable waste and chaos. His belief in panaceas like corn growing was almost superstitious. Yet Khrushchev must be given credit for alleviating the rigors and drabness of the *kolkhoz* life and for supplying at least a trickle of consumer goods to the average Soviet citizen. Not the least of his achievements was a vast program of housing construction. Poor in quality, these hastily prefabricated dwellings soon turned into slums; but in comparison with the gross neglect of the problem

under Stalin, even this was noteworthy progress.

Scientists, scholars, and intellectuals in general also owe a debt to Khrushchev, his bitter anti-intellectualism notwithstanding. Under his rule cultural exchanges with the West were resumed after two decades of Stalin's ban on such contacts. Gradually, communication channels were reopened. The subsequent declassfication of some selected subject matter allowed for a great flow of professional information on many levels. At least some Soviet scholars and artists were once again permitted to publish and travel abroad, and their renewed participation in international scientific conferences like that at Pugwash (beginning in July 1957) contributed in a small way to a partial reintegration of Soviet scholarship into the world academic community. These were modest gains, but they have to be judged against the nightmare of domestic thought control and the almost complete isolation from abroad that Stalin had imposed.

Starting in 1914 the Russian people had been exposed to a series of shocks. The murderous war of 1914–1918 was followed by a double upheaval and a bloody civil war. After seven years of this ordeal, and after a short respite in the form of the NEP (1921–1928), came the nightmare of the Stalin revolution. Hardly was it over when the USSR faced an external challenge to its very existence on both its Asiatic and European approaches. The four years of World War II, with its devastation and 20 to 30 million victims, strained every fiber of the Soviet people. This unprecedented sequence of traumatic experiences—a continuum of excruciating suffering stretching over three generations—profoundly scarred the psyche of the Soviet people. Khrushchev, in spite of all his limitations and idiosyncrasies, gave the Russian people some relief from their sufferings and tried to heal their wounds as best a former Stalinist could. Despite his mistakes and even follies, he left Soviet Russia a better place than it had been under his predecessor.

---

[4] Khrushchev died of a heart attack on September 11, 1971. Before his death, he managed to smuggle abroad two volumes of his memoirs, which were published in the United States under the title *Khrushchev Remembers*. For publishing his *Doctor Zhivago* abroad, Leonid Pasternak was sharply reprimanded by Khrushchev and suffered years of ostracism and chicanery.

SUGGESTED READING

BLOCH, SIDNEY, and PETER REDDAWAY, *Psychiatric Terror*. New York: Basic Books, 1977.

BLOOMFIELD, LINCOLN P., et al., *Khrushchev and the Arms Race: Soviet Interests in Arms Control and Disarmament, 1954–1964*. Cambridge, Mass.: MIT Press, 1966.

BOFFA, GIUSEPPE, *Inside the Khrushchev Era*. New York: Marzani & Munsell, 1963.

BROMKE, ADAM, ed., *The Communist States at the Crossroads: Between Moscow and Peking*. New York: Praeger, 1965.

BROWN, J. F., *The New Eastern Europe: The Khrushchev Era and After*. New York: Praeger, 1966.

BRZEZINSKI, ZBIGNIEW, ed., *Africa and the Communist World*. Stanford, Calif.: Stanford University Press, 1963.

———, *Dilemmas of Change in Soviet Politics*. New York: Columbia University Press, 1969.

CLEMENS, WALTER C., Jr., *The Arms Race and Sino-Soviet Relations*. Stanford, Calif.: Hoover Institution, 1968.

COHEN, STEPHEN F. ed., *An End of Silence: Uncensored Opinion in the Soviet Union. From Roy Medvedev's Underground Magazine. Political Diary*. Translated by George Saunders. New York: Norton, 1982.

CONQUEST, ROBERT, ed., *Agricultural Workers in the USSR*. New York: Praeger, 1969.

———, *Russia after Khrushchev*. New York: Praeger, 1965.

CRANKSHAW, EDWARD, *The New Cold War, Moscow vs. Peking*. Plainview, N.Y.: Books for Libraries, 1963.

DALLIN, ALEXANDER, et al, eds., *Diversity in International Communism: A Documentary Record, 1961–1963*. New York: Columbia University Press, 1963.

DINERSTEIN, HERBERT S., *The Making of a Missile Crisis: October 1962*. Baltimore, Md.: Johns Hopkins University Press, 1976.

FEIFER, GEORGE, *Justice in Moscow*. New York: Simon & Schuster, 1964.

FISCHER-GALATI, STEPHEN, *Eastern Europe in the Sixties*. New York: Praeger, 1963.

———, *The New Rumania: From People's Democracy to Socialist Republic*. Cambridge, Mass.: MIT Press, 1967.

GRIFFITH, WILLIAM, E., *Cold War and Coexistence: Russia, China, and the United States*. Englewood Cliffs, N.J.: Prentice-Hall, 1971.

JOHNSON, PRISCILLA, *Khrushchev and the Arts: The Politics of Soviet Culture, 1962–1964*. Cambridge, Mass.: MIT Press, 1965.

KASER, MICHAEL, *Comecon: Integration Problems of the Planned Economies*. (2nd ed.). New York: Oxford University Press, 1965.

LAPIDUS, GAIL W., ed., *Women in Soviet Society*. Berkeley: California University Press, 1978.

MACGWIRE, MICHAEL, KEN BOOTH, and JOHN McDONNELL, *Soviet Naval Policy: Objectives and Constraints*. Center for Foreign Policy Studies, Department of Political Sciences, Dalhousie University. New York: Praeger, 1975.

McCAULEY, MARTIN ed., *Khrushchev and Khrushchevism*. London: MacMillan, 1987.

McNEAL, ROBERT H., *The Bolshevik Tradition: Lenin, Stalin, Khrushchev and Brezhnev* (2nd ed.). Englewood Cliffs, N.J.: Prentice-Hall, 1975.

MEDVEDEV, ROY, *Khrushchev*, trans. Brian Pearce. Garden City, N.Y.: Doubleday, 1983.

PLOSS, SIDNEY L., *Conflict and Decision-Making Process in Soviet Russia: A Case Study of Agricultural Policy, 1953–1963*. Princeton, N.J.: Princeton University Press, 1965.

ROT, YAACOV, *From Encroachment to Involvement: A Documentary Study of Soviet Policy in the Middle East, 1945–1973* New York: Halsted Press, and Jerusalem: Israel Universities Press, 1974.

RUSH, MYRON, *Political Succession in the USSR* (2nd ed.). New York: Columbia University Press, 1965.

SALISBURY, HARRISON E., *War between Russia and China*. New York: Norton, 1969.

TATU, MICHEL, *Power in the Kremlin: From Khrushchev to Kosygin*. New York: Viking, 1969.

ULAM, ADAM B., *The Rivals: America and Russia Since World War II*. New York: Viking, 1971.

VALKENIER, ELIZABETH K., *The Soviet Union and the Third World: An Economic Bind*. New York: Praeger, 1983.

ZAGORIA, DONALD S., *Vietnam Triangle: Moscow, Peking, Hanoi*. New York: Pegasus, 1967.

CHAPTER 23

Soviet Russia Under Brezhnev's Leadership

The Khrushchev spoils were divided between his ungrateful protégé Leonid I. Brezhnev, who took over the post of the Party's First Secretary, and Alexei Kosygin, a former Finance and Consumer Goods Industry Minister and First Vice-Premier who now became Prime Minister. The new leadership pledged itself not to follow in the dictatorial footsteps of their predecessor and to observe the tenets of collective leadership. For about three or four years their promise was kept fairly scrupulously. Gradually, however, the logic of the Soviet political mechanism and the Russian tradition, perhaps shaped by a deep psychological need for a single strong father figure, began to reassert itself. During the late 1960s the more exuberant and dynamic Brezhnev began to overshadow his partner.

Son of Russian working-class parents, Leonid Ilich Brezhnev was born in December 1906 in Kamenskoe (later renamed Dneprodzerzhinsk), in the Northern

Ukraine. According to his official biography, he was a graduate of a classical high school. In 1923, the young Brezhnev joined the Komsomol and was sent to take a land surveyor's course, which enabled him to enter public administration in 1927. In 1931, he joined the Party and entered the metallurgical institute, from which he graduated in four years. In 1938, Brezhnev became "director of a department" in the Party organization of his home town.

Serving as a political commissar in World War II under Khrushchev, Brezhnev left the military service in 1946 as a decorated major-general. Soon he had become Party chief in Zaporozhe, where his energy and efficiency in rebuilding a hydroelectric station and a steel plant. In the early 1950s, he served as Party chief in Moldavia and then in Kazakhstan, both good schools of political-administrative work. While Party boss in Kazakhstan, Brezhnev was very helpful to Khrushchev in launching the virgin lands scheme. The excellent harvest of 1956, to which these lands contributed to a marked degree, rescued the First Secretary from his predicament. To reward him for this service, Khrushchev made Brezhnev a Secretary of the Central Committee and a member of the Politburo. In 1960, he became titular president of the USSR, which enabled him to travel abroad and familiarize himself with foreign affairs. In June 1963, Brezhnev was replaced as president by Mikoyan and restored to his role in the Secretariat.

BREZHNEV'S ASCENT

Brezhnev's ascent to supreme power was more rapid than that of Khrushchev. The Twenty-third Party Congress (March–April 1966) recognized Brezhnev's preeminence by awarding him the prestigious title of Secretary-General, which had not been in use since Stalin's death. By the early 1970s, Brezhnev was also a leading spokesman in

Leonid Brezhnev, an official picture in 1964

foreign affairs. On state visits abroad he began to be received everywhere with the ceremonial protocol due a head of state. By the fall of 1967, he dominated celebrations of the fiftieth anniversary of Bolshevik power. The Twenty-fourth Party Congress (March–April 1971) confirmed Brezhnev's personal control over the whole Party as well as the governmental apparatus.

From the middle 1970s on, Brezhnev's unquestioned supreme power has been underlined by a series of exceptional honors bestowed on him by the Supreme Soviet. On May 8, 1976, he was elevated from the rank of five-star general of the army to marshal. Despite his fast-rising prestige, Brezhnev on the whole has been careful to respect the process of group decision making, and, unlike Khrushchev, has never made any radical assaults on the Party's institutional structure. Moreover, while often blowing the traditional trumpet of Communist propaganda, Brezhnev has tried to avoid his predecessor's ebullient boasts about the instant achievement of fantastic goals. Yet a cult of personality has also gradually developed around Brezhnev.

In 1973, the Politburo's composition was changed. Genady I. Voronov, a former Minister of Agriculture, and Pyotr Shelest, a former Party boss in the Ukraine, were replaced by Marshal Andrei Grechko (Defense Minister), Yuri Andropov (security police chief) and Andrei Gromyko (Foreign Minister) Andropov's ascent to the Presidium marked the first time since Beria's fall in June 1953 that the chief of security was represented in the top Party body. Soon fear of the growing military preponderance was reflected in the appointment of a civilian, Dmitri Ustinov, to replace Marshal Andrei Grechko, who died at the end of April 1976. A Politburo member who for well over thirty years had been in charge of Russia's armaments industry, Ustinov became the first civilian to head the Soviet military since Leon Trotsky was named Commissar for the Army and Navy in 1918.

Gradually, Kosygin reconciled himself to his role as technocrat and stuck to the task of acting as Brezhnev's transmission belt to the governmental apparatus, with special emphasis on economic matters. The partnership ended only in 1980 with the resignation of Kosygin because of ill health.

BREZHNEV AND KOSYGIN'S ATTEMPTED REFORMS

The paramount initial task of the collective leadership was to put some order into the administrative chaos inherited from Khrushchev. The new rulers had to discard, first of all, his most unpopular policies, starting with the split of the Party into two sections. The Khrushchev-initiated campaign to transform eventually all collective farms into State farms was suspended. Private plots owned by collective farmers were restored to their previous size, assistance was again offered to collective farmers in acquiring livestock, and the tax on cattle owned by city dwellers was repealed. Yet in 1965 the proposed doubling of state investment in agriculture was shelved, while a sizable increase in price was paid by the State for purchases from collective farms. In 1966, collective farmers were offered a guaranteed monthly wage, and a unified social security system was extended to them.

In 1965, Kosygin tried to decentralize Soviet industrial planning by allowing more play in the forces of supply and demand. Wages for both managers and workers would depend on profitability, that is, on the sale of products, not on the fulfillment of prescribed quantitative norms. As in Yugoslavia, the Soviet economy would be a "market socialism" where supply and demand would again play their role, and suppliers and manufacturers would deal directly with one another rather than going through central economic ministries.

Soon, however, by the beginning of 1966, the innovations were sabotaged by opposition from conservative Party elements. First, they watered down the reforms by reinstating the principle of central planning; then they slowed down their implementation and reasserted the role of the Party. The conservative opposition realized that to free managers from central tutelage would reduce the power of the Party bureaucracy. The local Party boss exercises his power the same way the old Tammany Hall man did his, simply by virtue of the fact that his word was law. The Party chieftain has the final say on jobs, rents, and who gets what reward in his bailiwick. Every far-reaching economic reform raises the issue of how far the Party can allow liberalization to go without losing the political control necessary to maintain its hold on the country. One may imagine the following case: a factory director who under a new decentralized system has authority to hire and fire, uses his power and dismisses a man who had obtained his job as a reward for Party work. Who is to decide whether the man is to go or to retain his job? Consequently, the old pattern, which strongly favored heavy industry, had to be altered only slightly. The Ninth Five-Year Plan (1971–1975) approved at the Twenty-fourth Party Congress favored consumer goods to some extent. Considerable investments were slated for agriculture, passenger cars, and other consumer durables. The chief future task, noted the plan, was "to insure a significant increase in the material and cultural standard of living." For the first time since 1928, consumer goods output was to rise somewhat faster than heavy industry.

Despite large investment in machinery and fertilizers, agriculture has remained the Achilles heel of the Soviet economy. The annual harvest has continued to fluctuate. A poor crop in 1972 depressed the rate of economic growth to 1.7 percent; the good harvest of 1973 raised it momentarily to 7.5 percent. Crop failures in 1963 and 1972 resulted in repeated shortages of bread and flour. In 1972, the USSR purchased as much as $750 million worth of grain from the United States. Despite an excellent harvest of 222.5 million tons of grain in 1973, the USSR has not achieved self-sufficiency in grain, and later harvests have been much poorer. Actually, since 1953, per capita agricultural production in the USSR has risen only about 1 percent annually. Small private plots still provide about one-third of gross Soviet agricultural output.[1]

ARMS AND SPACE RACE

Under the Brezhnev–Kosygin team, the growth of the Soviet conventional armed forces continued. The defense budget increased steadily. Altogether, between 1966 and 1982, the Soviet military budget expanded from 13 billion rubles to well over 20 billion rubles. These official figures are incomplete, however, because the published defense expenditures have included only a portion of the overall Soviet military expenditure. The actual figure for defense, space, and nuclear-energy programs may be as high as 20 to 25 percent of the country's gross national product. As a result of their continuous allocation of huge funds to defense and defense-oriented heavy industry, the Soviets have also increased their stockpiles of intercontinental ballistic missiles. They have been able to build up their conventional forces into the world's largest standing army, achieve nuclear parity with the United States, as well as to make of the Soviet Union the world's second naval power.

The new leadership continued the space effort of its predecessor and tried to overtake the United States in space accomplishments. One of the more spectacular Soviet space achievements was the September 1970 soft landing and return of a robot craft; not only did it land on the moon, but it also brought back three and a half ounces of its surface dust. This was followed in November of the same year by the soft landing of an eight-wheeled moon-rover (*Lunakhod* in Russian), the first self-propelled vehicle to ride on the lunar surface. In July 1975, the USSR and the United States staged a joint space venture; the Soviet space ship *Soyuz* (Union) had a rendezvous with an American ship, *Apollo*. In 1983, two Soviet astronauts established the world endurance record in space by orbiting the earth for 185 days.

The impressive Soviet successes in space have been due to a variety of factors. The Russians, traditionally good in theoretical mathematics, have also been paying a great deal of attention to rocketry since the beginning of the century. The Soviet government has taken over and continued this tradition. It was quick to perceive the connection between rockets and their development for military purposes and to put considerable resources into further research in the field. Because the program is defense related, it has been provided all the financial support it has needed. Prestige and propaganda considerations have also played a major role in furthering the ambitious space program. The enormous defense and space effort, however, resulted in sacrifices in all non-defense-oriented branches of the economy.

DOMESTIC RECOMPRESSION

The duumvirate that succeeded Khrushchev also had to cope with the manifold consequences of his de-Stalinization campaign. By destroying the legend of Stalin, Khrushchev destroyed the myth of Party infallibility and thus weakened its hold on the people's minds. Some of the more daring individuals who had not lost the capacity to ask questions, especially the youth, began to query the hitherto unquestionable dogmas and practices. This ferment was especially striking in intellectual circles, where the liberalization process had considerably loosened the ideological pressure on artists, writers, and scholars, who were no longer required to pay homage to socialist realism and dialectical materialism in their work.

The mounting political unrest made the new leadership increasingly apprehensive.

---

[1] Soviet peasants till land areas about 70 percent greater than that in the United States. They have more than seven times the manpower but only about one-third the tractors and trucks and 60 percent of the grain combines.

Bent on conservative restoration, they were very concerned with the effect of intellectual opposition to Party discipline and ideological orthodoxy. By 1965 the trend of de-Stalinization had been reversed; for instance, memoirs of leading World War II military leaders began to praise Stalin's contribution to the task of "socialist construction" and even his wartime achievements; and Brezhnev has made repeated laudatory references to the role played by the late dictator. Alexander M. Nekrich's book about the initial military catastrophe entitled *June 22, 1941* was banned. In 1970, Stalin's grave at the Kremlin wall was provided with a marble bust.

The trend toward partial revindication of Stalin as a meritorious statesman has in turn encountered outspoken criticism among an important segment of the Soviet community. Chief spokesmen for the opposition, which has manifested itself especially strongly in academic circles and among the technological intelligentsia, have been some of the leading minds of the USSR. The critics of the new trend include Pyotr Kapitsa, the dean of Soviet physicists; Andrei D. Sakharov, the father of Soviet-controlled thermonuclear bombs; and Zhores A. Medvedev, a geneticist and the author of a major work in the sociology of science.

The most daring, courageous, and persistent critic of the re-Stalinization attempts has been Dr. Andrei Sakharov, who in 1968 published a significant document entitled "Thoughts on Progress, Peaceful Coexistence and Intellectual Freedom." In this eloquent manifesto he advocated permitting genuine freedom of thought and discussion in the Soviet Union. According to Sakharov, such freedom is necessary for the full development of science and hence for solving the most pressing problems facing Soviet society. He pleaded for an end to bureaucratic despotism and censorship and favored a liberal-democratic reform of the Soviet regime based on a multiparty system. He repeatedly condemned the monopoly of power by the Communist Party, dominated by "hypocrites and demagogues." He

criticized the Party's continued preaching of class struggle and the Marxist-Leninist assumption that world ideologies and nations must remain incompatible. Stressing the danger of nuclear war to mankind, Sakharov urged Soviet-American cooperation to save civilization. He argued that the Soviet and American systems, borrowing from each other, were actually converging and would end up with democratic socialism. Sakharov bluntly warned Soviet leaders that unless secrecy were removed from science, culture, and technology, the USSR would become a second-rate power.

THE DISSENT MOVEMENT

Late in 1970, Sakharov established the Human Rights Committee in the USSR. The declared aim of the committee has been "to give consultative aid to the organs of power in applying guarantees of the rights of man," rights theoretically granted by the Soviet Constitution of 1936 but, as a rule, not respected in practice by the authorities. In 1975, Sakharov was awarded the Nobel Peace Prize, but was refused permission to leave his country to receive the prize.

While the opposition in top scientific circles has been less exposed to traditional Soviet "administrative measures"—not only because of international pressure but also because of the continuing need of the regime for the expertise of some of the leading dissenters—this has not been the case with other protesters. The artistic and literary wing of the opposition originally was centered around a former inmate of concentration camps, Alexander Solzhenitsyn, author of *One Day in the Life of Ivan Denisovich*, *Cancer Ward*, and *The First Circle*, and the recipient of the 1970 Nobel Prize for literature. His bold and blunt criticism, not only of the Soviet regime but of Marxism as alien and harmful to the Russian ethos, soon made him subject to harassment and persecution. When in 1974 he began to publish abroad his monumental, multivolume work *The Concentration Camps*, about the Gulag

Archipelago, the domestic uproar reached its peak. In 1975, Solzhenitsyn was expelled from the USSR. Eventually, he settled in the United States, where he has continued his bitter criticism of the Soviet Party and of Communism in general, while presenting his own vision of Russia's future.

Hampered by a rigid censorship, the dissenters have tried to spread their ideas in a variety of ways, ranging from protest demonstrations and the circulation of privately printed, uncensored publications, to the smuggling of literary works abroad. Among the most significant phenomena in this sphere has been the emergence of an underground periodical entitled *Chronicle of Current Events,* which made its debut in the spring of 1968. The bimonthly *Chronicle* carried information on the latest arrests, interrogations, trials, and imprisonments of anti-Soviet dissenters, and printed texts of vital documents and letters of protest about official persecution of ethnic and religious minorities (Jews, Ukrainians, Crimean Tatars, Lithuanians, Estonians, Baptists).[2] Until his confinement to an insane asylum in February 1969, one of the most prominent contributors to the *Chronicle* was former Major General Pyotr Grigorenko, a highly decorated World War II hero who once taught cybernetics at Frunze Military Academy. In the spring of 1978, while visiting the United States, he was deprived by Moscow of his Soviet citizenship, military rank, and medals, and thus became a political exile.

Soviet authorities have treated dissenters either as undesirable elements and deported them abroad (as in the case of Solzhenitsyn and Vladimir Bukovsky), or as traitors (as in the case of General Gri-

gorenko), or as mentally deranged persons requiring treatment in mental institutions. This last has been the fate of an increasing number of dissenters, including Alexander Yesenin-Volpin. According to a statement by Yuri Andropov, Chairman of the Soviet State Security Committee and therefore boss of the entire KGB apparatus, the failure to endorse Soviet Communism is in itself a sign of a serious mental illness and can only be cured by intense psychiatric treatment. In January 1980, Dr. Sakharov, who had signed a dissident's protest against the Soviet invasion of Afghanistan, was banished from the capital to the city of Gorky, 250 miles east of Moscow.

ETHNIC FERMENT

Closely related to the political and intellectual dissent has been the surfacing of a new wave of national awareness among non-Russian ethnic minorities. Constituting nearly half of the total population, these minorities have been trying to claim those rights that the Soviet Constitution grants them. The predominance of Great Russians in most top Party and Government posts, the pressure to impose Great Russian culture on non-Russians under the guise of Sovietization, and the unwillingness of Moscow's leadership to live up to its many promises to non-Russian minorities have been increasingly criticized. A significant external factor which has stimulated unrest has been the creation of new independent states in Asia and Africa out of the ruin of Western colonial empires.

Ethnic ferment was apparent even in the Khrushchev era. After the Twentieth Party Congress of 1956, several national minorities formerly accused of collaboration with the Germans and banished from their homelands (Kalmyks, Chechens, Kabardinians, Balkarians, Ingush, Volga Germans, and Crimean Tatars) were rehabilitated and partly allowed to return to their national territories. This was done immediately for

---

[2] The underground publications are usually referred to by the Russian term of *samizdat. Samizdat* is a play on words. *Gosizdat* is a telescoping of *Gosudarstvennoye Izdatelstvo,* the name of the monopoly-wielding State Publishing House. The *sam* part of the new word means "self." The whole—*samizdat*—translates as "we publish ourselves"—that is, not the State, but we the people.

the Kalmyks, Chechens, Kabardinians, Balkarians, and Ingush, who were sent back to their former settlements. The rehabilitation of the Volga Germans and the Crimean Tatars, however, dragged on until 1967.

In the vanguard of the agitation for the implementation of human rights for all ethnic groups has been the Jewish minority, which numbers nearly two million people. Stalin never openly preached anti-Semitism as a theory, but it was inherent in his practice and, as his daughter Svetlana testified, in private he often gave vent to his violent anti-Semitic sentiments. Khrushchev here followed Stalin's lead in repeatedly denying the existence of anti-Semitism in the Soviet Union and refusing to admit that the Jewish population had been a special target of Hitler's genocidal policy. The publication in 1962 of Yevtushenko's poem "Babi Yar," dedicated to over 100,000 thousand Kiev Jews massacred during the war, revived the issue, which was then publicly debated. This precipitated Khrushchev's angry insistence that "We do not have a Jewish question." Nevertheless, he maintained that it is better for Jews not to hold high posts in government, for this only stirs up popular resentment.

This attitude, perpetuated by Khrushchev's successors, has been reflected in the increasing exclusion of Jews not only from politically sensitive posts, but also from most good jobs in general. There is considerable evidence that, like their Tsarist counterparts, Soviet officials have singled out Jewish, as well as Ukrainian and Baltic dissenters, for unusually harsh treatment. Anti-Semitic policies have in turn created increasing resentment on the part of Soviet Jews and led many of them to press loudly for strict application of those human rights that the Soviet constitution promised them. The focal point of the Jewish demands has been the right to emigrate to Israel. Initially, the Soviet authorities denied this right, describing it as a form of treason and "desertion of the Soviet fatherland." Under pressure of world opinion, however, Moscow has allowed thousands of Jewish dissenters to leave the country. The emigration reached its peak in 1979 when 51,320 Jews left the USSR. Thereafter, it dropped below 22,000 in 1980 and to 894 in 1984.

While the Jewish agitation, despite its unpleasant international repercussions, has not threatened the internal stability of the USSR, the ferment in the western borderland union republics, especially in the Ukraine and the Baltic countries, has been treated as a potential threat to the integrity of the USSR. Hence a series of purges of leading spokesmen of the "bourgeois nationalistic" deviationists. The reprisals hit especially hard the leading Ukrainian freedom fighters, including Valentin Moroz, Ivan Dziuba, Viacheslav Chornovil, and Ivan Svetlichny. In April 1966, two Ukrainian critics, Svetlichny and Dziuba, were accused of smuggling "nationalist" verses to the West. Chornovil, a courageous journalist who denounced the Russification reflected in shocking discrimination against the Ukrainian language and culture, has been incarcerated under terribly harsh conditions and sentenced to forced labor. In the early 1960s, similar purges took place in the Latvian, Azerbaijan, and Kazakh republics and in the Estonian, Latvian, Lithuanian, Ukrainian, Armenian, and Georgian SSRs in 1972 and 1973.

RELIGIOUS AND INTELLECTUAL UNREST

The ferment among the ethnic minorities has been paralleled by the protest movement of the religious believers, estimated at 30 to 50 million, who feel that their constitutional rights have also been violated by the Soviet authorities. While the official hierarchy of the predominant Greek Orthodox Church has adopted a rather conformist attitude, many Roman Catholics, especially the Lithuanians, and some Protestant sects have assumed an increasingly defiant attitude. A militant minority, ranging from dissident Baptists to Pentecostals who contend that their faith is none of the State's business, has been singled out by the authorities for especially harsh reprisals. Congregations have been required to register with a Government watchdog agency, the Council on Religious Affairs, and to accept constraints placed on them, including denial of religious instruction for children.

Many Soviet dissenters have adhered to the Russian tradition of oppositionists as lonely, morally motivated fighters, ready for endless, and perhaps hopeless, sacrifices to satisfy their inner compulsion. While most dissenters, including Sakharov, have not emphasized religion, a large segment of the dissent movement does have a strong religious coloring. A considerable segment of that movement, especially its Social Christian wing, has revealed a deep interest in the Russian past, including prerevolutionary art, especially ikons and old architecture. The rediscovery of the old Russia, partly through field trips to remote places to study the surviving historic monuments and old handwritten documents, has been a passion with many dissenters, for it has provided them with a live contact with the roots of their native culture.

The emergence of a half-tolerated, half-repressed opposition has been accompanied by an increasing number of political defections. During the last decade and a half, a number of prominent Soviet citizens have defected from the USSR and have sought political asylum in the West. The most sensational among them was Stalin's only daughter, Svetlana Alliluyeva, who, after settling in the United States, published several revealing accounts of her life, especially of her relations with her father. Other prominent defectors who have reinforced the ranks of the emigration include the two leading Russian writers, Solzhenitsyn and Siniavsky; a leading Soviet ballet star, Rudolph Nureyev; a young writer, Anatoly V. Kuznetsov; and Natalia Markarova, the prime ballerina of the Leningrad Kirov Ballet.

BREZHNEV–KOSYGIN FOREIGN POLICY

While in domestic politics the new leadership rejected many of their predecessor's measures, in the field of foreign policy there was no significant break with the line pursued by Khrushchev. After having criticized him for the break with China, neither Brezhnev nor Kosygin, who visited Mao in 1965 and again in 1969, was able to improve relations with Peking. Early in 1965, Sino-Soviet relations became strained by the increased military involvement of the United States in South Vietnam. In April 1965, in an effort to make their military assistance to North Vietnam more effective, Moscow asked Peking for the use of two airfields in southwestern China for air transit rights, and for the right to use harbor facilities in southern China. All the Soviet requests were turned down by Peking as allegedly violating Chinese sovereignty.

During the period of the Chinese Cultural Revolution (1965–1969), Sino-Soviet relations deteriorated still further. Symptomatic of the tension was a series of border incidents, accompanied by charges and countercharges that each side was massing military forces along the frontiers to launch an armed attack.

In March 1969, the Moscow–Peking dispute erupted in a violent clash between Soviet and Chinese armed forces along the Ussuri River and later extended to other points along the extensive 4,000-mile Sino-Soviet frontier. Both sides suffered heavy casualties and, as in the past, each held the other responsible for starting the conflict. To control this dangerous escalation, early in 1970 both sides appointed top diplomats to work out arrangements for quieting the dispute. Protracted negotiations produced no concrete results except the decision to exchange ambassadors and to tone down the intensity of the mutual propaganda campaigns, a stipulation not always observed.

Chinese dialogue with the United States

since 1971 and Peking's admission to the United Nations later that year have not improved Sino-Soviet relations either. Quite the contrary, it embittered them still further by inciting both sides to accusations of plotting an armed conflict against one another with the tacit support of an "imperialist silent partner." Neither the death of Mao in September 1976 nor the message of greetings sent by the People's Republic of China to the Soviet Union on the sixtieth anniversary of the Bolshevik revolution produced even a limited accommodation between the two Communist giants.

The necessity of deploying some forty army divisions as well as considerable nuclear forces along the Sino-Soviet border has only slightly diminished Soviet pressure on Western Europe. However, the specter of a possible two-front war altered Moscow's tactics and made legal confirmation of the territorial status quo in Europe a major and pressing objective of its foreign policy. In pursuit of that goal, Moscow renewed the call for a European conference to be followed by a European security pact that would reaffirm the frontiers established after World War II. The first step in that direction was the signing in September 1970 of a Treaty of Friendship with the government of West Germany. The treaty, followed by a similar pact between Warsaw and Bonn concluded in December of that year, ratified the 1945 status quo in Eastern and Central Europe. But the new Soviet leaders refused to rest on their laurels and continued to press for broader and more solemn confirmation of their wartime territorial gains by a European Security Conference. This they obtained through the Helsinki agreement in 1975.

Meanwhile, Moscow has expressed interest in becoming a major participant in West European trade, has concluded several agreements for marketing Soviet oil abroad as well as natural gas, and has participated in many trade fairs. For instance, Moscow signed an agreement with the Italian Fiat Company for a plant to be built in a new town called Togliatti to triple Soviet output of passenger cars.

THE SOVIET UNION AND EAST-CENTRAL EUROPE

The Soviet leaders, continuing Khrushchev's policy, have been working by various means to strengthen and make permanent their control over East-Central Europe. One

Soviet oil pipeline in construction

form of consolidating their hold has been the establishment within the framework of the Council of Mutual Economic Assistance (CMEA or COMECON) of several supra-national corporations to integrate the East European economies with that of the USSR. Other Soviet steps aimed at making the hegemonial sphere in East Central Europe more dependent on the USSR include the foundation of the International Bank for Economic Cooperation and the construction of the "Friendship Oil Pipe Line," which supplies Soviet oil to East Germany, Poland, Czechoslovakia, and Hungary.

The Soviet attempts to integrate East European economies with that of the USSR have been problematic. The foremost difficulty has been an inability to resolve satisfactorily the problem of joint investment, prices, currency, and convertibility. The increasing pressure on Moscow's satellites has resulted in two upsets. One of them has been Romanian opposition to Moscow's integrative drive. This opposition, which had already manifested itself in 1963, assumed new forms during the middle and late 1960s. The Romanians, especially their ambitious leader Nicolas Ceausescu, refused to submit to many Soviet demands, not only in the economic but also in the military sphere. While tightening its domestic controls, Bucharest pursued a largely independent line of foreign policy. Romania has maintained a policy of noncomment in the raging Sino-Soviet dispute and has even gone so far as to openly support Peking's point of view from time to time. In June 1967, after the Arab-Israeli war, Romania, unlike the USSR and all its dependents, continued to maintain diplomatic and trade relations with the Israelis, while pressing them for a peaceful accommodation with the Arabs.

Another country that came to oppose the tightening of the Soviet controls over its hegemonial sphere during the late 1960s was Czechoslovakia. Quiescent and submissive until 1964, the Czechs and especially the Slovaks gradually began to be affected by the political winds coming first from Tito's Yugoslavia, then from Gomułka's Poland after 1956, then from Kadar's reformist Hungary with its modernizing new Economic Model, and eventually from Ceausescu's Romania. In 1964, the huge statue of Stalin, which for well over a decade had spoiled the beautiful panorama of "golden Prague," was toppled. Public opinion began to force partial concessions from the reluctant regime of the staunch Stalinist Antonin Novotny. He tried for four years to channel the mounting discontent, but in December 1967 he was dismissed from his post as First Secretary of the Czechoslovak Party. In January 1968, after a long intra-party struggle, Novotny was replaced by a compromise candidate, Alexander Dubček, a reform-minded Slovak. Under the mounting pressure of public opinion, Dubček tried to liberalize the system and replace the lingering Stalinism with what he called "socialism with a human face." He abolished censorship, rehabilitated many victims of "the past period of mistakes," and even toyed with the idea of legalizing non-Communist political groups. He also showed considerable sympathy for various projects directed at loosening the Warsaw Treaty Organization and putting the Czechoslovak-Soviet military and economic relations on a more equitable basis. All this was accompanied by improving relations with the West, including the Federal Republic of Germany, from which Dubček expected large credits and technical aid to modernize the faltering economy of his country. The series of liberalizing concessions and incipient democratic reforms constituted the essence of what came to be called the "Prague Spring." Dubček's efforts immediately aroused the suspicions of Moscow, which saw in them a threat to three pillars of its control: the "leading role" of the Communist Party, the Warsaw Pact, and the CMEA, or COMECON.

Soviet response to the Prague Spring escalated through a series of stern warnings and preparatory military moves. At first Moscow tried to confidentially persuade the Czechslovak leaders to slow down the tempo of the reforms, as well as to alter their direction. When that failed they issued strong public warnings and sought, in a series of top-level meetings, to persuade Dubček and his associates to stop the avalanche of changes that were affecting both the internal structure of Czechoslovakia and its international position as an integral segment of the socialist camp. When all this failed, on August 21, 1968 the Soviets struck. With impressive speed and efficiency, Soviet, East German, Polish, Hungarian, and Bulgarian forces invaded and occupied Czechoslovakia. Dubček and his immediate associates and supporters were arrested and brought to Moscow in chains. There they were branded as traitors to international Communism and blackmailed into surrender.

Meanwhile, the invading forces encountered no active organized resistance and occupied the whole country. Partly owing to the Western, as well as the much stronger Chinese, condemnation of the invasion, the Soviets momentarily reinstated Dubček and his associates on the condition that they alter their reforms to the Soviets' satisfaction. A few weeks later Moscow forced Dubček to resign and imposed upon Czechoslovakia a new government run by Dr. Gustav Husák.

Like Jánŏs Kádár in Hungary, Husák was a former victim of the Stalinist purges. Husák's government soon signed a "Treaty of Friendship" that gave the Soviet forces the right of indefinite presence as well as the freedom to enter and leave Czechoslovakia at will.

An important factor behind the Soviet intervention was Moscow's fear that the triumph of the "liberals" in Czechoslovakia would destabilize the rest of its hegemonial sphere and eventually affect the Western fringes of the Soviet Union, especially Ukraine. The downfall of Novotny and the emergence of Dubček were for Brezhnev a signal of a gathering storm in East Central Europe. Despite Czech and West German protestations that the rapprochement between Prague and Bonn was merely an innocent case of economic cooperation, Brezhnev remained suspicious of the eventual effects of the West German *Ostpolitik* on Prague. All the Czech assurances of loyalty to the Warsaw Pact and the CMEA notwithstanding, Brezhnev, as a man schooled in Marxist dialectics, must have interpreted Prague's "economic opening to the West" as the first step toward broader and deeper cooperation between Czechoslovakia and

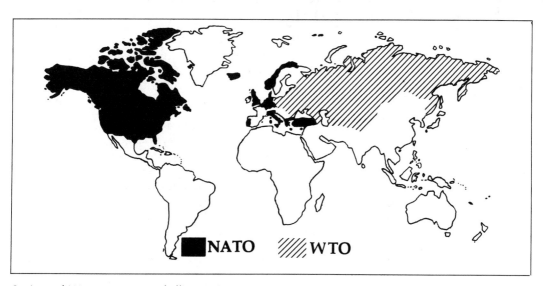

Soviet and Western systems of alliances in 1968

the strongest European member of NATO. Consequently, Brezhnev must have viewed Czechoslovakia's evolution as representing not only the danger of "revisionist" contamination, but also a potential threat to the existence of the Soviet-East European system of alliances.

At the Polish Party Congress of December 1968 in Warsaw, Brezhnev justified the military intervention as an exercise of the Soviet Union's right to protect "the achievements of the socialist construction" in other Communist states when they are threatened. This concept has been often called in the West "the Brezhnev doctrine."

MOSCOW AND THE THIRD WORLD

After World War II, as European colonial empires collapsed one after another, the bitter and complex conflicts among nations and tribes in Africa provided fertile ground for Moscow's support of the newly established, mostly unstable governments. The Soviet backing of a mosaic of third-world regimes, "one-party democracies," guerrillas, and "national liberation movements" allowed the Kremlin to project its image as the main champion of colonial peoples and their developing states. While Stalin had limited his expansion to the countries adjacent to the Soviet Union, which he could control with the bayonets of the Red Army, Khrushchev and his successors began to venture far afield into the most remote corners of the globe, offering economic as well as military aid to a plethora of developing nations.

Until 1965, Moscow continued to supply Indonesia with credits and economic assistance as well as liberal quantities of all sorts of weapons. The 1965 military coup which overthrew President Sukarno was paralleled by a massive purge of the Indonesian Communists, then the largest nonruling Communist Party in the world. The establishment of a Western-oriented regime ended the seemingly irreversible growth of Com-

munist influence in this oil-rich archipelago. Also, in Ghana the pro-Soviet regime of Nkrumah was replaced by an anti-Communist military government in 1965. Neither this double defeat, nor a similar blow that in 1973 overthrew the Marxist coalition government of Dr. Salvador Allende in Chile, stopped Soviet attempts to penetrate the developing countries of the Third World.

Until 1972, the focal points of Soviet penetration in the Near and Middle East were Iraq, Syria, and Egypt, particularly the last. Strategically situated at the juncture between the African and Asian continents and controling the Suez canal, Egypt's role in the Soviet strategy was initially paramount. To strengthen Egypt's dependence on the USSR, a team of Soviet engineers helped to complete the Aswan Dam on the Nile and the Helwan iron and steel complex near Cairo and prospected for oil and iron ore. Success in both fields bolstered Moscow's prestige considerably. While helping Egypt's economy, the Soviets also supplied the country with tanks, planes, and rockets, as well as several thousand Soviet military advisers. After the large-scale destruction of the Egyptian arsenal during the Arab-Israeli war of June 1967, Moscow not only resupplied them, but also installed many sophisticated surface-to-air missiles and radar stations and provided Soviet crews to man them. Operating from Egyptian naval and air bases, the Soviets could challenge American control of the Eastern Mediterranean and move easily to Aden, Sudan, or Libya.

The death of President Gamal Nasser in 1970 and his replacement by Colonel Anwar Sadat profoundly altered the Soviet position in Egypt. Sadat believed that he could achieve his objectives—modernizing his country and regaining some of the Egyptian land lost to Israel—only with American diplomatic support. Consequently, in July 1972 Sadat expelled most of the Soviet advisory personnel from his country and made overtures to Washington to gain its moral as well as material support for his cause. Despite this gesture, Moscow tried to maintain its position in Egypt, if only to assure the advantages its treaty of friendship with Cairo had given it at the Alexandria naval base. Soviet reluctance to rearm fully the Egyptian armed forces with the most sophisticated weapons plus Moscow's insistence on prompt payment of the old debts caused still further strains in the relations of the formerly close partners. President Sadat's cancellation of Egypt's friendship treaty with the Soviet Union and the subsequent liquidation of the Soviet naval bases in March 1976 caught Moscow by surprise. The Soviet Mediterranean squadron was suddenly compelled to anchor in international waters.

A major point of friction between the Soviet Union and the United States has been their conflicting attitudes toward the state of Israel. This has repeatedly resulted in highly explosive situations. For instance, at the peak of the Yom Kippur War of 1973 in the Middle East, the Soviets readied an airborne division as Israeli troops broke across the Suez Canal and encircled an entire Egyptian Army corps. Washington's response was a worldwide alert of American military forces. This confrontation was only gradually diffused, thanks to the restraint shown by both sides and owing to the existence of the direct hot line between the Kremlin and the White House. The Russians, while basically recognizing the existence of Israel, have supported the Arabs' demands: total withdrawal from Arab territories occupied in the 1967 war, acceptance of Palestinian rights, including the right to statehood, and recognition of the Palestine Liberation Organization as the sole legitimate representative of the Palestinian people.

Although Moscow has given the Arab cause a great deal of diplomatic and military support, its real political influence in the Arab world has been in the long run rather precarious. Russia's principal partners have been Syria and Libya, with whom it has billion-dollar arms agreements. Iraq has been also linked with the Soviet Union by a Treaty of Friendship and Cooperation, but

the ruling Socialist Baath Party has barely tolerated the Communist Party and gave open support to Somali guerrillas in their struggle against Soviet-backed Ethiopia.

During the 1970s, the Soviet Union, with a gain here or a loss there, continued its quest for greater influence on the African continent. This trend was punctuated by the Soviet-Cuban intervention in the former Portuguese colonies of Angola and Mozambique, and by the grand design which Moscow tried to implement in Northeast Africa.[3] Seldom in history has a great power made a bolder bid for establishing its influence than Moscow did in 1977–1978, when it attempted to control the whole of the Suez Canal–Red Sea trade routes between Europe and Asia. At the end of 1976, with Libya and Somalia under their control and with military advisers and technicians in Sudan and Ethiopia, the Soviets began to press into Chad in the heart of Africa. By the summer of 1977, they were threatening the defiant Egypt with encirclement and had a chance to bring the whole Northeastern African region within their sphere of influence. Brezhnev's gamble, supported by Cuba, staked Soviet prestige and billions in arms to build a pro-Soviet coalition out of the volatile national materials in Africa's Horn, a bloc that would offset the weak, conservative Arab regimes in the Red Sea area. Moscow's plan called for forging Ethiopia, Somalia, Sudan, Djibuti, and South Yemen into a pro-Soviet constellation. Meanwhile, however, through a combination of excessive ambition and ineptness, the Russians sustained a sharp diplomatic setback. On November 15, 1977, Somalia ordered all Soviet advisers to leave the country, ended the Soviet use of naval facilities on the Indian Ocean, and broke off diplomatic relations with Cuba. Not since 1972,

---

[3] During the 1970s, the USSR and Eastern European nations provided almost 90 percent of the military technicians in Africa, but Cuba won out with its massive presence in Angola, estimated at some 15,000 men by 1977. In the 1970s, the USSR emerged as one of the most important exporters of arms in the world.

when the Egyptians similarly expelled the Russians, had Moscow been dealt such a rebuff. Another area of Soviet diplomatic activities was the Indian subcontinent. Trying to bolster India as a bulwark against China, Moscow viewed with unease the Indo-Pakistani war of 1965 and successfully mediated its prompt end. Early in 1966 Premier Kosygin met with leaders of both states in the capital of the Soviet Uzbek republic, Tashkent, and arranged a peaceful settlement that greatly enhanced the Russian image in Asia. While putting the main emphasis on India, which the Soviets had supplied with economic as well as military aid, Moscow also sought to establish good relations with Pakistan, whose friendship with Peking and proximity to Soviet borders are significant strategic factors. During the early 1970s, under Indira Gandhi's premiership, India's dependence upon Soviet industrial, militarty, and diplomatic support reached its zenith. In 1971, following the Sino-American rapprochement, the USSR and India signed a twenty-year treaty of peace, friendship, and cooperation. Soviet support for India during the 1971 war that gave birth to Bangladesh, which had seceded from Pakistan with India's backing, was motivated by Pakistan's alliance with the United States and China and by Moscow's efforts to offset Chinese influence in the area. Using Indian naval bases, Soviet warships in the Indian Ocean were able to challenge the Western preponderance in that crucial area and to outflank China.

In addition to India and the Arab countries, Africa and South America have become prime recipients of new Soviet military and economic aid. Soviet military sales to Africa have increased nearly twenty-fold since 1970. In addition to military assistance in Libya, Angola, and Mozambique, arms and technical assistance, including Cuban technicians, have been flowing to "national liberation" movements in southern Africa, and military aid has continued to Uganda, Somalia, and Ethiopia.

After the withdrawal of the Soviet ICBMs from Cuba, the regime of Fidel Castro continued to receive not only liberal financial subsidies and economic aid from Moscow, but also military assistance. In return, Castro sided with the Soviets in their quarrel with the Chinese, opened Cuban ports to Soviet naval units, and assisted Soviet efforts to establish a foothold in Angola by sending his troops to successfully support the local socialist and pro-Soviet "national liberation movement" against its rivals in the civil war that broke out when the Portuguese withdrew in 1975. Cuba's acceptance as a member of CEMA in 1972 marked its further integration onto the Soviet camp.

TOWARD DETENTE

Despite these various ventures in the Third World, and in spite of other obstacles it has encountered, the Brezhnev–Kosygin team continued Khrushchev's post-Cuban crisis attempts to seek the relaxation of tensions with Washington, or a detente. Until early 1972, the Soviet search for detente was restrained by a variety of obstacles, one of which was the American involvement in Vietnam; another was the diametrically divergent policies of the two superpowers in the Near East. Still another has been the problem of the arms race, a key to the relations between the two superpowers. To cope with these controversial issues, in July 1967 Kosygin met with President Johnson at Glassboro, New Jersey, and the two leaders exchanged views on the main problems dividing them. Partly as a result of these talks, in August the two governments signed a treaty to check the spread of nuclear weapons.

The Soviet-led invasion of Czechoslovakia in August 1968 put a momentary damper on Soviet-American relations. Early in 1969, however, relations again improved when Moscow suggested ratification of the nuclear nonproliferation treaty and proposed that the two powers begin discussions on a strategic arms limitation treaty (SALT). A new phase in the attempted detente was reached as a result of the visit of President

Richard Nixon to the USSR in May 1972. The most significant result of the Nixon–Brezhnev summit in Moscow was the signing of a document called "Basic Principles of Relations between the USA and the USSR." By this declaration the two leaders agreed to develop normal relations "based on the principles of sovereignty, equality, [and] noninterference in internal affairs" while exercising restraint in order to avoid military confrontations. The two superpowers promised to cooperate in defusing dangerous tensions, to exchange views on mutual problems, and to limit their armaments. The Moscow summit meeting also included agreements that pledged the two countries to develop close economic relations and to cooperate in scientific, technological, and cultural fields. Other agreements signed by Brezhnev and Nixon in Moscow called for a joint space rendezvous (which took place in July 1975) and the establishment of a Soviet-American commission to plan long-term economic ties between the rivals.

Implementing the 1972 Moscow declaration, the two superpowers then signed a treaty limiting antiballistic-missiles systems (SALT I) and an interim agreement limiting strategic offensive arms. Under the terms of these two documents, the Soviets secured numerical advantage over the United States in ICBMs (1,618 to 1,054), in missile-launching submarines (62 to 44), and in submarine-launched ballistic missiles (950 to 710), while the United States still led in the number of warheads. Following President Nixon's Moscow visit, Soviet-American relations continued to improve throughout 1973 and 1974. In June 1973, Brezhnev visited the United States and approved an "Agreement on the Prevention of Nuclear War." The two governments also established a Soviet-American committee for the peaceful uses of atomic energy and for agricultural and oceanographic cooperation. Soviet-American relations were further strengthened by Nixon's June 1974 visit to the USSR and by President Gerald R. Ford's meeting with Brezhnev in Vladivostok that November. At Vladivostok the

two powers set the ceiling on the number of offensive missiles for each side at 2,400. Soviet-American cooperation also increased in space and environmental research.

Late in 1974, Soviet-American relations hit a large snag when the United States Senate refused to approve credits to finance Soviet purchases in this country and attached to the 1972 trade agreement an amendment calling for liberalization of the Soviet emigration policy, mainly pertaining to Jews. Moscow interpreted the Senate's action as flagrant interference in Soviet domestic affairs, canceled their Lend-Lease obligations, terminated several trade deals, and assumed a tough line in the SALT II negotiations.

Meanwhile, in July and August 1975, thirty-five countries from Europe and North America convened at Helsinki and signed a document entitled the "Final Act of the Helsinki Conference on Security and Cooperation in Europe." In effect, the signing of this document amounted to official Western recognition of the inviolability of the existing boundaries in Europe, thus legalizing the frontiers of Europe as established in 1945.

Initially, the Helsinki conference seemed to the Soviet leaders like the fulfillment of their dreams, an unmixed blessing. Yet, to obtain this coveted prize, they reluctantly accepted the so-called *third basket* of the Helsinki declaration. It included respect for human rights, the flow of information across borders, the right to travel, and even promises to extend "freedom of thought, conscience, religion or belief," as well as "the freedom of the individual to profess and practice, alone or in community with others, religion or belief, acting in accordance with the dictates of his own conscience." The *third basket* gave a considerable stimulus to the Soviet dissent movement.

THE CONSTITUTION OF 1977

On November 7, 1977, Soviet Russia celebrated its sixtieth anniversary with pride, pageantry, and fanfare. The huge, carefully orchestrated birthday party thrown by the triumphant regime was marked by three gifts from the rulers to their subjects: a new constitution, a new head of state, and a new national anthem that eliminated all mention of Stalin.[4] The preamble of the 1977 Constitution describes the USSR as "a society of mature socialist social relations" in which "the concern of all for the welfare of each and the concern of each for the welfare of all" is a guiding principle. Thus, the USSR is no longer defined as a dictatorship of the proletariat. A new section on foreign policy incorporated into the constitutional law of the USSR such principles as "inviolability of borders, renunciation of the use of force or the threat of force," and "non-interference in the internal affairs of other states." Thus the section echoes the language of the final act of the Helsinki conference on European security and cooperation. "Peaceful coexistence of states with different social systems" is declared to be a guiding norm of Soviet policy, but so is the support of "the struggle of peoples for national liberation and social progress." Another proviso affirms the principle of "socialist internationalism and comradely mutual aid" as a basic tenet of the Soviet Charter. Soviet intervention in Czechoslovakia in 1968 was justified according to this proviso, often called "the Brezhnev doctrine," and it is now written into the new Constitution.

After thirteen years of leadership of the Party, while promulgating the new Constitution, Leonid Brezhnev was vested with the position of Chairman of the Supreme Soviet, or nominal Chief of State, while remaining the Party's Secretary General. No such precedent had existed in the Soviet Union. Both Stalin and Khrushchev at one time combined the top jobs of Party boss and premier. After Khrushchev was overthrown in October 1964, the Party resolved that the two posts could not be held simultaneously, but this restriction was not extended to the chairmanship of the Supreme

Soviet. Thus Brezhnev became the first to be both Soviet Chief of State and Chief of the Party.

Another significant change that bolstered the role of the Party was the creation of a new post of first deputy chairman of the Presidium of the Supreme Soviet, or in effect, a "first vice-president."

While ambiguities abound in the section on foreign policy, in one domestic matter the new Constitution was much clearer than its predecessor: It formally endorsed the leading role of the Communist Party. In the 1936 document, the Party was mentioned almost in passing in Article 126. A new preamble, as well as Article 6, now enshrines the Party as the guiding spirit in Soviet state and society. While stating that "all power in the USSR is vested in the people," the new Constitution stressed that it is the Party that is the driving force behind all state and public bodies. This means that all power comes from the Party. Another novelty of the Brezhnev Constitution was the spelling out of the important role of the military establishment. A new section on national security stressed that, to insure the defense of the country, the State will equip the armed forces with everything necessary to fulfill their task. This development is in keeping with the main thrust of recent Soviet history. Since World War II, the Red Army has enjoyed a most honorable reputation in the minds of the people.

DEATH OF THE DETENTE

The early and middle 1970s were the years of detente, which culminated in the Helsinki declaration of 1975, and the signing of the SALT II agreements in Vienna in 1979. While the West understood the term detente as "relaxation of international tensions," followed by expansion of trade and cultural exchange, Moscow has adopted a much more restricted interpretation of the slogan. The Kremlin used the accompanying euphoria as an opportunity to expand in the Third World and undermine the United

---

[4] To date, the USSR has had four constitutions, proclaimed successively in 1918, 1922, 1936, and 1977.

The military parade at the Red Square in Moscow during the Sixtieth Anniversary of the Bolshevik Revolution

States position in Western Europe. The Soviets intensified their attempts to weaken Western Europe's ties with NATO with the purpose of turning one European country after another into neutral, non-committed buffer states. Their belief has been that these countries would eventually develop more intimate ties with the USSR.

These efforts, along with repeated Soviet intervention in Africa, strained the detente, but did not ruin it altogether. What dealt the fatal blow and escalated international tensions again was the chain of dramatic events of 1979. The chain started with the installation of the newest Soviet medium range SS-20 missiles in the Western regions of the USSR, as well as in East Germany and Czechoslovakia. Targeted on the main urban and industrial centers of Western Europe, the SS-20 more than doubled the Soviet strike capacity. Their installation meant that from well inside the Soviet orbit the Soviets could reach the NATO command posts and launching sites, while their own were out of reach of NATO's intermediate range missiles. Together with the marked Soviet superiority in conventional weapons, the SS-20 rockets further destabilized the military situation in Europe.

The worsening of the strategic balance in Europe was paralleled by the overthrow of the Shah Riza Pahlevi in the beginning of 1979. The upheaval in Iran unsettled the Western position in the Middle East. Suddenly, the pro-American establishment in Tehran was replaced by a fiercely anti-Western regime headed by a radical, fanatical Muslim leader, the Ayatollah Khomeini. His supporters not only sent the American military advisors packing, but also captured the United States embassy and kept its personnel as hostages for many months. The Ayatollah was certainly not pro-Soviet, but his predecessor was so pro-Western that his replacement resulted in a serious setback to the United States. As a result of the upheaval in Iran, a dangerous power-vacuum was created around the Persian Gulf. The damage of the West's position in the region represented an advantage to the Russians. They were doubtlessly pleased at the blow dealt to United States prestige in Iran and saw a new opportunity to enhance their influence in the oil-bearing and strategically vital area adjacent to their southern border. This is why the Kremlin initially supported the Islamic revolution, even though it feared its impact on its Muslim Central Asiatic provinces. It was hoped in Moscow that the Tudeh Communist Party, banned under the Shah, could gain enough popular support to play a dominant role once the Ayatollah Khomeini, already over 80 years old, was no longer in control. The Khomeini forces initially exploited the Communist support, but they saw it as a danger to themselves. That is why the Ayatollah struck out at the Tudeh Communist Party, banning it in May 1983 while half of the Soviet embassy staff in Tehran was forced to leave the country.

Meanwhile, in December 1979, with Iran hovering on the brink of chaos, and before SALT II could be ratified by the U.S. Senate, Soviet troops occupied Afghanistan. In Kabul, a government was established that was to be more directly controlled by Moscow and more firmly committed to the Marxist course than the one that had been already in power in Afghanistan since 1978. The reasons for the Kremlin's military move

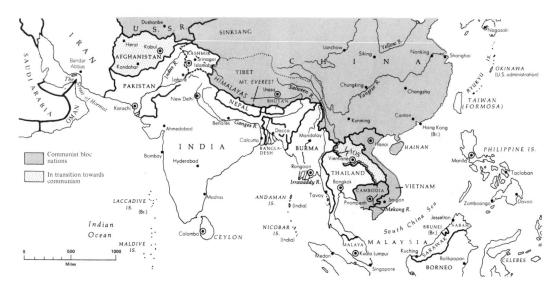

at that particular moment are still unclear. Did Brezhnev order the move into Afghanistan because he calculated that the power vacuum created by the downfall of the pro-American Shah was too good an opportunity to be missed? If American forces were to establish in Iran a military dictatorship replacing that of the Shah, Brezhnev may have reasoned, the result could be the bolstering of United States bases on the Soviet border, with a hostile China stretching along most of the remaining Soviet frontier in Asia, and only a shaky, turbulent Afghanistan in between. On the other hand, Russian troops poised in Afghanistan would ensure best that any potential American move into the Persian Gulf would be met, and Russian direct control of Afghanistan could bring about a partition of Iran into spheres of influence, as had been the case in 1907 and during World War II. Or did the Kremlin fear the birth of a radical Islamic fundamentalist regime in Afghanistan, the regime that could undermine its own Central Asiatic republics?

Whatever the motives, the invasion of Afghanistan, a region that the Russians had sought to take over several times before, seemed to fulfill a century-old Russian dream to dominate that country. To the Soviets, Afghanistan appeared to offer a stepping stone to the warm waters of the Arabian Sea and the Indian Ocean and a land rich in iron ore, copper, uranium, and natural gas. The Soviet military control of Afghanistan could considerably improve Moscow's strategic position both toward the West as well as China while threatening directly Iran and Pakistan. A substantial Soviet military presence would be placed not only at the Khyber Pass (the gateway from Central to South Asia) but beyond it. Second, Soviet ground and air forces could advance over the great divide of the Hindu Kush to within less than 500 miles from the Persian Gulf and the critical Strait of Hormuz leading into the Arabian Sea.

Since the invasion, ruthless "pacification operations" were waged by the Soviet occupation army of over 100,000 men against the widespread Afghan resistance movement. The construction of numerous military bases and large, modern airfields seemed to indicate that the Soviet forces were originally planning to stay for quite a while. At the same time, they engaged in a major effort to train Afghans in the Soviet Union to run their new satellite. Moscow's propaganda machine has tried to explain its "pacification" of Afghanistan as a fight against an "imperialist" attempt to overturn the "people's revolution."

Despite its obvious advantages, the Soviet invasion of Afghanistan had several negative effects for the USSR. First, President Carter reacted to the invasion by shutting off the flow of high-technology items and grain to the Soviets and he proclaimed a boycott of the 1980 Olympic games in Moscow. In addition, the invasion entrapped considerable Soviet forces in tricky guerrilla warfare, resembling the United States involvement in Vietnam. Like the United States in Vietnam, the Soviet soldiers were able to hold cities and control main lines of communication and carry out their own version of search-and-destroy missions and yet remain far short of "pacifying" the entire countryside despite killing some 9 percent of the Afgan population and exiling some nearly 5 million, mostly to Pakistan and Iran. The invasion has alerted Washington to recognize the necessity of improving American military readiness in the Persian Gulf and Indian Ocean areas. To the naval and air base of Diego Garcia, the United States has added new military facilities in Egypt, Oman, Somalia, and Kenya.

The agressive move in Afghanistan has pushed the United States to develop closer ties with Peking, which has included supplying American military-related technology to the Chinese armed forces. Moreover, the invasion destroyed any hope that the United States Senate would ratify the SALT II treaty, signed in Vienna in the summer of 1979 by President Carter. The Soviet aggression also resulted in a far-reaching alienation of public and government opinion in much of the Third World, particularly in Muslim countries. Last, but not least, the invasion of Afghanistan helped to elect the militantly anti-Communist Ronald Reagan to the office of president. He called the USSR "the focus of evil in the modern world" and stimulated an abrupt rise in U.S. defense spending, which included considerable aid to the Afgan guerrillas. Thus, even from the Soviet point of view, the balance

sheet of the invasion of Afghanistan has been definitely negative.

To the end of his rule, Brezhnev continued with increasing boldness Krushchev's policy of exploiting the local, indigenous forces to extend Soviet influence deep into the Third World. This has included not only Asia and Africa, but also Central America and the Caribbean region. In Latin America, Moscow focused its attention primarily on San Salvador and Nicaragua and on the little Caribbean island of Grenada, thus threatening the United States position in the vital region of the Panama Canal.

On the African continent, in 1975, Soviet weapons, technical and economic aid, as well as contingents of Cuban soldiers, brought Marxist revolutionaries to power in the former Portuguese colony of Angola. In Ethiopia, they have helped the Fidel Castro-type Communist military regime to consolidate its control over rebels in Eritrea and the Ogadan desert. Thanks to Soviet and Cuban allies, by 1979 Ethiopia was able to reverse the initially unfavorable tide of rebellion and secure control over Eritrea, a strategically vital region at the Red Sea.[5]

For Moscow, the setback of the anti-Ethiopian rebellion in Eritrea has been an important step forward in a high-risk gamble, which had involved a sudden shift of Soviet support from the equally Marxist rebels in Eritrea and Ogadan to the central government of Ethiopia, considered a more important ally of the USSR. Once Ethiopia had secured Eritrea's Red Sea ports, Massawa and Assab, the Soviets had acquired two excellent naval bases along a 1,000 mile coastline. These harbors more than compensated the Soviets for their expulsion from the Somali port of Berbera in 1978. Thus, by scoring another victory by proxy, the Soviet Union has become a leading maritime power in the Indian Ocean, across

---

[5] Eritrea, an Italian colony from 1890 to 1941, was joined to Ethiopia in a United Nations-sponsored federation in 1952. Without the Eritrean ports of Massawa and Assab, Ethiopia would have no access to the sea. In 1962, the Ethiopians simply annexed Eritrea.

which so much of the West's oil must travel. In November 1978, the Soviet Union signed a "friendship" treaty with Vietnam that committed the countries for 25 years, and turned it virtually into a full-scale political and military alliance. Moscow agreed not only to consult with Vietnam in all matters pertaining to its region, but also to take "appropriate effective measures" if either partner is attacked or threatened with at-tack. A similar clause had been included into the Soviet-Indian Treaty of 1979. Although in both cases the agreements seem aimed against China, the treaty with Vietnam is more similar to the one with India. This reflects Vietnam's status as a fellow socialist country, assigned the role of containing the Chinese influence in Southeast Asia.

Meanwhile, the United States, feeling threatened by the Soviet expansion in Asia and Africa, continued its policy of improving relations with China, which President Nixon initiated in 1972. At the end of January 1979, the Chinese Deputy Prime Minister, Teng Hsiao-ping, arrived in Washington to meet with President Carter and he brought a long list of goods and services that they wished to obtain from the United States, as well as advice on how the United States should proceed in its dealings with the Soviet Union. The talks resulted in some U.S. assistance to help China in its modernization programs. On April 3, 1979, Peking, whose treaty with Moscow dated back to 1950, gave notice of its formal cancellation.

THE POLISH CRISIS

What further aggravated the East–West tension was the long smoldering crisis in Poland, which eventually surfaced during the summer of 1980. Ever since 1956, Poland has been a maverick of the Soviet camp. With the agricultural land overwhelmingly in the hands of individual farmers, the Polish People's Republic has sharply contrasted with all of its Communist partners. Moreover, Poland has had relatively liberal cultural policies, and the Catholic Church has played an increasingly prominent role. In exchange for the loyal support given by the Polish leaders first to Khrushchev and then to Brezhnev in all matters of foreign policy, Moscow has tolerated these peculiarities as unavoidable evils.

Encouraged by this tolerance Edward Gierek, Party boss since the end of 1970, ventured even further. He framed an economic policy that was to use Western technology, which was to lead to a rapid expansion of Polish exports to the West, while, at the same time, supplying enough consumer goods to appease the restless population. Gierek's strategy was based on heavy borrowing from the West—this was to help Polish industries in producing goods for export in Western markets to pay for the foreign loans. His scheme also involved improving wages, which prompted a short-term boom. By the mid-1970s, however, difficulties began to mount. The higher personal incomes generated by politically motivated higher earnings could not be offset by adequate supplies of goods, especially food, for the domestic market, thus leading to inflation.

Opposition to Gierek's policies first surfaced in 1975 when he proposed amendments to the Polish Constitution that would ensure the leading role of the Party and the "unshakeable bonds with the Soviet Union." Faced with widespread protests, the Polish Party was forced to modify these amendments. The protest movement, stimulated by the recent signing of the Helsinki Declaration, continued to mount and demands for genuine respect for human rights, especially freedom of expression, intensified, however.

By the summer of 1980, the deepening economic crisis and food shortages had become so acute that the government made an attempt to impose drastic price increases. As a reply, in mid-August, workers in the Gdansk shipyards conducted a sit-down strike. By the end of August, spontaneously organized strikes spread throughout the country and soon received backing from the

Church hierarchy and many intellectuals. Led by a dynamic electrical worker, Lech Wałęsa, representatives of various regional striking committees formed a trade union independent of the state.

On August 31, 1980, Gierek was forced to concede to the workers not only the right to strike, but also to form an autonomous trade union free from government and Party control, known as "Solidarity." Gierek was eventually replaced by General Wojciech Jaruzelski, Minister of Defense and Commander-in-Chief of Poland's armed forces. Thus, for the third time in the history of Communist Poland, a workers' revolt resulted in a change in leadership. On this occasion, however, unlike in 1956 and 1970, the workers did so by nonviolent means.

Soon Solidarity's influence spread from industrial centers to the countryside, where farmers emulated the example of their urban comrades and proclaimed the formation of "Rural Solidarity." By the beginning of 1981, the autonomous trade unions had about 10 million members enrolled, which represented, with their families, the great majority of Poland's population of 36 million. Nearly one-third of the Polish United Workers' Party (PUWP) members joined the Solidarity movement.

The rise of a powerful, autonomous, democratically elected, non-Communist trade union in a key country of the Warsaw Pact confronted the Kremlin with an agonizing problem. Here was a classical, spontaneous, massive proletarian movement led by a genuine working class people, who were antagonistic to Communism and were permeated with a religious spirit. The cherished Soviet myth, that there are no conflicts between a working class party and the workers, was dramatically exploded. The Kremlin was alarmed. All verbal warnings and threatening gestures made by Moscow, including military demonstrations, proved ineffective: The Solidarity movement continued to get stronger and more militant. Although its moderate leaders professed loyalty to Poland's alliance with its eastern neighbors, the movement was regarded by the Kremlin as a threat to the Soviet control of Eastern Europe.

Confronted with the choice of either open military intervention following the Czechoslovakian model or allowing things to drift, the Soviet leadership hesitated. While the rest of the world was wondering what Moscow would do next, martial law was declared throughout the country by General Jaruzelski. On December 31, 1981, with the tacit approval of Moscow, he assumed virtual dictatorial power at the head of a Military Council, not unlike a South American *junta*. Personal freedoms were drastically curtailed, universities were closed, activities of all organizations were suspended, and starting with the Solidarity leadership, over 5,000 persons were interned. Addressing the nation, Jaruzelski, in veiled language, justified the crackdown as having been necessary to forestall Soviet intervention in Poland.

THE END OF THE BREZHNEV ERA

On November 10, 1982, the long ailing Brezhnev died at the age of 75 from a "heart disease and respiratory troubles." His period of 18 years in office was second longest after that of Stalin. The Brezhnev era covered the length of five American presidencies: those of Johnson, Nixon, Ford, Carter and part of Reagan's. In domestic politics, Brezhnev was a consensus man, a senior oligarch in a collective leadership who tended to consult his Politbureau colleagues in most important matters and avoided challenging vested interests of the established elite, whether civilian or military. He had seized power with the support of the military establishment, kept it largely thanks to their backing, and loyally repaid his debt of gratitude. Defense spending nearly doubled, increasing by some four percent a year up to 1976 and decreasing only after that period.

The growing prestige and influence of the Soviet defense establishment was a striking phenomenon of Brezhnev's rule. Since the 1960s, Soviet policy—and especially its overall strategy—has been based increasingly influenced by the advice of the military establishment. While the Politbureau made final decisions, the leading marshals were consulted first. As far as we know, the marshals barely failed to push Brezhnev over toward a nuclear showdown with China and they triggered the Afghan adventure.

The price of the systematic increase of military investments resulted, however, in serious economic strains and eventual stagnation. Agriculture, despite attempts to streamline the existing system, has remained the weakest area of the system. Supplying the population with food, especially meat, has continued to be an acute problem. Four disastrous grain harvests in a row have forced huge purchases abroad. Food imports cost $700 million in 1970 and as much as over $12 billion, in the early 1980s. Increased export of gold and oil paid for the import of grain and animal feed.[6]

In some ways, Brezhnev was Stalin's epigone: He, too, emphasized national power over ideology and industry over agriculture. Brezhnev selectively rehabilitated Stalin, mainly in terms of the Soviet victories over Germany and World War II. On the other hand, Brezhnev himself went far beyond Stalin's continental diplomacy and Khrushchev's fitful attempt at extending Soviet power beyond the confines of the Eurasian continent. He was the first Soviet ruler to conduct a truly global policy and project his country's power to four corners of the world.

Brezhnev's era was crowded with contradictions. He was an architect both of detente and of a massive Soviet military build-up. While preaching "peaceful co-existence," he ordered the invasion of both Czechoslovakia and Afghanistan. He signed both the Helsinki Accord and deployed the Soviet Union's advanced medium-range missiles against Western Europe. He was instrumental in making the USSR a superpower rivaling the United States, but he also presided over an ailing economy that was losing its momentum and showing signs of stagnation. His name is more likely to go down in history as the father of the "Brezhnev doctrine" rather than as a domestic reformer. To sum up the hallmarks of the Brezhenv era, one should say that it combined an expansive foreign policy, based on a formidable military build-up, with virtual immobility toward the end of his rule.

SUGGESTED READING

ANDRLE, VLADIMIR, *Managerial Power in the Soviet Union*. Lexington, Mass.: Lexington Books, 1976.

BARGHOORN, FREDERICK C., *Détente and the Democratic Movement in the USSR*. New York: Free Press, 1976.

BROWN, ARCHIE, and MICHAEL KASER, eds., *The Soviet Union Since the Fall of Khrushchev*. New York: Free Press, 1976.

BROWN, J. F., *Relations between the Soviet Union and Its Eastern European Allies*. Santa Monica, Calif.: Rand Corporation, 1975.

CHERNOVIL, VIACHESLAV, *The Chernovil Papers*. New York: McGraw-Hill, 1968.

DORNBERG, JOHN, *Brezhnev: the Mask of Power*. New York: Basic Books, 1974.

DUNLOP, JOHN B., *The New Russian Revolutionaries*. Belmont, Mass.: Nordland, 1976.

DZIUBA, IVAN, *Internationalism or Russification?* London: Weidenfeld and Nicolson, 1968.

FREEDMAN, ROBERT O., *Soviet Policy toward the Middle East Since 1970*. New York: Praeger, 1975.

GOLAN, GALIA, *The Soviet Union and the PLO*. Jerusalem: Hebrew University Soviet and Eastern European Research Center, 1977.

GOLDMAN, MARSHALL I., *The Enigma of Soviet Petroleum, Half Empty or Half Full?* Winchester, Mass.: Allen & Unwin, 1980.

---

[6] Soviet grain production is hard to assess since the USSR stopped reporting it in 1981. In 1981, the last year for which firm figures are available, the Soviets spent over $6.3 billion of hard currency on imported grain, or fully 50 percent of their hard-currency earnings from oil exports. The imported grain is not for bread alone. It is largely used for animal feed, which in turn increases meat production.

GRIGORENKO, PETR GRIGOR'EVICH, *The Grigorenko Papers: Writings by General P. Grigorenko and Documents on His Case.* Boulder, Colo.: Westview Press, 1976.

HAMMOND, THOMAS T., *Red Flag over Afghanistan. The Communist Coup, the Soviet Invasion, and the Consequences.* Boulder, Colo.: Westview Press, 1983.

HAYWARD, MAX, ed., *On Trial: The Soviet State versus Abram Tertz and Nikolai Arzhak.* New York: Harper & Row, 1966.

———, and WILLIAM C. FLETCHER, eds., *Religion and the Soviet State: A Dilemma of Power.* New York: Praeger, 1969.

JAIN, P. G., *Soviet Policy towards Pakistan and Bangladesh.* New Delhi: Radiant Publishers, 1974.

KHODOROVICH, TATYANA, ed., *The Case of Leonid Plyushch.* Boulder, Colo.: Westview Press, 1976.

KLINGHOFFER, ARTHUR J., *The Soviet Union and International Oil Politics.* New York: Columbia University Press, 1977.

LANE, CHRISTEL, *Christian Religion in the Soviet Union.* Albany: State University of New York Press, 1983.

LAPIDUS, GAIL W. ed., *Women, Work and Family in the Soviet Union.* Armonk, N.Y.: M. E. Sharpe, 1982.

LISANN, MAURY, *Broadcasting to the Soviet Union: International Politics and Radio.* New York: Praeger, 1975.

LOWENTHAL, RICHARD, *Model or Ally? The Communist Powers and the Developing Countries.* New York: Oxford University Press, 1976.

MORTON, HENRY W., and RUDOLPH L. TÖKES, *Soviet Politics and Society in the 1970's.* New York: Free Press, 1974.

NOVE, ALEC, *Stalinism and After.* London: Crane-Russak, 1975.

PANISH, PAUL, *Exit Visa: The Emigration of the Soviet Jews.* New York: Coward, McCann and Geoghegan, 1981.

PORTER, BRUCE D., *The USSR in Third World Conflicts. Soviet Arms and Diplomacy in Local Wars, 1945–1980.* New York: Cambridge University Press, 1984.

POTICHNY, PETER J., and JANE P. SHAPIRO, eds., *From the Cold War to Detente.* New York: Praeger, 1976.

RUBINSTEIN, ALVIN Z., *Red Star on the Nile.* Princeton, N.J.: Princeton University Press, 1977.

RYWKIN, MICHAEL, *Moscow's Muslim Challenge: Soviet Central Asia.* Armonk, N.Y.: M. E. Sharpe, 1982.

SAKHAROV, ANDREI A., *Progress, Coexistence and Intellectual Freedom.* New York: Norton, 1968.

SHEVCHENKO, ARKADY N., *Breaking with Moscow.* New York: Knopf, 1985.

SIMMONDS, GEORGE, ed., *Nationalism in the USSR and Eastern Europe in the Era of Brezhnev and Kosygin.* Detroit: University of Detroit Press, 1977.

STARR, S. FREDERICK, *Red and Hot: The Fate of Jazz in the Soviet Union, 1917–1980.* New York: Oxford University Press, 1983.

TOMA, PETER A., *The Changing Face of Communism in Eastern Europe.* Tucson: University of Arizona Press, 1970.

YANOV, ALEXANDER, *The Russian New Right: Right-Wing Ideologies in the Contemporary USSR.* Berkeley: University of California Press, 1978.

CHAPTER 24

Soviet Russia Since Brezhnev

Within forty-eight hours after Brezhnev's death, Yuri V. Andropov, age 68, was chosen as the Party's General Secretary. The transition was surprisingly smooth. On June 15, 1983, he assumed also the Soviet presidency in addition to the leadership of the Communist Party. In comparison, it had taken Brezhnev 13 years as party leader to achieve the same position.

Andropov's career was unusual. From 1953 to 1957 he was the ambassador to Hungary, and in the decade following 1957 he directed the Socialist countries' sector of the Central Committee. From 1967 to 1982, he was head of the KGB. Since 1973, he was also a member of the Politburo. On May 25, 1982, he stepped down as chief of the KGB, two days after being appointed one of the ten permanent secretaries of the Central Committee. Although Andropov's tenure of fifteen years was not marked by the bloody mass terror of the Stalinist type, the KBG expanded its functions and became a more

sophisticated means of enforcing nearly absolute political control, effectively emasculating the lingering Soviet dissent movement. Even jokes critical of the regime became a risky thing. As a contemporary saying went: "Comrade Andropov collects not only political stories: he also collects people who tell them."

Andropov began his top position with a call for prompt action to streamline the existing economic system. On November 22, 1982, in his first major policy speech, he emphasized the need to raise labor productivity and for the rewarding of industriousness; he also tried to tighten labor discipline and control drunkenness.[1]

Following Brezhnev's indicated willingness to rebuild closer ties with China, An-

---

[1] Unofficial sources speak of 40 to 45 million alcoholics in the Soviet Union (out of a population of 285 million), and total damage caused by alcohol-related problems is estimated at 180 billion rubles—nearly one-third of the country's GNP.

dropov continued with a series of friendly gestures toward Peking. He insisted on conducting the negotiations on a state-to-state, rather than party-to-party, basis. Peking's primary requirements for *rapprochement* have centered around security issues—the concentration of some forty Soviet divisions deployed along their borders, the Moscow-supported Vietnamese expansionist drive in Cambodia, and the withdrawal of Soviet troops from Afghanistan.

With regard to the crucial arms control problem, Andropov has proved to be a much tougher negotiator than Brezhnev. When the November 1981 Intermediate-range Nuclear Force (INF) talks began in Geneva, Moscow claimed that Soviet and NATO medium-range nuclear delivery vehicles were approximately balanced. With Andropov's ascent to power, the Soviets changed their approach and insisted on including the French and British medium-range warheads as part of the bargain. Andropov has maintained that if one included these three hundred warheads, NATO would enjoy a definite superiority. The United States delegation, on the other hand, argued that the 1979 establishment of the SS-20 in Eastern Europe had tipped the balance. Consequently, NATO decided to introduce at least 572 Pershing II rockets and cruise missiles to Britain, West Germany, and Italy to counterbalance Soviet superiority.

Andropov, however, firmly opposed any deployment of the new American medium-range missiles. He condemned them as a "dangerous provocation" because the Pershing IIs in West Germany and the cruise missiles in Britain and Italy would be able to reach well into the Soviet Union, covering an arc that extended from the mouth of the Dnieper to Leningrad. Consequently, they could hit Soviet military bases and command centers just short of Moscow. The shooting down of the South Korean airliner by a Soviet fighter on September 1, 1983, killing 269 passengers, did not improve the already tense international situation. The belligerent Soviet explanation hardly helped its image as a peace-loving country bent on relaxation of dangerous international tensions.

In December 1983, the Soviet delegation left the Superpower's Strategic Arms Reduction Talks (START) in Geneva and ended the mutual and balanced force reduction negotiations in Vienna. As a result, the world entered an uncharted period in which no nuclear arms control talks were going on for the first time in two years.

Suffering for a long time from diabetes and kidney disease, Andropov was absent from official functions from the end of August 1983. His death was officially announced on February 5, 1984. Thus, Andropov remained in power for fifteen months, and for over five months of that period was either bedridden or at least incapable of appearing in public. During his brief stewardship, Andropov achieved no more than a marginal improvement of Soviet productivity, without a fundamental shift in investment patterns away from heavy industry and high military spending. Managing to marginally bolster labor discipline and uncover the worst abuses of rampant corruption in high places left behind by the nepotic Brezhnev, he failed to shake the existing overcentralized bureaucratic structure. However, in foreign affairs Andropov was firm. He held tightly to Soviet positions in Vietnam and Afghanistan, thus failing to improve relations with China.

THE CHERNENKO INTERLUDE

Andropov was succeeded by seventy-two year old Konstantin V. Chernenko, Second Secretary of the Central Committee and the second ranking member of the Politburo. Chernenko, Brezhnev's closest aide throughout the leader's declining years, and considered his heir apparent, was passed over by his peers in 1982, who eventually voted for Andropov. The protracted illness of his rival gave Chernenko his second chance. This time the elderly Politburo did elect him over some younger candidates, such as Mikhail S. Gorbachev and Grigory V. Romanov, then fifty-two and sixty-one years of age, respectively. The reasons for the choosing an elderly, ailing, and rather undistinguished candidate over a set of obviously more vigorous and able rivals were puzzling. Most probably, no younger candidate commanded sufficient backing among the senior members of the Politburo. Or, perhaps, the selection of Chernenko may have been the only way to avoid a dangerous struggle for power—the Soviet leaders opted for a safer, compromise candidate who would act as a caretaker until the younger contenders could sort out their claims for supreme leadership. With the selection of Chernenko as their top boss, the old guard had reasserted itself. Gerontology at the Kremlin reached its peak.[2]

Continuing his predecessor's negative attitude toward the West, Chernenko rolled himself into the defensive posture of the porcupine—all bristles on the outside. He decided to boycott the 1984 Olympic games in Los Angeles. He clamped down on pro-Western learning in the arts and fired Yuri Lyubimov as artistic director of the popular Taganka Theater in Moscow. Lyubimov had funded and operated the Taganka Theater for twenty years and created its experimental style and the bulk of its repertoire. His defection to the West in 1983 was the biggest blow to Moscow's cultural life since Maksim Shostakovich, Soviet Russia's leading conductor, defected in 1981. In the arms control process, Chernenko also followed in the footsteps of his predecessor. When the White House sent General Brent Scowcroft to Moscow with a personal letter from President Reagan, Chernenko simply refused to receive the envoy.

Chernenko died on March 11, 1985, after barely thirteen months in office. He was a bureaucratic nonentity with no objective qualities for leadership, let alone an ability to develop a "personality cult." As a younger Party comrade remarked: "There can be no personality cult where there is no personality." The debilitating effect of the ridiculously inept handling of State affairs, domestic as well as international, by a senile man at the helm was striking. On the following day, March 12, a mere four hours after the news of Chernenko's death, Radio Moscow interrupted solemn music to announce the election of a much younger man, Mikhail S. Gorbachev, as General Secretary of the CPSU. The decisions favoring Andropov (November 1982) and Chernenko (February 1984) had not been announced until several days after their respective predecessors' demise. This was the quickest and smoothest transition of power in Soviet history. "The General Secretary is dead. Long live the General Secretary!"

THE RISE OF GORBACHEV

Mikhail S. Gorbachev, born in March 1931, is a son of a *kolkhoz* peasant in the Stavropol region in Northern Caucasus. He is the first Soviet leader not to have actively participated in World War II; he studied law and agriculture and joined the Party in 1952, starting his career already in the post-Stalin era. At his job of regional Party boss at Stavropol, he gained the reputation of an efficient administrator. In 1971, he became a member of the Party's Central Committee. Northern Caucasus was favored by the Kremlin elite because of several exclusive summer resorts with warm springs that were patronized by the Soviet elite. As the local Party boss, Gorbachev often played host to Andropov; befriended him, and turned him into his ally. In 1979, on his patron's initiative, Gorbachev was called to Moscow and joined the Politburo, where he first took charge of agriculture, as its nonvoting candidate member. In October 1980, he became a full member.

---

[2] Until 1985, the average age of Politburo members had constantly gone up. In 1919, the average age of Politburo members was about forty years; in 1934, it had risen to forty-eight years. In the last years of the Brezhnev era and during the Andropov and Chernenko interludes, the average age of Politburo members was around seventy years.

In the summer of 1983, supported by Andropov and taking advantage of the senile passivity of his colleagues, Gorbachev gradually took over responsibility for cadres, ideologies, and consumer industries in addition to agriculture. This was a formidable accumulation of power, unrivaled by any other member of the Politburo. Once elected General Secretary, Gorbachev lost no time in starting to reshape the country's ailing economy in alliance with a new Party team. On April 22, 1985, the 115th anniversary of Lenin's birth, the Politburo met in the Kremlin's Congress Palace in accordance with a carefully arranged hierarchical order. But, by the next day, this order was upset by the addition of three new men. Two of them, Yegor Ligachev and Nikolai Ryzhkov, had not even been candidate members of the Politburo. The third, Viktor Chebrikov, head of the KGB, had become a candidate member not long before.

The next big change came on July 1, nine weeks later, when Gorbachev's rival, Grigori Romanov, until then a full Politburo member and Central Committee Secretary for Heavy and Defense Industries, as well as the Leningrad Party boss, was forced into retirement. The very next day, July 2, the twenty-eight year career of the world's longest-serving Foreign Minister came to an end, when seventy-six year old Andrei Gromyko was kicked upstairs to the symbolic post of Chairman of the Presidium of the Supreme Soviet, or the nominal President of the USSR. At the same time, one of Gorbachev's confidants from his *Komsomol* days in the Caucasus, Edvard Shevardnadze, previously Party boss of Georgia and candidate member of the Politburo, was promoted to its full membership and became the new Foreign Minister. Aleksander Yakovlev, former ambassador to Canada, a man with broad Western experience, became the person in charge of propaganda. For the first time since 1961, a woman was allowed to join the top leadership when Aleksandra Biryukova was added to the Central Committee Secretariat. On September 27, the seventy-nine year old Prime Minister Nikolai Tikhonov retired and was replaced by Gorbachev's younger supporter and economic expert, Nikolai I. Ryzhkov.

Hardly two and a half weeks later, on October 14, the new General Secretary removed the Chairman of the State Planning Commission, who was one of the greatest stumbling blocks to his plans. Nikolai Baybakov was retired after twenty years in office. Whereas Baybakov had only been Deputy Prime Minister, his successor, Nikolai Talyzin, took on the office of First Deputy Chairman of the Council of Ministers and also became a Candidate Member of the Politburo. Thus, in seven months, Gorbachev restructured and rejuvenated the Soviet top leadership more quickly than any of his predecessors, Stalin not excluded.

The opening stages of Gorbachev's drive were marred by three accidents that badly reflected on both Soviet technology and management practices. The first was the near meltdown at the Chernoble (Ukraine) nuclear energy station in late April 1986; the second was the collision and sinking of the Soviet passenger ship "Admiral Nakhimov" in the Black Sea on August 31, 1986, with the loss of more than one hundred lives. October 3, the third blow to Soviet pride came in the form of the acknowledgment that a Soviet submarine, carrying ballistic missiles, had caught fire and sunk off the coast of Bermuda. Gorbachev was undisturbed by these blows. In a vigorous barnstorming campaign, he outlined the reasons for his reformatory zeal. Surrounded by his handpicked team of coworkers, most of them trained engineers and economists, Gorbachev went on with his plans to lift the Soviet Union from the bog of stagnation and corruption that had marked the late 1970s and early 1980s.

GORBACHEV'S PLANS

Gorbachev's reasoning was brutally frank. He declared that the present overcentralized economic model no longer works. This he illustrated with numerous facts and figures demonstrating the corruption and inefficiency of the overgrown bureaucratic apparatus. Since the late 1970s, the growth of the Soviet GNP, which in 1966–1970 exceeded 5 percent, has had a steady, diminishing tendency and reached 1.4 in 1986. Moreover, he argued, the resources of the western parts of the Soviet Union were yielding less and less. For instance, oil production showed a steady decline in 1984 and 1985. As a consequence, the processing industry could not expect investment on only a limited scale as more and more capital has to be applied for the extraction of raw materials in increasingly inaccessible parts of Siberia. The birth rate in the most heavily industrialized western segments has been declining for years and the problem has been compounded by the poor health of young workers. The lower productivity of Soviet workers he ascribed to inefficient management and rampant alcoholism, a truly national catastrophe. The balance between heavy and light industries was badly upset. Whereas in 1960 only 18 percent of heavy industry work was for the military establishment, by 1976–1977 it drained much of the industrial production of the Soviet Union, thus starving the supply consumer goods and vital services. This allowed the USSR to remain a military superpower,

but threatened its overall global position. To save it, the country must modernize. "We don't have much time left," he concluded.

It is true that, despite the general technological retardation, in selected military and space fields the Soviet Union was capable of impressive achievements. For instance, on December 29, 1987, three Soviet cosmonauts set a world record of 326 days in space. In the same year, the USSR registered ninety-one launches against none in the United States. These flights have given Soviet scientists an edge in researching space medicine and biology. But these records, as well as many other similar achievements, were very costly because resources were overwhelmingly concentrated only on a few selected goals. In the long run, such a policy drained the vital resources from the earth into outer space. According to conservative estimates, the Soviets spend from 14 to 16 percent of their GNP on military items; this is about twice the amount of the corresponding figure for the United States. The Soviet space budget is about three times higher than that of the United States— about $16 billion a year. But superiority in space, even combined with virtual nuclear parity with its main rival, is not a remedy for the host of common problems pestering the Soviet people on a daily basis. The economic

Gorbachev, at the Moscow I. Likhachev Auto works, discusses the factory's retooling.

reforms in China that significantly lifted the standard of living of its population, together with the simultaneous rise of Japan as an economic giant, made the Soviet decline more striking. The drop in the prices of oil and natural gas, two of the most important Soviet sources of hard currency next to gold, have further worsened the USSR's global status. Unlike his predecessors, Gorbachev has fully grasped the dangers inherent in these phenomena. His determination to prevent the Soviet Union from losing its position as a superpower has been reflected in the scope of his modernization plans and the intensity of his efforts.

At the Twenty-seventh Party Congress (February 25–March 6, 1986), Gorbachev launched his scheme of a "radical reform of the economy" by decentralizing and streamlining its management, while providing workers with proper incentives. He promised to give the enterprises more independence and to increase their interest in the final products "within the framework of the planned economy." By 1991, Gorbachev intends to achieve a major redistribution of power from central planning bodies and ministries to factories and enterprises. The *Gosplan* will only lay down general guidelines, while local managers will make their own detailed plans and set their own wages. Inefficient installations will be allowed to go bankrupt. State-dictated pricing systems are to be eliminated; the maze of subsidies and controls, which has distorted the whole economy, making it cheaper for Russian farmers to feed pigs with bread than grain, is to be dropped. The reform was to affect some 60 percent of all enterprises and to start on January 1, 1988. By 1990, price reform should have been carried out, cutting back sharply on the 50 billion rubles ($72.5 billion) worth of annual subsidies on food and services. Thus, Gorbachev's economic reform stresses the change in the system of management without altering basic property relations, especially in the countryside; his plans include only limited toleration of private enterprise and market-oriented mechanisms in agriculture, small

industry, and the service sector. The state ownership of the means of production, including the land, and the state's central role in economic planning are still unshakable dogmas of the Soviet system. This means that Gorbachev's economic plans are far less extensive than Lenin's NEP or the Chinese reforms.

Reshaping a system that currently employs over 20 million bureaucrats who set the prices of 200,000 products and control production and distribution is daunting and the political risks are tremendous. Gorbachev's plan of radical economic reconstruction (*perestroika* in Russian) cannot be carried out without far-reaching political changes. The reform means curtailment of many superfluous jobs and restructuring of the central administration. *Gosplan* itself is a gigantic bureaucracy with thousands of employees who control the operation of no fewer than 37,000 industrial enterprises. The lurking opposition of the huge bureaucratic machinery has been formidable. Such a resistance is nothing new in Russian history. A report presented to Tsar Alexander II in 1855 described the bureaucrats as "a savage and greedy horde which has taken possession of Russia and enjoys without inhibition the rights of conquerors . . . having bound the hands of ministers by centralization, paper formalism, and countless signatures." In this respect, very little has changed in Russia, as was demonstrated by the bureaucratic abortion of the attempted 1965 Kosygin reform.

In addition to the highly privileged Party *aparat*, the military establishment, or "steel eaters" as Khrushchev called them, is bound to be affected by Gorbachev's scheme of shifting his priority away from heavy industry toward more consumer goods. The growing power of the Soviet military establishment has been reflected in the constantly expanding defense appropriations; for more than a decade, the USSR has been increasing its defense spending by 3 to 4 percent a year in real terms. The military establishment's slogan has been: "the more weapons the better." What Gorbachev wants is a leaner armed forces that would cost less. His message to the military establishment seems to be: make better use of what you've got before you come asking for more.

The Soviet armed forces are a formidable opponent; they emerged from World War II with a greatly enhanced prestige. Stalin tried to play down this esteem for the military by attributing the victory in "the Great Patriotic War" to his own unique strategic genius. His successors, however, could not ignore the prestige of the military establishment. Members of the armed forces consider themselves legitimate bearers of the national will and guardians of its destiny. This group is the only organized body of people with an *esprit de corps* comparable to that of the Party. The "new class" of high officials shares with the top of the military establishment numerous privileges that are threatened by Gorvachev's stress on austerity. An entire department of the Party Central Committee provides for a variety of services and their families. The department operates and equips exclusive apartment hourse, country dachas, government palaces, special rest homes, car pools, and maintains squads of security-trained servants. A network of unmarked stores without display windows caters to the Soviet top hierarchy, offering choice delicacies like caviar, smoked salmon, export brandies, vodka, exotic wines, and liquours. These stores also carry foreign goods such as French cognac and perfumes, German and American cigarettes, and Japanese tape recorders—all at discount prices. The Soviet elite enjoys many of the privileges of the former ruling Tsarist aristocracy; chauffeur-driven cars, country villas, servants, as well as access to the top academic institutions for their children. The main difference is that these privileges are not hereditary.

To deal with the lingering opposition to his bold plans, Gorbachev has resorted to another slogan, that of *glasnost*, which in Russian means both openness and publicity. *Glasnost* allowed the Soviet media and intellectuals to debate and even criticze many ills of the Soviet society. This included even the military establishment, covering its role in the Afghanistan war—an increasingly unpopular venture. Thanks to *glasnost*, the press has begun to attack not only the civilian bureaucracy but also the complacency and inefficiency in the military establishment: poorly disciplined units, elite military schools that are simply camps for the privileged, favoritism in appointments, and the need for younger people in top command posts. In dealing with the military lobby, Gorbachev was helped by an accident. On May 27, 1987, a West German amateur flier, Matthias Rust, evading allegedly impregnable Soviet air defense systems, landed in Moscow's Red Square, near the Kremlin's walls, after an audacious five-hour flight. This was an unheard of scandal that gave the General Secretary his chance to rejuvenate the military chain of command. The aging Defense Minister, Marshal Sergei Sokolov, was dismissed and replaced by sixty-three year old General Dmitry T. Yazov. The suddenness of his appointment suggests that he was already in line to get the job. The fact that he was elevated over twenty more obvious candidates indicates that he was recruited especially by Gorbachev, who, as Chairman of the Defense Council, is roughly equivalent to commander-in-chief. Yazov has headed two of the Soviet Union's sixteen military districts, the Far East and Central Asia, and commanded Soviet troops in Czechoslovakia. His commands have thus far faced both NATO and China, giving him unique breadth of experience. These field experiences did not prevent him from writing numerous theoretical articles stressing the value of new technology in modern warfare. Especially valuable for Gorbachev's purposes, was that since January 1987 Yazov has been Deputy Minister of Defense in charge of personnel, and thus was already engaged in streamlining the mammoth military forces and making room for abler and younger high commanders.

REFORMING SOVIET AGRICULTURE

By far the greatest obstacle to reforming the entire economy is its agricultural sector in which Gorbachev has taken a special interest for years. Although its output increased by about 10 percent during the 1970s, Soviet agriculture has been an economic disaster in relation to the enormous amount of resources devoted to it since the mid-1960s. The 27,000 collective farms and 21,000 gigantic State farms are both organized in a way that hampers personal initiative and, as a result, effective production. As in industry, the collective and State farms are shackled by a system of norms set arbitrarily by the bureaucrats appointed by the Party.

Enormous funds have been invested in the modernization of the Soviet collective State farms by providing them with new machinery. Yet, it is widely admitted that the quality of the agricultural machines is often catastrophic. Many farms cannot start sowing on time because the necessary machines stand around idle for want of spare parts. A large part of the agricultural produce is spoiled as a result of delays, long transportation routes and lack of proper storage. In the eleventh five-year plan (1981–1985), 40 percent of all investments in agriculture were allocated to the construction of grain silos and other storage facilities. Most of this money was wasted through inefficiency, however. No wonder productivity is correspondingly low and the grain harvest per hectare is only about one-third of that achieved in the United States. As a result, over the years grain imports from the United States, Canada, Argentina, Australia, Brazil, and the EEC countries have accummulated a Soviet hard currency debt of about $40 billion. A leading economist, Nikolai P. Shmelev, recently estimated that more than $100 billion gained from oil exports was wasted on the purchase of foreign grain alone. It has been currently estimated that about 20 percent of the value of all foodstuffs consumed in the Soviet Union is imported.

Gorbachev, while in charge of agriculture, tried to remedy some of these shortcomings. For instance, in March 1983, he sanctioned breaking up large farms into small autonomous units or "brigades". It is now official policy to pay these groups according to their output, allowing them to be responsible for large segments of agricultural production and large tracts of land. In August 1987, agricultural contracting was expanded to include family contracts. Moreover, family contracting has been broadened to include the leasing of land to individual families; a new law permits leasing for twelve to fifteen years and includes provisions for acquiring tools. Leasing operates outside the collective farm contract structure, but employing workers from outside the family unit is still illegal. The long-term leasing of land represents a homage to the suppressed Social Revolutionary Party that had advocated a similar program. In essence, it is Gorbachev's policy to tolerate small-scale private agriculture under the heading of leasing, while basically sticking to its taboo—collectivized farming.

Agriculture contracts are a significant step forward, but thus far they have worked inadequately. Not all farm operations can be easily handled by small groups, and contract observance has been a problem in terms of the provision of supplies to the contract group, both from collective farms and from industrial suppliers. Moreover, there have been many reports that peasants who grow vegetables for sale in markets have frequently been victimized by jealous bureaucrats. The old habits die hard.

QUALITY OF LIFE

Besides quoting the disquieting figures about the steadily declining average annual rates of GNP, Gorbachev and the liberalized Soviet media have revealed some menacing symptoms of the rapidly deteriorating quality of life. After rising steadily since 1953, the standard of life began to level off in the late 1970s and has stagnated ever since. This was camouflaged by the official Soviet statistics until *glasnost* allowed publication of some shocking figures. For instance, the February 17, 1988 issue of the daily *Socialist Industry* noted that the education budget constituted 6.7 percent of the national budget in 1964, but had declined to 4.2 by 1982. The same article noted that in 1953, UNESCO had ranked the Soviet Union third in a table indicating the proportion of young people engaged in higher education. It now occupies 42nd position. It has been also officially admitted that air, soil, and water pollution have reached frightening dimensions, especially in some urban areas, and threaten ecological disaster. Another menacing factor has been the demographic trends, mainly among Slavic groups of the population. The traditionally strong Russian family has been undermined by the changing morals, as well as socioeconomic factors. The main threats have been the alarmingly high growth of alcoholism and divorce and the lack of adequate housing. The national divorce rate has reached 40 percent, and exceeded 50 percent in large urban areas. In almost half of the cases, the husband's drunkenness is cited among the reasons for divorce. Among the other causes mentioned are adultery, violence, "incompatibility," and cramped living conditions. In 1983, about 80 percent of the urban population lived in individual apartments, but the remainder lived in communal dwellings and lacked suitable accommodations for raising a family. Moreover, there are far more women than men, while an increasing number of single males refuse to marry for one reason or another.

Meanwhile, the reservoir of the available labor force has been practically exhausted. The fact that Soviet men are permitted to retire at 60 and women at 55 does not help matters; various incentives offered to workers by the authorities to remain in the work force have produced only limited results. At the same time, the Soviet population has been aging very fast. The median age was 24 in 1950 but exceeded 30 by 1986. The

declining birth rate has been paralleled by a growing number of abortions. In 1983, it was officially admitted that the number of abortions was exceeding that of live births. What was not revealed at that time was the fact that there were about twice as many abortions as live births, up to six million annually. No information was published on infant mortality in the USSR for more than a decade following the reported 20 percent increases of the 1971–1974 period. However, in October 1986, the Soviet press revealed that infant mortality rates are now higher than they were in 1971. On November 9, 1987, Minister of Health Evgenii Chazov complained that the USSR currently stands fiftieth in the world in terms of infant mortality, behind many countries of the Third World.

One factor behind the demographic crisis is the sorry state of medical services, once the pride of the Soviet regime. The right to free medical care was written into the 1977 Soviet Constitution. Statistically, in the USSR there are three times as many hospital beds and twice as many doctors per 10,000 people as there are in the United States. Yet Soviet spending on health care *per capita* has been the smallest among the industrialized nations. As a result, the overall death rate increased from 6.8 per thousand in 1964 to 10.3 in 1980. Males born in 1965 could expect an average life span of 66.2 years, while for those born in 1980 it is only 61.9 years; this is nearly a decade less than the life spans of males born in the United States. In 1980, life expectancy in the USSR was 11.5 years fewer for males than females. Some sociologists attributed this unusually wide gap to the much higher rates of alcoholism and tobacco smoking among the Soviet men. In addition, a sharp increase in deaths among urban residents from hypertension, coronary heart disease, and cancer has also been a striking phenomenon. The declining quality of health care is one of the by-products of the high level of defense spending, which strips resources away from the civilian sector of the economy. This is the crux of the dilemma facing Gorbachev in his effort to modernize: a country with a GNP about half that of the United States cannot afford to invest nearly a quarter of its resources on military and space budgets while at the same time supporting very extensive welfare benefits.

WOMEN AND YOUTH

The declining quality of life hits the female majority of the Soviet population harder than the males for a variety of reasons. Traditionally, Russian women had always performed heavy, dirty tasks both on the farm and in the urban households. The Soviet regime, while proclaiming equality of women before the law and in all spheres of activity, has not lightened their tasks. Quite the contrary. From 1928 on, Stalin sent them to construction sites to build factories and dams, to operate drill presses and lathes, to pour cement and asphalt, and to dig ditches and canals. Millions of them paid for this with their health and often lives. After Stalin's death, voices were raised in protest against this cruel exploitation of women at the expense of their family duties. In 1981, decrees were enacted banishing the employment of women in 460 heavy and hazardous jobs. Despite this, Soviet women still work harder and longer than their male counterparts. In the early 1980s, nearly 70 percent of all Soviet women, 16 or older, worked full-time, while a similar figure for the United States was 51 percent. By 1985, over 72 percent of all professional people were women; they have dominated such professions as teaching, medical services, and, of course, all sorts of secretarial and lower administrative duties. On the other hand, men held nearly three-quarters of the important pedagogical, medical, and political posts in the country.

In addition to their regular work at the offices, schools, hospitals, and factories,

Street sweeping Moscow style

married women usually spend some thirty to thirty-five hours per week on various household chores including shopping, often a most exhausting and intricate task. Their life is so crowded with everyday chores, from standing in lines to buy necessities to finding practically nonexistent electricians or plumbers, that they have no time for large-scale organizing and forming effective pressure groups. Feminism of the Western type, let alone women's liberation movements, hardly exist in the Soviet Union. Soviet women think simply in terms of survival. Nevertheless, under the seemingly placid surface, discontent has been brewing, especially among the younger generation of women. Here we find the link connecting the youth ferment with the women problem.

It was easier to seal the Soviet boundaries against foreign invaders during World War II than to prevent the gradual infiltration of Western culture fads and mores into the USSR. Jamming foreign broadcasts, strict censorship, all sorts of "administrative measures" and intense propaganda drives by the Party and its branch, the *Komsomol,* proved of no avail, and Western concepts and attitudes have continued to affect the people. Even the *Komsomol* leaders have privately admitted that Communist ideology is losing its hold on Soviet youth. This has been reflected in *Komsomol's* dwindling membership; its rank and file, taking advantage of *glasnost,* have openly criticized the top strata of the organization as too stuffy, doctrinaire, and bureaucratic. Another consequence of *glasnost* is the emergence of unofficial political clubs, which have been springing up throughout the country. Dissatisfaction with the war in Afghanistan is spreading more rapidly among the youth who are facing the draft than among the older generation.

Moreover, since the mid-1950s, Western literature, painting, and music have been creeping into the Soviet Union, especially its Western segments. Banned in the Stalin period, jazz has resurfaced after 1955 and has won grudging official toleration. Yet rock music, with its external paraphenalia, remained taboo. Despite this, during the 1960s and 1970s, rock groups sprang up all over the country and, again, the Party had to soften its opposition to it, while occasionally denouncing it as a "pollution of Russian culture," "pornography in music," and a symptom of "Western degeneration." With music came blue jeans, long hair, and other trappings of Western urban civilization. Rock was followed by Western videocassettes, pornographic magazines, and, eventually, all sorts of drugs. Warnings and penalties proved of no avail. By the 1980s, the international urban youth culture, including its slogans about equality of sexes, swept the Soviet Union. The success of various visitng Western rock groups and other artistic ensembles has been proof of the enthusiastic response to it by the youth.

Young women have fully participated in this cultural revolt against traditional standard, including economic exploitation of female labor and social inferiority of women. Being better educated than their male counterpart, they have been in the vanguard of the spontaneous movement that threatens to upset whatever remains of the established values of the male-dominated Russian society. Yet the translation of women's mounting discontent and the expression of their growing intellectual as well as economic power into political leverage is hedged by many obstacles. One principal obstacle is the fact that the Communist Party is itself a mighty bastion of male hegemony. Only a handful of women are members of the Central Committee; only one ever reached the Politburo. But the emergence of a Soviet women's liberation movement may be closer than one generally anticipates. The increasingly enthusiastic reception of the Western values among the young generation of both sexes is one of the principal factors behind the changes brewing beneath the surface.

RELIGION

Another latent problem hardly mentioned in Gorbachev's speeches is religion. Yet the question is of long-range paramount significance for the future of the country. It is a well-documented fact that a considerable number of Soviet subjects, despite over seventy years of persecution or at least harsh discrimination, believe in God and carry on religious practices. The Russian Orthodox Church is by far the largest denomination with a membership estimated at about 50 million. One should point out that large segments of the nominally Orthodox population of the Western Ukraine, annexed from Poland by the Soviet Union after World War II, were Greek Catholics or Uniates who recognized the supremacy of the Pope of Rome. They were forced to submit to the Moscow Patriarchate in 1945–1946. Yet most Ukrainians regard the suppression of their church as one of many aspects of a Moscow-inspired policy of Russification and many of them remain Uniates at heart.

The next largest religious group is the Muslims, numbering 45 to 50 million and located mostly in Soviet Central Asia and the Caucasus, in the vicinity of other Muslim countries, Turkey, Iran, and Afghanistan. There are an estimated 5.5 million Roman Catholics, mostly in the western borderlands, Lithuania, Latvia, and the former eastern provinces of Poland, now known as Western Belorussia and Western Ukraine. Protestants number altogether between 4 and 5 million. The other religious groups are much smaller. There are about 2 million Jews scattered all over the USSR, but living mainly in the cities, and some 0.5 million Buddhists in the Soviet Far East. Other localized groups include the Georgian Orthodox church in Georgia, the Armenian Church in Armenia, and Lutherans, largely living in the Baltic provinces of the USSR. There is an unknown number of sects mostly of Orthodox origin.

Thus, out of some 285 million Soviet subjects, over 100 million people, that is, well over one-third of the entire population, are in opposition to the atheistic principles professed and vigorously propagated by the State. It is true that by 1927 the hierarchy of the largest segment, the Russian Orthodox Church, did officially accept the Soviet Communist regime; it is true that during the "Great Patriotic War" the Church displayed extraordinary zeal in helping to save it from defeat in the name of patriotism; but the large body of the Orthodox faithful simply continue to persist in their sullen suspicion of most of their bishops and consider them either as hired agents or, at least, as captives of their mistaken submissive tactics. There is no doubt that the spiritual vitality and heroic courage of a considerable segment of the Orthodox Church is undimmed. In general, despite the repeated waves of persecution, a large body of believers of most denominations has continued to persist in their practices and has been expanding rather than contracting their ranks.

Gorbachev's ascent to power, despite his liberalizing reforms in many other fields, has, thus far, changed little in the ecclesiastical policy of the Kremlin. The permission to import 100,000 copies of the Bible is but a small concession when viewed against the background of continued harsh, discriminatory measures victimizing religious groups. Although some paragraphs of the Criminal Code are being revised to increase civil rights, there seems to be no immediate plan to radically revise restrictions on cults. The existing laws forbid activity by any congregation until it is registered with and approved by the authorities and prohibit teaching religion to children outside the family. Most important, membership of a religious group remains an obstacle to advancement. Only professed atheists may join the Communist Party, and without a Party card a Soviet citizen has almost no chance at senior jobs in government, the military and the police, education, or journalism. We shall see whether the 1988 celebration of the millennium of the conversion of Kieva Rus to Christianity will reveal further changes in the attitude of the Soviet regime toward over one third of its discriminated subjects.

GLASNOST

Gorbachev's bold reform plans have won only hesitant support of the broad masses of people; they fear that the changes in business management and alteration of work norms may result not only in lower wages and higher prices, but also unemployment and inflation. Only a tangible rise in the standard of life might persuade the silent majority to alter its attitude. Thus far, the most consistent supporters of the *perestroika* are to be found among Soviet intellectuals, university professors, writers, and artists. Although rather pampered economically, for decades they had been smarting under the tight censorship. Consequently, they greeted *glasnost* with enthusiasm. The slight relaxation of censorship, the cessation of jamming foreign broadcasts, the permission to publish Pasternak's novel, *Dr. Zhivago*, the rehabilitation of a few victims of Stalin, like Nicholas Bukharin, or of the popular singer, Vladimir Vysotsky, and a few other similar gestures have made some Soviet intellectuals ecstatic.

The euphoria of the educated strata of the Soviet society for the cultural liberalization has been reflected in the circulation of some of the leading Soviet newspapers and periodicals. The ones that have been more hesitant in their approval of the Gorbachev reforms, like the chief Party daily, *Pravda*, lost popularity and had to reduce circulation. On the other hand, the two leading literary and political journals, *Novy Mir* (New World) and *Znamya* (Banner), which side wholeheartedly with the *perestroika*, have doubled their readership. Both journals have led the way in publishing long-forbidden works. They have also printed some of the most vivacious discussions of the need for economic and political changes. The biggest winner in the circu-

lation states, however, has been *Druzhba Narodov* (Friendship Among Nations). Its circulation suddenly jumped from 150,000 to 800,000. The main reason for this seems to be the serializing of Anatoly Rybakov's novel *Children of the Arbat*, which describes realistically life during Stalin's purges. The novel instantly became the big hit. The fiercest indictments of Stalin's crimes have been Tengiz Abuladze's movie *Repentance*, depicting the times when the secret police chief, Beria, raged unbridled. The screenplay was written in 1982, produced in 1984 and first shown in Moscow only in January 1987. At the beginning of 1988, another literary taboo disappeared with the publication of Yevgeny Zamyatin's novel *We*, the forerunner of Aldous Huxley's *Brave New World* and George Orwell's *1984*. *We* was written in 1921, 11 years before Huxley's book and 28 years before Orwell's. The novel was fiercely attacked by Soviet critics and it was first published abroad in 1924. Zamyatin's world of the future is the "One State," a technocratic dictatorship ruled by the "Great Benefactor." Citizens have numbers instead of names and live in transparent glass boxes. Conformity is enforced by vigilant and everpresent "Guardians," whose weapons include sophisticated bugging devices. Hunger has been eliminated at the expense of eight tenths of the world's population, the family abolished, and love "conquered."

Although the relatively fast tempo of *glasnost* has outdistanced the tempo of the economic reform, even in this field the Party has been cautious. It is facing the dilemma of how to allow people more say without destabilizing its rule. Gorbachev himself has been rather ambivalent in his attitude toward the past. In February 1987, he told a meeting of mass media editors that the Soviet Union should have "no forgotten names and no blank pages in descriptions of the years of industrialization and collectivization." On the other hand, in his speech on the seventieth anniversary of the Bolshevik revolution, Gorbachev, facing the conservative opposition, also stressed the positive points of Stalin's rule. "We must see both Stalin's indisputable contribution to the struggle for Socialism, his defense of its gains, and [his] crude political mistakes and arbitrary behavior." Gorbachev went so far as to defend Stalin's industrialization and collectivization of agriculture by saying that Stalin's policy was "the only possible" path, given conditions at the time.

As far as the past is concerned, two schools of thought have emerged, one stressing the need to analyze frankly past mistakes in order not to repeat them, another expressing fear that an overly radical repudiation of the past will destroy the Communist Party's legitimacy and thus undermine the very existence of the regime. Yegor Likhachev, the second ranking member of the Politburo, has been the principal restraining spokesman for the Party. For him, Soviet history has been more than "a chain of unrelieved errors and mistakes." He has called for emphasizing the achievements of Communism, patriotism, "social optimism," and "respect for talented and honored people." Another signal of disapproval came from Viktor Chebrikov, member of the Politburo and Chief of the KGB. In his September 1987 speech commemorating the 110th anniversary of the birth of Felix Dzerzhinsky, the founder of the Cheka, Chebrikov warned that Western intelligence services were trying to sow discord among Soviet people and encouraging dissident activities among the intellectuals to subvert the cohesiveness of the country. He stressed especially the mounting dissent among ethnic minorities in the Caucasus and in the Western borderlands of the USSR, like Lithuania, Latvia, and Ukraine. The 1988 violent clashes in Armenia and Azerbaijan bolstered his hand.

ETHNIC AND DEMOGRAPHIC PROBLEMS

And, indeed, intellectual, religious, and political dissent is much stronger among the multinational regions of the USSR than among the Russians; the latter tend to be proportionately stronger in the ranks of the CPSU and identify themselves more with the Communist regime than do members of national minorities. Despite the denials of some leaders of the reemerging great Russian nationalistic movement, the Russians do represent the privileged and ruling stratum of the population. Among the twenty-three members of the two top bodies, the Politburo and the Secretariat, there are nineteen Russians. Three others are Slavs: Vladimir V. Shcherbitsky and Oleg D. Baklanov, who are Ukrainians, and Nikolai N. Slyunkov, a Byelorussian. Foreign Minister, Eduard A. Shevardnadze, a Georgian, is the only non-Slavic member of these two leading Party organs. The Central Committee, numbering over three hundred members is about two-thirds Russian.

The Constitution of 1977 stresses that the USSR is a voluntary union of equal nations working harmoniously to consolidate the already well established socialist society. In the days of Lenin, it was widely assumed among Communists that Marxism would be the doctrine that would unite in common purpose the plethora of one hundred or so different peoples, who live on one-sixth of the earth's surface, in equality, harmony, and brotherhood. Despite the claims of Soviet leaders that Communism has solved all ethnic problems, everyday practice belies these boasts. There is no doubt that the largest nationality, the Great Russians, continues to dominate the smaller ethnic groups. Russian nationalism has been on the rise since the "Great Patriotic War"—a victory that Stalin attributed to the unique, superior qualities of the Great Russian stock: courage, persistence, and singleness of purpose. The mounting trend toward Russian chauvinism has provoked strong criticism, especially among the Western periphery of the USSR, among the Ukrainians, as well as the Armenians, Georgians, and the Baltic peoples, Lithuanians, Latvians, and Estonians.

Leaders of many of the Soviet ethnic groups, the Jews being the most vocal, insist on the political equality and racial justice promised to them by the Constitution. Despite these promises, anti-Semitism, which had been originally condemned as a crime, is now endemic. Tsarist Russia was the traditional home of this prejudice, witnessing hundreds of pogroms, and many of Hitler's anti-Semitic fables were partly drawn from Muscovite sources. The USSR is the only major country that does not acknowledge the fact that Jews were a special target of Nazi crimes. Since the war, anti-Semitism has been encouraged by official propaganda that suggests that it is merely opposing the racially inspired ideology of "Zionism." Efforts of Soviet Jews to leave the Soviet Union are denounced as treason.

The ethnic issue is the USSR's most dangerous internal problem, because the Great Russian stock is gradually losing its numerical preponderance. Moreover, the Baltic peoples and the Ukrainians resent the fact that the Russians still dominate the political structure and try to impose their language and culture on the subject peoples. Many of the Asiatic minorities, faced with the pressures of modernization and the example of the Muslim revival in the Middle East, are also potentially an explosive force by virtue of their fast multiplying numbers and the vicinity of the dynamic, fundamentalist Iran. In central Asia, social stratification is assuming a racial aspect: Slavs versus non-Slavs. Muslim Asians are usually recruited for the lower jobs in industry and the armed forces.

The Stalinist ethnic policy, operating under the slogan that each culture must be "national in form but socialist in content," was largely successful if measured in terms of its objectives. Stalin ruthlessly eradicated "feudal" and "national bourgeois" elites and brought many areas of the USSR, particularly the non-European ones, "into the twentieth century" through forcible industrialization and the spread of literacy. By this means, however, Stalin created both socioeconomic and cultural preconditions for the emergence of truly modern nations where they had not previously existed.

While destroying the traditional native political elites, usually very small and isolated from the masses, he created new Communist elites. But they are skillfully manipulated by the Center. The Central Committee Secretariat in Moscow makes sure that the Russians (or at least loyal Ukrainians or Belorussians) are placed in key positions in the Union republics. Since Stalin, a pattern has been established that the first secretary in each Union republic is to be a member of the local nationality, while the second secretary and the head of the KGB are mostly Russian or at least Slavs. The second secretary is usually in charge of cadres, and it is he whose influence is usually decisive. While the Russians tend to dominate the USSR politically and culturally, their numerical predominance is threated by the demographic realities. The declining birth rate severely affects all of Russia, but it is most dramatic among the Great Russians.[3]

The Muslim population of Central Asia is less affected by consumerism, secularization, and the spread of contraception, and has retained its traditional high fertility rate as well as cohesiveness. The Muslim people are relatively young; in 1980 some 52 percent of them were under fifteen years of age, while the corresponding figure for the Russians was only 28 percent. With 45 to 50 million Muslims, the USSR is the fifth largest agglomeration of this religious group after Indonesia, India, Pakistan, and Bangladesh. By the year 2000, every second child born in the USSR will be a Muslim. The present demographic trend, if unchecked (and there is no indication that it could change in the near future), is bound to have a far-reaching impact on the ethnic makeup of the USSR, including its ruling

---

[3] For a perceptive evaluation of Soviet demographic changes, see Helen Carrère d'Encausse, *Decline of an Empire: The Soviet Socialist Republics in Revolt* (New York: Newsweek Books, 1979.) By the year 2000, the Russians will increase about 10 percent to 142 million. Although they will retain a plurality of 44.3 percent, they will lose their majority and will outnumber the Asians by less than two to one.

Party, its governmental bureaucracy, and the composition of its armed forces. This, in turn, may affect the very coherence of the USSR. By establishing national republics and providing them with political and cultural institutions and by quickly industrializing, the Soviet regime unwittingly released elemental forces of social integration and nation-building—forces that have developed a powerful momemtum of their own. Although the new national elites are by and large corrupt, obsequious, and compelled to pay lip service to Russian hegemony, they have, in many cases, deep, native roots. Here Georgia, Armenia, and Azerbaijan are good examples. Given all these centrifugal tensions, political liberalization and economic decentralization might allow ethnic separatism to disrupt the USSR. The student riots that took place in December 1986 in Alma Ata, the capital of Kazakhstan, in protest of the replacement of D. A. Kunayev, a Kazakh as the local Party boss, by a Russian are another illustration of this fact.

One of the paradoxes of the present-day international situation of the USSR is that it pursues a strongly anticolonialist policy while being itself the last great colonial empire. It not only encapsulates within its borders well over a hundred ethnic groups, but also dominates about 100 million people of East Central Europe who are increasingly dissatisfied and restless. Since Yugoslavia's expulsion from the Cominform in 1948, the Soviet hegemonial sphere in Europe has been shaken by a series of revolts. The first was the uprising of the East German workers in 1953; this was followed by the revolts of the Poles and Hungarians in 1956; then came the defection of the Albanians in 1960, followed by the persistent Romanian independent line in foreign policy that surfaced in 1963. The Czechoslovak Prague Spring of 1968 and finally the deep and protracted Polish crisis of the 1980s, triggered by the birth of the "Solidarity" movement, complete the picture of the continuous turmoil. A prominent American scholar, Robert F. Byrnes, called the Soviet

domination of East Central Europe "hegemony without security."

FOREIGN POLICY

The Soviet invasion of Afghanistan in December 1979 had far-reaching consequences for the international position of the USSR; they were discussed in some detail in the previous chapter. The net result was virtual diplomatic isolation of Moscow and the worsening of relations with the United States, China, Western Europe, and most Muslim countries. Gorbachev has been trying to end this isolation and started his campaign with Asia. During his July–August 1986 trip to India, he demonstrated his strong interest in Asian affairs and his willingness to assert Moscow's Asiatic position.

From the point of view of Gorbachev's reforms the most crucial consequence of the Afghanistan war, however, was losing access to Western technology; hence his efforts to improve Soviet-American relations and to restrain the increasingly costly arms race. He rightly reasons that the burden of the defense budget is the heaviest single ballast preventing the Soviet Union from moving forward again. This helps explain Gorbachev's persistent arms control initiatives directed in all main directions, the United States, Western Europe and China. All Moscow's efforts to improve relations with Peking were frustrated, however, by the relentless Chinese insistence on three preconditions: withdrawal of Soviet troops from Afghanistan, withdrawal of Vietnamese contingents from Cambodia, and reduction of Soviet garrisons armed with nuclear weapons deployed along the 4,000 miles of the Sino-Soviet border.

Repeatedly rebuffed by Peking, Gorbachev turned westward. Hoping that spectacular goodwill gestures would influence public opinion in the West and pressure their governments to pursue arms control on terms favorable to Moscow, Gorbachev has launched another spectacular peace

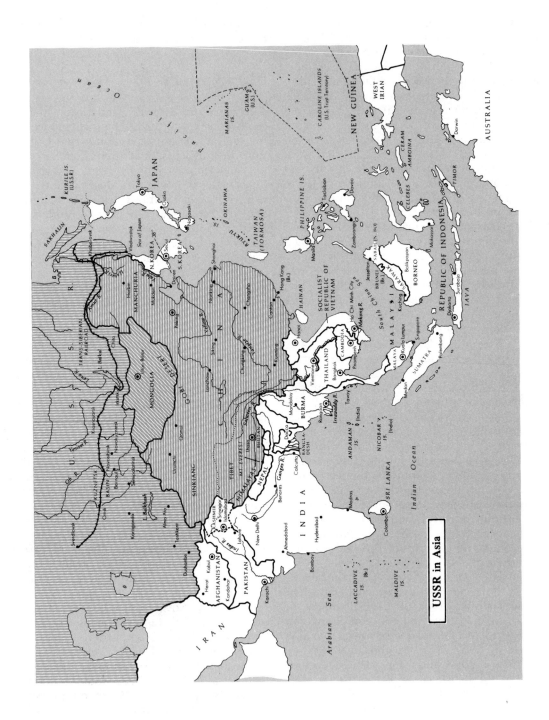

USSR in Asia

campaign. He has tried to promote broader East–West cultural contacts, allowed more Jews, Germans, and Armenians to leave the Soviet Union, and even dangled the prospect of an early withdrawal of Soviet troops from Afghanistan under certain conditions. Some political dissidents, for instance, Anatoly Sharansky, were released from prison and allowed to emigrate to Israel.[4] Andrei Sakharov was permitted to return to Moscow from internal exile and hold talks with the General Secretary himself. Many leading dissidents, however, remain incarcerated either in prisons or in psychiatric hospitals; whether their well-being has been lightened by application of the new regulations concerning their treatment is still a matter of controversy.

Parallel with these propagandistic gestures, Gorbachev has not only resumed the broken-off arms control negotiations in Geneva and Vienna, but also pressed for a series of summit meetings with President Reagan to finalize his partial disarmament efforts. The first of these summits held in Geneva, Switzerland, in November 1985 ended in failure. The second took place in Reykjavik, Iceland, in October 1986. Initially, the meeting seemed to produce sensational progress in arms reduction or even total elimination of nuclear weapons. Eventually, however, the negotiations dissolved into a public relations battle between Washington and Moscow. In both cases the stumbling block was Gorbachev's sly efforts to insert a set of paralyzing constraints on President Reagan's scheme of deploying over the United States a protective umbrella against a possible Soviet first-strike capacity. Officially, this space shield has been known as Strategic Defense Initiative (SDI), but denounced by its opponents as "Star War."

Not discouraged by the two failures to emasculate the SDI, Gorbachev, eager for an international success to bolster his still shaky internal position, did not relent on his pressure for another summit. Taking advantage of President Reagan's vulnerability caused by the revelation of the secret US-Iranian deals concerning trading arms for hostages, deals known as "Irangate," and a series of other domestic American scandals, Gorbachev managed to arrange for the third meeting with President Reagan in Washington. On December 8, 1987, one day after the forty-sixth anniversary of Pearl Harbor, the heads of the two superpowers signed a treaty limiting the intermediate-range nuclear force (INF). The treaty obliged the signatories to eliminate all intermediate nuclear warheads from their respective inventories. The document also contains a detailed scheme of on-the-spot verification: it allows United States and Soviet inspectors broad access to each other's territories at short notice, to verify that the terms of the treaty are being observed. Another feature of the INF treaty is the asymmetrical cuts in weaponry to arrive at the same final, equal total of 4,900 missiles each. The Soviets agreed to destroy four times as many missiles than the United States in order to reach that level. The destruction of the ground-launched missiles with a range between 300 and 3,600 miles does not significantly reduce the nuclear potential for the two global rivals: the intermediate rockets make up only about three to four percent of the superpower nuclear arsenal. Yet the treaty was hailed mainly for its symbolic significance. It marked the first time that the superpowers have agreed to eliminate an entire class of nuclear weapons.

From the very beginning, the Washington INF agreement has been a subject of bitter controversies. Its supporters have hailed it as great triumph of President Reagan's far-sighted defense strategy. In 1983, they have argued, he began the deployment of all Pershing 2-s in response to the Soviet deployment of SS-20 intermediate missiles in Europe. This he did despite Moscow's efforts at intimidation and the Soviet walk-

---

[4] About 8,010 Soviet Jews emigrated in 1987, more than eight times the number in the previous year. It was the highest number of people allowed to leave the Soviet Union since 1981. Also, about 4,500 people of German descent and some 2,000 Armenians were allowed to leave. The outlook for some 400,000 Jews who wish to emigrate is still bleak.

out from the Geneva and Vienna arms control negotiations, as well as considerable public opinion pressure in Western Europe. This resolve not only brought the Soviets back to the table but imposed on them triple concessions. First, they agreed to assymetrical reductions by agreeing to destroy many more missiles than the Americans; second, they agreed to leave French and British missiles intact; third, for the first time they accepted the principle of a rigid on-the-spot foreign inspection by allowing thirty to forty American experts to stay among them for thirteen years and watch what goes in and what comes out of their most important weapon systems.

Why was Gorbachev, "a man with a sweet smile but teeth of iron," willing to pay such a high price for the Washington agreement? There are several possible explanations for this unprecedented series of Soviet concessions. The first is strictly military. The United States Pershing 2 and the ground-based cruise missiles are much more accurate than the Soviet SS-20 missile. The American cruise missiles, for example, are able to come within 20 meters (about 21.8 yards) of their target in half the time. The accuracy of the Soviet SS-20 is rated at only 400 meters. The US rockets and missiles to be withdrawn had the presumed capability of taking out any Soviet military headquarters, munition dumps, concentration of guns, tanks, or planes between Western Europe and Moscow.

The second possible explanation of Gorbachev's conciliatory step is economic. To modernize his economy, Gorbachev eagerly desires to cut down on the military spending and free up money and manpower to be shifted to the civilian economy. Moreover, he wants to join the world trading community to facilitate a massive transfer of advanced technology that the Soviets are unable to generate themselves. Consequently, to catch up with the advanced countries, like the United States, Japan, and Western Europe, the USSR must return to the policy of detente; its essence is arms control, refraining from new belicose moves, like the invasion of Afghanistan, and a more civilized approach to human rights. Without a new detente, the USSR cannot hope to be admitted to the General Agreement on Tariffs and Trade (GATT), the International Monetary Bank, and the World Bank.

The third explanation for the Soviet concessions are the anticipated long-range strategic advantages Moscow hopes to derive from the INF agreement. By agreeing to dismantle nuclear-tipped Pershing 2 missiles that are able to hit Moscow from West Germany in thirteen minutes, argue the American as well as the West European opponents of the INF treaty, President Reagan has been ensnarled by the Soviet super-salesman. The treaty has exposed Western Europe to the Soviet conventional forces, three or four times more numerous than those of NATO, and thus undermined the defensive value of this vital organization. This line of reasoning has been summed up by General Bernard Rogers, former NATO Commander. According to him, by diminishing a vital part of the US nuclear arsenal, while leaving intact the greatly superior Soviet conventional forces, the INF treaty "puts NATO on the slipperty slope toward denuclearization of Western Europe, which is what the Soviets want." This weakening of the Western nuclear deterrent would accelerate the Soviets achieving their key objectives, which are "to intimidate, coerce and blackmail West European nations without having to fire a shot." This intimidation would allow Moscow "to enjoy the fruits of victory without the pains of war," concluded General Rogers.

Only the future can reveal whether this pessimistic assessment is correct. There is no doubt, however, that the Soviet ruling circles have greeted the agreement more unanimously and enthusiastically than even American supporters of President Reagan. It was significant that Gorbachev, during his Washington visit, vigorously pushed the problem of abolishing strategic nuclear weapons or the main American deterrent to any potential Soviet aggressive move.

Moreover, he rejected any linkage of the INF agreement with three other vital problems: Afghanistan, Nicaragua, and human rights. One has also to bear in mind that the slogan of a "nuclear-free world" has been a standard Soviet objective since Stalin. As long as the Russians preserve their superiority in conventional weapons, a complete denuclearization would ruin the strategic balance by depriving NATO of its main weapon. Meanwhile, in February 1988 new Soviet proposals were presented in Geneva at arms control talks. They do not clarify, however, the crucial problems of verification and other differences mainly in the Strategic Arms Reduction Talks (START).

Meanwhile, after his return from Washington Gorbachev altered his stand on Afghanistan. On April 14, 1988, the Soviet Union agreed in Geneva to pull all its troops out of Afghanistan within 9 months, beginning on May 15. Under the agreement one-half of the Soviet contingent of 115,000 soldiers should be withdrawn by August 15, and all troops by February 15, 1989. What would be a longe range impact of such a withdrawal on the regime whose legitimacy rests largely on its claim to political infallibility and military invincibility of its armed forces, is difficult to calculate.

GORBACHEV'S PROSPECTS

Despite the approval of Gorbachev's reform plans by the Party conference held in Moscow from June 28 to July 1, 1988, it is too early to say whether his experiment is destined to succeed. The problems he is facing are stupendous and the obstacles numerous. So far the tinkering with a punctured, listless economy has not been encouraging. In 1987, the yearly plan called for 4.1 percent growth in the net material product, a Soviet measure of national output; the actual growth was a mere 2.3 percent. Gorbachev's fatal flaw has been his failure, under pressure of the conservative faction, to put radical restructure in agriculture on the back burner. In contrast, the Chinese put farm

reform at the top of their program and obtained quick and most impressive economic results. It is expected that structural changes in the Soviet economy, planned by Gorbachev, would eliminate some 16 million jobs over the next 15 years. These unemployed people would either be absorbed by the expanding private sector or be retrained by the State and given new jobs because the Soviet Constitution guarantees everyone work. Nothing would undermine Gorbachev more quickly than mass unemployment or serious inflation.

Moreover, the scope and tempo of his reforms raise a number of questions. Is economic liberalization compatible with the centralized Communist political system? Is it possible to have economic freedom without political pluralism? Another big question mark is the strength and determination of Gorbachev's supporters. Is his political power basis firm enough? Thus far, as he has been barnstorming the country to whip up grass-roots support for his *perestroika*, he has found whole-hearted support only among intellectuals and some groups of enlightened technocrats. On the whole, he has faced indifference among the broad masses of the Soviet people, who have remain rather apathetic and even cynical about his efforts. Both Lenin and Stalin started with a small, but highly dedicated teams ready to risk anything fighting for their cause. Both Lenin and Stalin brutally removed large numbers of their opponents and replaced them with loyal partisans of the new order. Both massively promoted their supporters into administrative and political jobs. This created the "new class" of Soviet *apparatchiki*. In both cases the process was protracted, violent, and bloody.

Historically, Russian people have respected and followed only the rulers they feared and before whom they trembled. Bear in mind that Gorbachev has to face not only seventy years of Soviet history but also centuries of Muscovite-Russian heritage. The long legacy has been that of absolutist rule and centralization. Is Gorbachev ruthless enough to press his struggle with the lurking opposition to the bitter end? Will he go down in history as another Peter the Great or Khrushchev or, perhaps, another Alexander II?

SUGGESTED READING

BEICHMAN, ARNOLD, AND MIKHAIL S. BERNSTRAM, *Andropov: New Challenge to the West, A Political Biography*. New York: Stein & Day, 1983.

BIALER, SEWERYN, *Stalin's Successors: Leadership, Stability and Change in the Soviet Union*. New York: Columbia University Press, 1980.

BRESLAUER, GEORGE W., *Fire Images of Soviet Future: A Critical Review and Synthesis*. Berkeley: University of California Press, 1978.

BUKOVSKY, VLADIMIR, *To Choose Freedom*. Stanford, Calif.: Hoover Institution, 1987.

BYRNES, ROBERT F., ed., *After Brezhnev. Sources of Soviet Conduct in the 1980s*. Bloomington: Indiana University Press, 1983.

CAMPBELL, ROBERT W., *Trends in the Soviet Oil and Gas Industry*. Baltimore, Md.: Johns Hopkins University Press, 1976.

COCKS, PAUL, ROBERT V. DANIELS, AND NANCY W. HEER, eds., *The Dynamics of Soviet Politics*, Cambridge, Mass.: Harvard University Press, 1977.

COHEN, STEPHEN F., ed., *An End to Silence. Uncensored Opinion in the Soviet Union. From Roy Medvedev's Underground Magazine "Political Diary."* New York: Norton, 1982.

——, ALEXANDER RABINOWITCH, AND ROBERT SHARLET, eds., *The Soviet Union Since Stalin*. Bloomington: Indiana University Press, 1980.

DIBB, PAUL, *The Soviet Union: The Incomplete Superpower*. Foreword by Robert O'Neill. Urbana: University of Illinois Press, 1986.

DOUGLASS, JOSEPH D., JR., AND AMORETTA M. HOEBER, *Soviet Strategy for Nuclear War*. Stanford, Calif.: Hoover Institution, 1979.

DUNLOP, JOHN, *The Faces of Contemporary Russian Nationalism*. Princeton, N.J.: Princeton University Press, 1984.

EBON, MARTIN, *The Andropov File. The Life and Ideas of Yuri V. Andropov, General Secretary of the Communist Party of the Soviet Union*. New York: McGraw-Hill, 1983.

ELLIS, JANE, *The Russian Orthodox Church, a Contemporary History*. Bloomington: Indiana University Press, 1986.

FESHBACH, MURRAY, *The Soviet Union: Population Trends and Dilemmas*. Washington, D.C.: Population Reference Bureau, 1982.

GOLDMAN, MARSHALL I., *USSR in Crisis: The Failure of an Economic System*. New York: Norton, 1983.

——, *Gorbachev's Challenge. Economic Reform in the Age of High Technology*. New York: Norton, 1987.

GORBACHEV, MIKHAIL, *Perestroika: New Thinking for Our Country and the World*. New York: Harper & Row, 1987.

GOURÉ, LEON, *The Role of Nuclear Forces in Current Soviet Strategy*. Washington, D.C.: Center for Advanced International Studies, 1974.

——, *War and Survival in Soviet Strategy*. Washington, D.C.: Center for Advanced International Studies, 1976.

HARVEY, MOSE L., ET AL., *Science and Technology as an Instrument of Soviet Policy*. Washington, D.C.: Center for Advanced International Studies, 1972.

KANET, ROGER E., AND DONNA BAHRY, eds., *Soviet Economic and Political Relations with the Developing World*. New York: Praeger, 1975.

LANE, CHRISTEL, *Christian Religion in the Soviet Union, a Sociological Study*. Albany: State University of New York Press, 1978.

LEE, WILLIAM T. AND RICHARD F. STAAR, *Soviet Military Policy Since World War II*. Stanford, Calif.: Hoover Institution Press, Stanford University, 1986.

LEONHARD, WOLFGANG, *The Kremlin and the West, a Realistic Approach*, translated from German by Houchang E. Chehabi. New York: Norton, 1986.

MEDVEDEV, ZHORES A., *Soviet Science*. New York: Norton, 1978.

——, *Andropov*. New York: Norton, 1983.

——, *Soviet Agriculture*. New York: Norton, 1987.

SCHMIDT-HÄEUR, CHRISTIAN, *Gorbatchev. The Path to Power*. London: I. B. Tauris, 1986.

SINGLETON, FRED, ed., *Environmental Misuse in the Soviet Union*. New York: Praeger, 1976.

SOLOVYOV, VLADIMIR, AND ELENA KLEPIKOVA, *Yuri Andropov. A Secret Passage into the Kremlin*. New York: Macmillan, 1983.

SOLZHENITSYN, ALEXANDER, ET AL., *From Under*

Rubble, trans. A. M. Brock under the direction of Michael Scammell. New York: Bantam, 1976.

SPECHLER, DINA, *International Influences on Soviet Foreign Policy: Elite Opinion and the Middle East.* Jerusalem: Soviet and East European Research Center, Hebrew University, 1976.

SWEARINGEN, RODGER ed., *Siberia and the Soviet Far East: Strategic Dimensions in Multinational*

Perspective. Stanford, Calif.: Hoover Institution, 1987.

WILCZYNSKI, JOSEF, *The Multinationals and East–West Relations: Towards Transideological Collaboration.* Boulder, Colo.: Westview Press, 1976.

YANOV, ALEXANDER, *Detente after Brezhnev: The Domestic Roots of Soviet Foreign Policy.* Berkeley: University of California Press, 1977.

Appendix

EMPERORS OF RUSSIA, HOUSE OF ROMANOV

Peter I (Emperor in 1721)	1682–1725	Catherine II	1762–1796
Catherine I	1725–1727	Paul	1796–1801
Peter II	1727–1730	Alexander I	1801–1825
Anna	1730–1740	Nicholas I	1826–1855
Ivan VI	1740–1741	Alexander II	1855–1881
Elizabeth	1741–1761	Alexander III	1881–1894
Peter III	1761–1762	Nicholas II	1894–1917

PRIME MINISTERS OF THE PROVISIONAL GOVERNMENT

Prince G. E. Lvov	March–July 1917
A. F. Kerensky	July–November 1917

CHAIRMEN OF THE COUNCIL OF PEOPLE'S COMMISSARS (PRIME MINISTERS AFTER 1946)

V. I. Lenin	1917–1924	N. S. Khrushchev	1958–1964
A. I. Rykov	1924–1930	A. N. Kosygin	1964–1980
V. M. Molotov	1930–1941	N. A. Tikhonov	1980–1985
J. V. Stalin	1941–1953	N. I. Ryzhkov	1985–
G. M. Malenkov	1953–1955		
N. A. Bulganin	1955–1958		

GENERAL AND FIRST SECRETARIES OF THE PARTY'S CENTRAL COMMITTEE

J. V. Stalin, General Secretary, April 1922–March 5, 1953

G. M. Malenkov, First Secretary, March 5, 1953–March 15, 1953

N. S. Khrushchev, First Secretary, March 15, 1953–October 14, 1964

L. I. Brezhnev, First Secretary, October 14, 1964–March 1966; General Secretary, April 8, 1966–November 10, 1982

Y. V. Andropov, First Secretary, November 11, 1982–February 5, 1984

K. V. Chernenko, First Secretary, February 13, 1984–March 11, 1985

M. S. Gorbachev, General Secretary, March 12, 1985–

Congresses of the Russian Social Democratic Workers' Party (RSDWP), Russian Communist Party (Bolshevik) (RCP-B) since March 1918, Communist Party of the Soviet Union (Bolshevik) (CPSU-B) since December 1955, and Communist Party of the Soviet Union (CPSU) since October 1952.

RSDWP

I Congress	Minsk	March 1–3, 1898 (Old Style)
II Congress	Brussels and London	July 17–August 10, 1903
III Congress	London	April 12–27, 1905
(Bolshevik faction only)		
IV Congress	Stockholm	April 10–25, 1906
V Congress	London	April 30–May 19, 1907

RSDWP (Bolshevik)

VI Congress	Petrograd	July 26–August 3, 1917

RCP (Bolshevik)

VII Congress	Petrograd	March 6–8, 1918 (New Style)
VIII Congress	Moscow	March 18–23, 1919
IX Congress	Moscow	March 29–April 5, 1920
X Congress	Moscow	March 8–16, 1921
XI Congress	Moscow	March 27–April 2, 1922
XII Congress	Moscow	April 17–25, 1923
XIII Congress	Moscow	May 23–31, 1924

CPSU (Bolshevik)

XIV Congress	Moscow	December 18–31, 1925
XV Congress	Moscow	December 2–19, 1927
XVI Congress	Moscow	June 26–July 13, 1930
XVII Congress	Moscow	January 26–February 10, 1934
XVIII Congress	Moscow	March 10–21, 1939

CPSU

XIX Congress	Moscow	October 5–15, 1952
XX Congress	Moscow	February 14–25, 1956
XXI Congress	Moscow	January 27–February 5, 1959
XXII Congress	Moscow	October 17–31, 1961
XXIII Congress	Moscow	March 29–April 8, 1966
XXIV Congress	Moscow	March 30–April 9, 1971
XXV Congress	Moscow	February 24–29, 1976
XXVI Congress	Moscow	March, 1981
XXVII Congress	Moscow	February–March, 1986

CONGRESSES OF THE COMMUNIST INTERNATIONAL (COMINTERN)

First	March 2–6, 1919	Moscow
Second	July 19–August 7, 1920	Moscow–Petrograd
Third (United Front)	June 22–July 12, 1921	Moscow
Fourth	November 5–December 5, 1922	Moscow
Fifth	June 17–July 8, 1924	Moscow
Sixth (Ultra-left tactics)	July 17–September 1, 1928	Moscow
Seventh (Popular Front)	July 25–August 20, 1935	Moscow

ETHNIC COMPOSITION OF THE USSR:
THE LARGEST NATIONALITY
GROUPS (IN THOUSANDS)

Nationalities	Census of 1926 147.028	Percent of the Population	Census of 1979 262.085	Percent of the Population
Russians	77.791	52.9	137.397	52.4
Ukrainians	31.195	21.2	42.347	16.2
Uzbeks	3.989	2.7	12.456	4.8
Belorussians	4.739	3.2	9.463	3.6
Kazaks	3.989	2.7	6.556	2.5
Tartars	3.331	2.3	6.317	2.4
Azerbijanis	1.713	1.2	5.477	2.1
Armenians	1.568	1.1	4.151	1.6
Georgians	1.821	1.2	3.571	1.4
Moldavians	279	0.2	2.968	1.1
Tadziks	981	0.7	2.989	1.1
Lithuanians	41	0.0	2.851	1.1
Turkmanians	764	0.5	2.008	0.8
Germans	1.239	0.8	1.936	0.7
Kirgizians	763	0.5	1.906	0.7
Jews	2.672	1.8	1.811	0.7
Chuvashi	1.117	0.8	1.751	0.7
Ten ethnic groups of Dagestan	698	0.5	1.657	0.6
Latvians	151	0.1	1.439	0.5
Bashkirs	714	0.5	1.371	0.5
Mordvinians	1.340	0.9	1.192	0.5
Poles	782	0.5	1.151	0.4
Estonians	155	0.1	1.020	0.4

Source: 1984 supplement to Paul E. Lydolph, *Geography of the USSR: Topical Analysis* (Elkhart Lake, Wis.: Misty Valley Publishing, 1979).

Index